THE 1995-96 CHRISTIAN WRITERS' MARKET GUIDE

S0-BAU-230

SALLY E. STUART

CHRISTIAN WRITERS'
MARKET GUIDE
1995-1996

Harold Shaw Publishers
Wheaton, Illinois

Copyright © 1995 by Sally E. Stuart

All rights reserved. No part of this book may be reproduced or transmitted in any form or by any means, electronic or mechanical, including photocopying, recording, or any information storage and retrieval system without written permission from Harold Shaw Publishers, Box 567, Wheaton, Illinois 60189. Printed in the United States of America.

International Standard Serial Number: 1080-3955

ISBN 0-87788-118-9

Cover design by David LaPlaca

02 01 00 99 98 97 96 95

10 9 8 7 6 5 4 3 2

CONTENTS

INTRODUCTION

This year marks at least two significant milestones for this market guide. The first is an anniversary—this is the 10th annual edition. When I started all this 10 years ago, I had no idea this book would reach the level of prominence and prestige that it has. At this point most Christian writers consider it their primary tool for marketing, and it is recommended to aspiring and professional writers by many of the leading book and periodical publishers.

And the second is that for the first time it will be published by Harold Shaw Publishers, which will expand its influence and distribution in secular as well as Christian bookstores across the country. I am thankful for its continued and growing ministry in Christian publishing.

I am often asked how the market guide got its start. I actually never started out to write a market guide. Ten years ago I was visiting the office in Florida of what was then *The Christian Writer* magazine. I was preparing for a conference later that year and was hoping to convince the editor to pay for a mailing to a few publishers so I could make up a sheet of markets to hand out in one of my classes.

He was happy to do so since I could also use the information in my marketing column for his magazine. As the day progressed, and we talked about the possibilities, he said if I wanted to send out a few more questionnaires and put them into a book (or did he say booklet?), he would publish it for me. I thought that might be a good idea—I had no concept at the time what a really good idea it was.

That first edition, which came out in 1986, was 235 pages with large type and lots of white space. There were 129 book publishers (now 233), 437 magazines (now 593), 70 book topics (now 102), and 42 magazine topics (now 112). Back then most of the listings were only 2-6 lines, with the most basic information.

The first edition was written on a typewriter. By the time I was ready to start the second, I'd had a computer for six months that I'd never turned on. I was scared to death of it, but the thought of doing the market guide on a typewriter again was enough incentive. I turned on the computer and started the market guide the same day. And the rest—as they say—is history.

In this tenth edition you will find 76 periodicals, 32 book publishers, and 26 greeting card/specialty product publishers that were not in the previous edition. In the alphabetical listings, new additions are marked with a (+) plus sign before the title.

In addition, there are six new periodical topics and eight new book topics. Those are marked with an asterisk in the table of contents and the topical listings. Included in the new book topics are those publishers who publish booklets, pamphlets and tracts. In the magazine topics, you will find a listing of take-home papers and publishers who sponsor contests. The specialty product listings now include videos, computer games and computer programs.

This year we have expanded the list of Christian newspapers to over 50, and those are listed under "Newspapers" in the periodical topics. The agent list has dropped a few and added a few as that new and changing segment of the industry matures.

In the primary listings for both book and periodical publishers, I have continued to expand the descriptive information and tips to help you better understand the slant of each publisher. For the first time, the listings indicate which publishers accept fax queries, which ones prefer or require submissions on disk, and which periodicals use sidebars.

Again I want to thank those who have offered suggestions for additions or improvements in the past (some I've already implemented), and encourage all of you to send ideas that might improve content or format in the future.

As with any new reference book, I suggest you spend some quality time becoming familiar with its contents and structure. Discover the supplementary lists available throughout the book. Read through the glossary and spend a few minutes learning terms you are not familiar with. Review the lists of writers' groups and conferences and mark those you might be interested in pursuing during the coming months. The denominational listing will help you start making the important connection between periodicals and book publishers associated with different denominations.

A unique feature of this market guide is the extensive topical or subject listings included for both periodicals and book publishers. They will give you clear indications of which publishers are interested in articles or books on which topics.

Be sure to carefully study the "How to Use This Book" section. It will save you a lot of time and frustration in trying to understand the meaning of all the notations in the primary listings. Remember to send for sample copies (or catalog) and guidelines for any of these publishers or periodicals you are not familiar with. Then study those carefully before submitting anything to that publisher.

Editors tell me repeatedly that they are looking for writers who understand them, their periodical or publishing house, and most of all, their unique approach to the marketplace. One of the biggest complaints I am still getting from publishers is that the material they receive routinely is not appropriate for their needs. With a little time and effort, you can fulfill all their expectations, distinguish yourself as a professional, and sell what you write.

I wish you well as you embark on this exciting road to publication, whether for the first time or as a long-time veteran. And as I remind you every year, each of us has been given a specific mission in the field of writing. We often feel inadequate to the task, but I learned a long time ago that the writing assignments God has given me cannot be written quite as well by anyone else.

Sally E. Stuart
1647 SW Pheasant Dr.
Aloha OR 97006
(503)642-9844

P.S. For information on how to receive the market guide automatically every year and freeze the price at $18.99 for all future editions, or to get information on getting the guide at a discounted group rate, or getting books on consignment for your next seminar or conference, contact me at the address or phone number above.

HOW TO USE THIS BOOK

The purpose of this market guide is to make your marketing job easier and more targeted. However, it will serve you well only if you put some time and effort into studying its contents and using it as a springboard for discovering and becoming an expert on those publishers best suited to your writing topics and style.

Below you will find information on its general set-up and instructions for its use. In order to help you become more of an expert on marketing, I am including an explanation of each entry in the alphabetical listings for both the book section and the periodical section. Be sure to study these before trying to use this book.

1. Spend some time initially getting acquainted with the contents and set-up of this resource book. You cannot make the best use of it until you know exactly what it has to offer.

2. Study the Contents pages, where you will find listings of all the periodical and book topics. When selecting a topic, be sure to check related topics as well. Some cross-referencing will often be helpful. For example, if you have a novel that deals with doctor-assisted suicide, you might find the list for adult novels and the list for controversial issues and see which publishers are on both lists. Those would be good potential markets. In the topical sections you will find a letter "R" following publishers that accept reprints (pieces that have been printed in other publications, but you retain the rights).

3. The Primary/Alphabetical Listings for book and periodical publishers contain those publishers who answered the questionnaire and those who did not. The listings preceded by an asterisk (*) are those publishers who didn't respond and I was unable to update from other sources. Those with a number symbol (#) were updated from their guidelines or other sources. Since the information in those two groups was not verified by the publisher, you are encouraged to send for sample copies or catalogs and writers' guidelines before submitting to them.

4. In each **book-publisher listing** you will find the following information (as available), in this format:

a) Name of publisher

b) Address, phone and fax numbers.

c) Denomination or affiliation.

d) Name of editor - This may include the senior editor's name, followed by the name of another editor to whom submissions should be sent. In a few cases several editors are named with the type of books each is responsible for. Address to appropriate editor.

e) Sometimes a statement of purpose.

f) Sometimes a list of imprint names.

g) Number of inspirational/religious titles published per year.

h) Number of submissions received annually.

i) Percentage of books from first-time authors.

j) Whether or not they will accept books through agents. "Accepts ms through agents" means they are open to that, not that they require it.

k) The percentage of books from freelance authors they subsidy publish (if any).

l) Whether they reprint out-of-print books from other publishers.

m) Preferred manuscript length in words or pages.

n) Average amount of royalty, if provided. If royalty is a percentage of wholesale or net, it is based on price paid by bookstores or distributors. If it is on retail price, it is based on cover price of the book.

o) Average amount paid for advances - Whether a publisher pays an advance or not is noted in the listing; if they did not answer the question, there is no mention of it.

p) Whether they make any outright purchases and amount paid.

q) Average first printing (number of books usually printed for a first-time author).

r) Average length of time between acceptance of a manuscript and publication of the work.

s) Whether they consider simultaneous submissions. This means you can send a query or complete manuscript simultaneously to more than one publisher, as long as you advise everyone involved that you are doing so.

t) Length of time it should take them to respond to a query/proposal or to a complete manuscript (when two lengths of time are given, the first generally refers to a query and the latter to a complete manuscript). Give them a one-month grace period beyond that and then send a polite follow-up letter if you haven't heard from them.

u) Availability and cost for writers' guidelines and book catalogs - If the listing says "Guidelines," it means they are available for a #10 (business-sized) SASE with a first-class stamp. The cost of the catalog (if any), the size of envelope, and amount of postage are given, if specified (affix stamps to envelope, don't send loose). Tip: If postage required is more than $1.24, I suggest you put $1.24 in postage on the envelope and clearly mark it "Special 4th Class Rate." (That is enough for up to 1#). If the listing says "free catalog," it means you need only request it, they do not ask for payment or SASE. Note: If sending for both guidelines and catalog, it is not necessary to send both envelopes; guidelines will be sent with catalog.

v) Nonfiction Section - Preference for query letter, book proposal, or complete manuscript, and whether they accept phone or fax queries (new this year). If they want a query letter, send just a letter describing your project. If they want a query letter/proposal, you can add a chapter-by-chapter synopsis and the number of sample chapters indicated. If not specified, send one to three chapters. This is often followed by a quote from them about their needs, or what they don't want to see. This year there is also an indication of whether or not they will accept fax queries.

w) Fiction Section - Same information as nonfiction section.

x) Special Needs - If they have specific topics they need that are not included in the subject listings, they are indicated here.

y) Ethnic Books - Usually specifies which ethnic groups they target or any particular needs.

z) Tips - Specific tips provided by the editor/publisher.

Note: No information is included on acceptance of books on computer disk. Most publishers now do accept or even require that books be sent on a computer disk (usually along with a hard copy), but since each publisher's needs are different, that information will be supplied to you by the publisher who accepts your book or manuscript.

5. In each **periodical listing** you will find the following information (as available), in this format:

a) Name of periodical.

b) Address, phone number and fax number.

c) Denomination or affiliation.

d) Name of editor and editor to submit to (if different).

e) Theme of publication - This will help you understand their particular slant.

f) Format of publication, frequency of publication, number of pages and size of circulation - Tells whether magazine, newsletter, journal, tabloid, newspaper, or take-home paper. Frequency of publication indicates quantity of material needed. Number of pages usually indicates how much material they can use.

Circulation indicates the amount of exposure your material will receive, and often indicates how well they might pay or probability that they will stay in business.

g) Subscription rate - Amount given is for a one-year subscription in the country of origin. I suggest you subscribe to at least one of your primary markets every year to become better acquainted with its specific focus.

h) Date established - Included only if 1991 or later.

i) Openness to freelance; percentage freelance written. If they buy only a small percentage, it often means they are open but receive little that is appropriate. The percentage freelance written indicates how great your changes are of selling to them. When you have a choice, choose those with the higher percentage, but only if you have done your homework and know they are an appropriate market for your material.

j) Preference for query or complete manuscript, whether they want a cover letter with complete manuscripts, and whether they will accept phone or fax queries.

k) Payment schedule; payment on acceptance or publication; and rights purchased.

l) If a publication does not pay, or pays in copies or subscription, that is indicated in bold, capital letters.

m) If a publication is not copyrighted, it is indicated. That means that you should ask for your copyright notice to appear on your piece when they publish it, so your rights will be protected.

n) Preferred word lengths and average number of manuscripts purchased per year (in parentheses).

o) Response time - The time they usually take to respond to your query or manuscript submission (add mail time).

p) Seasonal material (also refers to holiday) - If sending holiday or seasonal material it should reach them at least the specified length of time in advance.

q) Acceptance of simultaneous submissions and reprints - If they accept simultaneous submissions, it means they will look at submissions (usually timely topic or holiday material) sent simultaneously to several publishers. Best to send to non-overlapping markets (such as denominational), and be sure to always indicate that it is a simultaneous submission. Reprints are pieces you have sold previously, but to which you hold the rights (which means you sold only first or one-time rights to the original publisher and the rights reverted to you as soon as they were published).

r) New this year is an indication of whether they prefer or require submissions on disk, and whether there is extra compensation for that. Most of them seem to want a disk after the piece is accepted, but want a query or hard copy first.

s) Average amount of kill fee, if they pay one.

t) Also new this year is an indication of whether they use sidebars (see glossary for definition).

u) Availability and cost for writer's guidelines, theme list, and sample copies - If the listing says "Guidelines," it means they are available for a #10 SASE (business-sized) with a first-class stamp. The cost for a sample copy, the size of envelope, and number of stamps required are given, if specified (affix stamps to envelope, don't send loose). Tip: If postage required is more than $1.24, I suggest you put $1.24 in postage on the envelope and clearly mark it "Special 4th Class Rate." (That is enough for up to 1#). If the listing says "Free sample copy" it means you need only to request them; they do not ask for payment or SASE. Note: If sending for both guidelines and sample copy, it is not necessary to send both envelopes; guidelines will be sent with sample copy. If a listing doesn't mention guidelines or a catalog, they probably don't have them.

v) Poetry - Name of poetry editor (if different). Average number of poems bought each year. Types of poetry; number of lines. Payment rate. Maximum number of poems you may submit at one time.

w) Fillers - Name of fillers editor (if different). Types of fillers accepted; word length. Payment rate.

x) Columns/Departments - Name of column editor. Names of columns in the periodical (information in parentheses gives focus of column); word length requirements; payment. Be sure to see sample before sending ms or query. Most columns require a query.

y) Special Issues or Needs - Indicates topics of special issues they have planned for the year, or unique topics not included in regular subject listings.

z) Ethnic - Any involvement they have in the ethnic market.

aa) Tips - Tips from the editor on how to break into this market or how to be successful as an author.

bb) At the end of some listings you will find a notation as to where that particular periodical placed in the Top 50 Plus Christian Periodical list in 1994, and/or their place in 1993. This list is compiled annually to indicate the most writer-friendly publications. To receive a complete listing, plus a prepared analysis sheet and writer's guidelines for the top 50 of those markets, send $21 (includes postage) to: Sally Stuart, 1647 SW Pheasant Dr., Aloha OR 97006, or call (503)642-9844 for more information.

Some listings also include EPA winners. These awards are made annually by the Evangelical Press Association (a trade organization for Christian periodicals).

6. It is important that you adhere closely to the guidelines set out in these listings. If a publisher asks for a query only, do not send a complete manuscript. Following these guidelines will mark you as a professional.

7. If your manuscript is completed, select the proper topical listing and target audience, and make up a list of possible publishers. Check first to see which ones will accept a complete manuscript (if you want to send it to those that require a query, you will have to write a query letter or book proposal to send first). Please do not assume that your manuscript will be appropriate for all those on the list. Read the primary listing for each and if you are not familiar with a publisher, read their writers'guidelines and study one or more sample copies or book catalog. (The primary listings contain information on how to get these.) Be sure the slant of your manuscript fits the slant of the publisher.

8. If you have an idea for an article, short story, or book but you have not written it yet, a reading of the appropriate topical listing will help you decide on a possible slant or approach. Select some publishers to whom you might send a query about your idea. If your idea is for an article, do not overlook the possibility of writing on the same topic for a number of different periodicals listed under that topic, either with the same target audience, or another from the list that indicates an interest. For example you could write on money management for a general adult magazine, a teen magazine, women's publication, or for pastors. Each would require a different slant, but you would get a lot more mileage from that idea.

9. If you do not have an idea, simply start reading through the topical listings or the primary listings. They are sure to trigger any number of book or magazine ideas you could go to work on.

10. If you run into words or terms you are not familiar with, check the glossary at the back of the book for definitions.

11. If you need someone to look at your material to evaluate it or to give it a thorough editing, look up the section on editorial services and find someone to send it to for such help. That often will make the difference between success or failure in publishing.

12. If you are a published author with other books to your credit, you may be interested in finding an agent. Unpublished authors generally don't need or won't be able to find an agent. However, some agents will consider unpublished authors, but you must have a completed manuscript before you approach an agent (see agent list).

13. Check the group list to find a group to join in your area. Go to the conference list to find a conference you might attend this year. Attending a conference every year or two is almost essential to your success as a writer.

14. **ALWAYS SEND AN SASE WITH EVERY QUERY OR MANUSCRIPT.**

15. **DO NOT RELY SOLELY ON THE INFORMATION PROVIDED IN THIS MARKET GUIDE.** It is just that—a guide—and is not intended to be complete in itself. It is important to your success as a freelance writer that you learn how to use writers' guidelines and study book catalogs or sample copies before submitting to any publisher. Be a professional!

ADDITIONAL RESOURCES TO HELP WITH YOUR WRITING AND MARKETING

1. **Top 50+ Christian Periodical Publishers Packet** - Includes a list of the Top 50+ "writer-friendly" periodicals, pre-prepared analysis sheets and publisher's guidelines for each of the top 50, and a master form for analyzing your own favorite markets. Saves more than $30 in postage and 25-30 hours of work. $21, postpaid.

2. **The 1995-96 Christian Writers' Market Guide on computer disk** in Word Perfect 5.1 Text on 5¼" or 3½"HD disk, for quick marketing reference. $28 postpaid.

3. **A Market Plan for More Sales** - A step-by-step plan to help you be successful in marketing. Includes 5 reproducible forms. $4.75, postpaid.

4. **The Complete Guide to Christian Writing and Speaking** - A handbook for beginning and advanced writers and speakers written by the 19 members of the editorial staff of *The Christian Communicator*. $12, postpaid.

5. **Permissions Packet** - A compilation of over 20 pages of information directly from publishers on how and when to ask permission to quote from other people's material or from Bible paraphrases. Information not available elsewhere in printed form. $5, postpaid.

6. **Keeping Track of Your Periodical Manuscripts** - This 8-page booklet can be duplicated to keep track of every step involved in sending out your periodical manuscripts to publishers. $4.75, postpaid.

7. **Keeping Track of Your Book Manuscripts** - A similar booklet adapted to the steps in tracking a book manuscript from idea to publication. $4.75, postpaid.

8. **How to Submit a Book Proposal to a Publisher** - This 8-page packet contains all you need to know to present a professional looking book proposal to a publishing house. $4.75 postpaid.

9. **How to Submit an Article or Story to a Publisher** - This 8-page booklet shows how to write a query, prepare a professional-looking manuscript, and more. $4.75 postpaid.

10. **Inside Religious Publishing** - Features chapters by 32 of the top people in the industry, on all aspects of Christian publishing. Includes a chapter by Sally Stuart on "Selling Your Book." $25 postpaid.

All of the above resources are available from Sally E. Stuart, 1647 SW Pheasant Dr., Aloha OR 97006, tel. (503)642-9844. Send a #10 SASE for a complete listing of resources available.

11. **The Writer's Edge** - A service that links book writers and Christian publishers. The writer fills out a book information form and sends that along with 3 sample chapters, a synopsis, and a check for $45. The writer receives a brief critique of the manuscript and, if the manuscript is accepted by The Writer's Edge, a synopsis of the manuscript will appear in a newsletter that goes to over 40 Christian publishers who use The Writer's Edge as a screening tool for unsolicited manuscripts. *For further information send an SASE to The Writer's Edge, P.O. Box 1266, Wheaton, IL 60189.*

TOPICAL/SUBJECT LISTINGS OF BOOK PUBLISHERS

One of the most difficult aspects of marketing is trying to determine which publishers might be interested in the book you want to write. This topical listing was designed to help you do just that.

First, look up your topic of interest in the following lists. If you don't find the specific topic, check the list of topics in the table of contents and find any related topics. Once you have discovered which publishers are interested in a particular topic, the next step is to secure writers' guidelines and book catalogs from those publishers. Don't assume that just because a particular publisher is listed under your topic that it would automatically be interested in your book. It is your job to determine whether your approach to the subject will fit within the unique scope of that publisher's catalog. It is also helpful to visit a Christian bookstore to actually see some of the books produced by each publisher you are interested in pursuing.

Note, too, that the primary listings for each publisher indicate what the publisher prefers to see in the way of a query, book proposal, or complete manuscript.

R - Indicates which publishers reprint out-of-print books from other publishers.

APOLOGETICS

Baker Books - R
Brentwood - R
Bridge Publishing - R
Broadman & Holman
Christian Classics
Christian Lit. Crusade - R
Christian Univ. Press - R
College Press - R
Companion Press - R
Concordia
Cornerstone Press
Cross Cultural
Crossway Books
Eerdmans Publishing - R
Franciscan Press - R
Franciscan Univ. Press - R
HarperSanFrancisco - R
Harvard House
Hensley, Virgil W. - R
Howard Publishing - R
Huntington House - R
ICAN Press - R
InterVarsity Press

Kregel - R
Liguori Publications
Loyola Univ. Press - R
Master Books - R
Morehouse - R
Nelson, Thomas - R
Oxford University
Pillar Books - R
Presbyterian/Reformed - R
PROBE Ministries
Proclaim Publishing
Revell, Fleming H.
Review & Herald - R
St. Paul Books - R
Scarecrow Press
Servant - R
Son-Rise
Star Song - R
Still Waters Revival - R
Trinity Foundation - R
Tyler Press - R
Tyndale House - R
Victor Books - R
Victory House - R
World Bible - R

Zondervan/Trade - R
Zondervan/Academic

ARCHAEOLOGY

Baker Books - R
Blue Dolphin - R
Bob Jones - R
Brentwood - R
Broadman & Holman
Christian Univ. Press - R
Christopher Publishing
Cliffside Publishing
College Press - R
Companion Press - R
Concordia
Eerdmans Publishing - R
HarperSanFrancisco - R
Franciscan Press - R
ICAN Press - R
Kregel - R
Morning Star Press - R
Nelson, Thomas - R
New Leaf Press - R
Oxford University

Proclaim Publishing
Review & Herald - R
Scarecrow Press
Trinity Press Intl. - R
Tyler Press - R
University Press/America - R
Westminster/John Knox
Winston-Derek - R
World Bible - R
Yale Univ. Press - R
Zondervan/Trade - R
Zondervan/Academic

AUTOBIOGRAPHY

Bantam Books
Bethany House
Bethel Publishing - R
Brentwood - R
Bridge Publishing - R
Christian Lit. Crusade - R
Christopher Publishing
Companion Press - R
Cross Cultural
DaBaR Services - R
Eerdmans Publishing - R
Fairway Press - R
Friends United Press - R
HarperSanFrancisco - R
Huntington House - R
ICAN Press - R
Living Flame Press
Living Sacrifice - R
LuraMedia
Moorings
Nelson, Thomas - R
OMF Books
Prescott Press - R
Proclaim Publishing
Regnery Publishing - R
St. Bede's - R
Son-Rise
Southern Baptist Press - R

Still Waters Revival - R
Trinity Press Intl. - R
Tyler Press - R
Tyndale House - R
Upper Room Books - R
VESTA
Victory House - R
Westminster/John Knox
Windflower - R
Zondervan/Trade - R

BIBLE/BIBLICAL STUDIES

Accent Publications
ACTA Publications
Alba House - R
AMG Publishers - R
Baker Books - R
Bethany House
Bethel Publishing - R
Bible Discovery
Bosco Multimedia, Don
Brentwood - R
Bridge Publishing - R
Brown-ROA
Chalice Press
Christian Classics
Christian Ed Pub.
Christian Lit. Crusade - R
Christopher Publishing
Church Growth Inst.
Cliffside Publishing
College Press - R
Collier-Macmillan
Companion Press - R
Concordia
Contemporary Drama Service
Cornell Univ Press - R
Creation House
Cross Cultural
CSS Publishing
DaBaR Services - R
Discipleship Resources

Editorial Evangelica
Eerdmans Publishing - R
Fairway Press - R
Franciscan Press - R
Franciscan Univ. Press - R
Gospel Publishing
Group Publishing
HarperSanFrancisco - R
Harrison House - R
Hendrickson Publishers - R
Hensley, Virgil W. - R
Herald Press
Honor Books
Howard Publishing - R
Huntington House - R
ICAN Press - R
InterVarsity Press
Kindred Press
Kregel - R
Liguori Publications
Liturgical Press
Living Flame Press
LuraMedia
Morehouse - R
Morning Star Press - R
Nazarene Pub. House
Nelson, Thomas - R
New Hope - R
Novalis
Our Sunday Visitor - R
Oxford University
Paraclete Press - R
Pastoral Press
Paulist Press
Pillar Books - R
Presbyterian/Reformed - R
Proclaim Publishing
Regal Books
Resource Publications
Revell, Fleming H.
Review & Herald - R
Roper Press - R
St. Anthony Messenger - R

St. Bede's - R
St. Paul Books - R
Shaw Publishers, Harold - R
Sheed & Ward - R
Shining Star
Son-Rise
Southern Baptist Press - R
Standard (sm.group)
Trinity Press Intl. - R
Tyler Press - R
Tyndale House - R
United Church Press
United Church Pub.
United Methodist
University Press/America - R
Upper Room Books - R
VESTA
Victor Books - R
Victory House - R
Wadsworth - R
Warner Press
Westminster/John Knox
Woman's Miss. Union - R
Wood Lake Books - R
World Bible - R
Yale Univ. Press - R
Zondervan/Trade - R
Zondervan/Academic

BIOGRAPHY

Alba House - R
Bantam Books
Bethany House
Bethel Publishing - R
Blue Dolphin - R
Bob Jones - R
Brentwood - R
Bridge Publishing - R
Broadman & Holman
Catholic Univ/America - R
Christian Classics
Christian Lit. Crusade - R

Christian Univ. Press - R
Christopher Publishing
College Press - R
Companion Press - R
Cornell Univ. Press - R
Cross Cultural
CSS Publishing
Dimension Books - R
Eerdmans Publishing - R
Fairway Press - R
Franciscan Press - R
Friends United Press - R
HarperSanFrancisco - R
Howard Publishing - R
Huntington House - R
ICAN Press - R
ICS Publications - R
InterVarsity Press
Kindred Press
Kregel - R
Lifetime Book - R
Living Sacrifice - R
Loyola Univ. Press - R
Morehouse - R
Morrow and Co., Wm
Mt. Olive College Press
Nelson, Thomas - R
OMF Books
Our Sunday Visitor - R
Oxford University
Proclaim Publishing
Questar - R
Regnery Publishing - R
Review & Herald - R
St. Bede's - R
Scarecrow Press
Servant - R
Son-Rise
Southern Baptist Press - R
Star Song - R
Still Waters Revival - R
Trinity Press Intl. - R
Tyler Press - R

Tyndale House - R
United Church Press
Upper Room Books - R
VESTA
Victory House - R
Warner Press
Westminster/John Knox
Windflower - R
Woman's Miss. Union - R
Yale Univ. Press - R
Zondervan/Trade - R

*BOOKLETS

Bosco Multimedia, Don
Christian Lit. Crusade - R
Discipleship Resources
Editorial Evangelica
Forward Movement - R
Gospel Publishing
Huntington House - R
InterVarsity Press
Kindred Press
Master Books - R
Moody Press (series only)
Morehouse - R
Our Sunday Visitor - R
TEACH Services - R
Tyler Press - R
Wood Lake Books - R

CELEBRITY PROFILES

Christopher Publishing
Collier-Macmillan
Companion Press - R
Howard Publishing - R
Lifetime Books - R
Moorings
Morning Star Press - R
Nelson, Thomas - R
New Leaf Press - R
Our Sunday Visitor - R

Prescott Press - R
Proclaim Publishing
Servant - R
Shaw Publishers, Harold - R
Starburst Publishers
Star Song - R
Tyndale House - R
Victory House - R
Wood Lake Books - R
W.R.S. Publishing - R
Zondervan/Trade - R

CHILDREN'S PICTURE BOOKS

Alba House - R
Ave Maria Press
Barbour & Co. - R
Bay Public., Mel - R
Bridge Publishing - R
Chariot Books
Concordia
Eerdmans Publishing - R
Emerald Books
Fairway Press - R
Gibson, C.R. - R
Gold'N'Honey Books
Herald Press
Hunt & Thorpe
Huntington House - R
Kindred Press
Living Flame Press
Moorings
Morehouse - R
Morris, Joshua
MML Company
National Baptist - R
Nelson, Thomas - R
Our Sunday Visitor - R
Pacific Press
Pelican Publishing - R
Prescott Press - R
Proclaim Publishing

Questar - R
Regina Press
Roper Press - R
St. Paul Books - R
Seaside Press
Son-Rise
Standard
Upper Room Books - R
Victor Books - R
Victory House - R
Zondervan/Trade - R

CHRISTIAN EDUCATION

Accent Publications
Alba House - R
Ave Maria Press
Baker Books - R
Bantam Books
Bosco Multimedia, Don
Brentwood - R
Bridge Publishing - R
Bristol House - R
Broadman & Holman
Brown-ROA
Chalice Press
Christian Classics
Christopher Publishing
Church Growth Inst.
Concordia
Contemporary Drama Service
Cross Cultural
CSS Publishing
Discipleship Resources
Editorial Evangelica
Educational Ministries
Eerdmans Publishing - R
Fairway Press - R
Gospel Publishing
Group Publishing
Harrison House - R
Hensley, Virgil W. - R
Honor Books

Howard Publishing - R
Hunt & Thorpe
Huntington House - R
ICAN Press - R
Judson Press - R
Kindred Press
Kregel - R
Liguori Publications
Liturgical Press
Loyola Univ. Press - R
Master Books - R
Morehouse - R
Morning Star Press - R
National Baptist - R
Nelson, Thomas - R
New Hope - R
New Leaf Press - R
Omega Publications
Our Sunday Visitor - R
Presbyterian/Reformed - R
Prescott Press - R
PROBE Ministries
Proclaim Publishing
Questar - R
Rainbow Books (CA)
Rainbow Books (FL)
Regal Books
Regnery Publishing - R
Religious Education
Resource Publications
Review & Herald - R
St. Paul Books - R
Scripture Press
Shining Star
Southern Baptist Press - R
Standard
Still Waters Revival - R
Tabor Publishing
TEACH Services - R
Trinity Foundation - R
Tyler Press - R
United Church Press
United Church Pub.

VESTA
Victor Books - R
Warner Press
Westminster/John Knox
Windflower - R
Winston-Derek - R
Woman's Miss. Union - R
Wood Lake Books - R
Zondervan/Trade - R

CHRISTIAN HOME SCHOOLING

AMG Publishers - R
Baker Books - R
Bantam Books
Bay Public., Mel - R
Bethel Publishing - R
Brentwood - R
Brown-ROA
College Press - R
Christopher Publishing
Crossway Books
CSS Publishing
Eerdmans Publishing - R
Fairway Press - R
Focus on the Family - R
Hensley, Virgil W. - R
Hunt & Thorpe
Huntington House - R
Nelson, Thomas - R
Prescott Press - R
Proclaim Publishing
Questar - R
Rainbow Books (FL)
Regnery Publishing - R
Review & Herald - R
Son-Rise
Starburst Publishers
Still Waters Revival - R
TEACH Services - R
Trinity Foundation - R
Tyler Press - R

Tyndale House - R
Victory House - R

CHRISTIAN LIVING

ACTA Publications
Alba House - R
AMG Publishers - R
Augsburg Fortress - R
Ave Maria Press
Baker Books - R
Bantam Books
Barclay Press - R
Bethany House
Bethel Publishing - R
Brentwood - R
Bridge Publishing - R
Bristol House - R
Broadman & Holman
Cameron Press
Chalice Press
Chosen Books
Christian Classics
Christian Lit. Crusade - R
Christian Publications - R
Christopher Publishing
Church Growth Inst.
Cistercian - R
College Press - R
Collier-Macmillan
Companion Press - R
Concordia
Covenant Publishers
Creation House
Cross Cultural
Crossway Books
DaBaR Services - R
Eerdmans Publishing - R
Element Books - R
Emerald Books
Fairway Press - R
Focus on the Family - R
Forward Movement - R

Friends United Press - R
Good Book
Gospel Publishing
Greenlawn Press - R
HarperSanFrancisco - R
Harrison House - R
Harvest House
Haworth Press - R
Herald Press
Horizon House - R
Howard Publishing - R
Huntington House - R
ICAN Press - R
InterVarsity Press
Judson Press - R
Kregel - R
Life Cycle Books - R
LifeJourney Books
Liguori Publications
Liturgical Press
Living Flame Press
Loyola Univ. Press - R
LuraMedia
Moody Press
Moorings
Morehouse - R
Morning Star Press - R
Nazarene Pub. House
Nelson, Thomas - R
New Hope - R
New Leaf Press - R
Omega Publications
Pacific Press
Paraclete Press - R
Pillar Books - R
Presbyterian/Reformed - R
Prescott Press - R
Proclaim Publishing
Questar - R
Regal Books
Regnery Publishing - R
Resurrection Press - R
Revell, Fleming H.

Review & Herald - R
Roper Press - R
St. Anthony Messenger - R
St. Paul Books - R
Servant - R
Shaw Publishers, Harold - R
Sheed & Ward - R
Son-Rise
Starburst Publishers
Star Song - R
Still Waters Revival - R
TEACH Services - R
Tyler Press - R
Tyndale House - R
United Church Press
United Methodist
Upper Room Books - R
VESTA
Victor Books - R
Victory House - R
Warner Press
Wellness
Westminster/John Knox
Woman's Miss. Union - R
Zondervan/Trade - R

CHRISTIAN SCHOOL BOOKS

Baker Books - R
Bridge Publishing - R
Christopher Publishing
Concordia
Fairway Press - R
Hensley, Virgil W. - R
Howard Publishing - R
Hunt & Thorpe
ICAN Press - R
Morehouse - R
Our Sunday Visitor - R
Proclaim Publishing
Rainbow Books (CA)
Rainbow Books (FL)

Son-Rise
Southern Baptist Press - R
Trinity Foundation - R
Tyler Press - R
Victory House - R

CHURCH LIFE

ACTA Publications
Alban Institute
Baker Books - R
Bethany House
Bethel Publishing - R
Brentwood - R
Bristol House - R
Broadman & Holman
Chalice Press
Christian Publications - R
Christian Univ. Press - R
Christopher Publishing
Church Growth Inst.
Companion Press - R
Concordia
Creation House
Cross Cultural
Crossway Books
CSS Publishing
Discipleship Resources
Eerdmans Publishing - R
Fairway Press - R
Franciscan Press - R
Gospel Publishing
HarperSanFrancisco - R
Harrison House - R
Herald Press
Howard Publishing - R
Huntington House - R
ICAN Press - R
InterVarsity Press
Judson Press - R
Kindred Press
Kregel - R
Liguori Publications

Living Flame Press
Loyola Univ. Press - R
Moody Press
Moorings
Morehouse - R
Nelson, Thomas - R
New Leaf Press - R
Our Sunday Visitor - R
Pillar Books - R
Presbyterian/Reformed - R
Proclaim Publishing
Questar - R
Regal Books
Regnery Publishing - R
Review & Herald - R
St. Bede's - R
Sheed & Ward - R
Tyler Press - R
Tyndale House - R
United Church Press
Upper Room Books - R
VESTA
Victory House - R
Warner Press
Woman's Miss. Union - R
Zondervan/Trade - R

CHURCH RENEWAL

ACTA Publications
Alban Institute
Ave Maria Press
Baker Books - R
Barclay Press - R
Bethany House
Bethel Publishing - R
Brentwood - R
Bridge Publishing - R
Bristol House - R
Broadman & Holman
Chalice Press
Christian Classics
Christopher Publishing

Church Growth Inst.
Companion Press - R
Concordia
Creation House
Cross Cultural
Crossway Books
DaBaR Services - R
Dimension Books - R
Discipleship Resources
Eerdmans Publishing - R
Fairway Press - R
Forward Movement - R
Franciscan Press - R
Franciscan Univ. Press - R
Gospel Publishing
Greenlawn Press - R
HarperSanFrancisco - R
Harrison House - R
Hensley, Virgil W. - R
Herald Press
Howard Publishing - R
Huntington House - R
InterVarsity Press
Judson Press - R
Kregel - R
Liguori Publications
Living Flame Press
Loyola Univ. Press - R
LuraMedia
Moorings
Morehouse - R
Morning Star Press - R
Nelson, Thomas - R
Omega Publications
Our Sunday Visitor - R
Pastoral Press
Pastor's Choice
Presbyterian/Reformed - R
Proclaim Publishing
Questar - R
Regal Books
Regnery Publishing - R
Renewal Press

Resurrection Press - R
Review & Herald - R
Servant - R
Sheed & Ward - R
Southern Baptist Press - R
Star Song - R
Tyler Press - R
Tyndale House - R
United Church Press
VESTA
Victory House - R
Westminster/John Knox
Windflower - R
Zondervan/Trade - R
Zondervan/Academic

CONTROVERSIAL ISSUES

Baker Books - R
Bantam Books
Brentwood - R
Chalice Press
Chosen Books
Cliffside Publishing
Companion Press - R
Cross Cultural
Crossway Books
Element Books - R
Forward Movement - R
Franciscan Univ. Press - R
HarperSanFrancisco - R
Harvest House
Howard Publishing - R
Hunt & Thorpe
Huntington House - R
ICAN Press - R
InterVarsity Press
Lifetime Books - R
LuraMedia
Moorings
Morehouse - R
Nelson, Thomas - R
New Society - R

Our Sunday Visitor - R
Pilgrim Press
Pillar Books - R
Presbyterian/Reformed - R
Prescott Press - R
PROBE Ministries
Proclaim Publishing
Questar - R
Regnery Publishing - R
Review & Herald - R
Still Waters Revival - R
Starburst Publishers
Trinity Foundation - R
Tyler Press - R
Victory House - R
Windflower - R
Winston-Derek - R
Wood Lake Books - R

COOKBOOKS

Bantam Books
Blue Dolphin - R
Brentwood - R
Fairway Press - R
Herald Press
ICAN Press - R
Moorings
Morrow & Company, Wm.
Mt. Olive College Press
Our Sunday Visitor - R
Prescott Press - R
Proclaim Publishing
Rainbow Books (FL)
Son-Rise
Southern Baptist Press - R
Starburst Publishers
TEACH Services - R
Tyler Press - R
University of NC Press
Victory House - R

COUNSELING AIDS

Accent Publications
ACTA Publications
Baker Books - R
Bethany House
Brentwood - R
Brown-ROA
Chosen Books
Christopher Publishing
Concordia
Dimension Books - R
Eerdmans Publishing - R
Emerald Books
Fairway Press - R
Franciscan Press - R
Good Book
Gospel Publishing
HarperSanFrancisco - R
Haworth Press - R
Hensley, Virgil W. - R
Herald Press
Howard Publishing - R
ICAN Press - R
InterVarsity Press
Judson Press - R
Kregel - R
Life Cycle Books - R
Liguori Publications
Living Flame Press
Loyola Univ. Press - R
LuraMedia
Morehouse - R
Neibauer Press - R
Nelson, Thomas - R
New Leaf Press - R
Pastor's Choice
Pilgrim Press
Pillar Books - R
Presbyterian/Reformed - R
Prescott Press - R
Proclaim Publishing
Questar - R

Rainbow Books (FL)
Rainbow's End
Regal Books
Resource Publications
Resurrection Press - R
Review & Herald - R
Servant - R
Shining Star
Son-Rise
Southern Baptist Press - R
Trinity Press Intl. - R
Tyler Press - R
Tyndale House - R
VESTA
Victory House - R
Warner Press
Westminster/John Knox
W.R.S. Publishing - R
Zondervan/Trade - R
Zondervan/Academic

CULTS/OCCULT

AMG Publishers - R
Baker Books - R
Bantam Books
Bethany House
Bridge Publishing - R
Broadman & Holman
Christian Lit. Crusade - R
Christopher Publishing
Concordia
Crossway Books
HarperSanFrancisco - R
Harvard House
Harvest House
Howard Publishing - R
Huntington House - R
InterVarsity Press
Kregel - R
Living Flame Press
Morning Star Press - R
Nelson, Thomas - R

New Hope - R
New Leaf Press - R
Open Court - R
Our Sunday Visitor - R
Pilgrim Press
Presbyterian/Reformed - R
Prescott Press - R
PROBE Ministries - R
Proclaim Publishing
Revell, Fleming H.
Review & Herald - R
Servant - R
Son-Rise
Starburst Publishers
TEACH Services - R
Trinity Press Intl. - R
Tyler Press - R
Tyndale House - R
VESTA
Victory House - R
Woman's Miss. Union - R
Zondervan/Trade - R
Zondervan/Academic

CURRENT/SOCIAL ISSUES

ACTA Publications
Alba House - R
Alba House - R
AMG Publishers - R
Baker Books - R
Barclay Press - R
Bethany House
Bethel Publishing - R
Brentwood - R
Bridge Publishing - R
Bristol House - R
Chalice Press
Chosen Books
Christian Univ. Press - R
Christopher Publishing
Collier-Macmillan
Companion Press - R

Concordia
Cornell Univ. Press - R
Cross Cultural
Crossway Books
DaBaR Services - R
Eerdmans Publishing - R
Element Books - R
Fairway Press - R
Forward Movement - R
Franciscan Press - R
Friendship Press
HarperSanFrancisco - R
Haworth Press - R
Herald Press
Horizon House - R
Howard Publishing - R
Huntington House - R
ICAN Press - R
InterVarsity Press
Judson Press - R
Kregel - R
Life Cycle Books - R
Lifetime Books - R
Liguori Publications
Loyola Univ. Press - R
LuraMedia
Moorings
Morehouse - R
Nelson, Thomas - R
New Hope - R
New Society - R
Our Sunday Visitor - R
Oxford University
Paulist Press
Pilgrim Press
Presbyterian/Reformed - R
Prescott Press - R
Proclaim Publishing
Questar - R
Regal Books
Regnery Publishing - R
Resurrection Press - R
Review & Herald - R

Servant - R
Shaw Publishers, Harold - R
Son-Rise
Starburst Publishers
Star Song - R
Still Waters Revival - R
Trinity Press Intl. - R
Tyler Press - R
Tyndale House - R
University Press/America - R
Upper Room Books - R
VESTA
Victor Books - R
Victory House - R
Westminster/John Knox
Windflower - R
Woman's Miss. Union - R
Zondervan/Trade - R

CURRICULUM

Accent Bible Curric.
Christian Ed Pub.
Christian Univ. Press - R
Christopher Publishing
Church Growth Inst.
Companion Press - R
Concordia
CSS Publishing
Editorial Evangelica
Educational Ministries
Franciscan Press - R
Friends United Press - R
Group's Hands-On
Hensley, Virgil W. - R
Master Books - R
Morehouse - R
New Society - R
Novalis
Our Sunday Visitor - R
Regal Books
Scripture Press
Trinity Foundation - R

Tyler Press - R
United Church Press
Wellness
Winston-Derek - R
Wood Lake Books - R

DEVOTIONAL BOOKS

Alba House - R
Augsburg Fortress - R
Barbour & Co. - R
Barclay Press - R
Bible Discovery
Brentwood - R
Bridge Publishing - R
Broadman & Holman
Chosen Books
Chrjstian Classics
Christian Lit. Crusade - R
Christopher Publishing
Companion Press - R
Concordia
Contemporary Drama Service
CSS Publishing
DaBaR Services - R
Eerdmans Publishing - R
Emerald Books
Fairway Press - R
Forward Movement - R
Gibson, C.R. - R
Gilgal
Gospel Publishing
HarperSanFrancisco - R
Harrison House - R
Harvest House
Herald Press
Honor Books
Howard Publishing - R
Hunt & Thorpe
ICAN Press - R
Kindred Press (juv)
Kregel - R
Liguori Publications

Living Flame Press
Loyola Univ. Press - R
Moody Press
Moorings
Morehouse - R
Morning Star Press - R
Nelson, Thomas - R
New Leaf Press - R
Novalis
OMF Books
Our Sunday Visitor - R
Pacific Press
Paraclete Press - R
Praxis Institute - R
Proclaim Publishing
Questar - R
Regal Books
Resurrection Press - R
Revell, Fleming H.
Review & Herald - R
St. Paul Books - R
Servant - R
Sheed & Ward - R
Sheer Joy! Press
Son-Rise
Standard (for kids)
Starburst Publishers
Star Song - R
TEACH Services - R
Trinity Press Intl. - R
Tyler Press - R
Tyndale House - R
United Church Pub.
United Methodist
Upper Room Books - R
VESTA
Victor Books - R
Victory House - R
Warner Press
Westminster/John Knox
World Bible - R
Zondervan/Trade - R

DISCIPLESHIP

Accent Publications
AMG Publishers - R
Baker Books - R
Barclay Press - R
Bethany House
Brentwood - R
Bridge Publishing - R
Bristol House - R
Broadman & Holman
Chalice Press
Chosen Books
Christian Classics
Christian Lit. Crusade - R
Christopher Publishing
Church Growth Inst.
Companion Press - R
Concordia
Creation House
Crossway Books
DaBaR Services - R
Discipleship Resources
Eerdmans Publishing - R
Fairway Press - R
Gospel Publishing
HarperSanFrancisco - R
Harvest House
Hensley, Virgil W. - R
Herald Press
Horizon House - R
Howard Publishing - R
Huntington House - R
ICAN Press - R
InterVarsity Press
Judson Press - R
Kindred Press
Kregel - R
Liguori Publications
Living Flame Press
LuraMedia
Moody Press
Moorings

Morehouse - R
Neibauer Press - R
Nelson, Thomas - R
New Hope - R
New Leaf Press - R
Our Sunday Visitor - R
Paraclete Press - R
Pillar Books- R
Presbyterian/Reformed - R
Proclaim Publishing
Questar - R
Regal Books
Regnery Publishing - R
Revell, Fleming H.
Review & Herald - R
Roper Press - R
St. Paul Books - R
Scarecrow Press
Servant - R
Sheed & Ward - R
Southern Baptist Press - R
Tyler Press - R
Tyndale House - R
United Church Press
VESTA
Victor Books - R
Victory House - R
Westminster/John Knox
Zondervan/Trade - R

DIVORCE

AMG Publishers - R
Ave Maria Press
Baker Books - R
Bantam Books
Bethany House
Brentwood - R
Bridge Publishing - R
Broadman & Holman
Chalice Press
Christopher Publishing
Collier-Macmillan

Companion Press - R
Concordia
Discipleship Resources
Forward Movement - R
Franciscan Press - R
Gilgal
Gospel Publishing
HarperSanFrancisco - R
Harvest House
Haworth Press - R
Herald Press
Howard Publishing - R
Huntington House - R
ICAN Press - R
InterVarsity Press
Kregel - R
Liguori Publications
Living Flame Press
LuraMedia
Morehouse - R
Nelson, Thomas - R
Presbyterian/Reformed - R
Proclaim Publishing
Questar - R
Resurrection Press - R
Review & Herald - R
Servant - R
Sheer Joy! Press
Southern Baptist Press - R
Starburst Publishers
TEACH Services - R
Tyler Press - R
Tyndale House - R
VESTA
Victor Books - R
Victory House - R
Zondervan/Trade - R

DOCTRINAL

AMG Publishers - R
Ave Maria Press
Baker Books - R

Bethany House
Brentwood - R
Broadman & Holman
Christian Classics
Christian Lit. Crusade - R
Christian Univ. Press - R
Christopher Publishing
Church Growth Inst.
Collier-Macmillan
Concordia
Cross Cultural
Crossway Books
Discipleship Resources
Eerdmans Publishing - R
Fairway Press - R
Franciscan Press - R
Franciscan Univ. Press - R
Friends United Press - R
Gospel Publishing
HarperSanFrancisco - R
Harrison House - R
Howard Publishing - R
ICAN Press - R
InterVarsity Press
Kregel - R
Liguori Publications
Liturgical Press
Living Flame Press
Loyola Univ. Press - R
Nelson, Thomas - R
Novalis
Omega Publications
OMF Books
Our Sunday Visitor - R
Paulist Press
Pillar Books - R
Praxis Institute - R
Presbyterian/Reformed - R
Proclaim Publishing
Questar - R
Regnery Publishing - R
Review & Herald - R
St. Bede's - R

St. Paul Books - R
Scarecrow Press
Sheed & Ward - R
Southern Baptist Press - R
Star Song - R
Still Waters Revival - R
Trinity Foundation - R
Tyler Press - R
Tyndale House - R
VESTA
Victor Books - R
Westminster/John Knox
World Bible - R
Zondervan/Trade - R

DRAMA

AD Players
Baker Books - R
Brentwood - R
Chalice Press
Concordia
Contemporary Drama Service
CSS Publishing
Fairway Press - R
ICAN Press - R
Lillenas
Loyola Univ. Press - R
Meriwether - R
Proclaim Publishing
Resource Publications
Sheer Joy! Press
Shining Star
Southern Baptist Press - R
Standard
Tyler Press - R

ECONOMICS

Brentwood - R
Broadman & Holman
Christopher Publishing
Collier-Macmillan

Concordia
Dimension Books - R
Eerdmans Publishing - R
Franciscan Press - R
HarperSanFrancisco - R
Haworth Press - R
Howard Publishing - R
Huntington House - R
Nelson, Thomas - R
New Society - R
Oxford University
Paulist Press
Pilgrim Press - R
Proclaim Publishing
Regnery Publishing - R
Review & Herald - R
Trinity Foundation - R
Trinity Press Intl. - R
Tyler Press - R
University Press/America - R
W.R.S. Publishing - R
Zondervan/Trade - R

ENVIRONMENTAL ISSUES

Bantam Books
Blue Dolphin - R
Broadman & Holman
Chalice Press
Chosen Books
Christopher Publishing
Concordia
Eerdmans Publishing - R
Element Books - R
Forward Movement - R
Franciscan Press - R
Friendship Press
HarperSanFrancisco - R
Huntington House - R
InterVarsity Press
Liguori Publications
Morehouse - R
New Society - R

Oxford University
Paulist Press
Pilgrim Press
Prescott Press - R
Proclaim Publishing
Questar - R
Rainbow Books (FL)
Regnery Publishing - R
Resurrection Press - R
Shining Star
Southern Baptist Press - R
Starburst Publishers
Tyler Press - R
University Press/America - R
Victor Books - R
W.R.S. Publishing - R
Zondervan/Trade - R

ETHICS

Alba House - R
Baker Books - R
Bantam Books
Bethany House
Brentwood - R
Broadman & Holman
Chalice Press
Christian Classics
Christian Univ. Press - R
Christopher Publishing
Collier-Macmillan
Companion Press - R
Concordia
Cornell Univ. Press - R
Creation House
Cross Cultural
Crossway Books
Eerdmans Publishing - R
Forward Movement - R
Franciscan Press - R
Franciscan Univ. Press - R
Friendship Press
HarperSanFrancisco - R

Haworth Press - R
Herald Press
Howard Publishing - R
Huntington House - R
ICAN Press - R
InterVarsity Press
Life Cycle Books - R
Lifetime Books - R
Liguori Publications
Loyola Univ. Press - R
Morehouse - R
Nelson, Thomas - R
New Leaf Press - R
New Society - R
Omega Publications
Open Court - R
Our Sunday Visitor - R
Oxford University
Paulist Press
Pilgrim Press
Presbyterian/Reformed - R
PROBE Ministries
Proclaim Publishing
Questar - R
Regnery Publishing - R
Resource Publications
Review & Herald - R
St. Anthony Messenger - R
St. Paul Books - R
Sheed & Ward - R
Star Song - R
Still Waters Revival - R
Trinity Foundation - R
Trinity Press Intl. - R
Tyler Press - R
University Press/America - R
VESTA
Victor Books - R
Wadsworth - R
Westminster/John Knox
Windflower - R
Yale Univ. Press - R
Zondervan/Trade - R

Zondervan/Academic

ETHNIC BOOKS

Augsburg Fortress - R
August House
Baker Books - R (black)
Chalice Press
Christian Univ. Press - R
College Press - R
Concordia
Cross Cultural
DaBaR Services - R
Discipleship Resources
Eerdmans Publishing - R
Editorial Evangelica
Forward Movement - R
Franciscan Univ. Press - R
Gospel Publishing
Guernica Editions - R
Herald Press
Judson Press - R
Kregel - R
Liguori Publications
Living Sacrifice - R
MML Company (children's)
National Baptist - R
Pacific Press (some)
Pelican Publishing - R
Pilgrim Press
Proclaim Publishing
St. Anthony Messenger - R
Star Song - R
Tyndale House
United Church Press
United Methodist
VESTA Publications
Winston-Derek - R
Woman's Miss. Union - R
World Bible - R
W.R.S. Publishing - R

EVANGELISM/WITNESSING

Accent Publications
Baker Books - R
Bethany House
Bethel Publishing - R
Brentwood - R
Bridge Publishing - R
Bristol House - R
Broadman & Holman
Chalice Press
Chosen Books
Christian Lit. Crusade - R
Christopher Publishing
Church Growth Inst.
Collier-Macmillan
Companion Press - R
Concordia
Creation House
Crossway Books
Discipleship Resources
Editorial Evangelica
Eerdmans Publishing - R
Fairway Press - R
Forward Movement - R
Franciscan Press - R
Gospel Publishing
HarperSanFrancisco - R
Harrison House - R
Hensley, Virgil W. - R
Herald Press
Horizon House - R
Howard Publishing - R
Huntington House - R
ICAN Press - R
InterVarsity Press
Jews for Jesus (Jewish)
Judson Press - R
Kregel - R
Langmarc
Liguori Publications
Morehouse - R
Morning Star Press - R

Neibauer Press - R
Nelson, Thomas - R
New Hope - R
New Leaf Press - R
Omega Publications
Pillar Books - R
Presbyterian/Reformed - R
Proclaim Publishing
Questar - R
Regal Books
Resurrection Press - R
Review & Herald - R
Sheer Joy! Press
Son-Rise
Southern Baptist Press - R
Star Song - R
Still Waters Revival - R
TEACH Services - R
Tyler Press - R
Tyndale House - R
United Church Press
VESTA
Victor Books - R
Victory House - R
Warner Press
Westminster/John Knox
Woman's Miss. Union - R
Zondervan/Trade - R
Zondervan/Academic

EXPOSÉS

Brentwood - R
Harvest House
Huntington House - R
Lifetime Books - R
Nelson, Thomas - R
Open Court - R
Prescott Press - R
Questar - R
Regnery Publishing - R
Southern Baptist Press - R
Starburst Publishers

Trinity Foundation - R
Tyler Press - R
Zondervan/Trade - R

FAMILY LIFE

ACTA Publications
Alba House - R
AMG Publishers - R
Augsburg Fortress - R
Ave Maria Press
Baker Books - R
Bantam Books
Bethany House
Bethel Publishing - R
Bosco Multimedia, Don
Brentwood - R
Broadman & Holman
Chalice Press
Christian Classics
Christopher Publishing
Church Growth Inst.
College Press - R
Collier-Macmillan
Companion Press - R
Concordia
Crossway Books
Discipleship Resources
Eerdmans Publishing - R
Emerald Books
Fairway Press - R
Focus on the Family - R
Forward Movement - R
Garborg's
Gibson, C.R. - R
Gospel Publishing
HarperSanFrancisco - R
Harrison House - R
Harvest House
Haworth Press - R
Hensley, Virgil W. - R
Herald Press
Honor Books

Howard Publishing - R
Huntington House - R
ICAN Press - R
InterVarsity Press
Kindred Press
Kregel - R
Langmarc
Life Cycle Books - R
LifeJourney Books
Liguori Publications
Living Flame Press
LuraMedia
Moody Press
Moorings
Morehouse - R
Nelson, Thomas - R
New Hope - R
New Leaf Press - R
Novalis
Our Sunday Visitor - R
Pelican Publishing - R
Pillar Books - R
Presbyterian/Reformed - R
Prescott Press - R
PROBE Ministries (values)
Proclaim Publishing
Questar - R
Rainbow Books (FL)
Rainbow's End
Regal Books
Regnery Publishing - R
Resurrection Press - R
Revell, Fleming H.
Review & Herald - R
St. Paul Books - R
Servant - R
Shaw Publishers, Harold - R
Shining Star
Son-Rise
Southern Baptist Press - R
Starburst Publishers
Star Song - R
Still Waters Revival - R

TEACH Services - R
Tyler Press - R
Tyndale House - R
United Methodist
Upper Room Books - R
VESTA
Victor Books - R - R
Warner Press
Wellness
Westminster/John Knox
Wood Lake Books - R
W.R.S. Publishing - R
Zondervan/Trade - R

FICTION: ADULT

Baker Books - R
Barbour & Co. - R
Bethany House
Bethel Publishing - R
Bridge Publishing - R
Cameron Press
Christian Classics
Christian Publications - R
Christopher Publishing
Companion Press - R
Cornerstone Press
Creation House
Crossway Books
Emerald Books
Friendship Press
Friends United Press - R
Harvest House
Heartsong Presents
Herald Press
Horizon House - R
Howard Publishing - R
ICAN Press - R
InterVarsity Press
LifeJourney Books
Moody Press
Moorings
Morrow & Company, Wm.

Mt. Olive College Press
Nazarene Pub. House
Nelson, Thomas - R
Pacific Press (true)
Proclaim Publishing
Questar - R
Regency Press
Revell, Fleming H.
Roper Press - R
Servant - R
Sheer Joy! Press
Starburst Publishers
Star Song - R
VESTA
Victor Books - R
Victory House - R
Windflower - R
Wood Lake Books - R
Zondervan/Trade - R

FICTION: ADVENTURE

Bantam Books
Bethany House
Bethel Publishing - R
Brentwood - R
Broadman & Holman
Christian Publications - R
Christopher Publishing
Companion Press - R
Concordia
Crossway Books
Eerdmans Publishing - R
Emerald Books
ICAN Press - R
LifeJourney Books
Moody Press
Moorings
Morehouse - R
Morris, Joshua
Morrow & Company, Wm. (juv)
Nelson, Thomas - R
Omega Publications

Prescott Press - R
Proclaim Publishing
Questar - R
Regency Press
Southern Baptist Press - R
Starburst Publishers
Victor Books - R
Victory House - R
Zondervan/Trade - R

FICTION: ALLEGORY

Bridge Publishing - R
Christopher Publishing
Creation House
Eerdmans Publishing - R
ICAN Press - R
Morris, Joshua
Morehouse - R
Proclaim Publishing
Questar - R
Star Song - R
Victory House - R
Wood Lake Books - R

FICTION: BIBLICAL

Bethel Publishing - R
Brentwood - R
Bridge Publishing - R
Christopher Publishing
College Press - R
Companion Press - R
Concordia
Creation House
CSS Publishing
Eerdmans Publishing - R
Fairway Press - R
Friends United Press - R
Herald Press
ICAN Press - R
Living Flame Press
Morehouse - R

Moorings
Morris, Joshua
Nazarene Pub. House
Proclaim Publishing
Questar - R
Regency Press
Sheer Joy! Press
Shining Star (juv)
Southern Baptist Press - R
Standard
Tyndale House - R
United Church Press
Victory House - R
Windflower - R
Wood Lake Books - R
Zondervan/Trade - R

FICTION: CONTEMPORARY

Baker Books - R
Bantam Books
Bethany House
Bethel Publishing - R
Brentwood - R
Broadman & Holman
Christian Publications - R
Christopher Publishing
Companion Press - R
Concordia
Creation House
Crossway Books
Eerdmans Publishing - R
Gibson, C.R. - R
HarperSanFrancisco - R
Herald Press
ICAN Press - R
Kindred Press
LifeJourney Books
Living Flame Press
Moorings
Morehouse - R
Morris, Joshua

Mt. Olive College Press
National Baptist - R
Nelson, Thomas - R
Proclaim Publishing
Questar - R
Regency Press
Southern Baptist Press - R
Standard
Star Song - R
Victor Books - R
Victory House - R
Windflower - R
Wood Lake Books - R
Zondervan/Trade - R

FICTION: FANTASY

Christopher Publishing
Companion Press - R
Eerdmans Publishing - R
ICAN Press - R
InterVarsity Press
Proclaim Publishing
Questar - R
Starburst Publishers
Victor Books - R
Victory House - R
Zondervan/Trade - R

FICTION: FRONTIER

Bantam Books
Bethany House
Bethel Publishing - R
Brentwood - R
Broadman & Holman
Christian Publications - R
Christopher Publishing
Eerdmans Publishing - R
ICAN Press - R
Moody Press
Moorings
Nazarene Pub. House

Nelson, Thomas - R
Proclaim Publishing
Questar - R
Regency Press
Roper Press - R
Servant - R
Southern Baptist Press - R
Victor Books - R
Victory House - R
Zondervan/Trade - R

FICTION: FRONTIER/ROMANCE

Bantam Books
Bethany House
Bethel Publishing - R
Brentwood - R
Christian Publications - R
Eerdmans Publishing - R
Heartsong Presents
ICAN Press - R
Moody Press
Nelson, Thomas - R
Pacific Press (true)
Proclaim Publishing
Questar - R
Regency Press
Revell, Fleming H.
Roper Press - R
Servant - R
Southern Baptist Press - R
Starburst Publishers
Victory House - R
Zondervan/Trade - R

FICTION: HISTORICAL

Bantam Books
Bethany House
Bethel Publishing - R
Brentwood - R
Broadman & Holman

Christian Publications - R
Christopher Publishing
Companion Press - R
Cornerstone Press
Crossway Books
Eerdmans Publishing - R
Friends United Press - R
HarperSanFrancisco - R
Herald Press
Horizon House - R
ICAN Press - R
LifeJourney Books
Misty Hill Press
Moody Press
Moorings
Morehouse - R
Morris, Joshua
Morrow & Company, Wm.
Nazarene Pub. House
Nelson, Thomas - R
Proclaim Publishing
Questar - R
Regency Press
Servant - R
Son-Rise
Southern Baptist Press - R
Starburst Publishers
Star Song - R
Victor Books - R
Victory House - R
Windflower - R
Zondervan/Trade - R

FICTION: HISTORICAL/ROMANCE

Bantam Books
Bethany House
Bethel Publishing - R
Brentwood - R
Christian Publications - R
Creation House
Crossway Books

Eerdmans Publishing - R
Emerald Books
Friends United Press - R
Harvest House
Heartsong Presents
Horizon House - R
ICAN Press - R
LifeJourney Books
Moody Press
Nazarene Pub. House
Nelson, Thomas - R
Proclaim Publishing
Questar - R
Regency Press
Revell, Fleming H.
Servant - R
Southern Baptist Press - R
Starburst Publishers
Victory House - R
Zondervan/Trade - R

FICTION: HUMOR

Bethel Publishing - R
Bridge Publishing - R
Broadman & Holman
Christian Publications - R
Christopher Publishing
Companion Press - R
Emerald Books
Fairway Press - R
ICAN Press - R
InterVarsity Press
LifeJourney Books
Morehouse - R
Morris, Joshua
Nazarene Pub. House
Nelson, Thomas - R
Prescott Press - R
Proclaim Publishing
Questar - R
Sheer Joy! Press
Standard

Star Song - R
Victor Books - R
Victory House - R

FICTION: JUVENILE
(Ages 8-12)

AMG Publishers - R
Bay Public., Mel - R
Bethany House
Bethel Publishing - R
Bob Jones - R
Broadman & Holman
Christian Publications - R
Concordia
Crossway Books
Eerdmans Publishing - R
Emerald Books
Fairway Press - R
Friendship Press
Friends United Press - R
Gold 'n' Honey
Herald Press
Horizon House - R
ICAN Press - R
InterVarsity Press
Kindred Press
Misty Hill Press
Moody Press
Morehouse - R
Morris, Joshua
Nelson, Thomas - R
Pacific Press (true)
Prescott Press - R
Proclaim Publishing
Questar - R
Roper Press - R
St. Paul Books - R
Sheer Joy! Press
Shining Star
Tyler Press - R
United Church Press
Upper Room Books - R

Victor Books - R
Victory House - R
Zondervan/Trade - R

FICTION: LITERARY

Baker Books - R
Christian Publications - R
Christopher Publishing
Gibson, C.R. - R
Guernica Editions - R
Herald Press
ICAN Press - R
InterVarsity Press
Moorings
Morrow & Company, Wm.
Mt. Olive College Press
Pelican Publishing - R
Proclaim Publishing
Questar - R
Star Song - R
VESTA
Victor Books - R
Victory House - R
Windflower - R

FICTION: MYSTERY

Baker Books - R
Bantam Books
Bethany House
Bethel Publishing - R
Broadman & Holman
Christian Publications - R
Christopher Publishing
Companion Press - R
Concordia
Crossway Books
ICAN Press - R
InterVarsity Press
LifeJourney Books
Moody Press
Moorings

Morehouse - R
Morrow & Company, Wm.
Nelson, Thomas - R
Prescott Press - R
Proclaim Publishing
Questar - R
Regency Press
Roper Press - R
Servant - R
Victor Books - R
Victory House - R
Zondervan/Trade - R

FICTION: MYSTERY/ROMANCE

Bantam Books
Bethany House
Bethel Publishing - R
Brentwood - R
Christian Publications - R
Heartsong Presents
ICAN Press - R
LifeJourney Books
Moody Press
Nelson, Thomas - R
Proclaim Publishing
Questar - R
Regency Press
Revell, Fleming H.
Roper Press - R
Servant - R
Southern Baptist Press - R
Victory House - R

FICTION: PLAYS

Bay Public., Mel - R
Brentwood - R
Creatively Yours
CSS Publishing
Eldridge Publishing (& musicals)
Fairway Press - R

Lillenas
Meriwether - R
Mt. Olive College Press
National Baptist - R
Pacific Theatre - R
Proclaim Publishing
Resource Publications
Sheer Joy! Press
Shining Star (juvenile)
Southern Baptist Press - R
Standard
Victory House - R

FICTION: ROMANCE

Christian Publications - R
Companion Press - R
Crossway Books
Heartsong Presents
ICAN Press - R
LifeJourney Books
Morrow & Company, Wm.
Nelson, Thomas - R
Proclaim Publishing
Regency Press
Sheer Joy! Press
Starburst Publishers
Victory House - R
Zondervan/Trade - R

FICTION: SCIENCE FICTION

Bethel Publishing - R
Christopher Publishing
Companion Press - R
ICAN Press - R
InterVarsity Press
Morrow & Company, Wm.
Nelson, Thomas - R
Prescott Press - R
Proclaim Publishing
Starburst Publishers

Victory House - R

FICTION: SHORT STORY COLLECTION

AMG Publishers - R
Christopher Publishing
Concordia
CSS Publishing
Emerald Books
Gibson, C.R. - R
Herald Press
ICAN Press - R
Morehouse - R
National Baptist - R
Proclaim Publishing
Victory House - R

FICTION: TEEN/YOUNG ADULT

AMG Publishers - R
Bay Public., Mel - R
Bethany House
Bob Jones - R
Christian Publications - R
Companion Press - R
Crossway Books
Eerdmans Publishing - R
Emerald Books
Fairway Press - R
Friendship Press
Herald Press
Horizon House - R
LifeJourney Books
Living Flame Press
Moody Press
Moorings
Morris, Joshua
Nelson, Thomas - R
Pacific Press (true)
Proclaim Publishing
St. Paul Books - R

Sheer Joy! Press
Victory House - R
Zondervan/Trade - R

GAMES/CRAFTS

Bay Public., Mel - R
Brown-ROA (religious)
Concordia
Contemporary Drama Service
CSS Publishing
Educational Ministries
Garborg's
Group Publishing
Harvest House
Meriwether - R
Morehouse - R
Our Sunday Visitor - R
Proclaim Publishing
Rainbow Books (CA)
St. Paul Books - R
Shining Star
Standard
TEACH Services - R
Tyler Press - R
United Methodist
Zondervan/Trade - R

GIFT BOOKS

Augsburg Fortress - R
Baker Books - R
Berrie, Russ
Bridge Publishing - R
Calligraphy Collection
Christopher Publishing
Companion Press - R
Contemporary Drama Service
Current Inc.
Eerdmans Publishing - R (art)
Element Books - R
Franciscan Press - R
Garborg's

Gibson, C.R. - R
HarperSanFrancisco - R
Harvest House
Herald Press
Honor Books
Howard Publishing - R
Hunt & Thorpe
Image Craft
Living Flame Press
Mailaways
Manhattan Greeting Card
MML Company
Moorings
Morehouse - R.
Morning Star Press - R
Mt. Olive College Press
Nelson, Thomas - R
New Leaf Press - R
Painted Hearts & Friends
Paraclete Press - R
Proclaim Publishing
Questar - R
Regnery Publishing - R
Resurrection Press - R
Revell, Fleming H.
St. Paul Books - R
Starburst Publishers
Star Song - R
Sunrise Publications
United Methodist
Upper Room Books - R
Victor Books - R
Victory House - R
Warner Press
Westminster/John Knox
Zondervan/Trade - R

GROUP STUDY BOOKS

Alban Institute
AMG Publishers - R
Baker Books - R
Bosco Multimedia, Don

Brentwood - R
Chalice Press
Christopher Publishing
Church Growth Inst.
Companion Press - R
Concordia
DaBaR Services - R
Discipleship Resources
Fairway Press - R
Gospel Publishing
HarperSanFrancisco - R
Hensley, Virgil W. - R
Herald Press
Howard Publishing - R
Judson Press - R
Langmarc
Liguori Publications
LuraMedia
Morehouse - R
Morning Star Press - R
Nelson, Thomas - R
New Hope - R
New Leaf Press - R
Our Sunday Visitor - R
Paraclete Press - R
Presbyterian/Reformed - R
Proclaim Publishing
Questar - R
Regnery Publishing - R
Resource Publications
Review & Herald - R
St. Anthony Messenger - R
Sheed & Ward - R
Southern Baptist Press - R
Standard
Star Song - R
Tyler Press - R
United Methodist
VESTA
Victor Books - R
Victory House - R
Woman's Miss. Union - R
World Bible - R

Zondervan/Trade - R

HEALING

Ave Maria Press
Baker Books - R
Bantam Books
Bethany House
Bethel Publishing - R
Brentwood - R
Bridge Publishing - R
Chosen Books
Christian Classics
Christian Lit. Crusade - R
Christopher Publishing
Companion Press - R
Concordia
Creation House
DaBaR Services - R
Eerdmans Publishing - R
Elder Books - R
Element Books - R
Fairway Press - R
Gilgal
Good Book
Gospel Publishing
HarperSanFrancisco - R
Harrison House - R
Haworth Press - R
Howard Publishing - R
ICAN Press - R
InterVarsity Press
Lifetime Books - R
Liguori Publications
Living Flame Press
Loyola Univ. Press - R
LuraMedia
Moorings
Morehouse - R
Morning Star Press - R
Nelson, Thomas - R
Our Sunday Visitor - R
Pillar Books - R

Prescott Press - R
Proclaim Publishing
Questar - R
Rainbow's End
Regnery Publishing - R
Resource Publications
Resurrection Press - R
Review & Herald - R
St. Paul Books - R
Servant - R
Son-Rise
Southern Baptist Press - R
Starburst Publishers
TEACH Services - R
Tyler Press - R
VESTA
Victory House - R
W.R.S. Publishing - R

HEALTH

Alba House - R
Baker Books - R
Bantam Books
Bethany House
Bethel Publishing - R
Blue Dolphin - R
Bob Jones - R
Brentwood - R
Broadman & Holman
Christopher Publishing
Concordia
Eerdmans Publishing - R
Elder Books - R
Element Books - R
Fairway Press - R
Good Book
HarperSanFrancisco - R
Howard Publishing - R
Huntington House - R
ICAN Press - R
InterVarsity Press
Life Cycle Books - R

Lifetime Books - R
Loyola Univ. Press - R
LuraMedia
Moorings
Morehouse - R
Nelson, Thomas - R
Omega Publications
Prescott Press - R
Proclaim Publishing
Rainbow Books (FL)
Regnery Publishing - R
Review & Herald - R
Son-Rise
Southern Baptist Press - R
Starburst Publishers
TEACH Services - R
Tyler Press - R
VESTA
Victory House - R
Wellness
W.R.S. Publishing - R
Zondervan/Trade - R

HISTORICAL

Bantam Books
Bethany House
Blue Dolphin - R
Bob Jones - R
Brentwood - R
Catholic Univ./America - R
Chalice Press
Christian Classics
Christian Univ. Press - R
Christopher Publishing
Cistercian - R
Cliffside Publishing
College Press - R
Concordia
Cornell Univ. Press - R
Cross Cultural
Custom Communications
Dimension Books - R

Eerdmans Publishing - R
Element Books - R
Franciscan Press - R
Friends United Press - R
Good Book
HarperSanFrancisco - R
Harrison House - R
Huntington House - R
ICAN Press - R
InterVarsity Press
Loyola Univ. Press - R
Morehouse - R
Morning Star Press - R
Morrow & Company, Wm.
Nelson, Thomas - R
Omega Publications
Our Sunday Visitor - R
Oxford University
Pillar Books - R
Prescott Press - R
Proclaim Publishing
Regnery Publishing - R
Review & Herald - R
St. Bede's - R
Scarecrow Press
Seaside Press
Son-Rise
Southern Baptist Press - R
Star Song - R
Still Waters Revival - R
TEACH Services - R
Trinity Foundation - R
Trinity Press Intl. - R
Tyler Press - R
United Church Press
University of NC Press
VESTA
Victor Books - R
Victory House - R
Windflower - R
Winston-Derek - R
World Bible - R
Zondervan/Trade - R

Zondervan/Academic

HOW-TO/SELF-HELP

Accent Publications
ACTA Publications
Alba House - R
Augsburg Fortress - R
Ave Maria Press
Baker Books - R
Bantam Books
Bethany House
Bethel Publishing - R
Blue Dolphin - R
Brentwood - R
Bridge Publishing - R
Broadman & Holman
Brown-ROA
Chosen Books
Christopher Publishing
Cliffside Publishing
Collier-Macmillan
Companion Press - R
Concordia
DaBaR Services - R
Elder Books - R
Element Books - R
Emerald Books
Fairway Press - R
Focus on the Family - R
Gibson, C.R. - R
Gilgal
Good Book
HarperSanFrancisco - R
Harrison House - R
Harvest House
Hensley, Virgil W. - R
Herald Press
Honor Books
Howard Publishing - R
Huntington House - R
ICAN Press - R
InterVarsity Press

Lifetime Books - R
Liguori Publications
Living Flame Press
Loyola Univ. Press - R
Meriwether - R (how-to only)
Moorings
Morehouse - R
Morning Star Press - R
Morrow & Company, Wm.
Mt. Olive College Press
Nelson, Thomas - R
New Hope - R
New Leaf Press - R
Omega Publications
OMF Books
Our Sunday Visitor - R
Paraclete Press - R
Prescott Press - R
Proclaim Publishing
Rainbow Books (FL)
Rainbow's End
Resource Publications
Resurrection Press - R
Revell, Fleming H.
Review & Herald - R
St. Paul Books - R
Seaside Press
Servant - R
Shaw Publishers, Harold - R
Son-Rise
Southern Baptist Press - R
Standard
Starburst Publishers
Star Song - R
Still Waters Revival - R
Tyler Press - R
Tyndale House - R
United Methodist
Victor Books - R
Victory House - R
Westminster/John Knox
Woman's Miss. Union - R
Wood Lake Books - R

World Bible - R
Zondervan/Trade - R

HUMOR

August House
Bethel Publishing - R
Blue Dolphin - R
Bob Jones - R
Brentwood - R
Broadman & Holman
Christopher Publishing
Companion Press - R
Concordia
CSS Publishing
Dimension Books - R
Emerald Books
Fairway Press - R
Focus on the Family - R
Friends United Press - R
Gibson, C.R. - R
HarperSanFrancisco - R
Harvest House
Howard Publishing - R
Hunt & Thorpe
Huntington House - R
ICAN Press - R
InterVarsity Press
Liguori Publications
Living Flame Press
LuraMedia
Meriwether - R
Moody Press
Moorings
Morehouse - R
Nelson, Thomas - R
New Leaf Press - R
Prescott Press - R
Proclaim Publishing
Questar - R
Regnery Publishing - R
Review & Herald - R
Servant - R

Son-Rise
Southern Baptist Press - R
Star Song - R
Tyler Press - R
United Methodist
Victor Books - R
Wood Lake Books - R
Zondervan/Trade - R

INSPIRATIONAL

Augsburg Fortress - R
August House
Bantam Books
Bethany House
Bethel Publishing - R
Blue Dolphin - R
Brentwood - R
Bridge Publishing - R
Broadman & Holman
Christian Classics
Christian Lit. Crusade - R
Christopher Publishing
Companion Press - R
Concordia
Crossway Books
DaBaR Services - R
Elder Books - R
Element Books - R
Fairway Press - R
Focus on the Family - R
Franciscan Press - R
Friends United Press - R
Garborg's
Gibson, C.R. - R
Gilgal
Good Book
Gospel Publishing
HarperSanFrancisco - R
Herald Press
Honor Books
Howard Publishing - R
Huntington House - R

ICAN Press - R
ICS Publications - R
Langmarc
Lifetime Books - R
Liguori Publications
Living Flame Press
Loyola Univ. Press - R
LuraMedia
Moody Press
Moorings
Morehouse - R
Morning Star Press - R
Nazarene Pub. House
Nelson, Thomas - R
New Leaf Press - R
Our Sunday Visitor - R
Pacific Press
Paraclete Press - R
Pelican Publishing - R
Proclaim Publishing
Questar - R
Rainbow's End
Resurrection Press - R
Review & Herald - R
St. Anthony Messenger - R
St. Paul Books - R
Servant - R
Shaw Publishers, Harold - R
Sheed & Ward - R
Sheer Joy! Press
Shining Star
Son-Rise
Southern Baptist Press - R
Starburst Publishers
Star Song - R
TEACH Services - R
Tyler Press - R
Tyndale House - R
United Church Press
United Methodist
VESTA
Victor Books - R
Victory House - R

Wellness
Westminster/John Knox
Winston-Derek - R
Wood Lake Books - R
World Bible - R
Zondervan/Trade - R

*LEADERSHIP

Baker Books - R
Bethel Publishing - R
Bosco Multimedia, Don
Church Growth Inst.
College Press - R
Creation House
Discipleship Resources
Forward Movement - R
Gospel Publishing
Harvest House
Hensley, Virgil W. - R
Herald Press
Howard Publishing - R
Huntington House - R
ICAN Press - R
InterVarsity Press
Kregel - R
Lifetime Books - R
Moody Press
Moorings
Morehouse - R
New Leaf Press - R
Paulist Press
Regal Books
Standard
Tyler Press - R
Wood Lake Books - R

LITURGICAL STUDIES

Alba House - R
Ave Maria Press
American Cath. Press - R
Brentwood - R

Chalice Press
Christian Classics
Christian Univ. Press - R
Christopher Publishing
Concordia
Cornell Univ. Press - R
Cross Cultural
CSS Publishing
Discipleship Resources
Eerdmans Publishing - R
Fairway Press - R
Franciscan Press - R
Franciscan Univ. Press - R
HarperSanFrancisco - R
Hensley, Virgil W. - R
Liguori Publications
Living Flame Press
Morehouse - R
Morning Star Press - R
Novalis
Our Sunday Visitor - R
Oxford University
Pastoral Press
Paulist Press
Pillar Books - R
Presbyterian/Reformed - R
Proclaim Publishing
Resource Publications
St. Anthony Messenger - R
St. Bede's - R
Scarecrow Press
Sheed & Ward - R
Southern Baptist Press - R
Star Song - R
Tyler Press - R
VESTA
Westminster/John Knox

MARRIAGE

Alba House - R
AMG Publishers - R
Ave Maria Press

Baker Books - R
Bethany House
Bethel Publishing - R
Bantam Books
Bosco Multimedia, Don
Brentwood - R
Broadman & Holman
Chalice Press
Christian Classics
Christopher Publishing
College Press - R
Collier-Macmillan
Companion Press - R
Concordia
Crossway Books
CSS Publishing
DaBaR Services - R
Discipleship Resources
Eerdmans Publishing - R
Fairway Press - R
Focus on the Family - R
Forward Movement - R
Franciscan Press - R
Franciscan Univ. Press - R
Garborg's
Gibson, C.R. - R
Gospel Publishing
HarperSanFrancisco - R
Harrison House - R
Harvest House
Haworth Press - R
Hensley, Virgil W. - R
Herald Press
Honor Books
Howard Publishing - R
Huntington House - R
ICAN Press - R
InterVarsity Press
Kregel - R
LifeJourney Books
Lifetime Books - R
Liguori Publications
Living Flame Press

Loyola Univ. Press - R
LuraMedia
Moorings
Morehouse - R
Nelson, Thomas - R
New Leaf Press - R
Novalis
Pacific Press
Pillar Books - R
Presbyterian/Reformed - R
Proclaim Publishing
Questar - R
Rainbow Books (FL)
Regal Books
Resource Publications
Resurrection Press - R
Revell, Fleming H.
Review & Herald - R
St. Paul Books - R
Servant - R
Shaw Publishers, Harold - R
Sheed & Ward - R
Sheer Joy! Press
Southern Baptist Press - R
Starburst Publishers
Star Song - R
Still Waters Revival - R
Tyler Press - R
Tyndale House - R
United Methodist
Upper Room Books - R
VESTA
Victor Books - R
Victory House - R
Westminster/John Knox
Zondervan/Trade - R

MEN'S BOOKS

Augsburg Fortress - R
Baker Books - R
Bethel Publishing - R
Blue Dolphin - R

Chosen Books
Christopher Publishing
Concordia
Crossway Books
Discipleship Resources
Focus on the Family - R
Forward Movement - R
Franciscan Univ. Press - R
Gospel Publishing
Harvest House
Hensley, Virgil W. - R
Howard Publishing - R
Huntington House - R
ICAN Press - R
InterVarsity Press
Kregel - R
Moody Press
Moorings
Morehouse - R
Nelson, Thomas - R
New Leaf Press - R
Pacific Press
Pilgrim Press
Proclaim Publishing
Questar - R
Rainbow Books (FL)
Regal Books
Resource Publications
Resurrection Press - R
Shaw Publishers, Harold - R
SonRise
Starburst Publishers
Star Song - R
Tyler Press - R
United Church Press
United Methodist
Victor Books - R
Victory House - R
WinstonDerek - R
Wood Lake Books - R

MIRACLES

Baker Books - R
Bethel Publishing - R
Brentwood - R
Bridge Publishing - R
Broadman & Holman
Chosen Books
Christian Classics
Christopher Publishing
Fairway Press - R
Franciscan Press - R
Gospel Publishing
HarperSanFrancisco - R
Harrison House - R
Howard Publishing - R
ICAN Press - R
InterVarsity Press
Liguori Publications
Living Flame Press
LuraMedia
Moorings
Morning Star Press - R
Nelson, Thomas - R
Our Sunday Visitor - R
Pillar Books - R
Proclaim Publishing
Questar - R
Review & Herald - R - R
Servant - R
Southern Baptist Press - R
Tyler Press - R
VESTA
Victory House - R

MISSIONARY

Bethel Publishing - R
Bob Jones - R
Brentwood - R
Chosen Books
Christian Lit. Crusade - R
Christian Publications - R

Christian Univ. Press - R
Christopher Publishing
Church Growth Inst.
Concordia
Crossway Books
Eerdmans Publishing - R
Fairway Press - R
Franciscan Press - R
Friendship Press
Friends United Press - R
Gospel Publishing
HarperSanFrancisco - R
Horizon House - R
Howard Publishing - R
Huntington House - R
ICAN Press - R
InterVarsity Press
Liguori Publications
Nelson, Thomas - R
New Hope - R
OMF Books
Pillar Books - R
Prescott Press - R
Proclaim Publishing
Questar - R
Review & Herald - R
Southern Baptist Press - R
TEACH Services - R
Tyler Press - R
VESTA
Westminster/John Knox
Woman's Miss. Union - R
Zondervan/Academic

MONEY MANAGEMENT

Alban Institute
Baker Books - R
Barbour & Co. - R
Bethany House
Brentwood - R
Broadman & Holman
Christopher Publishing

Church Growth Inst.
Collier-Macmillan
Concordia
Fairway Press - R
Focus on the Family - R
HarperSanFrancisco - R
Harvest House
Haworth Press - R
Hensley, Virgil W. - R
Honor Books
Howard Publishing - R
Lifetime Books - R
Nelson, Thomas - R
New Leaf Press - R
Omega Publications
Pelican Publishing - R
Pillar Books - R
Prescott Press - R
Proclaim Publishing
Questar - R
Regnery Publishing - R
Review & Herald - R
Servant - R
Southern Baptist Press - R
Starburst Publishers
Tyler Press - R
Tyndale House - R
Victor Books - R
Victory House - R
Winston-Derek - R
Zondervan/Trade - R

MUSIC-RELATED BOOKS

American Cath. Press - R
Bay Public., Mel - R
Christian Media
Christopher Publishing
Companion Press - R
Concordia
Contemporary Drama Service
Cornell Univ. Press - R
Cornerstone Press

Dimension Books - R
Discipleship Resources
Eerdmans Publishing - R
HarperSanFrancisco - R
Hunt & Thorpe
Lifetime Books - R
Lillenas
Morehouse - R
Nelson, Thomas - R
Our Sunday Visitor - R
Pastoral Press
Pillar Books - R
Prescott Press - R
Proclaim Publishing
Star Song - R
Tyler Press - R
Wood Lake Books - R

*PAMPHLETS

American Cath. Press - R
Bosco Multimedia, Don
Christian Univ. Press - R
Editorial Evangelica
Forward Movement - R
Kindred Press
Life Cycle Books
Liguori Publications
Master Books - R
Neibauer Press - R
Our Sunday Visitor - R
TEACH Services - R
Trinity Foundation - R

PARENTING

Augsburg Fortress - R
Ave Maria Press
Baker Books - R
Bantam Books
Bethany House
Bosco Multimedia, Don
Brentwood - R

Broadman & Holman

Chalice Press

Chosen Books

Christopher Publishing

College Press - R

Collier-Macmillan

Companion Press - R

Concordia

Crossway Books

CSS Publishing

DaBaR Services - R

Eerdmans Publishing - R

Fairway Press - R

Focus on the Family - R

Garborg's

Gospel Publishing

HarperSanFrancisco - R

Harrison House - R

Harvest House

Haworth Press - R

Hensley, Virgil W. - R

Herald Press

Honor Books

Horizon House - R

Howard Publishing - R

Huntington House - R

ICAN Press - R

InterVarsity Press

LifeJourney Books

Liguori Publications

Living Flame Press

Loyola Univ. Press - R

LuraMedia

Moorings

Morehouse - R

Nelson, Thomas - R

New Leaf Press - R

Omega Publications

Our Sunday Visitor - R

Pacific Press

Pillar Books - R

Presbyterian/Reformed - R

Prescott Press - R

Proclaim Publishing

Questar - R

Rainbow Books (FL)

Regal Books

Resurrection Press - R

Revell, Fleming H.

Review & Herald - R

St. Paul Books - R

Servant - R

Shaw Publishers, Harold - R

Sheed & Ward - R

Shining Star

Starburst Publishers

Still Waters Revival - R

Tabor Publishing

TEACH Services - R

Tyler Press - R

Tyndale House - R

United Church Press

United Methodist

Upper Room Books - R

VESTA

Victor Books - R

Victory House - R

Westminster/John Knox

Wood Lake Books - R

Zondervan/Trade - R

PASTORS' HELPS

Accent Publications

Alba House - R

Alban Institute

AMG Publishers - R

Ave Maria Press

Baker Books - R

Bethany House

Bethel Publishing - R

Brentwood - R

Bristol House - R

Broadman & Holman

Brown-ROA

Chalice Press

Christian Lit. Crusade - R

Christopher Publishing

Church Growth Inst.

Cliffside Publishing

Companion Press - R

Concordia

Crossway Books

CSS Publishing

Discipleship Resources

Eerdmans Publishing - R

Fairway Press - R

Franciscan Press - R

Gospel Publishing

Greenlawn Press - R

HarperSanFrancisco - R

Harrison House - R

Haworth Press - R

Hensley, Virgil W. - R

Herald Press

Huntington House - R

Judson Press - R

Kindred Press

Langmarc

Liguori Publications

Meriwether - R

Morehouse - R

Nazarene Pub. House

Neibauer Press - R

Nelson, Thomas - R

New Leaf Press - R

Our Sunday Visitor - R

Pastor's Choice

Paulist Press

Pillar Books - R

Presbyterian/Reformed - R

Proclaim Publishing

Questar - R

Regal Books

Resurrection Press - R

Review & Herald - R

Southern Baptist Press - R

Standard

Tyler Press - R

Tyndale House - R
United Church Press
Victor Books - R
Victory House - R
Wellness
Westminster/John Knox
Wood Lake Books - R
World Bible - R
Zondervan/Trade - R

PERSONAL EXPERIENCE

Brentwood - R
Chosen Books
Christopher Publishing
Companion Press - R
Concordia
Cross Cultural
DaBaR Services - R
Eerdmans Publishing - R
Fairway Press - R
Friends United Press - R
Gilgal
HarperSanFrancisco - R
Herald Press
Howard Publishing - R
Huntington House - R
ICAN Press - R
Kindred Press
Living Flame Press
Loyola Univ. Press - R
LuraMedia
Moorings
Nelson, Thomas - R
Omega Publications
Our Sunday Visitor - R
Pacific Press
Prescott Press - R
Proclaim Publishing
Rainbow's End
Review & Herald - R
Son-Rise
Southern Baptist Press - R

Tyler Press - R
Tyndale House - R
Upper Room Books - R
VESTA
Victory House - R
W.R.S. Publishing - R
Zondervan/Trade - R

*PERSONAL RENEWAL

Ave Maria Press
Baker Books - R
Creation House
Eerdmans Publishing - R
Friends United Press - R
Howard Publishing - R
Hunt & Thorpe
ICAN Press - R
Moorings
Our Sunday Visitor - R
Regal Books
Regnery Publishing - R
Tyler Press - R

PHILOSOPHY

Alba House - R
Brentwood - R
Catholic Univ./America - R
Christian Classics
Christian Univ. Press - R
Christopher Publishing
Concordia
Cornell Univ. Press - R
Cornerstone Press
Cross Cultural
Crossway Books
Eerdmans Publishing - R
Element Books - R
Fairway Press - R
Franciscan Press - R
Franciscan Univ. Press - R
Friends United Press - R

HarperSanFrancisco - R
Huntington House - R
ICAN Press - R
InterVarsity Press
Loyola Univ. Press - R
Open Court - R
Our Sunday Visitor - R
Oxford University
Paulist Press
Proclaim Publishing
Rainbow Books (FL)
Regnery Publishing - R
St. Bede's - R
Seaside Press
Star Song - R
Still Waters Revival - R
Tabor Publishing
Trinity Foundation - R
Trinity Press Intl. - R
University Press/America - R
VESTA
Wadsworth - R
Winston-Derek - R
World Bible - R
W.R.S. Publishing - R
Yale Univ. Press - R
Zondervan/Trade - R
Zondervan/Academic

POETRY

Blue Dolphin - R
Brentwood - R
Christopher Publishing
Companion Press - R
Cornerstone Press
Cross Cultural
Fairway Press - R
Garborg's
Gibson, C.R. - R
HarperSanFrancisco - R
Huntington House - R
ICAN Press - R

Morrow & Company, Wm.
Mt. Olive College Press
Poets Cove Press
Proclaim Publishing
Rainbow's End
Regnery Publishing - R
Star Song
Southern Baptist Press - R
TEACH Services - R
Tyler Press - R
Upper Room Books - R
VESTA
Wesleyan Univ. Press
Westminster/John Knox

POLITICAL THEORY

Brentwood - R
Catholic Univ./America - R
Christian Univ. Press - R
Christopher Publishing
Concordia
Franciscan Press - R
Friendship Press
HarperSanFrancisco - R
Huntington House - R
ICAN Press - R
Loyola Univ. Press - R
New Society - R
Open Court - R
Pilgrim Press
PROBE Ministries
Proclaim Publishing
Questar - R
Regnery Publishing - R
Starburst Publishers
Star Song - R
Still Waters Revival - R
Trinity Foundation - R
Tyler Press - R
University Press/America - R
University of NC Press
VESTA

W.R.S. Publishing - R

PRAYER

Alba House - R
Augsburg Fortress - R
Ave Maria Press
Baker Books - R
Bantam Books
Barclay Press - R
Bethany House
Bethel Publishing - R
Brentwood - R
Bridge Publishing - R
Bristol House - R
Broadman & Holman
Brown-ROA
Chalice Press
Chosen Books
Christian Classics
Christian Lit. Crusade - R
Christopher Publishing
Church Growth Inst.
Companion Press - R
Concordia
Creation House
CSS Publishing
DaBaR Services - R
Eerdmans Publishing - R
Emerald Books
Fairway Press - R
Forward Movement - R
Franciscan Press - R
Franciscan Univ. Press - R
Friends United Press - R
Gospel Publishing
Greenlawn Press - R
HarperSanFrancisco - R
Harrison House - R
Hensley, Virgil W. - R
Howard Publishing - R
Huntington House - R
ICAN Press - R

ICS Publications - R
InterVarsity Press
Kregel - R
Liguori Publications
Living Flame Press
Loyola Univ. Press - R
LuraMedia
Moody Press
Moorings
Morehouse - R
Morning Star Press - R
Nelson, Thomas - R
New Hope - R
New Leaf Press - R
Novalis
Our Sunday Visitor - R
Pacific Press
Paraclete Press - R
Pastoral Press
Pillar Books - R
Praxis Institute - R
Presbyterian/Reformed - R
Proclaim Publishing
Questar - R
Regal Books
Regina Press
Regnery Publishing - R
Resource Publications
Resurrection Press - R
Revell, Fleming H.
Review & Herald - R
St. Anthony Messenger - R
St. Bede's - R
St. Paul Books - R
Servant - R
Sheed & Ward - R
Southern Baptist Press - R
Starburst Publishers
Star Song - R
Still Waters Revival - R
Trinity Press Intl. - R
Tyler Press - R
Tyndale House - R

United Church Press
United Methodist
VESTA
Victor Books - R
Victory House - R
Warner Press
Westminster/John Knox
Winston-Derek - R
Woman's Miss. Union - R
Zondervan/Trade - R

PROPHECY

AMG Publishers - R
Brentwood - R
Bridge Publishing - R
Chosen Books
Christian Classics
Christian Media
Christopher Publishing
Cliffside Publishing
Companion Press - R
Creation House
Element Books - R
Fairway Press - R
Gospel Publishing
HarperSanFrancisco - R
Harvard House
Hensley, Virgil W. - R
Huntington House - R
ICAN Press - R
Kregel - R
Moorings
Morning Star Press - R
Nelson, Thomas - R
New Leaf Press - R
Pillar Books - R
Proclaim Publishing
Questar - R
Regal Books
Southern Baptist Press - R
Starburst Publishers
Still Waters Revival - R

TEACH Services - R
Trinity Press Intl. - R
Tyler Press - R
VESTA
Victory House - R
World Bible - R
Zondervan/Trade - R

PSYCHOLOGY

Alba House - R
Baker Books - R
Bantam Books
Bethany House
Blue Dolphin - R
Brentwood - R
Broadman & Holman
Christopher Publishing
Collier-Macmillan
Concordia
Cross Cultural
Dimension Books - R
Eerdmans Publishing - R
Elder Books - R
Element Books - R
Fairway Press - R
Focus on the Family - R
Franciscan Press - R
HarperSanFrancisco - R
Haworth Press - R
Huntington House - R
ICAN Press - R
InterVarsity Press
Living Flame Press
Loyola Univ. Press - R
LuraMedia
Morehouse - R
Morning Star Press - R
Nelson, Thomas - R
Open Court - R
Oxford University
Pilgrim Press
Proclaim Publishing

Rainbow Books (FL)
Regnery Publishing - R
Religious Education
Resurrection Press - R
Review & Herald - R
Servant - R
Southern Baptist Press - R
Starburst Publishers
Tabor Publishing
Trinity Press Intl. - R
Tyler Press - R
Tyndale House - R
University Press/America - R
VESTA
Victor Books - R
Victory House - R
World Bible - R
Yale Univ. Press - R
Zondervan/Trade - R
Zondervan/Academic

*RECOVERY BOOKS

Baker Books - R
Church Growth Inst.
Elder Books - R
Gospel Publishing
HarperSanFrancisco - R
Hensley, Virgil W. - R
Herald Press
Howard Publishing - R
ICAN Press - R
InterVarsity Press
Moorings
Morehouse - R
Our Sunday Visitor - R
Pilgrim Press
Rainbow's End
Resource Publications
St. Paul Books - R
Starburst Publishers
Tyler Press - R
Victor Books - R

REFERENCE BOOKS

AMG Publishers - R
Baker Books - R
Bethany House
Brentwood - R
Broadman & Holman
Christian Lit. Crusade - R
Christian Univ. Press - R
Christopher Publishing
Cliffside Publishing
Companion Press - R
Concordia
Crossway Books
CSS Publishing
Eerdmans Publishing - R
Element Books - R
Fairway Press - R
Good Book
HarperSanFrancisco - R
Hendrickson Publishers - R
Howard Publishing - R
ICAN Press - R
InterVarsity Press
Kregel - R
Lifetime Books - R
Moorings
Morehouse - R
Nelson, Thomas - R
OMF Books
Our Sunday Visitor - R
Oxford University
Pillar Books - R
Prescott Press - R
Review & Herald - R
Scarecrow Press
Southern Baptist Press - R
Star Song - R
Still Waters Revival - R
TEACH Services - R
Trinity Press Intl. - R
Tyler Press - R
Tyndale House - R

University Press/America - R
VESTA
Victory House - R
Westminster/John Knox
World Bible - R
Zondervan/Trade - R
Zondervan/Academic

RELIGION

Alba House - R
AMG Publishers - R (world)
Baker Books - R
Bantam Books
Bethany House
Bethel Publishing - R
Blue Dolphin - R
Brentwood - R
Bridge Publishing - R
Catholic Univ./America - R
Chalice Press
Christian Classics
Christian Univ. Press - R
Christopher Publishing
Cliffside Publishing
Concordia
Cornell Univ. Press - R
Cross Cultural
Crossway Books
CSS Publishing
Dimension Books - R
Eerdmans Publishing - R
Element Books - R
Fairway Press - R
Franciscan Press - R
Friendship Press
Friends United Press - R
Good Book
Gospel Publishing
Guernica Editions - R
HarperSanFrancisco - R
Hendrickson Publishers - R
Howard Publishing - R

Huntington House - R
ICAN Press - R
InterVarsity Press
Kregel - R
Liguori Publications
Living Flame Press
Loyola Univ. Press - R
More Press, Thomas
Morehouse - R
Morning Star Press - R
Morrow & Co, Wm.
Mt. Olive College Press
Nelson, Thomas - R
Open Court - R
Our Sunday Visitor - R
Oxford University
Paulist Press
Pilgrim Press
Praxis Institute - R
Proclaim Publishing
Questar - R
Regnery Publishing - R
Religious Education
Resurrection Press - R
Review & Herald - R
St. Anthony Messenger - R
St. Bede's - R
St. Paul Books - R
Seaside Press
Sheed & Ward - R
Sheer Joy! Press
Southern Baptist Press - R
Star Song - R
Still Waters Revival - R
Tabor Publishing
TEACH Services - R
Trinity Press Intl. - R
Tyler Press - R
Tyndale House - R
United Church Press
United Church Pub.
University of NC Press
University Press/America - R

VESTA
Victory House - R
Wadsworth Publishing
Westminster/John Knox
World Bible - R
Yale Univ. Press - R
Zondervan/Trade - R
Zondervan/Academic

RETIREMENT

Baker Books - R
Bethany House
Broadman & Holman
Christopher Publishing
College Press - R
Concordia
Elder Books - R
Fairway Press - R
HarperSanFrancisco - R
Nelson, Thomas - R
Proclaim Publishing
Questar - R
Regnery Publishing - R
Review & Herald - R
Southern Baptist Press - R
Starburst Publishers
Tyler Press - R
VESTA
Westminster/John Knox
Zondervan/Trade - R

*SCHOLARLY

Baker Books - R
Christian Univ. Press - R
Cliffside Publishing
Cross Cultural
Crossway Books
Eerdmans Publishing - R
Friends United Press - R
Good Book
Hendrickson Publishers - R

Huntington House - R
ICAN Press - R
Kregel - R
Morehouse - R
Our Sunday Visitor - R
Oxford University
Paulist Press
Pilgrim Press
Rainbow Books (FL)
St. Bede's - R
TEACH Services - R
Trinity Foundation - R
Tyler Press - R
University Press/America - R
Victor Books - R

SCIENCE

Bob Jones - R
Christopher Publishing
Cornell Univ. Press - R
Cross Cultural
Eerdmans Publishing - R
HarperSanFrancisco - R
Harvard House
Huntington House - R
ICAN Press - R
InterVarsity Press
Master Books - R
Open Court - R
Oxford University
Proclaim Publishing
Regnery Publishing - R
Review & Herald - R
Trinity Foundation - R
Tyler Press - R
World Bible - R

SENIOR ADULT CONCERNS

Augsburg Fortress - R
Baker Books - R
Bethany House

Broadman & Holman Publishers
Chalice Press
Christian Classics
Christopher Publishing
Church Growth Inst.
Concordia
Fairway Press - R
Gospel Publishing
HarperSanFrancisco - R
Haworth Press - R
Hensley, Virgil W. - R
Herald Press
Horizon House - R
Howard Publishing - R
ICAN Press - R
Judson Press - R
Langmarc
Living Flame Press
Loyola Univ. Press - R
LuraMedia
Morehouse - R
Nelson, Thomas - R
New Leaf Press - R
Prescott Press - R
Proclaim Publishing
Questar - R
Rainbow Books (FL)
Review & Herald - R
Southern Baptist Press - R
Star Song - R
Tyler Press - R
United Methodist
Westminster/John Knox
Woman's Miss. Union - R
Zondervan/Trade - R

SERMONS

AMG Publishers - R
Brentwood - R
Christian Classics
Christian Univ. Press - R
Christopher Publishing

Companion Press - R
Concordia
CSS Publishing
Eerdmans Publishing - R
Fairway Press - R
Franciscan Press - R
Gospel Publishing
HarperSanFrancisco - R
Herald Press
Huntington House - R
Kregel - R
Liturgical Press
Meriwether - R
Morning Star Press - R
Nelson, Thomas - R
Our Sunday Visitor - R
Pastor's Choice
Pillar Books - R
Proclaim Publishing
Review & Herald - R
Southern Baptist Press - R
Still Waters Revival - R
TEACH Services - R
Trinity Press Intl. - R
Tyler Press - R
Tyndale House - R
United Church Press
VESTA

Focus on the Family - R
Gospel Publishing
HarperSanFrancisco - R
Haworth Press - R
Hensley, Virgil W. - R
Herald Press
Horizon House - R
Howard Publishing - R
Huntington House - R
Langmarc
Living Flame Press
LuraMedia
Morehouse - R
Nelson, Thomas - R
New Leaf Press - R
Pillar Books - R
Proclaim Publishing
Questar - R
Revell, Fleming H.
Review & Herald - R
Shaw Publishers, Harold - R
Tyler Press - R
Tyndale House - R
VESTA
Victor Books - R
Wood Lake Books - R
W.R.S. Publishing - R
Zondervan/Trade - R

Forward Movement - R
Franciscan Press - R
Friendship Press
HarperSanFrancisco - R
Herald Press
Huntington House - R
ICAN Press - R
InterVarsity Press
Life Cycle Books - R
Lifetime Books - R
Loyola Univ. Press - R
LuraMedia
Morehouse - R
Nelson, Thomas - R
New Society - R
Oxford University
Paulist Press
Pilgrim Press
Proclaim Publishing
Questar - R
Regnery Publishing - R
Resurrection Press - R
Review & Herald - R
Sheed & Ward - R
Star Song - R
Still Waters Revival - R
Trinity Press Intl. - R
Tyler Press - R
United Church Pub.
VESTA
Westminster/John Knox
Windflower - R
Winston-Derek - R
Wood Lake Books - R
W.R.S. Publishing - R
Zondervan/Trade - R
Zondervan/Academic

SINGLES ISSUES

Baker Books - R
Bethany House
Brentwood - R
Broadman & Holman
Chalice Press
Christian Classics
Christopher Publishing
Church Growth Inst.
Collier-Macmillan Books
Concordia
DaBaR Services - R
Discipleship Resources

SOCIAL JUSTICE ISSUES

Alban Institute
Barclay Press - R
Bethany House
Brentwood - R
Chalice Press
Chosen Books
Christian Classics
Christopher Publishing
Collier-Macmillan
Concordia
Crossway Books
Eerdmans Publishing - R

SOCIOLOGY

Alba House - R
Baker Books - R
Bethany House

Brentwood - R
Christopher Publishing
Cross Cultural
Franciscan Press - R
HarperSanFrancisco - R
Haworth Press - R
Huntington House - R
ICAN Press - R
InterVarsity Press
Loyola Univ. Press - R
New Society - R
Oxford University
Paulist Press
Prescott Press - R
Proclaim Publishing
. Review & Herald - R
Still Waters Revival - R
University of NC Press
University Press/America - R
W.R.S. Publishing - R
Zondervan/Trade - R
Zondervan/Academic

SPIRITUALITY

Alba House - R
Alban Institute
Augsburg Fortress - R
Ave Maria Press
Baker Books - R
Bantam Books
Barclay Press - R
Bethany House
Bethel Publishing - R
Brentwood - R
Bridge Publishing - R
Broadman & Holman
Chalice Press
Chosen Books
Christian Classics
Christopher Publishing
Collier-Macmillan
Companion Press - R

Cross Cultural
Crossway Books
DaBaR Services - R
Dimension Books - R
Eerdmans Publishing - R
Elder Books - R
Element Books - R
Fairway Press - R
Forward Movement - R
Franciscan Press - R
Franciscan Univ. Press - R
Friends United Press - R
Gospel Publishing
HarperSanFrancisco - R
Howard Publishing - R
Hunt & Thorpe
Huntington House - R
ICAN Press - R
InterVarsity Press
Judson Press - R
Liguori Publications
Living Flame Press
Loyola Univ. Press - R
LuraMedia
Moorings
More Press, Thomas
Morehouse - R
Morning Star Press - R
Nazarene Pub. House
Nelson, Thomas - R
New Society - R
Novalis
Omega Publications
Our Sunday Visitor - R
Oxford University
Pacific Press
Paraclete Press - R
Pastoral Press
Pilgrim Press
Pillar Books - R
Praxis Institute - R
Presbyterian/Reformed - R
Proclaim Publishing

Questar - R
Regal Books
Regnery Publishing - R
Resurrection Press - R
Revell, Fleming H.
Review & Herald - R
St. Anthony Messenger - R
St. Bede's - R
St. Paul Books - R
Servant - R
Shaw Publishers, Harold - R
Sheed & Ward - R
Southern Baptist Press - R
Trinity Press Intl. - R
Tyler Press - R
Tyndale House - R
United Church Press
VESTA
Victor Books - R
Victory House - R
Westminster/John Knox
Winston-Derek - R
World Bible - R
Zondervan/Trade - R
Zondervan/Academic

SPORTS

Christopher Publishing
Howard Publishing - R
ICAN Press - R
Lifetime Books - R
Moorings
New Leaf Press - R
Prescott Press - R
Proclaim Publishing
Starburst Publishers
Star Song - R
Tyler Press - R
W.R.S. Publishing - R
Zondervan/Trade - R

*STEWARDSHIP

Baker Books - R
Bethel Publishing - R
Church Growth Inst.
Creation House
Discipleship Resources
Eerdmans Publishing - R
Forward Movement - R
Gospel Publishing
Hensley, Virgil W. - R
Herald Press
Huntington House - R
ICAN Press - R
Kregel - R
Morehouse - R
Presbyterian/Reformed - R
TEACH Services - R
Tyler Press - R

THEOLOGICAL

Alba House - R
AMG Publishers - R
Baker Books - R
Bethany House
Brentwood - R
Bridge Publishing - R
Broadman & Holman
Catholic Univ./America - R
Chalice Press
Christian Classics
Christian Univ. Press - R
Christopher Publishing
Cistercian - R
Cliffside Publishing
Collier-Macmillan
Companion Press - R
Concordia
Cross Cultural
Crossway Books
Dimension Books - R
Editorial Evangelica

Eerdmans Publishing - R
Fairway Press - R
Franciscan Press - R
Franciscan Univ. Press - R
Gospel Publishing
HarperSanFrancisco - R
Hendrickson Publishers - R
Hensley, Virgil W. - R
Herald Press
Howard Publishing - R
Huntington House - R
ICAN Press - R
InterVarsity Press
Kregel - R
Liturgical Press
Loyola Univ. Press - R
Moorings
Morehouse - R
Morning Star Press - R
Nelson, Thomas - R
New Leaf Press - R
Novalis
Omega Publications
OMF Books
Open Court - R
Our Sunday Visitor - R
Oxford University
Pastoral Press
Paulist Press
Pilgrim Press
Pillar Books - R
Praxis Institute - R
Presbyterian/Reformed - R
Proclaim Publishing
Regnery Publishing - R
Religious Education
Resurrection Press - R
Review & Herald - R
St. Paul Books - R
Servant - R
Sheed & Ward - R
Southern Baptist Press - R
Star Song - R

Still Waters Revival - R
Trinity Foundation - R
Trinity Press Intl. - R
Tyler Press - R
Tyndale House - R
United Church Press
United Church Pub.
University Press/America - R
Upper Room Books - R
VESTA
Victor Books - R
Victory House - R
Westminster/John Knox
World Bible - R
Zondervan/Trade - R
Zondervan/Academic

*TRACTS

American Tract Society
Christian Missions
Editorial Evangelica
Faith, Prayer & Tract
Forward Movement - R
Good News Publishers
Neibauer Press - R
St. Hilda's Press
TEACH Services - R
Trinity Foundation - R

TRAVEL

Bob Jones - R
Brentwood - R
Bridge Publishing - R
Christopher Publishing
Eerdmans Publishing - R
Morehouse - R
Mt. Olive College Press
Pelican Publishing - R
Prescott Press - R
Proclaim Publishing
Rainbow Books (FL)

WOMEN'S ISSUES

Alban Institute
AMG Publishers - R
Augsburg Fortress - R
Baker Books - R
Bantam Books
Bethany House
Bethel Publishing - R
Blue Dolphin - R
Bridge Publishing - R
Broadman & Holman
Chalice Press
Chosen Books
Christian Univ. Press - R
Christopher Publishing
Church Growth Inst.
Collier-Macmillan
Concordia
Cornell Univ. Press - R
Cross Cultural
Crossway Books
DaBaR Services - R
Eerdmans Publishing - R
Elder Books - R
Element Books - R
Emerald Books
Fairway Press - R
Forward Movement - R
Franciscan Press - R
Franciscan Univ. Press - R
HarperSanFrancisco - R
Harvest House
Haworth Press - R
Hensley, Virgil W. - R
Herald Press
Honor Books
Horizon House - R
Howard Publishing - R
Huntington House - R
ICAN Press - R
InterVarsity Press
Judson Press - R

Kregel - R
Life Cycle Books - R
Liguori Publications
LuraMedia
Moody Press
Morehouse - R
Morning Star Press - R
Nelson, Thomas - R
New Hope - R
New Leaf Press - R
New Society - R
Pacific Press
Pastoral Press
Pelican Publishing - R
Pilgrim Press
Pillar Books - R
Prescott Press - R
Proclaim Publishing
Questar - R
Rainbow Books (FL)
Regal Books
Resurrection Press - R
Review & Herald - R
St. Paul Books - R
Servant - R
Shaw Publishers, Harold - R
Sheed & Ward - R
Son-Rise
Southern Baptist Press - R
Starburst Publishers
Star Song - R
Still Waters Revival - R
Trinity Press Intl. - R
Tyler Press - R
United Church Press
United Church Pub.
United Methodist
University Press/America - R
Upper Room Books - R
VESTA
Victor Books - R
Victory House - R
Westminster/John Knox

Windflower - R
Winston-Derek - R
Woman's Miss. Union - R
Wood Lake Books - R
Zondervan/Trade - R
Zondervan/Academic

WORLD ISSUES

Bethany House
Bridge Publishing - R
Christopher Publishing
Companion Press - R
Cross Cultural
Crossway Books
Franciscan Press - R
Guernica Editions - R
HarperSanFrancisco - R
Herald Press
Howard Publishing - R
Huntington House - R
ICAN Press - R
InterVarsity Press
Loyola Univ. Press - R
Morehouse - R
Nelson, Thomas - R
New Leaf Press - R
New Society - R
Orbis Books
Pilgrim Press
Pillar Books - R
Prescott Press - R
PROBE Ministries
Proclaim Publishing
Questar - R
Regal Books
Regnery Publishing - R
Still Waters Revival - R
Trinity Foundation - R
Trinity Press Intl. - R
Tyler Press - R
University Press/America - R
VESTA

Victory House - R
Wood Lake Books - R
Zondervan/Trade - R

WORSHIP RESOURCES

AMG Publishers - R
Baker Books - R
Bethany House
Bridge Publishing - R
Broadman & Holman
Chalice Press
Christian Classics
Christopher Publishing
Collier-Macmillan
Companion Press - R
Concordia
CSS Publishing
Discipleship Resources
Editorial Evangelica
Educational Ministries
Eerdmans Publishing - R
Emerald Books
Fairway Press - R
Franciscan Press - R
Gospel Publishing
HarperSanFrancisco - R
Hensley, Virgil W. - R
Herald Press
Howard Publishing - R
Huntington House - R
Judson Press - R
Kregel - R
Liguori Publications
Liturgical Press
Loyola Univ. Press - R
Meriwether - R
Morehouse - R
Nelson, Thomas - R
Our Sunday Visitor - R
Pastoral Press
Pillar Books - R
Proclaim Publishing

St. Anthony Messenger - R
Sheed & Ward - R
Standard
Star Song - R
Tyler Press - R
Tyndale House - R
United Church Press
United Church Pub.
Upper Room Books - R
VESTA
Victory House - R
Westminster/John Knox
Wood Lake Books - R
Zondervan/Trade - R

YOUTH BOOKS (Nonfiction)

Note: Listing denotes books for 8-
    12-year olds, Junior Highs or
    Senior Highs. If all three, it
    will say "all".
Augsburg Fortress - R (8-12)
Baker Books - R (all)
Bethany House (all)
Bible Discovery (all)
Bob Jones - R (all)
Bosco Multimedia, Don (Jr/Sr
    High)
Bridge Publishing - R
Broadman & Holman (all)
Chariot Books (8-12)
Concordia (all)
Contemporary Drama Service
Creation House (Sr High)
Cross Cultural (Sr High)
Eerdmans Publishing - R (8-12/Jr
    High)
Emerald Books (all)
Fairway Press - R (all)
Forward Movement - R (all)
Hensley, Virgil W. - R (all)
Honor Books
Horizon House - R (Jr/Sr High)

Hunt & Thorpe (all)
Huntington House - R
Langmarc (Jr/Sr High)
Liguori Publications (all)
Morehouse - R (all)
Morris, Joshua (all)
Nelson, Thomas - R (all)
New Hope - R
Novalis (all)
OMF Books (all)
Our Sunday Visitor - R (all)
Proclaim Publishing (all)
Questar - R (all)
Rainbow Books (CA) (8-12)
Regal Books (Jr/Sr High)
Resurrection Press - R
Review & Herald - R (all)
St. Paul Books - R (all)
Son-Rise (all)
So. Baptist Press - R (all)
Still Waters Revival - R (all)
TEACH Services - R (8-12/Jr
    High)
Tyler Press - R (all)
United Church Press (all)
Upper Room Books - R
Victor Books - R (all)
Victory House - R
Woman's Miss. Union - R
Zondervan/Trade - R (all)

YOUTH PROGRAMS

Baker Books - R
Bosco Multimedia, Don
Bridge Publishing - R
Church Growth Inst.
Concordia
Contemporary Drama Service
Discipleship Resources
Educational Ministries
Fairway Press - R
Group Publishing

Hensley, Virgil W. - R
Huntington House - R
Judson Press - R
Kregel - R
Langmarc

Liguori Publications
Meriwether - R
Morehouse - R
Morris, Joshua
Nelson, Thomas - R

Proclaim Publishing
Regal Books
Resurrection Press - R
St. Anthony Messenger - R
Sheer Joy! Press

ALPHABETICAL LISTINGS OF BOOK PUBLISHERS

(*) An asterisk before a listing indicates no or unconfirmed information update.

(#) A number symbol before a listing indicates it was updated from their guidelines or other sources.

(+) A plus sign before a listing indicates it is a new listing.

ABINGDON PRESS - See The United Methodist Publishing House.

ACCENT BIBLE CURRICULUM, P.O. Box 36640, Colorado Springs CO 80936-3664. Cook Communications Ministries. Mary B. Nelson, mng. ed. Buys all rts as work for hire of assigned projects. Writers must be Baptist or baptistic. Submit query letter explaining qualifications to write curriculum; experience; published works. No freelance submissions.

> **Special Needs:** Writers for Kindergarten, Junior and Adult.

ACCENT PUBLICATIONS, P.O. Box 36640, Colorado Springs CO 80936-3664. (719)536-0100. Imprint of Cook Communications Ministries. Mary B. Nelson, mng. ed. Publishes 6-8 titles/yr. Receives 1,000-1,500 submissions annually. 75% of books from first-time authors. Accepts mss through agents (reluctantly). Royalty on retail; no advance. Publication within 1 yr. Responds in 8-12 wks. Guidelines; catalog for 9x12 SAE/5 stamps.

> **Nonfiction:** Query letter only; no phone/fax query. Christian education and church resources only.
>
> **Special Needs:** Books that would be resources for the local church.
>
> **Tips:** "Think in terms of series or complementary books which can be produced as a series (especially in even numbers of 2 or 4). Books sell better when the two reinforce each other's sales."

ACTA PUBLICATIONS, 4848 N. Clark St., Chicago IL 60640. (312)271-1030. Fax: (312)271-7399. Catholic. Gregory F. Augustine Pierce, co-pub. Resources for the "end-user"of the Christian faith. Publishes 10 titles/yr. Receives 50 submissions annually. 50% of books from first-time authors. No mss through agents. **SUBSIDY PUBLISHES 50%.** Prefers 125 pgs or 50,000 wds. Royalty 10% of net; no advance. Average first printing 2,000-3500. Publication within 12-18 mos. Responds in 4 wks. Guidelines; catalog for 9x12 SAE/3 stamps.

> **Nonfiction:** Query; no phone/fax query.
>
> **Tips:** "Most open to books that are useful to a large number of average Christians. Read our catalog and one of our books first."

A.D. PLAYERS, 2710 W. Alabama, Houston TX 77098. (713)526-2721. Fax: (713)522-5475. Christian. Martha Doolittle, literary mngr. Professional theater company that produces plays. Produces 12-15 plays/season. Receives 50 submissions annually. 1% of scripts from first-time authors. Accepts scripts through agents. Negotiable royalty; no advance. Production in 1 mo. to 3 yrs. Considers simultaneous submissions. Responds in 6-12 mos. Guidelines.

> **Special Needs:** Children's shows with 4-6 actors only; full-length plays with family values and contemporary issues.
>
> **Plays:** Query with synopsis. Any genre; also biographical or on social issues.

#ALBA HOUSE, 2187 Victory Blvd., Staten Island NY 10314. (718)761-0047. Fax: (718)761-0057. Catholic/Society of St. Paul. Aloysius Milella, ed; Edmund C. Lane, mng. ed. Publishes 30 titles/yr. Receives 1,000 submissions annually. 50% of books from first-time authors. Accepts mss through agents. Reprints books. Royalty 10% on retail; no advance. Publication within 9 mos. Considers simultaneous submissions. Responds in 1 month. Guidelines; catalog for SASE.

   Nonfiction: Query.

#THE ALBAN INSTITUTE, INC., 4550 Montgomery Ave., Ste. 433N, Bethesda MD 20814-3341. (301)718-4407. Fax: (301)718-1958. Episcopal Church. Celia A. Hahn, ed-in-chief. Publishes 10 titles/yr. Receives 100 submissions annually. No mss through agents. Prefers 100 pgs. Royalty 7-10% of net; advance $100. Publication within 1 yr. Responds in 2 mos. Guidelines; catalog for 9x12 SAE/3 stamps.

   Nonfiction: Proposal only first. Books for clergy and laity.

   Tips: "Books on congregational issues: problems and opportunities in congregational life; the clergy role and career; the ministry of the laity in church and world." Intelligent/liberal audience.

#AMERICAN CATHOLIC PRESS, 16160 S. Seton Dr., South Holland IL 60473-1863. (708)331-5485. Catholic worship resources. Father Michael Gilligan, ed. dir. Publishes 8 titles/yr. Reprints books. Pays $25-100 for outright purchases only. Publication within 8 mos. Considers simultaneous submissions. Responds in 2 mos.

   Nonfiction: Query first.

   Tips: "We publish only materials on the Roman Catholic liturgy. Especially interested in new music for church services."

*AMG PUBLISHERS, 6815 Shallowford Rd., Box 22000, Chattanooga TN 37422. (615)894-6060. Fax: (615)894-6863. Evangelical/AMG Intl. Dale Anderson, dir. Publishes 10 religious titles/yr. Receives 30 submissions annually. 20% of books from first-time authors. Accepts ms through agents. Reprints books. Prefers 150-250 pgs. Royalty 8% on retail (negotiable); no advance. Average first printing 2,500. Publication within 6 mos. Considers simultaneous submissions. Responds in 8-12 wks. No guidelines; free catalog.

   Nonfiction: Proposal/sample chapters.

   Fiction: Query first. Juvenile/teen-young adult.

   Tips: "Must be a needed subject. Our focus is on pastoral helps."

AUGSBURG FORTRESS, 426 S. 5th St., Box 1209, Minneapolis MN 55440. (612)330-3300. Fax: (612)330-3215. Evangelical Lutheran Church in America. Ron Klug, dir. of publishing; Alice Peppler, children's acq. ed; Robert Klausmeier, acq. ed. Publishes 35 titles/yr. Receives 1,500 submissions annually. 10% of books from first-time authors. Accepts mss through agents. Reprints books. Prefers 32-160 pgs. Royalty; advance. Average first printing 4,000. Publication within 12-18 mos. Considers simultaneous submissions. Responds in 3 mos. Guidelines; catalog for 9x12 SAE/5 stamps.

   Nonfiction: Query only; fax query ok.

   Fiction: Query only. Juvenile only.

   Special Needs: Historical fiction for 10-14 year olds; books on spirituality, family, and for over 50s.

   Ethnic Books: African-American, Hispanic, Asian-American, native American; contextual theology.

   Tips: "Query us first. Describe the project, the readership, how you think the book meets a need, your credentials for writing, how your book differs from similar books already published."

AUGUST HOUSE PUBLISHERS, INC., P.O. Box 3223, Little Rock AR 72203. (501)372-5450. Fax: (501)372-5579. Methodist. Ted Parkhurst, pres. Imprint: American Storytelling from August House. Publishes 0-2 titles/yr. Receives 200-300 submissions annually. 20% of books from first-time authors. Accepts mss through agents. **SUBSIDY PUBLISHES some books.** Prefers 192 pgs. Negotiable royalty; advance. Publication within 18 mos. Considers simultaneous submissions. Responds in 90 days. Guidelines; catalog for 9x12 SAE/5 stamps.

> **Nonfiction:** Query only; no phone queries.
>
> **Special Needs:** "The only religious books we are looking for are those that contain stories for retelling in church, Sunday school, or as devotions; or tell how to use a story in those settings."
>
> **Ethnic Books:** African-American; Mexican-American; other multicultural titles.

#AVE MARIA PRESS, Notre Dame IN 46556. (219)287-2831. Fax: (219)239-2904. Catholic. Rev. David E. Schlaver, CSC, pub.. Publishes 17 titles/yr. Receives 250 submissions annually. 50% of books from first-time authors. Accepts mss through agents. Royalty on retail; occasional advance. Average first printing 12,000. Publication within 8 mos. Considers simultaneous submissions. Responds as soon as necessary. Guidelines; catalog for 9x12 SAE/5 stamps.

> **Nonfiction:** Proposal/3 chapters or complete ms; no phone query.

BAKER BOOKS, Box 6287, Grand Rapids MI 49516. (616)676-9185. Fax: (616)676-9573. Evangelical. Allan Fisher, dir. of publications; submit to Jane Dekker, asst. Publishes 140 titles/yr. Receives 2,000 submissions annually. 3% of books from first-time authors. Accepts mss through agents. Reprints books. Prefers 150-300 pgs. Royalty from 14% of net; some advances. Average first printing 5,000. Publication within 1 yr. Considers simultaneous submissions. Responds in 2-6 wks. Guidelines; catalog for 9.5x12.5 SAE/5 stamps.

> **Nonfiction:** Proposal/3 chapters; phone/fax query not preferred. "Request our brochure on how to prepare a proposal."
>
> **Fiction:** Proposal/3 chapters only. "We are interested in mysteries and contemporary women's fiction from a Christian world view without being preachy. Our fiction is more literary than popular. Request summary of contemporary women's fiction."
>
> **Ethnic Books:** Would be interested in publishing specifically for the African-American market.
>
> **Tips:** "Please prepare a complete, well-organized proposal. Request our guidelines for guidance."

#BANTAM BOOKS, 1540 Broadway, New York NY 10036. (216)354-6500. General trade publisher with a religious/inspirational list. Submit to Religious Book Editor. Accepts mss only through agents. Prefers at least 80,000-100,000 wds. Royalty 4-15%; advance. Publication within 1 yr. Considers simultaneous submissions. Responds in 2 mos. No guidelines/catalog.

> **Nonfiction:** Proposal/1-2 chapters. "Want all types of religious/inspirational books." No humor, no triumph over tragedy unless subject is well-known or a celebrity.
>
> **Fiction:** Proposal/2-3 chapters. "Books must cross over into the trade market."
>
> **Tips:** "We want books that appeal to a large, general audience and fresh ideas. Be sure to investigate the competition and include an author bio. The author's relevant experience and authority is very important to us."

#BARBOUR & CO., INC., 1810 Barbour Dr., P.O. Box 719, Uhrichsville OH 44683. (614)922-6045. Fax: (614)922-5948. Stephen Reginald, V.P. editorial. Imprints: Barbour Books (nonfiction) and Heartsong Presents (fiction). Publishes 75 titles/yr. Receives 450 submissions annually. 40% of books from first-time authors. Accepts mss through agents. Reprints books. Prefers 50,000 wds. Royalty 5-10% of net; or outright purchases $1,000-2,500; advance $250-500. Average first printing 10,000. Publication within 6 mos. Considers simultaneous submissions. Responds in 1-3 mos. Guidelines; catalog $2.

Nonfiction: Proposal/3 chapters; phone query ok.

Fiction: See separate listing for Heartsong Presents.

Tips: "A great idea is more important than a great agent here."

*BARCLAY PRESS, 110 Elliott Rd., Newberg OR 97132-2120. (503)538-7345. Fax: (503)538-7033. Friends/Quaker. Dan McCracken, general manager. Publishes 2 titles/yr. Receives 15 submissions annually. 50% of books from first-time authors. Accepts mss through agents. Reprints books. Prefers 100-200 pgs. Royalty 10%; no advance. Average first printing 1,500. Publication within 18 mos. Considers simultaneous submissions. Responds in 2 wks-2 mos. No guidelines; free catalog.

Nonfiction: Proposal/2 chapters. "Looking for books on spirituality and current social issues."

*MEL BAY PUBLICATIONS, INC., #4 Industrial Dr., Pacific MO 63069. (314)257-3970. William Bay, V.P.; submit to L. Dean Bye, gen mgr. Publishes 25 inspirational/religious titles/yr. Accepts mss through agents. Reprints books. Royalty 10% on retail; no advance. Publication within 6-9 mos. Responds in 1-6 wks. Free guidelines/catalog.

Nonfiction: Proposal/chapters (photocopy only).

Fiction: Complete ms or proposal. Children's picture books, juvenile, plays.

Tips: Specializes in music books. "In case of musical submissions, we appreciate a cassette recording."

BEACON HILL PRESS OF KANSAS CITY - see NAZARENE PUBLISHING HOUSE

BETHANY HOUSE PUBLISHERS, 11300 Hampshire Ave. S, Minneapolis MN 55438. (612)829-2500. A Division of Bethany Fellowship, Inc. Sharon Madison, ms review ed. Publishes 80 titles/yr. Receives 3,000 submissions annually. 8% of books from first-time authors. Accepts mss through agents. Standard royalty & advance. Publication within 18 mos. Considers simultaneous submissions. Responds in 8-10 wks. Guidelines for fiction/nonfiction/juvenile; catalog for 9x12 SAE/5 stamps.

Nonfiction: Cover letter, synopsis, 3 chapters. "No music, cookbooks, diet books, prophecy, poetry, exercise books, textbooks, or personal experiences."

Fiction: Cover letter/synopsis/3 chapters. Children's (no picture books), teen/young adult, adult. "Go easy on romance angle. Include solid Christian teaching without preaching. Create believable characters with imperfections and strengths."

BETHEL PUBLISHING, 1819 S. Main, Elkhart IN 46516. (219)293-8585. Fax: (800)230-8271. Missionary Church. Rev. Richard Oltz, pres.; submit to Senior Editor. Publishes 3-6 titles/yr. Receives 600-800 submissions annually. 90% of books from first-time authors. Accepts mss through agents. Reprints books. Prefers 30,000-50,000 wds. Royalty 5-10% of net; no advance. Average first printing 10,000. Publication within 12 mos. Considers simultaneous submissions. Responds in 30 days. Guidelines; catalog for 9x12 SAE/3 stamps.

Nonfiction: Query; no phone query; fax query ok.

Fiction: Query. Adult/teen/juvenile. "Looking for teen/YA fiction."

BIBLE DISCOVERY, Chariot Family Publishing, 20 Lincoln Ave., Elgin IL 60120. (708)741-0800. Fax: (708)741-0499. Cook Communications Ministries. To acquaint children of all ages (1-14 yrs) with the truths of God's Word. See Chariot Family Publishing for details.

Nonfiction: Summary of idea and sample; complete ms for books for very young children; no phone query. "Most open to accurate, quality Bible stories and devotional material that effectively bridges Scripture to a child's life. We look for unique ideas that are clear, concise, and age-appropriate."

Special Needs: Bible portions/devotional material; new ways to utilize Scripture for 8-14 year olds. Bible storybooks; product ideas for using Scripture text; devotional; Bible portions for 0-3s and 3-8 year olds.

#BLUE DOLPHIN PUBLISHING, INC., P.O. Box 1920, Nevada City CA 95959-1920. (916)265-6925. Fax: (916)265-0787. Paul M. Clemens, pres. Imprint: Pelican Pond. Publishes 12-15 titles/yr. Receives 2,500 submissions annually. 75% of books from first-time authors. Accepts mss though agents. Reprints books. Prefers about 60,000 wds or 200 pgs. Royalty 10% of net; no advance. Average first printing 5,000. Publication within 4-8 mos. Considers simultaneous submissions. Responds in 1-2 mos. Guidelines; free catalog.

> **Nonfiction:** Complete ms; no phone query. "We will accept most categories, depending on preferences at the time and presentation of the work."
>
> **Special Needs:** Books on early Christianity, personal mysticism, relationships, self-help/inspirational, men's and women's issues. Poetry only from previously published poets.
>
> **Tips:** "Our emphasis is on health and ecology; self-growth."

BOB JONES UNIVERSITY PRESS, Light Line and Pennant Books Imprints (for children & youth only), Greenville SC 29614. (803)242-5100x4315. George Collins, ed-in-chief; Gloria Repp, acq. ed. for Light Line and Pennant books. Goal is to publish books for children that excel in both literary and moral content. Publishes 6-10 titles/yr. Receives 400 submissions annually. 30% of books from first-time authors. Accepts mss through agents. Reprints books. Prefers 3,000-60,000 wds (depends on age group). Outright purchases of $1,000-1,500; no advance. Average first printing 5,000. Publication within 12-18 months. Considers simultaneous submissions. Responds in 2 mos. Guidelines; catalog for 9x12 SAE/2 stamps.

> **Nonfiction:** Query or proposal/5 chapters; no phone query. "Looking for juvenile biography and history books."
>
> **Fiction:** Proposal/5 chapters or complete ms. "Looking for humor; problem realism; historical fiction."
>
> **Tips:** "Most open to realistic or historical fiction for upper elementary through teens; biography with a good moral tone."

DON BOSCO MULTIMEDIA, 475 North Ave., New Rochelle NY 10801. (914)576-0122. Fax: (914)654-0443. Catholic. Dr. James T. Morgan, ed. Books for youth and family ministries. Publishes 6 titles/yr. Receives 20 submissions annually. 60% of books from first-time authors. No mss through agents. Prefers 128 pgs. Royalty on net; no advance. Publication within 1 yr. Responds in 1 mo. Free guidelines/catalog.

> **Nonfiction:** Query. "Looking for books directed towards young people in order to develop life skills as Christians."
>
> **Also does:** Pamphlets & booklets.

BRENTWOOD CHRISTIAN PRESS, 4000 Beallwood Ave., Columbus GA 31904. (404)576-5787. Mainline. Jerry L. Luquire, exec. ed. Publishes 267 titles/yr. Receives 2,000 submissions annually. Accepts mss through agents. Reprints books. **SUBSIDY PUBLISHES 95%.** Prefers 120 pgs. Average first printing 500. Publication within 2 mos. Considers simultaneous submissions. Responds in 2 days. Guidelines; no catalog.

Nonfiction: Complete ms. "Collection of sermons on family topics; poetry; relation of Bible to current day."

Fiction: Complete ms. "Stories that show how faith helps overcome small, day-to-day problems. Prefer under 200 pgs."

Tips: "Keep it short; support facts with reference."

#BRIDGE PUBLISHING, INC., 2500 Hamilton Blvd., South Plainfield NJ 07080. (908)754-0745. Fax: (908)754-0613. Catherine J. Barrier, ed. Imprints: Bridge, Logos, Haven, and Open Scroll. Publishes 20 titles/yr. Receives 1,300 submissions annually. 50% of books from first-time authors. Accepts mss through agents. **SUBSIDY PUBLISHES 20%**. Reprints books. Prefers 200-300 pgs. Royalty 10-20% of net; advance $1,000-2,500. Average first printing 10,000. Publication within 4 mos. Considers simultaneous submissions. Responds in 3 mos. Free guidelines/catalog.

Nonfiction: Proposal/3 chapters; phone query ok. "Most open to evangelism, spiritual growth, self-help and education."

Fiction: Proposal/3 chapters or complete ms. For all ages.

Tips: "Call us. We are always ready to give specific advice depending on the circumstances."

*BRISTOL HOUSE, LTD., P.O. Box 4020, Anderson IN 46013-0020. (317)644-0856. Fax: (317)622-1045. Sara Anderson, sr. ed; submit to James S. Robb, ed. Imprint: Bristol Books. Publishes 6 titles/yr. Receives 35-55 submissions annually. 33-50% of books from first-time authors. Accepts mss through agents. Reprints books. **Some SUBSIDY**. Prefers 160-240 pgs. Royalty 14% of net; no advance. Average first printing 3,000. Publication within 6-9 mos. No simultaneous submissions. Responds in 3 mos. No guidelines; catalog for 9x12 SAE/2 stamps.

Nonfiction: Proposal/2 chapters; phone query ok (606)273-7142. "Looking for books on renewal."

*BROADMAN & HOLMAN PUBLISHERS, 127 9th Ave. N, Nashville TN 37234. (615)251-2401. Southern Baptist. Vicki Crumpton, acq/dev. ed. Publishes 65 titles/yr. Receives 1,500+ submissions annually. 20-30% of books from first-time authors. Accepts mss through agents. Length varies. Variable royalty on net & advance. Average first printing 3,000-5,000. Publication within 9-12 mos. Considers simultaneous submissions. Responds in 6-8 wks. Guidelines; catalog for 9x12 SAE/3 stamps.

Nonfiction: Proposal/2 chapters (see guidelines for format); no phone query. "Looking for men's books and practical theology."

Fiction: Proposal (complete synopsis)/2 chapters. Only publishes juvenile fiction in a series.

Tips: "Follow guidelines when submitting. Be informed about the market in general and specifically related to the book you want to write."

#BROWN PUBLISHING-ROA MEDIA, P.O. Box 539, Dubuque IA 52004. (319)588-1451. Fax: (319)589-4705. Catholic. Ernest T. Nedder, pub.; Mary Jo Graham, sr. ed. Publishes 50-100 titles/yr. Receives 100-300 submissions annually. Accepts mss through agents. Variable royalty or outright purchase; rarely pays advance. Average first printing 1,000-3,000. Publication within 1 yr. Considers simultaneous submissions. Responds in 2 mos. No guidelines; free catalog.

Nonfiction: Complete ms. "Looking primarily for school and parish text books and easy-to-use help books."

+CAMERON PRESS, INC., 155 Thornwood Dr., Marlton NJ 08053. (609)983-5937. Fax: (609)983-5331. Evangelical. Lynn Guise, ed. Publishes 10 titles/yr. Royalties 10% of net. Guidelines.

Nonfiction: "Need Christian living books."

Fiction: Adult fiction suitable for series.

Tips: "We do not deal in children's books or topics."

+CATHOLIC ANSWERS, INC., P.O. Box 17490, San Diego CA 92177. (619)541-1131. Fax: (619)541-1154. Karl Keating, ed. Will not be publishing until 1996.

#THE CATHOLIC UNIVERSITY OF AMERICA PRESS, 620 Michigan Ave. NE, Washington DC 20064. (202)319-5052. Fax: (202)319-5802. Catholic. Dr. David J. McGonagle, dir. Publishes 15-20 titles/yr. Receives 100 submissions annually. 50% of books from first-time authors. No mss through agents. Reprints books. Prefers 80,000-200,000 wds. Variable royalty on net; no advance. Average first printing 750. Publication within 1 yr. Considers simultaneous submissions. Responds in 3 mos. Guidelines; catalog for SASE.

    Nonfiction: Proposal/1 chapter, bio & credits; phone query ok. "Looking for history, literature, philosophy, political theory and theology."

    Tips: "We publish only works of original scholarship of interest to practicing scholars and academic libraries; works that are aimed at college and university classrooms. We do not publish for the popular religious audience."

*CHALICE PRESS, Box 179, St. Louis MO 63166. (314)231-8500. Fax: (314)231-8524. Christian Church (Disciples of Christ). Dr. David P. Polk, ed. Books for a thinking, caring church. Publishes 12 titles/yr. Receives 200 submissions annually. 25% of books from first-time authors. No mss through agents. Rarely reprints books. Prefers 150 pgs. Royalty 14-17% of net; no advance. Average first printing 2,500. Publication within 9 mos. Considers simultaneous submissions. Responds in 3 mos. Guidelines; catalog for 9x12 SAE/2 stamps.

    Nonfiction: Proposal/2 chapters; no phone query. "Looking for informed treatments of current social issues; preaching; stewardship."

    Tips & Ethnic Books: "We want to publish a greater number of female and ethnic minority writers."

CHARIOT BOOKS (juvenile books), Imprint of Chariot Family Publishing, Cook Communications Ministries, 20 Lincoln Ave., Elgin IL 60120. (708)741-9558. "Chariot Books (children's imprint), will not be accepting unsolicited manuscripts. We're overwhelmed with mss, and have cut back on editorial staff."

    Tips: They will look at manuscripts recommended by current authors, or those submitted through The Writer's Edge Manuscript Service (see listing in Editorial Services).

CHARIOT FAMILY PUBLISHING, 20 Lincoln Ave., Elgin IL 60120. (708)741-0800. Fax: (708)741-0499. Cook Communications Ministries. Imprints: Chariot Books (children) & LifeJourney Books (adults), and Bible Discovery. Karl Schaller, dir. of product development. Publishes 80 titles/yr. Receives 1,500 submissions annually. 5% of books from first-time authors. Accepts mss through agents. Royalty or outright purchases; advance. Average first printing 10,000. Publication within 18 mos. considers simultaneous submissions. Responds in 3 mos. Guidelines; no catalog.

    Nonfiction: Accepts no manuscripts except through The Writer's Edge (see listing in Editorial Services).

    Fiction: All unsolicited mss returned with guidelines.

#CHOSEN BOOKS, Division of Baker Book House, 3985 Bradwater St., Fairfax VA 22031-3702. (703)764-8250. Fax: (703)764-3995. Charismatic. Jane Campbell, ed. Publishes 6-8 titles/yr. Receives 600 submissions annually. 15% of books from first-time authors. Accepts mss through agents. Prefers 60,000 wds or

200 pgs. Royalty 14% of net; advance. Average first printing 5,000. Publication within 1-2 yrs. Considers simultaneous submissions. Responds in 2-3 mos. Guidelines; no catalog.

> **Nonfiction:** Proposal/2 chapters; no phone query. "Looking for books with a charismatic Christian orientation."
>
> **Tips:** "Narratives must have a strong theme and reader benefits."

CHRISTIAN CLASSICS, INC., Box 30, Westminster MD 21158-0930. (410)848-3065. Fax: (410)857-2805. Catholic. Was bought out by Thomas More, a division of Tabor Publishing, 200 E. Bethany Dr., P.O. Box 7000, Allen TX 75002.

CHRISTIAN ED. PUBLISHERS, Box 2789, La Jolla CA 92038. (619)578-4700. Carol Rogers, mng. ed. An evangelical publisher of Bible Club materials for ages two through high school. Publishes 28 titles/yr. 25% of books from first-time authors. No mss through agents. Outright purchases for .02-.03 per wd; no advance. Publication within 9 mos. Responds in 30 days. Guidelines; catalog for 9x12 SAE/2 stamps.

> **Nonfiction:** Query first. Bible studies, curriculum and take-home papers.
>
> **Fiction:** Query first. Juvenile fiction for take-home papers. "Each story is divided into 4-5 sections of about 300 wds ea."
>
> **Tips:** "All writing done on assignment. Send letter with age level you want to write for, with your qualifications."

CHRISTIAN LITERATURE CRUSADE, Box 1449, Fort Washington PA 19034. (215)542-1240. Fax: (215)542-7580. Ken Brown, pub. mng.; Willard Stone, submissions ed. Publishes 6-8 new titles/yr; 40-50 reprints. Receives 100 submissions annually. Few books from first-time authors. No mss through agents. Reprints books. Royalty 5-10% on retail; $500 advance. Average first printing 2,500-5,000. Publication within 18 mos. Considers simultaneous submissions. Responds in 1-3 wks. Free guidelines/catalog.

> **Nonfiction:** Query letter; phone/fax query ok. "Looking for mission biographies for young people."
>
> **Also does:** Booklets.
>
> **Tips:** "Send only a proposal and three chapters. You are less likely to get a favorable notice if you send the complete manuscript unasked."

CHRISTIAN MEDIA, Box 448, Jacksonville OR 97530. (503)899-8888. Fax: on request. James Lloyd, ed/pub. Publishes 4 titles/yr. Query. Considers simultaneous submissions. Responds in 90 days. No guidelines; catalog $1.

> **Tips:** "Interested in media-oriented materials with a specific focus on Christian music, video, film, broadcasting or drama. Includes manuals, instructional or otherwise. Also books of prophetic interpretation, end times, eschatology, interpolations of political events, etc. Rapture proponents should stick with fiction."

+CHRISTIAN MISSIONS PRESS, Box 675, Waynesboro GA 30830. Tracts only. No information on openness to freelance submissions.

CHRISTIAN PUBLICATIONS, 3825 Hartzdale Dr., Camp Hill PA 17011. (717)761-7044. Christian and Missionary Alliance. David E. Fessenden, ed. Publishes 35-40 titles/yr. Receives 400 submissions annually. 5-10% of books from first-time authors. Accepts mss through agents. **SUBSIDY PUBLISHES 2%**. Reprints books. Prefers 160 pgs. Royalty 5-10% of net; outright purchases $100-2,000; advance $500. Average first printing 5,000. Publication within 12-16 mos. Considers simultaneous submissions. Responds in 1-4 mos. Guidelines; catalog for 9x12 SAE/3 stamps.

Nonfiction: Proposal/2 chapters; no phone/fax query. "Looking for books on contemporary Christian living that have a solid biblical base."

Fiction: Proposal/2 chapters. Adult, teen, children. "Something that could be a series. No 'end times'or science fiction please!"

Tips: "Most open to a well-written, contemporary-sounding book that moves the reader toward a deeper relationship with Jesus Christ."

+**CHRISTIAN UNIVERSITIES PRESS,** 781 Woodmont #345, Bethesda MD 20814. (301)654-7414. Fax: (301)654-7336. An imprint of International Scholar's Publications. Dr. Robert West, ed-in-chief. Mainstream scholarship with a Christian theme. Publishes 30 titles/yr. Receives 120+ submissions annually. 30-35% of books from first-time authors. No mss through agents. Reprints books. Prefers 250+ pgs. Royalty 5-10% of net; no advance. Average first printing 1,000. Publication within 6 mos. Considers simultaneous submissions. Responds in 1 mo. Guidelines; copy for 9x12 SAE/2 stamps.

Nonfiction: Proposal/2 chapters; phone/fax query ok. "Looking for theology, reference, missionary and renewal books."

Ethnic Books: Hispanic.

Also Does: Pamphlets.

Tips: "Most open to scholarly monograph/dissertation."

THE CHRISTOPHER PUBLISHING HOUSE, 24 Rockland St., Hanover MA 02339. (617)826-7474. Fax: (617)826-5556. Nancy A. Lucas, mng. ed. Publishes 12 titles/yr. Receives over 1,200 submissions annually. 30% of books from first-time authors. Accepts mss through agents. **SUBSIDY PUBLISHES 15%.** Prefers 100+ pgs. Royalty 10-30% of net; no advance. Average first printing 2,000. Publication within 12-14 mos. Considers simultaneous submissions. Responds in 4-6 wks. Guidelines; catalog for #10 SAE/2 stamps.

Nonfiction: Complete ms; no phone/fax query. Most topics; no juvenile material.

Fiction: Complete ms. Adult only. About 100 pgs.

CHURCH GROWTH INSTITUTE, Box 7000, Forest VA 24551. (804)525-0022. Fax: (804)525-0608. Conservative/evangelical. Cindy G. Spear, ed. Publishes 14 titles/yr. Receives 30 submissions annually. 20% of books from first-time authors. No mss through agents. Prefers 200 pgs. Royalty on retail or outright purchase. Average first printing 5,000. Publication within 6-12 mos. Considers simultaneous submissions. Responds in 60 days. Guidelines; catalog for 9x12 SAE/5 stamps.

Nonfiction: Proposal/2+ chapters; fax query ok.

Special Needs: Fresh material re: stewardship and attendance campaigns; how to start or develop various ministries in the church; small group curriculum.

Tips: "Book must be able to fit in an entire resource packet as part of a theme related to church growth or ministry. Our products are educational tools for pastors or churches. Books are lay-oriented, while related packets are leadership-oriented."

*****CISTERCIAN PUBLICATIONS INC.,** Wallwood Hall, WMU Station, Kalamazoo MI 49008. (616)387-8920. Fax: (616)387-8921. Catholic/Order of Cistercians of the Strict Observance. Dr. E. Rozanne Elder. ed. dir. Publishes 8-10 titles/yr. Receives 25-50 submissions annually. No mss through agents. Reprints books. Prefers 204-286 pgs. No payment. Average first printing 1,500. Publication within 18-48 mos. Responds in 3 mos. Free guidelines/catalog.

Nonfiction: Proposal/2 chapters; no phone query. Christian living, historical and theology.

Tips: "Christian monastic studies only."

+CLIFFSIDE PUBLISHING HOUSE, 11535 Old Hwy 16, Grassy Creek NC 28631. (910)982-9285. New publisher. Brodrick Shepherd, pres. Specializes in books on the return of Christ/end of the world. Publishes 3 titles/yr. Accepts mss through agents. Prefers 200 pgs. Royalty 5-10% on retail; negotiable advance. Average first printing 3,000. Publication in 8-12 mos. Considers simultaneous submissions. Responds in 1 month. Guidelines; no catalog yet.

> **Nonfiction:** Query or proposal/2-3 chapters; no phone/fax query.
>
> **Special Needs:** Manuscripts dealing with apocalyptic studies, prophecy, and related commentaries or specialty works concerning end-time theories.
>
> **Tips:** "Most open to a book addressing a biblical subject with a refreshing twist that incorporates works of biblical scholarship in a format suitable for lay persons; or highly specialized reference works."

COLLEGE PRESS PUBLISHING CO., INC., 223 W. Third St., Box 1132, Joplin MO 64802. (417)623-6280 or (800)289-3300. Fax: (417)623-8250. Christian Church/Church of Christ. John M. Hunter, ed. Imprint: Forerunner Books. Publishes 30 titles/yr. Receives 400+ submissions annually. 1-5% of books from first-time authors. Accepts mss through agents. Reprints books. Prefers 250-300 pgs or 40,000-60,000 wds. Royalty 10% of net; no advance. Average first printing 2,000. Publication within 6 mos. Considers simultaneous submissions. Responds in 2-3 mos. Guidelines; catalog for 9x12 SAE/5 stamps.

> **Nonfiction:** Query only; no phone query. "Looking for apologetics and preparation for life in the 21st century."
>
> **Ethnic Books:** Reprints their own books in Spanish.
>
> **Tips:** "Most open to conservative, biblical exposition with an 'Arminian' view and/or 'amillenial' slant."

*COLLIER-MACMILLAN PUBLISHING CO., 866 Third Ave., New York NY 10022. (212)702-9865. Trade book publisher with a religious line. Stephen Wilburn, dir., religious books. Publishes 8-12 titles/yr. Prefers 50,000 wds & up. Royalty & advance.

> **Nonfiction:** Proposal/3-5 chapters.

*COMPANION PRESS, 167 Walnut Bottom Rd., Shippenburg PA 17257. (717)532-3040. Fax: (717)532-9291. Inter-denominational. Imprint: Destiny Image Books. Keith Carroll, pub. Publishes 38 titles/yr. Receives 300 submissions annually. 80% of books from first-time authors. Accepts mss through agents. Reprints books. **SUBSIDY PUBLISHES 80%.** Prefers 60,000 wds. Royalty 4-8% on retail; for subsidy, purchase books at 70% of retail price; no advance. Average first printing 5,000. Publication within 3 mos. Considers simultaneous submissions. Responds in 4 wks. Free guidelines & catalog.

> **Nonfiction & Fiction:** Query or complete ms.

CONCORDIA PUBLISHING HOUSE, 3558 S. Jefferson Ave., St. Louis MO 63118-3968. (314)268-1000. Fax: (314)268-1329. Lutheran Church/Missouri Synod. Ruth Geisler, family/children's ed; Rev. Bruce Cameron, academic/theological ed. Publishes 75 titles/yr. Receives 1,200+ submissions annually. 25% of books from first-time authors. Accepts mss through agents. Royalty 6-10% on retail; some outright purchases. Publication within 10-12 mos. Frowns on simultaneous submissions. Responds in 8 wks. Free guidelines/catalog, as available.

> **Nonfiction:** Proposal/2 chapters; no phone query.
>
> **Fiction:** Proposal/2 chapters. For children or teens only; also picture books. Fiction guidelines available on request. Christian fiction only.
>
> **Ethnic Books:** Publishes books for Hispanic, Chinese, African-American, Hmong, and Vietnamese.

Tips: "Most open to family, inspirational/devotional, or children's books."

CONTEMPORARY DRAMA SERVICE - See Meriwether Publishing, Ltd.

COOK COMMUNICATIONS MINISTRIES - See Chariot Family Publishing, Chariot Books, LifeJourney Books and Bible Discovery.

DAVID C. COOK PUBLISHING CO. - See Cook Communications Ministries.

*CORNELL UNIVERSITY PRESS, Box 250, 124 Roberts Pl., Ithaca NY 14851. (607)257-7000. Fax: (607)257-3552. Nondenominational. Bernard Kendler & Roger Hayden, eds. Publishes 6-8 titles/yr. Receives 20 submissions annually. 50% of books from first-time authors. Accepts mss through agents. Reprints books. Prefers 100,000 wds. Royalty 5-10%; rarely pays advance. Average first printing 1,250. Publication within 1 yr. May consider simultaneous submission. Responds in 3 mos. Free guidelines/catalog.

> **Nonfiction:** Query first. "Looking for historical (esp. medieval and early modern) and philosophical books."

+CORNERSTONE PRESS, 939 W. Wilson Ave., Chicago IL 60640. (312)989-6361. Fax: (312)989-2076. Jane Hertenstein, assoc. ed. Publishes 10-15 titles/yr. Receives 30-50 submissions annually. Prefers 200-250 pgs. Royalty 12%.

> **Nonfiction:** Proposal/chapters.

*COVENANT PUBLISHERS, Box 26361, Philadelphia PA 19141. (215)638-4324. Mainline Protestant. Dr. Matthew Sadiku, exec. ed. Publishes 2 titles/yr. Receives 4 submissions annually. 50% of books from first-time authors. Prefers 250 pgs. Royalty 10% of net; no advance. Publication within 6 mos. Responds in 2 wks. Catalog for SASE.

> **Nonfiction:** Complete ms. "Looking for Christian living topics."

CREATION HOUSE, 190 N. Westmonte Dr., Altamonte Springs FL 32714. (407)862-7565. Fax: (407)869-6051. Strang Communications Co. Deborah Poulalion, mng. ed; submit to Kelli L. Bass. Publishes 20 titles/yr. Receives 600 submissions annually. 5% of books from first-time authors. Accepts mss through agents. Prefers 40,000 wds. Royalty on net; advance. Average first printing 5,000. Publication within 6-9 mos. Considers simultaneous submissions. Responds in 2+ mos. Free guidelines/catalog.

> **Nonfiction:** Proposal/3 chapters; no disks or phone query. "Need books of special interest to charismatics and pentecostals; also practical Christian living."

*CREATIVELY YOURS, 2906 W. 64th Pl., Tulsa OK 74132. Publishes individual scripts and books of plays, poems and related material; general religious. Jill Morris, pub. Send complete ms. Responds in 2 mos or less. Pays $25 for plays; $5 for poems (4-20 lines/action), and $10 for choral readings. Buys all rts. Guidelines; free brochure.

> **Tips:** "Try the material on children—if they don't like it, don't send it to us. Use humor whenever possible. The plays we publish can be used with puppets or children, so don't overload on characters, props or setting—keep it simple."

> **Note:** Since this publisher wants individual plays or poems, it is listed in the topical section for periodicals.

+CROSS CULTURAL PUBLICATIONS, INC., P.O. Box 506, Notre Dame IN 46556. (219)272-0899. Fax: (219)273-5973. Cyriac K. Pullapilly, gen. ed. Promotes intercultural and interfaith understanding. Publishes 3-5 titles/yr. Receives 3000+ submissions annually. 85% of books from first-time authors. Accepts mss through agents. Prefers 150-200 pgs. Royalty 10% of net; no advance. Publication within 4 mos. Considers simultaneous submissions. Responds in 4-6 wks. No guidelines; free catalog.

Nonfiction: Query/proposal/1 chapter; phone/fax query ok.

Special Needs: Intercultural topics.

Ethnic Books: "Yes, if they meet out standards."

Tips: "Most open to solidly researched, well-written books on serious issues. Send a well-written summary to get our attention."

CROSSWAY BOOKS, 1300 Crescent St., Wheaton IL 60187. (708)682-4300. Fax: (708)682-4785. A division of Good News Publishers. Leonard G. Goss, editorial dir. Publishes 50-60 titles/yr. Receives 4,500 submissions annually. 10-15% of books from first-time authors. Accepts mss through agents. Rarely reprints books. Royalty 15-21% of net; advance. Publication within 7-9 mos. Considers simultaneous submissions. Responds in 6-8 wks. Guidelines; catalog for 9x12 SAE/6 stamps.

Nonfiction: Query only; no phone query; fax query ok.

Fiction: Query/proposal/2 chapters. Also takes western novels.

Tips: "Most open to books that are consistent with what the Bible teaches and stand within the stream of historic Christian truth; books that give a clear sense that the author is a genuine Christian seeking to live a consistent Christian life."

#C.S.S. PUBLISHING CO., P.O. Box 4503, Lima OH 45802-4503. (419)227-1818. Fax: (419)228-8184. Protestant. Fred Steiner, ed. dir. Publishes 50 titles/yr. Receives 300 submissions annually. 65% of books from first-time authors. No mss through agents. **SUBSIDY PUBLISHES 20% through Fairway Press.** Prefers 100-125 pgs. Outright purchases for $25-400. Average first printing 2,000. Publication within 1-2 yrs. Considers simultaneous submissions. Responds in 3 mos. Guidelines; free catalog.

Nonfiction: Complete ms; phone query ok. "Need worship resources, sermon illustrations."

Fiction: Complete ms. plays (Advent/Christmas) and short story collections.

*CUSTOM COMMUNICATIONS SERVICES, INC./SHEPHERD PRESS/CUSTOMBOOK, 77 Main St., Tappan NJ 10983. (914)365-0414. Norman Shaifer, pres. Publishes 50-75 titles/yr. 50% of books from first-time authors. No mss through agents. Royalty on net; some outright purchases for specific assignments. Publication within 6 mos. Responds in 1 month. Guidelines; no catalog.

Nonfiction: Query/proposal/chapters. "Histories of individual congregations, denominations, or districts."

Tips: "Find stories of larger congregations (750 or more households) who have played a role in the historic growth and development of the community or region."

*DABAR SERVICES, P.O. Box 35377, Detroit MI 48235. (313)861-2806. Fax: (313)864-9444. Diane Reeder, content ed. Publishes 1-2 titles/yr. Receives 3 submissions annually. 100% of books from first-time authors. No mss through agents. Open to subsidy publishing, especially of established speakers. Would reprint books. Royalty 10-15% on retail; no advance. Average first printing 3,000. Publication time undetermined. Considers simultaneous submissions. Responds in 3 mos. No guidelines/catalog.

Nonfiction: Query first. "We look for books that speak to the specific needs of African-American women while not necessarily excluding the needs of other women."

Ethnic Books: "Black women are our target audience."

Tips: "Explore and exhaust all other avenues. We're small and new. But if a book is burning within and no other doors have opened, contact us. The book needs to have a strong, scriptural base."

#DIMENSION BOOKS, INC., 1 Summit St., Rockaway NJ 07866. (201)627-4334. Catholic. Thomas P. Coffey, ed. Publishes 11 titles/yr. Receives hundreds of submissions annually. 20% of books from first-time authors. Accepts mss through agents. Reprints books. Prefers 200 pgs. Royalty on retail; advance.

Average first printing 10,000. Publication within 6 mos. Considers simultaneous submissions. Responds in 2-5 wks. No guidelines; catalog for #10 SAE/1 stamp.

Nonfiction: Query; no phone query. Christian spirituality, music, biography and psychology.

DIMENSIONS FOR LIVING - See **THE UNITED METHODIST PUBLISHING HOUSE.**

DISCIPLESHIP RESOURCES, Box 840, Nashville TN 37202. (615)340-7068. (800)814-7833. Fax: (615)340-7006. United Methodist. Craig Gallaway, ed. dir. Publishes 20-30 titles/yr. Receives 250-300 submissions annually. 40% of books from first-time authors. Accepts mss through agents. Prefers 96-144 pgs. Royalty 10% of net; no advance. Average first printing 4,000. Publication within 4 mos. Responds in 6-8 wks. Guidelines; catalog for 9x12 SAE/3 stamps.

Nonfiction: Proposal/2 chapters; phone/fax query ok. "Looking for leadership in ministry in the 21st century; ministry of laity—spiritual gifts."

Ethnic Books: Produces titles related to ministries for African-American, Hispanic, and Asian American.

Also does: Some booklets.

Tips: "Most open to a book that examines a specific area of ministry in the church and understands that leading this area is part of the total system of ministry in the church. Stay in touch with the real needs in the church."

*****DISCOVERY PUBLISHING HOUSE**, Box 3566, Grand Rapids MI 49501. Radio Bible Class. Robert DeVries, pub.; submit to Carol Holquist, assoc. pub. Guidelines. Not included in topical listings.

+EDITORIAL EVANGELICA, P.O. Box 4138, Cleveland TN 37320. (615)468-7655. Fax: (615)478-7825. Church of God (TN). Robert A. Rivera, ed. of Spanish Publications. Mostly curriculum material for Hispanics. Publishes 1-2 titles/yr. Receives 4 submissions annually. No books from first-time authors. No mss through agents. Prefers 200 pgs. Royalty 10% on retail; no advance. Mostly in-house projects. Publication with 6 mos. No guidelines or catalog.

Nonfiction: Query only; no phone/fax queries. "Looking for biblical exegesis, Christian education and theology."

Ethnic Books: Spanish only.

Also does: Pamphlets, booklets and tracts.

*****EDUCATIONAL MINISTRIES, INC.**, 165 Plaza Dr., Prescott AZ 86303-5549. (602)771-8601. Fax: (602)771-8621. Christian education publisher/Mainline Protestant. Robert Davidson, ed.; Suzanne Rood Cox, project ed. Publishes 10 titles/yr. Prefers 40-100 pgs. Royalty 10% on retail; some outright purchases $500. Responds in 3 mos. Guidelines; catalog for 9x12 SAE/4 stamps.

Nonfiction: Complete ms. Christian education resource books.

WM B. EERDMANS PUBLISHING CO., 255 Jefferson Ave. SE, Grand Rapids MI 49503. (616)459-4591. Fax: (616)459-6540. Protestant/Academic/Theological. Jon Pott, ed-in-chief; Amy Eerdmans, children's book ed.; Nueva Creacion, Spanish imprint. Publishes 100 titles/yr. Receives 1,100-1,400 submissions annually. 10% of books from first-time authors. Accepts mss through agents. Reprints books. Royalty 7.5-10% on retail; occasional advance, $1,000. Average first printing 5,000. Publication within 1 yr. Considers simultaneous submissions. Responds in 1 wk to 6 mos. Free guidelines/catalog.

Nonfiction: Proposal/1 chapter; no phone/fax query. "Looking for religious approaches to contemporary issues; spiritual growth; scholarly works; biography for middle readers through young adults; children's picture books expressing positive family values."

Fiction: Proposal/1 chapter. Children/teen; limited amount for adults.

Ethnic Books: Spanish imprint.

Tips: "Most open to material with general appeal, but well researched, cutting-edge material that bridges the gap between evangelical and mainline world."

+**ELDER BOOKS**, P.O. Box 490, Forest Knolls CA 94933. (415)488-9002. Fax: (415)488-4720. Susan Sullivan, dir. New publisher. All books from first-time authors. Accepts mss through agents. Reprints books. Prefers 130 pgs. Royalty 7% of net; advance. Average first printing 3,000. Publication with 12 months. Considers simultaneous submissions. Responds in 6 wks. No guidelines; catalog for #10 SAE/1 stamp.

Nonfiction: Query; fax query ok. "Most open to books on aging."

+**ELEMENT BOOKS**, 42 Broadway, Rockport MA 01966. (508)546-1044. Fax: (508)546-9882. Paul Cash, acq. ed. Books for broad religious market. Publishes 25 titles/yr. Receives hundreds of submissions annually. 15% of books from first-time authors. Accepts mss through agents. Reprints books. Prefers 125-250 pgs. Variable royalty & advance. Average first printing 3,000-5,000. Publication within 18 mos. Considers simultaneous submissions. Responds in 6-8 wks. Free guidelines & catalog.

Nonfiction: Query only; no phone/fax query.

Tips: "Try to reach a broad-based market—no books on very scholarly or limited-interest subjects."

+**ELDRIDGE PUBLISHING**, P.O. Box 1595, Venice FL 34284. (800)HI-STAGE. Fax (800)453-5179. Independent Christian drama publisher. Nancy Vorhis, sr. ed. To provide superior religious drama to enhance preaching and teaching, whatever your Christian faith. Publishes 20 plays/yr. Receives 300 plays annually. 50% of plays from first-time authors. Accepts mss through agents. One-act to full-length plays. Outright purchases of $200-500; no advance. Publication within 6 months. Considers simultaneous submissions. Responds in 2 mos. Guidelines; free play catalog.

Plays: Complete ms; phone/fax queries not preferred. For children, teens and adults.

Special Needs: Prefers plays and musicals set around Christmas and Easter. Other religious holidays and "anytime"Christian plays also considered.

Tips: "Have play produced at your church and others prior to submissions, to get out the bugs. At least try a stage reading."

*****EMERALD BOOKS**, P.O. Box 635, Lynnwood WA 98046. (206)771-1153. Fax: (206)775-2383. Non-denominational. Warren Walsh, owner/ed. Publishes 4-6 titles/yr. Receives 20-30 submissions annually. Accepts mss through agents. **SUBSIDY PUBLISHES 5%.** Prefers 150-200 pgs. Royalty 15% of net; seldom pays an advance. Average first printing 7,500. Publication within 6 mos. Considers simultaneous submissions. Responds in 30-60 days. Guidelines; free catalog.

Nonfiction: Proposal/2 chapters. "Looking for solid Christian living books and solid books for youth."

Fiction: Proposal/2-4 chapters. For all ages.

*****FAIRWAY PRESS**, Subsidy Division for C.S.S. Publishing Company, 517 S. Main St., Box 4503, Lima OH 45802. (419)227-1818. Fax: (419)228-9184. Niki C. Dunham, gen. mgr. Publishes 60-75 titles/yr. Receives 365 submissions annually. 98% of books from first-time authors. Accepts mss through agents. Reprints books. **SUBSIDY PUBLISHES 100%.** Royalty; no advance. Average first printing 2,000. Publication within 8-9 mos. Considers simultaneous submissions. Responds in up to 1 month. Free guidelines/catalog for 9x12 SAE.

Nonfiction: Complete ms. "Looking for mss with a Christian theme, and seasonal material."

Fiction: Complete ms. For adults, teens, or children.

+FAITH, PRAYER & TRACT LEAGUE, Grand Rapids MI 49504-1390. Tracts only. No information on openness to freelance submissions.

FOCUS ON THE FAMILY PUBLISHERS, 8605 Explorer Dr., Colorado Springs CO 80920-1051. (719)531-3400. Fax: (719)531-3484. Gwen Weising, mng. ed. Publishes 15 titles/yr. Receives 1,200 submissions annually. One book/yr from first-time authors. Accepts mss through agents. Occasionally reprints books. Prefers 225 pgs. Royalty on retail; advance. Average first printing 20,000. Publication within 18 mos. Considers simultaneous submissions. Responds in 2-4 wks. Guidelines; no catalog.

Nonfiction: Query only.

Tips: "Because we are cross-marketing, we need writers who also have a public ministry—speaking, teaching—experience in verbal as well as written communication."

FORWARD MOVEMENT PUBLICATIONS, 412 Sycamore St., Cincinnati OH 45202. (513)721-6659. Fax: (513)421-0315. Episcopal. Seeking new editor. Publishes 8 books; 32 booklets/yr. Receives 150-200 submissions annually. 50% of books from first-time authors. No mss through agents. Occasionally reprints books. Prefers short mss. One-time honorarium; no advance. Average first printing 6,000. Considers simultaneous submissions. Responds in 1-2 mos. Guidelines; catalog for #10 SAE/3 stamps.

Nonfiction: Complete ms/query/proposal (depends on length); no phone/fax query. "We really aren't looking for books although we publish about 8 a year. We need short works for pamphlets and booklets."

Ethnic Books: Pamphlets in Spanish.

#FRANCISCAN PRESS, 1800 College Ave., Quincy IL 62301-2670. (217)228-5670. Fax: (217)228-5672. Catholic/Franciscan. Imprints: Franciscan Herald Press and Franciscan Press. Est. 1991. Dr. Terrence J. Riddell, dir. Publishes 5-10 titles/yr. Receives 50-100 submissions annually. 10% of books from first-time authors. No mss through agents. Reprints books. Royalty 5-10% of net; outright purchases negotiated; no advance. Average first printing 2,500. Publication within 12-18+ mos. Considers simultaneous submissions. Responds in up to 6 mos. No guidelines; free catalog.

Nonfiction: Query first. "Looking for moral theology; Franciscan history; works on life and writings of SS, Francis, Clare, Bonaventure."

Tips: "Please observe our somewhat specific subject area limitations."

FRANCISCAN UNIVERSITY PRESS, University Blvd., Steubenville OH 43952. (614)283-6357. Fax: (614)283-6442. Catholic. Celeste Gregory, ed. Publishes 10 titles/yr. Receives 30 submissions annually. 5% of books from first-time authors. No mss through agents. Reprints books. Prefers 250 pgs. Royalty 5-15% on retail; no advance. Average first printing 1,000-2,000. Publication within 1 yr. Considers simultaneous submissions. Responds in several mos. Guidelines; free catalog.

Nonfiction: Proposal/1 chapter; author vita; table of contents; no phone query; fax query ok. "Looking for Catholic apologetics and biblical studies."

Ethnic Books: "Spanish translations of our best-selling devotional works."

Tips: "Most of our books are solicited from university professors and associates."

*FRIENDSHIP PRESS, 475 Riverside Dr., Room 860, New York NY 10115. (212)870-2496. Fax: (212)870-2550. National Council of Churches of Christ. Margaret Larom, ed.; submit to Audrey A. Miller, dir. Publishes 12-20 titles/yr. Receives 35 submissions annually. 50% of books from first-time authors. Accepts mss through agents. Prefers 40-130 pgs. Royalty; some outright purchases; advance. Average first printing 10,000. Publication within 9-12 mos. Occasionally considers simultaneous submissions. Responds in 1-3 mos. Guidelines; catalog for 9x12 SAE.

Nonfiction: Complete ms; no phone query. "Looking for books on life in a multicultural society, the churches, and the United Nations."

Fiction: Complete ms. For all ages.

Special Needs: Global perspective, mission education and political and religious issues, peace and justice education, cultural understanding and appreciation, spiritual reflection and development related to mission and social action.

Tips: "Most open to a book that fits a theme stated in our guidelines (one global/one topical), or one with a secured market. Church people primary audience."

FRIENDS UNITED PRESS, 101 Quaker Hill Dr., Richmond IN 47374. (317)962-7573. Fax: (317)966-1293. Friends United Meeting (Quaker). Ardith Talbot, ed. To energize and equip persons to live an abundant life in God. Publishes 6-8 titles/yr. Receives 50-60 submissions annually. 75% of books from first-time authors. Accepts mss through agents. **SUBSIDY PUBLISHES 5%.** Reprints books. Prefers 250-300 pgs. Royalty 7.5% of net (after printing costs are recouped); no advance. Average first printing 1,000-1,500. Publication within 6 mos. Considers simultaneous submissions. Responds in 4-6 mos. Free guidelines/catalog.

Nonfiction: Proposal or complete ms; phone/fax query ok. "Looking for books on Quaker history and spirituality."

Fiction: Complete ms. For all ages.

Special Needs: Quaker history and spirituality.

Tips: "We are restricted to Quaker authors, history, doctrine, etc."

+GARBORG'S HEART 'N HOME, 2060 W. 98th St., Bloomington MN 55431. (612)888-5727. Fax: (612)888-4775. Joan Garborg, ed. Produces DayBrighteners—encouraging, inspirational daily thoughts for different audiences. Publishes 20 titles/yr. Receives 100 submissions annually. 5% of books from first-time authors. Accepts mss through agents. Prefers 366 pgs (60 wds/pg). Royalty 5% of net or outright purchase; no advance. Publication within 6-12 mos. Considers simultaneous submissions. Responds in 1 mo. Guidelines; catalog for 9x12 SAE/2 stamps.

Nonfiction: Send a sample of 30 days of thoughts or quotes.

Special Needs: Gift books for female relationships: friends, mother, daughter, sister, grandmother. Inspirational gift books having crossover appeal to the secular market.

#C.R. GIBSON CO., 32 Knight St., Norwalk CT 06856. (203)847-4543. Julie Mitchell, ed. Publishes 15 titles/yr. Receives 700 submissions annually. 20% of books from first-time authors. Accepts mss through agents. Reprints books. **SUBSIDY PUBLISHES 20%.** Prefers 40-60 pgs. Royalty 6% of net or outright purchase of $100-3,000; advance $500-5,000. Average first printing 10,000. Publication within 18 mos. Considers simultaneous submissions. Responds in 4 mos. Guidelines.

Nonfiction: Proposal/1 chapter. Specializes in gift books.

Fiction: Proposal/1 chapter. Adult and children's picture books. Poetry books (complete ms).

*GILGAL PUBLICATIONS, Box 3386 or 3399, Sunriver OR 97707. (503)593-8639. Fax: (503)593-5604. Judy Osgood, exec. ed. Publishes 1 title/yr. Receives 100 submissions annually. No mss through agents. Pays $10 for each short article accepted for the anthologies, plus royalties. Pays on acceptance. Responds in 3-13 wks (only if SASE is included). Guidelines when available for new book projects.

Nonfiction: Complete ms (after reading guidelines). "Our books are all anthologies on coping with stress and resolving grief. Not interested in other book mss."

#GOLD 'N' HONEY BOOKS, Box 1720, Sisters OR 97759. (503)549-1144. Children's book imprint Thomas Womack, ed. Publishes 20 titles/yr. Receives 500 submissions annually. 5% of books from first-time authors. Prefers not to work with agents. Royalty 5-18% of net. Publication with 10 mos. Responds in 2 mos. Catalog $2.

> **Nonfiction:** Query. Illustrated books.

> **Fiction:** Query. Religious picture books.

GOOD BOOK PUBLISHING COMPANY, 2747 S. Kihei Rd., #D110, Kihei, Maui HI 96753. Tel./Fax: (808)874-4876. Christian/Protestant Bible Fellowship. Ken Burns, pres. Researches and publishes books on the biblical/Christian roots of Alcoholics Anonymous. Publishes 3 titles/yr. Receives 2 submissions annually. No books from first-time authors. No mss through agents. Prefers 200 pgs. Royalty 10%; no advance. Average first printing 1,000. Publication within 3 mos. Considers simultaneous submission. Responds in 2 wks. No guidelines; catalog for #10 SAE/2 stamps.

> **Nonfiction:** Query letter only; no phone/fax query. Books on the spiritual history of A.A.

+GOOD NEWS PUBLISHERS, 1300 Crescent St., Wheaton IL 60187. (708)682-4300. Fax: (708)682-4785. Tracts only. Want 2½ manuscript pages, 40 characters/line. Send to Tract Editor. Responds in 4 wks. Guidelines.

GOSPEL LIGHT PUBLICATIONS - See REGAL BOOKS.

+GOSPEL PUBLISHING HOUSE, 1445 Boonville Ave., Springfield MO 65802. (417)831-8000. Fax: (417)862-7566. Assemblies of God. David A. Womack, mngr. Imprints: CHRISM and Logion Press. Denominational publisher that also sells in the trade market. Publishes 12-15 titles/yr. Receives 400 submissions annually. 75% of books from first-time authors. Accepts mss through agents. Prefers 160-280 pgs. Royalty on retail; negotiable advance. Average first printing 5,000. Publication within 1 yr. Immediate response. Free guidelines/catalog.

> **Nonfiction:** Proposal/outline/1 chapter; phone/fax query ok.

> **Also Does:** Booklets.

> **Ethnic Books:** Some Spanish materials.

+GREENLAWN PRESS, 107 S. Greenlawn, South Bend IN 46617. (219)234-5088. Fax: (219)236-6633. Interdenominational/Mainline Christian. Dan Decelles, pub. Published 2 titles/yr. Receives 6 submissions annually. 10% of books from first-time authors. Accepts mss through agents. Reprints books. Prefers 150 pgs. Royalty; no advance. Average first printing 3,500. Publication within 9 mos. Responds in 3 mos. Guidelines; catalog for 9x12 SAE/2 stamps.

> **Nonfiction:** Query; no phone query; fax query ok. "Looking for books on Christian daily life."

GROUP PUBLISHING, INC., Box 481, Loveland CO 80539. (303)669-3836. Fax: (303)669-3269. Imprint: Group Books. Mike Nappa, acq. ed. Publishes 24-30 titles/yr. Receives 300-500 submissions annually. 10-25% of books from first-time authors. No mss through agents. Prefers 200 ms pgs. Royalty to 10% of net; some outright purchases; advance $1,000. Average first printing 7,000. Publication within 18 mos. Considers simultaneous submissions. Responds in 3-6 mos. Guidelines; catalog for 9x12 SAE/2 stamps.

> **Nonfiction:** Proposal/2 chapters; no phone/fax query. "Looking for new, creative, active and inter-active craft books and other types of programming books for children's ministry and youth ministry."

Tips: "Study our line of books before you approach us. Read *Why Nobody Learns Much of Anything in Church and How to Fix It*, by Thom & Joani Schultz, then present a proposal that fits the standards outlined in that book."

+GROUP'S HANDS-ON BIBLE CURRICULUM, Box 481, Loveland CO 80539. (303)669-3836. Fax: (303)669-3269. Mike Nappa, acq. ed. Publishes 24 titles/yr. Receives 200 submissions annually. 40% of books from first-time authors. No mss through agents. Outright purchase. Publication within 12-18 mos. Considers simultaneous submissions. Responds in 3-6 mos. Trial assignment guidelines/catalog for 9x12 SAE/2 stamps.

   Nonfiction: Query requesting a trial assignment. Produces curriculum for preschoolers, 1st-2nd, 3rd-4th, and 5th-6th graders.

#GUERNICA EDITIONS, Box 117, Stn. P, Toronto ON M5S 2S6 Canada. Fax: (416)657-8885. Antonio D'Alfonso, ed. Publishes 2 religious titles/yr. Receives 1,000 submissions annually. 5% of books from first-time authors. Accepts mss through agents. Reprints books. Prefers 128 pgs. Royalty 3-10% on retail; outright purchases $200-5,000. Average first printing 1,000. Publication within 18 mos. Responds in 3 mos. No guidelines; for catalog send money order for stamps (if from US).

   Nonfiction: Query first. "Looking for books on world issues."

   Fiction: Query first. Interested in ethnic and translations.

   Ethnic Books: Concentration on Italian culture. "We are involved in translations and ethnic issues."

+HANNIBAL BOOKS, 921 Center, Hannibal MO 63401. Tel/Fax: (314)221-2464. Hefley Communications. Marti Hefley, ed. To impact readers for Christ. Publishes 4-6 titles/yr. Receives 40 submissions annually. Almost no books from first-time authors. Accepts mss through agents. Prefers 200 pgs. Variable royalty on net; no advance. Average first printing 4,000.

   Nonfiction: Query letter only. Phone queries only if you know editor.

   Fiction: Query letter only. Rarely does fiction.

   Tips: "Most open to a crossover book. Send an intelligent query."

#HARPERSANFRANCISCO, 1160 Battery St., San Francisco CA 94111-1213. (415)477-4400. Fax: (415)477-4444. Religious division of a general trade publisher (HarperCollins). Tom Grady, pub. Publishes 180 titles/yr. Receives 10,000 submissions annually. 5% of books from first-time authors. Accepts mss through agents. Reprints books. Prefers 160-256 ms pgs. Royalty 10-15% on cloth, 7.5% on paperback, on retail; advance. Average first printing 7,500-10,000. Publication within 18 mos. Considers simultaneous submissions. Responds in 2 mos. Free guidelines/catalog.

   Nonfiction: Query or proposal/chapters.

*HARRISON HOUSE PUBLISHERS, Box 35035, Tulsa OK 74153. (918)582-2126. Evangelical/Charismatic. Submit to Editorial Asst. Publishes 36 titles/yr. Receives 1,500 submissions annually. 1% of books from first-time authors. No books through agents. Reprints books. Prefers 128-160 pgs. Royalty on net; no advance. Average first printing 10,000. Publication within 18 mos. Considers simultaneous submissions. Responds in 6 wks. Guidelines; no catalog.

   Nonfiction: Query only; no phone query. "Looking for charismatic teaching books from active ministers. Historical books should be on revivalists."

   Tips: "Books should teach the power of the Name of Jesus, the authority of the believer and a revelation of God's grace for mankind."

+HARVARD HOUSE, P.O. Box 24221, Denver CO 80224. (303)369-8596. Fax: (303)751-4686. Donald Webster, ed. Publishes 2-3 titles/yr. Receives 10 submissions annually. All books from first-time authors. No mss through agents. **SUBSIDY PUBLISHES 70%.** Prefers 80-200 pgs. Royalty 8-15% of net. Average first printing 1,000. Publication within 6 mos. Considers simultaneous submissions. Responds in 2 mos. Guidelines; catalog $1.

> **Nonfiction:** Proposal/up to 5 chapters or complete ms; fax query ok. "Looking for apologetics, prophecy, science/religion interface that appeals to both religious and secular. Must be marketable to secular talk shows."
>
> **Tips:** "Author must be capable/willing to do radio/TV interviews."

HARVEST HOUSE PUBLISHERS, 1075 Arrowsmith, Eugene OR 97402. (503)343-0123. Fax: (503)342-6410. Evangelical. Eileen L. Mason, ed-in-chief; submit to Manuscript Coordinator. Books that help the hurts of people. Publishes 80 titles/yr. Receives 4,000 submissions annually. 3-5% of books from first-time authors. Accepts mss through agents. Prefers 200 pgs. Royalty 14-18% of net; no advance. Average first printing 10,000. Publication within 2-8 wks. Considers simultaneous submissions. Responds in 5-6 wks. Guidelines; catalog for 9x12 SAE/3 stamps.

> **Nonfiction:** Proposal/3 chapters; no phone/fax query.
>
> **Fiction:** Proposal/3 chapters. Adult historical romance.

#THE HAWORTH PASTORAL PRESS, An imprint of The Haworth Press, 10 Alice St., Binghamton NY 13904-1580. (607)722-5857. Fax: (607)722-8465. Dr. William Clements, sr. ed. Publishes 5-10 titles/yr. Receives 25-50 submissions annually. 20% of books from first-time authors. Prefers no mss through agents. Reprints books. Prefers up to 250 pgs. Royalty 7.5-12% of net; no advance. Average first printing 1,500. Publication within 18 mos. Prefers no simultaneous submissions. Responds in 3 mos. Free guidelines/catalog.

> **Nonfiction:** Proposal/2 chapters; no phone query. "Looking for books on psychology/social work, etc., with a pastoral perspective."

#HEARTSONG PRESENTS, Imprint of Barbour and Company, Inc., P.O. Box 719, 1810 Barbour Dr., Uhrichsville, OH 44683. (614)922-6045. Fax: (614)922-5948. Rebecca Germany, ed. Publishes 48 titles/yr. Receives 100-200 submissions annually. 20% of books from first-time authors. Accepts mss through agents. Prefers 45,000-50,000 wds. Royalty 5-10% of net; outright purchases; $500 advance. Average first printing 20,000. Publication within 6-8 months. Considers simultaneous submissions. Responds in 3-5 wks. Guidelines; no catalog.

> **Fiction:** Proposal/3 chapters or complete ms. All types of inspirational romances.

HENDRICKSON PUBLISHERS, INC., 137 Summit St./Box 3473, Peabody MA 01961-3473. (508)632-6546. Fax: (508)531-8146. Patrick Alexander, sr. academic ed; submit to Dr. Philip H. Anderson, acq. ed. An academic press specializing in Biblical studies. Publishes 12-15 titles/yr. Receives 100-125 submissions annually. 3% of books from first-time authors. No mss through agents. Reprints books. Prefers 200-500 pgs. Royalty 14% of net; no advance. Average first printing 1,500-2,000. Publication within 1 yr. Considers simultaneous submissions. Responds in 3 mos. Free guidelines/catalog.

> **Nonfiction:** Proposal/chapters; no phone query. "Looking for biblical studies and reference works."
>
> **Tips:** "A well-organized, thought provoking, clear and accurate proposal has the best chance of being read."

VIRGIL W. HENSLEY, INC., 6116 E. 32nd St., Tulsa OK 74135. (918)644-8520. Fax: (918)664-8562. Terri Kalfas, ed. Publishes 5-10 titles/yr. Receives 700 submissions annually. 50% of books from first-time authors. Accepts mss through agents. Reprints books. Prefers 65,000 wds for fiction; Bible studies vary. Royalty 5% on retail; no advance. Average first printing 5,000. Publication within 12-18 mos. Considers simultaneous submissions. Responds in 8 wks. Guidelines; catalog for 9x12 SAE/4 stamps.

> **Nonfiction:** Proposal/1st 3 chapters; no phone/fax query. "If it's good we'll consider it even if it doesn't fit the categories we've indicated."
>
> **Special Needs:** Bible studies that teach students how to apply biblical principles to their lives.

HERALD PRESS, 616 Walnut Ave., Scottdale PA 15683. (412)887-8500. Fax: (412)887-3111. Canadian Address: Herald Press Canada, 490 Dutton Dr., Waterloo ON N2L 6H7 Canada. Mennonite Church. S. David Garber, book ed. To publish books consistent with scriptures interpreted in the Anabaptist/Mennonite tradition. Publishes 30 titles/yr. Receives 1,300 submissions annually. 15% of books from first-time authors. Accepts mss through agents. Rarely reprints books. Prefers 160-192 pgs. Royalty 10-12% on retail; no advance. Average first printing 3,500-5,000. Publication within 10 mos. Dislikes simultaneous submissions. Responds in 2 mos. Free guidelines; catalog for 9x12 SAE/2 stamps.

> **Nonfiction:** Proposal/2 chapters; fax query ok.
>
> **Fiction:** Query first. Juvenile/teen/adult.
>
> **Special Needs:** Bible study books; peace and social concerns, conflict resolution.
>
> **Ethnic Books:** Native American (California focus); Amish and Mennonite.
>
> **Tips:** "Most open to books promoting peace and justice."

*HIGLEY PUBLISHING CORPORATION, Box 5398, Jacksonville FL 32247. (904)396-1918. Wesley C. Reagan, ed. Publishes 1 title/yr. No mss through agents. Outright purchase of $900-3,600. Average first printing 70,000. Not in topical listings. Guidelines; no catalog.

> **Tips:** "Our purpose is to publish an annual undenominational resource for adult teachers, based on International Sunday school outlines."

HOLMAN BIBLE PUBLISHERS - See **BROADMAN & HOLMAN PUBLISHERS**.

*HONOR BOOKS, Box 55388, Tulsa OK 74155. (918)585-5033. Evangelical. Submit to Acquisitions. Publishes 12 titles/yr. 0% of books from first-time authors. Accepts mss through agents. Prefers 192 pgs. Royalty on net; no advance. Publication within 2 yrs. Considers simultaneous submissions. Responds in 6 wks. Guidelines; no catalog.

> **Nonfiction:** Query or proposal/2 chapters. "Looking for motivational books for the Christian professional who balances a relationship with God with responsibilities to family, church and work; business-related books; books on personal excellence."
>
> **Tips:** "Also need holiday-focused gift books and books to strengthen families."

HORIZON HOUSE PUBLISHERS, Subsidiary of Christian Publications, 3825 Hartzdale Dr., Camp Hill PA 17011. (717)761-7044. David Fessenden, ed. See listing for Christian Publications for details.

+HOWARD PUBLISHING, 3117 N 7th St., West Monroe LA 71291. (318)396-3122. Fax: (318)397-1882. Philis Boultinghouse, ed; submit to Gary Myers. Inspiring holiness in the lives of believers. Publishes 6-10 titles/yr. Receives 50 submissions annually. 10% of books from first-time authors. Accepts mss through agents. Reprints books. Prefers 150-400 pgs. Royalty 10% of net or outright purchase for $500-4,000; no advance. Average first printing 3,000-15,000. Publication within 6-12 mos. Considers simultaneous submissions. Free catalog.

> **Nonfiction:** Proposal or complete ms.

Fiction: Complete ms. Adult.

Tips: "Most open to a book that meets a serious and relevant need. Research potential audience."

+HUNT AND THORPE, Bowland House, Alresford, Hants, UK. (UK)962 735320. John Hunt, ed. Children's books for the international Christian market. Publishes 20 titles/yr. Receives 100 submissions annually. 5% of books from first-time authors. Accepts mss through agents. Prefers 20-40 pgs. Royalty on net; advance. Average first printing 20,000. Publication within 1 yr. Considers simultaneous submissions.Responds in 1 wk. Free catalog.

Nonfiction: Proposal/1 chapter.

Fiction: Proposal/1 chapter. "Suitable for colour publishing."

HUNTINGTON HOUSE PUBLISHERS, Box 53788, Lafayette LA 70505-3788. (318)237-7049. Mark Anthony, ed-in-chief. Publishes 25-30 titles/yr. Receives 2,000 submissions annually. 90-95% of books from first-time authors. Accepts mss through agents. Reprints books. Prefers 50,000-60,000 wds or 208-224 pgs. Royalty 10% on retail; negotiable advance. Average first printing 5,000-10,000. Publication within 6 mos. Considers simultaneous submissions. Responds in 10-12 wks. Free guidelines/catalog.

Nonfiction: Proposal/synopsis; no chapters.

Fiction: Proposal/synopsis. Rarely does fiction.

Also Does: Occasionally does booklets.

Tips: "We focus on current issues-related themes, mostly religious, politically conservative, and philosophical."

Note: Has absorbed Prescott Press.

+ICAN PRESS BOOK PUBLISHERS, INC., ICAN Press Bldg., 616 Third Ave., Chula Vista CA 91910. (619)425-8945. Fax: (619)425-2829. Dr. Dahk Knox, ed-in-chief; submit to Scott Romney. New in Christian books. Receives 1000+ submissions annually. 90+% of books from first-time authors. Accepts mss through agents. **SUBSIDY PUBLISHES 30%.** Reprints books. Prefers 100+ pgs; 300 average. Royalty 75% of net; no advance. Average first printing 1,000-2,500. Publication within 6 months. Considers simultaneous submissions. Responds in 2-3 wks. Free guidelines/catalog.

Nonfiction: Query, proposal or ms; phone/fax query ok. "Looking for inspirational, real life success stories, and Christian children's stories."

Fiction: Query, proposal or ms. "Needs morals—keep pace moving—simple style—quick reads—no flat characters."

Tips: "Most open to prophecy, inspirational, fiction based on end times events, identifying cults."

+ICHTHUS PUBLICATIONS, 2348 Third Pl. NW, Birmingham AL 35215. (205)853-5183. David Hudson, ed. Royalties 50%. Send ms on 3.5"disk in text format.

Fiction: For young teens to age 20. No children's.

#ICS PUBLICATIONS, 2131 Lincoln Rd NE, Washington DC 20002. (202)832-8489. Fax: (202)832-8967. Catholic/Institute of Carmelite Studies. Steven Payne, OCD, ed. dir. Publishes 8 titles/yr. Receives 20-30 submissions annually. 10% of books from first-time authors. Accepts mss through agents. Reprints books. Prefers 200 pgs. Royalty 2-6% on retail; some outright purchases; advance $500. Average first printing 3,000-7,000. Publication within 12-24 mos. Considers simultaneous submissions. Responds in 2 mos. Guidelines; catalog for 7x10 SAE/2 stamps.

Nonfiction: Query or outline/1 chapter; phone query ok. "Most open to translation of Carmelite classics; popular introductions to Carmelite themes which show a solid grasp of the tradition."

Special Needs: Popular commentaries on Carmelite authors—John of the Cross, Teresa of Avila, Therese of Lisieux, etc.

INTERVARSITY PRESS, Box 1400, Downers Grove IL 60515. (708)964-5700. Fax: (708)964-1251. Andrew T. Le Peau, ed. dir. Publishes 80 titles/yr. Receives 1,800 submissions annually. 15% of books from first-time authors. Accepts mss through agents. Prefers 120-240 pgs; 35,000-70,000 wds. Negotiable royalty on retail; outright purchases of $1000 & up; negotiable advance. Average first printing 6,000. Publication within 1 yr. Considers simultaneous submissions. Responds in 8-12 wks. Guidelines; catalog for 9x12 SAE/6 stamps.

Nonfiction: All unsolicited mss (from people they have had no previous contact with) are referred to The Writer's Edge (see their listing under Editorial Services - IL); no phone query; fax query ok.

Fiction: See Nonfiction above. Children/adult. "Fiction need not be explicitly Christian or religious, but should arise out of a Christian perspective."

Also Does: Booklets.

Tips: "Looking for books for the Christian market which fill empty niches in the marketplace with quality books that help people grow personally; includes Bible studies, reference books, textbooks."

JEWS FOR JESUS BOOKS, 60 Haight St., San Francisco CA 94102. (415)864-2600. Fax: (415)552-8325. Steven Lawson, Director of Publications. Imprint: Purple Pomegranate. Publishes 3-5 titles/yr. No mss through agents. Royalty; no advance. No guidelines/catalog.

Nonfiction: Query; no phone/fax query. "We only do Jewish evangelism or messianic topics."

Note: They are not generally open to submissions, but they did say: "We would like to hear from Jewish believers who are writers. We do have a need from time to time for editing and freelance ghost writing, and on a rare occasion have published a book by someone who is not on our staff. But we would like to establish a relationship with such a person, rather than seeing a manuscript without any previous contact."

#JUDSON PRESS, Box 851, Valley Forge PA 19482-0851. (610)768-2118. Fax: (610)768-2056. American Baptist Churches U.S.A. Harold Rast, pub; Mary Nicol, mng. ed. Publishes 15-20 titles/yr. Receives 750 submissions annually. 50% of books from first-time authors. Accepts mss through agents. Reprints books. Prefers 30,000-80,000 wds or 128-160 pgs. Royalty 10% on retail or flat fee; advance $250. Average first printing 5,000. Publication within 15 mos. Considers simultaneous submissions. Responds in 6 mos. Guidelines; catalog for 9x12 SAE/4 stamps..

Nonfiction: Proposal/1 chapter; phone query ok (but not preferred). "Looking for practical how-to for local church leaders and pastors."

Ethnic Books: African-American.

Tips: "Develop a proposal before you write the whole ms."

KINDRED PRESS, 4-169 Riverton Ave., Winnipeg MB R2L 2E5 Canada. (204)669-6575. Fax: (204)654-1865. Mennonite Brethren. Marilyn Hudson, dir. To resource the churches within the denomination. Publishes 3-4 titles/yr. Receives 30 submissions annually. 95% of books from first-time authors. No mss through agents. **SUBSIDY PUBLISHES 25%**. Prefers 200 pgs. Royalty 15% on retail; no advance. Average first printing 2,000. Publication within 1 yr. Considers simultaneous submissions. Responds in 2 mos. Guidelines; free catalog.

Nonfiction: Proposal/3 chapters; no phone/fax query. Also does pamphlets & booklets. "Looking for Bible studies and juvenile devotionals."

Fiction: Proposal/2-3 chapters. For all ages. Limited.

Tips: "Most open to books in keeping with our tenets of faith. Follow our guidelines."

KREGEL PUBLICATIONS, P.O. Box 2607, Grand Rapids MI 49333. (616)451-4775. Dennis R. Hillman, sr. ed. To provide tools for ministry and Christian growth from a conservative, evangelical prospective. Publishes 60 titles/yr. Receives 150 submissions annually. 20% of books from first-time authors. Accepts mss through agents. Reprints books. Length open. Royalty 8-14% of net; negotiable advance. Average first printing 5,000. Publication within 12 mos. Considers simultaneous submissions. Responds in 2 mos. Guidelines; free catalog.

> **Nonfiction:** Proposal/2 chapters; no phone/fax query. "Most open to biblically-based, study or expositional books for pastors or students; church or ministry-related issues books."

> **Ethnic Books:** Spanish Division: Editorial Portaroz.

*LANGMARC PUBLISHING, P.O. Box 33817, San Antonio TX 78265. (210)822-2521. Fax: (210)822-5014. Lutheran. Renee Hermanson, ed. Focuses on spiritual growth of readers. Publishes 5 titles/yr. Receives 50-60 submissions annually. 50% of books from first-time authors. No mss through agents. Prefers 150-300 pgs. Royalty 8-10% on retail; no advance. Average first printing 1,500. Publication within 9-12 mos. No simultaneous submissions. Responds in 1 mo. Brochure for #10 SAE/1 stamp.

> **Nonfiction:** Query or proposal/3 chapters; phone query ok. "Most open to inspirational, congregational helps, or materials for teens."

*LIFE CYCLE BOOKS, Box 420, Lewiston NY 14092. (416) 690-5860. Fax: (416)690-5860. Paul Broughton, gen. mgr. Publishes 1-3 inspirational/religious titles/yr. Receives 50 submissions annually. 50% of books from first-time authors. Accepts mss through agents. Reprints books. Royalty 8% of net; outright purchase of brochure material, $250; advance $100-300. **SUBSIDY PUBLISHES 10%.** Publication within 10 mos. Responds in 6 wks. Guidelines; free catalog.

> **Nonfiction:** Query or complete ms. "Our emphasis is on pro-life and pro-family titles."

> **Tips:** "We are most involved in publishing leaflets of about 1,500 wds, and welcome submissions of mss of this length."

LIFEJOURNEY BOOKS (adult books) Imprint of Chariot Family Publishing, Cook Communications Ministries. See Chariot Family Publishing for details.

> **Nonfiction:** Books on Christian living or marriage.

> **Fiction:** Submissions only through The Writers Edge.

LIFETIME BOOKS, Fell Publishers, Inc., 2131 Hollywood Blvd., Hollywood FL 33020. (305)925-5242. Brian Feinblum, sr. ed. General publisher that publishes 2-4 religious titles/yr. Receives 50 submissions annually. 80% of books from first-time authors. No mss through agents. Reprints books. Prefers 60,000 wds or 250-300 pgs. Royalty 7-15% on retail; no advance. Average first printing 10,000. Publication within 8-10 mos. Considers simultaneous submissions. Responds in 1 month. Guidelines; catalog for 9x12 SAE/5 stamps.

> **Nonfiction:** Query first; no phone query; fax query ok.

> **Tips:** "Spirituality is fine, but books predicting world doom, God's powers, or interpretations of the Bible won't sell. Include a clear marketing and promotional strategy."

#LIGUORI PUBLICATIONS, 1 Liguori Dr., Liguori MO 63057-9999. (314)464-2500. Catholic/Redemptionists. Robert Pagliari, CSSR, ed-in-chief; Audrey Vest, mng. ed. Publishes 50 titles/yr. Receives 200 submissions annually. 20% of books from first-time authors. Accepts mss through agents. Prefers 20-200 pgs. Royalty 9% on retail; outright purchase of 20-page pamphlets for $400; advance varies. Average first printing 5,000 on books, 10,000 on pamphlets. Publication within 2 yrs. Responds in 2-3 mos. Free guidelines/catalog.

Nonfiction: Proposal/3 chapters (complete ms for pamphlets). "Looking for pastoral, practical material targeted to parishes and individuals with specific needs."

Ethnic Books: Publishes books in Spanish.

Tips: "Manuscripts accepted by us must have a strong, practical application."

#LILLENAS PUBLISHING CO., (Drama Division of Beacon Hill Press), Program Builder Series and Other Drama Resources, Box 419527, Kansas City MO 64141. (816)931-1900. Fax: (816)753-4071. Church of the Nazarene. Paul M. Miller, ed. Publishes 15 drama resource books and 5 program builders/yr. Royalties for drama resources; outright purchase of program builder material. Considers simultaneous submissions. Responds in 8-12 wks. Guidelines; catalog.

Nonfiction: Query (preferred) or complete ms. Accepts readings, plays, puppet scripts, program and service features.

Tips: "We have added a new line of full-length plays for use in schools and dinner theater that are wholesome but not specifically religious."

*LION PUBLISHING, 20 Lincoln Ave., Elgin IL 60120. (708)741-4256. Cook Communications Ministries. Contact Neil Cuthbert. "Generally not considering unsolicited manuscripts or proposals." Catalog.

#THE LITURGICAL PRESS, P.O. Box 7500, St. John's Abbey, Collegeville MN 56321. (612)363-2213. Fax: (800)445-5899. St. John's Abbey (a Benedictine group). Imprints: Michael Glazier Books and Pueblo Books. Mark Twomey, mng. ed. Publishes 100 titles/yr. Prefers 100-600 pgs. Royalty 10% of net; some outright purchases; no advance. Responds in 2 mos. Guidelines; free catalog.

Nonfiction: Query/proposal. Adult only.

Tips: "We publish liturgical, scriptural, and pastoral resources."

*LIVING FLAME PRESS, 325 Rabro Dr., Hauppauge NY 11788. (516)348-5251. Catholic/ecumenical. Nancy Benvenga & Emily Teutshman, eds. Publishes 10 titles/yr. Receives 50 submissions annually. 25% of books from first-time authors. No mss through agents. Royalty 5% on retail (negotiable). Publication within 24 mos. Responds in 1 week on query. Guidelines; free catalog.

Nonfiction: Proposal/chapters. Needs theology and liturgy.

Fiction: Proposal/chapters. No "biblical" novels based on outdated or literal understandings of Scripture.

Tips: "Most open to a well-researched, well-written book on timely pastoral issues."

*LIVING SACRIFICE BOOK CO., A division of Voice of the Martyrs, Inc., 200 E. Frank Phillips Blvd., P.O. Box 443, Bartlesville OK 74005. (918)337-8015. Fax: (918)337-9185. Tom White, C.E.O. Publishes 2 titles/yr. Accepts mss through agents. Reprints books. Prefers 200 pgs. Terms negotiable. Average first printing 5,000. Publication within 8 mos. Considers simultaneous submissions. Responds in 1 month. No guidelines; free catalog.

Nonfiction: Complete mss; phone query ok. "Books related to the subject of the persecuted church in Communist/Moslem countries."

Ethnic Books: Publishes some titles in Spanish.

Tips: "Most open to biographies or autobiographies on Christians who are persecuted for their faith, or informational books relating to Islam or Communism."

#LOYOLA UNIVERSITY PRESS, 3441 N. Ashland Ave., Chicago IL 60657. (312)281-1818. Fax: (312)281-0555. Catholic. Rev. Joseph F. Downey, S.J., ed. dir. Publishes 12-15 titles/yr, Campion Books Imprint (trade books), Values & Ethics Series (Dr. Rugh McGugan, ed). Receives 150 submissions annually. 60% of books from first-time authors. No mss through agents. Reprints books. Prefers 60,000-80,000 wds or 180-230 pgs. Royalty 10% of net; no advance. Average first printing 1,500-2,000. Publication within 1 yr. Considers simultaneous submissions. Responds in 2 mos. Free guidelines/catalog.

Nonfiction: Query or proposal/chapters. "Most open to professionally written mss, more or less in the Catholic tradition (but not conservative), written out of solid field training and experience."

Tips: "Review our catalog, sample our published books from the last five years, and find a match there to your book in treatment and viewpoint."

#LURA MEDIA, INC., 7060 Miramar Rd., Ste. 104, San Diego CA 92121. (619)578-1948. Fax: (619)578-7560. Ecumenical. Lura Jane Geiger, ed-in-chief. Specializes in books on personal growth with spiritual and feminine dimensions. Publishes 6-8 titles/yr. Receives 250 submissions annually. 60% of books from first-time authors. Accepts mss through agents. Prefers 125-225 pgs. Royalty 10% of net; seldom offers advance, $500. Average first printing 3,000. Publication within 15 mos. Considers simultaneous submissions. Responds in 3 mos. Guidelines: catalog for 9x12 SAE/2 stamps.

Nonfiction: Book proposal/1 chapter; no phone query. "Looking for books on spirituality, women's issues, and personal experience."

Tips: "Most open to books on renewal for body, mind and spirit that are relational, creative, and well integrated."

MASTER BOOKS, Box 26060, Colorado Springs CO 80936-6060. (719)591-0800. Fax: (719)591-1446. Creation Life Publisher, Inc. Ron Hillestad, gen. mngr. Publishes 8-10 titles/yr. Receives 100 submissions annually. 10% of books from first-time authors. No mss through agents. **SUBSIDY PUBLISHES 5-15%.** Reprints books. Royalty 10-15% of net; no advance. Average first printing 5,000. Publication within 6 mos. Considers simultaneous submissions. Responds in 7-10 days. No guidelines; free catalog.

Nonfiction: Query; no phone query. "Looking for biblical creationism; biblical science; creation/evolution debate material."

Also Does: Pamphlets and booklets; computer games.

MERIWETHER PUBLISHING LTD., 885 Elkton Dr., Colorado Springs CO 80907. (719)594-4422. Fax: (719)594-9916. General trade publisher that does some religious titles. Ted Zapel, ed. Publishes 3-4 titles/yr; 35 plays/yr. Receives 700 submissions annually (mostly plays). 80% of books from first-time authors. Accepts mss through agents. Reprints books. Prefers 200 pgs. Royalty 10% on retail for books; plays are a 10% royalty to a (varying) fixed amount. Average first printing 5,000. Publication within 12-18 mos. Considers simultaneous submissions. Responds in 4-6 wks. Guidelines; catalog for 9x12 SAE/3 stamps.

Nonfiction: Proposal/1 chapter. "Looking for creative worship books, i.e., drama, using the arts in worship, how-to books with ideas for Christian education.

Fiction: Plays only, including religious plays. Send complete ms.

Tips: "No religious titles with fundamentalist themes or approaches; we prefer mainstream religion titles. Most open to drama-related books."

*MISTY HILL PRESS, 5024 Turner Rd., Sebastopol CA 95472. (707)823-7437. Small press that does some religious titles. Sally C. Karste, ed. Publishes 1 title/yr. Negotiable royalty. Responds in 1 week. Guidelines; catalog for 9x12 SAE/2 stamps.

Fiction: Query first. Historical fiction for children.

+THE MML COMPANY, P.O. Box 3426, Greenville SC 29602. (803)370-1900. Fax: (803)370-2038. George Brock, pres. Publishes 1 title/yr. Receives 3 submissions annually. All books from first-time authors. No mss through agents. **SUBSIDY PUBLISHES some.** Royalty 15%; no advance. No guidelines; catalog.
    Nonfiction: Only children's picture books and gift books.
    Ethnic: Hispanic.

MOODY PRESS, 820 N. LaSalle Blvd., Chicago IL 60610. (312)329-2101. Fax: (312)329-8062. Imprint: Northfield Publishing. Submit to Moody Press Editor. To provide books that evangelize, edify the believer, and educate concerning the Christian life. Publishes 60-65 titles/yr. Receives 2,000 submissions annually. 5% of books from first-time authors. No mss through agents. Royalty on net; variable advance. Average first printing 10,000. Publication within 18-24 mos. Considers simultaneous submissions. Responds in 6-8 wks. Guidelines; free catalog.
    Nonfiction: Proposal/2-3 chapters; no phone/fax query.
    Fiction: Complete ms. Children/teen/adult.
    Also Does: Booklets in series only.
    Tips: "Become well-informed (investigate thoroughly) the need in the book marketplace before attempting to write a book—and then target that need."

+MOORINGS, 555 Marriott Dr., Ste. 800, Nashville TN 37214-1000. (615)231-6720. Fax: (231-6730). Nondenominational. Timothy Jones, mng. ed. Publishes books that offer stability and security to a church and culture in need of both. Publishes 25-30 titles/yr. Accepts mss through agents. Considers simultaneous submissions. Responds in 4-6 wks. Guidelines; no catalog.
    Nonfiction: Proposal/2-3 chapters or complete ms; fax query ok.
    Fiction: Proposal/2-3 chapters or complete ms. Children/teen/adult.
    Tips: "We look for fiction, nonfiction, and juvenile books that are consistent with historic, biblical Christian faith; they must be creative, well-written, theologically sound, relevant to today's needs, and appeal to a wide audience."

#THOMAS MORE PRESS, 205 W. Monroe, 6th Floor, Chicago IL 60606. (312)609-8880. Fax: (312)609-8891. Catholic/Thomas More Assn. Joel Wells, ed. Publishes 2-6 titles/yr. Prefers 40,000 wds. Royalty 7.5% on retail; advance. Responds in 2 wks. Guidelines; free catalog.
    Nonfiction: Complete ms or proposal/chapters. Religion and spirituality.
    Tips: "Looking for books on theology, commentary, reflection, spirituality and reference—for the serious, but non-scholarly reader."

MOREHOUSE PUBLISHING CO., 871 Ethan Allen Hwy., Ste. 204, Ridgefield CT 06877. (203)431-3927. Fax: (203)431-3964. Episcopal/ecumenical. Deborah Grahame-Smith, sr. ed. Publishes 15-20 titles/yr. Receives 650-700 submissions annually. 40% of books from first-time authors. Accepts mss through agents. Reprints books. Prefers 80-150 pgs. Royalty 6-12% on retail; advance $350-700. Average first printing 2,500-3,500. Publication within 6-9 mos. Considers simultaneous submissions. Responds in 6-8 wks. Guidelines; catalog for 9x12 SAE/4 stamps.
    Nonfiction: Proposal/2 chapters; no phone/fax query. "Looking for books on marriage, parenting, singles, youth, seniors, and current social issues."
    Fiction: Proposal/2 chapters. For children/teens.
    Also does: Booklets.

Tips: "Most open to a book aimed at a specific market/readership, which has perhaps evolved from a workshop or study program (field-tested and fine-tuned by interested Christians); a book that answers a specific need or fills a specific gap in the bookstores."

*MORNING STAR PRESS, Box 1095, Grand Central Station, New York NY 10163. (212)661-4304. Morning Star Chapel. Rev. Kathleen Shedaker, pub. Publishes 2 titles/yr. Receives 3 submissions annually. 50% of books from first-time authors. No books through agents. Reprints books. Prefers 120 pgs. Royalty 10% on retail; no advance. Publication within 6 mos. Considers simultaneous submissions. Responds in 3-6 wks. No guidelines/catalog.

Nonfiction: Query first. "Only religious/inspirational books."

Tips: "We encourage members of all denominations to live a more Christian life."

JOSHUA MORRIS PUBLISHING, 206 Danbury Rd., Wilton CT 06897. (203)834-9878. Fax: (203)834-0811. Anglican/Evangelical. Sally Lloyd Jones, editorial dir. A Christian children's book packager. Publishes 75-100 titles/yr. Receives 200 submissions annually. 5% of books from first-time authors. Accepts mss through agents. Makes outright purchases. Average first printing 25,000-50,000. Publication within 1 yr. Considers simultaneous submissions. Responds in 3-4 mos. No guidelines or catalog.

Nonfiction: Proposal/1 chapter; no phone query. "Looking for educational books on biblical or general theme with a Christian approach."

Fiction: Proposal/1 chapter. Children/teens.

Special Needs: Produces board games and all kinds of novelty books for children.

Tips: "Most open to novelty books for children ages 3-5 based on biblical themes." Prefers series of 2 or more.

#WILLIAM MORROW AND CO., 1350 Avenue of the Americas, New York NY 10019. (212)261-6500. Fax: (212)261-6595. General trade publisher that does a few religious titles. Debbie Mercer-Sullivan, mng. ed. Publishes 5 religious titles/yr. Receives 10,000 submissions annually. 30% of books from first-time authors. Accepts most mss through agents. Prefers 50,000-100,000 wds. Standard royalty on retail; advance varies. Publication within 1-2 yrs. Considers simultaneous submissions. Responds in 3 mos. No guidelines/catalog.

Nonfiction & Fiction: Query only through agent.

+MOUNT OLIVE COLLEGE PRESS, 634 Henderson St., Mount Olive NC 28365. (919)658-2502. Dr. Pepper Worthington, ed. Publishes 5 titles/yr. Receives 500 submissions annually. 60% of books from first-time authors. No mss through agents. **SUBSIDY PUBLISHES 35%.** Publication within 2 yrs. Responds in 6 mos. Free guidelines/catalog.

Nonfiction: Proposal/1 chapter. Religion.

Fiction: Synopsis/1 chapter. Religious. For poetry submit 6 sample poems.

MULTNOMAH BOOKS - See **Questar Publishers.**

*NATIONAL BAPTIST PUBLISHING BOARD, 6717 Centennial Blvd., Nashville TN 37209. (615)350-8000. Fax: (615)350-9018. National Missionary Baptist Convention of America. Rev. Kenneth H. Dupree, dir. of publications. To provide quality Christian education resources to be used by African-American churches. Receives 200 submissions annually. 30% of books from first-time authors. Accepts mss through agents. Reprints books. Prefers 130 pgs. Outright purchases; advance. Average first printing 20,000. Publication within 1 yr.

Nonfiction: Complete ms; phone query ok.

Fiction: Complete ms. "We need biblically based fiction for children."

Ethnic Books: African-American publisher.

Tips: "Most open to religious books that can be used for Christian education."

*NAVPRESS/PINON PRESS, Box 35001, Colorado Springs CO 80935. (719)548-9222. Debby Weaver, submissions ed. "We are no longer accepting *any* unsolicited submissions, proposals, queries, etc."

NAZARENE PUBLISHING HOUSE/BEACON HILL PRESS OF KANSAS CITY, 6401 The Paseo, Kansas City MO 64131. (816)333-7000x2447. Fax: (816)333-1748. Church of the Nazarene. Shona Fisher, ed. coordinator. Publishes 50 titles/yr. Receives 400+ submissions annually. 40% of books from first-time authors. No mss through agents. Prefers 200 pgs. Royalty 12-16% of net; or outright purchase; no advance. Average first printing 3,000-5,000. Publication within 9 mos. Considers simultaneous submissions. Responds in 2-3 mos. Free guidelines/catalog.

  Nonfiction: Proposal/2 chapters; no phone/fax query.

  Fiction: Proposal/2 chapters. For adults.

  Ethnic Books: Spanish division—Casa Nazarena De Publicaciones.

  Tips: "Most open to practical, lay-oriented books on personal growth and applied Christianity. Inspirational and devotional books also considered."

*NEIBAUER PRESS, 20 Industrial Dr., Warminster PA 18974. (215)322-6200. Fax: (215)322-2495. Evangelical/Protestant clergy and church leaders. Nathan Neibauer, ed. Publishes 8 titles/yr. Receives 100 submissions annually. 5% of books from first-time authors. No mss through agents. Reprints books. Prefers 200 pgs. Royalty on net; some outright purchases. **SOME SUBSIDY.** Publication within 6 mos. Considers simultaneous submissions. Responds in 2 wks. No guidelines; catalog for 9x12 SAE.

  Nonfiction: Query first.

  Tips: "Need religious books on stewardship and church enrollment, and bulletin fillers. Also tracts and pamphlets."

#THOMAS NELSON PUBLISHERS, P.O. Box 141000, 506 Nelson Pl., Nashville TN 37214. (615)889-9000. Evangelical. Imprints: Oliver-Nelson, Janet Thoma, and Jan Dennis Books. Submit to Book Editorial. Publishes 250 titles/yr. Receives over 2,000 submissions annually. 15% of books from first-time authors. Accepts mss through agents. Reprints books. **SUBSIDY PUBLISHES 10%.** Prefers 250 pgs. Variable royalty or outright purchase; advance. Average first printing 7,500. Publication within 1 yr. Considers simultaneous submissions. Responds in 8 wks. Guidelines; catalog for 9x12 SAE.

  Nonfiction: Proposal/3 chapters. "Looking for books on seniors and aging; biblical reference; career planning; biblical counseling; singles; and theology."

  Fiction: Proposal/3 chapters. Needs Christian themes for adults and teens.

  Tips: "Any books for children must be a complete package; we don't supply illustrations."

NEW HOPE, Box 12065, Birmingham AL 35202-2065. (205)991-8102. Fax: (205)991-4990. Woman's Missionary Union; Auxiliary to Southern Baptist Convention. Cindy McClain, ed. Publishes 10 titles/yr. Receives 80 submissions annually. 85% of books from first-time authors. Accepts mss through agents. Reprints books. Prefers 150-250 pgs. Royalty or outright purchases; no advance. Average first printing 5,000-10,000. Publication within 12-18 mos. Considers simultaneous submissions. Responds in 6 mos. Guidelines; free catalog for 9x12 SAE.

  Nonfiction: Proposal/3 chapters or complete ms; no phone query. "All that we publish must have a missions/ministry emphasis."

  Tips: "Most open to books which lead to spiritual growth toward a missions lifestyle or that lead to involvement in missions or support of missions."

NEW LEAF PRESS, Box 311, Green Forest AR 72638. (501)438-5288. Fax: (501)438-5120. Pentecostal/Charismatic. Jim Fletcher, acq. ed. Publishes 35 titles/yr. Receives 1,500 submissions annually. 10% of books from first-time authors. Accepts mss through agents. Reprints books. Prefers 100-400 pgs. Royalty on net; no advance. Average first printing 5,000. Publication within 10 mos. Considers simultaneous submissions. Responds in 30-90 days. Guidelines; catalog for 9x12 SAE/2 stamps.

> **Nonfiction:** Query, proposal or complete ms; phone/fax query ok. "Looking for devotional gift books and Christian living."

> **Tips:** "Tell us why this book is marketable and why it will be a blessing and fulfill the needs of others."

*NEW SOCIETY PUBLISHERS, 4527 Springfield Ave., Philadelphia PA 19143. (215)382-6543. (Canadian Address: Box 189, Gabriola Island BC V0R 1X0 Canada) Barbara Hirshkowitz, ed. mgr. Publishes 1-2 titles/yr. Receives dozens of submissions annually. 90% of books from first-time authors. Accepts mss through agents. Reprints books. Prefers up to 220 pgs. Royalty 10-15% of net; advance to $3,000 (if needed). Average first printing 3,000. Publication within 6 mos. Considers simultaneous submissions. Guidelines; free catalog.

> **Nonfiction:** Query only; no phone query. "Looking for nonviolent traditions in religions other than Christianity or Judaism (we have those). Also economics or environmental issues."

> **Tips:** "We publish books about fundamental social change through nonviolent action. We emphasize success stories and tool books."

*NOVALIS, 223 Main St., Ottawa ON K1S 1C4 Canada. (612)236-1393. Fax: (613)236-1393. University of St. Paul. Michael O'Hearn, acq. ed. Publishes 18 titles/yr. Prefers 200 pgs. Royalty & outright purchases; no advance. Considers simultaneous submissions. Responds in 12 wks. No guidelines/catalog.

> **Nonfiction:** Query or proposal/chapters.

> **Special Needs:** Sacramental preparation, materials on the revised rite of Christian funerals.

OMEGA PUBLICATIONS, P.O. Box 4130, Medford OR 97501. (503)826-1030. Jeani McKeever, ed. Publishes 2 titles/yr. Responds in 2 wks. Prefers 150-200 pgs. Open to freelance.

> **Nonfiction & Fiction:** Query first.

*OMF BOOKS, 1058 Avenue Rd., Toronto ON M5N 2C6 Canada. (416)483-0427. Overseas Missionary Fellowship. Edyth Banks, pub. mngr. Publishes 6-12 titles/yr. **SUBSIDY PUBLISHES 20%**. Prefers up to 200 pgs. Royalty about 7.5%; advance. Responds in 10 wks. No guidelines.

> **Nonfiction:** Query. "Must relate to mission work or Christian living in East Asia." Most books written by OMF members.

#OPEN COURT PUBLISHING CO., 332 S. Michigan Ave., Ste. 2000, Chicago IL 60604-9968. David Ramsey Steele, ed. dir. Publishes 4 religious titles/yr. Receives 600 submissions annually. 20% of books from first-time authors. Accepts mss through agents. Reprints books. Prefers 350-400 pgs. Royalty 5-12% of net; advance $1,000-2,000. Average first printing 500 (cloth), 1,500 (paperback). Publication within 1-3 yrs. Considers simultaneous submissions. Responds in 6 mos. Free catalog.

> **Nonfiction:** Query or proposal/2 chapters. "We're looking for works of high intellectual quality for a scholarly or general readership on comparative religion, philosophy of religion, and religious issues. We have special interest in religions of other cultures, notably oriental."

#ORBIS BOOKS, P.O. Box 308, Maryknoll NY 10545-0308. (914)941-7636. Fax: (914)945-0670. Catholic Foreign Mission Society. Robert Ellsberg, ed. Publishes 50-55 titles/yr. Receives 2,200 submissions annually. 2% of books from first-time authors. Accepts few mss through agents. Prefers 250-350 pgs. Royalty

10-15% of net; advance $500-3,000. Publication within 15 mos. Responds in 2 mos. Free guidelines/catalog.

> **Nonfiction:** Proposal/2 chapters. "Global justice and peace; religious development in Asia, Africa, and Latin America; Christianity and world religions."

OUR SUNDAY VISITOR, INC., 200 Noll Plaza, Huntington IN 46750. (219)356-8400. Fax: (219)356-8472. Catholic. Jacquelyn M. Murphy, ed. To assist Catholics to be more aware and secure in their faith and capable of relating their faith to others. Publishes 30 titles/yr. Receives 300 submissions annually. 10% of books from first-time authors. Accepts mss through agents. Reprints books. Royalty on retail; advance. Average first printing 5,000. Publication within 12-18 mos. Considers simultaneous submissions. Responds within 6 mos. Free guidelines/catalog.

> **Nonfiction:** Complete ms; no phone/fax query. "Most open to books on saints, prayer and family."
> **Also Does:** Pamphlets & booklets.
> **Tips:** "All books published must relate to the Catholic church. Give as much background information as possible on why the topic was chosen."

OXFORD UNIVERSITY PRESS, 200 Madison Ave., New York NY 10016. (212)679-7300. Academic press. Cynthia Read, sr. ed. Service to academic community. Publishes 60+ titles/yr. Receives hundreds of submissions annually. 10% of books from first-time authors. Accepts mss through agents. Prefers 300 pgs. Negotiable royalty & advance. Average first printing 1,500. Publication within 1 yr. Considers simultaneous submissions. Responds in 3 mos. No guidelines; free catalog.

> **Nonfiction:** Proposal/2 chapters; no phone/fax query. "Most open to academic books."

#PACIFIC PRESS PUBLISHING ASSN., Box 7000, Boise ID 83707-7000. (208)465-2595. Fax: (208)465-2531. Seventh-day Adventist. Russell Holt, ed. Publishes 35 titles/yr. Receives 600 submissions annually. 35% of books from first-time authors. No mss through agents. Prefers 33,000-85,000 wds or 128-256 pgs. Royalty 8-16% of net; advance $300-500. Average first printing 5,000. Publication within 6-10 mos. Considers simultaneous submissions. Responds in 3 mos. Guidelines; catalog for 9x12 SAE/3 stamps.

> **Nonfiction:** Query or proposal/1-2 chapters; complete ms ok; phone queries ok. "Looking for inspirational, devotional, family life and Christian living books."
> **Fiction:** Query, proposal/2 chapters, or complete ms. "Stories must be based on events that actually happened but written in good fiction style."
> **Ethnic Books:** Occasionally publishes for ethnic market.
> **Tips:** "Most open to inspirational/devotional book that focuses on a specific type of person and his/her needs—singles, parents of various age children, people struggling with specific issues/addictions, etc."

PACIFIC THEATRE PRESS, 1440 W. 12th Ave., Vancouver BC V6H 1M8 Canada. (604)731-5483. Fax: (604)733-3880. Ron Reed, artistic dir. Publishes 10 plays/yr. Reprints plays. Prefers full-length or one-act plays and sketches. Royalty 15% on retail for plays, flat fee for sketches; advances only on commissioned work. Considers simultaneous submissions. No guidelines.

> **Plays:** Query/summary & sample scene or complete script/summary pg.
> **Special Needs:** "Producible plays by Christians, but not necessarily religious, for college or community theater; strong or unusual sketches for church/street/youth/revue settings."

PARACLETE PRESS, P.O. Box 1568, Orleans MA 02653. (508)255-4685. Fax: (508)255-5705. Ecumenical. David Manuel, editor; submit to Pam Jordan. Publishes 3-4 titles/yr. Receives 30 submissions annually.

85% of books from first-time authors. Accepts mss through agents. Reprints books. Prefers less than 300 pgs (typeset). Royalty on net; no advance. Average first printing 3,000 or 10,000. Publication within 4 mos. No simultaneous submissions. Responds in 4-6 mos. No guidelines; free catalog.

Nonfiction: Proposal/2 chapters; fax query ok. "Looking for books on deeper spirituality that appeal to all denominations."

Tips: "Looking for anything that would encourage a non-believer to make a commitment to Christ, or believers to strengthen their commitment."

*THE PASTORAL PRESS, 225 Sheridan St. NW, Washington DC 20011. (202)723-1254. Fax: (202)723-2262. Catholic/National Assn. of Pastoral Musicians. Lawrence Johnson, dir. Publishes 16 titles/yr. Receives 12 submissions annually. 60% of books from first-time authors. Accepts mss through agents. Prefers 250 pgs. Royalty 10% of net; no advance. Publication within 10 mos. Considers simultaneous submissions. Responds in 2 mos. No guidelines; free catalog.

Nonfiction: Complete ms.

Tips: "Most open to theology and planning of Roman Catholic liturgies."

PASTOR'S CHOICE PRESS, 4000 Beallwood Ave., Columbus GA 31904. (404/706)576-5787. Subsidiary of Brentwood Publishers Group. Jerry Luquire, exec. dir. **SUBSIDY PUBLISHES 100%**. Focus is on sermon notes, outlines, illustrations, plus news that pastors would find interesting. Publishes 300-500 copies. Cost of about $3-4/book. Publication in 45 days. Same day response.

PAULIST PRESS, 997 Macarthur Blvd., Mahwah NJ 07430. (201)825-7300. Fax: (201)825-7345. Catholic. Donald Brophy, mng. ed. Publishes 90-100 titles/yr. Receives 400 submissions annually. 20% of books from first-time authors. Accepts mss through agents. Royalty 10% on retail; advance $500. Average first printing 3,500. Publication within 10 mos. Responds in 2-3 mo. Guidelines; no catalog.

Nonfiction: Query, then proposal/1 chapter; no phone query. "Looking for theology (Catholic and ecumenical Christian), popular spirituality, liturgy, and religious education texts."

Tips: "Most open to progressive, world-affirming, theologically sophisticated, growth-oriented, well-written books. Have strong convictions but don't be pious. Stay well-read. Pay attention to contemporary social needs."

PELICAN PUBLISHING CO., INC., P.O. Box 3110, Gretna LA 70054-3110. (504)368-1175. Nina Kooij, ed. Publishes 8 titles/yr. Receives 400 submissions annually. 10% of books from first-time authors. Accepts books through agents. Reprints books. Prefers 300 pgs. Royalty 10%; some advances. Average first printing 6,000. Publication within 9-18 mos. Responds in 1 mo. Guidelines; catalog for 9x12 SAE/9 stamps.

Nonfiction: Proposal/2 chapters; no phone/fax query. "We only consider submissions from established speakers."

Fiction: Proposal/2 chapters. Children/adults. "Material must reflect a particular faith or a particular place/time (Eastern Germany, World War II, etc.)."

Ethnic Books: Fiction for blacks, Hispanics, Native Americans, Asian-Americans, etc. Ethnic history for above groups.

PILGRIM PRESS, 700 Prospect Ave. E., Cleveland OH 44115. (216)736-3700. Fax: (216)736-3703. United Church of Christ. Richard E. Brown, ed. Publishes 18-20 titles/yr. Receives 275-300 submissions annually. 5% of books from first-time authors. Accepts mss through agents. Prefers 50,000 wds or 175-250 pgs. Royalty 8% of net; negotiable advance. Average first printing 3,000. Publication within 9-12 mos. Considers simultaneous submissions. Responds in 8-10 wks. Free guidelines/catalog.

Nonfiction: Query/proposal/1-2 chapters; no phone/fax query. "Looking for academic trade books on social issues and the moral life; gender studies; spirituality; counseling/self-help."

Ethnic Books: Occasional title for African-American and Native-American audience.

Also Does: Journal/calendar for women.

Tips: "Read journals and magazines in the field to see what topics are being discussed."

*PILLAR BOOKS AND PUBLISHING CO., INC., 5840 S. Memorial Dr., Ste. 111, Tulsa OK 74145. (918)665-3240. Fax: (918)663-7690. Elizabeth Sherman, ed. Publishes 5 titles/yr. Receives 50 submissions annually. No mss through agents. **SUBSIDY PUBLISHES 100%** . Reprints books. Prefers 150-200 pgs. Royalty 10-15% of net; no advance. Average first printing 15,000. Publication within 2-3 mos. Considers simultaneous submissions. Responds in 4 wks. Free guidelines & catalog.

Nonfiction: Complete ms or query; phone query ok. "Looking for Bible teaching materials, commentaries on scripture or areas of study, scholarly studies on topical subjects."

Tips: "Most open to powerful biblically-based ideas comprised of sound doctrine, ideas that will edify, exhort, admonish, and build up the body of Christ."

POETS COVE PRESS, 4000 Beallwood Ave., Columbus GA 31904. (404/706)576-5787. Subsidiary of Brentwood Publishers Group. Jerry Luquire, exec. dir. Publishes 125 titles/yr. **SUBSIDY PUBLISHES 100%.** Specializes in self-publishing books of religious or inspirational poetry, in small press runs of under 500 copies. Publication in 45 days. Same day response.

Tips: "Type one poem per page; include short bio and photo with first submission."

*PRAXIS INSTITUTE PRESS, 275 High Rd., Newbury MA 01951. (508)462-0563. Non-denominational. Robin Amis, dir. Publishes 3 titles/yr. No mss through agents. Reprints books. Prefers 100-300 pgs. Does mostly translations. Royalty 10% of net; no advance. Average first printing 3,000. Publication within 12-16 mos. Considers simultaneous submissions. Responds slowly. No guidelines; free catalog.

Nonfiction: Query only; phone query ok. "Most open to translations within the tradition of spirituality; or original works by living authors only if based on actual experience."

PRESBYTERIAN AND REFORMED PUBLISHING CO., Box 817, Phillipsburg NJ 08865. (908)454-0505. Fax: (908)859-2390. Not a denominational house. Thom E. Notaro, ed. Publishes 6-10 titles/yr. Receives 150 submissions annually. 20% of books from first-time authors. Accepts mss through agents. Reprints books. Royalty 10-14% of net. Publication within 6-10 mos. Considers simultaneous submissions. Responds in 4-8 wks. Free guidelines/catalog.

Nonfiction; Proposal/3 chapters.

Tips: "Clear, engaging, and insightful applications of reformed theology to life. Offer us fully developed proposals and polished sample chapters."

#PRESCOTT PRESS PUBLISHERS - See HUNTINGTON HOUSE.

PROBE MINISTRIES INTL., 1900 Firman Dr., Ste. 100, Richardson TX 75081-6796. (214)480-0240. Fax: (214)644-9664. Evangelical Council for Financial Accountability. Louis D. Whitworth, sr. ed. To support goals of the ministry and to equip Christians to respond to challenges of our culture. Publishes 2-3 titles/yr. No mss through agents. Prefers 120-250 pgs. Pays variable royalty; no advance. Average first printing 2,000. Publication within 6-9 mos. Considers simultaneous submissions. Responds in 2 mos. No guidelines; free copy.

Nonfiction: Query only; phone query ok; no fax query. "Christian approaches to all the academic disciplines; national issues: political, social, medical; education; family values."

Tips: "Most open to a popular level book on apologetics with sound theology and a Christian world view written by a well-educated person of credible reputation and scholarship."

*PROCLAIM PUBLISHING, 12500 Marion Ln. W., Ste. 4110, Minnetonka MN 55305-1327. Jo Reaves, pub. Publishes 24 titles/yr. Receives 200 submissions annually. 80% of books from first-time authors. Accepts mss through agents. **SUBSIDY PUBLISHES 100%.** Prefers 100-250 pgs (any length ok). Average first printing 2,500. Publication within 2-3 mos. Considers simultaneous submissions. Responds in 2-4 wks. Guidelines; no catalog.

Nonfiction: Query only; no phone query. Any topic.

Fiction: Query only. Juvenile, teen, adult. Any genre.

Ethnic Books: Interested in publishing some.

Tips: "We are now able to offer a total marketing program, as well as warehousing and order-fulfillment services with an 800 number. Our services are affordable."

PROMISE PUBLISHING, 2324 N. Batavia #105, Orange CA 92665. (714)282-1199. Fax: (714)997-5545. M.B. Steele, ed./V.P. Publishes 6 titles/yr. Receives few submissions annually. 50% of books from first-time authors. Accepts mss through agents. **100% COOPERATIVE PUBLISHING.** Royalty 10-15% on retail (negotiable); no advance. Average first printing 5,000. Publication within 6 mos. Considers simultaneous submissions. Pre-acceptance talks determine acceptance. No guidelines; free catalog.

Nonfiction: Query; phone/fax query ok.

Fiction: They might consider fiction under the same terms, but it's seldom feasible under their cooperative publishing approach.

Special Needs: "We are interested in whatever topics fall within the parameters of our 'cooperative publishing'approach, if it is not contradictory to the Bible." Not included in topical listings.

*QUESTAR PUBLISHERS, Box 1720, Sisters OR 97759. (503)549-1144. Fax: (503)549-2044. Brenda Saltzer, editorial asst. Multnomah Books is their imprint for youth and adult books; Gold 'n'Honey is imprint for children's books. Publishes 35-40 titles/yr. Receives 1,800-2,000 submissions annually. 1% of books from first-time authors. Prefers not to work with agents. Reprints few books. Length depends on book. Negotiable royalty and advance. Average first printing 10,000-15,000. Publication within 6-12 mos. Considers simultaneous submissions. Responds in 2 mos. Guidelines; catalog for 9x12 SAE/3 stamps.

Nonfiction: Proposal/2-3 chapters; no phone query.

Fiction: Proposal/2-3 chapters. "Looking for clean, moral, uplifting fiction—not necessarily religious."

Tips: "We evaluate specifically on a book-by-book basis. Most books are shaped by our editors based on input from our marketing and sales departments. We use about 1% or less of our unsolicited mss."

+QUINTESSENTIAL BOOKS, P.O. Box 2566, Shawnee Mission KS 66201. (913)384-8871. Fax: (913)831-3663. Nondenominational. Janette L. Jasperson, VP of Editorial. Est 1994. Will focus initially on reprinting books out of print from non-subsidy publishers. Publishes 4-6 titles/yr. Reprints books. Prefers 175-250 pgs. Royalty on net; no advance. Average first printing 1,000-2,500. Publication within 18 mos. No simultaneous submissions. Reports in 6-8 wks. Not included in topical listings.

Nonfiction: Cover letter with history of the book, number of copies printed, sales to date, and a brief summary of marketing efforts. "Any topic except cults or eschatology."

Fiction: Same initial submission. "Any genre except romance or children's books."

Tips: "We are looking for hard-hitting books that are based squarely on Scripture. No fluff."

RAINBOW BOOKS, Box 2789, La Jolla CA 92038. (619)578-4700. Carol Rogers, ed. dir. Publishes 12 titles/yr. Receives 100 submissions annually. 40% of books from first-time authors. No mss through agents. Prefers 64 pgs. Outright purchases $500. Publication within 12-24 mos. Considers simultaneous submissions. Responds in 3-5 mos. Guidelines; catalog for 9x12 SAE/2 stamps.

> **Nonfiction:** Proposal/2-3 chapters or complete ms; phone query ok. "Looking for 64-pg. activity books (reproducible) for teachers to use in teaching the Bible to children."
>
> **Tips:** "Most open to book of creative activities that encourage Bible learning for Christian educators to use with children age 2 through grade 6."

RAINBOW BOOKS, P.O. Box 430, Highland City FL 33846-0430. Phone/Fax: (813)648-4420. Betsy A. Lampe, ed. dir. Publishes 2 titles/yr. Receives 50-100 submissions annually. 100% of books from first-time authors. No mss through agents.'Prefers 64+ pgs. Royalty 4-10% of net; advance $500. Average first printing 2,000-5,000. Publication within 6 mos. Considers simultaneous submissions. Responds in 1 mo. Guidelines; copy for 6x9 SAE/4 stamps.

> **Nonfiction:** Query only. Well-targeted self-help, how-to or educational.
>
> **Tips:** "No religious titles with a doomsday thrust."

*RAINBOW'S END COMPANY, 354 Golden Grove Rd., Baden PA 15005. (412)266-4997. Judith Blanarik, sr. ed.; submit to Wayne P. Brumagin. Publishes 5-10 titles/yr. Receives 50+ submissions annually. 80% of books from first-time authors. No mss through agents. **SUBSIDY PUBLISHES (author pays half) for 95%.** Prefers 150-250 pgs. After initial investment (@ $3,500), author gets all profits from first printing. Average first printing 1,000. Publication within 10-15 mos. Considers simultaneous submissions. Responds in 4-6 wks. Guidelines; no catalog; book samples $3 ea.

> **Nonfiction:** Complete ms; no phone query. "All books must make a difference in lives—that difference being Jesus Christ."
>
> **Special Needs:** Books on recovery from addictions.
>
> **Tips:** "We are offering Christian writers a reputable way of getting their work into print through a reasonably-priced publishing program. Standards are high. Don't be too wordy. Make sure Scripture quotes are accurate. Stay within specified length."

REGAL BOOKS, 2300 Knoll Dr., Ventura CA 93003. (805)644-9721. Gospel Light Publications. Kyle Duncan, ed. dir.; Jean Daly, curriculum ed. Publishes 15-20 titles/yr. Receives 800 submissions annually. 5% of books from first-time authors. No mss through agents. Prefers 200-300 pgs. Royalty 10-15% of net (10% on curriculum books); advance $1,500-5,000. Average first printing 10,000-15,000. Publication within 12-18 mos. Responds in 4-8 wks. No guidelines/catalog.

> **Nonfiction:** NOT ACCEPTING MSS OR QUERIES AT THIS TIME. All unsolicited mss will be returned unopened; no phone/fax queries.

#REGENCY PRESS, P.O. Box 2306, Bandera TX 78003. (210)796-7215. Gayle Buck, ed. No mss through agents. Prefers 70,000-75,000 wds. Royalty 7-10% on retail; no advance. Publication within 18 mos. Considers simultaneous submissions. Responds ASAP. Guidelines; no catalog.

> **Fiction:** Proposal/3 chapters or complete ms. "Romantic adventure preferred, either contemporary or historical, with believable characters. Must include Christian, Bible-based teaching without preaching—character's lives show growth in Christian principles."

Tips: "Make it professional; no haphazard, lazy format. Biblical and historical references must be accurate."

#THE REGINA PRESS, 145 Sherwood Ave., Farmingdale NY 11735. (516)694-8600. Fax: (516)694-2205. Catholic/Christian. George Malhame, juvenile ed. Publishes 5-10 titles/yr. Royalty on net; some outright purchases; some advances. No guidelines; sometimes sends free catalog.

Fiction: Query/proposal. Children's picture books for ages 3-8; coloring books.

REGNERY PUBLISHING (formerly **REGNERY GATEWAY, INC.**), 422 1st St. SE, #300, Washington DC 20003-1803. (202)546-5005. Fax: (202)546-8759. Trade publisher that does scholarly Catholic books and evangelical Protestant books. Richard Vigilante, exec. ed. Publishes 1-2 religious titles/yr. Receives 20 submissions annually. 20% of books from first-time authors. Accepts mss through agents. Reprints books. Prefers 200-300 pgs. Royalty 10% on retail; advances to $50,000. Average first printing 5,000. Publication within 6-9 mos. Considers simultaneous submissions. Responds in 4-6 mos. Free catalog.

Nonfiction: Proposal/1-2 chapters & cover letter; no phone/fax query.

Tips: "Religious books should relate to politics, history, current affairs, biography, and public policy."

*RELIGIOUS EDUCATION PRESS, 5316 Meadow Brook Rd., Birmingham AL 35242. (205)991-1000. Fax: (205)991-9669. Nancy J. Vickers, mng. ed. Publishes 5-6 titles/yr. Receives 280 submissions annually. 40% of books from first-time authors. Accepts mss through agents. Prefers 250-300 pgs. Royalty 10% on retail; no advance. Average first printing 2,000. Publication within 9 mos. Responds in 2 mos. Guidelines; free catalog.

Nonfiction: Query first. "Serious, scholarly books of special interest to professional religious educators and pastoral ministers."

Tips: "Personally examine 2-4 of our books first to see if your book fits representative specifications."

*REMNANT PUBLICATIONS, 272 Union City Rd., Coldwater MI 49036. (517)278-4011/2665. Seventh-day Adventist. Bill Smith, dir. Publishes 11 titles/yr. This is a new company only reprinting books at this time. Not in topical listings.

*RENEWAL PRESS, INC., 1117 Hellmers Ln., Ocean Springs MS 39564. (601)875-4128. Southern Baptist. Grant Shipp, pres. Publishes 1 title/yr. Receives 1 submission annually. 100% of books from first-time authors. No mss through agents. Prefers 175 pgs. Average first printing 2,000. Publication within 3 mos. Responds in 2 wks. Free guidelines/brochure.

Nonfiction: Query first. "Information and procedures concerning church renewal, and small groups."

RESOURCE PUBLICATIONS, INC., Ste. 290, 160 E. Virginia St., San Jose CA 95128. (408)286-8505. Fax: (408)287-8748. Kenneth E. Guentert, ed. dir. Publishes 15 titles/yr. Receives 250 submissions annually. 20% of books from first-time authors. Accepts mss through agents. Prefers 50,000 wds. Royalty 8% of net; no advance. Average first printing 3,000. Publication within 1 yr. Responds in 3 mos. Guidelines; catalog for 9x12 SAE/2 stamps.

Nonfiction: Query; phone/fax query ok.

Fiction: Query. Adult/teen/children. Only short skits or read-aloud stories for storytellers. "Must be useful in ministerial, counseling, or educational settings."

Also Does: Computer Programs; aids to ministry or education.

Tips: "Know our market. We cater to ministers in Catholic and mainstream Protestant settings. We are not an evangelical house or general interest publisher."

#RESURRECTION PRESS LTD, Box 248, Williston Park NY 11596. (516)742-5686. Fax: (516)746-6872. Catholic. Imprint: Spirit Life Series. Emilie Cerar, sr. ed. Publishes 10-12 titles/yr. Receives 130 submissions annually. 50% of books from first-time authors. Accepts mss through agents. Reprints books. Prefers 150 pgs. Royalty 5-10% of net; advance $250-2,000. Average first printing 3,000. Publication within 1 yr. Considers simultaneous submissions. Responds in 1-2 mos. Free guidelines & catalog.

Nonfiction: Query only; no phone query. "Most open to pastoral resources, self-help, and spirituality for the active Christian."

*FLEMING H. REVELL CO., Box 6287, Grand Rapids MI 49516. (616)676-9185. Fax: (616)676-9573. Subsidiary of Baker Book House. Imprint: Spire Books. William J. Petersen, ed. dir. Publishes 60 titles/yr. Receives 1,750 submissions annually. 10% of books from first-time authors. Accepts mss through agents. Prefers 192 pgs. Royalty 14% of net; advance $2,000. Average first printing 5,000. Publication within 1 yr. Considers simultaneous submissions. Responds in 2 mos. Guidelines.

Nonfiction: Proposal/2 chapters.

Fiction: Synopsis/2 chapters. Adult.

REVIEW AND HERALD PUBLISHING ASSN., 55 W. Oak Ridge Dr., Hagerstown MD 21740-7390. (301)791-7000. Fax: (301)790-9734. Seventh-day Adventist. Tim Crosby, acq. ed. Publishes 40 titles/yr. Receives 450 submissions annually. 2-3% of books from first-time authors. Accepts mss through agents. Reprints books. Prefers 128-160 pgs or 45,000 wds. Royalty 14-16% of net; advance $500. Average first printing 5,000. Publication within 12-18 mos. Considers simultaneous submissions. Responds in 3-4 mos. Guidelines; catalog $3.

Nonfiction: Proposal/2-3 chapters or complete ms.

ROPER PRESS, 4737 A Gretna, Dallas TX 75207. (214)630-4808. Fax: (214)630-4822. Evangelical. Billy O. Hoskins, pres. Publishes 4-6 titles/yr. Receives 300-500 submissions annually. 10% of books from first-time authors. Accepts mss through agents. Reprints books. Royalty on net; no advance. Average first printing varies. Publication within 12-18 mos. Considers simultaneous submissions. Responds in 1-2 mos. Guidelines; catalog for 9x12 SAE/2 stamps.

Nonfiction: Proposal/3 chapters; no phone/fax query. "Most interested in Bible study and Bible stories."

Fiction: Proposal/3 chapters. Adult. "Christian principles must be integral to the story, not a tacked-on afterthought."

Tips: "Finish the title before submission; have an independent reader evaluate it; provide complete background on author."

ST. ANTHONY MESSENGER PRESS, 1615 Republic St., Cincinnati OH 45210. (513)241-5615. Toll-free: (800)488-0488. Fax: (513)241-0399. Catholic. Lisa Biedenbach, mng. ed. Publishes 12-15 titles/yr. Receives 250 submissions annually. 10% of books from first-time authors. Accepts mss through agents. Reprints books. Prefers 100-250 pgs. Royalty 10-12% of net; advance $600-1,000. Average first printing 5,000. Publication within 12-18 mos. Responds in 4-6 wks. Guidelines; catalog for 9x12 SAE/4 stamps.

Nonfiction: Query; no phone/fax query. "Looking for books about Catholic identity; books for pastoral ministry; Catholic history; and Scripture study resources."

Tips: "Most open to spirituality books that help reader live a Catholic Christian life in our culture."

ST. BEDE'S PUBLICATIONS, Box 545, Petersham MA 01366. (508)724-3407. Fax: (508)724-3574. Catholic. Sr. Scholastica Crilly, OSB, ed. Publishes 10 titles/yr. Receives 250 submissions annually. 5% of books from first-time authors. Accepts mss through agents. Reprints books. Prefers 100-250 pgs. Royalty 5-7.5% on retail; no advance. Average first printing 1,500. Publication within 2 yrs. Considers simultaneous submissions. Responds in 6 wks. Guidelines; catalog for 9x13 SAE/2 stamps.

Nonfiction: Query first; no phone query.

Tips: "Just state what you've got simply without gimmicks or attention-getting ploys that usually turn off editors before they've even read your proposal. If your work is worthy of publication, it will stand on its own."

*ST. HILDA'S PRESS, c/o Longstreet Press, 2150 Newmarket Parkway, Ste. 102, Marietta GA 30067. (404)980-1488. Episcopal Press of the western NC diocese. Gail Godwin, ed. Publishes artistic and spiritual books, tracts, and music. Not included in topical listings.

ST. PAUL BOOKS AND MEDIA, 50 St. Paul's Ave., Boston MA 02130. (617)522-8911. Fax: (617)541-9805. Catholic. Sr. Mary Mark Wickenhiser, ed. dir. To help clarify Catholic belief and practice for the average reader. Publishes 30 titles/yr. Receives 750 submissions annually. 30% of books from first-time authors. Accepts ms through agents. Reprints books. Royalty 5% (for children's) up to 12% of net; negotiable outright purchases; negotiable advance. Average first printing 5,000. Publication within 18-24 mos. Responds in 4-8 weeks. Guidelines; catalog for 9x12 SAE/5 stamps.

Nonfiction: Query; no phone/fax query.

Fiction: Query. Juvenile (8-12 yrs) & teen.

Tips: "Most open to easy reading books—not too technical or too wordy—written for the average busy person."

#SCARECROW PRESS INC., 52 Liberty St., Box 4167, Metuchen NJ 08840-1279. (908)548-5767. Division of Grolier that does a few religious titles. Norman Horrocks, V.P., Editorial. Publishes 5 religious titles/yr. Receives 600-700 submissions annually. 70% of books from first-time authors. Accepts mss through agents. Prefers 250+ pgs. Royalty 10-15% of net; no advance. Average first printing 1,000. Publication within 6-18 mos. Considers simultaneous submissions. Responds in 1 month. Guidelines; catalog for 9x12 SAE/4 stamps.

Nonfiction: Query first. "Only looking for reference material of interest to libraries."

SCRIPTURE PRESS - Dewey Bertolini, New Product Developer, Youth Level. See **VICTOR BOOKS.**

+SEASIDE PRESS, 1506 Capitol Ave., Plano TX 75074. (214)423-0090. Imprint of Wordware Publishing, Inc. Russell A. Stultz, pres. Publishes 50-70 titles/yr. Receives 60-75 submissions annually. 40% of books from first-time authors. Accepts mss through agents. Royalty 8-12% of net. Publication within 6 mos. Considers simultaneous submissions. Responds in 1 mo. Free guidelines; catalog.

Nonfiction: Proposal/2 chapters. Religion.

SERVANT PUBLICATIONS/VINE BOOKS/CHARIS BOOKS, 840 Airport Blvd., Ann Arbor MI 48107. (313)761-8505. Imprints: Vine Books for Evangelical Christians; Charis Books for Catholics. Heidi Hess, mng. ed.; submit to Peg VandeVoorde. Publishes 35-40 titles/yr. 3% of books from first-time authors. Accepts mss through agents. Reprints books. Prefers 80,000-100,000 wds. Royalty & advance. Publication within 9-12 mos. Considers simultaneous submissions. Responds in 60-90 days. Guidelines; catalog for 9x12 SAE/5 stamps.

Nonfiction: "We will accept non-fiction proposals only from agents or previously published authors."

Fiction: Query/proposal/2 chapters. Adult.

HAROLD SHAW PUBLISHERS, Box 567, Wheaton IL 60189. (708)665-6700. Fax: (708)665-6793. Joan Guest, mng. ed; Mary Horner, Bible study ed. Publishes 40 titles/yr. Receives 1,200 submissions annually. 10-20% of books from first-time authors. Accepts mss through agents. Reprints books. Prefers 150-245 pgs. Royalty on retail; outright purchases $1,000-2,500 (for Bible Study guides and compilations); advance. Average first printing 5,000. Publication within 12-18 mos. Responds in 6-8 wks. Free guidelines; catalog for 9x12 SAE/6 stamps.

> **Nonfiction:** Proposal/2-3 chapters; no phone/fax query. "Looking for practical books on personal/spiritual growth issues."

> **Tips:** "Most open to well-written, practical books from evangelical world view. Avoid sensational or highly sectarian topics. Interested in mental health issues and books that fill a void in the marketplace."

*SHEED & WARD, Box 419492, Kansas City MO 64141. (816)531-0538. Fax: (816)931-5082. Catholic/ecumenical. Robert Heyer, ed-in-chief. Publishes 30 titles/yr. Receives 200 submissions annually. 10% of books from first-time authors. No mss through agents. **SUBSIDY PUBLISHES 2%.** Reprints books. Prefers 100-200 pgs. Royalty 6% on retail; work-for-hire; no advance. Average first printing 2,000. Publication within 4-7 mos. Responds in 3 mos. Guidelines; catalog for 7x11 SAE/2 stamps.

> **Nonfiction:** Complete ms. "Looking for euthanasia, health care, spirituality, leadership, sacraments, small group or priestless parish facilitating books."

> **Tips:** "Be in touch with needs of progressive/changing parishes."

*SHEER JOY! PRESS/PROMOTIONS, Rt 1 Box 110E, Pink Hill NC 28572. (919)568-6101. Fax: (919)568-4171. Protestant. James R. Adams, pres.; submit to Patricia Adams, ed. Publishes 1-2 titles/yr. Receives 5-10 submissions annually. No mss through agents. **SUBSIDY PUBLISHES 85%.** Prefers 20,000-30,000 wds (200 pgs). Royalty on retail; no advance. Average first printing 1,000. Publication within 6 mos. Considers simultaneous submissions. Responds in 3-4 wks. No guidelines/catalog.

> **Nonfiction:** Complete ms. "Need Bible-based dramatic readings."

> **Fiction:** Complete ms. "Need Bible-based puppet skits."

> **Tips:** "Be very illustrative and forceful in writing Christian drama."

+SHILOH PRESS, 422 Larkfield Center #252, Santa Rosa CA 95403. (707)545-5371. Mary Busha, publisher. "Seeking inspirational and devotional witers, poets, and experienced compiler-editors for future projects. Unpublished, unagented, and inexperienced writers are welcome and should be encouraged by the opportunity to work with an experienced and nurturing book-production team. For a writer's presentation package, including information regarding topics and titles, guidelines, samples, deadlines, terms of publication, publishing opportunities, and submission procedures, send $3.50." Not included in topical listings.

*SHINING STAR PUBLICATIONS, Box 299, Carthage IL 62321. (800)435-7234; (217)357-3981. Fax: (217)357-3987. Good Apple, Inc. Becky Daniel, ed. Publishes 20 titles/yr. Receives 1,000 submissions annually. 50% of books from first-time authors. Accepts mss through agents. Prefers 64-144 pgs. Outright purchases $640-1,440 ($10.50/page for ideas). Average first printing 3,000. Publication within 1 yr. Considers simultaneous submissions. Responds in 6 wks. Guidelines; free catalog.

Nonfiction: Proposal/2 chapters or complete ms. "We do reproducible workbooks to teach scriptures and Christian values."

Fiction: Book proposal or complete ms. "Biblical fiction: retell story using only Scripture facts."

Tips: "Teachers appreciate things that can be presented in a short time. We have new 3-Minute and 5-Minute Bible stories series. Most open to crafts, bulletin board ideas. etc."

*SON-RISE PUBLICATIONS, 143 Greenfield Rd., New Wilmington PA 16142. (800)358-0777. Fax: (412)946-8700. Florence W. Biros, acq. ed. Publishes 5-6 titles/yr. Receives 20 submissions annually. 50% of books from first-time authors. Accepts mss through agents. **SUBSIDY PUBLISHES 50%.** Prefers 25,000-40,000 wds or 90-196 pgs. Royalty 7.5-10% on retail; no advance. Average first printing 3,000. Publication within 8-9 mos. No simultaneous submissions. Responds ASAP. No guidelines or catalog.

Nonfiction: Query; no phone query. "Most open to Christian teaching and testimony combined."

Fiction: Query. "Looking for an historical novel series."

*SOUTHERN BAPTIST PRESS, 4000 Beallwood, Columbus GA 31904. (404)576-5787. Jerry L. Luquire, exec. ed. Publishes 42 books/yr. Receives 600 submissions annually. Accepts mss through agents. Reprints books. **SUBSIDY PUBLISHES 95%.** Prefers 120 pgs. Average first printing 500. Publication within 2 mos. Considers simultaneous submissions. Responds in 1 week. Guidelines; no catalog.

Nonfiction: Complete ms. "Collections of sermons on family topics; poetry; relation of Bible to current day."

Fiction: Complete ms. "Stories that show how faith helps overcome small, day-to-day problems. Prefers under 200 wds."

Tips: "Keep it short; support facts with reference."

STANDARD PUBLISHING, 8121 Hamilton Ave., Cincinnati OH 45231. (513)931-4050. Fax: (513)931-0904. Theresa Hayes, acq. ed. An evangelical Christian publisher of curriculum, classroom resources, and children's books. Publishes 75 titles/yr. Receives 1,500 submissions annually. 40-50% of books from first-time authors. Accepts mss through agents. Royalty 4-10% of net; outright purchases $500-2,000; advance $500. Average first printing 20,000. Publication within 12 mos. Considers simultaneous submissions. Responds in 1 mo. Guidelines; catalog $2.

Nonfiction: Complete ms; no phone/fax query. "Looking for tips for teachers, training material, bulletin board helps, classroom activity books."

Fiction: Complete ms. Children's picture books.

Tips: "Most open to a well-written (fun to read) story that teaches, in a unique and clever manner, something about living for God."

STARBURST PUBLISHERS, Box 4123, Lancaster PA 17604. (717)293-0939. Ellen Hake, ed. dir. Publishes 7-10 titles/yr. Receives 500 submissions annually. 50% of books from first-time authors. Accepts mss through agents. Prefers 60,000-70,000 wds. Royalty 6-15% of net; advances only to top prospects. Average first printing 5,000. Publication within 12 mos. Considers simultaneous submissions. Responds in 4-6 wks. Guidelines; catalog for 9x12 SAE/4 stamps.

Nonfiction: Query or proposal/3 chapters; no phone/fax query. "Looking for health, cookbooks and parenting books."

Fiction: Query only. Adult. "Must be very unique or by established author."

Tips: "Most open to nonfiction and self-help books."

#STAR SONG PUBLISHING GROUP, 2325 Crestmoore, Nashville TN 37215. (615)269-0196. Fax: (615)385-2708. Matthew A. Price, VP. Serving those who serve the church. Publishes 20-25 titles/yr.

Receives 300 submissions annually. 10% of books from first-time authors. Accepts mss through agents. Reprints books. Prefers 75,000-125,000 words or 224 pgs. Royalty 15-20% of net; advance $1,500. Average first printing 5,000. Publication within 1 yr. Considers simultaneous submissions. Responds in 4 mos. Free guidelines/catalog.

Nonfiction: Query; no phone query. "Looking for reference books."

Fiction: Query. For all ages. Contemporary. Query for poetry.

Ethnic Books: African-American.

Tips: "Send a cover letter, summary, brief marketing proposal and vita."

*STILL WATERS REVIVAL BOOKS, 4710 - 37A Ave., Edmonton AB T6L 3T5 Canada. (403)450-3730. Reformed Church. Reg Barrow, pres. Publishes 15 titles/yr. Receives few submissions. Very few books from first-time authors. Accepts mss through agents. Reprints books. Prefers 128-160 pgs. Negotiated royalty or outright purchase. Considers simultaneous submissions. No guidelines; catalog for 9x12 SAE/2 stamps.

Nonfiction: Proposal/2 chapters. "Reformed and Reconstructionistic books of scholarly value, for the use of educated laymen." No non-Reformed or pre-millennial.

Tips: "Most open to books based on the system of doctrine found in the Westminster confession of faith, as it applies to our contemporary setting."

*TABOR PUBLISHING, 25115 Avenue Stanford, Ste. 130, Valencia CA 91355. Catholic/mainline Christian. Cullen W. Shippe, pres.; Carol Prochaska, mng. ed. Publishes 15-20 titles/yr. Receives 150 submissions annually. 75% of books from first-time authors. Accepts mss through agents. Prefers up to 75,000 wds. Royalty 4-12% of net; some outright purchases for $500-2,000; advance $1,000. Publication within 18 mos. Responds in 1 mo.

Nonfiction: Query only. All unsolicited mss returned unopened. Textbooks.

TEACH SERVICES, INC., RR 1 Box 182, Brushton NY 12916. (518)358-2125. Fax: (518)358-3028. Frances Hullquist, ed; submit to Wayne Reid. Publishes 20-26 titles/yr. Receives 45 submissions annually. 50% of books from first-time authors. No mss through agents. **SUBSIDY PUBLISHES 20%.** Reprints books. Prefers 96 pgs. Royalty 10% on retail; no advance. Average first printing 3,000. Publication within 4 mos. Responds in 1 wk. No guidelines; catalog for 9x12 SAE/3 stamps.

Nonfiction: Proposal/2 chapters; phone/fax query ok. "Looking for books on prophecy."

Also Does: Pamphlets, booklets and tracts. IBM (music typesetting).

THE TRINITY FOUNDATION, P.O. Box 1666, Hobbs NM 88240. John W. Robbins, pres. Advocates a systematic presentation of the whole doctrine of God. Publishes 6 titles/yr. Receives 12 submissions annually. Accepts mss through agents. Reprints books. Prefers 200 pgs. Outright purchase; free books; no advance. Average first printing 3,000. Publication within 1 yr. Considers simultaneous submissions. Responds in 2 mos. No guidelines; catalog for #10 SAE/1 stamp.

Nonfiction: Query; no phone/fax query.

Also Does: Pamphlets & tracts.

Tips: "Most open to well-written, biblical books. Read Gordon Clark first."

*TRINITY PRESS INTERNATIONAL, Box 851, Valley Forge PA 19482. (215)768-2120. Fax: (215)768-2056. Dr. Harold W. Rast, dir./ed. Publishes 20-25 titles/yr. Receives 150-200 submissions annually. 3% of books from first-time authors. Accepts mss through agents. Reprints books. Royalty 7.5-10% on retail; advance $500 & up. **SUBSIDY PUBLISHES 10%.** Publication within 8 mos. Responds in 8 wks. Guidelines; free catalog.

Nonfiction: Complete ms or proposal/1 chapter. "Religious material only in the area of Bible studies, theology, ethics, etc."No dissertations or essays.

Tips: "Give small amount of information for first submission."

TYLER PRESS, 1221 W.S.W. Loop 323, Tyler TX 75701. (903)581-2255. Fax: (903)581-7841. J. A. Johnson, sr. ed. A self-publisher's service bureau that will lend its imprint to selected titles for co-published distribution. Publishes 20 titles/yr. Receives 250+ submissions annually. 98% of books from first-time authors. **SUBSIDY PUBLISHES 100%.** Reprints books. Prefers 204 pgs & up. Works on a joint publishing venture with the author; no advance. Average first printing 1,500-2,000. Publication within 2 mos. Considers simultaneous submissions. Responds in 3-4 wks. No guidelines/catalog.

Nonfiction: Query; fax query ok. "We enthusiastically promote self-help/how-to, historical, creation science, current social and political issues, biographies, autobiographies, marriage and family, and women's issues."

Fiction: Query. For children only.

Also Does: Booklets.

TYNDALE HOUSE PUBLISHERS, 351 Executive Dr., Box 80, Wheaton IL 60189-0080. (708)668-8300. Fax: (708)668-6685. Ronald Beers, V.P editorial; submit to Marilyn Dellorto. Publishes 100 titles/yr. Receives 3,000 submissions annually. 5-10% of books from first-time authors. Accepts mss through agents. Reprints books. Royalty; outright purchase of some children's books up to $1,000; advance up to $5,000. **SUBSIDY PUBLISHES 30%.** Average first printing 5,000-10,000. Publication within 12-18 mos. Considers simultaneous submissions. Responds in up to 3 mos. Guidelines (separate guidelines for children's books—request specifically); catalog for 9x12 SAE/9 stamps.

Nonfiction: Query/synopsis.

Fiction: Query. Also children's books, especially for ages 10-14.

Ethnic Books: Publishes Echoes Sunday School Curriculum for African-American churches.

UNITED CHURCH PRESS, 700 Prospect Ave. E., Cleveland OH 44115-1100. (216)736-3700. Fax: (216)736-3703. United Church of Christ/Board for Homeland Missions. Kim M. Sadler, ed. Publishes 12-15 titles/yr. Receives 60+ submissions annually. 50% of books from first-time authors. Accepts mss through agents. Royalty 8-12% of net; work for hire, one-time fee; advance negotiable. Average first printing 3,000. Publication within 9-12 mos. Rarely considers simultaneous submissions. Responds in 10-12 wks. Free guidelines/catalog.

Nonfiction: Proposal/2 or more chapters or complete ms. No phone query.

Fiction: Proposal/2 or more chapters or complete ms. Biblical, for children or teens.

Special Needs: Children's sermons, worship resources, youth materials, religious materials for ethnic groups.

Ethnic Books: African-American, Native-American, Asian-American, Pacific Islanders, and Hispanic.

Tips: "Most open to well-written mss that are United Church of Christ specific and/or religious topics that cross denominations. Use inclusive language and follow the Chicago Manual of Style."

THE UNITED CHURCH PUBLISHING HOUSE, 85 St. Clair Ave. E., Toronto ON M4T 1M8 Canada. (This address will change in March 1995.) (416)925-4850. Fax (416)925-9692. The United Church of Canada. Peter Gordon White, ed-in-chief; Elizabeth Phinney, mng. ed. Publishes 10-15 titles/yr. Receives 60 submissions annually. 15% of books from first-time authors. Accepts mss through agents. Prefers 200 pgs. Royalty 8-10% on retail; advance $100-300. Average first printing 2,000. Publication within 4-6 mos. Responds in 2 mos. Guidelines; catalog for 9x12 SASE.

Nonfiction: Query; no phone query. "Must be of interest to Canadians and address some aspect of Canadian living." Publishes books by Canadian authors only.

UNITED METHODIST PUBLISHING HOUSE, Box 801, Nashville TN 37202. (615)749-6000. United Methodist. Imprints: Abingdon Press and Dimensions for Living. Editors: Mary Catherine Dean or Sally Sharpe. To provide resources that help others know, love and serve God and neighbor. Publishes 12-15 titles/yr. Receives 500-700 submissions annually. 3% of books from first-time authors. Accepts mss through agents. Prefers 128 pgs. Negotiable royalty & advance (rare). Publication within 10-15 mos. No simultaneous submissions. Responds in 6-8 wks. Guidelines; catalog for 9x12 SAE/5 stamps.

Nonfiction: Proposal/2 chapters; no phone query; fax query ok. "Looking for books on parenting, marriage and family."

Ethnic Books: African-American, Native-American, and Asian-American.

Tips: "Most open to books different than similar books in the market. Include detailed information in the proposal regarding competitive books and what sets yours apart."

#UNIVERSITY OF NORTH CAROLINA PRESS, Box 2288, Chapel Hill NC 27515-2288. (919)966-3561. Academic publisher that does a few books of religious studies. Kate Douglas Torrey, dir. Publishes 65 titles/yr. 70% of books from first-time authors. Accepts mss through agents. Prefers 75,000-125,000 wds. Royalty varies; occasional advance. Publication within 1 yr. Responds in 5 mos. Guidelines; free catalog.

Nonfiction: Proposal/chapters. Religious studies.

UNIVERSITY PRESS OF AMERICA, 4720 Boston Way, Lanham MD 20706. (301)459-3366. Fax: (301)459-2118. Academic press. Michelle R. Harris, acq. ed. Publishes scholarly works in the social sciences and humanities. Publishes 50 religious titles/yr. Receives 600+ submissions annually. Accepts mss through agents. Reprints books. Prefers 250 pgs. Royalty 5-15% of net; no advance. Average first printing 500-1,000. Publication within 3-6 mos. Considers simultaneous submissions. Responds in 4-6 wks. No guidelines; catalog for 9x12 SAE/4 stamps.

Nonfiction: Proposal/1-2 chapters. "Looking for scholarly monographs."

Tips: "We publish a wide range of religion works from theology to religious psychology to sufism."

*UPPER ROOM BOOKS, 1908 Grand Ave., Box 189, Nashville TN 37202. (615)340-7332. United Methodist. Janice Grana, ed. Publishes 20-25 titles/yr. Receives 100 submissions annually. 10% of books from first-time authors. Accepts mss through agents. Reprints books. Royalty on retail; advance. Considers simultaneous submissions. Responds in 6-8 wks. Guidelines; catalog for 9x12 SAE/3 stamps.

Nonfiction: Proposal/3 chapters or complete ms.

Tips: "Need books that are well written with a high literary value; books that focus on spirituality, spiritual formation, and related themes."

#VESTA PUBLICATIONS, LTD., Box 1641, Cornwall ON K6H 5V6 Canada. (613)932-2135. Fax: (613)932-7735. General trade publisher that does a few religious titles. Stephen Gill, ed. Publishes 4 titles/yr. Receives 350 submissions annually. 80% of books from first-time authors. No mss through agents. **SUBSIDY PUBLISHES 5%** (author pays about 50% of cost). Prefers 75,000 wds & up. Royalty 10% of net; no advance. Publication within 2 mos. Considers simultaneous submissions if noted. Responds in 1 mo. Catalog for SAE/IRCs.

Nonfiction & Fiction: Query; phone query ok. Literary fiction.

Ethnic Books: Ethnic fiction.

VICTOR BOOKS, 1825 College Ave., Wheaton IL 60187. (708)668-6000. Fax: (708)668-3806. Scripture Press Publications, Inc. David Horton, sr. acq. ed.; Liz Duckworth, mng. ed. for Children's Products and SonPower Youth Resources. Publishes over 100 titles/yr. Receives 2,000 submissions annually. 5% of books from first-time authors. Accepts mss through agents. Reprints books (name authors only). Prefers 80,000-100,000 wds. Royalty 10-12% on retail; advance $2,000-3,000. Average first printing 7,500-10,000. Publication within 9-15 mos. Considers simultaneous submissions. Responds in 60-90 days. Guidelines; catalog for 9x12 SAE/5 stamps.

> **Nonfiction:** Proposal/2 chapters; no phone query. "Most open to fresh, marketable concepts; well-thought-out, and well-written books."
>
> **Fiction:** Proposal/2-3 chapters. Children/adult; picture books.
>
> **Tips:** "Develop your writing skill; develop a platform; know the industry."

#VICTORY HOUSE, INC., Box 700238, Tulsa OK 74170. (918)747-5009. Fax: (918)747-1970. Lloyd B. Hildebrand, mng. ed. Publishes 5 titles/yr. Receives 850 submissions annually. 5% of books from first-time authors. Accepts mss through agents. **SUBSIDY PUBLISHES 10%.** Reprints books. Prefers 250 pgs. Royalty negotiable; rarely pays advance. Average first printing 5,000. Publication within 1 yr. Considers simultaneous submissions. Responds in 3-6 mos. Guidelines/catalog for #10 SAE/1 stamp.

> **Nonfiction:** Complete ms; sometimes accepts phone query. "Looking for books on prayer, Christian living, and contemporary issues."
>
> **Fiction:** Complete ms. For all ages.
>
> **Tips:** "Most open to a well-written book with substance and a fresh approach. Keep the writing simple and direct. Show, don't tell. Avoid preachiness. Illustrate teaching with personal examples. Don't overwrite."

WADSWORTH PUBLISHING COMPANY, 10 Davis Dr., Belmont CA 94002. (415)595-2350. Fax: (415)637-7544. Secular publisher that does some religious books. Tammy Goldfeld, ed. Publishes 5-10 higher education religious textbooks/yr. Receives 200 submissions annually. 20% of books from first-time authors. No mss through agents. Reprints books. Royalty 10-50%; no advance. Average first printing 5,000. Publication within 1 yr. Considers simultaneous submissions. Responds in 2-4 mos. Free guidelines/catalog.

> **Nonfiction:** Proposal/no chapters; no phone query; fax query ok. "Looking for college textbooks, especially on world religions; anthologies."

*WARNER PRESS, Box 2499, Anderson IN 46018-2499. (317)644-7721. Church of God. David C. Schultz, ed-in-chief; Dan Harman, book ed. Publishes 10-15 titles/yr. Receives 200 submissions annually. 5% of books by first-time authors. Accepts mss through agents. Prefers 120 pgs. Royalty 15% of net; seldom makes advances. Average first printing 5,000. Publication within 8 mos. Responds in 2 wks. No guidelines; free catalog.

> **Nonfiction:** Query only; no phone query.

*WELLNESS PUBLICATIONS, Box 2397, Holland MI 49423. (616)335-5553. Darrell Franken, pres. Specializes in health and faith books. Publishes 1 title/yr. Receives 25 submissions annually. All books from first-time authors. Accepts mss through agents. Prefers 250 pgs. Royalty 10% on retail; no advance. Average first printing 2,000. Publication within 3 mos. Responds in 3 mos. No guidelines; free catalog.

> **Nonfiction:** Complete ms.

Tips: "Most open to self-help books, especially dealing with marriage and family life."

*WESLEYAN UNIVERSITY PRESS, 110 Mt. Vernon St., Middletown CT 06457. Peter J. Potter, ed. Royalty. **Nonfiction:** Complete ms. Books of poetry, 64-80 pgs.

#WESTMINSTER/JOHN KNOX PRESS, 100 Witherspoon St., Louisville KY 40202-1396. (502)569-5043. Fax: (502)569-5018. Presbyterian Church (U.S.A.). Stephanie Egnotovich, mng. ed.; Davis Perkins, ed. dir; Walter Sutton & Alexa Smith, professional and general books; Cynthia Thompson & Jeffries Hamilton, academic books; Harold Twiss, general books. Publishes 80-100 titles/yr. Prefers 200 pgs. Royalty 7-10%; negotiable advance. Responds in 2-3 mos. Prefers disk copy. Guidelines; free catalog.

> **Nonfiction:** Proposal/chapters. Emphasizes ethics and theology.

+WINDFLOWER COMMUNICATIONS, 67 Flett Ave., Winnipeg MB R2K 3N3 Canada. (204)668-7475. Fax: (204)661-8530. Non-denominational. Susan B. Brandt, ed; submit to Alissa J. Brandt Murenzi. Publishes quality, wholesome literature for family reading, pleasure and learning. Publishes 4-5 titles/yr. Receives 50-60 submissions annually. 85% of books from first-time authors. Accepts mss through agents. Reprints books. Prefers 150-200 pgs. Royalty or outright purchase; no advance. Average first printing 1,000. Publication within 1 yr. Considers simultaneous submissions. Responds within 2 mos. Free guidelines/catalog.

> **Nonfiction:** Proposal/3 chapters; phone/fax queries ok. "Looking for historical, Canadiana and current issue books."
>
> **Fiction:** Proposal/3 chapters. Teen/adult.
>
> **Tips:** "Try to focus on an original component—something that sticks out."

+WINSTON-DEREK PUBLISHERS, P.O. Box 90883, Nashville TN 37209. (615)321-0535. Fax: (615)329-4824. Maggie Staton, ed. Imprints: Scythe Publications; James C. Winston (religious trade division); One Horn Press. Publishes 50-60 titles/yr. Receives 200+ submissions annually. 40% of books from first-time authors. Accepts mss through agents. **SUBSIDY PUBLISHES 10-15%.** Reprints books. Prefers 80,000-100,000 wds or 300-400 pgs. Royalty 10-15% of net; advance $5,000-10,000. Average first printing 15,000. Publication within 15 mos. Responds in 8 wks. Guidelines; catalog for 9x12 SAE/4 stamps.

> **Nonfiction:** Complete ms/synopsis/introductory author letter; no phone/fax query. "We are looking for titles that are unique in any phase of religious studying. They must be theologically sound (Christian), well-researched, and written for the general market."
>
> **Fiction:** Proposal or complete ms. "No occult, science fiction or New Age."
>
> **Ethnic Books:** African-American; Native-American. Fiction & nonfiction; Black studies.
>
> **Tips:** "Most open to documentaries. Know our format and what we are seeking."

WOMAN'S MISSIONARY UNION, P.O. Box 830010, Birmingham AL 35283-0010. (205)991-8100. Fax: (205)991-4990. Southern Baptist. Cindy McClain, editorial group mngr. A Missions publisher. Publishes 40 titles/yr (many are work for hire). Receives 80 submissions annually. 85% of books from first-time authors. Accepts mss through agents. Reprints books. Prefers 150-250 pgs. Royalty on retail or outright purchase; no advance. Average first printing 5,000-10,000. Publication within 12-18 mos. Considers simultaneous submissions. Responds in 6 mos. Guidelines; copy for 9x12 SAE.

> **Nonfiction:** Proposal/3 chapters or complete ms. (Mss considered in the spring and fall only.) "All that we produce must have a missions/ministry emphasis."
>
> **Ethnic Books:** Publishes books for Hispanic market.
>
> **Tips:** "Most open to how-to for missions involvement or books that address involvement in missions or lead persons into involvement."

+WOOD LAKE BOOKS, INC., 10162 Newene Rd., Winfield BC V4V 1R2 Canada. (604)766-2778. Fax: (604)766-2736. Ecumenical/Mainline. David Cleary, ed. Publishes 10 titles/yr. Receives 120 submissions annually. 80% of books from first-time authors. Accepts mss through agents. **SUBSIDY PUBLISHES 10%.** Reprints books. Prefers 144-166 pgs. Royalty 7-12% on retail; some advances. Average first printing 3,000. Publication within 8-12 mos. Considers simultaneous submissions. Responds in 1-4 mos. Free guidelines/catalog.

> **Nonfiction:** Proposal/2-3 chapters; phone query ok. "Looking for books related to the seasons of the church year; resources for clergy."
>
> **Fiction:** Proposal/2-3 chapters. Children/teen/adult.
>
> **Also Does:** Booklets and a magazine. Interested in religious computer games.
>
> **Tips:** "We publish Canadian authors only."

*WORD PUBLISHING, 1501 LBJ Freeway Ste 650,Dallas TX 75234-6069. (214)488-9673. Fax: (214)488-1311.

*WORLD BIBLE PUBLISHERS, INC., 1500 Riverside Dr., P.O. Box 370, Iowa Falls IA 50126. (515)648-4271. Fax: (515)648-4801. Dan Penwell, Dir. of New Product Development. Seeks to make the Bible more understandable to the masses. Publishes 6-10 titles/yr. 25% of books from first-time authors. Accepts mss through agents. **Some SUBSIDY PUBLISHING.** Reprints books. Prefers 200-300 pgs. Royalty 10-15% of net; some outright purchases; some advances. Average first printing 5,000-7,500. Publication within 6 mos. Considers simultaneous submissions. Responds in 2-4 wks. No guidelines; catalog for 9x12 SAE/$2.90 postage.

> **Nonfiction:** Query or book proposal; phone query ok. "Most open to popular-style reference book or popular-style Bible study book."
>
> **Ethnic Books:** African-American and Spanish.
>
> **Tips:** "Have a well-defined statement of purpose; a well-developed outline of the book with a good summary of each chapter; and actual formatted page layouts of what author perceives the book should look like."

#W.R.S. PUBLISHING, 701 N. New Rd., Waco TX 76710. (817)776-6461. Fax: (817)757-1454. Ann Page, acq. dir. Publishes 6 titles/yr. Receives 600 submissions annually. 20% of books from first-time authors. Accepts mss through agents. Reprints books. Prefers 75,000 wds. Royalty 15% of net; negotiable advance. Publication within 1 yr. Considers simultaneous submissions. Responds in 1 mo. Guidelines; catalog for 9x12 SAE.

> **Nonfiction:** Query or proposal/chapters; no phone query. "Looking for biographical and inspirational books—ordinary people with extraordinary accomplishments. Impossible dream stories."
>
> **Ethnic Books:** For African-Americans.
>
> **Tips:** "Most open to promotable author or subject."

*YALE UNIVERSITY PRESS, 92A Yale Station, New Haven CT 06520. (203)432-0900. Charles Grench, exec. ed. Publishes 10 religious titles/yr. Receives 175 submissions annually. 15% of books from first-time authors. Accepts mss through agents. Reprints books. Prefers up to 100,000 wds or 400 pgs. Royalty to 15% on retail; advances as needed. Average first printing 1,500. Publication within 1 yr. Responds in 2-13 wks. No guidelines; free catalog.

> **Nonfiction:** Query first. "Excellent and saleable scholarly books."

#ZONDERVAN PUBLISHING HOUSE, General Trade Books, 5300 Patterson S.E., Grand Rapids MI 49530-0002. (616)698-6900. HarperCollins. Submit to Editorial Coordinator. Publishes 130 trade titles/yr. Receives 3,000 submissions annually. 20% of books from first-time authors. Accepts mss through agents. Reprints books. Royalty 12-14% of net; variable advance. Average first printing 5,000. Publication within 14 mos. Considers simultaneous submissions. Responds in 3 mos. Guidelines; no catalog. For a recording about submissions, call (616)698-3447.

Nonfiction: Proposal/1 chapter (follow guidelines); no phone query.

Fiction: Query or proposal/2 chapters. "Looking for series for adults and juveniles."

Tips: "Send something unique, distinctive in content. Proposal must show strong understanding of competition and audience."

*ZONDERVAN PUBLISHING HOUSE, Academic and Professional Books, 5300 Patterson Ave. SE, Grand Rapids MI 49530. (616)698-6900. Division of HarperCollins Publishers. Rachel Berrens, ed. Publishes 40-45 academic titles/yr. Accepts mss through agents. Seldom reprints books or dissertations. Royalty 14% of net; usually pays advance. Publication within 3 months. Free guidelines/catalog.

Nonfiction: Query or proposal/1-2 chapters. Academic books only.

Tips: "Includes books on preaching, counseling, discipleship, worship, and church renewal for pastors, professionals, and lay leaders in ministry."Wesleyan perspective.

BOOK PUBLISHERS NOT INCLUDED

Following is a list of book publishers who did not return a questionnaire, have gone out of business, or asked to be deleted for various reasons. Their inclusion on this list indicates a lack of interest in freelance submissions. The following codes indicate the reason for each: OB - Out of business, ABD - Asked to be deleted, NF - No freelance, NQ - Did not return questionnaire, or BA - Bad address.

Abbey Press (ABD)

Affirmation Books (OB)

Aglow (OB)

Anglican Book Centre, The (NQ)

Arbuta House (NQ)

Arnold Publications (NF)

A.S. Barnes (BA)

Back To the Bible Books (OB)

Banner of Truth Trust (NF)

Bethesda Press (NF)

Bible Temple Publishing (NF)

Bookmates Intl., Inc. (NF for now)

Brethren Press (NF)

Brownlow Publishing Co. (NQ)

Canec Publishing House (NQ)

Canyonview Press (NF)

Center for Learning (ABD)

Chosen People Ministries (NF)

Christian Schools Intl (NF)

Church & Synagogue Library (NQ)

Doubleday (ABD)

Evergreen Publication (OB for now)

Falcon Press (NQ)

Gazelle Publications (NF for now)

Michael Glazier Inc (BA)

Great Ocean Publishers (NQ)

Guideposts Books (ABD)

Harpers Ferry Press (BA)

Helmers & Howard (NQ)

Here's Life Publishers (OB)

Holman Bible Publishers (now Broadman & Holman)

Hope Publishing House (NQ)

Ideals Publishing Corp (NQ)

Krieger Publishing (NF)

Life Books (NQ)

LifeCare Books (ABD)

Life Enrichment (bad phone #)

Loizeaux Brothers (NF)

Magnificat Press (OB)

Majestic Books (ABD)

Ministry Pub Co (OB)

Morse Press (BA)

Mott Media (NF)
Multi-Language Media (NF)
Mustard Seed Books (NF)
Nelson-Hall Publishers (ABD)
Parthenon Press (NQ)
Pastoral Fisherman (BA)
Pathway Press (NQ)
People of Destiny, Intl. (NF)
Peregrine Press (NF for now)
Pine Mt Press (BA)
Pointe Publishers (NQ)
Polaris Press (NF)
Prometheus Books (NQ)
Provident Press (OB)
Randall House Publications (NF)
Regular Baptist Press (NQ)
Russell House (BA)
Rutledge Hill Press (ABD)

William H. Sadlier (NF)
Scroll Publishing (NF for now)
Silver Burdett Ginn Inc. (ABD)
Skipjack Press (NF)
Sparrow Press (NF)
Sherwood Sugden (NQ)
Star Books (OB)
Sweetwater Publications (NF)
Today's Christian Woman Books (NF)
Triumph Books (NF)
Twenty-Third Publications (NF)
Union Gospel Press (NF)
Welch Publishing Co (OB)
Westport Publishers (ABD)
Whitaker House (NF for now)
Windy Willow Press (OB)
Wolgemuth & Hyatt (OB)

MARKET ANALYSIS

TOP 26 BOOK PUBLISHERS IN ORDER OF MOST BOOKS PUBLISHED PER YEAR

1. Thomas Nelson 250
2. HarperSanFrancisco 180
3. Baker Book House 140
4. Zondervan 130
5. Victor Books 100+
6. Wm. B. Eerdmans 100
7. Liturgical Press 100
8. Tyndale House 100
9. Paulist Press 90-100
10. Westminster/John Knox 80-100
11. Bethany House 80
12. Chariot Family Pub. 80
13. Harvest House 80
14. InterVarsity Press 80
15. Joshua Morris 75-100
16. Barbour & Co. 75
17. Concordia 75
18. Standard Publishing 75
19. Broadman & Holman 65
20. University of NC 65
21. Moody Press 60-65
22. Oxford University 60+
23. Kregel 60
24. Fleming H. Revell 60
25. Brown/ROA 50-100
26. Custom Commun. 50-75

ALL PUBLISHERS IN ORDER OF MOST BOOKS PUBLISHED PER YEAR

Thomas Nelson 250
HarperSanFrancisco 180
Baker Book House 140
Zondervan 130
Victor Books 100+
Wm. B. Eerdmans 100

Liturgical Press 100
Tyndale House 100
Paulist Press 90-100
Westmin./John Knox 80-100
Bethany House 80
Chariot Family Publishing 80
Harvest House 80
InterVarsity Press 80
Joshua Morris 75-100
Barbour & Co. 75
Concordia 75
Standard Publishing 75
Broadman & Holman 65
University of NC 65
Moody Press 60-65
Oxford University 60+
Kregel 60
Fleming H. Revell 60
Brown/ROA 50-100
Custom Commun. 50-75
Seaside Press 50-70
Crossway 50-60
Winston-Derek 50-60
Orbis Books 50-55
CSS Publishing 50
Liguori Publications 50
Nazarene Pub House 50
Univ. Press of America 50
Heartsong Presents 48
Zondervan Academic 40-45
Forward Movement 40
Review and Herald 40
Woman's Missionary Union 40
Harold Shaw 40
Harrison House 36
Christian Publications 35-40
Questar 35-40
Servant Publications 35-40
Augsburg Fortress 35

Bridge Publishing 35

Meriwether (plays) 35

New Leaf Press 35

Pacific Press 35

Alba House 30

Christian Univer Press 30

College Press 30

Herald Press 30

Our Sunday Visitor 30

Sheed & Ward 30

Christian Ed Publishers 28

Our Sunday Visitor 30

St. Paul Books 30

Huntington House 25-30

Moorings 25-30

Mel Bay Publications 25

Element Books 25

New Leaf Press 25

GROUP Publishing 24-30

Group's Hands-On 24

Discipleship Resources 20-30

TEACH Services 20-26

Star Song 20-25

Trinity Press Intl. 20-25

Upper Room Books 20-25

Bridge Publishing 20

Creation House 20

Eldridge Publishing 20

Garborg's 20

Gold'n'Honey 20

Hunt and Thorpe 20

Shining Star 20

Pilgrim Press 18-20

Novalis 18

Pastoral Press 16

Catholic Univ of America 15-20

Focus on the Family 15-20

Judson Press 15-20

Morehouse Publishing 15-20

Rainbow Books (FL) 15-20

Regal Books 15-20

Tabor Publishing 15-20

Lillenas 15+

C.R. Gibson 15

Joy Publishing 15

New Hope 15

Resource Publications 15

Still Waters 15

United Church Publishing Hs 15

Church Growth Institute 14

United Church Publishing 13

Friendship Press 12-20

Ave Maria Press 12-15

Blue Dolphin 12-15

Gospel Publishing House 12-15

Hendrickson Publishers 12-15

Loyola University Press 12-15

St. Anthony Mess. Press 12-15

United Methodist 12-15

Chalice Press 12

Christopher Pub Hs 12

Honor Books 12

Pastoral Press 12

Rainbow Books (CA) 12

Dimension Books 11

Remnant Publications 11

Cornerstone Press 10-15

Prescott Press 10-15

Warner Press 10-15

Resurrection Press 10-12

ACTA Publications 10

Alban Institute 10

AMG Publishers 10

Christian Classics 10

Educational Ministries 10

Franciscan Univ Press 10

Living Flame 10

New Hope 10

Pacific Theatre (plays) 10

St. Bede's Publications 10

Wood Lake Books 10

Yale University Press 10

Collier-MacMillan 8-12

Cistercian Publications 8-10

Master Books 8-10

American Catholic Press 8

ICS Publications 8
Neibauer Press 8
Pelican Publishing 8
Starburst Publishers 7-10
OMF Books 6-12
Howard Publishing 6-10
Bob Jones University Press 6-10
Presbyterian/Reformed 6-10
World Bible 6-10
Accent Publications 6-8
Chosen Books 6-8
Christian Literature Crusade 6-8
Cornell University Press 6-8
Friends United Press 6-8
Lura Media 6-8
Don Bosco Multimedia 6
Bristol House 6
Promise Publishing 6
Trinity foundation 6
WRS Publishing 6
Franciscan Press 5-10
Haworth Press 5-10
Hensley, Virgil W. 5-10
Rainbow's End 5-10
Regina Press 5-10
Wadsworth Publishing 5-10
Religious Education Press 5-6
Son-Rise 5-6
Langmarc Publishing 5
Mt. Olive College Press 5
Scarecrow Press 5
Victory House 5
Emerald Books 4-6
Hannibal Books 4-6
Roper Press 4-6
Windflower Communications 4-5
Christian Media 4
Covenant Publishers 4
Open Court 4
VESTA Publications 4
Bethel Publishing 3-6
Jews for Jesus 3-5
Meriwether Publishing 3-4

Paraclete Press 3-4
Cliffside Publishing 3
Good Book 3
Praxis Institute 3
Thomas More Press 2-6
Cross Cultural 2-5
Lifetime Books 2-4
Harvard House 2-3
Kindred Press 2-3
Probe Ministries 2-3
Barclay Press 2
Covenant Publishers 2
Greenlawn Press 2
Guernica Editions 2
Krieger Publishing 2
Living Sacrifice 2
Morning Star Press 2
Omega Publications 2
Rainbow Books (FL) 2
Life Cycle Books 1-3
DaBaR Services 1-2
Editorial Evangelica 1-2
New Society Publishers 1-2
Regnery Publishing 1-2
Elder Books 1
Gilgal Publications 1
Higley Publishing 1
MML Company 1
Renewal Press 1
Wellness Publications 1
August House 0-2

SUBSIDY PUBLISHERS:

Brentwood 267
Poet's Cove 125
Fairway Press 60-75
Southern Baptist Press 42
Companion Press 38
Proclaim Publishing 24
Tyler Press 20
Pillar Books 5
Sheer Joy! Press 1-2

BOOK PUBLISHERS WITH THE MOST BOOKS ON THE BEST SELLER LIST FOR THE LAST YEAR

Note: This tally is based on actual sales in Christian bookstores for January-November 1994. The list is broken down by types of books, i.e., children's, fiction, paperback and cloth. Numbers behind the names indicate the number of titles each publisher had on that best-seller list during the year. The combined list indicates the total number a particular publisher had on all the lists combined. It is interesting to note that last year only 26 publishers had books on the best seller list; this year 35 publishers made the list. Not listed here are 5 or 6 additional secular publishers who had books that crossed over into Christian bookstores.

Fiction Books

1. Bethany House 18
2. Multnomah Books 8
3. Thomas Nelson 7
4. Tyndale House 7
5. Harvest House 5
6. Crossway Books 3
7. Macmillan 3
8. Zondervan 1
9. NavPress 1
10. Victor 1

Nonfiction - Cloth

1. Word 13
2. Zondervan 7
3. Thomas Nelson 7
4. Focus on the Family 4
5. Questar 4
6. HarperCollins 2
7. Revell 2
8. Tyndale House 2
9. Creation House 2
10. Discovery House 2
11. Harvest House 2
12. Baker Books 1
13. Bethany House 1
14. Crossway Books 1
15. Moody Press 1
16. Servant 1
17. Sparrow 1

Nonfiction - Paperback

1. Word 8
2. Multnomah Books 5
3. Harvest House 3
4. NavPress 3
5. Barbour Books 2
6. Broadman & Holman 2
7. Focus on the Family 2
8. Honor Books 2
9. Moody Press 2
10. Pinon Press 2
11. Regal Books 2
12. Tyndale House 2
13. Augsburg Fortress 1
14. Destiny Image 1
15. Harrison House 1
16. Living Truth 1
17. Macmillan 1
18. Thomas Nelson 1
19. Revell 1
20. Rutledge Hill 1
21. Standard 1
22. Victor Books 1
23. Whitaker House 1
24. Zondervan 1
Plus 5 secular publishers

Children's Books

1. Gold 'N' Honey 9
2. Crossway 7
3. Tyndale House 6
4. Thomas Nelson 5
5. Zondervan 4
6. Bethany House 4
7. Chariot Books 3
8. Focus on the Family 3
9. Regina 2
10. Victor 2

11. Baker Books 1
12. HarperCollins 1
13. Macmillan 1
14. Regal Books 1
15. Star Song 1
16. World Bible 1

Combined Best-Seller Lists
(Combination of four lists above)
1. Bethany House 23
2. Word 21
3. Thomas Nelson 20
4. Tyndale House 17
5. Questar 13
6. Multnomah Books 13
7. Zondervan 13
8. Crossway 11
9. Focus on the Family 9
10. Harvest House 8
11. Macmillan 5
12. NavPress 4
13. Victor Books 4
14. Chariot Books 3
15. HarperCollins 3
16. Moody Press 3
17. Regal Books 3
18. Revell 3
19. Baker Books 2
20. Barbour Books 2
21. Broadman & Holman 2
22. Creation House 2
23. Discovery House 2
24. Honor Books 2
25. Pinon Press 2
26. Regina 2
27. Augsburg Fortress 1
28. Destiny Image 1
29. Harrison House 1
30. Living Truth 1
31. Rutledge Hill 1
32. Servant 1
33. Sparrow 1
34. Standard 1

35. Whitaker House 1

Comment:
Unfortunately, of the publishers listed above with best-selling books, a number are not open to freelance submissions. However, some of them can be reached through The Writer's Edge (see listing under Editorial Services - Illinois).

BOOK TOPICS MOST POPULAR WITH PUBLISHERS

Note: The numbers following the topics indicate how many publishers said they were interested in seeing a book on that topic. To find the list of publishers interested in each topic, go to the Topical Listings for books (see Table of Contents).

1. Christian Living 108
2. Bible/Biblical Studies 101
3. Family Life 95
4. Prayer 93
5. Women's Issues 91
6. Spirituality 87
7. Religion 86
8. How-to/Self-help 84
9. Marriage 83
10. Christian Education 82
11. Inspirational 81
12. Theological 81
13. Devotional Books 80
14. Parenting 78
15. Current/Social Issues 77
16. Church Renewal 73
17. Evangelism/Witnessing 72
18. Discipleship 71
19. Ethics 67
20. Biography 66
21. Pastor's Helps 66
22. Historical 63
23. Church Life 62
24. Counseling Aids 61
25. Doctrinal 61
26. Healing 59

27. Psychology 53
28. Gift Books 52
29. Apologetics 51
30. Social Justice Issues 50
31. Worship Resources 50
32. Group Study Books 49
33. Youth Books 49
34. Divorce 48
35. Reference Books 48
36. Humor 47
37. Health 46
38. Philosophy 46
39. Fiction: Adult 45
40. Cults/Occult 44
41. Men's Books 44
42. Controversial Issues 43
43. Liturgical Studies 42
44. Children's Picture Books 41
45. Missionary 41
46. Singles Issues 40
47. Autobiography 39
48. Money Management 39
49. Personal Experience 39
50. Fiction: Juvenile 38
51. Prophecy 38
52. Sr. Adult Concerns 38
53. Ethnic Books 37
54. World Issues 37
55. Fiction: Contemporary 36
56. Fiction: Historical 36
57. Environmental Issues 35
58. Archaeology 34
59. Sermons 34
60. Christian Home Schooling 33
61. Miracles 33
62. Fiction: Biblical 32
63. Fiction: Adventure 29
64. Curriculum 28
65. Political 28
66. Economics 27
67. Music-Related Books 27
68. Poetry 27
69. Youth Programs 26

70. *Leadership 27
71. Fiction: Historical/Romance 26
72. Fiction: Mystery 26
73. Sociology 25
74. Fiction: Teen/Young Ad. 24
75. Fiction: Humor 23
76. *Scholarly 23
77. Celebrity Profiles 22
78. Fiction: Frontier 22
79. Cookbooks 21
80. Fiction: Frontier/Romance 21
81. Games/Crafts 21
82. Christian School Books 20
83. Drama 20
84. Retirement 20
85. Science 20
86. Fiction: Literary 19
87. *Recovery Books 19
88. Fiction: Plays 18
89. Fiction: Mystery/Romance 17
90. *Stewardship 17
91. *Booklets 16
92. Exposés 15
93. Fiction: Romance 14
94. *Personal Renewal 13
95. Sports 13
96. Fiction: Allegory 12
97. Fiction: Short Story Coll. 12
98. *Pamphlets 12
99. Fiction: Science Fiction 11
100. Fiction: Fantasy 11
101. Travel 11
102. *Tracts 10

Comments:

If you are a fiction writer, you are more likely to sell adult fiction (44 possible publishers—3 more than last year), than you are juvenile fiction (38 publishers—two more than last year) or teen fiction (24 publishers—2 less than last year & 5 less than 2 years ago). The most popular genres with publishers are (1) Contemporary Fiction (4th last yr) and (2) Historical Fiction (1st last yr), both with 36 markets, (3) Biblical Fiction with 32 markets (tied for

3rd last year), (4) Adventure Fiction with 29 markets (tied for 3rd last year), and (5) Historical/Romance and Mystery, both with 26 markets (Historical/Romance was 5th last year, and Mystery has moved up to tie). Interest in both adult and juvenile fiction increased this year, while teen fiction dropped. Interest also dropped in Frontier/Romance, Mystery/Romance, Allegory, Short-Story Collections, Science Fiction, and Fantasy; Frontier and Romance remained the same, while interest increased in Humorous, Literary, and Plays.

Good news for poets this year: While there were only 16 book publishers who published poetry books last year (up two from the previous year), this year there are 27—a significant gain of over 47% over the last two years. Even though the market is improving, many will still want to consider self-publishing (look for cooperative publishers or subsidy publishers in this book), or sell to periodicals. Go to the topical listings in this book to find periodical markets for poetry.

Compared to last year, the top five topics are exactly the same, but of those between six and 20, only two stayed in the same slot. Spirituality, Christian Education, How-to/Self-help, Inspirational, and Church Renewal increased in interest, while Theological, Devotional Books, Parenting, Current/Social issues, Evangelism, Discipleship, and Counseling Aids showed a slight decrease in interest. Counseling Aids dropped out of the top 20 (to #24) and Ethics moved into the top 20 (from #24).

In a general comparison to last year, the following topics showed a significant increase or decrease in interest among the publishers. The topics are listed under each heading with those making the greatest change in position at the top. The numbers indicate the number of places that topic moved up or down on the list since last year.

Decreased in interest:
Fiction: Historical 13
Fiction: Adventure 11

Economics 10
Fiction: Biblical 9
Christian Home Schooling 9
Fiction: Frontier/Romance 9
Retirement 9
Autobiography 8
Children's Picture Books 8
Drama 7
Fiction: Mystery/Romance 7
Devotional Books 6
Fiction: Teen/Young Adult 6
Money Management 6
Singles Issues 6
Theological 6

Increased in interest:
Men's Books 24
Controversial Issues 22
Gift Books 18
Poetry 17
Music-Related Books 11
Philosophy 11
Health 10
Ethnic 7
Curriculum 6

Comments:
The following topics showed a significant decrease in interest for the second year in a row: Fiction: Teen/Young Adult (down 3 years), Drama (down 3 years), and Fiction: Mystery/Romance.

The following topics were down last year, but up this year: Health, Controversial Issues, and Gift Books.

The following topic showed an increase in interest for the second year in a row: Curriculum.

The following topics were up last year, but down this year: Economics, Children's Picture Books, Fiction: Frontier/Romance, and Fiction: Historical.

SUMMARY OF INFORMATION ON CHRISTIAN BOOK PUBLISHERS FOUND IN THE ALPHABETICAL LISTINGS

Note: The following numbers are based on the maximum total estimate for each company. For example, if a company gave a range of 5-10, the averages were based on the higher number, 10. This information will be valuable in determining if the contract offered by your publisher is in line with other publishers in some of these areas. For further help, check the section on editorial services to find those who offer contract evaluations, which are most valuable.

TOTAL MANUSCRIPTS RECEIVED:

One hundred seventy-six publishers indicated they received a combined total of over 117,000 manuscripts during the year. That is an average of 665 manuscripts per editor, per year (that's a 6% increase over last year). The actual number of manuscripts received ranged from one to 10,000 per editor.

NUMBER OF BOOKS PUBLISHED:

One hundred ninety-eight publishers reported that they will publish a combined total of nearly 5,750 titles during the coming year. That is an average of 29 books per publisher (an increase of nearly 7% over last year). The actual number per publisher ranges from two to 250. Of those who responded to the question this year, 39% will publish more books than last, 30% will publish about the same number, and 31% will publish fewer. If each publisher actually publishes his maximum estimate of books for the year, just under 5% of the manuscripts submitted will be published (that's a decrease of a half a percent from last year).

AVERAGE FIRST PRINT RUN:

Based on 147 book publishers who indicated their average first print run, the average first printing of a book for a new author is about 5,620 books. That's an increase of just over 1% over last year. Actual print runs ranged from 500 to 20,000 copies.

ROYALTIES:

Of the 183 publishers who reported that they paid royalties, 57 (31.1%) pay on the retail price; 90 (49.2%) pay on the wholesale price or net; and 36 (19.7%) didn't tell which. (Those percentages indicate that the number paying on the retail price has dropped 5.4% and those paying on net has increased 2.5%) The average royalty based on the retail price of the book was 8.25% to 10.5%. (Actual royalties varied from 2% to 15%.) The average royalty based on net varied from 9.25% to 12.75%. (Actual royalties varied from 4-30%.) The recommended royalty based on net is 18%, but only 10% of the Christian publishers counted here are paying 18% or higher.

ADVANCES:

One hundred seventy-six publishers responded to the question about whether or not they paid advances. Of those, 50.6% say they pay advances (down from 55% last year and 59% the year before) and 49% (up from 45% last year) say they do not. Of those who pay advances, only 18% (32 publishers) gave a specific amount. The average advance for those 32 was $934–1836 (that was an average increase of about 24%). The actual range was from $100 to $10,000. Of course, a number of these publishers pay more than that for established authors or potentially best-selling books. It is not unusual for a first author to get no advance or a small one. Once you have one or more books published, feel free to ask for an advance, and raise the amount for each book. Don't be afraid to ask for an advance, even on a first book, if you need the money to support you while you finish the manuscript. Although more publishers are saying they don't give an advance, or are reluctant to name an amount, the truth is many publishers do give advances when warranted, but are reluctant to advertise that fact or to divulge an amount.

REPORTING TIME:

Waiting for a response from an editor is often the hardest part of the writing business. Of the 191 editors who indicated how long you should have to wait for a response from them, the average time was just under 8-10 weeks. However, since the times they actually gave ranged from one to 52 weeks, be sure to check the listing for the publisher you are interested in. Give them a two-week grace period, then feel free to write a polite letter asking about the current status of your manuscript. Give them another month to respond, and if you don't hear anything, you can call as a last resort.

TOPICAL LISTINGS OF PERIODICALS

As soon as you have an article or story idea, look up that topic in the following topical listings (see Table of Contents for a full list of topics). Study the appropriate periodicals in the primary/alphabetical listings (as well as their writers'guidelines and sample copies), and select those that are most likely targets for the piece you are writing.

Note that most ideas can be written for more than one periodical if you slant them to the needs of different audiences; for example, current events for teens, or pastors, or women. Have a target periodical and audience in mind before you start writing. Each topic is divided by age-group/audience, so you can pick appropriate markets for your particular slant.

If the magazine prefers or requires a query letter, be sure to write that letter first and then follow any guidelines or suggestions they make if they give you a go-ahead.

R - TAKES REPRINTS
(*) - Indicates new topic this year.

BIBLE STUDIES

ADULT/GENERAL
ADVOCATE - R
America
Annals of St. Anne
Baptist Beacon - R
Baptist Informer
Bible Advocate - R
Bible Today
Biblical Reflections - R
Canadian Catholic
Catholic Digest - R
Catholic Twin Circle - R
Charisma/Christian Life
Christian Standard - R
Church Herald - R
Church Herald/Holiness - R
Compass
Connecting Point - R
Cresset
Emphasis/Faith & Living - R
Evangel - R
Evangelical Baptist - R
Evangelical Friend

Foursquare World - R
God's Revivalist
Good News Journal - R
Hallelujah! - R
Head to Head - R
Hearing Hearts - R
Highway News - R
Inspirer, The - R
It's Your Choice - R
John Milton - R
Liguorian
Living Church
Lutheran, The
Lutheran Digest - R
Lutheran Layman
Lutheran Witness
Maranatha - R
Mennonite, The - R
MESSAGE
MESSAGE/Open Bible - R
Messenger, The (NC) - R
Messenger/St. Anthony
Ministry Today - R
Morning Glory - R
North American Voice

Our Family - R
Our Sunday Visitor
Pentecostal Evangel - R
Pentecostal Homelife - R
Plowman, The - R
Pourastan - R
Prayerworks - R
Praying
Presbyterian Outlook
Presbyterian Record - R
Presbyterian Survey - R
Rural Landscapes
St. Willibrord Journal
Signs of the Times - R
Silver Wings - R
U.S. Catholic
Wesleyan Advocate - R
Witness, The

CHILDREN
Crusader - R

CHRISTIAN
EDUCATION/LIBRARY
CE Connection - R

Christian School
Church Educator - R
GROUP
Leader - R
Lutheran Education
Shining Star
Youth Leader - R

MISSIONS
Childlife
New World Outlook
Urban Mission - R

PASTORS/LEADERS
Christian Century
Five Stones, The - R
Group's Jr High
Jour/Biblical Ethics - R
Journal/Christian Healing - R
Liturgy - R
Lutheran Forum - R
Lutheran Partners - R
Preacher's Magazine - R
Priest, The
PROCLAIM - R
Pulpit Helps - R
Quarterly Review
Review for Religious
Single Ad. Ministries Jour.
Word & World

TEEN/YOUNG ADULT
Conqueror - R
Cross Walk
Edge, The - R
Kiln, The - R
Magazine/Youth! - R
Pathway I.D. - R
Student, The
Student Leadership - R
Teenage Christian - R
Teen Life - R
Young Adult Today

Young Salvationist - R

WOMEN
Anna's Journal - R
Church Woman
Co-Laborer - R
Contempo
Daughters of Sarah - R
Horizons - R
Journey - R
Joyful Woman - R
Lutheran Woman Today
Response
Royal Service
Salt and Light - R
Wesleyan Woman - R
Woman's Touch - R

BOOK EXCERPTS

ADULT/GENERAL
Advent Christian Witness
African Amer. Heritage - R
Aspire
AXIOS - R
Better Tomorrow, A
Bible Advocate - R
Biblical Reflections - R
Canadian Catholic
Caregivers Connection - R
Celebrate Life - R
Charisma/Christian Life
Christian Edge - R
Christian Event - R
Christian Parenting - R
Christian Reader - R
Christian Single - R
Christianity Today - R
Church Herald/Holiness - R
Columbia - R
Conquest
Cresset
Door, The - R

Emphasis/Faith & Living - R
Evangelical Friend
Expression Christian
Focus on the Family
Gospel Tidings - R
Home Life
Home Times - R
Indian Life - R
InterVarsity
It's Your Choice - R
John Milton - R
Jour/Christian Nursing - R
Kansas City Christian - R
Living - R
Maranatha - R
MESSAGE/Open Bible - R
Ministry Today - R
Moody
Morning Glory - R
New Covenant - R
New Heart, A - R
New Thought - R
ParentLife - R
Parents of Teenagers - R
Pentecostal Evangel - R
Plus - R
Pourastan - R
Praying
Presbyterian Outlook
Presbyterian Record - R
Puzzler's Digest - R
SCP Journal - R
Signs of the Times - R
Sunday Digest - R
Today's Better Life
Urban Family
U.S. Catholic
Vista - R
Witness, The

CHILDREN
Focus/Clubhouse
High Adventure - R

Touch - R

CHRISTIAN
EDUCATION/LIBRARY
CE Connection - R
Changing Lives
Christian School
GROUP
Leader - R
Memos - R
Resource - R

MISSIONS
Aeropagus - R
Intl. Journal/Frontier - R
World Vision - R

PASTORS/LEADERS
Christian Century
Diaconalogue - R
Five Stones, The - R
Ivy Jungle Report - R
Jour/Biblical Ethics - R
Journal/Christian Healing - R
Ministries Today
Networks - R
Single Ad. Ministries Jour.
Worldwide Challenge - R
Youthworker - R

TEEN/YOUNG ADULTS
Breakaway - R
Edge, The - R
Freeway - R
Kiln, The - R
Teenage Christian - R
Teen Life - R

WOMEN
Co-Laborer - R
Conscience - R
Horizons - R
Journey - R

Joyful Woman - R
Link & Visitor - R
Salt and Light - R
Today's Christian Woman
Wesleyan Woman - R

WRITERS
Inklings - R
Writers Connection - R
Writing Right - R

BOOK REVIEWS

ADULT/GENERAL
AGAIN - R
Anglican Journal - R
Aspire
AXIOS - R
Better Tomorrow, A
Biblical Reflections - R
Burning Light - R
Canadian Baptist - R
Canadian Catholic
Caregivers Connection - R
Cathedral Age - R
Catholic Twin Circle - R
Celebrate Life - R
Charisma/Christian Life
Christian Courier (Canada) - R
Christian Edge - R
Christian Event - R
Christian Parenting - R
Christian Reader - R
Christian Renewal - R
Christian Research
Christianity/Arts
Christianity Today - R
Church Advocate, The - R
Comments from the Friends - R
Commonweal
Compass
Connecting Point - R
Cornerstone - R

Cresset
Discovery - R
Dovetail - R
Evangelical Baptist - R
Expression Christian
First Things
Friends Journal - R
Good News Journal
Good News Reporter - R
Head to Head - R
Hearing Hearts - R
Home Life
Home Times - R
Impact Magazine - R
Indian Life - R
Interim - R
It's Your Choice - R
Joyful Noise
Jour/Christian Nursing - R
Living Church
Mennonite, The - R
John Milton - R
Minnesota Christian - R
National Catholic
New Thought - R
New Trumpet - R
Parenting Treasures - R
ParentLife - R
Pentecostal Testimony - R
Perspectives on Science
Plowman, The - R
Pourastan - R
Praying
Presbyterian Record - R
Presbyterian Survey - R
Professional Parents - R
Psychology for Living - R
Puzzler's Digest - R
Ratio
Religious Education
Rural Landscapes
St. Anthony Messenger
SCP Journal - R

Shantyman, the - R
Smart Dads
Social Justice - R
Spiritual Life
Inland Northwest
Touchstone
Upsouth - R
Urban Family

CHRISTIAN
EDUCATION/LIBRARY
CE Counselor - R
Christian Librarian - R
Christian School
Leader - R
Librarian's World - R
Memos - R
Resource - R
Today's Catholic Teacher - R
Vision - R
Youth & CE Leadership - R
Youth Leader - R

MISSIONS
Areopagus - R
Intl. Journal/Frontier - R
Missiology
New World Outlook
World Christian - R
World Vision - R

MUSIC
Hymn, The - R

PASTORS/LEADERS
Advance - R
Bethany Choice - R
Catechumenate
Christian Century
Christian Management - R
Christian Ministry
Christian Sentinel
Church Growth Network - R

Clergy Journal
Five Stones, The - R
Jour/Biblical Ethics - R
Journal/Christian Healing - R
Lutheran Partners - R
Ministries Today
Networks - R
Preacher's Magazine - R
Quarterly Review
Resource - R
Review for Religious
Search
Single Ad. Ministries Jour.
Word & World

TEEN/YOUNG ADULT
Edge, The - R
Insight - R
Magazine/Youth! - R
Student Leadership - R
Teenage Christian - R
Teen Life - R
You! - R

WOMEN
Co-Laborer - R
Conscience - R
Daughters of Sarah - R
Esprit - R
Journey - R
Wesleyan Woman
Woman's Touch - R

WRITERS
Canadian Writer's Jour - R
Cross & Quill - R
Gotta Write
Inklings - R
Writers Anchor - R
Writers Connection
Writer's Guidelines
Writer's Infor Network
Writer's Nook News

Writing Right - R

CELEBRITY PIECES

ADULT/GENERAL
American Tract Soc. - R
Better Tomorrow, A
AXIOS - R
Bookstore Journal - R
Canada Lutheran - R
Canadian Catholic
Catholic Digest - R
Catholic Twin Circle - R
Celebrate Life - R
Charisma/Christian Life
Christian Event - R
Christian Media - R
Christian Reader - R
Christian Single - R
Christianity Today - R
Columbia - R
Companion
Critic, The
Door, The - R
Emphasis/Faith & Living - R
Expression Christian
Family Journal - R
Good News, Etc - R
Good News Journal - R
Guideposts
Hayden Herald - R
Head to Head - R
Hearing Hearts - R
Herald of Holiness - R
Home Life
Home Times - R
John Milton - R
Kansas City Christian - R
Kootenai Courier - R
Indian Life - R
Living - R
Lutheran Layman
Maranatha - R

Mature Years - R
MESSAGE
Messenger, The (NC) - R
Minnesota Christian - R
Ministry Today - R
New Thought - R
Our Sunday Visitor
Parents of Teenagers
Pentecostal Evangel - R
Plus - R
Positive Approach, A - R
Prayerworks - R
Presbyterian Record - R
Pursuit - R
Puzzler's Digest - R
St. Anthony Messenger
Signs of the Times - R
Sports Spectrum
Standard - R
Sunday Digest - R
United Methodist Reporter
Upsouth - R
Urban Family
Vibrant Life - R
Vital Christianity - R

CHILDREN
Counselor - R
Crusader - R
Guideposts for Kids
Pockets - R
Touch - R
Venture (IL) - R

CHRISTIAN
EDUCATION/LIBRARY
Changing Lives
Resource - R

MISSIONS
IMPACT
Worldwide Challenge - R

PASTORS/LEADERS
Journal/Christian Camping - R

TEEN/YOUNG ADULT
Breakaway - R
Brio
Edge, The - R
Insight - R
Insight/Out - R
Magazine/Youth! - R
Spirit
Straight - R
Teenage Christian - R
Teen Life - R
You! - R
Young Salvationist - R

WOMEN
Today's Christian Woman
Wesleyan Woman - R

WRITERS
Christian Communicator - R
Exchange
Gotta Write
Writer's Forum - R
Writer's Infor Network

CHRISTIAN BUSINESS

ADULT/GENERAL
Annals of St. Anne
Aspire
AXIOS - R
Biblical Reflections - R
Bookstore Journal - R
Canada Lutheran - R
Catholic Digest - R
Catholic Sentinel - R
Catholic Twin Circle - R
Charisma/Christian Life
Christian Courier (Canada) - R
Christian Event - R

Christian Media - R
Christian Retailing - R
Christian Single - R
Christianity Today - R
Decision
Discovery - R
Emphasis/Faith & Living - R
Evangel - R
Evangelical Visitor - R
Expression Christian
Family, The - R
Good News Journal - R
Good News Reporter - R
Guideposts
Hearing Hearts - R
Herald of Holiness - R
Highway News - R
Home Times - R
InterVarsity
Kansas City Christian
Maranatha - R
Mature Years - R
Mennonite, The - R
MESSAGE
Messenger, The (NC) - R
Ministry Today - R
Minnesota Christian - R
New Covenant - R
New Trumpet - R
PCA Messenger - R
Pentecostal Evangel - R
Pentecostal Homelife - R
Pentecostal Testimony - R
Praying
Presbyterian Record - R

MISSIONS
Childlife
Worldwide Challenge - R

PASTORS/LEADERS
Advance - R
Christian Century

Christian Management - R
Clergy Journal
Nat/Intl Religion Report
Today's Parish
Your Church - R

TEEN/YOUNG ADULT
Teenage Christian - R

WOMEN
Lutheran Woman Today
Salt and Light - R
Wesleyan Woman - R
Woman's Touch - R

CHRISTIAN EDUCATION

ADULT/GENERAL
America
Anglican Journal - R
Annals of St. Anne
AXIOS - R
Baptist Informer
B.C. Catholic - R
Bible Advocate - R
Biblical Reflections - R
Canadian Baptist - R
Canada Lutheran - R
Canadian Catholic
Cathedral Age - R
Catholic Accent
Catholic Digest - R
Catholic Forester - R
Catholic Parent
Catholic Sentinel - R
Catholic Twin Circle - R
Charisma/Christian Life
Christian C.L. RECORD - R
Christian Courier (Canada) - R
Christian Edge - R
Christian Home & School
Christianity Today - R
Church Herald/Holiness - R

Columbia - R
Compass
Covenant Companion - R
Cresset
Decision
Discovery - R
Emphasis/Faith & Living - R
Evangel - R
Evangelical Baptist - R
Evangelical Beacon
Evangelical Friend
Evangelical Visitor - R
Focus on the Family
Foursquare World - R
Friends Journal - R
God's Revivalist
Good News, Etc - R
Good News Journal - R
Good News Reporter - R
Herald of Holiness - R
Home Times - R
John Milton - R
Joyful Noise
Kansas City Christian - R
Liguorian
Living Church
Lookout - R
Lutheran Digest - R
Maranatha - R
Mature Years - R
Mennonite, The - R
Mennonite Brethren - R
MESSAGE
Messenger, The (Canada) - R
Messenger, The (NC) - R
Ministry Today - R
Minnesota Christian - R
New Covenant - R
New Trumpet - R
North American Voice
NW Christian Journal - R
Northwestern Lutheran - R
Our Family - R

Our Sunday Visitor
Parenting Treasures - R
ParentLife - R
Parents of Teenagers
PCA Messenger - R
Pentecostal Evangel - R
Pentecostal Homelife - R
Pentecostal Testimony - R
Plowman, The - R
Pourastan - R
Prayerworks - R
Presbyterian Outlook
Presbyterian Record - R
Religious Education
Salt Shaker - R
SCP Journal - R
Social Justice - R
United Church Observer
Upsouth - R
U.S. Catholic
Vista - R
Witness, The

CHRISTIAN
EDUCATION/LIBRARY
(See Alphabetical listings)

MISSIONS
Compassion
Partners

PASTORS/LEADERS
Advance - R
Christian Century
Christian Ministry
Church Administration
Church Business - R
Discipleship Training
Five Stones, The - R
Groups's Jr High
Liturgy - R
Lutheran Partners - R
Ministries Today

Nat/Intl Religion Report
Networks - R
Preacher's Magazine - R
Pulpit Helps - R
Quarterly Review
Resource - R
Review for Religious
Search
Today's Parish
Word & World
Youthworker - R

TEEN/YOUNG ADULT
Conqueror - R
Cross Walk
You! - R

WOMEN
Esprit - R
Lutheran Woman Today
Response
Woman's Touch - R

CHRISTIAN LIVING

ADULT/GENERAL
ADVOCATE - R
Alive! - R
alive now! - R
America
American Tract Soc. - R
Annals of St. Anne
Arkansas Catholic
Aspire
At Ease - R
AXIOS - R
Baptist Beacon - R
B.C. Catholic - R
Better Tomorrow, A
Bible Advocate - R
Biblical Reflections - R
Canadian Baptist - R
Canada Lutheran - R

Canadian Catholic
Catholic Digest - R
Catholic Forester - R
Catholic New York
Catholic Parent
Catholic Sentinel - R
Catholic Twin Circle - R
Charisma/Christian Life
Christian Courier (WI) - R
Christian Courier (Canada) - R
Christian Edge - R
Christian Event - R
Christian Home & School
Christian Living - R
Christian Renewal - R
Christian Single - R
Christian Standard - R
Christianity Today - R
Church Herald - R
Church Herald/Holiness - R
Church of God EVANGEL
Columbia - R
Commonweal
Companion
Companions - R
Connecting Point - R
Conquest
Covenant Companion - R
Crossway/Newsline
Decision
Discipleship Journal - R
Emphasis/Faith & Living - R
Evangel - R
Evangelical Baptist - R
Evangelical Beacon - R
Evangelical Friend
Evangelical Visitor - R
Explorer
Family, The - R
Family Digest, The - R
Fellowship Today - R
Focus on the Family - R
Foursquare World - R

Gem, The - R
God's Revivalist
Good News - R
Good News Journal - R
Good News Reporter - R
Gospel Tidings - R
Guideposts
Head to Head - R
Hearing Hearts - R
Herald of Holiness - R
Highway News - R
Home Life
Home Times - R
Impact Magazine - R
Indian Life - R
Inspirer, The - R
Interim - R
InterVarsity
John Milton - R
Jour/Christian Nursing - R
Kansas City Christian - R
Lifeglow - R
Light and Life
Liguorian
Live - R
Living - R
Living Church
Lookout - R
Lutheran, The
Lutheran Digest - R
Lutheran Layman
Maranatha - R
Marian Helpers - R
Mature Years - R
Mennonite, The - R
Mennonite Brethren - R
MESSAGE
Messenger, The (Canada) - R
Messenger, The (NC) - R
Messenger/St. Anthony
Messenger of the Sacred Heart
Ministry Today - R
Moody

Morning Glory - R
New Covenant - R
New Oxford Review
News Network Intl.
New Trumpet - R
North American Voice
Northwestern Lutheran - R
Our Family - R
Our Sunday Visitor
Parenting Treasures - R
Parents of Teenagers
PCA Messenger - R
Pentecostal Evangel - R
Pentecostal Homelife - R
Pentecostal Messenger - R
Pentecostal Testimony - R
Plus - R
Positive Approach - R
Pourastan - R
Power for Living - R
Prayerworks - R
Praying
Presbyterian Record - R
Presbyterian Survey - R
PROGRESS - R
Psychology for Living - R
Purpose - R
Rural Landscapes
St. Anthony Messenger
Salt Shaker - R
SCP Journal - R
Seek - R
Sharing - R
Signs of the Times - R
Social Justice - R
Spiritual Life
Standard - R
Sunday Digest - R
Today's Better Life
United Church Observer
Upsouth - R
U.S. Catholic
Vision (MO) - R

Vista - R
Vital Christianity - R
War Cry
Wesleyan Advocate - R
Witness, The

CHILDREN
BREAD/God's Children - R
CLUBHOUSE - R
GUIDE - R
Guideposts for Kids
High Adventure - R
Junior Trails - R
Partners - R
Power & Light - R
Primary Pal
R-A-D-A-R - R
Venture (IL) - R
Wonder Time

CHRISTIAN
EDUCATION/LIBRARY
Brigade Leader - R
Changing Lives
Church Educator - R
Leader - R
Lutheran Education
Perspective - R
Resource - R
Shining Star
Youth Leader - R

MISSIONS
American Horizon - R
Worldwide Challenge - R

PASTORS/LEADERS
Advance - R
Christian Management Report - R
Diaconalogue - R
Discipleship Training
Eucharistic Minister - R
Five Stones, The - R

Jour/Biblical Ethics - R
Journal/Christian Healing - R
Ministries Today
Nat/Intl Religion Report
Preacher's Illus. Service - R
Preacher's Magazine - R
Pulpit Helps - R
Review for Religious
Word & World

TEEN/YOUNG ADULT
Certainty
Challenge (IL)
Conqueror - R
Edge, The - R
Freeway - R
Insight - R
Insight/Out - R
Kiln, The - R
Magazine/Youth! - R
Student Leadership - R
Teenage Christian - R
Teen Life - R
Teen Power - R
Teen Quest - R
With - R
YOU! - R
Young Adult Today
Young & Alive - R
Young Salvationist - R
Youth World - R

WOMEN
Co-Laborer - R
Daughters of Sarah - R
Esprit - R
Helping Hand - R
Horizons - R
Joyful Woman - R
Link & Visitor - R
Lutheran Woman Today
Salt and Light - R
Sisters Today

Today's Christian Woman
Virtue - R
Wesleyan Woman - R
Woman's Touch - R

CHURCH MANAGEMENT

ADULT/GENERAL
Acts 29
AXIOS - R
Biblical Reflections - R
Canada Lutheran - R
Canadian Catholic
Christian Edge - R
Church of God EVANGEL
Emphasis/Faith & Living - R
Evangelical Baptist - R
Hearing Hearts - R
John Milton - R
Joyful Noise
Kansas City Christian - R
Living Church
Lutheran Digest - R
MESSAGE/Open Bible - R
Ministry Today - R
Northwestern Lutheran - R
U.S. Catholic
Our Sunday Visitor
Pourastan - R
Wesleyan Advocate - R

CHRISTIAN
EDUCATION/LIBRARY
CE Connection - R
CE Counselor - R
Leader - R
Leader/Church School Today
Resource - R

PASTORS/LEADERS
Advance - R
Christian Century
Christian Management - R

Christian Ministry
Church Growth Network- R
Group's Jr High
Leadership Journal - R
Lutheran Partners - R
Nat/Intl Religion Report
Preacher's Magazine - R
Priest, The
Pulpit Helps - R
Resource - R
Word & World
Worship Leader
Your Church - R
Youthworker - R

CHURCH OUTREACH

ADULT/GENERAL
Acts 29
Advent Christian Witness
ADVOCATE - R
Alive! - R
America
At Ease - R
AXIOS - R
Baptist Beacon - R
Baptist Informer
Bible Advocate - R
Canada Lutheran - R
Canadian Baptist - R
Canadian Catholic
Catholic Sentinel - R
Catholic Twin Circle - R
Charisma/Christian Life
Christian Edge - R
Christian Event - R
Christianity Today - R
Church Herald - R
Church Herald/Holiness - R
Columbia - R
Companion
Companions - R
Conquest

Decision
Dovetail - R
Emphasis/Faith & Living - R
Episcopal Life - R
Evangel - R
Evangelical Baptist - R
Evangelical Beacon - R
Evangelical Friend
Evangelical Visitor - R
Expression Christian
Fellowship Today - R
God's Revivalist
Good News - R
Good News Journal - R
Good News Reporter - R
Home Times - R
Inspirer, The - R
Interchange
John Milton - R
Kansas City Christian - R
Liguorian
Living Church
Lookout - R
Lutheran, The
Lutheran Digest - R
Lutheran Layman
Maranatha - R
Mature Years - R
Mennonite, The - R
Mennonite Brethren - R
Mennonite Reporter
MESSAGE
Messenger, The (Canada) - R
Messenger, The (NC) - R
Ministry Today - R
Moody
New Covenant - R
New Oxford Review
News Network Intl.
North American Voice
Our Family - R
Our Sunday Visitor
Pentecostal Evangel - R

Pentecostal Messenger - R
Pentecostal Testimony - R
Positive Approach - R
Pourastan - R
Presbyterian Outlook
Presbyterian Record - R
Presbyterian Survey - R
Purpose - R
Religious Broadcasting
Religious Education
Rural Landscapes
St. Joseph's Messenger - R
SCP Journal - R
Seek - R
Sharing - R
United Church Observer
Urban Family
U.S. Catholic
Vista - R
Wesleyan Advocate - R

CHILDREN
Focus/Clubhouse
High Adventure - R

CHRISTIAN
EDUCATION/LIBRARY
CE Connection - R
CE Counselor - R
Changing Lives
Church Educator - R
Insight - R
Leader - R
Lutheran Education
Perspective - R
Resource - R
Youth & CE Leadership - R
Youth Leader - R

MISSIONS
American Horizon - R
Catholic Near East
Childlife

Compassion
IMPACT
Urban Mission - R
World Vision - R
Worldwide Challenge - R

PASTORS/LEADERS
Advance - R
Christian Management - R
Christian Ministry
Church Administration
Church Growth Network - R
Five Stones, The - R
Group's Jr High
Leadership Journal - R
Liturgy - R
Lutheran Partners - R
Ministries Today
Nat/Intl Religion Report
Preacher's Magazine - R
Priest, The
Pulpit Helps - R
Resource - R
Review for Religious
Search
Single Ad. Ministries Jour.
Today's Parish
Word & World

TEEN/YOUNG ADULT
Freeway - R
Insight - R
Insight/Out - R
Magazine/Youth! - R
Teen Life - R
Teen Power - R
YOU! - R
Young Adult Today

WOMEN
Esprit - R
Horizons - R
Lutheran Woman Today

Wesleyan Woman
Woman's Touch - R

*CONTESTS

CHILDREN'S
It's Your Choice
Pockets

FICTION
Canadian Writer's Jour
Felicity

NONFICTION
Felicity
It's Your Choice
CWI Florida Conference

POETRY
Canadian Writer's Jour
Felicity
Tickled By Thunder
Time of Singing
Writer's Journal

CONTROVERSIAL ISSUES

ADULT/GENERAL
AFA Journal - R
American Tract Soc. - R
Aspire
At Ease - R
AXIOS - R
Bible Advocate - R
Biblical Reflections - R
Canada Lutheran - R
Canadian Baptist - R
Canadian Catholic
Celebrate Life - R
Charisma/Christian Life
Christian Courier (Canada) - R
Christian Media - R
Christian Research

Christian Social Action - R
Christianity Today - R
Columbia - R
Commonweal
Compass
Cornerstone - R
Cresset
Critic, The
Door, The - R
Dovetail - R
Episcopal Life - R
Evangelical Baptist - R
Evangelical Friend
Expression Christian
Faith Today
Family Journal - R
First Things
Focus on the Family
Friends Journal - R
Good News, Etc - R
Good News Journal - R
Good News Reporter - R
Hallelujah! - R
Head to Head - R
Hearing Hearts - R
Home Times - R
John Milton - R
Jour/Christian Nursing - R
Joyful Noise
Kansas City Christian - R
Light and Life
Liguorian
Living Church
Lookout - R
Lutheran, The
Lutheran Witness
Maranatha - R
Mature Years - R
Messenger, The (NC) - R
Messenger/St. Anthony
Minnesota Christian - R
Moody
New Oxford Review

Newsline - R
News Network Intl.
New Trumpet - R
Our Family - R
Pentecostal Evangel - R
Presbyterian Outlook
Presbyterian Record - R
Presbyterian Survey - R
Religious Education
Religious Broadcasting
Rural Landscapes
St. Anthony Messenger
Salt Shaker - R
SCP Journal - R
Seek - R
Social Justice - R
U.S. Catholic
Vista - R
Upsouth - R
Urban Family
Vital Christianity - R
War Cry
Wesleyan Advocate - R
Witness, The

CHILDREN
Guideposts for Kids
Skipping Stones - R

CHRISTIAN
EDUCATION/LIBRARY
CE Connection - R
CE Counselor - R
Leader - R
Resource - R
Today's Catholic Teacher - R
Youth Leader - R

MISSIONS
American Horizon - R
Worldwide Challenge - R

PASTORS/LEADERS
Bethany Choice - R
Christian Century
Christian Ministry
Christian Sentinel
Cross Currents - R
Diaconalogue - R
Group's Jr High
Jour/Biblical Ethics - R
Journal/Christian Camping - R
Lutheran Forum - R
Lutheran Partners - R
Ministries Today
Nat/Intl Religion Report
Networks - R
Search
Single Ad. Ministries Jour.
Word & World
Youthworker - R

TEEN/YOUNG ADULT
Brio
Certainty
Conqueror - R
Edge, The - R
Freeway - R
Insight/Out - R
Issues & Answers - R
Kiln, The - R
Magazine/Youth! - R
Straight - R
Student Leadership - R
Teenage Christian - R
Teen Life - R
With - R
You! - R
Young Adult Today
Young Salvationist - R

WOMEN
Conscience - R
Daughters of Sarah- R
Esprit - R

Horizons - R
Today's Christian Woman
Virtue - R

WRITERS
Inklings - R
Writer's Forum - R

CULTS/OCCULT

ADULT/GENERAL
Acts 29
America
American Tract Soc. - R
AXIOS - R
Baptist Beacon - R
Bible Advocate - R
Biblical Reflections - R
Canada Lutheran - R
Catholic Digest - R
Catholic Twin Circle - R
Charisma/Christian Life
Christian Event - R
Christian Information
Christian Research
Christianity Today - R
Church Herald/Holiness - R
COMMENTS - R
Conquest
Cornerstone - R
Evangelical Baptist - R
Evangelical Friend
Faith Today
God's Revivalist
Good News, Etc - R
Good News Journal - R
Highway News - R
It's Your Choice - R
John Milton - R (sects)
Jour/Christian Nursing - R
Jour/Church & State
Kansas City Christian - R
Lutheran Digest - R

Maranatha - R
MESSAGE/Open Bible - R
Messenger, The (NC) - R
Minnesota Christian - R
New Heart, A - R
New Oxford Review
New Trumpet - R
Our Sunday Visitor
Parents of Teenagers - R
Pentecostal Evangel - R
Pentecostal Messenger - R
Power for Living - R
Psychology for Living - R
SCP Journal - R
Sunday Digest - R
Vista - R
VISION (CA) - R
Wine Castles (occult)

CHILDREN
Crusader - R

CHRISTIAN
EDUCATION/LIBRARY
Team - R
Youth Leader - R

MISSIONS
American Horizon - R
Areopagus - R
IMPACT
World Christian - R

PASTORS/LEADERS
Christian Sentinel
Discipleship Training
Jour/Biblical Ethics - R
Journal/Christian Healing - R
Lutheran Partners - R
Nat/Intl Religion Report
Word & World

TEEN/YOUNG ADULT
Brio
Certainty
Challenge (IL)
Edge, The - R
Freeway - R
Insight - R
Insight/Out - R
Issues & Answers - R
Kiln, The - R
Magazine/Youth! - R
Pathway I.D. - R
Straight - R
Student, The
Teenage Christian - R
Teen Life - R
Teen Power - R
Teen Quest - R
YOU! - R
Young Adult Today
Youth Update

WOMEN
Woman's Touch - R

CURRENT/SOCIAL ISSUES

ADULT/GENERAL
ADVOCATE - R
AFA Journal - R
AGAIN - R
Alive! - R
alive now! - R
America
American Tract Soc. - R
Anglican Journal - R
Arlington Catholic
Aspire
AXIOS - R
Baptist Informer
B.C. Catholic - R
Bible Advocate - R
Biblical Reflections - R

Bookstore Journal - R

Canada Lutheran - R

Canadian Catholic

Cathedral Age - R

Catholic Courier

Catholic Forester - R

Catholic New York

Catholic Sentinel - R

Catholic Twin Circle - R

Celebrate Life - R

Charisma/Christian Life

Christian American

Christian Courier (WI) - R

Christian Courier (Canada) - R

Christian Crusade

Christian Event - R

Christian Home & School

Christian Living - R

Christian Parenting - R

Christian Reader - R

Christian Renewal - R

Christian Single - R

Christian Social Action - R

Christian Standard - R

Christianity Today - R

Church & State - R

Church Herald - R

Church Herald/Holiness - R

Church of God EVANGEL

Columbia - R

Commonweal

Compass

Conquest

Cornerstone - R

Critic, The

Discipleship Journal - R

Door, The - R

Emphasis/Faith & Living - R

Episcopal Life - R

Evangel - R

Evangelical Baptist - R

Evangelical Friend

Evangelical Visitor - R

Faith Today

Fellowship Today - R

First Things

Focus on the Family

Foursquare World - R

Friends Journal - R

Good News - R

Good News, Etc - R

Good News Journal - R

Good News Reporter - R

Gospel Tidings - R

Hallelujah! - R

Hayden Herald - R

Head to Head - R

Herald of Holiness - R

Highway News - R

Home Life

Home Times - R

Impact Magazine - R

Interim - R

InterVarsity

It's Your Choice - R

John Milton - R

Jour/Christian Nursing - R

Jour/Church & State

Kansas City Christian - R

Kootenai Courier - R

Liberty - R

Light and Life

Liguorian

Live - R

Living Church

Lookout - R

Lutheran, The

Lutheran Journal - R

Lutheran Layman

Maranatha - R

Marion Helpers Bulletin

Mature Living

Mennonite, The - R

Mennonite Brethren - R

Mennonite Reporter

MESSAGE

MESSAGE/Open Bible - R

Messenger, The (NC) - R

Messenger/St. Anthony

Ministry Today - R

Minnesota Christian - R

Montana Catholic - R

Moody

New Covenant - R

New Heart, A - R

New Oxford Review

New Thought - R

New Trumpet - R

North American Voice

Our Family - R

Our Sunday Visitor

ParentLife - R

Parents of Teenagers - R

Pentecostal Evangel - R

Pentecostal Homelife - R

Pentecostal Messenger - R

Pentecostal Testimony - R

Plowman, The - R

Pourastan - R

Power for Living - R

Presbyterian Outlook

Presbyterian Record - R

Presbyterian Survey - R

Psychology for Living - R

Purpose - R

Puzzler's Digest - R

Quiet Revolution - R

Religious Broadcasting

Religious Education

Rural Landscapes

St. Anthony Messenger

St. Joseph's Messenger - R

Salt

Salt Shaker - R

SCP Journal - R

Seek - R

Signs of the Times - R

Social Justice - R

Standard - R

Star of Zion
Touchstone
Urban Family
Vista - R
Vital Christianity - R
War Cry
Wesleyan Advocate - R
Witness, The
World

CHILDREN
Crusader - R
God's World Today
GUIDE - R
Guideposts for Kids
High Adventure - R
R-A-D-A-R - R
Skipping Stones - R
Touch - R

CHRISTIAN
EDUCATION/LIBRARY
Brigade Leader - R
CE Connection - R
CE Counselor - R
Memos - R
Resource - R
Teachers in Focus - R (education)
Team - R
Today's Catholic Teacher - R
Vision - R
Youth Leader - R

MISSIONS
American Horizon - R
Areopagus - R
Childlife - R
Compassion
IMPACT
P.I.M.E. World - R
Urban Mission - R
World Christian - R
Worldwide Challenge - R

PASTORS/LEADERS
Advance - R
Christian Century
Christian Ministry
Cross Currents - R
Diaconalogue - R
Discipleship Training
Five Stones, The - R
Ivy Jungle Report - R
Jour/Biblical Ethics - R
Liturgy
Lutheran Forum - R
Lutheran Partners - R
Ministries Today
Nat/Intl Religion Report
Preacher's Magazine - R
Resource - R
Review for Religious
Search
Single Ad. Ministries Jour.
Word & World
Youthworker - R

TEEN/YOUNG ADULT
Brio
Certainty
Conqueror - R
Edge, The - R
Freeway - R
Insight - R
Insight/Out - R
Issues & Answers - R
Kiln, The - R
Magazine/Youth! - R
Pathway I.D. -R
Pioneer - R
Straight - R
Student, The
Student Leadership - R
Teenage Christian - R
Teen Life - R
Teen Power - R
Teen Quest - R

Today's Christian Teen
With - R
YOU! - R
Young Adult Today
Young Salvationist - R
Youth Update

WOMEN
Co-Laborer - R
Conscience - R
Contempo
Daughters of Sarah - R
Esprit - R
Horizons - R
Jour/Women's Ministries
Journey - R
Link & Visitor - R
Lutheran Woman Today
Response
Royal Service
Salt and Light - R
Sisters Today
Today's Christian Woman
Virtue - R
Wesleyan Woman
Woman's Touch - R

WRITERS
Inklings - R

**DEVOTIONALS/
MEDITATIONS**

ADULT/GENERAL
Acts 29
Advocate - R
alive now! - R
Annals of St. Anne
At Ease - R
Baptist Beacon - R
Baptist Informer
Bible Advocate - R
Broken Streets

Canadian Catholic
Caregivers Connection - R
Catholic Digest - R
Catholic Forester - R
Catholic Twin Circle - R
Charisma/Christian Life
Christian Event - R
Christian Living - R
Christian Renewal - R
Christianity Today - R
Companion
Companions - R
Emphasis/Faith & Living - R
Evangel - R
Evangelical Baptist - R
Evangelical Friend
Explorer
Family Digest, The - R
Fellowship Today - R
Foursquare World - R
God's Revivalist
Good News Journal - R
Gospel Tidings - R
Head to Head - R
Hearing Hearts - R
Inspirer, The - R
John Milton - R
Kansas City Christian - R
Lifeglow - R
Light and Life
Liguorian
Living Church
Lookout - R
Lutheran Journal - R
Lutheran Witness
Maranatha - R
Mennonite Brethren - R
MESSAGE
MESSAGE/Open Bible - R
Messenger, The (Canada) - R
Messenger, The (NC) - R
Messenger of the Sacred Heart
Morning Glory - R

New Covenant - R
New Heart, A - R
New Trumpet - R
North American Voice
Our Sunday Visitor
ParentLife - R
Pentecostal Evangel - R
Pentecostal Homelife - R
Pentecostal Messenger - R
Pourastan - R
Prayerworks - R
Praying
Presbyterian Record - R
Presbyterian Survey - R
Prism - R
Rural Landscapes
Salt Shaker - R
Seek - R
Sharing - R
Silver Wings - R
Standard - R
Today's Single - R
Upsouth - R
U.S. Catholic
Vital Christianity - R
War Cry
Wine Castles

CHILDREN
High Adventure - R
Keys for Kids - R
My Friend
Power & Light - R
Primary Pal
R-A-D-A-R - R
Touch - R

CHRISTIAN
EDUCATION/LIBRARY
Church Worship
Leader - R
Lutheran Education
Shining Star

Today's Catholic Teacher - R

DAILY DEVOTIONAL
(See alphabetical list)

MISSIONS
Areopagus - R

PASTORS/LEADERS
Christian Century
Christian Ministry
Diaconalogue - R
Emmanuel
Five Stones, The - R
Journal/Christian Healing - R
Priest, The
Pulpit Helps - R
Review for Religious

TEEN/YOUNG ADULT
Breakaway - R
Brio
Challenge (IL)
Conqueror - R
Cross Walk
Insight - R
Insight/Out - R
Magazine/Youth! - R
Straight - R
Take Five
Teenage Christian - R
Teen Life - R
With - R
YOU! - R
Young Adult Today
Young Salvationist - R

WOMEN
Co-Laborer - R
Daughters of Sarah - R
Horizons - R
Jour/Women's Ministries
Journey - R

Lutheran Woman Today
Response
Salt and Light - R
Virtue - R
Wesleyan Woman - R
Woman's Touch - R

WRITERS

Christian Author
Cross & Quill - R
Inklings - R

DISCIPLESHIP

ADULT/GENERAL

Acts 29
Advocate - R
American Tract Soc. - R
At Ease - R
Baptist Beacon - R
Bible Advocate - R
Canada Lutheran - R
Canadian Baptist - R
Canadian Catholic
Catholic Digest - R
Christian Event - R
Christian Living - R
Christianity Today - R
Church Herald/Holiness - R
Companion
Conquest
Cornerstone - R
Decision
Discipleship Journal - R
Emphasis/Faith & Living - R
Evangel - R
Evangelical Baptist - R
Gospel Tidings - R
Hallelujah! - R
Head to Head - R
Herald of Holiness - R
Highway News - R
Indian Life - R

Inspirer, The - R
John Milton - R
Kansas City Christian - R
Light and Life
Liguorian
Living Church
Lookout - R
Lutheran Digest - R
Maranatha - R
Mature Years - R
Mennonite, The - R
Messenger, The (Canada) - R
Ministry Today - R
Moody
New Covenant - R
New Oxford Review
New Trumpet - R
Our Family - R
Parents of Teenagers
Pentecostal Evangel - R
Pentecostal Homelife - R
Pentecostal Messenger - R
Pentecostal Testimony - R
Power for Living - R
Prism - R
Purpose - R
Religious Education
St. Joseph's Messenger - R
Seek - R
Silver Wings - R
Standard - R
Sunday Digest - R
Upsouth - R
U.S. Catholic
Vision (MO) - R
Vista - R
Vital Christianity - R
Wesleyan Advocate - R
Witness, The

CHILDREN

BREAD/God's Children - R
High Adventure - R

CHRISTIAN EDUCATION/LIBRARY

Brigade Leader - R
CE Connection - R
CE Counselor - R
Changing Lives
Christian School
Church Educator - R
Leader - R
Team - R
Youth & CE Leadership - R
Youth Leader - R

MISSIONS

American Horizon - R
Urban Mission - R
Worldwide Challenge - R

PASTORS/LEADERS

Advance - R
Christian Century
Christian Management - R
Church Growth Network - R
Group's Jr High
Ivy Jungle Report - R
Journal/Christian Camping - R
Journal/Christian Healing - R
Lutheran Partners - R
Ministries Today
PROCLAIM - R
Pulpit Helps - R
Quarterly Review
Review for Religious
Word & World
Youthworker - R

TEEN/YOUNG ADULT

Certainty
Challenge (TN)
Conqueror - R
Freeway - R
Insight - R
Kiln, The - R

Magazine/Youth! - R
Student Leadership - R
Teenage Christian - R
Teen Life - R
Teen Power - R
With - R
Young Salvationist - R

WOMEN
Co-Laborer - R
Esprit - R
Helping Hand - R
Journey - R
Link & Visitor - R
Sisters Today
Today's Christian Woman
Virtue - R
Wesleyan Woman - R
Women Alive! - R

WRITERS
Inklings - R

DIVORCE

ADULT/GENERAL
America
Aspire
At Ease - R
Bible Advocate - R
Canada Lutheran - R
Canadian Baptist - R
Catholic Digest - R
Catholic Twin Circle - R
Charisma/Christian Life
Christian Event - R
Christian Home & School
Christian Parenting - R
Christian Single - R
Church Herald/Holiness - R
Companions - R
Evangelical Baptist - R
Focus on the Family - R

Friends Journal - R
Good News, Etc - R
Good News Journal - R
Good News Reporter - R
Hallelujah! - R
Hayden Herald - R
Highway News - R
Home Life
Impact Magazine - R
John Milton - R
Kansas City Christian - R
Kootenai Courier - R
Liguorian
Living - R
Living Church
Lookout - R
Lutheran Digest - R
Maranatha - R
Mature Years - R
MESSAGE
MESSAGE/Open Bible - R
Messenger, The (NC) - R
Minnesota Christian - R
Moody
New Covenant - R
New Heart, A - R
New Trumpet - R
Our Family - R
Parents of Teenagers
PCA Messenger - R
Pentecostal Evangel - R
Pentecostal Messenger - R
Power for Living - R
Praying
Presbyterian Record - R
Presbyterian Survey - R
Psychology for Living - R
Purpose - R
Seek - R
Signs of the Times - R
Single-Parent Family
Standard - R
Today's Single - R

Upsouth - R
U.S. Catholic
VISION (CA) - R
Vista - R
Wine Castles

CHILDREN
Guideposts for Kids
R-A-D-A-R - R

CHRISTIAN
EDUCATION/LIBRARY
Leader - R
Lutheran Education

MISSIONS
Worldwide Challenge - R

PASTORS/LEADERS
Chicago Studies
Christian Ministry
Lutheran Partners - R
Ministries Today
PROCLAIM - R
Pulpit Helps - R
Single Ad. Ministries Jour.
Word & World

TEEN/YOUNG ADULT
Insight - R
Insight/Out - R
Magazine/Youth! - R
Straight - R
With - R
YOU! - R
Young Adult Today
Youth Update

WOMEN
Journey - R
Joyful Woman - R
Lutheran Woman Today
Salt and Light - R

Today's Christian Woman
Virtue - R
Wesleyan Woman - R
Woman's Touch - R
Women Alive - R

DOCTRINAL

ADULT/GENERAL
ADVOCATE - R
America
Anglican Journal - R
At Ease - R
Baptist Beacon - R
Baptist Informer
B.C. Catholic - R
Bible Advocate - R
Biblical Reflections - R
Canadian Catholic
Catholic Digest - R
Christian Media - R
Christian Renewal - R
Christianity Today - R
Church Herald/Holiness - R
Church of God EVANGEL
Companions - R
Compass
Conquest
Cornerstone - R
Cresset
Critic, The
Emphasis/Faith & Living - R
Evangelical Baptist - R
Evangelical Friend
Evangelical Visitor - R
Good News - R
Hallelujah! - R
Hearing Hearts - R
Interim - R
John Milton - R
Journal of Church & State
Kansas City Christian - R
Liguorian

Living Church
Lutheran Layman
Lutheran Witness
Maranatha - R
Messenger, The (NC) - R
Ministry Today - R
North American Voice
Our Family - R
Our Sunday Visitor
Pentecostal Evangel - R
Pourastan - R
Presbyterian Outlook
Presbyterian Record - R
Presbyterian Survey - R
Queen of All Hearts
St. Willibrord Journal
Salt Shaker - R
SCP Journal - R
Sharing - R
Signs of the Times - R
Silver Wings - R
Social Justice - R
This Rock
Upsouth - R
U.S. Catholic

CHILDREN
R-A-D-A-R - R

CHRISTIAN EDUCATION/LIBRARY
CE Counselor - R
Leader - R
Lutheran Education
Youth Leader - R

MISSION
Intl Jour/Frontier - R
Urban Mission - R
Worldwide Challenge - R

PASTORS/LEADERS
Advance - R

Chicago Studies
Christian Century
Discipleship Training
Homiletic & Pastoral Review
Jour/Biblical Ethics - R
Lutheran Forum - R
Lutheran Partners - R
Nat/Intl Religion Report
Preacher's Magazine - R
Priest, The
PROCLAIM - R
Pulpit Helps - R
Review for Religious
Word & World

TEEN/YOUNG ADULT
YOU! - R
Young Adult Today
Youth Update

WOMEN
Daughters of Sarah - R
Esprit - R
Lutheran Woman Today
Woman's Touch - R
Wesleyan Woman - R

WRITERS
Inklings

ECONOMICS

ADULT/GENERAL
America
AXIOS - R
Better Tomorrow, A
Biblical Reflections - R
Bookstore Journal - R
Canadian Catholic
Catholic Forester - R
Catholic Twin Circle - R
Christian C.L. RECORD - R
Christian Courier (Canada) - R

Christian Retailing - R
Christian Single - R
Christian Social Action - R
Christianity Today - R
Compass
Discovery - R
Evangelical Friend
Expression Christian
Faith Today
Friends Journal - R
Good News, Etc - R
Good News Journal - R
Hayden Herald - R
Home Life
Home Times - R
It's Your Choice - R
John Milton - R
Kansas City Christian - R
Kootenai Courier - R
Mennonite, The - R
Minnesota Christian - R
Our Sunday Visitor
PCA Messenger - R
Pentecostal Messenger - R
Praying
Prism - R
Professional Parents - R
Quiet Revolution - R
Rural Landscapes - R
SCP Journal - R
Single-Parent Family
Social Justice - R
Today's Better Life
U.S. Catholic
Vista - R
Vital Christianity - R
Witness, The

CHILDREN
Guideposts for Kids

MISSIONS
IMPACT

Urban Mission - R
World Vision - R

PASTORS/LEADERS
Christian Century
Christian Ministry
Five Stones, The - R
Jour/Biblical Ethics - R
Lutheran Partners - R
Nat/Intl Religion Report
Preacher's Magazine - R
Today's Parish
Word & World

TEEN/YOUNG ADULT
Issues & Answers - R
Young Adult Today
Youth Update

WOMEN
Horizons - R
Journey - R
Salt and Light - R
Woman's Touch - R

WRITERS
Writer's Forum - R
Writer's Nook News

ENVIRONMENTAL ISSUES

ADULT/GENERAL
Anglican Journal - R
Aspire
AXIOS - R
Biblical Reflections - R
Canada Lutheran - R
Canadian Catholic
Cathedral Age - R
Charisma/Christian Life
Catholic Exponent
Catholic Forester - R
Catholic Sentinel - R

Celebrate Life - R
Christian Courier (Canada) - R
Christian Living - R
Christian Single - R
Christian Social Action - R
Christianity Today - R
Church Herald - R
Commonweal
Companion
Compass
Cornerstone - R
Emphasis/Faith & Living - R
Evangelical Friend
Faith Today
Friends Journal - R
Good News Journal - R
Hayden Herald - R
Herald of Holiness - R
Home Life
Home Times - R
It's Your Choice - R
John Milton - R
Kansas City Christian - R
Kootenai Courier - R
Liguorian
Living - R
Living Church
Lookout - R
Lutheran, The
Lutheran Digest - R
Mature Years - R
Mennonite, The - R
Messenger, The (NC) - R
Messenger/St. Anthony
Ministry Today - R
Minnesota Christian - R
Moody
New Trumpet - R
NW Christian Journal - R
Our Family - R
Our Sunday Visitor
Parents of Teenagers - R
Pegasus Review - R

Plowman, The - R
Prairie Messenger
Praying
Presbyterian Record - R
Presbyterian Survey - R
Prism - R
Purpose - R
Puzzler's Digest - R
Rural Landscapes
St. Anthony Messenger
SCP Journal - R
Signs of the Times - R
Total Health
United Church Observer
Vital Christianity - R
War Cry
Witness, The

CHILDREN
Crusader - R
Focus/Clubhouse
GUIDE - R
Guideposts for Kids
High Adventure - R
Pockets - R
Primary Days - R
R-A-D-A-R - R
Skipping Stones - R

CHRISTIAN
EDUCATION/LIBRARY
Christian School
Lutheran Education
Today's Catholic Teacher - R

MISSIONS
IMPACT
P.I.M.E. World - R
World Vision - R

PASTORS/LEADERS
Christian Century
Christian Ministry

Church Business - R
Cross Currents - R
Five Stones, The - R
Jour/Biblical Ethics - R
Journal/Christian Camping - R
Lutheran Partners - R
Nat/Intl Religion Report
Search
Word & World

TEEN/YOUNG ADULT
Challenge (TN)
Freeway - R
Insight/Out - R
Issues & Answers - R
Kiln, The - R
Magazine/Youth! - R
Straight - R
Student Leadership - R
Teenage Christian - R
Teen Life - R
Teen Power - R
Teen Quest - R
YOU! - R
With - R
Young Adult Today
Youth Update

WOMEN
Daughters of Sarah - R
Horizons - R
Journey - R
Sisters Today

ESSAYS

ADULT/GENERAL
African Amer. Heritage - R
alive now! - R
Aspire
AXIOS - R
Biblical Reflections - R
Burning Light - R

Catholic Answer
Catholic Parent
Catholic Twin Circle
Christian Event - R
Christianity/Arts
Christianity Today - R
Christmas - R
Church & State - R
Church Herald/Holiness - R
Columbia - R
Compass
Cornerstone - R
Critic, The
Emphasis/Faith & Living - R
Evangelical Friend
Evangelical Visitor - R
Explorer
Family Journal - R
First Things
Hayden Herald - R
Head to Head - R
Highway News - R
Home Times - R
Inspirer, The - R
John Milton - R
Kansas City Christian - R
Kootenai Courier - R
Liguorian
Living Church
Lookout - R
Messenger/St. Anthony
Ministry Today - R
Montana Catholic - R
National Catholic
New Oxford Review
New Thought - R
New Trumpet - R
Parents of Teenagers - R (teen)
Pegasus Review - R
Plenty Good Room
Poetry Forum
Pourastan - R
Power for Living - R

Presbyterian Outlook
Presbyterian Survey - R
Prism - R
Puzzler's Digest - R
Ratio
Religious Education
Salt Shaker - R
SCP Journal - R
Sharing - R
Social Justice - R
Touchstone
Upsouth - R
Vista - R
Wine Castles

CHILDREN
Nature Friend - R

MISSIONS
Areopagus - R
Catholic Near East
World Vision - R

PASTORS/LEADERS
Homiletic & Pastoral Review
Liturgy - R
Quarterly Review
Word & World
Youthworker - R

TEEN/YOUNG ADULT
Insight - R
Magazine/Youth! - R
Straight - R
Student Leadership - R
Teen Life - R
Young Adult Today
Youth Focus - R

WOMEN
Daughters of Sarah - R
Link & Visitor - R
Lutheran Woman Today

Virtue - R

WRITERS
Canadian Writer's Jour - R
Inklings - R
Writers Anchor - R
Writer's Infor Network
Writer's Nook News

ETHICS

ADULT/GENERAL
Aspire
At Ease - R
AXIOS - R
Bible Advocate - R
Biblical Reflections - R
Canadian Catholic
Catholic Digest - R
Catholic Exponent
Catholic Parent
Celebrate Life - R
Christian Courier (Canada) - R
Christian Research
Christian Single - R
Christian Social Action - R
Christianity Today - R
Church Herald/Holiness - R
Columbia - R
Commonweal
Compass
Conquest
Cornerstone - R
Emphasis/Faith & Living - R
Evangelical Baptist - R
Faith Today
Family Journal - R
First Things
Good News, Etc - R
Good News Reporter - R
Hayden Herald - R
Head to Head - R
Hearing Hearts - R

Herald of Holiness - R
Home Times - R
Impact Magazine - R
It's Your Choice - R
John Milton - R
Jour/Christian Nursing - R
Jour/Church & State
Kansas City Christian - R
Kootenai Courier - R
Liguorian
Living Church
Lookout - R
Maranatha - R
Mature Years - R
Mennonite Brethren - R
Messenger/St. Anthony
Ministry Today - R
Minnesota Christian - R
Moody
New Covenant - R
New Heart - R
New Oxford Review
New Thought - R
New Trumpet - R
Our Family - R
Our Sunday Visitor
Parents of Teenagers
PCA Messenger - R
Pegasus Review - R
Pentecostal Evangel - R
Pentecostal Testimony - R
Power for Living - R
Prism - R
Purpose - R
Religious Education
Rural Landscapes
Seek - R
Social Justice - R
Today's Better Life
United Church Observer
Upsouth - R
Vista - R
Vital Christianity - R

Witness, The

CHILDREN
Guideposts for Kids
High Adventure - R
R-A-D-A-R - R
Wonder Time

CHRISTIAN
EDUCATION/LIBRARY
CE Connection - R
Journal/Adventist Educ. - R
Vision - R

MISSIONS
Areopagus - R
Urban Mission - R
Worldwide Challenge - R

PASTORS/LEADERS
Bethany Choice - R
Christian Century
Christian Management - R
Christian Ministry
Cross Currents - R
Ivy Jungle Report - R
Jour/Biblical Ethics - R
Journal/Christian Healing - R
Lutheran Partners - R
Nat/Intl Religion Report
Priest, The
PROCLAIM - R
Resource - R
Review for Religious
Word & World
Your Church - R
Youthworker - R

TEEN/YOUNG ADULT
Certainty
Conqueror - R
Edge, The - R
Kiln, The - R

Student Leadership - R
Teen Life - R
With - R
Young Salvationist - R
Youth Update

WOMEN
Conscience - R
Daughters of Sarah - R
Esprit - R
Link & Visitor - R
Salt and Light - R
Today's Christian Woman
Virtue - R
Wesleyan Woman - R

WRITERS
Canadian Writer's Jour - R
Inklings - R

ETHNIC PIECES

ADULT/GENERAL
African Amer. Heritage - R
Baptist Informer
Bible Advocate - R
Canadian Baptist - R
Christian Living - R
Christian Single - R
Class
Common Boundary
Cornerstone - R
Dovetail - R
El Orador
Enlace Informativo
Focus on the Family
Foursquare World - R
Good News, Etc. - R
Hallelujah! - R
Home Times - R
Impact Magazine
Indian Life - R
Joyful Noise

Liguorian
MESSAGE/Open Bible - R
New Trumpet - R
Plenty Good Room
Plowman, The - R
Pourastan - R
Purpose - R
Star of Zion
Upsouth - R
Urban Family

CHILDREN
GUIDE - R
Guideposts for Kids
On the Line - R
Skipping Stones - R
Story Friends - R

CHRISTIAN
EDUCATION/LIBRARY
Leader - R
Student Leadership Journal - R
Vision - R

MISSIONS
Urban Mission

PASTORS/LEADERS
Liturgy - R
Lutheran Partners - R

TEEN/YOUNG ADULT
Certainty
Magazine/Youth! - R
Straight - R
Student Leadership Journal - R
Take Five (photos)
Teen Life - R
Young Adult Today
Young Salvationist - R
Youth Focus - R

WOMEN

Daughters of Sarah - R
Virtue - R

EVANGELISTIC

ADULT/GENERAL

Acts 29
Advent Christian Witness
ADVOCATE - R
American Tract Soc. - R
Anglican Journal - R
At Ease - R
Baptist Beacon - R
Baptist Informer
Bible Advocate - R
Canadian Baptist - R
Canadian Catholic
Catholic Accent
Catholic Digest - R
Charisma/Christian Life
Christian Chronicle
Christian Courier (WI) - R
Christian Event - R
Christian Reader - R
Church Herald/Holiness - R
Church of God EVANGEL
Companions - R
Conquest
Cornerstone - R
Decision
Discipleship Journal - R
Emphasis/Faith & Living - R
Evangel - R
Evangelical Baptist - R
Evangelical Visitor - R
Focus on the Family
God's Revivalist
Good News, Etc - R
Good News Journal - R
Good News Reporter - R
Hallelujah! - R
Hearing Hearts - R

Highway News - R
Home Times - R
Indian Life - R
Inspirer, The - R
InterVarsity
John Milton - R
Jour/Church & State
Kansas City Christian - R
Liguorian
Live - R
Living Church
Lutheran, The
Lutheran Digest - R
Lutheran Layman
Lutheran Witness
Maranatha - R
MESSAGE/Open Bible - R
Messenger, The (NC) - R
Ministry Today - R
Morning Glory - R
New Covenant - R
New Heart, A - R
New Oxford Review
News Network Intl.
New Trumpet - R
Parenting Treasures - R
Parents of Teenagers - R
Pentecostal Evangel - R
Pentecostal Messenger - R
Pentecostal Testimony - R
Positive Approach, A - R
Power for Living - R
Prayerworks - R
Presbyterian Record - R
Presbyterian Survey - R
Pursuit - R
Queen of All Hearts
Religious Broadcasting
Religious Education
Salt Shaker - R
Seek - R
Shantyman, The - R
Sharing - R

Silver Wings - R
Standard - R
Star of Zion
Sunday Digest - R
This Rock
Together - R
Upsouth - R
U.S. Catholic
Vision (MO) - R
Vista - R
Vital Christianity - R
War Cry
Wesleyan Advocate - R

CHILDREN

BREAD/God's Children - R
Counselor - R
GUIDE - R
High Adventure - R
R-A-D-A-R - R
Venture (IL) - R

CHRISTIAN EDUCATION/LIBRARY

CE Connection - R
Evangelizing Today's Child
Leader - R
Lutheran Education
Resource - R
Youth & CE Leadership - R
Youth Leader - R

MISSIONS

American Horizon - R
IMPACT
Intl Jour/Frontier - R
Partners
Urban Mission - R
World Christian - R
World Vision - R
Worldwide Challenge - R

PASTORS/LEADERS

Advance - R
Christian Ministry
Church Administration
Church Growth Network - R
Evangelism - R
Leadership Journal
Lutheran Partners - R
Nat/Intl Religion Report
Networks - R
Preacher's Magazine - R
Priest, The
PROCLAIM - R
Pulpit Helps - R
Resource - R
Search
Youthworker - R

TEEN/YOUNG ADULT

Freeway - R
Pathway I.D. - R
Student Leadership Journal - R
Teenage Christian - R
Teen Life - R
Teen Power - R
YOU! - R
Young Adult Today
Young Salvationist - R

WOMEN

Co-Laborer - R
Joyful Woman - R
Salt and Light - R
Today's Christian Woman
Wesleyan Woman - R
Woman's Touch - R

FAMILY LIFE

ADULT/GENERAL

Acts 29
Advent Christian Witness
ADVOCATE - R

AFA Journal - R
Alive! - R (grandparenting)
America
American Tract Soc. - R
Annals of St. Anne
Arlington Catholic
Aspire
At Ease - R
AXIOS - R
Baptist Beacon - R
Baptist Informer
B.C. Catholic - R
Better Tomorrow, A
Bible Advocate - R
Biblical Reflections - R
Canada Lutheran - R
Canadian Catholic
Catholic Digest - R
Catholic Exponent
Catholic Forester - R
Catholic Parent
Catholic Twin Circle - R
Celebrate Life - R
Charisma/Christian Life
Christian C.L. RECORD - R
Christian Courier (WI) - R
Christian Courier (Canada) - R
Christian Edge - R
Christian Event - R
Christian Home & School
Christian Living - R
Christian Parenting - R
Christian Reader - R
Christian Renewal - R
Church Herald/Holiness - R
Church of God EVANGEL
Columbia - R
Companion
Companions - R
Connecting Point - R
Conquest
Covenant Companion - R
Dovetail - R

Emphasis/Faith & Living - R
Evangel - R
Evangelical Baptist - R
Evangelical Beacon - R
Evangelical Friend
Evangelical Visitor - R
Expression Christian
Family, The - R
Family Digest, The - R
Family Journal - R
Fellowship Today - R
Focus on the Family - R
Foursquare World - R
Gem, The - R
God's Revivalist
Good News, Etc - R
Good News Journal
Good News Reporter - R
Gospel Tidings - R
Hayden Herald - R
Head to Head - R
Hearing Hearts - R
Herald of Holiness - R
Highway News - R
Home Life
Homeschooling Today
Home Times - R
Impact Magazine - R
Indian Life - R
Interim - R
It's Your Choice - R
John Milton - R
Kansas City Christian - R
Kootenai Courier - R
LA Catholic Agitator
Light and Life
Liguorian
Live - R
Living - R
Living Church
Lookout - R
Lutheran, The
Lutheran Digest - R

Lutheran Layman
Lutheran Witness
Maranatha - R
Mature Years - R
Mennonite, The - R
Mennonite Brethren - R
MESSAGE
MESSAGE/Open Bible - R
Messenger (KY)
Messenger, The (Canada) - R
Messenger, The (NC) - R
Messenger/St. Anthony
Ministry Today - R
Minnesota Christian - R
Moody
Morning Glory - R
New Oxford Review
New Trumpet - R
Northwestern Lutheran - R
Our Family - R
Our Sunday Visitor
Parenting Treasures - R
ParentLife - R
Parents of Teenagers
PCA Messenger - R
Pegasus Review - R
Pentecostal Evangel - R
Pentecostal Homelife - R
Pentecostal Messenger - R
Pentecostal Testimony - R
Plus - R
Positive Approach - R
Positive Living - R
Pourastan - R
Power for Living - R
Prayerworks - R
Praying
Presbyterian Record - R
Presbyterian Survey - R
Professional Parents - R
PROGRESS - R
Psychology for Living - R
Purpose - R

Puzzler's Digest - R
Religious Education
St. Anthony Messenger
Salt Shaker - R
Seek - R
Signs of the Times - R
Smart Dads
Social Justice - R
Standard - R
Sunday Digest - R
Table Talk
Today's Better Life
Together - R
United Church Observer
Upsouth - R
Urban Family
U.S. Catholic
VISION (CA) - R
Vision (MO) - R
Vista - R
Vital Christianity - R
Voice, The - R
War Cry
Wesleyan Advocate - R

CHILDREN
BREAD/God's Children - R
CLUBHOUSE - R
GUIDE - R
Guideposts for Kids
High Adventure - R
Junior Trails - R
R-A-D-A-R - R
Skipping Stones - R
Touch - R
Wonder Time
Young Crusader - R

CHRISTIAN
EDUCATION/LIBRARY
Brigade Leader - R
CE Connection - R
CE Counselor - R

Children's Ministry
Church Educator - R
GROUP
Leader - R
Lutheran Education
Shining Star
Youth Leader - R

MISSIONS
American Horizon - R
Childlife - R
IMPACT
World Christian - R
Worldwide Challenge - R

MUSIC
Tradition - R

PASTORS/LEADERS
Advance - R
Bethany Choice - R
Chicago Studies
Diaconalogue - R
Journal/Christian Healing - R
Lutheran Partners - R
Networks - R
Preacher's Illus. Service - R
PROCLAIM - R
Pulpit Helps - R
Today's Parish
Word & World
Youthworker - R

TEEN/YOUNG ADULT
Breakaway - R
Certainty
Challenge (IL)
Conqueror - R
Freeway - R
Insight - R
Insight/Out - R
Kiln, The - R
Magazine/Youth! - R

Pioneer - R
Straight - R
Teenage Christian - R
Teen Life - R
Teen Quest - R
With - R
YOU! - R
Young Adult Today

WOMEN
Co-Laborer - R
Contempo
Daughters of Sarah - R
Esprit - R
Helping Hand - R
Journey - R
Link & Visitor - R
Lutheran Woman Today
Royal Service
Today's Christian Woman
Virtue - R
Wesleyan Woman - R
Woman's Touch - R
Women Alive! - R

WRITERS
Housewife-Writers Forum - R
Writer's Forum - R

FILLERS: ANECDOTES

ADULT/GENERAL
Acts 29
African Amer. Heritage - R
Alive! - R
AXIOS - R
Catholic Digest - R
Christian Courier (WI) - R
Christian Event - R
Christian Info. Assoc.
Christian Parenting - R
Christian Retailing - R
Church Herald/Holiness - R

Companion
Companions - R
Conquest
Decision
Evangel - R
Family, The - R
Family Digest, The - R
Foursquare World - R
Good News Reporter - R
Guideposts
Hayden Herald - R
Head to Head - R
Home Times - R
Impact Magazine - R
Inspirer, The - R
John Milton - R
Kansas City Christian - R
Kootenai Courier - R
Live - R
Living - R
Lutheran Digest - R
Lutheran Journal - R
Maranatha - R
Mature Living
Morning Glory - R
New Heart - R
New Trumpet - R
Our Family - R
Parenting Treasures - R
ParentLife - R
Parents of Teenagers
Pentecostal Testimony - R
Power for Living - R
Presbyterian Record - R
Presbyterian Survey - R
Purpose - R
Puzzler's Digest - R
Salt Shaker - R
Table Talk
Wine Castles

CHILDREN
Focus/Clubhouse

High Adventure - R

CHRISTIAN
EDUCATION/LIBRARY
Christian School
Christian Librarian - R
Leader - R
Lutheran Education
Religion Teacher's Journal
Shining Star
Teachers In Focus - R
Vision - R

MUSIC
Church Pianist, etc.
Tradition

PASTORS/LEADERS
ArtPlus
Christian Management - R
Eucharistic Minister - R
Ivy Jungle Report - R
Journal/Christian Healing - R
Preacher's Magazine - R
Pulpit Helps - R
Resource - R

TEEN/YOUNG ADULT
Campus Life - R
Certainty
Challenge (IL)
Insight - R
Insight/Out - R
Kiln, The - R
Teenage Christian - R
YOU! - R
Young Salvationist - R

WOMEN
Anna's Journal
Co-Laborer - R
Esprit - R
Salt and Light - R

WRITERS

Byline
Cross & Quill - R
Canadian Writer's Jour - R
Christian Response - R
Felicity - R
Housewife-Writers Forum - R
Writers Anchor - R
Writer's Digest
Writer's Exchange - R
Writer's Resource - R
Write Touch - R

FILLERS: CARTOONS

ADULT/GENERAL

Alive! - R
alive now! - R
At Ease - R
AXIOS - R
Bookstore Journal - R
Canadian Baptist - R
Catholic Twin Circle - R
Christian Edge - R
Christian Event - R
Christian Information
Christian Retailing - R
Commonweal
Companion
Connecting Point - R
Cornerstone - R
Critic, The
Door, The - R
Evangel - R
Family Digest, The - R
Foursquare World - R
Good News Journal - R
Good News Reporter - R
Hayden Herald - R
Head to Head - R
Hearing Hearts - R
Herald of Holiness - R
Home Life

Home Times - R
Impact Magazine - R
Inside Journal
Kansas City Christian - R
Kootenai Courier - R
Liguorian
Live - R
Living - R
Lutheran, The
Lutheran Digest - R
Lutheran Journal - R
Lutheran Witness
Maranatha - R
Mature Living
Mature Years - R
Mennonite, The - R
Montana Catholic - R
New Heart - R
New Trumpet - R
NW Christian Journal - R
Our Family - R
Parenting Treasures - R
ParentLife - R
PCA Messenger - R
Pentecostal Testimony - R
Power for Living - R
Presbyterian Record - R
Presbyterian Survey - R
Prism - R
Purpose - R
Pursuit - R
Puzzler's Digest - R
Salt Shaker - R
Shantyman, The - R
Standard - R
Star of Zion
Table Talk
Together - R
Touchstone
United Church Observer
Vista - R
Whisper - R
World

CHILDREN

CLUBHOUSE - R
Counselor - R
Crusader - R
Focus/Clubhouse Jr
GUIDE - R
High Adventure - R
On the Line - R
Power & Light - R
R-A-D-A-R - R
Skipping Stones - R
Touch - R

CHRISTIAN
EDUCATION/LIBRARY

Baptist Leader - R
CE Counselor - R
Christian Librarian - R
Journal/Adventist Educ. - R
Leader - R
Leader/Church School Today
Teacher's Interaction
Team - R
Today's Catholic Teacher - R
Vision - R

MUSIC

Church Pianist, etc.
Creator
Glory Songs - R
Senior Musician - R

PASTORS/LEADERS

ArtPlus
Celebration
Christian Century
Christian Management - R
Christian Ministry
Christian Sentinel
Eucharistic Minister - R
Ivy Jungle Report - R
Journal/Christian Camping - R
Preacher's Magazine - R

Preaching
Reformed Worship- R
Resource - R
Your Church - R

TEEN/YOUNG ADULT
Breakaway - R
Brio
Challenge (TN)
Edge, The - R
Freeway - R
Insight - R
Insight/Out - R
Kiln, The - R
Magazine/Youth! - R
Teenage Christian - R
Teen Power - R
Teen Quest - R
With - R
YOU! - R
Young Salvationist - R

WOMEN
Esprit - R
Joyful Woman - R
Wesleyan Woman - R
Women Alive! - R

WRITERS
Byline
Canadian Writer's Jour - R
Christian Communicator - R
Cross & Quill - R
Felicity - R
Heaven - R
Housewife-Writers Forum - R
Writers Anchor - R
Writer's Exchange - R
Writer's Guidelines

FILLERS: FACTS

ADULT/GENERAL
African Amer. Heritage - R
Alive! - R
AXIOS - R
Bible Advocate - R
Canadian Baptist - R
Catholic Digest - R
Christian Courier (WI) - R
Christian Information
Church Herald/Holiness - R
Conquest
Cornerstone - R
God's Revivalist
Good News Reporter - R
Hallelujah! - R
Head to Head - R
Inspirer, The - R
Lutheran Digest - R
Maranatha - R
Mature Living
Mature Years - R
Mennonite, The - R
Morning Glory - R
New Trumpet - R
Parenting Treasures - R
PCA Messenger - R
Pourastan - R
Presbyterian Record - R
Professional Parents - R
Puzzler's Digest - R
Salt Shaker - R
Southwestern News - R
Standard - R
Vista - R

CHILDREN
CLUBHOUSE -R
Counselor - R
GUIDE - R
High Adventure - R
Junior Trails - R

My Friend
On the Line - R
Skipping Stones - R
Young Crusader - R

CHRISTIAN
EDUCATION/LIBRARY
Leader/Church School Today
Leader - R
Lutheran Education
Shining Star
Today's Catholic Teacher - R
Vision - R
Youth Leader - R

PASTORS/LEADERS
ArtPlus
Christian Ministry
Church Management - R
Ivy Jungle Report - R
Journal/Christian Healing - R
Single Ad. Ministries Jour.

TEEN/YOUNG ADULT
Breakaway - R
Brio
Campus Life - R
Certainty
Challenge (IL)
Insight - R
Insight/Out - R
Student Leadership - R
YOU! - R
Young Salvationist - R

WOMEN
Co-Laborer - R
Today's Christian Woman
Wesleyan Woman - R

WRITERS
Cross & Quill - R
Gotta Write

Home Office - R
Housewife-Writers Forum - R
Writers Anchor - R
Writers Connection
Writer's Exchange - R
Writer's Guidelines
Writer's Nook News
Writer's Resource - R
Write Touch - R

FILLERS: GAMES

ADULT/GENERAL
Alive! - R
Catholic Digest - R
Christian Edge - R
Connecting Point - R
Evangel - R
Family, The - R
Good News Journal - R
Good News Reporter - R
Head to Head - R
Hearing Hearts - R
Inspirer, The - R
Living - R
Maranatha - R
ParentLife - R
Smart Dads
Standard - R

CHILDREN
Attention Please! - R
CLUBHOUSE - R
Counselor - R
Crusader - R
Focus/Clubhouse Jr
GUIDE - R
Guideposts for Kids
High Adventure - R
Listen
Pockets - R
Power & Light - R
Primary Pal

R-A-D-A-R - R
Skipping Stones - R
Wonder Time
Young Crusader - R

CHRISTIAN
EDUCATION/LIBRARY
Leader - R
Leader/Church School Today
Perspective - R
Religion Teacher's Journal
Shining Star

TEEN/YOUNG ADULT
Certainty
Challenge (IL)
Challenge (TN)
Conqueror - R
Student Leadership - R
Teenage Christian - R
Young Salvationist - R

FILLERS: IDEAS

ADULT/GENERAL
Alive! - R
Caregivers Connection - R
Catholic Digest - R
Catholic Parent
Christian Drama - R
Christian Edge - R
Christian Parenting - R
Christian Retailing - R
Conquest
Evangel - R
God's Revivalist
Good News Reporter - R
Head to Head - R
Hearing Hearts - R
Home Times - R
John Milton - R
Kansas City Christian - R
Maranatha - R

New Trumpet - R
ParentLife - R
Pourastan - R
Presbyterian Record - R
Puzzler's Digest - R
St. Joseph's Messenger - R
Seek - R
Smart Dads
Table Talk

CHILDREN
Focus/Clubhouse
High Adventure - R
Listen
R-A-D-A-R - R
Young Crusader - R

CHRISTIAN
EDUCATION/LIBRARY
Church Worship
Leader - R
Leader/Church School Today
Lutheran Education
Parish Teacher - R
Religion Teacher's Journal
Shining Star
Team - R
Vision - R

MUSIC
Glory Songs - R
Senior Musician - R

PASTORS/LEADERS
Ivy Jungle Report - R
Journal/Christian Healing - R
Lutheran Partners - R
Preacher's Illus. Service - R
Preacher's Magazine - R
Single Ad. Ministries Jour.

TEEN/YOUNG ADULT
Brio

Campus Life - R
Certainty
Insight/Out - R
Magazine/Youth! - R
Teenage Christian - R
YOU! - R

WOMEN
Anna's Journal
Co-Laborer - R

WRITERS
Canadian Writer's Jour - R
Exchange
Felicity - R
Housewife-Writers Forum - R
Tickled By Thunder
Writers Anchor - R
Writers Connection (tips)
Writer's Exchange - R
Write Touch - R
Writing Right - R

FILLERS: JOKES

ADULT/GENERAL
Alive! - R
Catholic Digest - R
Christian Event - R
Good News Reporter - R
Hayden Herald - R
Home Times - R
Impact Magazine - R
Kootenai Courier - R
Liguorian
Lutheran, The
Lutheran Digest - R
Lutheran Journal - R
Maranatha - R
Mature Years - R
New Heart - R
Our Family - R
Puzzler's Digest - R

Salt Shaker - R
Seek - R

CHILDREN
CLUBHOUSE - R
Counselor - R
Guideposts for Kids
High Adventure - R
My Friend
On the Line - R
Pockets - R
R-A-D-A-R - R
Skipping Stones - R

CHRISTIAN
EDUCATION/LIBRARY
Lutheran Education

MUSIC
Tradition

PASTORS/LEADERS
ArtPlus
Ivy Jungle Report - R
Journal/Christian Healing - R
Preacher's Illus. Service - R

TEEN/YOUNG ADULT
Kiln, The - R
Teenage Christian - R
YOU! - R

WOMEN
Joyful Woman - R

WRITERS
Felicity - R
Writer's Exchange - R

FILLERS: NEWSBREAKS

ADULT/GENERAL
Anglican Journal - R

Arkansas Catholic
B.C. Catholic - R
Canada Lutheran - R
Catholic Telegraph
Celebrate Life - R
Christian Courier (WI) - R
Christian Event - R
Christian Information
Christian Renewal - R
Common Boundary
Conquest
Good News Reporter - R
Hallelujah! - R
Head to Head - R
Home Times - R
Indian Life - R
Interchange
Interim - R
John Milton - R
Kansas City Christian - R
Maranatha - R
Mennonite Weekly
Morning Glory - R
Professional Parents - R
Puzzler's Digest - R
Religious Broadcasting
Southwestern News

CHILDREN
GUIDE - R

CHRISTIAN
EDUCATION/LIBRARY
Christian Librarian - R
Vision - R
Youth Leader - R

PASTORS/LEADERS
Christian Management - R
Christian Ministry, The
Church Business - R
Ivy Jungle Report - R
Journal/Christian Healing - R

Preacher's Illus. Service - R
Single Ad. Ministries Jour.

TEEN/YOUNG ADULT
Certainty
Challenge (IL)
Insight - R
Magazine/Youth! - R
Teenage Christian - R

WOMEN
Conscience - R
Joyful Woman - R
Wesleyan Woman - R

WRITERS
Gotta Write
Writers Anchor - R
Writers Connection
Writer's Exchange - R
Writer's Guidelines
Writer's Nook News
Writer's Resource - R
Writing Right - R

FILLERS: PARTY IDEAS

ADULT/GENERAL
Hayden Herald - R
Head to Head - R
Hearing Hearts - R
Kootenai Courier - R
ParentLife - R
Puzzler's Digest - R

CHILDREN
Focus/Clubhouse
My Friend

CHRISTIAN
EDUCATION/LIBRARY
Leader - R
Perspective - R

Team - R

MUSIC
Glory Songs
Senior Musician - R

PASTORS/LEADERS
Ivy Jungle Report - R

TEEN/YOUNG ADULT
Conqueror - R
Insight - R
Insight/Out - R
Student Leadership - R

FILLERS: PRAYERS

ADULT/GENERAL
alive now!
Bible Advocate - R
Companions - R
Cornerstone - R
Explorer
Family, The - R
Good News Reporter - R
Head to Head - R
Inspirer, The - R
Morning Glory - R
Pourastan - R
Presbyterian Record - R
Salt Shaker - R
Southwestern News - R
Upsouth - R

CHILDREN

Pockets - R

CHRISTIAN
EDUCATION/LIBRARY
Baptist Leader - R
Leader - R
Religion Teacher's Journal

Vision - R

PASTORS/LEADERS
ArtPlus
Church Management - R

TEEN/YOUNG ADULT
Freeway - R
Straight - R
Teenage Christian - R
Young Salvationist - R

WOMEN
Anna's Journal - R
Co-Laborer - R
Esprit - R
Joyful Woman - R
Salt and Light - R

WRITERS
Cross & Quill - R

FILLERS: PROSE

ADULT/GENERAL
Bible Advocate - R
Broken Streets - R
Church Herald/Holiness - R
Companions - R
Conquest
Cornerstone - R
Decision
Discovery - R
Evangel - R
Explorer
Family, The - R
God's Revivalist
Hallelujah! - R
Head to Head - R
Inspirer, The - R
Live - R
New Trumpet - R
Presbyterian Record - R

Presbyterian Survey - R
Puzzler's Digest - R
Salt Shaker - R
Standard - R
Sunday Digest - R
Upsouth - R
Vital Christianity - R
Wesleyan Advocate - R
Wine Castles

CHILDREN
CLUBHOUSE - R
Partners - R

CHRISTIAN
EDUCATION/LIBRARY
Vision - R

PASTORS/LEADERS
Church Management - R
Preacher's Illus. Service - R
Preacher's Magazine - R
Pulpit Helps - R

TEEN/YOUNG ADULT
Brio
Certainty
Challenge (IL)
Conqueror - R
Freeway - R
Insight/Out - R
Magazine/Youth! - R
Teen Power - R

WOMEN
Anna's Journal - R
Co-Laborer - R
Esprit - R
Salt and Light - R
Today's Christian Woman

WRITERS
Chip Off Writer's Block - R

Writers Anchor - R
Writer's Exchange - R
Write Touch - R

FILLERS: QUIZZES

ADULT/GENERAL
Alive! - R
Catholic Digest - R
Catholic Twin Circle - R
Door, The - R
Evangel - R
Good News Journal - R
Hearing Hearts - R
Impact Magazine - R
Inspirer, The - R
John Milton - R
Living - R
Maranatha - R
Mature Living
Mature Years - R
MESSAGE
Power for Living - R
Puzzler's Digest - R
St. Willibrord Journal
Standard - R
Together - R

CHILDREN
CLUBHOUSE - R
Counselor - R
GUIDE - R
Guideposts for Kids
High Adventure - R
On the Line - R
Partners - R
Pockets - R
Skipping Stones - R
Story Mates - R
Young Crusader - R

CHRISTIAN
EDUCATION/LIBRARY
Leader - R

MUSIC
Glory Songs - R
Senior Musician - R

PASTORS/LEADERS
Ivy Jungle Report - R

TEEN/YOUNG ADULT
Breakaway - R
Brio
Conqueror - R
Freeway - R
Insight/Out - R
Magazine/Youth! - R
Student Leadership - R
Teenage Christian - R
Teen Power - R
Young Salvationist - R

WRITERS
Felicity - R
Writers Anchor - R

FILLERS: QUOTES

ADULT/GENERAL
Acts 29
Bible Advocate - R
Canadian Baptist - R
Christian Edge - R
Christian Information
Church Herald & Holiness Banner -
    R
Companion
Good News Journal - R
Guideposts
Hallelujah! - R
Head to Head - R
Home Times - R

John Milton - R
Kansas City Christian - R
Maranatha - R
Montana Catholic - R
Morning Glory - R
New Trumpet - R
Parenting Treasures - R
Pourastan - R
Puzzler's Digest - R
Seek - R
Smart Dads
Southwestern News - R
Together - R
Wine Castles

CHILDREN
Skipping Stones - R

CHRISTIAN
EDUCATION/LIBRARY
Shining Star
Youth Leader - R

PASTORS/LEADERS
ArtPlus
Christian Management - R
Ivy Jungle Report - R
Journal/Christian Healing - R
Single Adult Min Journal

TEENS/YOUNG ADULTS
Kiln, The - R
Teenage Christian - R

WOMEN
Anna's Journal - R
Co-Laborer - R
Esprit - R
Joyful Woman - R
Salt and Light - R

WRITERS
Christian Communicator - R

Exchange
Writers Anchor - R
Writer's Exchange - R

FILLERS: SHORT HUMOR

ADULT/GENERAL
Alive! - R
Annals of St. Anne
Better Tomorrow, A
Catholic Digest - R
Christian Event - R
Christian Parenting - R
Christian Reader - R
Companion
Conquest
Door, The - R
Evangel - R
Friends Journal - R
God's Revivalist
Good News Reporter - R
Guideposts
Hayden Herald - R
Head to Head - R
Home Times - R
Impact Magazine - R
John Milton - R
Kansas City Christian - R
Kootenai Courier - R
Liguorian
Live - R
Living - R
Lutheran, The
Lutheran Digest - R
Lutheran Journal - R
Lutheran Witness
Maranatha - R
Mature Living
Mature Years - R
Morning Glory - R
New Heart - R
New Trumpet - R
Our Family - R

Parenting Treasures - R
ParentLife - R
PCA Messenger - R
Pentecostal Testimony - R
Pourastan - R
Purpose - R
Presbyterian Record - R
Presbyterian Survey - R
Puzzler's Digest - R
St. Willibrord Journal
Seek - R
Southwestern News - R
Star of Zion
Upsouth - R
Vista - R

CHILDREN
Focus/Clubhouse
GUIDE - R
Junior Trails - R
Skipping Stones - R
Touch - R
Young Crusader - R

CHRISTIAN
EDUCATION/LIBRARY
Christian Librarian - R
Leader - R
Lutheran Education
Teachers in Focus
Team - R

MUSIC
Creator
Glory Songs - R
Senior Musician - R

PASTORS/LEADERS
ArtPlus
Christian Management - R
Ivy Jungle Report - R
Journal/Christian Healing - R
Eucharistic Minister - R

Preacher's Illus. Service - R
Resource - R

TEEN/YOUNG ADULT
Brio
Certainty
Freeway - R
Insight - R
Insight/Out - R
Kiln, The - R
Magazine/Youth! - R
Straight - R
Teenage Christian - R
Teen Power - R
YOU! - R
Young Salvationist - R

WOMEN
Co-Laborer - R
Joyful Woman - R
Salt and Light - R

WRITERS
Byline
Canadian Writer's Jour - R
Writers Anchor - R
Writer's Digest
Writer's Exchange - R
Write Touch - R

FILLERS: WORD PUZZLES

ADULT/GENERAL
Alive! - R
Christian Edge - R
Christian Event - R
Companion
Connecting Point - R
Conquest
Friends Journal - R
Good News Journal - R
Hayden Herald - R
Head to Head - R

Hearing Hearts - R
Impact Magazine - R
Inspirer, The - R
Kootenai Courier - R
Living - R
Maranatha - R
Mature Living
Mature Years - R
Power for Living - R
Standard - R
Today's Single
Together - R

CHILDREN
CLUBHOUSE - R
Counselor - R
Crusader - R
Focus/Clubhouse Jr
GUIDE - R
High Adventure - R
On the Line - R
Our Little Friend - R
Partners - R
Pockets - R
Power & Light - R
Primary Days - R
Primary Pal
R-A-D-A-R - R
Skipping Stones - R
Story Mates - R
Wonder Time
Young Crusader - R

CHRISTIAN
EDUCATION/LIBRARY
Leader - R
Parish Teacher - R
Shining Star

MUSIC
Young Musicians

TEEN/YOUNG ADULT
Certainty
Challenge (IL)
Challenge (TN)
Conqueror - R
Freeway - R
Teenage Christian - R
Teen Power - R
Young Salvationist - R

WOMEN
Esprit - R

WRITERS
Felicity - R
Heaven - R
Writers Anchor - R

FOOD/RECIPES

ADULT/GENERAL
Aspire
AXIOS - R
Better Tomorrow, A
Catholic Forester - R
Catholic Parent
Christian C.L. RECORD - R
Christian Parenting - R
Christian Single - R
Focus on the Family
Good News Reporter - R
Hayden Herald - R
Home Life
Home Times - R
Ideals - R
Kootenai Courier - R
Lutheran Digest - R
MESSAGE
ParentLife - R
Pentecostal Homelife - R
PROGRESS - R
Puzzler's Digest - R
Salt Shaker - R

Today's Better Life

CHILDREN
Focus/Clubhouse/Clubhouse Jr.
R-A-D-A-R - R
Skipping Stones - R
Touch - R

WOMEN
Helping Hand - R
Wesleyan Woman - R
Woman's Touch - R

HEALING

ADULT/GENERAL
Acts 29
ADVOCATE - R
At Ease - R
Biblical Reflections - R
Canadian Baptist - R
Catholic Digest - R
Catholic Twin Circle - R
Charisma/Christian Life
Christian Single - R
Church Herald/Holiness - R
Common Boundary
Connecting Point - R
Evangel - R
Evangelical Baptist - R
Explorer
Foursquare World - R
Friends Journal - R
Good News, Etc - R
Good News Journal - R
Guideposts
Head to Head - R
It's Your Choice
John Milton - R
Jour/Christian Nursing - R
Kansas City Christian - R
Liguorian
Live - R

Living - R
Living Church
Lutheran Digest - R
Maranatha - R
MESSAGE/Open Bible - R
Messenger, The (NC) - R
New Covenant - R
New Heart - R
New Oxford Review
Our Family - R
Pentecostal Evangel - R
Pentecostal Homelife - R
Pentecostal Messenger - R
Pentecostal Testimony - R
Presbyterian Record - R
Presbyterian Survey - R
Purpose - R
Puzzler's Digest - R
SCP Journal - R
Sharing - R
Today's Better Life
Total Health
Upsouth - R
VISION (CA) - R
Vision (MO) - R
Vital Christianity - R
Wine Castles

CHRISTIAN
EDUCATION/LIBRARY
Youth Leader - R

MISSIONS
American Horizon - R
Areopagus - R

PASTORS/LEADERS
Diaconalogue - R
Eucharistic Minister - R
Jour/Biblical Ethics - R
Journal/Christian Healing - R
Lutheran Partners - R
Ministries Today

Networks - R
Priest, The
Word & World

TEEN/YOUNG ADULT
Conqueror - R
Pathway I.D. - R
Sharing the VICTORY - R
Teen Life - R
YOU! - R
Young Adult Today

WOMEN
Daughters of Sarah - R
Helping Hand - R
Journey - R
Lutheran Woman Today
Response
Virtue - R
Woman's Touch - R

HEALTH

ADULT/GENERAL
Alive! - R
Anglican Journal - R
Aspire
B.C. Catholic - R
Better Tomorrow, A
Bible Advocate - R
Biblical Reflections - R
Canada Lutheran - R
Caregivers Connection - R
Catholic Digest - R
Catholic Exponent
Catholic Forester - R
Catholic Twin Circle - R
Charisma/Christian Life
Christian Courier (WI) - R
Christian Courier (Canada) - R
Christian Edge - R
Christian Event - R
Christian Living - R

Christian Single - R
Christian Social Action - R
Church Herald/Holiness - R
Companion
Discovery - R
Evangel - R
Evangelical Friend
Focus on the Family
Friends Journal - R
Good News Journal - R
Good News Reporter - R
Guideposts
Hayden Herald - R
Head to Head - R
Home Life
Home Times - R
Interim - R
John Milton - R
Jour/Christian Nursing - R
Kansas City Christian - R
Kootenai Courier - R
Lifeglow - R
Living - R
Lookout - R
Lutheran Digest - R
Lutheran Witness
Mature Years - R
MESSAGE
MESSAGE/Open Bible - R
Messenger, The (NC) - R
Montana Catholic - R
New Heart, A - R
New Trumpet - R
ParentLife - R
Pentecostal Evangel - R
Pentecostal Homelife - R
Plus - R
Poetry Forum
Positive Approach, A - R
Pourastan - R
Praying
Professional Parents - R
Puzzler's Digest - R

SCP Journal - R
Sharing - R
Single-Parent Family
Star of Zion
Today's Better Life
Today's Single - R
Total Health
Upsouth - R
Urban Family
Vibrant Life - R
Vital Christianity - R

CHILDREN
Focus/Clubhouse Jr.
GUIDE - R
Guideposts for Kids
On the Line - R

CHRISTIAN
EDUCATION/LIBRARY
CE Connection - R

MISSIONS
Areopagus - R
Childlife - R
Compassion

PASTORS/LEADERS
Chicago Studies
Jour/Biblical Ethics - R
Journal/Christian Camping - R
Journal/Christian Healing - R
Lutheran Partners - R
Word & World

TEEN/YOUNG ADULT
Conqueror - R
Insight - R
Insight/Out - R
Magazine/Youth! - R
Pioneer - R
Straight - R
Teenage Christian - R

Teen Life - R
YOU! - R
Young Adult Today
Young & Alive - R

WOMEN
Daughters of Sarah - R
Helping Hand - R
Journey - R
Lutheran Woman Today
Response
Today's Christian Woman
Virtue - R
Wesleyan Woman - R
Woman's Touch - R

HISTORICAL

ADULT/GENERAL
African Amer. Heritage - R
AGAIN - R
America
Annals of St. Anne
At Ease - R
AXIOS - R
Baptist History
Bible Advocate - R
Canadian Catholic
Catholic Answer
Catholic Digest - R
Catholic Heritage - R
Catholic Sentinel - R
Catholic Twin Circle - R
Celebrate Life - R
Charisma/Christian Life
Christian C.L. RECORD - R
Christian Courier (Canada) - R
Christian Edge - R
Christian History - R
Christian Renewal - R
Christianity Today - R
Church & State - R
Church Herald - R

Class

Compass

Conquest

Evangelical Baptist - R

Evangelical Friend

First Things

Friends Journal - R

Good News Reporter - R

Hayden Herald - R

Herald of Holiness - R

Home Times - R

Ideals - R

Indian Life - R

InterVarsity

It's Your Choice - R

John Milton - R

Jour/Christian Nursing - R

Jour/Church & State

Kootenai Courier - R

Lifeglow - R

Living Church

Lutheran Digest - R

Lutheran Journal - R

Lutheran Layman

Lutheran Witness

MESSAGE

Messenger, The (NC) - R

Messenger/St. Anthony

Methodist History

Minnesota Christian - R

Morning Glory - R

New Trumpet - R

Our Sunday Visitor

Pentecostal Evangel - R

Presbyterian Outlook

Presbyterian Record - R

Presbyterian Survey - R

Pourastan - R

Prayerworks - R

Purpose - R

Puzzler's Digest - R

Religious Education

Salt Shaker - R

SCP Journal - R

Sharing - R

Social Justice - R

Sunday Digest - R

Upsouth - R

Urban Family

CHILDREN

BREAD/God's Children - R

CLUBHOUSE - R

Guideposts for Kids

High Adventure - R

Junior Trails - R

My Friend

On the Line - R

Partners - R

Power & Light - R

R-A-D-A-R - R

CHRISTIAN
EDUCATION/LIBRARY

Changing Lives

Lutheran Education

Today's Catholic Teacher - R

Vision - R

MISSIONS

American Horizon - R

Areopagus - R

Catholic Near East

IMPACT

Urban Mission - R

World Vision - R

Worldwide Challenge - R

MUSIC

Church Pianist, etc.

Score - R

Tradition - R

PASTORS/LEADERS

Five Stones, The - R

Jour/Biblical Ethics - R

Journal/Christian Healing - R

Lutheran Forum - R

Lutheran Partners - R

Today's Parish - R

Word & World

TEEN/YOUNG ADULT

Challenge (IL)

Issues & Answers - R

Kiln, The - R

Magazine/Youth! - R

Pioneer - R

Student Leadership - R

Teenage Christian - R

Teen Life - R

Young Adult Today

Young & Alive - R

Youth Focus - R

WOMEN

Daughters of Sarah - R

Link & Visitor - R

Salt and Light - R

Virtue - R

Wesleyan Woman - R

WRITERS

Inklings - R

HOLIDAY THEMES

ADULT/GENERAL

Advent Christian Witness

ADVOCATE - R

Alive! - R

alive now! - R

American Tract Soc. - R

Annals of St. Anne

At Ease - R

AXIOS - R

Baptist Beacon - R

Bible Advocate - R

Canada Lutheran - R

Canadian Baptist - R
Canadian Catholic
Cathedral Age - R
Catholic Accent
Catholic Digest - R
Catholic New York
Catholic Parent
Catholic Sentinel - R
Catholic Twin Circle - R
Celebrate Life - R
Charisma/Christian Life
Christian C.L. RECORD - R
Christian Courier (WI) - R
Christian Edge - R
Christian Event - R
Christian Home & School
Christian Living - R
Christian Parenting - R
Christian Reader - R
Christian Single - R
Christian Standard - R
Christianity Today - R
Christmas - R
Church Herald/Holiness - R
Church of God EVANGEL
Companions - R
Connecting Point - R
Conquest
Covenant Companion - R
Decision
Discovery - R
Dovetail - R
Emphasis/Faith & Living - R
Evangel - R
Evangelical Baptist - R
Evangelical Friend
Evangelical Visitor - R
Explorer
Expression Christian
Family, The - R
Family Digest, The - R
Fellowship Today - R
Focus on the Family

Foursquare World - R
Gem, The - R
God's Revivalist
Good News, Etc - R
Good News Journal - R
Good News Reporter - R
Gospel Tidings - R
Hayden Herald - R
Hearing Hearts - R
Herald of Holiness - R
Highway News - R
Home Times - R
Ideals - R
Inspirer, The - R
John Milton - R
Kootenai Courier - R
Lifeglow - R
Light and Life
Liguorian
Live - R
Living - R
Living Church, The
Lookout - R
Lutheran Digest - R
Lutheran Witness
Maranatha - R
Mature Years - R
Mennonite Brethren - R
MESSAGE/Open Bible - R
Messenger (KY)
Messenger, The (Canada) - R
Messenger, The (NC) - R
Messenger/St. Anthony
Minnesota Christian - R
Ministry Today - R
Montana Catholic - R
Morning Glory - R
NW Christian Journal
Our Sunday Visitor
Parenting Treasures - R
ParentLife - R
Parents of Teenagers - R
PCA Messenger - R

Pegasus Review - R
Pentecostal Evangel - R
Pentecostal Homelife - R
Pentecostal Messenger - R
Plenty Good Room
Plus - R
Pourastan - R
Power for Living - R
Prayerworks - R
Presbyterian Outlook
Presbyterian Record - R
Presbyterian Survey - R
PROGRESS - R
Psychology for Living - R
Purpose - R
Puzzler's Digest - R
St. Anthony Messenger
St. Joseph's Messenger - R
Salt Shaker - R
Seek - R
Sharing - R
Standard - R
Star of Zion
Sunday Digest - R
Table Talk
Today's Single - R
United Church Observer
Urban Family - R
U.S. Catholic
Vista - R
Vital Christianity - R
Voice, The - R
War Cry
Wesleyan Advocate - R

CHILDREN
Attention Please!
CLUBHOUSE - R
Counselor - R
Focus/Clubhouse/Clubhouse Jr
Guideposts for Kids
High Adventure - R
Junior Trails - R

My Friend
On the Line - R
Pockets - R
Primary Pal
R-A-D-A-R - R
Skipping Stones - R
Touch - R
Wonder Time
Young Crusader - R

CHRISTIAN
EDUCATION/LIBRARY
Baptist Leader - R
CE Connection - R
Changing Lives
Church Educator - R
Cornerstone Connections - R
GROUP
Leader - R
Leader/Church School Today
Parish Teacher - R
Perspective - R
Religion Teacher's Journal
   (religious)
Shining Star
Today's Catholic Teacher - R
Vision - R

MISSIONS
Catholic Near East
Door of Hope
World Vision - R
Worldwide Challenge - R

MUSIC
Church Pianist
Music Leader
Quest - R
Score - R

PASTORS/LEADERS
Advance - R
Celebration

Christian Management - R
Christian Ministry
Lutheran Partners - R
Preacher's Magazine - R
Proclaim
Pulpit Helps - R
Youth Leader - R

TEEN/YOUNG ADULT
Breakaway - R
Certainty
Conqueror - R
Cornerstone - R
Edge, The - R
Freeway - R
Insight - R
Kiln, The - R
Mag/Christian Youth - R
Teenage Christian - R
Teen Life - R
Teen Power - R
With - R
Young & Alive - R

WOMEN
Anna's Journal - R
Co-Laborer - R
Helping Hand - R
Journey - R
Joyful Woman - R
Just Between Us
Link & Visitor - R
Probe
Salt and Light - R
Today's Christian Woman
Virtue - R
Wesleyan Woman - R

WRITERS
Inklings - R

HOME SCHOOLING

ADULT/GENERAL
Anglican Journal - R
Aspire
AXIOS - R
Charisma/Christian Life
Christian C.L. RECORD - R
Christian Parenting - R
Christian Reader - R
Evangelical Baptist - R
Expression Christian
Family, The - R
Family Journal - R
Focus on the Family
Friends Journal - R
Good News, Etc - R
Good News Journal - R
Good News Reporter - R
Gospel Tidings - R
Hayden Herald - R
Homeschooling Today
Home Times - R
Inspirer, The - R
Kansas City Christian - R
Kootenai Courier - R
Lookout - R
Lutheran Life - R
MESSAGE/Open Bible - R
Messenger, The (NC) - R
Minnesota Christian - R
Moody
NW Christian Journal - R
ParentLife - R
Parents of Teenagers
PCA Messenger - R
Pentecostal Homelife - R
Pentecostal Messenger - R
Positive Approach - R
Psychology for Living - R
Religious Education
Salt Shaker - R
Social Justice - R

Table Talk
Vista - R
Wesleyan Advocate - R
Writer's Forum - R

CHILDREN
BREAD/God's Children - R
GUIDE - R
R-A-D-A-R - R
Skipping Stones - R
Touch - R

CHRISTIAN
EDUCATION/LIBRARY
CE Connection - R
Christian Educators Jour - R
Christian School
Lutheran Education

PASTORS/LEADERS
Journal/Christian Camping - R
Nat/Intl Religion Report
Pulpit Helps - R

TEEN/YOUNG ADULT
Conqueror - R
You! - R

WOMEN
Esprit - R
Helping Hand - R
Journey - R
Today's Christian Woman
Virtue - R
Wesleyan Woman - R

WRITERS
Inklings - R

HOW-TO ACTIVITIES (JUV.)

ADULT/GENERAL
Christian Drama - R

Christian Event - R
Hearing Hearts - R
It's Your Choice - R
John Milton - R
Living - R
Lutheran Life - R
MESSAGE - R
Ministry Today - R
Parenting Treasures - R
Pentecostal Evangel - R
Salt Shaker - R

CHILDREN
Attention Please! - R
BREAD/God's Children - R
Counselor - R
Focus/Clubhouse/Clubhouse Jr.
God's World Today
High Adventure - R
Junior Trails - R
Listen
My Friend
Nature Friend - R
On the Line - R
Partners - R
Primary Days - R
Primary Pal
R-A-D-A-R - R
Touch - R
Venture (IL) - R
Wonder Time

CHRISTIAN
EDUCATION/LIBRARY
Evangelizing Today's Child
Junior Teacher - R
Memos - R
Perspective - R
Resource - R
Shining Star

PASTORS/LEADERS
Group's Jr High

Networks - R

TEEN/YOUNG ADULT
Breakaway - R
Freeway - R
Insight - R
Insight/Out - R
Teenage Christian - R
Teen Power - R
Magazine/Youth! - R
You! - R
Young Salvationist - R

HOW-TO/SELF-HELP

ADULT/GENERAL
Advent Christian Witness
Advocate - R
African Amer. Heritage - R
Alive! - R
Aspire
At Ease - R
Baptist Informer
Biblical Reflections - R
Canada Lutheran - R
Caregivers Connection - R
Catholic Digest - R
Catholic Twin Circle - R
Charisma/Christian Life
Christian Edge - R
Christian Event - R
Christian Home & School
Christian Living - R
Christian Parenting - R
Christian Retailing - R
Christian Single - R
Christian Standard - R
Church Herald - R
Columbia - R
Companion
Connecting Point - R
Conquest
Dovetail - R

Emphasis/Faith & Living - R
Family, The - R
Family Digest, The - R
Focus on the Family
Good News, Etc. - R
Gospel Tidings - R
Guideposts
Hayden Herald - R
Head to Head - R
Hearing Hearts - R
Home Life
Home Times - R
Indian Life - R
It's Your Choice - R
John Milton - R
Kootenai Courier - R
Light and Life
Liguorian
Living - R
Lookout - R
Lutheran Digest - R
Lutheran Journal - R
Lutheran Layman
Mature Living
Mature Years - R
Mennonite, The - R
MESSAGE
Messenger, The (NC) - R
Ministry Today - R
New Trumpet - R
Our Sunday Visitor
ParentLife - R
Parents of Teenagers - R
Pentecostal Evangel - R
Pentecostal Homelife - R
Plus - R
Positive Approach, A - R
Positive Living - R
Power for Living - R
Praying
Psychology for Living - R
Pursuit - R
Puzzler's Digest - R

Quiet Revolution - R
Sharing - R
Smart Dads
Standard - R
Sunday Digest - R
Today's Better Life
Today's Single - R
Total Health
Upsouth - R
Urban Family
Vista - R

CHILDREN
Attention Please! - R
Guideposts for Kids
High Adventure - R
My Friend
R-A-D-A-R - R

CHRISTIAN
EDUCATION/LIBRARY
Brigade Leader - R
CE Connection - R
CE Counselor - R
Children's Ministry
Christian School
Church & Synagogue Libraries - R
GROUP
Journal/Adventist Educ. - R
KEY - R
Librarian's World - R
Lollipops
Resource - R
Shining Star
Vision - R

MISSIONS
IMPACT

MUSIC
Church Music Report
Music Leader
Score - R

PASTORS/LEADERS
Christian Ministry
Church Administration
Church Business - R
Group's Jr High
Ivy Jungle Report - R
Jour/Biblical Ethics - R
Journal/Christian Camping - R
Journal/Christian Healing - R
Lutheran Partners- R
Networks - R
Priest, The
Resource - R
Youthworker - R

TEEN/YOUNG ADULT
Breakaway - R
Certainty
Challenge (IL)
Challenge (TN)
Edge, The - R
Insight - R
Insight/Out - R
Magazine/Youth! - R
Pioneer - R
Student Leadership - R
Teenage Christian - R
Teen Life - R
You ! - R

WOMEN
Co-Laborer - R
Just Between Us
Link & Visitor - R
Lutheran Woman Today
Probe
Salt and Light - R
Today's Christian Woman
Virtue - R
Wesleyan Woman - R
Woman's Touch - R

WRITERS

Byline
Canadian Writer's Jour - R
Chips Off Writer's Block - R
Christian Author
Christian Communicator - R
Cross & Quill - R
Exchange
Home Office - R
Tickled By Thunder
Writers Anchor - R
Writers Connection - R
Writer's Digest
Writer's Exchange - R
Writer's Forum (OH) - R
Writer's Guidelines
Writer's Infor Network

HUMOR

ADULT/GENERAL
African Amer. Heritage - R
Alive! - R
alive now! - R
Aspire
At Ease - R
AXIOS - R
Better Tomorrow, A
Biblical Reflections - R
Canada Lutheran - R
Canadian Baptist - R
Catholic Digest - R
Catholic Forester - R
Catholic Parent
Catholic Twin Circle - R
Celebrate Life - R
Christian C.L. RECORD - R
Christian Drama - R
Christian Edge - R
Christian Event - R
Christian Parenting - R
Christian Reader - R
Christian Single - R

Church Herald - R
Church of God EVANGEL
Companion
Connecting Point - R
Cornerstone - R
Covenant Companion - R
Critic, The
Door, The - R (satire)
Emphasis/Faith & Living - R
Evangel - R
Evangelical Visitor - R
Family, The - R
Family Digest, The - R
Family Journal - R
Focus on the Family - R
Good News, Etc. - R
Good News Journal - R
Good News Reporter - R
Hayden Herald - R
Head to Head - R
Hearing Hearts - R
Highway News - R
Home Life
Home Times - R
Impact Magazine - R
John Milton - R
Jour/Christian Nursing - R
Kootenai Courier - R
Light and Life
Liguorian
Live - R
Living Church
Lookout - R
Lutheran, The
Lutheran Digest - R
Lutheran Journal - R
Lutheran Layman
Lutheran Witness
Maranatha - R
Mature Living
Mature Years - R
Mennonite, The - R
MESSAGE

MESSAGE/Open Bible - R
Messenger, The (NC) - R
Ministry Today - R
Minnesota Christian - R
Morning Glory - R
New Trumpet - R
Our Family - R
ParentLife - R
Parents of Teenagers
PCA Messenger - R
Pegasus Review - R
Pentecostal Homelife - R
Pentecostal Testimony - R
Power for Living - R
Prayerworks - R
Praying
Presbyterian Outlook
Presbyterian Record - R
Presbyterian Survey - R
Progress - R
Pursuit - R
Puzzler's Digest - R
Salt
Salt Shaker - R
Single-Parent Family
Standard - R
Sunday Digest - R
Table Talk
Today's Single - R
Upsouth - R
Urban Family
Vista - R
Vital Christianity - R
Voice, The - R

CHILDREN
Crusader - R
Focus/Clubhouse Jr
GUIDE - R
High Adventure - R
My Friend
On the Line - R
Power & Light - R

R-A-D-A-R - R
Touch - R
Venture (IL) - R
Wonder Time
Young Crusader - R

CHRISTIAN
EDUCATION/LIBRARY
Brigade Leader - R
Christian School
Leader - R
Resource - R
Team - R
Today's Catholic Teacher - R
Vision - R

MISSIONS
Areopagus - R
World Christian - R
Worldwide Challenge - R

MUSIC
Church Pianist, etc.
Quest - R
Score - R

PASTORS/LEADERS
Five Stones, The - R
Journal/Christian Healing - R
Networks - R
Preacher's Illus. Service - R
Preacher's Magazine - R
Priest, The
Resource - R
Today's Parish
Your Church - R
YMR Today

TEEN/YOUNG ADULT
Breakaway - R
Brio
Certainty
Challenge (IL)

Conqueror - R
Freeway - R
Insight - R
Insight/Out - R
Kiln, The - R
Magazine/Youth! - R
Pioneer - R
Straight - R
Student, The
Teenage Christian - R
Teen Life - R
Teen Power - R
Teen Quest - R
YOU! - R
Young Adult Today
Young Salvationist - R
Youth Focus - R

WOMEN
Co-Laborer - R
Helping Hand - R
Horizons - R
Journey - R
Joyful Woman - R
Lutheran Woman Today
Today's Christian Woman
Wesleyan Woman - R
Woman's Touch - R

WRITERS
Byline
Canadian Writer's Jour - R
Exchange
Felicity - R
Housewife-Writers Forum - R
Inklings - R
Writers Anchor - R
Writer's Exchange - R
Writer's Guidelines
Writers Infor Network

INSPIRATIONAL

ADULT/GENERAL
Acts 29
ADVOCATE - R
African Amer. Heritage - R
Annals of St. Anne
Aspire
At Ease - R
Baptist Beacon - R
Better Tomorrow, A
Bible Advocate - R
Broken Streets
Canada Lutheran - R
Catholic Accent
Catholic Answer
Catholic Digest - R
Catholic Forester - R
Catholic Parent
Catholic Twin Circle - R
Celebrate Life - R
Charisma/Christian Life
Christian Edge - R
Christian Event - R
Christian Parenting - R
Christian Reader - R
Christian Single - R
Church Herald - R
Church Herald/Holiness - R
Church of God EVANGEL
Columbia - R
Companion
Companions - R
Connecting Point - R
Conquest
Covenant Companion - R
Discipleship Journal - R
Emphasis/Faith & Living - R
Evangel - R
Evangelical Baptist - R
Evangelical Beacon - R
Evangelical Friend
Evangelical Visitor - R

Explorer
Family, The - R
Family Digest, The - R
Fellowship Today - R
Foursquare World - R
Gem, The - R
God's Revivalist
Good News - R
Good News, Etc. - R
Good News Reporter - R
Gospel Tidings - R
Guideposts
Head to Head - R
Hearing Hearts - R
Herald of Holiness - R
Highway News - R
Home Times - R
Ideals - R
Indian Life - R
Inspirer, The - R
John Milton - R
Lifeglow - R
Light and Life
Liguorian
Live - R
Living - R
Living Church
Lookout - R
Lutheran, The
Lutheran Digest - R
Lutheran Journal - R
Lutheran Layman
Lutheran Witness
Maranatha - R
Marian Helpers - R
Mature Living
Mature Years - R
Mennonite Brethren - R
MESSAGE
MESSAGE/Open Bible - R
Messenger, The (Canada) - R
Messenger, The (NC) - R
Messenger of the Sacred Heart

Ministry Today - R
Morning Glory - R
New Covenant - R
New Heart, A - R
New Thought - R
New Trumpet - R
Oblates
Our Sunday Visitor
Parenting Treasures - R
ParentLife - R
PCA Messenger - R
Pegasus Review - R
Pentecostal Evangel - R
Pentecostal Homelife - R
Pentecostal Messenger - R
Plenty Good Room
Plus - R
Pourastan - R
Power for Living - R
Prayerworks - R
Praying
Presbyterian Outlook
Presbyterian Record - R
Presbyterian Survey - R
Progress - R
Purpose - R
Puzzler's Digest - R
Queen of all Hearts
St. Anthony Messenger
St. Joseph's Messenger - R
Salt Shaker - R
Seek - R
Shantyman, The - R
Sharing - R
Standard - R
Sunday Digest - R
Table Talk
Teaching Home, The
Today's Better Life
Today's Single - R
Total Health
Upsouth - R
U.S. Catholic

VISION (CA) - R
Vision (MO) - R
Vista - R
Voice, The - R
War Cry
Wesleyan Advocate - R
Wine Castles
Worldwide Challenge - R

CHILDREN
CLUBHOUSE- R
GUIDE - R
High Adventure - R
Partners - R
R-A-D-A-R - R
Skipping Stones - R
Venture (IL) - R
Wonder Time

CHRISTIAN
EDUCATION/LIBRARY
Brigade Leader - R
CE Connection - R
Changing Lives
Christian School
Junior Teacher - R
Leader - R
Librarian's World - R
Lutheran Education
Perspective - R
Resource - R
Shining Star
Vision - R
Youth Leader - R

MISSIONS
American Horizon - R
Areopagus - R
Message of the Cross - R
World Vision - R

MUSIC
Quest - R

Score - R

Senior Musician - R

PASTORS/LEADERS

Christian Century

Christian Management - R

Eucharistic Minister - R

Five Stones, The - R

Group's Jr High

Journal/Christian Healing - R

Lutheran Partners - R

Networks - R

Preacher's Magazine - R

Priest, The

PROCLAIM - R

Pulpit Helps - R

Review for Religious

TEEN/YOUNG ADULT

Breakaway - R

Certainty

Challenge (IL)

Conqueror - R

Freeway - R

Insight - R

Insight/Out - R

Kiln, The - R

Magazine/Youth! - R

Straight - R

Teenage Christian - R

Teen Life - R

Teen Power - R

Teen Quest - R

Young Adult Today

Young & Alive - R

Young Salvationist - R

WOMEN

Co-Laborer - R

Esprit - R

Helping Hand - R

Horizons - R

Journey - R

Joyful Woman - R

Lutheran Woman Today

Salt and Light - R

Sisters Today

Today's Christian Woman

Virtue - R

Wesleyan Woman - R

Woman's Touch - R

WRITERS

Byline

Canadian Writer's Jour - R

Felicity - R

Inklings - R

Writers Anchor - R

Writer's Forum (OH) - R

Writer's Forum - R

Writer's Guidelines

Writer's Infor Network

INTERVIEWS/PROFILES

ADULT/GENERAL

Acts 29

ADVOCATE - R

African Amer. Heritage - R

AGAIN - R

Alive! - R

Anglican Journal - R

Arkansas Catholic

Arlington Catholic

At Ease - R

AXIOS - R

Better Tomorrow, A

Biblical Reflections - R

Bookstore Journal - R

Burning Light - R

Canadian Catholic

Catholic Digest - R

Catholic New York

Catholic Parent

Catholic Sentinel - R

Catholic Twin Circle - R

Charisma/Christian Life

Christian C.L. RECORD - R

Christian Courier (WI) - R

Christian Courier (Canada) - R

Christian Edge - R

Christian Event - R

Christian Renewal - R

Christian Single - R

Christianity Today - R

Church & State - R

Church Herald/Holiness - R

Church of God EVANGEL

Class

Columbia - R

Companion

Cornerstone - R (music)

Critic, The

Door, The - R

Dovetail - R

Emphasis/Faith & Living - R

Episcopal Life - R

Evangel - R

Evangelical Baptist - R

Evangelical Friend

Expression Christian

Family, The - R

Family Digest, The - R

Family Journal - R

First Things

Focus on the Family

Friends Journal - R

Good News, Etc - R

Good News Reporter - R

Guideposts

Hayden Herald - R

Head to Head - R

Hearing Hearts - R

Herald of Holiness - R

Highway News - R

Home Life

Home Times - R

Impact Magazine - R

Indian Life - R

Interim - R

InterVarsity

John Milton - R

Jour/Christian Nursing - R

Joyful Noise

Kansas City Christian - R

Kootenai Courier - R

Lifeglow - R

Liguorian

Living - R

Living Church

Lookout - R

Lutheran, The

Lutheran Layman

Lutheran Witness

Maranatha - R

Mature Living

Mature Years - R

Mennonite, The - R

Mennonite Reporter

MESSAGE

Messenger (KY)

Messenger, The (NC) - R

Minnesota Christian - R

New Covenant - R

New Heart, A - R

New Trumpet - R

Our Sunday Visitor

ParentLife - R

Parents of Teenagers

Pentecostal Evangel - R

Pentecostal Testimony - R

Plenty Good Room

Positive Approach - R

Positive Living - R

Power for Living - R

Praying

Presbyterian Outlook

Presbyterian Record - R

Presbyterian Survey - R

Prism - R

Professional Parents - R

Pursuit - R

Puzzler's Digest - R

Quiet Revolution - R

St. Anthony Messenger

Salt

SCP Journal - R

Shantyman, The - R

Sharing - R

Signs of the Times - R

Single-Parent Family

Standard - R

Star of Zion

Sunday Digest - R

Today's Better Life

Touchstone

United Church Observer

Upsouth - R

Urban Family

U.S. Catholic

Vista - R

Whisper - R

Witness, The

CHILDREN

Attention Please!

Crusader - R

Skipping Stones - R

Touch - R

Venture (IL) - R

**CHRISTIAN
EDUCATION/LIBRARY**

CE Counselor - R

Changing Lives

Christian Educators Jour - R

Christian School

GUIDE - R

Lutheran Education

Perspective - R

Resource - R

Teachers in Focus

Vision - R

Youth & CE Leadership - R

Youth Leader - R

MISSIONS

American Horizon - R

Childlife - R

Compassion

IMPACT

Partners

P.I.M.E. World - R

Urban Mission - R

World Christian - R

World Vision - R

Worldwide Challenge - R

MUSIC

Church Music World

Quest - R

Score - R

PASTORS/LEADERS

Christian Century

Christian Management - R

Cross Currents - R

Diaconalogue - R

Five Stones, The - R

Ivy Jungle Report - R

Journal/Christian Camping - R

Journal/Christian Healing - R

Ministries Today

Networks - R

Preacher's Magazine - R

PROCLAIM - R

Search

Single Ad. Ministries Jour.

Worship Leader

Youthworker - R

TEEN/YOUNG ADULT

Breakaway - R

Freeway - R

Insight - R

Insight/Out - R

Issues & Answers - R

Magazine/Youth! - R

Pathway I.D. - R

Sharing the VICTORY - R
Spirit
Straight - R
Teenage Christian - R
Teen Life - R
Teen Power - R
Teen Quest - R
YOU! - R
Young Adult Today
Young & Alive - R
Young Salvationist - R
Youth Focus - R

WOMEN
Church Woman
Contempo
Daughters of Sarah - R
Esprit - R
Horizons - R
Jour/Women's Ministries
Link & Visitor - R
Lutheran Woman Today
Probe
Royal Service
Salt and Light - R
Today's Christian Woman
Virtue - R
Wesleyan Woman - R

WRITERS
Canadian Writer's Jour - R
Christian Communicator, The - R
Cross & Quill - R
Inklings - R
Writers Connection - R
Writer's Digest
Writer's Info
Writer's Infor Network

LEADERSHIP

ADULT/GENERAL
Acts 29

At Ease - R
Baptist Beacon - R
Bible Advocate - R
Biblical Reflections - R
Canada Lutheran - R
Canadian Baptist - R
Catholic Digest - R
Christian Edge - R
Christian Event - R
Christianity Today - R
Church Herald/Holiness - R
Columbia - R
Companion
Discipleship Journal - R
Emphasis/Faith & Living - R
Evangel - R
Evangelical Baptist - R
Faith Today
Foursquare World - R
Friends Journal - R
Good News, Etc - R
Hearing Hearts - R
Home Times - R
It's Your Choice - R
John Milton - R
Liguorian
Living Church
Lutheran Digest - R
Mennonite, The - R
MESSAGE/Open Bible - R
Ministry Today - R
New Trumpet - R
NW Christian Journal - R
Our Family - R
Our Sunday Visitor
Pentecostal Evangel - R
Pentecostal Homelife - R
Pentecostal Messenger - R
Purpose - R
Presbyterian Outlook
Religious Education
Upsouth - R
Urban Family

Vista - R

CHILDREN
High Adventure - R
R-A-D-A-R - R

CHRISTIAN
EDUCATION/LIBRARY
Baptist Leader - R
Brigade Leader - R
CE Connection - R
CE Counselor - R
Changing Lives
Church Educator - R
Church Worship
GROUP
Leader - R
Leader/Church School Today
Memos - R
Perspective - R
Resource - R
Team - R
Vision - R
Youth & CE Leadership - R
Youth Leader - R

MISSIONS
American Horizon - R
Urban Mission - R
Worldwide Challenge - R

MUSIC
Score - R

PASTORS/LEADERS
Advance - R
Christian Century
Christian Management - R
Christian Ministry
Church Business - R
Church Growth Network - R
Church Management - R
Group's Jr High

Ivy Jungle Report - R
Jour/Biblical Ethics - R
Journal/Christian Healing - R
Leadership Journal - R
Lutheran Partners - R
Ministries Today
Preacher's Magazine - R
Priest, The
Pulpit Helps - R
Resource - R
Word & World
Worship Leader
Your Church - R
Youthworker - R

TEEN/YOUNG ADULT
Kiln, The - R
Magazine/Youth! - R
Student Leadership - R

WOMEN
Esprit - R
Journey - R
Link & Visitor - R
Salt and Light - R
Virtue - R
Wesleyan Woman - R

WRITERS
Writers Anchor - R

LITURGICAL

ADULT/GENERAL
Acts 29
AGAIN - R
alive now! - R
Canada Lutheran - R
Canadian Catholic
Catholic Digest - R
Catholic Parent
Church Herald/Holiness - R
Commonweal

Companion
Cresset
Episcopal Life - R
Family Digest, The - R
John Milton - R
Liguorian
Living Church
Messenger (KY)
New Trumpet - R
North American Voice
Our Family - R
Our Sunday Visitor
Pourastan - R
Praying
Presbyterian Outlook
Presbyterian Record - R
Silver Wings - R
United Church Observer
Upsouth - R
U.S. Catholic

CHRISTIAN
EDUCATION/LIBRARY
Church Educator - R
Church Worship
Lutheran Education
Parish Teacher - R
Religion Teacher's Journal

MISSIONS
Areopagus - R
Catholic Near East

MUSIC
Church Pianist, etc.
Creator
Hymn, The

PASTORS/LEADERS
Catechumenate
Celebration
Chicago Studies
Christian Ministry

Church Administration
Eucharistic Minister - R
Five Stones, The - R
Journal/Christian Healing - R
Liturgy
Lutheran Forum - R
Lutheran Partners - R
Preaching
Preacher's Illus. Service - R
Preacher's Magazine - R
Priest, The
PROCLAIM - R
Quarterly Review
Reformed Worship - R
Review for Religious
Today's Parish
Word & World

TEENS/YOUNG ADULTS
You! - R
Youth Update

WOMEN
Daughters of Sarah - R
Horizons - R
Lutheran Woman Today
Sisters Today

WRITERS
Inklings - R

MARRIAGE

ADULT/GENERAL
Advent Christian Witness
ADVOCATE - R
Alive! - R
America
American Tract Soc. - R
Aspire
At Ease - R
AXIOS - R
Better Tomorrow, A

Bible Advocate - R
Biblical Reflections - R
Canada Lutheran - R
Canadian Baptist - R
Canadian Catholic
Catholic Digest - R
Catholic Parent
Catholic Twin Circle - R
Celebrate Life - R
Charisma/Christian Life
Christian C.L. RECORD - R
Christian Courier (Canada) - R
Christian Edge - R
Christian Event - R
Christian Home & School
Christian Living - R
Christian Parenting - R
Church Herald/Holiness - R
Church of God EVANGEL
Columbia - R
Companion
Companions - R
Conquest
Decision
Dovetail - R
Emphasis/Faith & Living - R
Evangel - R
Evangelical Baptist - R
Evangelical Beacon - R
Evangelical Friend
Evangelical Visitor - R
Expression Christian
Family, The - R
Family Digest, The - R
Fellowship Today - R
Focus on the Family - R
Foursquare World - R
Friends Journal - R
Good News, Etc - R
Good News Journal - R
Good News Reporter - R
Gospel Tidings - R
Guideposts

Hayden Herald - R
Head to Head - R
Hearing Hearts - R
Highway News - R
Home Life
Home Times - R
Impact Magazine - R
Indian Life - R
John Milton - R
Joyful Noise
Kansas City Christian - R
Kootenai Courier - R
Lifeglow - R
Light and Life
Liguorian
Live - R
Living - R
Living Church
Lookout - R
Lutheran, The
Lutheran Digest - R
Lutheran Witness
Mature Years - R
Mennonite, The - R
Mennonite Brethren - R
MESSAGE
MESSAGE/Open Bible - R
Messenger, The (Canada) - R
Messenger, The (NC) - R
Messenger/St. Anthony
Ministry Today - R
Minnesota Christian - R
Montana Catholic - R
Moody
New Covenant - R
New Oxford Review
New Trumpet - R
North American Voice
NW Christian Journal - R
Northwestern Lutheran - R
Our Family - R
Our Sunday Visitor
Parenting Treasures - R

Parents of Teenagers
PCA Messenger - R
Pegasus Review - R
Pentecostal Evangel - R
Pentecostal Homelife - R
Pentecostal Messenger - R
Pentecostal Testimony - R
Plus - R
Power for Living - R
Praying
Presbyterian Record - R
Presbyterian Survey - R
Progress - R
Psychology for Living - R
Purpose - R
St. Anthony Messenger
Salt Shaker - R
Seek - R
Signs of the Times - R
Smart Dads
Social Justice - R
Standard - R
Sunday Digest - R
Today's Better Life
Upsouth - R
Urban Family
U.S. Catholic
VISION (CA) - R
Vision (MO) - R
Vista - R
Vital Christianity - R
Voice, The - R
Wesleyan Advocate - R

CHRISTIAN
EDUCATION/LIBRARY
Brigade Leader - R
CE Connection - R
CE Counselor - R
Leader - R
Lutheran Education

MISSIONS
Worldwide Challenge - R

MUSIC
Score - R

PASTORS/LEADERS
Bethany Choice - R
Chicago Studies
Christian Century
Jour/Biblical Ethics - R
Journal/Christian Healing - R
Lutheran Partners - R
Ministries Today
Networks - R
Preacher's Illus. Service - R
PROCLAIM - R
Pulpit Helps - R
Search
Today's Parish
Word & World

TEEN/YOUNG ADULT
Insight - R
Student, The
YOU! - R
Young Adult Today
Young & Alive - R
Youth Update

WOMEN
Anna's Journal - R
Co-Laborer - R
Helping Hand - R
Journey - R
Joyful Woman - R
Link & Visitor - R
Lutheran Woman Today
Today's Christian Woman
Virtue - R
Wesleyan Woman - R
Woman's Touch - R
Women Alive! - R

WRITERS
Housewife-Writer's Forum - R
Writer's Forum - R

MEN'S ISSUES

ADULT/GENERAL
Annals of St. Anne
At Ease - R
AXIOS - R
Biblical Reflections - R
Canada Lutheran - R
Canadian Baptist - R
Catholic Parent
Celebrate Life - R
Christian Edge - R
Christian Event - R
Christian Living - R
Christian Parenting - R
Christian Single - R
Christian Social Action - R
Christianity Today - R
Church of God EVANGEL
Companion
Covenant Companion - R
Critic, The
Emphasis/Faith & Living - R
Evangelical Baptist - R
Expression Christian
Family, The - R
Family Journal - R
Focus on the Family
Foursquare World - R
Friends Journal - R
Good News, Etc - R
Good News Journal - R
Good News Reporter - R
Gospel Tidings - R
Hearing Hearts - R
Herald of Holiness - R
Highway News - R
Home Life
Home Times - R

Indian Life - R
Joyful Noise
Kansas City Christian - R
Liguorian
Light and Life
Mature Years - R
Mennonite, The - R
Ministry Today - R
Moody
Newsline - R
New Trumpet - R
Our Family - R
Pentecostal Evangel - R
Pentecostal Messenger - R
Pentecostal Testimony - R
Plus - R
Power for Living - R
Praying
Purpose - R
Smart Dads
Sunday Digest - R
Today's Better Life
Vibrant Life - R (health)
Vista - R
Vital Christianity - R
Witness, The

CHRISTIAN
EDUCATION/LIBRARY
Brigade Leader - R
Leader - R
Resource - R

MISSIONS
American Horizon - R
Brigade Leader - R
New World Outlook
Worldwide Challenge - R

MUSIC
Quest - R
Score - R

PASTORS/LEADERS
Bethany Choice - R
Jour/Biblical Ethics - R
Leadership Journal
Lutheran Partners - R
Ministries Today
Nat/Intl Religion Report
Word & World

WOMEN
Anna's Journal - R
Virtue - R

MIRACLES

ADULT/GENERAL
Acts 29
America
Annals of St. Anne
Aspire
At Ease - R
Biblical Reflections - R
Canadian Baptist - R
Canadian Catholic
Catholic Digest - R
Catholic Forester - R
Catholic Twin Circle - R
Charisma/Christian Life
Christian Event - R
Church Herald/Holiness - R
Companion
Connecting Point - R
Evangel - R
Explorer
Friends Journal - R
God's Revivalist
Good News, Etc - R
Good News Journal - R
Guideposts
Hearing Hearts - R
Home Times - R
Impact Magazine - R
Liguorian

Live - R
Lutheran Digest - R
Maranatha - R
Messenger, The (NC) - R
New Oxford Review
Pegasus Review - R
Pentecostal Evangel - R
Pentecostal Homelife - R
Pentecostal Messenger - R
Power for Living - R
Prayerworks - R
Puzzler's Digest - R
Queen of All Hearts
Sharing - R
Standard - R
Total Health
Upsouth - R
VISION (CA) - R
Vision (MO) - R
Vista - R
Vital Christianity - R
Wine Castles

CHILDREN
BREAD/God's Children - R
GUIDE - R
Guideposts for Kids
Touch - R

CHRISTIAN
EDUCATION/LIBRARY
Changing Lives

MISSIONS
American Horizon - R
Areopagus - R

MUSIC
Score - R

PASTORS/LEADERS
Journal/Christian Healing - R
Lutheran Partners - R

Ministries Today
Networks - R
Word & World

TEEN/YOUNG ADULT
Conqueror - R
Insight - R
Insight/Out - R
Pathway I.D. - R
Teen Life - R
YOU! - R
Young Adult Today

WOMEN
Joyful Woman - R
Lutheran Woman Today
Virtue - R
Woman's Touch - R

MISSIONS

ADULT/GENERAL
Acts 29
Alive! - R
Annals of St. Anne
Anglican Journal - R
At Ease - R
Baptist Informer
B.C. Catholic - R
Bible Advocate - R
Biblical Reflections - R
Canada Lutheran - R
Canadian Baptist - R
Canadian Catholic
Catholic Digest - R
Catholic Twin Circle - R
Charisma/Christian Life
Christian Event - R
Christian Reader - R
Christian Renewal - R
Christianity Today - R
Church Herald/Holiness - R
Columbia - R

Companion
Companions - R
Connecting Point - R
Conquest
Decision
Episcopal Life - R
Evangel - R
Evangelical Baptist - R
Evangelical Friend
Focus on the Family
Good News, Etc - R
Good News Reporter - R
Gospel Tidings - R
Hallelujah! - R
Hearing Hearts - R
Indian Life - R
InterVarsity
John Milton - R
Jour/Christian Nursing - R
Liguorian
Live - R
Living Church
Lookout - R
Lutheran, The
Lutheran Witness
Maranatha - R
Mennonite, The - R
Mennonite Brethren - R
Mennonite Reporter
MESSAGE/Open Bible - R
Messenger, The (NC) - R
Moody
New Heart, A - R (medical)
New Oxford Review
News Network Intl.
New Trumpet - R
North American Voice
Our Family - R
Our Sunday Visitor
Parents of Teenagers - R
Pentecostal Evangel - R
Pentecostal Homelife - R
Pentecostal Messenger - R

Pentecostal Testimony - R
Power for Living - R
Prayerworks - R
Presbyterian Outlook
Presbyterian Record - R
Presbyterian Survey - R
Psychology for Living - R
Purpose - R
Queen of All Hearts
Religious Broadcasting
Seek - R
Standard - R
Star of Zion
Sunday Digest - R
Upsouth - R
Vision (MO) - R
Vista - R
Vital Christianity - R

CHILDREN
BREAD/God's Children - R
CLUBHOUSE - R
GUIDE - R
Partners - R
Primary Pal
R-A-D-A-R - R

CHRISTIAN
EDUCATION/LIBRARY
Brigade Leader - R
Changing Lives
Church Educator - R
Evangelizing Today's Child
Leader - R
Shining Star
Youth Leader - R

MISSIONS
(see alphabetical listings)

MUSIC
Quest - R
Score - R

PASTORS/LEADERS
Christian Century
Christian Management - R
Church Administration
Discipleship Training
Evangelism - R
Five Stones, The - R
Journal/Christian Healing - R
Lutheran Partners - R
Ministries Today
Nat/Intl Religion Report
Networks - R
Preacher's Magazine - R
PROCLAIM - R
Pulpit Helps - R
Search
Word & World
Youthworker - R

TEEN/YOUNG ADULT
Challenge (IL)
Conqueror - R
Freeway - R
Insight - R
Insight/Out - R
Kiln, The - R
Magazine/Youth! - R
Pathway I.D. - R
Priest, The
Student, The
Student Leadership Jour - R
Teen Life - R
Teen Power - R
Teen Quest - R
YOU! - R
Young Adult Today
Young Salvationist - R

WOMEN
Co-Laborer - R
Contempo
Esprit - R
Joyful Woman - R

Link & Visitor - R
Lutheran Woman Today
Response
Royal Service
Virtue - R
Wesleyan Woman
Woman's Touch - R

MONEY MANAGEMENT

ADULT/GENERAL

Anglican Journal - R
Aspire
At Ease - R
AXIOS - R
Better Tomorrow, A
Biblical Reflections - R
Catholic Digest - R
Catholic Forester - R
Catholic Parent
Catholic Twin Circle - R
Charisma/Christian Life
Christian C.L. RECORD - R
Christian Edge - R
Christian Event - R
Christian Parenting - R
Christian Single - R
Church Herald/Holiness - R
Connecting Point - R
Discovery - R
Emphasis/Faith & Living - R
Evangel - R
Evangelical Baptist - R
Evangelical Friend
Evangelical Visitor - R
Expression Christian
Focus on the Family - R
Good News, Etc - R
Gospel Tidings - R
Guideposts
Hayden Herald - R
Head to Head - R
Hearing Hearts - R

Herald of Holiness - R
Highway News - R
Home Life
Home Times - R
Indian Life - R
John Milton - R
Kootenai Courier - R
Lookout - R
Lutheran Digest - R
Mennonite, The - R
MESSAGE
MESSAGE/Open Bible - R
Messenger, The (NC) - R
Ministry Today - R
New Trumpet - R
ParentLife - R
Parents of Teenagers
PCA Messenger - R
Pentecostal Evangel - R
Pentecostal Homelife - R
Pentecostal Messenger - R
Pentecostal Testimony - R
Power for Living - R
Professional Parents - R
Puzzler's Digest - R
Religious Broadcasting
Signs of the Times - R
Smart Dads
Sunday Digest - R
Today's Better Life
Urban Family
Vista - R

CHILDREN

Crusader - R
R-A-D-A-R - R

CHRISTIAN EDUCATION/LIBRARY

CE Connection - R
Christian School

MISSIONS

World Christian - R

MUSIC

Score - R

PASTORS/LEADERS

Advance - R
Christian Ministry
Church Business - R
Clergy Journal
Journal/Christian Camping - R
Journal/Christian Healing - R
Lutheran Partners - R
Ministries Today
Networks - R
Pastor's Tax & Money
Preacher's Magazine - R
Today's Parish
Your Church - R
Youthworker - R

TEEN/YOUNG ADULT

Kiln, The - R
Magazine/Youth! - R
Student, The
Teen Life - R
Young Adult Today

WOMEN

Esprit - R
Journey - R
Lutheran Woman Today
Salt and Light
Today's Christian Woman
Wesleyan Woman - R
Woman's Touch - R

WRITERS

Writers Anchor - R

MUSIC REVIEWS

ADULT/GENERAL
Canadian Catholic
Christian Edge - R
Christian Event - R
Christian Parenting - R
Christianity/Arts
Commonweal
Cornerstone - R
Expression Christian
Good News Journal - R
Good News Reporter - R
Hayden Herald - R
Head to Head - R
Home Life
Home Times - R
Impact Magazine - R
Kootenai Courier - R
Parents of Teenagers
Plowman, The - R
Presbyterian Record - R
Upsouth - R
Urban Family

**CHRISTIAN
EDUCATION/LIBRARY**
CE Counselor - R

MUSIC
Hymn, The - R
Quest - R

PASTORS/LEADERS
Christian Century

TEEN/YOUNG ADULT
Insight - R
Teenage Christian - R
With - R
Young Salvationist - R

WOMEN
Joyful Woman - R

NATURE

ADULT/GENERAL
Alive! - R
AXIOS - R
Canadian Catholic
Catholic Digest - R
Catholic Forester - R
Companion
Companions - R
Friends Journal - R
Hayden Herald - R
John Milton - R
Kootenai Courier - R
Lifeglow - R
Liguorian
Lutheran Digest - R
Mature Years - R
New Trumpet - R
Pegasus Review - R
Pentecostal Evangel - R
Pourastan - R
Prayerworks - R
Praying
Puzzler's Digest - R
Seek - R
Upsouth - R

CHILDREN
BREAD/God's Children - R
CLUBHOUSE - R
Crusader - R
High Adventure - R
Junior Trails - R
My Friend
Nature Friend
On the Line
R-A-D-A-R - R
Skipping Stones - R
Touch - R

Venture (IL) - R

**CHRISTIAN
EDUCATION/LIBRARY**
Shining Star

PASTORS/LEADERS
Journal/Christian Healing - R
Lutheran Partners - R
Word & World

TEEN/YOUNG ADULT
Insight - R
Magazine/Youth! - R
Teenage Christian - R
Teen Life - R
Young & Alive - R

WOMEN
Esprit - R
Virtue - R

NEWSPAPERS

Anglican Journal - R
Arkansas Catholic
Arlington Catholic
B.C. Catholic - R
Catholic Accent
Catholic Courier
Catholic Exponent
Catholic New York
Catholic Sentinel
Catholic Telegraph
Catholic Twin Circle - R
Christian American
Christian Chronicle
Christian Courier (WI) - R
Christian Courier (Canada) - R
Christian Crusade
Christian Edge - R
Christian Event - R
Christian Focus

Discovery - R
Encourager Provider - R
Enlace Informativo
Episcopal Life - R
Expression Christian
Family Journal, The
Good News, Etc. - R
Good News Journal
Hayden Herald - R
Home Times - R
Inland NW Christian
Inside Journal
Interchange
Interim - R
Issues & Answers - R
Kansas City Christian - R
Kootenai Courier - R
Maranatha - R
Mennonite Reporter
Mennonite Weekly
Messenger (KY)
Minnesota Chronicle - R
Montana Catholic - R
National Catholic
Northwest Christian Journal
Oblate World
Our Sunday Visitor
Probe
Pulpit Helps - R
Inland Northwest
Today's Single
World

OPINION PIECES

ADULT/GENERAL
Acts 29
African Amer. Heritage - R
Arlington Catholic
At Ease - R
AXIOS - R
B.C. Catholic - R
Bible Advocate - R

Biblical Reflections - R
Canadian Baptist - R
Canadian Catholic
Catholic New York
Celebrate Life - R
Charisma/Christian Life
Christian Chronicle
Christian Event - R
Christian Renewal - R
Christianity Today - R
Commonweal
Compass
Cornerstone - R
Door, The - R
Dovetail - R
Episcopal Life - R
Evangelical Baptist - R
Evangelical Friend
Expression Christian
Family Journal - R
Fellowship Today - R
First Things
Good News, Etc - R
Good News Reporter - R
Head to Head - R
Hearing Hearts - R
Home Times - R
Interim - R
It's Your Choice - R
John Milton - R
Jour/Christian Nursing - R
Kansas City Christian - R
Light and Life (600 wds)
Living Church
Lookout - R
Lutheran, The
Maranatha - R
Mennonite Brethren - R
Mennonite Reporter
Mennonite Weekly
MESSAGE/Open Bible - R
Messenger (KY)
Minnesota Christian - R

New Oxford Review
New Thought - R
New Trumpet - R
Pentecostal Messenger - R
Pourastan - R
Presbyterian Record - R
Presbyterian Survey - R
Prism - R
Puzzler's Digest - R
Quiet Revolution - R
Salt
Social Justice - R
Urban Family
U.S. Catholic
Vista - R

CHRISTIAN EDUCATION/LIBRARY
CE Connection - R
Lutheran Education

MISSIONS
American Horizon - R
Areopagus - R
World Vision - R

MUSIC
Score - R

PASTORS/LEADERS
Christian Ministry
Jour/Biblical Ethics - R
Journal/Christian Healing - R
Lutheran Partners - R
Ministries Today
Priest, The
Single Ad. Ministries Jour.
Word & World
Your Church - R

TEEN/YOUNG ADULT
Insight - R
Insight/Out - R

Magazine/Youth! - R
Teenage Christian - R
Teen Life - R
You! - R
Young Adult Today
Youth Focus - R

WOMEN
Anna's Journal - R
Conscience - R
Daughters of Sarah - R
Lutheran Woman Today

WRITERS
Canadian Writer's Jour - R
Exchange
Tickled By Thunder
Writers Anchor - R
Writers Infor Network

PARENTING

ADULT/GENERAL
Advent Christian Witness
American Tract Soc. - R
Annals of St. Anne
Aspire
AXIOS - R
Baptist Beacon - R
Better Tomorrow, A
Biblical Reflections - R
Canada Lutheran - R
Canadian Baptist - R
Catholic Digest - R
Catholic Forester - R
Catholic Parent
Catholic Sentinel - R
Charisma/Christian Life
Christian Courier (Canada) - R
Christian Edge - R
Christian Event - R
Christian Home & School
Christian Living - R

Christian Parenting - R
Church Herald/Holiness - R
Columbia - R
Companion
Companions - R
Dovetail - R
Emphasis/Faith & Living - R
Evangel - R
Evangelical Baptist - R
Evangelical Beacon - R
Evangelical Friend
Evangelical Visitor - R
Expression Christian
Family, The - R
Family Digest, The - R
Fellowship Today - R
Focus on the Family - R
Foursquare World - R
Friends Journal - R
God's Revivalist
Good News, Etc - R
Good News Journal - R
Good News Reporter - R
Gospel Tidings - R
Hayden Herald - R
Hearing Hearts - R
Herald of Holiness - R
Highway News - R
Home Life
Home Times - R
Impact Magazine - R
Indian Life - R
It's Your Choice - R
John Milton - R
Kansas City Christian - R
Kootenai Courier - R
Light and Life
Liguorian
Living - R
Lookout - R
Lutheran, The
Lutheran Digest - R
Mature Years - R

Mennonite, The - R
MESSAGE
MESSAGE/Open Bible - R
Messenger, The (Canada) - R
Messenger, The (NC) - R
Messenger/St. Anthony
Ministry Today - R
Moody
New Covenant - R
New Oxford Review
New Trumpet - R
Our Family - R
Our Sunday Visitor
Parenting Treasures - R
ParentLife - R
Parents of Teenagers
PCA Messenger - R
Pegasus Review - R
Pentecostal Evangel - R
Pentecostal Homelife - R
Pentecostal Messenger - R
Plus - R
Positive Approach - R
Pourastan - R
Power for Living - R
Praying
Presbyterian Survey - R
Progress - R
Psychology for Living - R
Purpose - R
Puzzler's Digest - R
Religious Education
St. Anthony Messenger
St. Joseph's Messenger - R
Salt Shaker - R
Seek - R
Single-Parent Family
Smart Dads
Social Justice - R
Standard - R
Sunday Digest - R
Table Talk
Today's Better Life

Today's Single - R
United Church Observer
Upsouth - R
Urban Family
U.S. Catholic
Vision (MO) - R
Vista - R
Vital Christianity - R
Wesleyan Advocate - R

CHRISTIAN EDUCATION/LIBRARY

Brigade Leader - R
CE Connection - R
Christian School
Church Educator - R
GROUP
Leader - R
Lutheran Education

MISSIONS

Worldwide Challenge - R

MUSIC

Score - R

PASTORS/LEADERS

Bethany Choice - R
Diaconalogue - R
Discipleship Training
Group's Jr High
Journal/Christian Healing - R
Lutheran Partners - R
Networks - R
Preacher's Illus. Service - R
Pulpit Helps - R
Single Ad. Ministries Jour.
Youthworker - R

WOMEN

Co-Laborer - R
Daughters of Sarah - R
Helping Hand - R

Joyful Woman - R
Lutheran Woman Today
Today's Christian Woman
Virtue - R
Wesleyan Woman - R
Women Alive! - R

WRITERS

Housewife-Writer's Forum - R
Writer's Forum - R

PERSONAL EXPERIENCE

ADULT/GENERAL

Acts 29
Advent Christian Witness
ADVOCATE - R
African Amer. Heritage - R
AGAIN - R
alive now! - R
Annals of St. Anne
At Ease - R
B.C.Catholic - R
Bible Advocate - R
Biblical Reflections - R
Canada Lutheran - R
Canadian Baptist - R
Catholic Digest - R
Catholic New York
Catholic Sentinel - R
Catholic Twin Circle - R
Celebrate Life - R
Charisma/Christian Life
Christian Courier (Canada) - R
Christian Edge - R
Christian Event - R
Christian Parenting - R
Christian Reader - R
Christian Renewal - R
Christian Single - R
Church Herald - R
Church Herald/Holiness - R
Commonweal

Companion
Companions - R
Compass
Conquest
Cornerstone - R
Crossway/Newsline
Decision
Door, The - R
Dovetail - R
Evangel - R
Evangelical Baptist - R
Evangelical Friend
Evangelical Visitor - R
Family Digest, The - R
Family Journal - R
Fellowship Today - R
Friends Journal - R
Gem, The - R
God's Revivalist
Good News - R
Good News, Etc - R
Good News Journal
Good News Reporter - R
Guideposts
Head to Head - R
Hearing Heart - R
Herald of Holiness - R
Highway News - R
Home Life
Home Times - R
Ideals - R
Impact Magazine - R
Indian Life - R
Inspirer, The - R
Interim - R
InterVarsity
It's Your Choice - R
John Milton - R
Jour/Christian Nursing - R
Light and Life
Liguorian
Living - R
Living Church

Lookout - R
Lutheran, The
Lutheran Digest - R
Lutheran Journal - R
Lutheran Layman
Maranatha - R
Marian Helpers - R
Mature Years - R
Mennonite, The - R
Mennonite Brethren - R
Mennonite Reporter
MESSAGE/Open Bible - R
Messenger, The (NC) - R
Minnesota Christian - R
Moody
Morning Glory - R
New Covenant - R
New Heart - R
Newsline - R
New Trumpet - R
Our Family - R
Parenting Treasures - R
Parents of Teenagers
Pentecostal Evangel - R
Pentecostal Homelife - R
Pentecostal Messenger - R
Plenty Good Room
Plus - R
Positive Approach, A - R
Power for Living - R
Praying
Presbyterian Record - R
Presbyterian Survey - R
PROGRESS - R
Psychology for Living - R
Purpose - R
Pursuit - R
Puzzler's Digest - R
Salt Shaker - R
SCP Journal - R
Seek - R
Shantyman, The - R
Sharing - R

Single-Parent Family
Standard - R
Star of Zion
Sunday Digest - R
Table Talk
Today's Single - R
Touchstone
United Church Observer
Upsouth - R
Urban Family
VISION - R
Vision (MO) - R
Vista - R
Vital Christianity - R
Voice, The - R
Wesleyan Advocate - R
Wine Castles

CHILDREN
Attention Please! - R
Counselor - R
GUIDE - R
R-A-D-A-R - R
Skipping Stones - R
Touch - R
Venture (MN)
Young Crusader - R

CHRISTIAN
EDUCATION/LIBRARY
Brigade Leader - R
CE Connection - R
CE Counselor - R
Changing Lives
Journal/Adventist Educ. - R
KEY - R
Lutheran Education
Perspective - R
Religion Teacher's Journal
Resource - R
Teachers in Focus - R (teacher)
Youth & CE Leadership - R

MISSIONS
American Horizon - R
Areopagus - R
Heartbeat - R
P.I.M.E. World - R
World Christian - R
Worldwide Challenge - R

MUSIC
Music Leader
Score - R

PASTORS/LEADERS
Christian Ministry
Church Business - R
Diaconalogue - R
Discipleship Training
Eucharistic Minister - R
Five Stones, The - R
Journal/Christian Healing - R
Ministries Today
Networks - R
Preacher's Illus. Service - R
Today's Parish
Youthworker - R

TEEN/YOUNG ADULT
Breakaway - R
Campus Life - R
Certainty
Challenge (IL)
Conqueror - R
Freeway - R
Insight - R
Insight/Out - R
Magazine/Youth! - R
Spirit
Straight - R
Student, The
Teenage Christian - R
Teen Life - R
Teen Power - R
Teen Quest - R

With - R (1st person teen)
You! - R
Young Adult Today
Young Salvationist - R
Youth Focus - R
Youth World - R

WOMEN

Anna's Journal - R
Contempo
Daughters of Sarah - R
Esprit - R
Journey - R
Jour/Women's Ministries
Joyful Woman - R
Just Between Us
Link & Visitor - R
Lutheran Woman Today
Probe
Response
Royal Service
Salt and Light - R
Sisters Today
Today's Christian Woman
Virtue - R
Wesleyan Woman - R
Woman's Touch - R

WRITERS

Byline
Chips Off Writer's Block - R
Exchange
Home Office - R
Housewife-Writer's Forum - R
Tickled By Thunder
Writer's Infor Network
Writer's Nook News

PHOTOGRAPHS

Note: "Reprint" indicators (R) have
been deleted from this section, and
"B" for black & white glossy prints

or "C" for color transparencies inserted. An asterisk (*) before a listing indicates they buy photos with
articles only.

ADULT/GENERAL

ABS RECORD
Advent Christian Witness - B
ADVOCATE - B & C
African-American Heritage - B
Alive! - B
alive now! - B
American Tract Soc.
Anglican Journal - B & C
Annals of St. Anne
Arlington Catholic - B & C
At Ease - B & C
*Better Tomorrow, A - C
Bible Advocate - B & C
Bible Today - B
Bookstore Journal - B & C
Burning Light - B
Calvinist Contact - B & C
Canada Lutheran - B
*Cathedral Age - B
Catholic Courier - B
Catholic Digest - B & C
Catholic Exponent - B
Catholic Forester - C
Catholic Heritage
Catholic New York - B
Catholic Parent
*Catholic Sentinel - B & C
Catholic Telegraph - B
Catholic Twin Circle
Celebrate Life - B & C
Charisma/Christian Life - C
Christian Chronicle - B
Christian Courier - B
Christian Crusade - B
Christian Drama - B
*Christian Event
*Christian History - B & C

Christian Home & School - B & C
*Christian Information
Christian Living - B
Christian Parenting Today - B & C
*Christian Reader - B & C
Christian Retailing - B & C
*Christian Single - C
Christian Social Action - B
Christian Standard - B & C
Christianity Today - B & C
Church & State
Church Herald - B & C
Church of God EVANGEL - C
Class
Columbia - C/prints
Comments From the Friends - B
Common Ground
*Commonweal - B & C
Companion - B
Connecting Point - B
*Conquest - B & C
Cornerstone - B & C
Covenant Companion - B
Discipleship Journal - C
Episcopal Life - B
Evangel - B
Evangelical Baptist - B & C
Evangelical Beacon - B & C
Evangelical Friend - B
Evangelical Visitor - B
Expression Christian - B
Faith Today - B
*Family, The - B & C
Fellowship Today - B
Focus on the Family - C
Foursquare World ADVANCE - C
Good News, Etc - B & C
Good News Journal - B
Gospel Tidings - B
Guideposts - B & C
Hallelujah - B
Head to Head - B & C
Herald of Holiness - B & C

Highway News - B
*Home Life - C
*Home Times - B
Ideals - C (No 35mm)
Impact Magazine - C
Indian Life - C
Inside Journal - B
Inspirer, The - B
Interchange - B
Interim
InterVarsity - B
*Journal/Christian Nursing - B/C
Joyful Noise
Liberty - B & C
*Lifeglow - B & C
Light and Life - B & C
Liguorian - B & C
Live - B & C
Living - B & C
Living Church - B & C
Lookout - B & C
Lutheran, The - B
Lutheran Journal - C
Lutheran Witness - B & C
Maranatha - B
Marian Helpers - B & C
Mature Living
Mature Years - C
Mennonite, The - B
Mennonite Brethren Herald - B
Mennonite Reporter - B & C
Mennonite Weekly - B
MESSAGE - B & C
MESSAGE/Open Bible - B/C
Messenger (KY) - B
Messenger, The (Canada) - B
Messenger, The (NC) - B
*Montana Catholic - B
Nat. Christian Reporter - B &
    C/prints
*New Heart - B
*News Network Intl. - C
New Thought Journal - B (cover)

*New Trumpet
Northwestern Lutheran
Our Family - B & C
Our Sunday Visitor - B & C
Parents of Teenager - B & C
PCA Messenger - B
Pentecostal Evangel - B & C
Pentecostal Messenger - C
Pentecostal Testimony - B & C
Plenty Good Room - B
Plowman, The - B
*Positive Approach, A
*Power for Living - B
Prairie Messenger - B
Praying - B
Presbyterian Outlook
Presbyterian Record - B & C
Presbyterian Survey - B & C
Prism
*Professional Parents - B & C
*Purpose - B
Pursuit - B
*Puzzler's Digest - B
Quiet Revolution - B
*Religious Broadcasting
Rural Landscapes - B
St. Anthony Messenger - B & C
Salt - B
SCP Journal - B & C
Seek - B
Signs of the Times - C
Southwestern News - B & C
Spiritual Life - B
Sports Spectrum - C
Standard - B
Star of Zion - B & C
Sunday Digest - C
Thema - B
Today's Better Life - C
Today's Single - B
Together - B & C
Total Health - B & C
Twin Cities Christian - B

United Church Observer - B & C
VISION - B & C
Vista - B & C
*Vital Christianity - C
War Cry - C
Wesleyan Advocate - C
Whisper
Witness, The

CHILDREN
*Counselor - B & C
*Focus/Clubhouse/Clubhouse Jr - C
God's World Today - C
Guideposts for Kids - C
Junior Trails - C
Listen - C (slides)
Nature Friend - B & C
My Friend
On the Line - B
Pockets - C (some)
Power & Light - B
Primary Days - B & C
R-A-D-A-R - B & C
*Skipping Stones - B
Story Friends - B
Together Time - C
Touch - B
Venture - B & C
Wonder Time - B & C

CHRISTIAN
EDUCATION/LIBRARY
Baptist Leader - B
Brigade Leader - B
CE Counselor - B & C
Children's Ministry - B
Christian Librarian - B
Christian School - C
Evang. Today's Child - B & C
GROUP - B
Journal/Adventist Education - B
Junior Teacher - B & C
KEY - B

Leader/Church School Today - B
Level C Teacher - B
*Librarian's World - B & C
Lollipops
Parish Teacher - B
Perspective - B & C
Religion Teacher's Journal - B & C
Teachers in Focus - C
Teachers Interaction - B
Team - B & C
Today's Catholic Teacher - B & C
Youth & CE Leadership - B & C

DAILY DEVOTIONALS
Daily Dev for Deaf - C
Light From the Word - C
Secret Place - B & C

MISSIONS
American Horizon
Areopagus - B & C
Catholic Near East - C
P.I.M.E. World - C
Childlife
Impact - B & C
Intl Jour/Frontier Missions
Message of the Cross - B & C
New World Outlook - B & C
Partners - C
*Wherever - B
World Christian - B & C
World Vision - C
Worldwide Challenge - C

MUSIC
Church Musician - B
Creator - B
Music Leader - B & C

PASTORS/LEADERS
Advance - B & C
Celebration - B & C
Christian Century - B

Christian Ministry - B
Discipleship Training - B
Environment & Art - B & C
Group's Jr High - B
*Journal/Christian Camping - B & C
*Leadership Journal - B & C
Liturgy - B
Lutheran Forum - B
*Lutheran Partners - B
Networks - B
Preacher's Magazine - B & C
Preaching - B & C
Resource - B & C
Today's Parish - B & C
*Your Church - B & C

TEEN/YOUNG ADULT
Breakaway - C
Brio - C
Campus Life - C
*Certainty - B
Challenge (IL) _ B
Challenge (TN) - B & C
The Conqueror - B & C
Edge, The
Freeway - B
Insight - B & C
Lighted Pathway - B & C
Magazine/Youth! - B & C
Pioneer - B
Sharing the VICTORY - C
Spirit - B & C
Straight - B & C
Student, The - B
Student Leadership - B & C
Take Five - B & C
*Teen Life
Teen Power - B
Teen Quest - B & C
Teens Today - B
Venture - B
With - B

YOU! - B & C
Young Adult Today - B
Young & Alive - B (prefer) & C
Young Salvationist - C
*Youth Focus

WOMEN
Anna's Journal - B
Conscience - B
Daughters of Sarah - B
*Esprit - B
Helping Hand - B
Horizons - B
Jour/Women's Ministries - B
Joyful Woman - C
Just Between Us
Link & Visitor - B
Lutheran Woman Today - B
Probe - B & C
Response - B & C
Sisters Today - B & C
Today's Christian Woman - C
Virtue - B & C
Wesleyan Woman
Woman's Touch - C
Women Alive! - B

WRITERS
Gotta Write - B
Home Office - B
Housewife-Writers Forum - B
Tickled By Thunder - B
*Writer's Digest

POETRY

ADULT/GENERAL
ADVOCATE - R
African Amer. Heritage - R
alive now! - R
America
At Ease - R
AXIOS - R

Baptist Beacon - R
Bible Advocate - R
Broken Streets - R
Burning Light
Caregivers Connection - R
Celebrate Life - R
Christian Courier (Canada) - R
Christian Drama - R
Christian Event - R
Christian Living - R
Christian Reader - R
Christian Single - R
Christianity/Arts
Christmas - R
Church Herald/Holiness - R
Class
Commonweal
Companion
Companions - R
Connecting Point - R
Cornerstone - R
Covenant Companion - R
Creatively Yours
Cresset
Decision
Door, The - R
Evangel - R
Explorer
Family Journal - R
First Things
Foursquare World - R
Friends Journal - R
God's Revivalist
Good News Reporter - R
Guideposts
Hallelujah! - R
Hayden Herald - R
Head to Head - R
Hearing Hearts - R
Herald of Holiness - R
Home Life
Home Times - R
Ideals - R

Impact Magazine - R
Inspirer, The - R
John Milton - R
Jour/Christian Nursing - R
Kootenai Courier - R
Liberty (little) - R
Light and Life
Lighthouse Fiction
Liguorian
Live - R
Living Church
Lutheran Digest - R
Lutheran Journal - R
Manna
Mature Living
Mature Years - R
Mennonite, The - R
Mennonite Brethren - R
Messenger, The (Canada) - R
Miraculous Medal
Morning Glory - R
New Heart - R
New Thought - R
New Trumpet - R
North American Voice
Oblates
Our Family - R
Parenting Treasures - R
PCA Messenger - R
Pegasus Review - R
Pentecostal Evangel - R
Pentecostal Messenger - R
Pentecostal Testimony - R
Plowman, The - R
Poetry Forum
Pourastan - R
Power for Living - R
Prayerworks - R
Presbyterian Record - R
Presbyterian Survey - R
Purpose - R
Queen of all Hearts
Ratio

St. Anthony Messenger
St. Joseph's Messenger - R
Salt Shaker - R
Shantyman, The - R
Sharing - R
Silver Wings - R
Standard - R
Star of Zion
Sunday Digest - R
Table Talk
Thema - R
Time of Singing - R
Today's Single - R
Touchstone
Upsouth - R
Vision (MO) - R
Vital Christianity - R
Voice, The - R
Wesleyan Advocate - R
Whisper - R
Wine Castles
Witness, The

CHILDREN
Attention Please! - R
CLUBHOUSE - R
Creatively Yours
Focus/Clubhouse Jr
Guideposts for Kids
Junior Trails - R
Listen
Mission
My Friend
Nature Friend - R
On the Line - R
Our Little Friend - R
Partners - R
Pockets - R
Primary Treasure - R
R-A-D-A-R - R
Skipping Stones - R
Story Friends - R
Story Mates - R

Together Time - R
Touch - R
Wonder Time
Young Crusader - R

CHRISTIAN
EDUCATION/LIBRARY
Baptist Leader - R
Christian Educators Jour - R
Christian School
Church Educator - R
Church Worship
Leader - R
Level C Teacher - R
Lollipops
Resource - R
Shining Star
Teacher Interaction - R
Today's Catholic Teacher - R
Vision - R

DAILY DEVOTIONALS
Living Words - R
Secret Place

MISSIONS
New World Outlook

MUSIC
Choir Herald, etc.
Church Musician - R
Church Pianist, etc.
Glory Songs - R
Hymn, The (hymns only) - R
Music Leader
Quest - R
Score - R
Senior Musician - R
Tradition

PASTORS/LEADERS
ArtPlus
Catechumenate

Christian Century
Cross Currents - R
Diaconalogue - R
Emmanuel
Journal/Christian Camping - R
Journal/Christian Healing - R
Liturgy
Lutheran Forum - R
Lutheran Partners - R
Networks - R
Preacher's Illus. Service - R
Review for Religious
Today's Parish

TEEN/YOUNG ADULT
Campus Life
Freeway - R
Insight - R
Insight/Out - R
Magazine/Youth! - R
Sharing the Victory - R
Straight - R
Student Leadership - R
Take Five - R
Teenage Christian - R
Teen Life - R
Teen Power - R (by teens)
Teen Quest - R (by teens)
With - R
Young Salvationist - R
Youth Focus - R
Youth World - R

WOMEN
Anna's Journal - R
Co-Laborer - R
Conscience - R
Daughters of Sarah - R
Esprit - R
Horizons - R
Jour/Women's Ministries
Joyful Woman - R
Link & Visitor - R

Lutheran Woman Today
Probe
Salt and Light - R
Sisters Today
Virtue - R
Wesleyan Woman - R
Woman's Touch - R
Women Alive! - R

WRITERS
Byline
Canadian Writer's Jour - R
Christian Communicator - R
Cross & Quill
Felicity - R
Gotta Write
Heaven - R
Housewife-Writers Forum - R
Inklings - R
My Legacy - R
Omnific - R
Tickled By Thunder
Writers Anchor - R
Writer's Digest
Writer's Exchange - R
Writer's Guidelines - R
Write Touch - R

POLITICAL

ADULT/GENERAL
AFA Journal - R
Anglican Journal - R
Apocalypse Chronicles - R
AXIOS - R
Bible Advocate - R
Biblical Reflections - R
Canadian Catholic
Catholic Courier
Celebrate Life - R
Charisma/Christian Life
Christian American
Christian C.L. RECORD - R

Christian Courier (WI) - R
Christian Courier (Canada) - R
Christian Crusade
Christian Event - R
Christian Media - R
Christian Renewal - R
Christian Social Action - R
Christianity Today - R
Commonweal
Compass
Cornerstone - R
Cresset
Critic, The
ESA Advocate
Evangelical Baptist - R
Evangelical Friend
Expression Christian
Faith Today
First Things
Friends Journal - R
Good News, Etc - R
Good News Reporter - R
Head to Head - R
Home Times - R
Interim - R
It's Your Choice - R
John Milton - R
Jour/Church & State
Kansas City Christian - R
Lookout - R
Messenger, The (NC) - R
Minnesota Christian - R
News Network Intl.
New Trumpet - R
Perspectives on Science
Praying
Presbyterian Outlook
Presbyterian Survey - R
Religious Broadcasting
Religious Education
SCP Journal - R
Social Justice - R
Upsouth - R

Witness, The
World

CHRISTIAN
EDUCATION/LIBRARY
Today's Catholic Teacher - R

MISSIONS
Areopagus - R

MUSIC
Score - R

PASTORS/LEADERS
Lutheran Forum - R
Lutheran Partners - R
Nat/Intl Religion Report
Networks - R
Preacher's Illus. Service - R
Word & World

TEEN/YOUNG ADULT
Issues & Answers - R
With - R
Young Adult Today

WOMEN
Conscience - R
Daughters of Sarah - R
Horizons - R
Virtue - R
Wesleyan Woman - R

PRAYER

ADULT/GENERAL
Acts 29
Advent Christian Witness
ADVOCATE - R
alive now! - R
Annals of St. Anne
Aspire
At Ease - R

Baptist Beacon - R
Baptist Informer
Bible Advocate - R
Broken Streets
Canadian Baptist - R
Canadian Catholic
Catholic Digest - R
Celebrate Life - R
Charisma/Christian Life
Christian Event - R
Christianity Today - R
Church Herald/Holiness - R
Church of God EVANGEL
Christian Living - R
Companion
Companions - R
Compass
Connecting Point - R
Conquest
Covenant Companion - R
Discipleship Journal - R
Emphasis/Faith & Living - R
Episcopal life - R
Evangel - R
Evangelical Baptist - R
Evangelical Beacon - R
Evangelical Friend
Evangelical Visitor - R
Family, The - R
Family Digest, The - R
Family Journal - R
Fellowship Today - R
Foursquare World - R
God's Revivalist
Good News, Etc - R
Good News Journal - R
Good News Reporter - R
Gospel Tidings - R
Guideposts
Hallelujah! - R
Head to Head - R
Hearing Hearts - R
Herald of Holiness - R

Highway News - R
Home Life
Home Times - R
Indian Life - R
Inspirer, The - R
John Milton - R
Jour/Christian Nursing - R
Kansas City Christian - R
Light and Life
Liguorian
Live - R
Living Church
Lookout - R
Lutheran, The
Lutheran Digest - R
Lutheran Layman
Lutheran Witness
Marian Helpers - R
Mature Years - R
Mennonite, The - R
Mennonite Brethren - R
MESSAGE
Messenger, The (NC) - R
Messenger/St. Anthony
Messenger of the Sacred Heart
Ministry Today - R
Moody
Morning Glory - R
New Covenant - R
New Oxford Review
New Trumpet - R
North American Voice
Our Family - R
Our Sunday Visitor
Pegasus Review - R
Pentecostal Evangel - R
Pentecostal Homelife - R
Pentecostal Messenger - R
Presbyterian Outlook
Plowman, The - R
Plus - R
Pourastan - R
Power for Living - R

Prayerworks - R
Praying
Presbyterian Record - R
Presbyterian Survey - R
Purpose - R
Queen of All Hearts
St. Anthony Messenger
Salt
Salt Shaker - R
Seek - R
Sharing - R
Silver Wings - R
Social Justice - R
Spiritual Life
Standard - R
Sunday Digest - R
Table Talk
Today's Better Life
Upsouth - R
U.S. Catholic
Vision (MO) - R
Vista - R
Vital Christianity - R
Wesleyan Advocate - R
Wine Castles

CHILDREN

Attention Please! - R
BREAD/God's Children - R
Counselor - R
Focus/Clubhouse
GUIDE - R
High Adventure - R
Primary Pal
R-A-D-A-R - R
Touch - R
Wonder Time

CHRISTIAN
EDUCATION/LIBRARY
Brigade Leader - R
CE Connection - R
Changing Lives

Church Educator - R
Church Worship
Evangelizing Today's Child - R
Leader - R
Lutheran Education
Religion Teacher's Journal
Resource - R
Shining Star
Vision - R
Youth Leader - R

MISSIONS

American Horizon - R
Areopagus - R
Childlife - R
Intl Jour/Frontier Missions - R
Message of the Cross - R
Worldwide Challenge - R

MUSIC

Quest - R
Score - R

PASTORS/LEADERS

Advance - R
Chicago Studies
Christian Ministry
Five Stones, The - R
Journal/Christian Healing - R
Leadership Journal
Liturgy - R
Lutheran Partners - R
Ministries Today
Networks - R
Preacher's Illus. Service - R
Preacher's Magazine - R
Priest, The
PROCLAIM - R
Pulpit Helps - R
Resource - R
Review for Religious
Search
Today's Parish

Word & World

TEEN/YOUNG ADULT
Certainty
Challenge (IL)
Conqueror - R
Freeway - R
Insight - R
Insight/Out - R
Magazine/Youth! - R
Pathway I.D. - R
Straight - R
Student, The
Student Leadership - R
Teenage Christian - R
Teen Life - R
Teen Power - R
YOU! - R
Vision - R
With - R
Young Adult Today
Young Salvationist - R
Youth Update

WOMEN
Anna's Journal - R
Co-Laborer - R
Contempo
Daughters of Sarah - R
Esprit - R
Helping Hand - R
Horizons - R
Journey - R
Joyful Woman - R
Lutheran Woman Today
Response
Royal Service
Sisters Today
Today's Christian Woman
Virtue - R
Wesleyan Woman - R
Women Alive! - R

WRITERS
Inklings - R

PROPHECY

ADULT/GENERAL
Acts 29
ADVOCATE - R
Apocalypse Chronicles - R
Baptist Beacon - R
Bible Advocate - R
Canadian Baptist - R
Charisma/Christian Life
Christian Information
Christian Media - R
Church Herald/Holiness - R
Evangelical Baptist - R
Evangelical Friend
Foursquare World - R
God's Revivalist
Good News, Etc - R
Hallelujah! - R
Home Times - R
John Milton - R
Kansas City Christian - R
MESSAGE/Open Bible - R
Messenger, The (NC) - R
New Trumpet - R
Our Family - R
Pentecostal Messenger - R
Pentecostal Testimony - R
Praying
Queen of All Hearts
SCP Journal - R
Signs of the Times - R
Silver Wings - R

**CHRISTIAN
EDUCATION/LIBRARY**
Youth Leader - R

PASTORS/LEADERS
Journal/Christian Healing - R

Ministries Today
PROCLAIM - R
Pulpit Helps - R
Word & World

TEEN/YOUNG ADULT
Challenge (IL)
Insight/Out - R
Issues & Answers - R
Pathway I.D. - R
Young Adult Today

WOMEN
Daughters of Sarah - R
Woman's Touch - R

PSYCHOLOGY

ADULT/GENERAL
Aspire
AXIOS - R
Biblical Reflections - R
Catholic Digest - R
Catholic Twin Circle - R
Common Boundary
Companion
Evangelical Friend
Good News, Etc - R
Home Times - R
John Milton - R
Jour/Christian Nursing - R
Lutheran Journal - R
Lutheran Layman
MESSAGE
MESSAGE/Open Bible - R
New Covenant - R
Parenting Treasures
Parents of Teenagers - R
Perspectives on Science
Praying
Professional Parents - R
Psychology for Living - R
Puzzler's Digest - R

Ratio
Religious Education
St. Anthony Messenger
SCP Journal - R
Social Justice - R
Today's Better Life
Total Health
Vista - R
Wine Castles - R

CHRISTIAN EDUCATION/LIBRARY
Church Educator - R
Lutheran Education
Resource - R

MUSIC
Score - R

PASTORAL/LEADERS
Advance - R
Christian Ministry
Eucharistic Minister - R
Group's Jr High
Jour/Biblical Ethics - R
Journal/Christian Healing - R
Lutheran Partners - R
Priest, The
Review for Religious
Single Ad. Ministries Jour.
Word & World

TEENS/YOUNG ADULTS
Teen Life - R

WOMEN
Daughters of Sarah - R
Esprit - R
Virtue - R
Woman's Touch - R

WRITERS
Inklings - R

Writer's Forum - R

*PUPPET PLAYS

CE Counselor - R
Creatively Yours
Focus/Clubhouse Jr
Lillenas
My Friend
Sheer Joy! Press
Shining STar
Touch - R

RELATIONSHIPS

ADULT/GENERAL
Aspire
At Ease - R
AXIOS - R
Better Tomorrow, A
Bible Advocate - R
Biblical Reflections - R
Canada Lutheran - R
Canadian Baptist - R
Catholic Digest - R
Catholic Forester - R
Christian Edge - R
Christian Event - R
Christian Living - R
Christian Parenting - R
Christian Single - R
Columbia - R
Companion
Conquest
Discipleship Journal - R
Dovetail - R
Evangel - R
Evangelical Baptist - R
Explorer
Family, The - R
Family Digest
Focus on the Family
Foursquare World - R

Friends Journal - R
Good News, Etc - R
Good News Journal - R
Good News Reporter - R
Head to Head - R
Hearing Hearts - R
Herald of Holiness - R
Highway News - R
Home Life
Home Times - R
Indian Life - R
It's Your Choice - R
Jour/Christian Nursing - R
Kansas City Christian - R
Lifeglow - R
Liguorian
Lutheran Digest - R
Mature Years - R
Mennonite, The - R
Ministry Today - R
Moody
New Trumpet - R
Parenting Treasures - R
Parents of Teenagers
Pegasus Review - R
Pentecostal Evangel - R
Pentecostal Messenger - R
Pentecostal Testimony - R
Plus - R
Positive Living - R
Power for Living - R
Praying
Professional Parents - R
Progress - R
Purpose- R
Pursuit - R
Puzzler's Digest - R
Silver Wings - R
Single-Parent Family
Sunday Digest - R
Today's Better Life
Upsouth - R
Urban Family

U.S. Catholic
Vista - R
Vital Christianity - R

CHILDREN
BREAD for God's Children
Focus/Clubhouse/Clubhouse Jr
GUIDE - R
Guideposts for Kids
R-A-D-A-R - R
Touch - R

CHRISTIAN
EDUCATION/LIBRARY
Brigade Leader - R
Church Educator - R
Resource - R

MISSIONS
American Horizon - R
Message of the Cross - R
Worldwide Challenge - R

MUSIC
Score - R

PASTORS/LEADERS
Christian Ministry
Ministries Today
Youthworker - R
Word & World

TEEN/YOUNG ADULT
Certainty
Challenge (TN)
Freeway - R
Insight - R
Magazine/Youth! - R
Student Leadership - R
Teenage Christian - R
Teen Life - R
Teen Power - R
Youth Update

WOMEN
Anna's Journal - R
Co-Laborer - R
Daughters of Sarah - R
Journey - R
Joyful Woman - R
Today's Christian Woman
Virtue - R
Wesleyan Woman - R

WRITERS
Inklings - R

RELIGIOUS FREEDOM

ADULT/GENERAL
AFA Journal - R
AGAIN - R
America
AXIOS - R
Bible Advocate - R
Biblical Reflections - R
Catholic Digest - R
Catholic Twin Circle - R
Celebrate Life - R
Charisma/Christian Life
Christian C.L. RECORD - R
Christian Courier (WI) - R
Christian Courier (Canada) - R
Christian Event - R
Christian Social Action - R
Christianity Today - R
Church & State - R
Church Herald/Holiness - R
Columbia - R
Connecting Point - R
Cornerstone - R
Cresset
Episcopal Life - R
Evangelical Friend
Family Journal - R
Faith Today
First Things

Focus on the Family
Friends Journal - R
God's Revivalist
Good News, Etc - R
Good News Journal - R
Good News Reporter - R
Hallelujah! - R
Hearing Hearts - R
Herald of Holiness - R
Home Times - R
John Milton - R
Jour/Church & State
Kansas City Christian - R
Liberty - R
Living Church
Lookout - R
Mature Years - R
MESSAGE
Messenger, The (NC) - R
MESSAGE/Open Bible - R
Minnesota Christian - R
Moody
Morning Glory - R
News Network Intl.
New Trumpet - R
Our Family - R
Our Sunday Visitor
Pegasus Review - R
Pentecostal Evangel - R
Pentecostal Messenger - R
Pourastan - R
Presbyterian Outlook
Presbyterian Survey - R
Prism - R
Religious Education
SCP Journal - R
Social Justice - R
United Church Observer
Upsouth - R
U.S. Catholic
Vista - R

CHILDREN
GUIDE - R
Skipping Stones - R

CHRISTIAN
EDUCATION/LIBRARY
CE Connection - R
Church Worship
Today's Catholic Teacher - R
Vision - R
Youth Leader - R

MISSIONS
Areopagus - R
Worldwide Challenge - R

MUSIC
Quest - R

PASTORS/LEADERS
Christian Century
Discipleship Training
Jour/Biblical Ethics - R
Journal/Christian Healing - R
Lutheran Partners - R
Ministries Today
Nat/Intl Religion Report
Networks - R
Pulpit Helps - R
Search
Word & World

TEEN/YOUNG ADULT
Conqueror - R
Issues & Answers - R
Kiln, The - R
Teen Life - R
Young Adult Today

WOMEN
Daughters of Sarah - R
Esprit - R
Response

Woman's Touch - R

WRITERS
Christian Response - R

SALVATION TESTIMONIES

ADULT/GENERAL
Acts 29
ADVOCATE - R
AGAIN - R
American Tract Soc. - R
At Ease - R
Bible Advocate - R
Broken Streets
Canadian Baptist - R
Charisma/Christian Life
Christian Event - R
Church Herald/Holiness - R
Companions - R
Connecting Point - R
Conquest
Crossway/Newsline
Decision
Emphasis/Faith & Living - R
Evangel - R
Evangelical Baptist - R
Evangelical Friend
Explorer
God's Revivalist
Good News - R
Good News, Etc - R
Good News Journal
Good News Reporter - R
Hallelujah! - R
Head to Head - R
Hearing Hearts - R
Herald of Holiness - R
Highway News - R
Home Times - R
Indian Life - R
Inspirer, The - R
Light and Life

Liguorian
Living Church, The
Maranatha - R
MESSAGE
MESSAGE/Open Bible - R
Messenger, The (NC) - R
Ministry Today - R
Moody
Morning Glory - R
New Covenant - R
New Heart, A - R
New Oxford Review
New Trumpet - R
Pentecostal Evangel - R
Pentecostal Messenger - R
Pentecostal Testimony - R
Power for Living - R
Prayerworks - R
PROGRESS - R
Pursuit - R
Salt Shaker - R
SCP Journal - R
Shantyman, The - R
Sharing - R
Silver Wings - R
Standard - R
Together - R
Upsouth - R
VISION (CA) - R
Vista - R
Vital Christianity - R
Voice, The - R
Wesleyan Advocate - R

CHILDREN
BREAD/God's Children - R
Counselor - R
GUIDE - R
Primary Days - R

CHRISTIAN
EDUCATION/LIBRARY
Evangelizing Today's Child

Youth Leader - R

MISSIONS
American Horizon - R
Childlife - R
Worldwide Challenge - R

PASTORS/LEADERS
Journal/Christian Healing - R
Networks - R

TEEN/YOUNG ADULT
Certainty
Challenge (IL)
Conqueror - R
Freeway - R
Insight - R
Pathway I.D. - R
Teen Life - R
Teen Power - R
Young Adult Today

WOMEN
Esprit - R
Joyful Woman - R
Virtue - R
Wesleyan Woman - R
Woman's Touch - R

SCIENCE

ADULT/GENERAL
AXIOS - R
Biblical Reflections - R
Canadian Catholic
Catholic Digest - R
Catholic Twin Circle - R
Christian C.L. RECORD - R
Christian Courier (Canada) - R
Christian Information
Companions - R
Compass
Family Journal - R

First Things
Home Times - R
John Milton - R
Kansas City Christian - R
Lutheran Journal - R
New Trumpet - R
Perspectives on Science
Prayerworks - R
Religious Education
Salt Shaker - R
SCP Journal - R

CHILDREN
Guideposts for Kids
My Friend
Nature Friend - R
Primary Days - R
Primary Pal
Venture (IL) - R

CHRISTIAN
EDUCATION/LIBRARY
Journal/Adventist Educ. - R
Today's Catholic Teacher - R
Vision - R

PASTORS/LEADERS
Jour/Biblical Ethics - R
Journal/Christian Healing - R
Lutheran Partners - R
Word & World

TEEN/YOUNG ADULT
Challenge (IL)
Edge, The - R
Issues & Answers - R
Teen Life - R
Young Adult Today

WOMEN
Esprit - R

SENIOR ADULT ISSUES

ADULT/GENERAL
Acts 29
ADVOCATE - R
Alive! - R
Anglican Journal - R
AXIOS - R
B.C. Catholic - R
Better Tomorrow, A
Bible Advocate
Biblical Reflections - R
Canada Lutheran - R
Canadian Baptist - R
Caregivers Connection - R
Cathedral Age - R
Catholic Digest - R
Catholic Exponent
Catholic Forester - R
Charisma/Christian Life
Christian Courier (Canada) - R
Christian Event - R
Christian Home & School
Christian Living - R
Church Herald/Holiness - R
Church of God EVANGEL
Columbia - R
Companion
Companions - R
Conquest
Covenant Companion - R
Decision
Discovery - R
Emphasis/Faith & Living - R
Evangel - R
Evangelical Baptist - R
Evangelical Friend
Expression Christian
Focus on the Family
Good News Journal - R
Hayden Herald - R
Hearing Hearts - R
Herald of Holiness - R

Home Times - R
Inspirer, The - R
John Milton - R
Jour/Christian Nursing - R
Kansas City Christian - R
Kootenai Courier - R
Light and Life
Liguorian
Lookout - R
Lutheran, The
Lutheran Digest - R
Mature Years - R
Mennonite, The - R
MESSAGE
Messenger, The (NC) - R
Minnesota Christian - R
Montana Catholic - R
Moody
New Trumpet - R
NW Christian Journal - R
Our Family - R
Our Sunday Visitor
PCA Messenger - R
Pentecostal Evangel - R
Pentecostal Messenger - R
Plus - R
Presbyterian Outlook
Presbyterian Record - R
Presbyterian Survey - R
Purpose - R
Puzzler's Digest - R
Resource - R
Salt Shaker - R
Standard - R
Star of Zion
Sunday Digest - R
Upsouth - R
U.S. Catholic
Vista - R
Wesleyan Advocate - R
Witness, The

CHRISTIAN EDUCATION/LIBRARY

CE Connection - R
CE Counselor - R
Church Educator - R
Leader - R
Leader/Church School Today

MISSIONS

Worldwide Challenge - R

MUSIC

Senior Musician - R

PASTORS/LEADERS

Christian Century
Diaconalogue - R
Jour/Biblical Ethics - R
Journal/Christian Healing - R
Lutheran Partners - R
Search
Single Ad. Ministries Jour.
Word & World

WOMEN

Co-Laborer - R
Link & Visitor - R
Today's Christian Woman
Virtue - R
Wesleyan Woman - R

SERMONS

ADULT/GENERAL

Baptist Beacon - R
Bible Advocate - R
Cathedral Age - R
Church Herald/Holiness - R
Cresset
Evangelical Baptist - R
God's Revivalist
Inspirer, The - R
John Milton - R

Joyful Noise
Maranatha - R
Messenger, The (NC) - R
Morning Glory - R
Pentecostal Evangel - R
Pourastan - R
Presbyterian Survey - R
Salt Shaker - R
Wine Castles

CHRISTIAN EDUCATION/LIBRARY

Church Worship
Youth Leader - R

PASTORS/LEADERS

Christian Ministry
Clergy Journal
In Season
Journal/Christian Healing - R
Lutheran Forum - R
Preacher's Illus. Service - R
Preaching
PROCLAIM - R
Pulpit Helps - R
Today's Parish

SHORT STORY: ADULT

African Amer. Heritage - R
Alive! - R
alive now! - R
Annals of St. Anne
Baptist Informer
Better Tomorrow, A
Burning Light - R
Byline
Canadian Writer's Jour - R
Catholic Forester
Chips Off Writer's Block - R
Christian Century
Christian Courier (Canada) - R
Christian Educators Journal

Christian Living - R
Christian Reader - R
Christian Renewal - R
Christian School
Christmas - R
Church Herald - R
Church Musician
Companion
Companions - R
Connecting Point - R
Conquest
Cornerstone - R
Critic, The
Daughters of Sarah - R
Emphasis/Faith & Living - R
Esprit - R
Evangel - R
Evangelical Visitor - R
Explorer
Family, The - R
Felicity - R
Friends Journal - R
God's Revivalist
Hayden Herald - R
Head to Head - R
Hearing Hearts - R
Helping Hand - R
Home Life
Home Office - R
Home Times - R
Horizons - R
Housewife-Writer's Forum - R
Ideals
Impact Magazine - R
Indian Life - R
Inklings - R
Inspirer, The - R
It's Your Choice - R
John Milton - R
Journal/Christian Healing - R
Kootenai Courier - R
Lighthouse Fiction
Liguorian

Live - R
Lookout - R
Lutheran Journal - R
Lutheran Partners - R
Lutheran Witness
Lutheran Woman Today
Maranatha - R
Mature Living
Mature Years - R
Mennonite Brethren - R
Messenger, The (NC) - R
Messenger of the Sacred Heart
Ministry Today - R
Miraculous Medal
Moody
My Legacy - R
New Trumpet - R
North American Voice
Parenting Treasures - R
Pegasus Review - R
Pentecostal Homelife - R
Plowman, The - R
Poetry Forum
Prayerworks - R
Praying
Presbyterian Record - R
Probe
Queen of all Hearts
Quest - R
Ratio
St. Anthony Messenger
St. Joseph's Messenger - R
Seek - R
Standard - R
Star of Zion
Sunday Digest - R
Thema - R
Tickled By Thunder
Today's Christian Woman
Today's Single - R
Touchstone
Upsouth - R
U.S. Catholic

Virtue - R
Vision - R
Vista - R (seniors)
Vital Christianity - R
Wesleyan Woman - R
Wherever
Women Alive! - R
Writer's Guidelines
Write Touch - R
Writing Right - R

SHORT STORY: ADVENTURE

CHILDREN
Attention Please! - R
BREAD/God's Children - R
CLUBHOUSE - R
Connecting Point - R
Counselor - R
Crusader - R
Discoveries - R
Focus/Clubhouse/Clubhouse Jr
GUIDE - R
Guideposts for Kids
Inklings - R
John Milton - R
Junior Trails - R
Lighthouse Fiction
Listen
Lollipops (young)
Power & Light - R
R-A-D-A-R - R
Shantyman, The - R
Touch - R
Venture (IL) - R
Young Crusader - R

TEEN/YOUNG ADULT
Breakaway - R
Challenge (IL)
Insight - R
Insight/Out - R

Lighthouse Fiction
John Milton - R
Magazine/Youth! - R
Teenage Christian - R
Straight - R
Student, The
Teen Life - R
Teen Life - R
Teen Quest - R
Teens Today - R
Young Adult Today
Youth World - R

ADULT
African Amer. Heritage - R
Alive! - R
Byline
Chip Off Writer's Block - R
Christian Courier (Canada) - R
Emphasis/Faith & Living - R
Evangel - R
Felicity - R
Hayden Herald - R
Home Life
Inklings - R
It's Your Choice - R
John Milton - R
Kootenai Courier - R
Lighthouse Fiction
Liguorian
Live - R
Miraculous Medal
My Legacy - R
New Trumpet - R
Pentecostal Testimony - R
Plowman, The - R
Standard - R
Thema - R
Tickled By Thunder
Vision (MO) - R
Whisper - R
Writer's Guidelines

SHORT STORY: ALLEGORY

CHILDREN
Focus/Clubhouse
GUIDE - R
Head to Head - R
Inklings - R
John Milton - R
Pockets - R
Salt Shaker - R
Touch - R

TEENS/YOUNG ADULT
Conqueror - R
Head to Head - R
I.D.
Magazine/Youth! - R
John Milton - R
Salt Shaker - R
Student Leadership - R
Teen Life - R
Youth World - R

ADULT
Burning Light - R
Chip Off Writer's Block - R
Discipleship Journal - R
Esprit - R
Evangel - R
Felicity - R
Head to Head - R
Hearing Hearts - R
Highway News - R
Home Times - R
Inklings - R
It's Your Choice - R
John Milton - R
Mennonite Brethren - R
My Legacy - R
New Thought - R
New Trumpet - R
Pentecostal Homelife - R
Pentecostal Testimony - R

Plowman, The - R
Ratio
Salt Shaker - R
Thema - R
Vision (MO) - R
Writer's Guidelines

SHORT STORY: BIBLICAL

CHILDREN
BREAD/God's Children - R
Church Educator - R
CLUBHOUSE - R
Discoveries - R
Focus/Clubhouse Jr
Gospel Tidings - R
Head to Head - R
Inklings - R
Messenger, The (NC) - R
My Friend (Christmas)
Pockets - R
Power & Light - R
Preacher's Illus. Service - R

TEEN/YOUNG ADULT
Conqueror - R
Gospel Tidings - R
Head to Head - R
Magazine/Youth! - R
Maranatha - R
Messenger, The (NC) - R
Preacher's Illus. Service - R
Student, The
Student Leadership - R
Teenage Christian - R
Teen Life - R
Young Adult Today

ADULT
Annals of St. Anne
Christian Courier (Canada) - R
Church Herald/Holiness - R
Church Worship

Connecting Point - R
Daughters of Sarah - R
Dreams & Visions
Esprit - R
Emphasis/Faith & Living - R
Evangel - R
Explorer
Five Stones, The - R
Head to Head - R
Hearing Hearts - R
Highway News - R
It's Your Choice - R
Helping Hand - R
Horizons - R
Impact Magazine - R
Inklings - R
Inspirer, The - R
Liguorian
Live - R
Lutheran Woman Today
Maranatha - R
Mature Years - R
Messenger, The (NC) - R
Ministry Today - R
Miraculous Medal
My Legacy - R
Pentecostal Homelife - R
Pentecostal Testimony - R
Plowman, The - R
Preacher's Illus. Service - R
Presbyterian Record - R
Ratio
Sharing - R
U.S. Catholic
Wesleyan Woman - R

SHORT STORY:
CONTEMPORARY

CHILDREN
BREAD/God's Children - R
Canada Lutheran - R
Focus/Clubhouse Jr

Head to Head - R
Inklings - R
Junior Trails - R
Listen
Power & Light - R
R-A-D-A-R - R
Shantyman, The - R
Story Friends - R
Touch - R

TEEN/YOUNG ADULT
BREAD/God's Children - R
Certainty
Challenge (IL)
Freeway - R
Head to Head - R
Insight - R
Insight/Out - R
Magazine/Youth! - R
Spirit
Straight - R
Teenage Christian - R
Teen Life - R
Teen Power - R
Teen Quest - R
Teens Today - R
Tradition - R

ADULT
Better Tomorrow, A
Burning Light
Byline
Canadian Lutheran - R
Chip Off Writer's Block - R
Christian Living - R
Christian Single - R
Companion
Connecting Point - R
Conquest
Cornerstone - R
Critic, The
Daughters of Sarah - R
Dreams & Visions

Esprit - R
Evangel - R
Felicity - R
Head to Head - R
Hearing Hearts - R
Highway News - R
Home Life
Housewife-Writers Forum - R
Inklings - R
Inspirer, The - R
It's Your Choice - R
Liguorian
Lookout - R
Lutheran Journal - R
Maranatha - R
Messenger/St. Anthony
Miraculous Medal
Moody
My Legacy - R
New Trumpet - R
Plowman, The - R
St. Anthony Messenger
St. Joseph's Messenger - R
Standard - R
Thema - R
Tickled By Thunder
Tradition - R
Upsouth - R
U.S. Catholic
Virtue - R
Vital Christianity - R
Writer's Guidelines

SHORT STORY: FANTASY

CHILDREN
Focus/Clubhouse
Guideposts for Kids
Inklings - R
John Milton - R
Lollipops (young)
Venture (MN)

TEEN/YOUNG ADULT
John Milton - R
Magazine/Youth! - R
Spirit
With - R
Young Adult Today
Young Salvationist - R

ADULT
Burning Light
Byline
Chip Off Writer's Block - R
Christian Courier (Canada) - R
Connecting Point - R
Cornerstone - R
Dreams & Visions
Esprit - R
Felicity - R
Housewife-Writers Forum - R
Inklings - R
It's Your Choice - R
John Milton - R
My Legacy - R
New Thought - R
New Trumpet - R
Plowman, The - R
Presbyterian Record - R
Ratio
Thema - R
Tickled By Thunder
Whisper - R
Writer's Guidelines

SHORT STORY: FRONTIER

CHILDREN
Focus/Clubhouse/Clubhouse Jr
Guideposts for Kids
High Adventure - R
Inklings - R
John Milton - R
Lighthouse Fiction
R-A-D-A-R - R

TEEN/YOUNG ADULT
Challenge (IL)
John Milton - R
Lighthouse Fiction
Magazine/Youth! - R
Teenage Christian - R

ADULT
Byline
Chip Off Writer's Block - R
Connecting Point - R
Felicity - R
Hayden Herald - R
Inklings - R
It's Your Choice - R
John Milton - R
My Legacy - R
Kootenai Courier - R
Lighthouse Fiction
Liguorian
Miraculous Medal
Plowman, The - R
Thema - R
Tickled By Thunder
Writer's Guidelines

SHORT STORY: FRONTIER/ROMANCE

Byline
Challenge (IL)
Chip Off Writer's Block - R
Connecting Point - R
Felicity - R
Inklings - R
It's Your Choice - R
Lighthouse Fiction
Miraculous Medal
My Legacy - R
Plowman, The - R
Teenage Christian - R
Writer's Guidelines

SHORT STORY: HISTORICAL

CHILDREN
BREAD/God's Children - R
CLUBHOUSE - R
Counselor - R
Focus/Clubhouse/Clubhouse Jr
Guideposts for Kids
High Adventure - R
Indian Life - R
Inklings - R
John Milton - R
Lighthouse Fiction
Messenger, The (NC) - R
My Friend
On the Line - R
R-A-D-A-R - R
Salt Shaker - R
Shantyman, The - R

TEEN/YOUNG ADULT
BREAD/God's Children - R
Challenge (IL)
Indian Life - R
John Milton - R
Lighthouse Fiction
Magazine/Youth! - R
Messenger, The (NC) - R
Salt Shaker - R
Teenage Christian - R
Teen Life - R
Tradition - R
Young Adult Today
Youth - R

ADULT
African Amer. Heritage - R
Alive! - R
Byline
Chip Off Writer's Block - R
Christian Courier (Canada) - R
Companions - R

Connecting Point - R
Conquest
Daughters of Sarah - R
Esprit - R
Explorer
Felicity - R
Hayden Herald - R
Home Times - R
Horizons - R
Housewife-Writers Forum - R
Indian Life - R
Inklings - R
It's Your Choice - R
John Milton - R
Kootenai Courier - R
Lighthouse Fiction
Liguorian
Live - R
Maranatha - R
Messenger, The (NC) - R
Miraculous Medal
My Legacy - R
New Trumpet - R
North American Voice
Plowman, The - R
Presbyterian Record - R
Ratio
Salt Shaker - R
Seek - R
Thema - R
Tickled by Thunder
Tradition - R
Upsouth - R
Wesleyan Woman - R
Writer's Guidelines

SHORT STORY:
HISTORICAL/ROMANCE

Byline
Chip Off Writer's Block - R
Connecting Point - R
Felicity - R

Inklings - R
It's Your Choice - R
Lighthouse Fiction
Liguorian
Miraculous Medal
My Legacy - R
Plowman, The - R
Teenage Christian - R
Writer's Guidelines

SHORT STORY:
HUMOROUS

CHILDREN
Attention Please! - R
Crusader - R
Focus/Clubhouse/Clubhouse Jr
GUIDE - R
Guideposts for Kids
High Adventure - R
Inklings - R
John Milton - R
Junior Trails - R
Lighthouse Fiction
Messenger, The (NC) - R
My Friend
On the Line - R
Preacher's Illus. Service - R
R-A-D-A-R - R
Salt Shaker - R
Touch - R
Venture (IL) - R
Wonder Time

TEEN/YOUNG ADULT
Breakaway - R
Brio - R
Campus Life - R
Challenge (IL)
Freeway - R
Insight - R
Insight/Out - R
John Milton - R

Lighthouse Fiction
Magazine/Youth! - R
Messenger, The (NC) - R
Preacher's Illus. Service - R
Salt Shaker - R
Student, The
Student Leadership - R
Teenage Christian - R
Teen Life - R
Teen Power - R
Teen Quest - R
Teens Today - R
Tradition - R
With - R
Young Adult Today

ADULT
African Amer. Heritage - R
Alive! - R
Better Tomorrow, A
Burning Light
Byline
Canada Lutheran - R
Catholic Forester - R
Chip Off Writer's Block - R
Christian Courier (Canada) - R
Companion
Connecting Point - R
Conquest
Dreams & Visions
Esprit - R
Evangel - R
Family, The - R
Felicity - R
Five Stones, The - R
Hayden Herald - R
Home Life
Home Times - R
Horizons - R
Housewife-Writers Forum - R
Impact - R
Inklings - R
Inspirer, The - R

It's Your Choice - R
John Milton - R
Kootenai Courier - R
Lighthouse Fiction
Live - R
Lookout - R
Lutheran Journal - R
Maranatha - R
Mature Years - R
Messenger, The (NC) - R
Miraculous Medal
My Legacy - R
New Trumpet - R
Pentecostal Homelife - R
Pentecostal Testimony - R
Plowman, The - R
Preacher's Illus. Service - R
Presbyterian Record - R
St. Joseph's Messenger - R
Salt Shaker - R
Seek - R
Standard - R
Thema - R
Tickled By Thunder
Tradition - R
Upsouth - R
Virtue - R
Vista - R (seniors)
Wesleyan Woman - R
Writer's Guidelines

SHORT STORY: JUVENILE

Attention Please! - R
BREAD/God's Children - R
Children's Church - R (6-8)
Christian Home & School
Christmas - R
Counselor - R
Crusader - R
Discoveries - R
Evangelizing Today's Child
Felicity - R

Focus/Clubhouse/Clubhouse Jr
Good News Journal - R
Gospel Tidings - R
GUIDE - R
Guideposts for Kids
Head to Head - R
High Adventure - R
Inklings - R
It's Your Choice - R
John Milton - R (8-12)
Junior Trails - R
Lighthouse Fiction
Listen (4-6)
Lollipops
Lutheran Woman Today
Magazine/Youth! - R
Messenger, The (NC) - R
My Friend
My Legacy - R
On the Line - R
Partners - R
Plowman, The
Pockets - R
Power & Light - R
Presbyterian Record - R
Primary Days - R
Primary Pal
R-A-D-A-R - R
Salt Shaker - R
Shantyman, The - R
Skipping Stones - R
Story Friends - R
Teenage Christian - R
Today's Catholic Teacher - R
Touch - R
Venture (IL) - R
Venture (MN)
Wonder Time
Write Touch
Young Crusader - R
Young Musicians

SHORT STORY: LITERARY

CHILDREN
Inklings - R
John Milton - R

TEEN/YOUNG ADULT
John Milton - R

ADULT
Burning Light - R
Byline
Chip Off Writer's Block - R
Christian Courier (Canada) - R
Christian Living - R
Compass
Conquest
Cornerstone - R
Critic, The
Daughters of Sarah - R
Dreams & Visions
Esprit - R
Felicity - R
Hayden Herald - R
Highway News - R
Home Times - R
Inklings - R
It's Your Choice - R
John Milton - R
Kootenai Courier - R
Liguorian
Live - R
Lutheran Journal - R
Mennonite Brethren Herald-R
Miraculous Medal
My Legacy - R
New Thought - R
Plowman, The - R
Ratio
Thema - R
Tickled By Thunder
Upsouth - R
Virtue - R

Writer's Guidelines

SHORT STORY: MYSTERY

CHILDREN
Attention Please! - R
BREAD/God's Children - R
CLUBHOUSE - R
Focus/Clubhouse/Clubhouse Jr
Guideposts for Kids
Inklings - R
John Milton - R
Junior Trails - R
On the Line - R
R-A-D-A-R - R
Salt Shaker - R
Touch - R
Venture (IL) - R

TEEN/YOUNG ADULT
Challenge (IL)
John Milton - R
Magazine/Youth! - R
Salt Shaker - R
Teenage Christian - R
Teen Life - R
Young Adult Today

ADULT
African Amer. Heritage - R
Burning Light - R
Byline
Chip Off Writer's Block - R
Christian Courier (Canada) - R
Connecting Point - R
Felicity - R
Housewife-Writers Forum - R
Inklings - R
It's Your Choice - R
John Milton - R
Miraculous Medal
My Legacy - R
New Trumpet - R

Plowman, The - R
Quest
Salt Shaker - R
Thema - R
Tickled By Thunder
Whisper - R
Writer's Guidelines

SHORT STORY: MYSTERY/ROMANCE

Byline
Chip Off Writer's Block - R
Christian Single - R
Connecting Point - R
Inklings - R
It's Your Choice - R
Miraculous Medal
Plowman, The - R
Standard - R
Teenage Christian - R
Writer's Guidelines

SHORT STORY: PARABLES

CHILDREN
Annals of St. Anne
CLUBHOUSE - R
Focus/Clubhouse
GUIDE - R
High Adventure - R
Indian Life - R
Inklings - R
Pockets - R
Preacher's Illus. Service - R
R-A-D-A-R - R
Salt Shaker - R
Touch - R

TEEN/YOUNG ADULT
Annals of St. Anne
Indian Life - R
Insight - R

Insight/Out - R
Magazine/Youth! - R
Preacher's Illus. Service - R
Salt Shaker - R
Straight - R
Student, The
Student Leadership - R
Teenage Christian - R
Teen Life - R
With - R
Young Adult Today

ADULT
alive now! - R
America
Annals of St. Anne
Burning Light - R
Catholic Twin Circle - R
Christian Courier (Canada) - R
Christian Living - R
Christian Single - R
Church Worship
Companion
Discovery - R
Emphasis/Faith & Living - R
Esprit - R
Evangel - R
Explorer
Five Stones, The - R
God's Revivalist
Hearing Hearts - R
Helping Hand - R
Highway News - R
Home Times - R
Horizons - R
Impact Magazine - R
Indian Life - R
Inklings - R
Inspirer, The - R
It's Your Choice - R
LA Catholic
Live - R
Lutheran

Maranatha - R
Mennonite Brethren - R
MESSAGE
Messenger/St. Anthony
Ministry Today - R
Pentecostal Testimony - R
Plowman, The - R
Preacher's Illus. Service - R
Presbyterian Record - R
Psychology for Living - R
Ratio
Response
Salt Shaker - R
Upsouth - R
U.S. Catholic
Wesleyan Woman - R
Woman's Touch - R

SHORT STORY: PLAYS

A.D. Players (book section)
Burning Light - R
Christian Drama - R
Church Worship
Creatively Yours
Esprit - R
Five Stones, The - R
Focus/Clubhouse Jr
Head to Head - R
Horizons - R
Inklings - R
It's Your Church - R
Music Leader
My Friend
Plowman, The - R
Ratio
Shining Star
Student, The
Thema - R (short)
Touch - R

SHORT STORY: ROMANCE

TEEN/YOUNG ADULT
Brio
Lighthouse Fiction
Teen Life - R
Teen Quest - R
Teens Today - R
Young Salvationist - R

ADULT
African Amer. Heritage - R
Alive! - R
Byline
Chip Off Writer's Block - R
Christian Single - R
Connecting Point - R
Helping Hand - R
Housewife-Writers Forum - R
Inklings - R
It's Your Choice - R
Lighthouse Fiction
Miraculous Medal
New Trumpet - R
Plowman, The - R
Ratio
St. Joseph's Messenger - R
Writer's Guidelines

SHORT STORY: SCIENCE FICTION

CHILDREN
Focus/Clubhouse/Clubhouse Jr
Guideposts for Kids
Inklings - R
John Milton - R

TEEN/YOUNG ADULT
Breakaway - R
John Milton - R
Magazine/Youth! - R
Teen Life - R

Teen Quest - R
Thema - R
With - R
Young Adult Today
Young Salvationist - R

ADULT
Burning Light - R
Byline
Chip Off Writer's Block - R
Christian Courier (Canada) - R
Connecting Point - R
Housewife-Writers Forum - R
Impact Magazine - R
Inklings - R
It's Your Choice - R
John Milton - R
New Trumpet - R
Plowman, The - R
Ratio
Thema - R
Tickled By Thunder
Whisper - R
Writer's Guidelines

SHORT STORY: SKITS

CHILDREN
Christian Drama - R
Head to Head - R
Inklings - R
Shining Star
Touch - R

TEEN/YOUNG ADULT
Christian Drama - R
Head to Head - R
Student Leadership - R

ADULT
Christian Drama - R
Church Worship
Esprit - R

Five Stones, The - R
Head to Head - R
Inklings - R
It's Your Choice - R
Plowman, The - R
Wesleyan Woman - R

SHORT STORY:
TEEN/YOUNG ADULT

BREAD/God's Children - R
Breakaway - R
Brio
Campus Life - R
Canada Lutheran - R
Catholic Forester - R
Certainty
Challenge (IL)
Companions - R
Conqueror - R
Evangel- R
Explorer
Freeway - R
Gospel Tidings - R
Hayden Herald - R
Head to Head - R
High Adventure - R
Insight - R
Insight/Out - R
It's Your Choice - R
John Milton - R
Kootenai Courier - R
Lighthouse Fiction
Magazine/Youth! - R
Messenger, The (NC) - R
Pentecostal Testimony - R
Plowman, The - R
Presbyterian Record - R
Quest - R
Skipping Stones - R
Spirit
Straight - R
Student, The

Student Leadership
Teenage Christian - R
Teen Life - R
Teen Life - R
Teen Power - R
Teens Today - R
Touch - R
With - R
Write Touch - R
Young Adult Today
Young Crusader - R
Young Salvationist - R
Youth World - R

SINGLES ISSUES

ADULT/GENERAL
Acts 29
American Tract Soc. - R
Aspire
At Ease - R
Biblical Reflections - R
Canadian Baptist - R
Catholic Digest - R
Charisma/Christian Life
Christian Courier (Canada) - R
Christian Event - R
Christian Living - R
Christian Parenting - R
Christian Reader - R
Christian Single - R
Christian Social Action - R
Church Herald/Holiness - R
Church of God EVANGEL
Columbia - R
Companion
Companions - R
Covenant Companion - R
Discipleship Journal - R
Emphasis/Faith & Living - R
Evangelical Baptist - R
Evangelical Friend
Expression Christian

Family, The - R
Family Journal - R
Focus on the Family
Foursquare World - R
Friends Journal - R
Good News, Etc. - R
Good News Journal - R
Good News Reporter - R
Hayden Herald - R
Hearing Hearts - R
Herald of Holiness - R
Home Times - R
John Milton - R
Kansas City Christian - R
Kootenai Courier - R
Light and Life
Liguorian
Live - R
Living - R
Lookout - R
Lutheran, The
Lutheran Digest - R
Mature Years - R
Mennonite, The - R
MESSAGE
Messenger, The (Canada) - R
Messenger, The (NC) - R
Ministry Today - R
Minnesota Christian - R
Moody
Newsline - R
New Trumpet - R
NW Christian Journal - R
PCA Messenger - R
Pentecostal Evangel - R
Pentecostal Messenger - R
Pentecostal Testimony - R
Power for Living - R
Presbyterian Record - R
Presbyterian Survey - R
Purpose - R
St. Anthony Messenger
Signs of the Times - R

Single-Parent Family
Standard - R
Urban Family
U.S. Catholic
Vista - R
Vital Christianity - R
Wesleyan Advocate - R

CHRISTIAN
EDUCATION/LIBRARY
CE Connection - R
CE Counselor - R
Leader - R
Resource - R

MISSIONS
Worldwide Challenge - R

MUSIC
Quest - R
Score - R

PASTORS/LEADERS
Church Administration
Journal/Christian Healing - R
Lutheran Partners - R
Ministries Today
Nat/Intl Religion Report
Pulpit Helps - R
Resource - R
Search
Single Ad. Ministries Jour.
Word & World

TEEN/YOUNG ADULT
Conqueror - R
YOU! - R
Young Adult Today

WOMEN
Co-Laborer - R
Joyful Woman - R
Salt and Light - R

Today's Christian Woman
Virtue - R
Wesleyan Woman - R

*SOCIAL JUSTICE

ADULT/GENERAL
Bible Advocate - R
Biblical Reflections - R
Canadian Baptist - R
Canadian Catholic
Cathedral Age - R
Catholic Sentinel - R
Christian Living - R
Christian Reader - R
Cornerstone - R
Covenant Companion - R
Cresset
Evangel - R
Faith Today
First Things
Foursquare World - R
Friends Journal - R
Hallelujah! - R
Hayden Herald - R
Head to Head - R
Home Times - R
It's Your Choice - R
Jour/Christian Nursing - R
Jour/Church & State
Kootenai Courier - R
Liguorian
Mennonite, The - R
Mennonite Brethren - R
Messenger/St. Anthony
Moody
New Trumpet - R
Pourastan - R
Praying
Purpose - R
Rural Landscapes
Social Justice - R
Upsouth - R

Urban Family
Vital Christianity - R

CHILDREN
Skipping Stones - R

PASTOR/LEADER
Jour/Biblical Ethics - R
Lutheran Partners - R

SOCIOLOGY

ADULT/GENERAL
Anglican Journal - R
Biblical Reflections - R
Catholic Digest - R
Christian Courier (Canada) - R
Compass
Critic, The
Evangelical Friend
Faith Today
Friends Journal - R
Herald of Holiness - R
It's Your Choice - R
John Milton - R
Jour/Church & State
Lutheran Journal - R
Moody
New Oxford Review
Quiet Revolution - R
Rural Landscapes
SCP Journal - R
Seek - R
Social Justice - R
Star of Zion
Upsouth - R
Vista - R
Vital Christianity - R
Witness, The

CHRISTIAN
EDUCATION/LIBRARY
CE Connection - R

Church Educator - R
Today's Catholic Teacher - R

MISSIONS
Areopagus - R
Urban Mission - R

MUSIC
Score - R

PASTORS/LEADERS
Christian Century
Christian Ministry
Eucharistic Minister - R
Five Stones, The - R
Group's Jr High
Jour/Biblical Ethics - R
Journal/Christian Healing - R
Lutheran Partners - R
Nat/Intl Religion Report
Single Ad. Ministries Jour.
Word & World

TEEN/YOUNG ADULT
Teen Life - R
Young Adult Today

WOMEN
Daughters of Sarah - R
Virtue - R
Wesleyan Woman - R

WRITERS
Inklings - R

SPIRITUALITY

ADULT/GENERAL
Acts 2
alive now! - R
American Tract Soc. - R
Annals of St. Anne
At Ease - R

Baptist Beacon - R
Bible Advocate - R
Bible Today
Biblical Reflections - R
Canada Lutheran - R
Canadian Catholic
Catholic Digest - R
Catholic Exponent
Catholic Parent
Christian Chronicle
Christian Event - R
Christian Home & School
Christian Living - R
Christian Reader - R
Christian Single - R
Christianity Today - R
Church Herald/Holiness - R
Church of God EVANGEL
Columbia - R
Common Boundary
Commonweal
Companion
Companions - R
Compass
Covenant Companion - R
Cresset
Discipleship Journal - R
Door, The - R
Dovetail - R
Emphasis/Faith & Living - R
Evangel - R
Evangelical Beacon - R
Episcopal Life - R
Evangelical Baptist - R
Evangelical Friend
Faith Today
Family Digest, The - R
Fellowship Today - R
First Things
Friends Journal - R
God's Revivalist
Good News Journal - R
Guideposts

Hearing Hearts - R
Herald of Holiness - R
Highway News - R
John Milton - R
Jour/Christian Nursing - R
Liguorian
Living - R
Living Church
Lookout - R
Lutheran, The
Lutheran Digest - R
Maranatha - R
Mature Years - R
Mennonite, The - R
Mennonite Brethren - R
MESSAGE
Messenger, The (Canada) - R
Messenger, The (NC) - R
Messenger/St. Anthony
Ministry Today - R
Morning Glory - R
New Covenant - R
New Oxford Review
Newsline - R
New Thought - R
New Trumpet - R
North American Voice
Our Family - R
Our Sunday Visitor
Parenting Treasures - R
Pegasus Review - R
Pentecostal Evangel - R
Pentecostal Homelife - R
Pentecostal Messenger - R
Praying
Presbyterian Outlook
Presbyterian Record - R
Presbyterian Survey - R
Purpose - R
Puzzler's Digest - R
Queen of All Hearts
Religious Education
Rural Landscapes

St. Anthony Messenger
St. Willibrord Journal
SCP Journal - R
Sharing - R
Signs of the Times - R
Social Justice - R
Spiritual Life
Standard - R
Table Talk
United Church Observer
Upsouth - R
U.S. Catholic
Vision (MO) - R
Vista - R
Vital Christianity
Wesleyan Advocate - R
Witness, The

CHILDREN
Focus/Clubhouse
GUIDE - R
Skipping Stones - R
Wonder Time

CHRISTIAN
EDUCATION/LIBRARY
Brigade Leader - R
CE Connection - R
Christian School
Church Educator - R
Church Worship
Leader - R
Lutheran Education
Religion Teacher's Journal
Resource - R
Vision - R
Youth & CE Leadership - R
Youth Leader - R

MISSIONS
Areopagus - R
Message of the Cross - R
World Vision - R

Worldwide Challenge - R

MUSIC
Quest - R
Score - R

PASTORS/LEADERS
Chicago Studies
Christian Century
Christian Ministry
Cross Currents - R
Diaconalogue - R
Eucharistic Minister - R
Five Stones, The - R
Homiletic & Pastoral Review
Jour/Biblical Ethics - R
Journal/Christian Healing - R
Lutheran Partners - R
Ministries Today
Preacher's Illus. Service - R
Priest, The
PROCLAIM - R
Pulpit Helps - R
Review for Religious
Search
Today's Parish
Word & World
Youthworker - R

TEEN/YOUNG ADULT
Conqueror - R
Insight - R
Kiln, The - R
Magazine/Youth! - R
Student, The
Student Leadership - R
Teenage Christian - R
Teen Life - R
With - R
YOU! - R
Young Adult Today
Young Salvationist - R
Youth Update

WOMEN
Daughters of Sarah - R
Esprit - R
Horizons - R
Journey - R
Joyful Woman - R
Lutheran Woman Today
Response
Sisters Today - R
Virtue - R
Wesleyan Woman - R
Women Alive! - R

WRITERS
Inklings - R

SPORTS

ADULT/GENERAL
American Tract Soc. - R
Aspire
AXIOS - R
Better Tomorrow, A
Christian Courier (WI) - R
Christian Courier (Canada) -R
Christian Event - R
Christian Single - R
Columbia - R
Connecting Point - R
   (Special Olympics)
Expression Christian
Good News, Etc - R
Good News Reporter - R
Hayden Herald - R
Hearing Hearts - R
Home Times - R
Indian Life - R
John Milton - R (for blind)
Kansas City Christian - R
Kootenai Courier - R
Lifeglow - R
Live - R
Lutheran Layman

Lutheran Witness
Messenger, The (NC) - R
Minnesota Christian - R
New Trumpet - R
NW Christian Journal - R
Parents of Teenagers - R
PCA Messenger - R
Power for Living - R
Sports Spectrum

CHILDREN
Counselor - R
Crusader - R
Focus/Clubhouse
GUIDE - R
High Adventure - R
On the Line - R
Primary Days - R
R-A-D-A-R - R
Touch - R
Venture (IL) - R

CHRISTIAN
EDUCATION/LIBRARY
Christian School

MISSIONS
Worldwide Challenge - R

MUSIC
Quest - R

PASTORS/LEADERS
Nat/Intl Religion Report
Preacher's Illus. Service - R

TEEN/YOUNG ADULT
Breakaway - R
Certainty
Challenge (IL)
Challenge (TN)
Edge, The - R
Freeway - R

Insight - R
Insight/Out - R
Issues & Answers - R
Magazine/Youth! - R
Pioneer - R
Sharing the VICTORY - R
Straight - R
Teenage Christian - R
Teen Life - R
Teen Power - R
Teen Quest - R
With - R
YOU! - R
Young Adult Today
Young & Alive - R
Young Salvationist - R

WOMEN
Esprit - R
Virtue - R

*STEWARDSHIP

ADULT/GENERAL
Advocate - R
Bible Advocate - R
Biblical Reflections - R
Canadian Baptist - R
Canadian Catholic
Catholic Forester - R
Christian Event - R
Christian Living - R
Church of God EVANGEL
Companions - R
Evangel - R
Hearing Hearts - R
Highway News - R
Liguorian
Living Church
Mennonite, The - R
Mennonite Brethren - R
Message/Open Bible
Moody

New Trumpet - R
Pentecostal Testimony - R
Praying
Rural Landscapes
Sunday Digest - R
Upsouth - R
U.S. Catholic

CHILDREN
R-A-D-A-R - R

CHRISTIAN
EDUCATION/LIBRARY
Brigade Leader - R
Church Educator - R
Leader - R
MUSIC
Score - R

PASTORS/LEADERS
Jour/Biblical Ethics - R
Lutheran Partners - R
Preacher's Magazine - R
Resource - R
Your Church - R

TEENS/YOUNG ADULTS
Teen Life - R
With - R

WOMEN
Esprit - R
Wesleyan Woman - R

*TAKE-HOME PAPERS

ADULT/GENERAL
Companions - R
Conquest
Evangel - R
Gem, The - R
Live - R
Lookout, The - R

Power for Living - R
Seek - R
Standard - R
Sunday Digest - R
Vision - R
Vista - R

CHILDREN
Counselor - R
Discoveries - R
Good News for Children
Junior Trails - R
On the Line - R
Our Little Friend - R
Partners
Power & Light - R
Primary Days - R
Primary Pal
Primary Treasure
Promise
R-A-D-A-R - R
Story Friends - R
Story Mates - R
Together Time - R
Venture (MN)

TEEN/YOUNG ADULT
Certainty
Challenge (IL)
Cross Walk
Freeway - R
Gem, The - R
Pathway I.D. - R
Straight - R
Teen Life (AG) - R
Teen Life (MO)- R
Teen Power - R
Visions
Youth World - R

THEOLOGICAL

ADULT/GENERAL
Acts 29
AGAIN - R
America
Anglican Journal - R
Annals of St. Anne
At Ease - R
Baptist Beacon - R
Baptist Informer
B.C. Catholic - R
Bible Advocate - R
Biblical Reflections - R
Canadian Catholic
Catholic Digest - R
Catholic Twin Circle - R
Charisma/Christian Life
Christian Renewal - R
Christian Research
Christian Social Action - R
Christianity Today - R
Church Herald - R
Church Herald/Holiness - R
Columbia - R
Commonweal
Companion
Companions - R
Compass
Conquest
Cornerstone - R
Critic, The
Emphasis/Faith & Living - R
Episcopal Life - R
Evangelical Baptist - R
Evangelical Friend
Evangelical Visitor - R
First Things
Good News - R
Hallelujah! - R
Hearing Hearts - R
Interim - R
John Milton - R

Jour/Church & State
Liguorian
Living Church
Lutheran, The
Lutheran Digest - R
Lutheran Layman
Maranatha - R
Mature Years - R
MESSAGE
MESSAGE/Open Bible - R
Messenger, The (NC) - R
Messenger/St. Anthony
Ministry Today - R
New Oxford Review
New Thought - R
North American Voice
Our Family - R
Our Sunday Visitor
Pentecostal Evangel - R
Plowman, The - R
Presbyterian Outlook
Presbyterian Record - R
Presbyterian Survey - R
Queen of All Hearts
Ratio
Religious Education
Rural Landscapes
St. Willibrord Journal
Salt Shaker - R
SCP Journal - R
Silver Wings - R
Social Justice - R
Spiritual Life
United Church Observer
Upsouth - R
U.S. Catholic
Voice, The - R
Witness, The

CHRISTIAN
EDUCATION/LIBRARY
CE Connection - R
Church Educator - R

Church Worship
Journal/Adventist Educ. - R
Lutheran Education
Resource - R
Today's Catholic Teacher - R
Youth Leader - R

MISSIONS
Areopagus - R
Urban Mission - R
Worldwide Challenge - R

MUSIC
Score - R

PASTORS/LEADERS
Catechumenate
Chicago Studies
Christian Century
Christian Ministry
Cross Currents - R
Eucharistic Minister - R
Five Stones, The - R
Homiletic & Pastoral Review
Jour/Biblical Ethics - R
Journal/Christian Healing - R
Lutheran Forum - R
Lutheran Partners - R
Ministries Today
Nat/Intl Religion Report
Networks - R
Preacher's Illus. Service - R
Preacher's Magazine - R
Priest, The
PROCLAIM - R
Pulpit Helps - R
Quarterly Review
Review for Religious
Search
Theology Today
Today's Parish
Word & World
Youthworker - R

TEEN/YOUNG ADULT
Student, The
Teen Life - R
Young Adult Today
Youth Update

WOMEN
Conscience - R
Daughters of Sarah - R
Esprit - R
Horizons - R
Jour/Women's Ministries
Lutheran Woman Today
Sisters Today - R
Virtue - R
Wesleyan Woman - R
Woman's Touch - R

WRITERS
Inklings - R
Writer's Forum - R

THINK PIECES

ADULT/GENERAL
American Tract Soc. - R
Annals of St. Anne
Aspire
AXIOS - R
Bible Advocate - R
Biblical Reflections - R
Canada Lutheran - R
Canadian Catholic
Catholic Digest - R
Catholic Forester - R
Catholic Twin Circle - R
Christian C.L. RECORD - R
Christian Courier (Canada) - R
Christian Edge - R
Christian Event - R
Christian Reader - R
Christian Retailing - R
Christianity Today - R

Church Herald - R
Commonweal
Companion
Compass
Door, The - R
Episcopal Life - R
Evangel - R
Evangelical Baptist - R
Evangelical Friend
Evangelical Visitor - R
Explorer
Family Journal - R
First Things
Good News, Etc - R
Hayden Herald - R
Head to Head - R
Hearing Hearts - R
Herald of Holiness - R
Home Times - R
Inspirer, The - R
John Milton - R
Jour/Christian Nursing - R
Kansas City Christian - R
Kootenai Courier - R
Liguorian
Lookout - R
Lutheran, The
Lutheran Digest - R
Lutheran Journal - R
Maranatha - R
Mature Years - R
MESSAGE/Open Bible - R
Messenger, The (NC) - R
Minnesota Christian - R
New Oxford Review
New Thought - R
New Trumpet - R
PCA Messenger - R
Pegasus Review - R
Pentecostal Homelife - R
Pentecostal Messenger - R
Prayerworks - R
Praying

Presbyterian Record - R
Presbyterian Survey - R
Purpose - R
Puzzler's Digest - R
Ratio
Religious Education
Rural Landscapes
Seek - R
Vista - R
Vital Christianity - R
Voice, The - R
Wesleyan Advocate - R

CHILDREN
CLUBHOUSE - R
Guideposts for Kids
R-A-D-A-R - R
Skipping Stones - R

CHRISTIAN
EDUCATION/LIBRARY
CE Connection - R
Changing Lives
Lutheran Education
Resource - R
Vision - R

MISSIONS
Areopagus - R
Catholic Near East
World Vision - R

MUSIC
Quest - R
Tradition - R

PASTORS/LEADERS
Christian Century
Eucharistic Minister - R
Jour/Biblical Ethics - R
Journal/Christian Healing - R
Lutheran Partners - R
Ministries Today

Networks - R
Priest, The
Word & World

TEEN/YOUNG ADULT
Conqueror - R
Freeway - R
Insight - R
Insight/Out - R
Kiln, The - R
Magazine/Youth! - R
Teenage Christian - R
Teen Life - R
Teen Quest - R
Vision - R
YOU! - R
Young Adult Today

WOMEN
Anna's Journal - R
Esprit - R
Horizons - R
Journey - R
Link & Visitor - R
Lutheran Woman Today
Virtue - R
Wesleyan Woman - R
Woman's Touch - R

WRITERS
Exchange
Inklings - R
Writers Anchor - R
Writer's Forum - R

TRAVEL

ADULT/GENERAL
African Amer. Heritage - R
Alive! - R
Aspire
Better Tomorrow, A
Catholic Digest - R

Catholic Twin Circle - R
Christian Courier (Canada) - R
Christian Single - R
Class
Columbia - R
Companion
Explorer
Family Digest, The - R
Hayden Herald - R
Home Times - R
John Milton - R
Joyful Noise
Kootenai Courier - R
Living - R
Lookout - R
Lutheran Layman
Mature I iving
Mature Years - R
New Trumpet - R
ParentLife - R
Pentecostal Homelife - R
Puzzler's Digest - R
Seek - R
Smart Dads
Star of Zion
Sunday Digest - R
Upsouth - R

CHILDREN
Skipping Stones - R

MISSIONS
Areopagus - R
Childlife - R

MUSIC
Score - R

PASTORS/LEADERS
Preacher's Illus. Service - R

TEEN/YOUNG ADULT
Conqueror - R

Teenage Christian - R
Young Adult Today
Young & Alive - R
Youth Focus - R

WOMEN
Virtue - R
Wesleyan Woman - R

TRUE STORIES

ADULT/GENERAL
Acts 29
ADVOCATE - R
AGAIN - R
Annals of St. Anne
Aspire
At Ease - R
Baptist Beacon - R
Canada Lutheran - R
Catholic Digest - R
Catholic Twin Circle - R
Charisma/Christian Life
Christian Edge - R
Christian Event - R
Christian Living - R
Christian Parenting - R
Christian Reader - R
Church Herald/Holiness - R
Companion
Conquest
Crossway/Newsline
Emphasis/Faith & Living - R
Evangel - R
Evangelical Friend
Evangelical Visitor - R
Family, The - R
Foursquare World - R
Gem, The - R
God's Revivalist
Good News, Etc - R
Good News Journal
Good News Reporter - R

Guideposts
Head to Head - R
Hearing Hearts - R
Herald of Holiness - R
Highway News - R
Home Times - R
Impact Magazine - R
Indian Life - R
Inspirer, The - R
InterVarsity
It's Your Choice - R
John Milton - R
Jour/Christian Nursing - R
Kansas City Christian - R
Lifeglow - R
Light and Life
Liguorian
Live - R
Living - R
Lookout - R
Lutheran, The
Lutheran Digest - R
Lutheran Journal - R
Lutheran Layman
Lutheran Witness
Maranatha - R
Mennonite, The - R
MESSAGE
MESSAGE/Open Bible - R
Messenger, The (NC) - R
Ministry Today - R
Minnesota Christian - R
Moody
Morning Glory - R
New Heart, A - R
New Trumpet - R
Our Family - R
Parenting Treasures - R
Pentecostal Evangel - R
Pentecostal Homelife - R
Pentecostal Messenger - R
Pentecostal Testimony - R
Plus - R

Power for Living - R
Prayerworks - R
Praying
Presbyterian Record - R
Professional Parents - R
Pursuit - R
Puzzler's Digest - R
Quiet Revolution - R
Salt Shaker - R
SCP Journal - R
Seek - R
Sharing - R
Signs of the Times - R
Standard - R
Together - R
Upsouth - R
Vision (MO) - R
Vista - R
Vital Christianity - R
Wesleyan Advocate - R
Wine Castles

CHILDREN
CLUBHOUSE - R
Counselor - R
Crusader - R
Focus/Clubhouse/Clubhouse Jr
GUIDE - R
High Adventure - R
Junior Trails - R
Listen
Mission
Nature Friend - R
On the Line - R
Our Little Friend - R
Partners - R
Primary Days - R
Primary Treasure - R
R-A-D-A-R - R
Skipping Stones - R
Touch - R
Young Crusader - R (family)

CHRISTIAN EDUCATION/LIBRARY
CE Connection - R
Changing Lives
Church Media Library - R
Lutheran Education
Perspective - R
Resource - R
Shining Star
Teacher Interaction - R
Youth Leader - R

MISSIONS
American Horizon - R
Areopagus - R
Childlife
Heartbeat - R
Urban Mission - R
World Christian - R
World Vision - R
Worldwide Challenge - R

MUSIC
Quest - R
Score - R

PASTORS/LEADERS
Eucharistic Minister - R
Five Stones, The - R
Networks - R
Preacher's Illus. Service - R

TEEN/YOUNG ADULT
Certainty
Challenge (IL)
Conqueror - R
Freeway - R
Insight - R
Insight/Out - R
Kiln, The - R
Magazine/Youth! - R
Pioneer - R
Straight - R

Teenage Christian - R
Teen Life - R
Teen Life - R
Teen Power - R
With - R
Young Adult Today
Young & Alive - R
Young Salvationist - R
Youth World - R

WOMEN
Anna's Journal - R
Helping Hand - R
Journey - R
Joyful Woman - R
Link & Visitor - R
Lutheran Woman Today
Today's Christian Woman
Virtue - R
Wesleyan Woman - R
Woman's Touch - R

WRITERS
Writers Anchor - R
Writer's Nook News

WITNESSING

ADULT/GENERAL
Acts 29
ADVOCATE - R
American Tract Soc. - R
Annals of St. Anne
At Ease - R
Baptist Beacon - R
Bible Advocate - R
Canada Lutheran - R
Canadian Baptist - R
Canadian Catholic
Catholic Digest - R
Charisma/Christian Life
Christian Event - R
Christian Information

Christian Research
Christian Social Action - R
Church Herald/Holiness - R
Church of God EVANGEL
Companion
Companions - R
Conquest
Crossway/Newsline
Decision
Discipleship Journal - R
Emphasis/Faith & Living - R
Evangelical Friend
Evangelical Baptist - R
Evangelical Visitor - R
God's Revivalist
Good News, Etc - R
Good News Journal - R
Good News Reporter - R
Hallelujah! - R
Hearing Hearts - R
Herald of Holiness - R
Highway News - R
Indian Life - R
InterVarsity
John Milton - R
Jour/Christian Nursing - R
Light and Life
Liguorian
Live - R
Lutheran Layman
Lutheran Witness
Maranatha - R
MESSAGE/Open Bible - R
Messenger, The (NC) - R
Ministry Today - R
Moody
Morning Glory - R
New Covenant - R
New Heart, A - R
New Oxford Review
New Trumpet - R
Our Family - R
Pentecostal Evangel - R

Pentecostal Messenger - R
Power for Living - R
Praying
Presbyterian Survey - R
Purpose - R
SCP Journal - R
Seek - R
Standard - R
Sunday Digest - R
Upsouth - R
Vision - R
Vista - R
Vital Christianity - R
Wesleyan Advocate - R

CHILDREN
Counselor - R
GUIDE - R
Primary Days - R
R-A-D-A-R - R
Touch - R

CHRISTIAN
EDUCATION/LIBRARY
CE Connection - R
Changing Lives
Church Media Library - R
Evangelizing Today's Child
Insight
Journal/Adventist Educ. - R
Lutheran Education
Resource - R
Shining Star
Youth & CE Leadership - R
Youth Leader - R

MISSIONS
American Horizon - R
IMPACT
Message of the Cross - R
Mission Frontier - R
Urban Mission - R
World Christian - R

Worldwide Challenge - R

MUSIC
Quest - R
Score - R

PASTORS/LEADERS
Advance - R
Church Administration
Discipleship Training
Eucharistic Minister - R
Evangelism - R
Journal/Christian Healing - R
Lutheran Partners - R
Ministries Today
Nat/Intl Religion Report
Networks - R
PROCLAIM - R
Pulpit Helps - R

TEEN/YOUNG ADULT
Certainty
Challenge (IL)
Conqueror - R
Freeway - R
Insight - R
Magazine/Youth! - R
Straight - R
Student, The
Teenage Christian - R
Teen Life - R
Teen Power - R
Teen Quest - R
YOU! - R
Young Adult Today
Young Salvationist - R

WOMEN
Co-Laborer - R
Esprit - R
Joyful Woman - R
Lutheran Woman Today
Salt and Light - R

Sisters Today - R
Virtue - R
Wesleyan Woman - R
Woman's Touch - R

WOMEN'S ISSUES

ADULT/GENERAL
Advent Christian Witness
Anglican Journal - R
Annals of St. Anne
Aspire
At Ease - R
Canada Lutheran - R
Canadian Baptist - R
Canadian Catholic
Cathedral Age - R
Catholic Digest - R
Catholic Exponent
Catholic Parent
Catholic Twin Circle - R
Celebrate Life - R
Charisma/Christian Life
Christian C.L. RECORD - R
Christian Courier (Canada) - R
Christian Edge - R
Christian Event - R
Christian Living - R
Christian Reader - R
Christian Single - R
Christian Social Action - R
Church of God EVANGEL
Columbia - R
Companion
Compass
Covenant Companion - R
Critic, The
Emphasis/Faith & Living - R
Episcopal Life - R
Evangelical Baptist - R
Evangelical Friend
Expression Christian
Focus on the Family

Foursquare World - R
Friends Journal - R
Good News, Etc - R
Good News Journal - R
Good News Reporter - R
Gospel Tidings - R
Hayden Herald - R
Hearing Hearts - R
Herald of Holiness - R
Highway News - R
Home Life
Home Times - R
Interim - R
It's Your Choice - R
John Milton - R
Jour/Christian Nursing - R
Joyful Noise
Kansas City Christian - R
Kootenai Courier - R
Light and Life
Liguorian
Live - R
Living - R
Lookout - R
Lutheran, The
Mature Years - R
Mennonite, The - R
MESSAGE
Messenger, The (NC) - R
Ministry Today - R
Minnesota Christian - R
Moody
Newsline - R
New Trumpet - R
Our Sunday Visitor
Pentecostal Evangel - R
Pentecostal Messenger - R
Plus - R
Power for Living - R
Prairie Messenger (church)
Praying
Presbyterian Outlook
Presbyterian Survey - R

Prism - R
Professional Parents - R
Progress - R
Purpose - R
Puzzler's Digest - R
Rural Landscapes
St. Joseph's Messenger - R
Salt
Signs of the Times - R
Standard - R
Sunday Digest - R
Total Health
Today's Better Life
United Church Observer
Upsouth - R
Urban Family
Vista - R
Vital Christianity - R
Witness, The

CHRISTIAN
EDUCATION/LIBRARY
Leader - R
Resource - R

MISSIONS
American Horizon - R
New World Outlook
Urban Mission - R
World Vision - R
Worldwide Challenge - R

PASTORS/LEADERS
Bethany Choice - R
Christian Century
Diaconalogue - R
Journal/Christian Healing - R
Lutheran Partners - R
Ministries Today (little)
Nat/Intl Religion Report
Single Ad. Ministries Jour.
Youthworker - R
Word & World

TEEN/YOUNG ADULT
Brio
Vision - R
Young Adult Today

WOMEN
(See alphabetical listing)

WRITERS
Housewife-Writer's Forum - R

WORLD ISSUES

ADULT/GENERAL
Alive!
America
Annals of St. Anne
Aspire
At Ease - R
AXIOS - R
Baptist Informer
Bible Advocate - R
Biblical Reflections - R
Canada Lutheran - R
Canadian Catholic
Catholic Twin Circle - R
Charisma/Christian Life
Christian Courier (Canada) - R
Christian Crusade
Christian Living - R
Christian Reader - R
Christian Single - R
Christian Social Action - R
Church Herald/Holiness - R
Columbia - R
Companion
Compass
Cresset
Critic, The
Emphasis/Faith & Living - R
Evangelical Baptist - R
Evangelical Friend
Evangelical Visitor - R

Expression Christian
First Things
Friends Journal - R
God's Revivalist
Good News, Etc. - R
Gotta Write
Hallelujah! - R
Home Times - R
Interchange
InterVarsity
John Milton - R
Kansas City Christian - R
Liberty - R
Lookout - R
Lutheran, The
Lutheran Layman
MESSAGE
MESSAGE/Open Bible - R
Messenger (KY)
Messenger, The (NC) - R
Messenger/St. Anthony
Ministry Today - R
Minnesota Christian - R
Moody
Morning Glory - R
News Network Intl.
New Trumpet - R
Our Sunday Visitor
PCA Messenger - R
Pentecostal Evangel - R
Pentecostal Messenger - R
Power for Living - R
Praying
Presbyterian Outlook
Presbyterian Record - R
Presbyterian Survey - R
Prism - R
Quiet Revolution - R
St. Anthony Messenger
SCP Journal - R
Social Justice - R
United Church Observer
Upsouth - R

Urban Family
Vision (MO) - R
Vital Christianity - R
Witness, The

CHILDREN
Counselor - R
God's World Today
R-A-D-A-R - R
Skipping Stones - R

MISSIONS
Areopagus - R
Catholic Near East
Childlife
Compassion
IMPACT
New World Outlook
P.I.M.E. World - R
Urban Mission - R
World Christian - R
World Vision - R
Worldwide Challenge - R

PASTORS/LEADERS
Christian Century
Lutheran Partners - R
Nat/Intl Religion Report
Networks - R
Preacher's Illus. Service - R
Preacher's Magazine - R
Word & World
Youthworker - R

TEEN/YOUNG ADULT
Challenge
Conqueror - R
Insight - R
Insight/Out - R
Issues & Answers - R
Magazine/Youth! - R
Student, The
Student Leadership - R

Teenage Christian - R
Teen Life - R
Young Adult Today

WOMEN
Contempo
Daughters of Sarah - R
Esprit - R
Helping Hand - R
Horizons - R
Link & Visitor - R
Lutheran Woman Today
Response
Royal Service
Sisters Today - R
Virtue - R
Wesleyan Woman - R
Woman's Touch - R

WORSHIP

ADULT/GENERAL
Acts 29
ADVOCATE - R
alive now! - R
Annals of St. Anne
At Ease - R
Baptist Beacon - R
Baptist Informer
Bible Advocate - R
Canada Lutheran - R
Canadian Baptist - R
Canadian Catholic
Cathedral Age - R
Catholic Digest - R
Charisma/Christian Life
Christian Event - R
Christian Living - R
Church Herald/Holiness - R
Companion
Companions - R
Covenant Companion - R
Cresset

Decision
Discipleship Journal - R
Emphasis/Faith & Living - R
Evangel - R
Evangelical Baptist - R
Evangelical Beacon - R
Evangelical Friend
Evangelical Visitor - R
Faith Today
Fellowship Today - R
Foursquare World - R
Friends Journal - R
Good News - R
Good News, Etc - R
Good News Journal - R
Hearing Hearts - R
Herald of Holiness - R
Highway News - R
Inspirer, The - R
John Milton - R
Joyful Noise
Liguorian
Living Church
Lookout - R
Lutheran, The
Maranatha - R
Mature Years - R
Mennonite, The - R
Mennonite Reporter
MESSAGE
Messenger, The (Canada) - R
Messenger, The (NC) - R
Ministry Today - R
Moody
Morning Glory - R
New Trumpet - R
North American Voice
NW Christian Journal - R
Our Family - R
Our Sunday Visitor
Pentecostal Evangel - R
Pentecostal Homelife - R
Pentecostal Messenger - R

Pentecostal Testimony - R
Plenty Good Room
Pourastan - R
Prayerworks - R
Praying
Presbyterian Outlook
Presbyterian Record - R
Presbyterian Survey - R
St. Willibrord Journal
Salt Shaker - R
Seek - R
Silver Wings - R
Sunday Digest - R
United Church Observer
Upsouth - R
U.S. Catholic
Vista - R
Vital Christianity - R
Wesleyan Advocate - R

CHILDREN
BREAD/God's Children - R
R-A-D-A-R - R
Wonder Time

CHRISTIAN
EDUCATION/LIBRARY
CE Connection - R
Changing Lives
Christian Ed Journal - R
Church Educator - R
Church Media Library - R
Church Worship
Journal/Adventist Educ. - R
Leader - R
Lutheran Education
Resource - R
Shining Star
Youth & CE Leadership - R
Youth Leader - R

MISSIONS
American Horizon - R

Areopagus - R
Catholic Near East
IMPACT
Worldwide Challenge - R

MUSIC
Church Pianist, etc.
Creator
Glory Songs - R
Hymn, The - R

PASTORS/LEADERS
Advance - R
Chicago Studies
Christian Management - R
Clergy Journal
Environment & Art
Five Stones, The - R
Journal/Christian Healing - R
Leadership Journal - R
Liturgy
Lutheran Forum - R
Lutheran Partners - R
Ministries Today
Networks - R
Preacher's Illus. Service - R
Preacher's Magazine - R
Priest, The
PROCLAIM - R
Pulpit Helps - R
Reformed Worship - R
Review for Religious
Search
Today's Parish
Word & World
Worship Leader
Youthworker - R

TEEN/YOUNG ADULT
Conqueror - R
Freeway - R
Insight - R
Pathway I.D. - R

Straight - R
Teenage Christian - R
Teen Life - R
Teen Power - R
Student Leadership - R
Young Adult Today
Young Salvationist - R
Youth Update

WOMEN
Daughters of Sarah - R
Horizons - R
Joyful Woman - R
Lutheran Woman Today
Sisters Today - R
Today's Christian Woman
Virtue - R
Wesleyan Woman - R

YOUTH ISSUES

ADULT/GENERAL
Acts 29
American Tract Soc. - R
Annals of St. Anne
AXIOS - R
Canada Lutheran - R
Canadian Baptist - R
Canadian Catholic
Cathedral Age - R
Catholic Digest - R
Catholic Exponent
Catholic Forester - R
Christian Courier (Canada) - R
Christian Edge - R
Christian Event - R
Christian Social Action - R
Church Herald/Holiness - R
Columbia - R
Companion
Companions - R
Covenant Companion - R
Decision

Emphasis/Faith & Living - R
Evangelical Baptist - R
Evangelical Friend
Expression Christian
Family, The - R
Focus on the Family
Foursquare World - R
Good News, Etc - R
Good News Journal - R
Good News Reporter - R
Gospel Tidings - R
Hearing Hearts - R
Herald of Holiness - R
Home Times - R
It's Your Choice - R
John Milton - R
Kansas City Christian - R
Light and Life
Living - R
Living Church
Lutheran, The
Lutheran Digest - R
Maranatha - R
Mennonite, The - R
Mennonite Brethren - R
MESSAGE
Messenger, The (Canada) - R
Messenger, The (NC) - R
Ministry Today - R
New Oxford Review
Our Family - R
PCA Messenger - R
Pentecostal Evangel - R
Pentecostal Messenger - R
Pentecostal Testimony - R
Pourastan - R
Praying
Presbyterian Outlook
Presbyterian Record - R
Presbyterian Survey - R
Religious Education
Rural Landscapes
Smart Dads

United Church Observer
Urban Family
U.S. Catholic
Vital Christianity - R
Witness, The

CHILDREN
BREAD/God's Children - R
CLUBHOUSE - R
Crusader - R
Focus/Clubhouse/Clubhouse Jr
GUIDE - R
Guideposts for Kids
High Adventure - R
Power & Light - R
R-A-D-A-R - R
Skipping Stones - R
Touch - R
Venture (IL) - R
Young Crusader - R

CHRISTIAN EDUCATION/LIBRARY
CE Connection - R
CE Counselor - R
Changing Lives
Church Educator - R
GROUP
Journal/Adventist Educ. - R
KEY - R
Leader - R
Leader/Church School Today
Lutheran Education
Parish Teacher - R
Perspective - R
Religion Teacher's Journal
Resource - R
Team - R
Vision - R
Youth & CE Leadership - R
Youth Leader - R

MISSIONS
American Horizon - R
New World Outlook
Worldwide Challenge - R

MUSIC
Quest - R
Score - R

PASTORS/LEADERS
Bethany Choice - R

Five Stones, The - R
Group's Jr High
Ivy Jungle Report - R
Journal/Christian Healing
Lutheran Partners - R
Ministries Today
Nat/Intl Religion Report
Pulpit Helps - R
Search
Word & World
YMR Today

Youthworker - R

TEEN/YOUNG ADULT
(See alphabetical listing)

WOMEN
Virtue - R
Wesleyan Woman - R

ALPHABETICAL LISTINGS OF PERIODICALS

Following are the listings of periodicals. They are arranged alphabetically by type of periodical (see Table of Contents for a list of types). Nonpaying markets are indicated in bold letters within those listings, e.g. **NO PAYMENT**.

If a listing is preceded by an asterisk (*), it indicates that publisher did not send updated information. If it is preceded by a number symbol (#) it was updated from available sources or by phone. If it is preceded by a (+) it is a new listing. It is important that freelance writers request writer's guidelines and a recent sample copy before submitting to any of these publications, but especially to those with the * and # symbols.

If you do not find the publication you are looking for, check the supplementary listings following this section for those periodicals that have ceased publication, changed names, or are not open to freelance submissions.

For a detailed explanation of how to understand and get the most out of these listings, as well as solid marketing tips, see the "How to Use This Book" section at the front of the book. Unfamiliar terms are explained in the Glossary at the back of the book.

(*) An asterisk before a listing indicates no or unconfirmed information update.
(#) A number symbol before a listing means it was updated from their current writer's guidelines or other sources.
(+) A plus sign means it is a new listing.

ADULT/GENERAL MARKETS

*ACTS 29, P.O. Box 4237, Evergreen CO 80439-3745. (303)674-9744. Fax: (303)674-9709. Episcopal Renewal Ministries. Tom Beckwith, ed. To report, support, and encourage parish renewal within the Anglican community and as a forum for apostolic teaching. Bimonthly mag; circ 55,000. Free subscription. 50% freelance. Complete ms/cover letter; no phone query. **NO PAYMENT**, for all rts. Articles 500-1,400 wds (24/yr); book & music reviews, 800 wds. Free copy.
>   **Fillers:** Anecdotes, quotes; 25-75 wds.
>   **Columns/Departments:** Personal Testimonies, 500 wds; Teaching Articles (doctrine/policy), 1,200-1,400 wds; Reports (Episcopal Parish Renewal), 800 wds; Parish Articles, 1,200 wds.
>   **Tips:** "Manuscripts from Episcopal lay people and clergy are welcome."

#ADVENT CHRISTIAN WITNESS, P.O. Box 23152, Charlotte NC 28227. (704)545-6161. Fax: (704)573-0712. Advent Christian General Conference. Robert J. Mayer, ed. Denominational. Monthly mag; 20 pgs; circ 3,700. Subscription $11. 10% freelance. Complete ms. Pays $15-25, on publication, for one-time rts. Articles 750-1,200 wds (4/yr). Responds in 8 wks. Seasonal 6 mos ahead. Considers simultaneous submissions. Guidelines; copy $2.

ADVOCATE, (International Pentecostal Holiness ADVOCATE), P.O. Box 12609, Oklahoma City OK 73157. (405)787-7110. Fax: (405)789-3957. International Pentecostal Holiness Church. Shirley Spencer, exec.

ed. Denominational; conservative in viewpoint; full-gospel. Monthly mag; 20 pgs; circ 3,700. Subscription $9.75. 10% freelance. Complete ms; no phone/fax query. Pays $15-25, on acceptance, for 1st, reprint, or simultaneous rts. Articles 500-1,200 wds. Responds in 8 wks. Seasonal 4 mos ahead. Considers simultaneous submissions & reprints. Sidebars ok. Guidelines; free copy.

Poetry: Buys 12/yr. Free verse, traditional; to 15 lines; $10-20. Submit max. 3 poems.

*****AFA JOURNAL**, P.O. Box 2440, 107 Parkgate Dr., Tupelo MS 38801. (601)844-5036. American Family Assn. Don Wildmon, exec. ed; Randall Murphree, articles ed. Urges people to become involved, as change agents, with social/moral issues, such as pornography, TV programming, abortion, and First Amendment rights. Monthly (11X) journal; 24 pgs; circ 400,000. 5% freelance. Query; phone query ok. **NO PAYMENT.** Not copyrighted. Articles 1,000 wds (2-3/yr). Considers simultaneous query & reprints. Responds in 2 mos. No guidelines; free copy.

Tips: "Most open to articles on social and moral issues with impact on the family."

#AFRICAN-AMERICAN HERITAGE, 8443 S. Crenshaw Blvd., Ste. 103, Inglewood CA 90305. (213)752-3706. General publication that includes inspirational and religious articles. Dennis DeLoach, ed. To cultivate self-esteem, pride and appreciation for ethnic heritage. Quarterly mag; circ 25,000. 30% freelance. Query. Pays $25-300 on publication; for 1st, one-time, or simultaneous rts. Articles 200-2,000 wds (6/yr); fiction 200-2,000 wds (6/yr). Responds in 1-2 mos. Seasonal 6 mos ahead. Considers simultaneous submissions & reprints. Kill fee 25%. Guidelines; copy for 9x12 SAE/4 stamps.

Poetry: Buys 60/yr. Any type; 4-36 lines; $10-25. Submit max. 5 poems.

Fillers: Buys 12/yr. Anecdotes, facts; 10-200 wds; $25-100.

Special Needs: February is Black History Month.

#AGAIN MAGAZINE, P.O. Box 76, Ben Lomond CA 95005. (408)336-5118. Fax: (408)336-8882. Orthodox/Conciliar Press. Weldon Hardenbrook, ed. A call to the people of God to return to their roots of historical orthodoxy once AGAIN. Quarterly mag; 32 pgs; circ 4,500. Subscription $12. 1% freelance. Query. **PAYS IN COPIES.** Considers simultaneous submissions & reprints. Articles 1,500-2,000 wds; fiction 1,500-2,500 wds; book reviews 500-700 wds. Responds in 4 mos. Seasonal 2 mos ahead. Serials 2 parts. Guidelines; copy $2.50/9x12 SAE/5 stamps.

#ALIVE! A MAGAZINE FOR CHRISTIAN SENIOR ADULTS, P.O. Box 46464, Cincinnati OH 45246-0464. (513)825-3681. Christian Seniors Fellowship. June Lang, office ed. Focuses on activities and opportunities for active, Christian senior adults, 55 and older; upbeat rather than nostalgic. Quarterly mag; 12-16 pgs; circ 6,000. Subscription/membership $10. 60% freelance. Complete ms/cover letter; no phone query. Pays .03-.05/wd ($18-75), on publication, for one-time rts. Articles 600-1,200 wds (25/yr); fiction 600-1,500 wds (12/yr- pays $20-60). Responds in 6 wks. Seasonal 6 mos ahead. Accepts reprints (pays less). Guidelines; copy for 9x12 SAE/3 stamps.

Poetry: Buys 6/yr. Free verse, light verse, traditional; $3-10. Submit max. 3 poems.

Fillers: Buys 15/yr. Anecdotes, cartoons, ideas, jokes, short humor, and word puzzles; 50-500 wds; $2-15.

Columns/Departments: Buys 50/yr. Heart Medicine (humor, grandparent/grandchild anecdotes), to 100 wds, $2.50-5; Games 'n Stuff (word puzzles/games), $2-25.

Tips: "No mss returned without SASE. Language must be consistent with Christian ethics. Need some articles/fiction from male point of view."

*****ALIVE NOW!** 1908 Grand Ave., Box 189, Nashville TN 37202-0189. (615)340-7218. Fax: (615)340-7006. United Methodist/The Upper Room. George Graham, ed. Short writings in attractive graphic setting for reflection and meditation. Bimonthly mag; 64 pgs; circ 65,000. 90% freelance. Complete ms/cover letter. Pays $15-20, on acceptance, for all, one-time or reprint rts. Articles 250 wds; fiction 250-750 wds. Responds in 2-3 wks. Seasonal 6-8 mos ahead. Guidelines/theme list; free copy.

Poetry: Free verse, traditional; to 25 lines.

Fillers: Cartoons, prayers.

#**AMERICA**, 106 W. 56th St., New York NY 10019. (212)581-4640. Catholic. Rev. George W. Hunt, S.J., ed. A national journal of opinion. Weekly mag; 24-32 pgs; circ 36,000. 100% freelance. Query or complete ms/cover letter. Pays $50-100, on acceptance, for all rts. Articles 1,500-2,000 wds. Responds in 3 wks. Seasonal 3 mos ahead. Free guidelines.

Poetry: Patrick Samway, S.J. Light verse, serious poetry, unrhymed; 15-30 lines; $7.50-25 (on publication). Submit max. 3 poems.

*****THE AMERICAN BAPTIST**, Box 851, Valley Forge PA 19482. American Baptist Church. Philip E. Jenks, ed. Denominational. Little freelance. Not in topical listings.

Tips: "Interested in denominational-oriented news and issues stories."

*****AMERICAN BIBLE SOCIETY RECORD**, 1865 Broadway, New York NY 10023. (212)408-1480. Fax: (212)408-1456. Clifford P. Macdonald, ed. Report of stewardship for ABS members. Monthly mag; 32 pgs; circ 275,000. 2% freelance. Query; phone query ok. Negotiable payment, on acceptance, for all rts. Not copyrighted. Articles 500-600 wds (1/yr). Considers simultaneous query & reprints. Not in topical listings. No guidelines; free copy.

Tips: "Only articles concerning the Bible or the work and mission of the ABS."

*****AMERICAN TRACT SOCIETY**, Box 462008, Garland TX 75046. (214)276-9408. Perry Brown, tract ed. Majority of tracts written to win unbeliever. Bimonthly tracts; 25 million produced annually. 10% freelance. Query or complete ms/cover letter; phone query ok. Pays $100-150, on publication, for simultaneous rts. Tracts 800-1,200 wds (3-6/yr). Responds in 4-6 wks. Seasonal 8-9 mos ahead. Accepts reprints. Guidelines; free samples.

Special Needs: Youth issues.

Tips: "Choose a subject that is very relevant and evident to potential readers."

*****ANGLICAN JOURNAL**, 600 Jarvis St., Toronto ON M4Y 2J6 Canada. (416)924-9192. Anglican Church of Canada. Carolyn Purden, ed; submit to Vianney Carriere, news ed. Informs Canadian Anglicans about the church at home and overseas. Newspaper (10x/yr); 24 pgs; circ 272,000. 25% freelance. Query; phone query ok. Pays $50-500 (Canadian), on publication, for 1st rts. Articles 200-800 wds. Responds in 2 wks. Seasonal 2 mos ahead. Accepts reprints. Guidelines.

THE ANNALS OF SAINT ANNE DE BEAUPRE, Box 1000, St. Anne de Beaupre QB G0A 3C0 Canada. (418)827-4538. Fax: (418)827-4530. Redemptorist Fathers. Father Roch Achard, C.Ss.R., ed. Promotes Catholic family values. Monthly (11X) mag; 32 pgs; circ 50,000. Subscription $8 U.S. 80% freelance. Complete ms/cover letter; phone query ok. Pays .03-.04/wd, on acceptance, for 1st NASR. Articles 500-1,500 wds (30/yr); fiction 500-1,500 wds (15/yr). Responds in 2 wks. Seasonal 3 mos ahead. Free guidelines/copy.

Poetry: Overstocked for now.

Tips: "Write something educational, inspirational, objective and uplifting. No articles without a spiritual thrust. Good, solid stories, no heavy or long quotes or citations, or borrowing from other authors."

THE APOCALYPSE CHRONICLES, Box 448, Jacksonville OR 97530. (503)899-8888. James Lloyd, ed/pub. Deals with the apocalypse exclusively. Quarterly tabloid; circ 1,000. Estab 1992. Query; no phone query. Payment negotiable for reprint rts. Articles. Responds in 9 wks. No guidelines; copy for #10 SAE/2 stamps.

*ARKANSAS CATHOLIC, P.O. Box 7417, Little Rock AR 72217. (501)664-0340. Catholic. Pete Hoelscher, ed. Regional newspaper for the local Diocese. Published 40x/yr; 16 pgs; circ 7,000. 5% freelance. Query/clips only. Pays $2.50/column inch, on publication, for 1st rts. Articles 500-1,300 wds. Responds in 3 wks. Considers simultaneous submissions. Guidelines; copy for 9x12 SAE/2 stamps.

   Columns/Departments: Viewpoint (issues-related opinion pieces); Scripture Speaks Today (Bible commentary); 500 wds.

   Tips: "Most open to news of the Diocese or pieces that inspire readers to consider what it means to be Catholic today."

*ARLINGTON CATHOLIC HERALD, 200 N. Glebe Rd., Ste. 614, Arlington VA 22203. (703)841-2590. Catholic. Michael Flach, ed. Regional newspaper for the local Diocese. Weekly newspaper; 24 pgs; circ 45,000. 20-25% freelance. Complete ms/cover letter. Pays $50-200, on publication, for one-time rts. Articles 500-2,000 wds. Responds in 2 mos. Guidelines; free copy.

   Columns/Departments: Sports; School News; Local Entertainments; 500 wds.

   Tips: "All submissions must be Catholic-related. Avoid controversial issues within the Church."

+ASPIRE, 404 BNA Dr. Ste. 600, Bldg. 200, Nashville TN 37217. (615)872-8080. Fax: (615)889-0437. Susan Salmon Trotman, sr. ed. A lifestyle magazine for Christians ages 35-45. Bimonthly mag; 84 pgs. 50% freelance. Query/clips; fax query ok. Pays, on acceptance, for first & reprint rts. Responds in 4-6 wks. Seasonal 6 mos ahead. Kill fee 20%. Sidebars ok. Guidelines; copy $3.50/9x12 SAE.

   Columns/Departments: Family Matters; Great Outdoors; Food for Thought; Bodywise; all 800-1,000 wds.

#AT EASE, 1445 Boonville Ave., Springfield MO 65802. (417)862-2781. Fax: (417)863-7276. Assemblies of God. Lemuel D. McElyea, ed; articles to Janet Walker, mng ed. Devotional articles for military personnel. Bimonthly mag; 4 pgs; circ 28,000. 90% freelance. Complete ms/cover letter; phone query ok. Pays .03/wd, on publication, for 1st or one-time rts. Articles to 400 wds (20/yr). Responds in 3-4 wks. Seasonal 6 mos ahead. Considers simultaneous submissions & reprints. Guidelines/copy for #10 SAE/1 stamp.

   Poetry: Buys 4/yr. Avant-garde, free verse, light verse, traditional; $10.

   Fillers: Buys 5/yr. Cartoons; $20-40.

   Tips: "Strong human interest; talk about real life. Make subject inspiring and uplifting. We want to win souls."

*AXIOS, 1501 E. Chapman Ave. #345, Fullerton CA 92631-4000. Orthodox Christian. Fr. Daniel John Gorham, ed. Review of public affairs, religion, literature and the arts, and is especially interested in the Orthodox Catholic Church and its world view. Bimonthly newsletter; 32 pgs; circ 15,672. Subscription $25. 90% freelance. Complete ms/cover letter; no phone query. Pays .04/wd & up ($25-500), on publication, for 1st rts. Articles, any length (29/yr); book reviews 2,000 wds. Responds in 4-8 wks. Seasonal 4 mos ahead. Considers simultaneous submissions & reprints. Kill fee 25%. Copy $4.20/9x12 SAE/$1.20 currency.

   Poetry: Buys 6/yr. Traditional; any length; $5-25. Submit max. 3 poems.

   Fillers: Buys 25/yr. Anecdotes, cartoons, facts.

Columns/Departments: Buys 80 religious book and film reviews/yr. Query.

Tips: "Most open to articles. Be sure you have an idea of who and what an orthodox Christian is."

** This periodical was #58 on the 1994 Top 50 Plus Christian Publishers list.

*THE BAPTIST BEACON, RR 1, Waterford ON N0E 1Y0 Canada. (519)443-8525. Baptist. Sterling Clark, ed. For adults, emphasizing biblical doctrine, evangelism, prophesy, and inspirational articles. Monthly mag; 20 pgs; circ 300. Subscription $12. 15% freelance. Complete ms/cover letter; phone query ok. **NO PAYMENT** for one-time use. Articles any length. Seasonal 3 mos ahead. Accepts reprints. Free copy.

Poetry: Accepts 24+/yr. Traditional; any length. Submit any number.

Tips: "Most open to devotional, inspirational and biblical teaching."

*BAPTIST HISTORY AND HERITAGE, 901 Commerce St., Ste. 400, Nashville TN 37203. (615)244-0344. Southern Baptist. Dr. Charles W. DeWeese, ed. A scholarly journal focusing on Baptist history. Quarterly journal; 64 pgs; circ 2,000. 15-20% freelance. Query. Pays $192 (for assigned only), for all rts. Articles to 4,000 wds. Responds in 2 mos. Guidelines; no copy.

Tips: "Most open to lesser known aspects of Baptist history based on primary sources."

*THE BAPTIST INFORMER, 603 S. Wilmington St., Raleigh NC 27601. (919)821-7466. Fax: (919)836-0061. General Baptist. Archie D. Logan, ed. Regional African-American publication. Monthly tabloid; 16 pgs; circ 10,000. 10% freelance. Query or complete ms/cover letter. **PAYS IN COPIES,** for one-time rts. Articles & fiction. Responds in 3 mos. Considers simultaneous submissions. No guidelines; free copy.

#THE B.C. CATHOLIC, 150 Robson St., Vancouver BC V6B 2A7 Canada. (604)683-0281. Fax: (604)683-8117. Catholic. Rev. Vincent Hawkswell, ed. News, education and inspiration for Canadian Catholics. Weekly (47X) newspaper; 16 pgs; circ 20,000. 70% freelance. Query; phone query ok. Pays variable rate, on publication, for 1st rts. Articles 400-500 wds. Responds in 6 wks. Seasonal 4 wks ahead. Considers simultaneous submissions & reprints. No guidelines or copy.

Tips: "We prefer to use Catholic writers."

*THE BEACON, P.O. Box 387, Live Oak FL 32060-0387. Submit to the Editor. Bimonthly newsletter. 20% freelance. Free subscription. Not in topical listings.

A BETTER TOMORROW, 404 BNA Dr., Ste. 600, Bldg. 200, Nashville TN 37217. (615)872-8080. Fax: (615)889-0437. Nondenominational. Vicki Huffman, assoc. ed. For Christian seniors who want to make the most of their later years (most 55-75). Bimonthly mag; 76 pgs; circ 50,000. Subscription $17.95. Estab 1992. 15% freelance. Query/clips; fax query ok. Pays .10-.15/wd, on acceptance, for 1st rts. Articles 800-2,000 wds (20/yr); fiction, 1,200-1,500 wds (3/yr); book reviews, 350 wds, $60. Responds in 6 wks. Seasonal 6 mos ahead. Considers simultaneous submissions. Kill fee 20%. No disk. Sidebars ok. Guidelines; copy $3.50/9x12 SAE.

Columns/Departments: Buys 20/yr. Good Sports (physical activity, how-to, equipment), 1,000 wds; Grandstand (grandchildren anecdotes), 50-100 wds; Snapshots (an over-50 making a difference), 350 wds; .15/wd. Query.

Tips: "Send ideas with published clips and show you know how to relate to our audience."

BIBLE ADVOCATE, Box 33677, Denver CO 80233. (303)452-7973. Fax: (303)452-0657. Church of God (Seventh Day). Roy Marrs, ed; Sherri Langton, asst ed. Mostly older adult readers; general reading. Monthly (11X) mag; 20 pgs; circ 12,600. Free subscription. 25% freelance. Complete ms/cover letter; fax query ok. Pays $10/printed pg, to $25; on publication; for 1st, one-time, reprint & simultaneous rts. Articles 1,000-2,500 wds (25-35/yr). Responds in 4-6 wks. Seasonal 6 mos ahead. Considers simultaneous submissions & reprints. Kill fee to $25. Disk or not. Sidebars ok. Guidelines; copy for 9x12 SAE/3 stamps.

Poetry: Accepts 10-20/yr. Free verse, traditional; 5-25 lines; $5. Submit max. 5 poems.

Fillers: Buys 5/yr. Facts, prayers, prose, quotes; 50-200 wds; $5-10.

Columns/Departments: Accepts 6/yr. Viewpoint (social or religious issues), to 700 wds; Pastor's Corner (devotional by pastors only), 300-350 wds; pays in copies.

Tips: "Viewpoint column and poetry most open. Keep your writing fresh. Have something different to say that is biblically sound and insightful, and stick to your focus."

*BIBLE REVIEW, 3000 Connecticut Ave. NW, #300, Washington DC 20008. (202)387-8888. Fax: (202)483-3423. Biblical Archaeological Society. Hershel Shanks, ed. Bimonthly mag; 80 pgs; circ 40,000. 5% freelance. Query only. Pays to $300, on publication, for one-time rts. Accepts reprints. Articles 700-1,500, to 5,000 wds. Responds in 1 yr. Not in topical listings. No guidelines or copy.

Tips: "Looking for interesting, historical, critical analysis of the Bible."

THE BIBLE TODAY, Saint John's Abbey, Collegeville MN 56321-7500. (612)363-2213. Fax: (800)445-5899. Catholic. Ms to: Rev. Leslie J. Hoppe, O.FM., ed., 5401 S. Cornell Ave., Chicago IL 60615. Explains the meaning and context of particular biblical passages and books and encourages a regular, prayerful reading of the Bible. Bimonthly mag; 64 pgs; circ 8,000. Subscription $22. 20% freelance. Complete ms/cover letter; phone/fax query ok. **PAYS 5 COPIES & 1 YR SUBSCRIPTION.** Articles to 2,000 wds (15/yr). Responds in 4-9 wks. Seasonal 6 mos ahead. No sidebars. Free guidelines/copy.

Tips: "Most open to general articles on the Bible or biblical themes, biblical archaeology, biblical spirituality."

+BIBLICAL REFLECTIONS ON MODERN MEDICINE, P.O. Box 14488, Augusta GA 30919. (706)736-0161. Dr. Ed Payne, ed. For all Christians interested in medical-ethical issues. Bimonthly newsletter; circ 1,100. Subscription $19. 20% freelance. Complete ms/cover letter. **PAYS IN COPIES & SUBSCRIPTION,** for 1st rts. Articles to 1,500 wds (5/yr). Responds in 1-4 wks. Considers simultaneous submissions & reprints. No sidebars. Guidelines/copy for #10 SAE/1 stamp.

*BOOKSTORE JOURNAL, Box 200, Colorado Springs CO 80901. (719)576-7880. Fax: (719)576-0795. Christian Booksellers Assn. Cindy Parolini, pub. dir. To provide Christian bookstore owners with professional retail skills, product information, and industry news. Monthly trade journal; 175 pgs; circ 10,000. Subscription $45. 50% freelance. Query/clips. Pays .11-.14/wd, on publication, for all or 1st rts. Articles 800-3,500 wds (12/yr). Responds in 6 wks. Seasonal 5 mos ahead. Considers simultaneous submissions & reprints. Kill fee 90%. Guidelines; copy $5/9x12 SAE/3 stamps.

Fillers: Buys 12/yr. Cartoons; $100.

Tips: "Know the Christian retail industry. Do your homework and get facts straight, quotes accurate, etc."

BROKEN STREETS, 57 Morningside Dr. E., Bristol CT 06010. (203)582-2943. Ron Grossman, ed. For Christian writers of poetry, especially new writers. Semiannual journal; 40-50 pgs; circ 500. Subscription $10. 100% freelance. Complete ms/cover letter; no phone query. **PAYS IN COPIES,** for one-time rts. Articles 100-500 wds (5-10/yr). Responds in 1 wk. Accepts reprints. Guidelines $1; copy $4.

Poetry: Accepts 200/yr. All types; no length limit. Submit max. 5 poems.

Fillers: Accepts 50/yr. Prose, devotionals, prayers, journal entries; 5-15 lines.

Tips: "Buy a sample, write a good cover letter, and pray for guidance."

BURNING LIGHT: A Journal of Christian Literature, 98 Constitution Way, Franklin NJ 07416-2151. (201)209-0365. Carl Simmons, ed/pub. A journal of writing by Christians, rather than 'Christian writing.' Quarterly jour; circ 300. Subscription $14. Estab 1993. 80% freelance. Complete ms/cover letter; phone query ok. **PAYS IN COPIES/SUBSCRIPTION**, for all rts (negotiable). Articles to 8,000 wds (4/yr); fiction to 8,000 wds, longer if serialized, (10-12/yr); book reviews, 150-500 wds. Responds in 2-4 wks. Seasonal 3 mos ahead. Considers simultaneous submissions & reprints (rarely). Prefers disk copy. No sidebars. Guidelines; copy $4.

> **Poetry:** Buys 30-40/yr. Avant-garde, free verse, haiku, traditional; to 500 lines. Submit max. 6 poems.

> **Tips:** "No nice recitals of sermons; we're about walking with Christ into a world with a lot of problems. We get lots of poetry; short stories and essays are harder to come by."

CANADA LUTHERAN, 1512 St. James St., Winnipeg MB R3H 0L2 Canada. (204)786-6707. Fax: (204)783-7548. Evangelical Lutheran Church in Canada. Kenn Ward, ed. Denominational. Monthly (11X) mag; 40 pgs; circ 23,000. Subscription $17 U.S. 45% freelance. Complete ms/cover letter; no phone query; fax query ok. Pays $40-120 (Canadian), on publication, for one-time rts. Articles 600-2,000 wds (15/yr); fiction 800-1,500 wds (4/yr). Responds in 1 wk. Seasonal 10 mos ahead. Considers simultaneous submissions & reprints. Guidelines.

> **Tips:** "Canadians/Lutherans receive priority, but not the only consideration. Want material that is clear, concise and fresh. Articles that talk about real life experiences of faith receive our best reader response."

+THE CANADIAN BAPTIST, 414-195 The West Mall, Etobicoke ON M3C 5K1 Canada. (416)622-8600. Fax: (416)622-0780. Baptist Convention of Ontario and Quebec/Western Canada. Dr. Larry Matthews, ed. Covers issues relevant to and events/stories about people in the Baptist community. Monthly (10X) mag; 32 pgs; circ 11,500. Subscription $18/Canadian. 90% freelance. Query; phone/fax query ok. Pays negotiable rates, on acceptance, for 1st NASR. Articles. Responds in 6 wks. Seasonal 3 mos ahead. Considers simultaneous submissions & reprints (occasionally). Kill fees negotiated. Prefers disk copy. Sidebars ok. Guidelines; copy for 9x13 SAE.

> **Fillers:** Commissioned. Cartoons, facts, quotes.

THE CANADIAN CATHOLIC REVIEW, St. Thomas More College, 1437 College Dr., Saskatoon SK S7N 0W6 Canada. (306)966-8959. Fax: (306)966-8904. Catholic. Rev. Daniel Callam, CSB, ed. For intelligent (but not scholarly) Catholics who take their faith seriously. Monthly (11X) mag; 40 pgs; circ 1,000. Subscription $25, U.S. 30% freelance. Query; phone/fax query ok. Pays $50-300, on publication, for 1st NASR. Articles 1,000-6,000 wds (10/yr); book reviews 500 wds/$25. Responds in 2-4 wks. Seasonal 6 mos ahead. No sidebars. No guidelines; copy $3.21/9x12 SAE.

> **Columns/Departments:** Buys 10/yr. Scripture; Liturgy; American Notes; The Church in Quebec; all 1,000 wds; $50.

> **Tips:** "Most open to columns and general articles. Be lucid, articulate, faithful and brief."

CAREGIVER'S CONNECTION (formerly **PARENT CARE**), Box 12624, Roanoke VA 24027. (703)342-7511 (also fax). Betty Robertson, mng ed. For caregivers of the disabled, ill or elderly. Monthly newsletter; 8 pgs; circ 100+. Subscription $19.95. 95% freelance. Complete ms; fax query ok. Pays $3-5, on acceptance, for one-time, reprint or simultaneous rts. Articles 750-1,200 wds (40-50/yr). Responds in 6 wks. Seasonal 3 mos ahead. Considers simultaneous submissions & reprints. Prefers disk copy. Guidelines; copy $2.50.

Poetry: Avant-garde, free verse, haiku, traditional; no payment.

Fillers: Recipes, care-giving tips and ideas; 25-200 wds; no payment.

Tips: "Be a caregiver; write practical, how-to articles."

CATHEDRAL AGE, Mount St. Alban, Massachusetts & Wisconsin Aves NW, Washington DC 20016-5098. (202)537-6200. Fax: (202)364-6600. Washington National Cathedral (Episcopal). Submit to the Editor. About what's happening in and to cathedrals and their programs. Quarterly mag; 32 pgs; circ 35,000. Subscription $20. 60% freelance. Query/clips; phone/fax query ok. Pays to $500, on publication, for all rts. Articles to 2,000 wds; book reviews 600 wds, $100. Responds in 4 wks. Seasonal 4 mos ahead. Accepts reprints. Prefers disk copy. Guidelines; copy $5/9x12 SAE/5 stamps.

> **Tips:** "We prefer to assign articles, so query/clips first. Always write from the viewpoint of an individual first, then move into a more general discussion of the topic. Human interest angle important."

#THE CATHOLIC ACCENT, P.O. Box 850, Greensburg PA 15601. (412)834-4010. Fax: (412)836-5650. Catholic. Alice Laurich, ed. Local news and inspiration for the Diocese of Greenburg PA (Western & Southwestern PA). Weekly newspaper; 20 pgs; circ 48,000. Complete ms/cover letter. Variable payment, for one-time rts. Articles 300-500 wds. Responds in 1-2 mos. No guidelines; copy .35.

> **Tips:** "Most open to inspirational articles."

*THE CATHOLIC ANSWER, 207 Adams St., Newark NJ 07105. (219)356-8400. Our Sunday Visitor/Catholic. Father Peter Stravinskas, mng. ed. Answers to questions of belief for orthodox Catholics. Bimonthly mag; 64 pgs; circ 60,000. 50% freelance. Query/clips. Pays $100, on publication, for 1st rts. Articles 1,200-2,200 wds (80/yr). Seasonal 6 mos ahead. Guidelines; free copy (from 200 Noll Plaza, Huntington IN 46750).

#CATHOLIC COURIER, 1150 Buffalo Rd., Rochester NY 14624. (716)328-4340. Fax: (328)8640. Catholic. Karen M. Franz, ed. Independent newspaper for the Diocese of Rochester NY. Weekly newspaper; 20 pgs; circ 48,000. Subscription $19.50. 5% freelance. Complete ms/cover letter. Pays $30-100, on publication, for one-time rts. Articles 1,200 wds. Responds in 1-2 mos. Considers simultaneous submissions.

> **Columns/Departments:** Et Cetera; Leisure; Opinion; Sports; Youth; 750 wds.

#CATHOLIC DIGEST, Box 64090, St. Paul MN 55164-0090. (612)962-6749. Fax: (612)962-6755. Catholic. Richard Reece, ed. Primarily for Catholic families with teens or grown children; most reprinted from other publications. Monthly mag; 128 pgs; circ 550,000. Subscription $16.97. 10% freelance. Complete ms (for original material)/cover letter, tear sheets for reprints; no phone query. Pays $100-400, on acceptance, for one-time or reprint rts. Articles 1,500-2,500 wds (75-100/yr). Responds in 4 wks. Seasonal 4-5 mos ahead. Accepts reprints. Guidelines; copy for 7x10 SAE/4 stamps.

> **Fillers:** Buys 250/yr. Anecdotes, facts, games, ideas, jokes, quizzes, short humor; 1 line to 150 wds; $4-50.

> **Columns/Departments:** Buys 50-100/yr. Open Door (personal stories of conversion to Catholicism); 300-500 wds; $20-50. See guidelines for full list.

> **Tips:** "We use a broad selection of articles."

> ** This periodical was #25 on the 1994 Top 50 Plus Christian Publishers list. (#5 in 1993)

#THE CATHOLIC EXPONENT, P.O. Box 6787, Youngstown OH 44501-6787. (216)744-5251. Fax: (216)744-8451. Catholic. Dennis Finneran, ed. Family-oriented paper for Catholics in northern OH Diocese. Biweekly newspaper; 24 pgs; circ 37,000. 20% freelance. Query. Pays variable rates, on publication, for one-time rts. Articles to 500 wds. Considers simultaneous submissions. No guidelines; free copy.

Tips: "Our emphasis is on moral/ethical issues."

+CATHOLIC FORESTER, Box 3012, Naperville IL 60566-7012. (708)983-4920. Fax: (708)983-5113. Catholic. Dorothy Deer, ed. For mixed audience, primarily parents and grandparents between the ages of 30 and 80. Bimonthly mag; 36 pgs; circ 103,000. Free/membership. 25% freelance. Complete ms/cover letter; phone/fax query ok. Pays $20, on acceptance, 1st or one-time rts. Articles 300-1,500 wds (prefers 1,000), 20/yr; fiction 1,000-2,000 wds (4/yr), pays .20/wd. Responds in 4 wks. Seasonal 9 mos ahead. Prefers disk copy. Accepts reprints. Sidebars ok. Guidelines; copy for 9x12 SAE/2 stamps.

#CATHOLIC HERITAGE, 200 Noll Plaza, Huntington IN 46750. (219)356-8400. Fax: (219)356-8472. Catholic. Robert Lockwood, ed. For those interested in Catholic history. Bimonthly mag; circ 25,000. 25% freelance. Query; no phone query. Pays $200, on acceptance, for 1st rts. Articles 1,000-2,000 wds (15/yr). Responds in 3-5 wks. Seasonal 6 mos ahead. Accepts reprints. Kill fee 33% or $50-75. No guidelines; free copy.

Tips: "Most open to general features."

#CATHOLIC NEW YORK, 1011 1st Ave, 17th Fl., New York NY 10022. (212)688-2399. Fax: (212)688-2642. Catholic. Anne Buckley, ed-in-chief. To inform New York Catholics. Weekly newspaper; 44 pgs; circ 130,000. Subscription $20. 10% freelance. Query or complete ms/cover letter. Pays $15-100, on publication, for one-time rts. Articles 500-800 wds. Responds in 1 mo. No guidelines; copy $1.

Columns/Departments: Comment; Catholic New Yorkers (profiles of unique individuals); 325 wds.

Tips: "Most open to articles that show how to integrate Catholic faith into work, hobbies or special interests."

CATHOLIC PARENT, 200 Noll Plaza, Huntington IN 46750. (800)348-2440. Catholic. Woodeene Koenig-Bricker, ed. Practical advice for Catholic parents, with a specifically Catholic slant. Bimonthly mag; 52 pgs; circ 30,000. Subscription $18. Estab 1993. 90% freelance. Query/clips or complete ms/cover letter; fax query ok. Pays variable rates, on acceptance, for 1st rts. Articles 250-1,000 wds (30-40/yr). Responds in 6-8 wks. Seasonal 6 mos ahead. Kill fee. Disks ok. Sidebars ok. Guidelines; copy $3/10x13 SAE/5 stamps.

Fillers: Mary Bazzett. Accepts 40/yr. Parenting tips, 100-200 wds, $25.

Tips: "Be practical in your advice. Read the publication to see how we use a blend of how-to and some personal experience."

** This periodical was #26 on the 1994 Top 50 Plus Christian Publishers list.

CATHOLIC SENTINEL, P.O. Box 18030, Portland OR 97218-0030. (503)281-1191. Fax: (503)282-3486. Catholic. Robert Pfohman, ed. For Catholics in the Archdiocese of western and eastern Oregon. Weekly tabloid; 16-24 pgs; circ 15,000. Subscription $22. 25% freelance. Query; phone/fax query ok (if timely). Pays $25-150, on publication, for one-time rts. Not copyrighted. Articles 800-1,800 wds (15/yr). Responds in 6 wks. Seasonal 1 month ahead. Accepts reprints (on columns, not news or features; tell them). Prefers disk copy or over modem. Kill fee 100%. Sidebars ok. Copy 50 cents/9x12 SAE/2 stamps.

Columns/Departments: Buys about 30/yr. Opinion Page, 600 wds, $10. Send complete ms.

Tips: "Find active Catholics living their faith in specific, interesting, upbeat, positive ways."

#CATHOLIC TELEGRAPH, 100 E. 8th St., Cincinnati OH 45202. (513)421-3131. Fax: (513)381-2242. Catholic. Tricia Hempel, gen. mng. Diocese newspaper for Cincinnati area. Weekly newspaper; 20 pgs; circ 27,000. 10% freelance. Send resume and writing samples for assignment. Pays varying rates, on publication, for all rts. Articles. Responds in 2-3 wks. Kill fee. Guidelines sent/acceptance; free copy.

Fillers: Newsbreaks (local).

#CATHOLIC TWIN CIRCLE, 15760 Ventura Blvd., Ste. 1201, Encino CA 91436-3001. (818)382-3636 or (800)421-3230. Fax: (818)382-3677. Catholic. Loretta G. Seyer, ed. Features writing for Catholics and/or Christian families of all ages. Weekly newspaper; 20 pgs; circ 30,000. 45% freelance. Complete ms/cover letter. Pays .10/wd; on publication; for all, 1st, one-time or reprint rts (.03-.05/wd). Articles 800-1,200 wds; book reviews 750 wds. Responds in 3 mos. Seasonal 3 mos ahead. Serials 3 parts. Guidelines; copy for 9x12 SAE/2 stamps or $2.

Fillers: Cartoons, quizzes.

Columns/Departments: Opinions/editorials on topics of interest to Catholic families; 600-800 wds; $50.

CELEBRATE LIFE (formerly **ALL ABOUT ISSUES**), Box 1350, Stafford VA 22555. (703)659-4171. Fax: (703)659-2586. American Life League. Steve Dunham, mng ed. A pro-life educational group. Bimonthly mag; 48 pgs; circ 145,000. Subscription $12.95. 75% freelance. Query. Pays $50/pg ($25/pg for reprints); on publication; for one-time rts. Articles 500-2,000 wds (50/yr); book reviews 250-500 wds, $25-50. Responds in 2-8 wks. Seasonal 6 mos ahead. Considers simultaneous query & reprints (please indicate). Kill fee. Query for sidebars. Guidelines/theme list; copy for 9x12 SAE/4 stamps.

Fillers: Buys 6+/yr. Newsbreaks (local or special pro-life news); 50-100 wds; $10.

Columns/Departments: Buys 6+/yr. Prayer and Fasting (personal spirituality), 500 wds; Voice Page (pro-life action written by students), 500 wds; $25-50.

Special Needs: Abortion, euthanasia, and natural family planning.

Tips: "Don't be too basic, e.g. don't write to prove abortion is wrong—our readers know that. Send feature articles to fit themes."

** This periodical was #66 on the 1994 Top 50 Plus Christian Publishers list. (#46 in 1993)

*CELEBRATION, 207 Hillsboro, Silver Spring MD 20902. (301)681-4927. Interdenominational. Bill Freburger, ed. To help Christian clergy prepare for Sunday celebrations (baptism, marriage, funerals, etc.). Monthly mag; 48 pgs; circ 9,000. Some freelance. Query. Pays .10/wd, on acceptance, for 1st rts. Articles any length. Responds in 2 wks. No guidelines; free copy.

Fillers: Cartoons.

#CHARISMA & CHRISTIAN LIFE, 600 Rinehart Rd., Lake Mary FL 32746. (407)333-0600. Fax: (407)333-9753. Strang Communications. Stephen Strang, ed: articles to John Archer. Primarily for the Pentecostal and Charismatic Christian community. Monthly mag; 100 pgs; circ 200,000. Subscription $19.97. 75% freelance. Query. Pays $75-400, on publication, for 1st rts. Articles 1,500-2,500 wds. Responds in 1 mo. Seasonal 8 mos ahead. Kill fee. Guidelines; copy for 9x12 SAE.

Tips: "Tell us in the cover letter why you are qualified to write the story. Ask yourself if the story would be of special interest to a charismatic/Pentecostal Christian audience."

+CHRISTIAN AMERICAN NEWSPAPER, 1801-L Sara Dr., Chesapeake VA 23321. (804)424-2630. Fax: (804)424-9068. Christian Coalition, Inc. Submit to The Editor. To provide a Christian perspective on the news, enabling them to be more effective citizens by being better informed. Newspaper published 9X/yr; circ 325,000. Subscription $24. Open to freelance.

*CHRISTIAN CHRONICLE, P.O. Box 11000, Oklahoma City OK 73136. (405)425-5070. Church of Christ. Glover Shipp, mng ed. Denominational; international; focus on evangelism. Monthly (10X) newspaper; 32 pgs; circ 112,000. 5% freelance. Complete ms/cover letter. Pays varying rates, on acceptance, for one-time rts. Articles to 1,000 wds. Responds in 2-3 wks. No guidelines; free copy.

Tips: "We prefer to get submissions from members of the Church of Christ."

*THE CHRISTIAN CIVIC LEAGUE OF MAINE RECORD, Box 5459, Augusta ME 04332. (207)622-7634. Jasper S. Wyman, ed. Focuses on church, public service and political action. Monthly newsletter; 12 pgs; circ 4,600. 10% freelance. Query. **NO PAYMENT** for one-time rts. Articles (10-12/yr). Responds in 4-8 wks. Seasonal 2 mos ahead. Considers simultaneous query & reprints. Free copy. Not in topical listings.

*THE CHRISTIAN COURIER, 1933 W. Wisconsin Ave., Milwaukee WI 53233. (414)344-7300. Fax: (414)344-7375. ProBuColls Assn. John M. Fisco, Jr., pub. To propagate the Gospel of Jesus Christ in the Midwest. Monthly newspaper; circ 10,000. 10% freelance. Query. **PAYS IN COPIES,** for one-time rts. Not copyrighted. Articles 300-1,500 wds (6/yr). Responds in 2-4 wks. Seasonal 2 mos ahead. Accepts reprints. Guidelines; free copy.

   Fillers: Anecdotes, facts, newsbreaks; 10-100 wds.

#CHRISTIAN COURIER, 4-261 Martindale Rd., St. Catherines ON L2W 1A1 Canada. (U.S. address: Box 110, Lewiston NY 14092). (905)682-8311. Fax: (905)682-8313. Independent (Protestant Reformed). Bert Witvoet, ed; Bob Vander Vennen, book review ed. To present Canadian and international news, both religious and secular, from a Reformed Christian perspective. Weekly (44X) newspaper; 20 pgs; circ 5,000. 25% freelance. Complete ms/cover letter; phone query ok. Pays .05-.10/wd, on publication, for one-time rts. Articles 700-1,000 wds (20/yr); fiction 1,000-2,000 wds (10/yr); book reviews 100-500 wds. Responds in 3 wks. Seasonal 1 yr ahead. Accepts reprints. Guidelines; copy for 9x12 SAE/IRC.

   Poetry: Buys 20/yr. Avant-garde, free verse, traditional; 10-30 lines; $15-30. Submit max. 5 poems.

*CHRISTIAN CRUSADE NEWSPAPER, P.O. Box 279, Neosho MO 64850. (918)438-4234. Fax: (417)451-4319. Interdenominational. Billy James Hargis, pub. A Christian, pro-American approach to current social and political issues. Monthly newspaper; 24 pgs; circ 25,000. 50% freelance. Query. Pays varying rates, on publication, for all rts. Articles. Responds in 2 mos. No guidelines; free copy.

*CHRISTIAN DRAMA MAGAZINE, 1824 Celestia Blvd., Walla Walla WA 99362-3619. (509)529-0089. Judy Tash, ed. For Christian dramatists; promoting the Gospel through drama. Quarterly mag; 28 pgs; circ 300. Subscription $5.50. Estab 1990. 40% freelance. Complete ms/cover letter; phone query ok. Pays $25; on publication; for 1st, one-time, reprint & simultaneous rts. Articles 300-1,000 wds (6/yr); plays/skits 50-1,500 wds (6/yr); play reviews 50-200 wds/$25. Responds in 4-12 wks. Seasonal 6 mos ahead. Considers simultaneous submissions & reprints. Guidelines; copy for 8x10 SAE/3 stamps.

   Poetry: Accepts 4-6/yr. Poetry appropriate for dramatic readings; $25.

   Fillers: Ideas (about Christian drama), news; to 100 wds; $5-10.

   Columns/Departments: Questions & Answers (drama production); 50-200 wds; $10-25.

   Special Needs: Drama, drama directing, script writing, acting, set design, special effects, puppetry, mime, sound design, play scripts, lighting, costumes, performance reviews, script reviews, news about Christian drama groups, publishers who buy scripts, Christian dance.

#THE CHRISTIAN EDGE, 6501 Branson Ln., Bakersfield CA 93009. (805)837-1378. Fax: (805)397-2661. Evangelical. Don Chase, pub/ed. Activity and resources guide; not an issues-driven publication. Monthly newspaper; circ 1,500. Subscription $15. 30% freelance. Query or complete ms/cover letter; no phone query. **PAYS IN COPIES,** for reprint rts. Articles 150-350 wds (20-30/yr); book & music reviews 350 wds. Responds in 2 wks. Seasonal 2 mos ahead. Considers simultaneous submissions & reprints. No guidelines; copy $1 + $1.25 postage (no SAE).

   Fillers: Cartoons, games, ideas, quotes, word puzzles; 50-150 wds.

+THE CHRISTIAN EVENT JOURNAL, 7127 Little River Turnpike #206, Annandale VA 22003. (703)914-0001. Fax: (703)914-1474. Evangelical. Kathie Nee, asst. ed. To inform, educate, inspire and encourage the Christian community in the greater Washington DC/Baltimore area. Monthly newspaper; 28-32 pgs; circ 50,000. Subscription $19.95. Estab 1994. 80% freelance. Query/clips or complete ms/cover letter; phone query ok. Pays $10-45, on publication, for 1st, one-time, reprint & simultaneous rts. Articles 200-1,500 wds (50/yr); book/music reviews, 300-500 wds, $10-20. Responds in 3-8 wks. Seasonal 3-4 mos ahead. Considers simultaneous submissions & reprints. Prefers disk copy. Sidebars ok. Guidelines; copy for 9x12 SAE/8 stamps.

    Poetry: Any type. Send any number.

    Fillers: Anecdotes, cartoons, jokes, newsbreaks, short humor, word puzzles.

    Columns/Departments: Open to column suggestions by freelancers.

    Tips: "Photos/illustrations to go along with articles would help."

+THE CHRISTIAN FOCUS, P.O. Box 2891, 725 Kingsley Ave., Orange Park CA 32067. (904)269-7362. Fax: (904)269-7362. Teresa D. Foster, ed. Committed to truth in Christian news around the world, nation and community. Newspaper. Circulation 15,000. Subscription $16. Open to freelance.

CHRISTIAN HISTORY, 465 Gundersen Dr., Carol Stream IL 60188. (708)260-6200. Fax: (708)260-0114. Christianity Today, Inc. Mark Galli, ed. To teach Christian history to educated readers in an engaging manner. Quarterly mag; 50 pgs; circ 80,000. Subscription $19.95. 75% freelance. Query or complete ms/cover letter; fax query ok. Pays .10/wd, on publication, for 1st & some reprint rts (anthology & online rts). Articles 1,000-3,000 wds. Responds in 4-6 wks. Kill fee 50%. Sidebars ok. Guidelines/theme list; copy $5/10x13 SAE/4 stamps.

    Tips: "Let us know your particular areas of specialization and any books or papers you have written in the area of Christian history."

    ** 1994 EPA Award of Merit - General.

CHRISTIAN HOME & SCHOOL, 3350 East Paris Ave. SE, Box 8709, Grand Rapids MI 49512. (616)957-1070. Fax: (616)957-5022. Christian Schools Intl. Dr. Gordon L. Bordewyk, ed; submit to Roger Schmurr, sr. ed. Focuses on parenting and Christian education; for parents who send their children to Christian schools. Bimonthly mag; 32 pgs; circ 52,000. Subscription $11.95. 50% freelance. Complete ms/cover letter; no phone query. Pays $75-150, on publication, for 1st rts. Articles 1,200-2,000 wds (40/yr); fiction 1,200-2,000 wds. Responds in 1 mo. Seasonal 4 mos ahead. Considers simultaneous query. Guidelines/theme list; copy for 9x12 SAE/4 stamps.

    Tips: Most open to features.

    ** 1994 EPA Award of Merit - Organizational.

+CHRISTIAN INFORMATION ASSOCIATES NEWSLETTER (C.I.A.), P.O. Box 55, Decatur AR 72722. W.B. Atwood, ed. For the Christian who wants specific information on Bible prophecy that is being fulfilled today; patriotic. Monthly newsletter; variable length. Free subscription (donation expected). Estab 1994. 100% freelance. Complete ms/cover letter. **PAYS IN SUBSCRIPTION,** for one-time rts. Considers simultaneous submissions. No disk. Sidebars ok. Theme list; copy $1.

    Fillers: Accepts 24-30/yr. Anecdotes, cartoons, facts, newsbreaks, prayers, Bible quotes; 60-150 wds.

CHRISTIAN LIVING, 616 Walnut Ave., Scottdale PA 15683-1999. (412)887-8500. Mennonite. Steve Kriss, ed. Denominational with emphasis on community, family and spirituality. Monthly (8X) mag; 36 pgs; circ 6,000. 50% freelance. Complete ms. Pays $30-60, on acceptance, for one-time rts. Articles 700-1,200 wds (50/yr); fiction 700-1,200 wds (4/yr). Responds in 3 wks. Seasonal 5 mos ahead. Considers simultaneous submissions & reprints. Guidelines; copy for 9x12 SAE/3 stamps.

Poetry: Buys 10-12/yr. Free verse, haiku; 3-24 lines; $10-30. Submit max. 6 poems.

Ethnic: Targets all ethnic groups involved in the Mennonite religion.

Tips: "We want well-written, non-formulaic fiction."

** This periodical was #56 on the 1994 Top 50 Plus Christian Publishers list. (#41 in 1993)

CHRISTIAN MEDIA, Box 448, Jacksonville OR 97530. (503)899-8888. James Lloyd, ed/pub. For emerging Christian songwriters, artists, and others professionals involved in music, video, film, print and broadcasting. Bimonthly newsletter; 8 pgs; circ 4,000. Query. Payment negotiable, on publication, for all rts. Articles. Accepts reprints. Prefers disk copy. No guidelines; copy $1.

Special Needs: Particularly interested in stories that expose dirty practices in the industry—royalty rip-offs, misleading ads, financial misconduct, etc.

#THE CHRISTIAN OBSERVER, 9400 Fairview Ave., Ste. 200, Manassas VA 22110. (703)335-2844. Fax: (703)368-4817. The Christian Observer, Inc.; Presbyterian Reformed. Edwin Elliott, ed. To encourage and edify God's people and families. Mag. published 2X/month; circ 2,000. Subscription $27. Not in topical listings.

CHRISTIAN PARENTING TODAY, P.O. Box 36630, Colorado Springs CO 80936. (719)531-7776. Fax: (719)535-0172. Brad Lewis, ed. Practical advice for parents, from a Christian perspective, that runs the whole gamut of needs: social, educational, spiritual, medical, etc. Bimonthly mag; 68-104 pgs; circ 225,000. Subscription $16.97. 90% freelance. Query; fax query ok. Articles to 2,500 wds (10/yr); book/music reviews (usually assigned), 500 wds, $35. Pays .15-.25/wd, on acceptance for assigned (on publication for unsolicited), for 1st rts. Responds in 8 wks. Seasonal 8 mos ahead. Considers simultaneous submissions & reprints. Kill fee 25%. Prefers disk on final. Sidebars ok. Guidelines; copy for 9x12 SAE/5 stamps.

Fillers: Buys 60-100/yr. Anecdotes, short humor, parenting tips; 25-100 wds; $25-40.

Columns/Departments: Buys 15/yr. Parent Exchange (parenting tips), 25-100 wds, $40; Life in Our House (humorous anecdotes), 25-100 wds, $25.

Tips: "Use the presence of people in your writing. Quotes from authorities and examples from real life make a strong article. No preaching."

** This periodical was #27 on the 1994 Top 50 Plus Christian Publishers list (#4 in 1993). Also 1994 EPA Award of Excellence - General.

THE CHRISTIAN READER, 465 Gundersen Dr., Carol Stream IL 60188. (708)260-6200. Fax: (708)260-0114. Christianity Today, Inc. Bonne Steffen, ed. A Christian "Readers Digest" that uses both reprints and original material. Monthly mag; 115 pgs; circ 250,000. Subscription $17.50. 20% freelance. Query/fax query ok. Pays $10-400 (.10/wd); on acceptance; for 1st & reprint rts. Articles 500-1,500 wds (50/yr). Responds in 2-6 wks. Seasonal 6 mos ahead. Considers simultaneous submissions & reprints. Kill fee. Prefers disk copy. Guidelines; copy for 6x9 SAE/2 stamps.

Poetry: Buys 2/yr. Free verse, light verse, traditional; 25-75 lines; $40-65. Submit max. 6 poems.

Fillers: Short humor (see Lite Fare).

Columns/Departments: Buys 2/yr. Lite Fare (adult church humor), 25-150 wds; Kids of the Kingdom (kids say and do funny things), 25-150 wds; Personally Speaking (quotes from well-known people), 250-500 wds; $25. Complete ms.

Tips: "Keep articles short; we edit everything. First-person non-fiction stories are a top priority editorially for final selection."

CHRISTIAN RENEWAL, Box 770, Lewiston NY 14092. (716)284-7784. Fax: (905)562-7828. Reformed (Conservative). John Van Dyk, mng. ed. Church-related and world news for members of the Reformed community of churches in North America. Biweekly tabloid; 20 pgs; circ 4,300. Subscription $28/yr. 25% freelance. Complete ms. **NO PAYMENT.** Articles 500-2,000 wds; fiction (6/yr). Responds in 4 wks. Seasonal 3 mos ahead. Accepts reprints.

CHRISTIAN RESEARCH JOURNAL, Box 500, San Juan Capistrano CA 92693-0500. (714)855-9926. Fax: (714)855-9927. Christian Research Institute. Elliot Miller, ed-in-chief. For those who have been affected by cults and the occult. Quarterly mag; 56 pgs; circ 34,000. Subscription $20. 3% freelance. Complete ms. Pays .15/wd, on publication, for 1st rts. Articles to 5,000 wds (1/yr); book reviews 1,000-2,500 wds. Responds in 16-20 wks. Kill fee up to 50%. Requires disk copy. Rarely uses sidebars. Guidelines; copy $5.

Columns/Departments: Witnessing Tips (evangelism), 1,000 wds; Viewpoint (opinion on cults, ethics, etc.), 875 wds.

Tips: "Be patient; we sometimes review mss only twice a year, but we will get back to you. Most open to features (on cults), book reviews, opinion pieces and witnessing tips."

#CHRISTIAN RETAILING, 600 Rinehart Rd., Lake Mary FL 32746. (407)333-0600. Fax: (407)333-9753. Strang Communications, Inc. Carol Chapman Stertzer, ed. Business/trade publication directed toward Christian retail/bookstore owners, managers and clerks. Monthly trade journal/tabloid; 72 pgs; circ 9,500. 60% freelance. Complete ms. Pays .10-.12/wd ($200-340); on publication; for all rts. Articles to 700-2,000 wds (36/yr). Responds in 2 mos. Seasonal 5 mos ahead. Kill fee. Accepts reprints. Guidelines; copy $3.

Fillers: Buys 5/yr. Anecdotes, cartoons, ideas; 50-300 wds; $20-50.

Tips: "Most open to features. Think about interesting subjects for Christian retailers."

CHRISTIAN SINGLE, 127 9th Ave. N, Nashville TN 37234. (615)251-5721. Fax: (615)251-5008. Southern Baptist. Stephen Felts, ed-in-chief; Leigh Neely, mng ed. For Christian singles, ages 25-45. Monthly mag; 52 pgs; circ 70,000. Subscription $13.30. 50% freelance. Query or complete ms/cover letter; phone/fax query ok. Pays $25 & up (negotiable); on acceptance; for all, 1st, one-time or reprint rts. Articles 500-2,000 wds (48/yr) & fiction 1,800-2,500 wds (6/yr—complete ms). Responds in 4-8 wks. Seasonal 6 mos ahead. Accepts reprints. Requires disk copy. Uses sidebars in most feature articles. Guidelines; copy for 9x12 SAE/4 stamps.

Poetry: Buys 12/yr. Traditional; any length; $25-100. Submit max. 3 poems.

Special Needs: "Anything related to Christian single lifestyle."

Tips: "Be aware of audience; they aren't all preparing for marriage. They're happy and secure with their single status. They are interested in travel, spiritual enrichment, and in-depth articles related to today's tough issues."

** This periodical was #47 on the 1994 Top 50 Plus Christian Publishers list.

#CHRISTIAN SOCIAL ACTION, 100 Maryland Ave. NE, Washington DC 20002. (202)488-5621. Fax: (202)488-5619. United Methodist. Lee Ranck, ed. Information and analysis of critical social issues from the perspective of Christian faith. Monthly (11X) mag; 48 pgs; circ 2,500. Subscription $13.50. 2% freelance. Query or complete ms/cover letter. Pays $75-125, on publication, for all rts. Articles 2,000 wds (25-30/yr). Responds in 4-5 wks (longer for accepted material). Sometimes accepts reprints. Guidelines/copy for #10 SAE.

Tips: "We look for experts on an issue who can write, instead of writers who can research an issue; know the issue well. Our audience is Christian social activists."

CHRISTIAN STANDARD, 8121 Hamilton Ave., Cincinnati OH 45231. (513)931-4050. Fax: (513)931-0904. Standard Publishing/Christian Churches/Churches of Christ. Sam E. Stone, ed. Devoted to the restoration of New Testament Christianity, its doctrines, its ordinances, and its fruits. Weekly mag; 24 pgs; circ 61,000. Subscription $17. 50% freelance. Complete ms/cover letter. Pays $10-80, on publication, for 1st rts. Articles 400-1,600 wds (200/yr). Responds in 4 wks. Seasonal 8-12 mos ahead. Accepts reprints. Guidelines; copy for 9x12 SAE/3 stamps.

+CHRISTIANITY AND THE ARTS, P.O. Box 118088, Chicago IL 60611. (312)642-8606. Nondenominational. Marci Whitney-Schenck, ed/pub. Emphasis is on Christian expression in art, dance, music, literature and film. Quarterly; circ 5,000. Subscription $15. Estab 1994. Query. **NO PAYMENT FOR NOW.** Uses articles, poetry, reviews and essays. No guidelines; sample copy for SASE.

#CHRISTIANITY TODAY, 465 Gundersen Dr., Carol Stream IL 60188-2498. (708)260-6200. Fax: (708)260-0114. Carol Thiessen, ed. For evangelical Christian thought leaders who seek to integrate their faith commitment with responsible action. Magazine published 15X/yr; 90 pgs; circ 200,000. Subscription $24.95. 80% freelance. Query/clips; no phone query. Pays .10/wd, on publication, for 1st rts. Articles 1,000-4,000 wds (60/yr); book reviews 500-750 wds, pays $75. Responds in 3 mos. Seasonal 8 mos ahead. Accepts reprints (payment 25% of regular rate). Kill fee. Guidelines; copy for 9x12 SAE/3 stamps.

    Columns/Departments: Buys 7/yr. Church in Action (profile of unusual person/ministry), 900-1,000 wds (query); Speaking Out (op/ed), 650 wds (complete ms); $75-150.

    Tips: "Most of our freelance material is assigned."

#CHRISTMAS, The Annual of Christmas Literature and Art, Box 1209, Minneapolis MN 55440. (612)330-3442. Augsburg Fortress. Kristine Oberg, ed. Birth of Christ central to celebration of Christmas. Annual book; 64 pgs; circ 40,000. 70-100% freelance. Complete ms/cover letter; no phone query. Pays $150-300, on acceptance, for one-time rts. Articles 1,500-2,500 wds (3-4/yr); fiction 1,000-2,000 wds (3-4/yr). Responds in 12 wks. Works 14-18 mos ahead. Accepts reprints. Guidelines/themes; copy $12.95 + postage (call 800-328-4648).

    Poetry: Buys 2-3/yr. Free verse, light verse, traditional; to 30 lines; $75-125. Submit max. 3 poems. Nothing on Santa Claus.

    Tips: "Short stories related to Christmas only." Using less freelance.

    ** #47 on the 1993 Top 50.

#CHURCH & STATE, 8120 Fenton St., Silver Springs MD 20910-4781. (301)589-3707. Fax: (301)495-9173. Americans United for Separation of Church and State. Joseph L. Conn, mng. ed. Emphasizes religious liberty and church/state relations matters. Monthly mag; 24-32 pgs; circ 33,000. 10% freelance. Query. Pays negotiable fee, on acceptance, for all rts. Articles 600-3,000 wds (11/yr), prefers 800-1,600 (11/yr). Responds in 2 mos. Considers simultaneous query & reprints. Guidelines; copy for 9x12 SAE/3 stamps.

    Tips: "We are not a religious magazine. You need to see our magazine before you try to write for it."

#THE CHURCH ADVOCATE, Box 926, 700 E. Melrose Ave., Findlay OH 45839. (419)424-1961. Fax: (419)424-3433. Churches of God General Conference. Linda M. Draper, ed. Denominational. Monthly mag; circ 6,660. Subscription $10. Little freelance. Query or complete ms. Pays $10/printed pg, on publication. Articles 1,000-2,500 wds. Accepts reprints. Free guidelines/copy.

#THE CHURCH HERALD, 4500 - 60th St. SE, Grand Rapids MI 49512-9642. (616)698-7071. Fax: (616)698-6606. Reformed Church in America. Jeffrey Japinga, mng. ed. We are seeking to relate the Christian faith to the problems and issues our denominational audience faces every day. Monthly mag; circ 108,000. Subscription $10. 5% freelance. Query only (complete ms for fiction). Pays $50-200 ($45-120 for fiction); on acceptance; for 1st, one-time, all, simultaneous & reprint rts. Articles 400-1,500 wds (15/yr); fiction 400-1,500 wds (1/yr). Responds in 1-2 mos. Seasonal 6 mos ahead. Considers simultaneous query & reprints. Kill fee 50%. Guidelines; copy $2/9x12 SAE.

> **Tips:** "Most open to feature articles."

*CHURCH HERALD AND HOLINESS BANNER, 7415 Metcalf, Box 4060, Overland Park KS 66204. (913)432-0331. Fax: (913)722-0351. Church of God (Holiness)/Herald and Banner Press. Ray Crooks, ed. Denominational; conservative/evangelical people. Biweekly mag; 20 pgs; circ 2,500. Subscription $10. 50% freelance. Complete ms/cover letter; no phone query. **NO PAYMENT**, for one-time rts. Not copyrighted. Articles 200-800 wds (25+/yr); fiction 500-1,000 wds. Responds in 2 mos. Seasonal 6 mos ahead. Considers simultaneous submissions & reprints. Guidelines; no copy.

> **Poetry:** Buys few. Traditional; 8-24 lines.
>
> **Fillers:** Anecdotes, facts, prose, quotes; 150-400 wds.
>
> **Tips:** "Most open to devotional articles. Must be concise, well-written, and get one main point across; 200-400 wds."

CHURCH OF GOD EVANGEL, 1080 Montgomery Ave., Cleveland TN 37311. (615)476-4512. Church of God (Cleveland, TN). Homer G. Rhea, ed-in-chief. Denominational. Monthly mag; 36 pgs; circ 50,000. Subscription $10. 40% freelance. Complete ms; no phone/fax query. Pays $10-50, on acceptance, for one-time rts. Articles 400-1,200 wds (25/yr). Responds in 2 wks. Seasonal 6 mos ahead. Considers simultaneous submissions. Seldom uses sidebars. Guidelines (2 stamps); copy for 9x12 SAE/4 stamps.

> **Tips:** "Always willing to buy thoughtful, well-written pieces that speak to people where they live. Always need humor with a point."

#CLASS, 900 Broadway, New York NY 10003. (212)677-3055. General publication that accepts religious articles. Denolyn Carroll, exec. ed. Geared toward Caribbean, Latin, and African-American readers, 18-49 years old. Monthly mag; circ 250,000. 25% freelance. Query/clips. Pays up to .10/wd, 45 days after publication, for 1st & reprint rts. Articles 500-1,300 wds. Responds in 6 wks. Seasonal 3 mos ahead. Guidelines; copy for 9x12 SAE/4 stamps.

> **Poetry:** Buys 10-20/yr; up to $10. Submit max. 5 poems.

#COLUMBIA, P.O. 1670, New Haven CT 06510. (203)772-2130. Fax: (203)777-0114. Knights of Columbus (Catholic). Richard McMunn, ed. Geared to a general Catholic family audience. Monthly mag; 92 pgs; circ 1.5 million. Subscription $6; foreign add $2. 50-60% freelance. Query; no phone query. Pays to $250-500, on acceptance, for 1st rts. Articles 1,000-1,500 wds (30/yr). Responds in 2-3 wks. Seasonal 4 mos ahead. Accepts reprints. Kill fee 20%. Free guidelines/copy.

> **Tips:** "Keep eye out for K of C activity in local area and send a query letter about it."
>
> ** This periodical was #19 on the 1994 Top 50 Plus Christian Publishers list.

COMMENTS FROM THE FRIENDS, Box 819, Assonet MA 02702. No calls. David A. Reed, ed. For ex-Jehovah's Witnesses, their relatives, Christians reaching out to them, and dissident Witnesses. Quarterly newsletter; 16 pgs; circ 1,500. Subscription $9. 5% freelance. Complete ms/cover letter. Pays $5-20 (sometimes copies), on publication, for one-time rts. Articles 50-2,000 wds (3/yr); book reviews 50-

1,000 wds. Responds in 4-8 wks. Seasonal 4 mos ahead. Considers simultaneous submissions & reprints. Macintosh disks only. No sidebars. Guidelines; copy $1/#10 SAE/2 stamps.

Columns/Departments: Witnessing Tips, 500-1,000 wds.

Special Needs: Articles about Jehovah's Witnesses; articles about changes in Watchtower governing body.

Tips: "Acquaint us with why you are qualified to write about J.W.'s. Write well-documented, concise articles relevant to J.W.'s today. We automatically reject all material not specifically about Jehovah's Witnesses."

COMMON BOUNDARY, 5272 River Rd., Ste. 650 Bethesda MD 20816. (301)652-9495. Ecumenical. Mark Judge, ed. asst. Explores relationship between psychotherapy and spirituality. Bimonthly mag; 64 pgs; circ 26,000. 50% freelance. Query. Pays varying rates, on publication, for 1st rts. Articles 3,000-4,000 wds. Responds in 3-6 mos. Considers simultaneous submissions. Kill fee 1/3. Guidelines; copy $5.

Fillers: Newsbreaks, 200-600 wds.

+COMMON GROUND, 5038 Dorsey Hall Dr., Ellicott City MD 21042. (41)740-5300. Fax: (410)5305. Division of Search Ministries. Mike Donohue, mng ed. Church bulletin insert for evangelical churches interested in lifestyle evangelism; 1 pg. Sells in quantities of 50, to churches. 10% freelance. Query/clips; phone query ok. Pays $400, on acceptance, for one-time rts. Articles 900-1,100 wds. Seasonal 3 mos ahead. Requires disk copy. Guidelines/theme list/copy for #10 SAE/1 stamp.

Tips: "Be practical, down-to-earth in writing. Incorporate stories into the articles to illustrate themes. Call me for themes before submitting."

COMMONWEAL, 15 Dutch St., New York NY 10038. (212)732-0800. Catholic. Patrick Jordan, mng ed. A review of public affairs, religion, literature and the arts. Biweekly mag; 32 pgs; circ 19,000. Subscription $39. 30% freelance. Query; phone query ok/no fax query. Pays $75-100, on publication, for all rts. Articles 750-3,000 wds (60/yr); fiction (2/yr); some book/music reviews, 750 wds, $75. Responds in 3-4 wks. Seasonal 3 mos ahead. Kill fee 2%. Occasional sidebars. Guidelines; copy for 10x13 SAE/3 stamps.

Poetry: Rosemary Deen. Buys 25/yr. Free verse, haiku, light verse traditional; to 75 lines; .50/line. Submit max. 5 poems.

Columns/Departments: Upfronts (brief, newsy facts and info behind the headlines), 750-1,000 wds; The Last Word (commentary based on insight from personal experience or reflection), 700 wds.

Tips: "Most open to meaningful articles on social, political, religious and cultural topics; or columns."

#COMPANION MAGAZINE, Box 535, Station F, Toronto ON M4Y 2L8 Canada. (416)463-5442. Fax: (416)463-4392. Catholic/Franciscan. Fr. R. Riccioli, ed; submit to Betty McCrimmon, man. ed. An adult, Catholic, inspirational, devotional family magazine. Monthly (11X) mag; 32 pgs; circ 5,000. 50% freelance. Complete ms, with cover letter. Pays .06/wd (Canadian funds), on publication, for 1st rts. Articles 500-1,500 wds (35/yr); fiction 500-1,000 wds (7/yr). Responds in 6 wks. Seasonal 5 mos ahead. Considers simultaneous submissions. Guidelines; copy for 7x10 SAE with IRCs.

Poetry: Free verse, light verse, traditional. Pays .60/line (Canadian).

Fillers: Anecdotes, cartoons, prayers, quotes, short humor, word puzzles.

Special Needs: Articles on St. Francis, Franciscan spirituality, and social justice.

Tips: Most open to human interest.

COMPANIONS, Box 1212, Harrisonburg VA 22801-1212. (703)434-0768. Mennonite. Roger L. Berry, ed. Consistent with conservative Mennonite doctrine: believer baptism, nonresistance, and nonconformity. Weekly take-home paper; 4 pgs; circ 8,000. Subscription $9.50. 80% freelance. Complete ms; no phone/fax query. Pays .02-.05/wd, on acceptance, for all, 1st, or reprint rts. Articles 200-800 wds (200/yr) & fiction 800-3,000 wds (30/yr). Responds in 6 wks. Seasonal 5 mos ahead. Accepts reprints. No disks. No sidebars. Guidelines; copy for 9x12 SAE/2 stamps.

> **Poetry:** Buys 40/yr. Traditional, 8-24 lines; .30-.50/line. Submit max. 5 poems.
>
> **Fillers:** Buys 15/yr. Anecdotes, prose, prayers; 50-150 wds.
>
> **Columns/Departments:** Buys 15/yr. Science and Scripture (creationist/Biblicist), and Archaeology and Scripture (archaeology that support biblical truths); 400-700 wds.
>
> **Tips:** "Study guidelines and get a feel for our very distinctive approach to Christian living. We now require prospective writers to complete our Writer's Questionnaire before we consider their writing."
>
> ** This periodical was #28 on the 1994 Top 50 Plus Christian Publishers list. (#32 in 1993)

#COMPASS: A Jesuit Journal, 10 St. Mary St. #300, Toronto ON M4Y 1P9 Canada. (416)921-0653. Fax: (416)921-1864. Catholic. Robert Chodos, ed. Ethical and ecumenical discussion of social and religious topics; for educated, but non-specialized readership. Bimonthly mag; 52 pgs; circ 3,700. Subscription $19. 10% freelance. Query/clips; no phone query. Pays $100-500 (Canadian), on publication, for 1st rts. Articles 1,000-2,000 wds (60/yr); fiction 1,000-2,500 wds/pays $100-250); book reviews 2,000 wds/$300. Responds in 8 wks. No seasonal. Considers simultaneous submissions. Kill fee 50%. Guidelines/theme list; copy $2/9x12 SAE/$1.35 postage (Canadian).

> **Fillers:** Accepts 60/yr. Short, pithy quotes from other writers; 10-150 wds. Pays 1-yr subscription.
>
> **Columns/Departments:** Buys 24/yr. Testament (contemporary application of scripture); Colloquy (theology & daily life); Saint (fresh perspective on a Saint); all 750 wds; $100-150. Query.
>
> **Tips:** "We are interested primarily in analytical and reflective articles. Write for themes."

*CONNECTING POINT, Box 685, Cocoa FL 32923. (407)632-0130. Linda G. Howard, ed. For and by the mentally challenged (retarded) community; primarily deals with spiritual and self-advocacy issues. Monthly mag; circ 1,000. Estab 1989. 75% freelance. Complete ms. **NO PAYMENT** for 1st rts. Articles (24/yr) & fiction (12/yr), 250-750 wds; book reviews 150 wds. Responds in 3-6 wks. Seasonal 3 mos ahead. Considers simultaneous submissions & reprints. Guidelines; copy for 9x12 SAE/6 stamps.

> **Poetry:** Accepts 4/yr. Any type; 4-66 lines. Submit max. 10 poems.
>
> **Fillers:** Accepts 12/yr. Cartoons, games, word puzzles; 50-250 wds.
>
> **Columns/Departments:** Accepts 24/yr. Devotion Page, 1,000 wds; Bible Study, 500 wds. Query.
>
> **Special Needs:** Record reviews, self-advocacy, integration/normalization, justice system.
>
> **Tips:** "All ms need to be in primary vocabulary."

CONQUEST, 1300 N Meacham Rd., Schaumburg IL 60173-4888. (708)843-1600. Regular Baptist. Joan E. Alexander, ed. Take-home paper for adults; conservative, fundamental. Weekly take-home paper; 4 pgs; circ 60,000. 50-60% freelance. Complete ms. Pays .03-.05/wd, on acceptance, for all, 1st or one-time rts. Articles 200-1,200 wds (25-35/yr); fiction 600-1,500 wds (some multi-part fiction), (20-30/yr). Responds in 4-8 wks. Seasonal 1 yr ahead. Sidebars ok. Guidelines; copy for #10 SAE/2 stamps.

> **Fillers:** Anecdotes, facts, ideas, newsbreaks, prose, short humor, word puzzles.
>
> **Tips:** Not everything that is Christian is suitable for readers in fundamental Baptist churches. Most open to fiction and nonfiction."

CORNERSTONE, 939 W. Wilson, Chicago IL 60640. (312)561-2450x2080. Fax: (312)989-2076. Evangelical Covenant Church. Jennifer Ingerson, submissions ed. For young adults, 18-35; covers contemporary issues in light of evangelical Christianity. Quarterly (3-4x) mag; 64 pgs; circ 30,000. Subscription $15. Up to 20% freelance. Complete ms/cover letter; fax query ok. Pays .08-.10/wd), on publication, for one-time rts. Articles to 2,700 wds (1-3/yr); fiction 250-2,500 wds (1-4/yr); book/music/film reviews 500-1,000 wds. Responds in 12-24 wks. Seasonal 6 mos ahead. Considers simultaneous submissions & reprints. Sidebars ok. Guidelines; copy for 9x12 SAE/5 stamps.

> **Poetry:** Tammy Boyd. Buys 15-24/yr. Any type; $10-25. Submit max. 5 poems.
>
> **Fillers:** Buys 1-4/yr. Cartoons, facts, prose, prayers, quotes; 500-1,000 wds.
>
> **Columns/Departments:** Buys 3-4/yr. Music Interviews to 2,700 wds. News items.
>
> **Tips:** "Issues pertinent to contemporary society seen with a biblical world view. No pornography, cheap shots about non-Christians, or unrealistic/sugar-sweet articles. Looking for high-quality fiction and book or music reviews."

THE COVENANT COMPANION, 5101 N. Francisco Ave., Chicago IL 60625. (312)784-3000. Fax: (312)784-4366. Evangelical Covenant Church. John E. Phelan, Jr., ed. Denominational. Monthly mag; 40 pgs; circ 22,000. Subscription $26. 20% freelance. Complete ms/cover letter. Pays $15-50; on publication; for 1st or one-time rts. Articles 300-1,000 wds (10-55/yr); book reviews 500-1,000 wds/$15-25. Responds in 4-6 wks. Seasonal 3-6 mos ahead. Considers simultaneous submissions & reprints. Sidebar ok. Guidelines; copy $2.25/9x12 SAE.

> **Poetry:** Buys 5-10/yr. Free verse; $15. Submit max. 3 poems.
>
> **Tips:** "Study guidelines and send general articles of universal interest and pertinence. Also open to church year/holiday material."

THE CRESSET, A Review of Arts, Literature & Public Affairs, Huegli Hall #29, Valpariaso IN 46383. (219)464-5274. Fax: (219)464-5496. Valpariaso University/Lutheran. Gail McGrew Eifrig, ed. For college educated, professors, pastors, lay people; serious review essays on religious-cultural affairs. Monthly mag; circ 4,300. Subscription $8.50. 100% freelance. Complete ms/cover letter. Pays $25, on publication, for all rts. Articles 1,500 wds & up (25/yr). Responds in 12 wks. Prefers disk copy. No sidebars. Copy for 9x12 SAE/5 stamps.

> **Poetry:** Rene Steinke, ed. Buys 25/yr. Avant-garde, free verse, traditional; $25.
>
> **Columns/Departments:** Buys 5/yr, $25.

THE CRITIC, 205 W. Monroe St., 6th Floor, Chicago IL 60606-5097. (312)609-8880. Fax: (312)609-8891. American Catholic Culture. John Sprague, ed. Emphasis on literature, arts and theology. Quarterly journal; 130 pgs; circ 2,000. Subscription $20. 80% freelance. Query (complete ms for fiction or poetry); no phone query. Pays $25-400, on acceptance, for one-time rts. No reprints. Articles (8/yr); fiction (8/yr). Responds in 6-8 wks. Prefers disk. No guidelines; copy $6.

> **Poetry:** Buys 15/yr. Submit max. 3 poems.
>
> **Fillers:** Cartoons.
>
> **Special Needs:** Literary profiles/interviews; ecumenical issues.

+CROSS ROADS, P.O. Box 3826-G, Silver Spring MD 20918-0826. Submit to The Editor. A place to share your gifts. **PAYS 5 COPIES.** Articles & short stories, to 1,500 wds. Accepts reprints. Does not return submissions. Guidelines.

+CROSSWAY/NEWSLINE, 103 Ambleside Rd., Lightwater, Surrey GU185UJ England. Tel. 02764 72724. Airline Aviation & Aerospace Christian Fellowship. J. Brown, gen. sec. Crossway is an annual magazine;

Newsline a quarterly booklet; 16 pgs. Free subscription. 100% freelance. **NO PAYMENT.** Articles on aviation to 2,000 wds. Sample copy.

#DECISION, 1300 Harmon Pl., Minneapolis MN 55440. (612)338-0500. Fax: (612)335-1299. Billy Graham Evangelistic Assn. Roger C. Palms, ed. Evangelism/Christian nurture. Monthly (11X) mag; 42 pgs; circ 1,800,000. Subscription $7. 25% freelance. Complete ms; no phone query. Pays $10-200, on publication, for all, 1st or reprint rts. Articles 1,400-1,600 wds (90/yr). Reports 1-2 wks. Seasonal 10-12 mos ahead. Kill fee. Guidelines/theme list; copy for 10x13 SAE/3 stamps.

> **Poetry:** Buys 40/yr. Free verse, light verse, traditional; 4-20 lines; .50/wd. Submit max. 7 poems.
>
> **Fillers:** Buys 30-40/yr. Anecdotes, prose; 400-1,000 wds; $50-75.
>
> **Columns/Departments:** Buys 11/yr. Where Are They Now? (people who have become Christian through Billy Graham ministries); 600-900 wds; $70.
>
> **Special Needs:** Vignettes—Concise narratives relating incidents from life written with a spiritual application; 400-1,000 wds.
>
> **Tips:** "Most open to first-person testimonies of people from all walks of life that clearly show how an individual committed life to Jesus Christ."
>
> ** This periodical was #59 on the 1994 Top 50 Plus Christian Publishers list.

#DISCIPLESHIP JOURNAL, Box 35004, Colorado Springs CO 80935. (719)531-3529. Fax: (719)598-7128. The Navigators. Susan Maycinik, ed. For motivated, maturing Christians desiring to grow spiritually and to help others grow; biblical and practical. Bimonthly mag; 80 pgs; circ 100,000. Subscription $18.97. 95% freelance. Query; no phone query. Pays .17/wd, on acceptance, for 1st or reprint rts. Articles 500-3,000 wds (50/yr); fiction published rarely. Responds in 4-6 wks. Seasonal 6 mos ahead. Considers simultaneous submissions. Kill fee. Guidelines/theme list; copy for 9x12 SAE/7 stamps.

> **Columns/Departments:** Buys 6/yr. On the Home Front (Q & A regarding family issues); 950 wds; $175.
>
> **Tips:** "Most open to non-theme articles."
>
> ** This periodical was #8 on the 1994 Top 50 Plus Christian Publishers list. (#36 in 1993)

*DISCOVERY, P.O. Box 607702, Orlando FL 32860-7702. (407)682-9494. Fax: (407)682-7005. Radio Station WTLN FM/AM. Janice Willis, ed. For Christian community in Central Florida. Bimonthly newspaper; circ 20,000. Subscription $3. Query. **NO PAYMENT.** Not copyrighted. Articles & book reviews. Seasonal 3 mos ahead. Accepts reprints.

> **Columns/Departments:** Christian Walk (general interest), 500 wds; Family Life (babies-seniors), 500 wds.
>
> **Tips:** "We've never used fiction but would be open to parables."

#THE DOOR, Box 118, N. 30th St., Waco TX 76710. (916)842-2701. Fax: (916)842-7729. Youth Specialties. Bob Darden, ed. (817)752-1468. Satire of evangelical church plus issue-oriented interviews. Bimonthly mag; 36 pgs; circ 11,000. Subscription $24. 50% freelance. Complete ms; no phone query. Pays $60-200, on publication, for 1st rts. Not copyrighted. Articles 750-1,500 wds (30/yr). Responds in 3 mos. Seasonal 6 mos ahead. Accepts reprints. Kill fee $40-50. Guidelines/theme list; copy $4.

> **Poetry:** Mike Yaconelli. Buys 2-3/yr. Avant-garde, free verse; $40-100. Submit max. 6 poems.
>
> **Fillers:** Buys 10/yr. Cartoons, quizzes, short humor, mock ads; 100-250 wds; $50-100.
>
> **Tips:** "We look for biting satire/humor—National Lampoon not Reader's Digest. You must understand our satirical slant. Read more than one issue to understand our 'wavelength.' "

+DOVETAIL: A Newsletter By and For Jewish-Christian Families, P.O. Box 19945, Kalamazoo MI 49019. (616)342-2900. Joan C. Hawkhurst, ed. Offers balanced, non-judgmental articles for interfaith families and the professionals who serve them. Bimonthly newsletter; 12-16 pgs; circ 800. Subscription $24.99. Estab. 1992. Complete ms/cover letter; no phone/fax query. Pays $20 or subscription, on publication, for one-time rts. Articles 800-1,200 wds (15/yr). Reports in 8 wks. Seasonal 4 mos ahead. Accepts simultaneous submissions & reprints. Prefers disk copy. Some sidebars. No guidelines; copy for 5x7 SAE/2 stamps.

#DREAMS & VISIONS, RR 1, Washago ON L0K 2B0 Canada. Skysong Press. Steve Stanton, ed. Quality fiction for Christian readers. Triannual journal; 52 pgs; circ 200. Subscription $12 U.S. 100% freelance. Complete ms. **NO PAYMENT** ($100 for Best of Year as chosen by subscribers), for 1st rts & one non-exclusive reprint. Fiction 2,000-6,000 wds (28/yr). Responds in 6-8 wks. Considers simultaneous submissions. Guidelines; copy $3.95.

> **Tips:** "Be concise, powerful and unique."

EMPHASIS ON FAITH AND LIVING, Box 9127, Fort Wayne IN 46899-9127. (219)747-2027. Fax: (219)747-5331. Missionary Church. Robert Ransom, mng ed. Denominational; for adults 40 and older. Bimonthly mag; 16 pgs; circ 13,000. Subscription free. 10% freelance. Complete ms/cover letter; no phone query. Pays .03-.04/wd; on publication; for 1st, one-time, reprint or simultaneous rts. Not copyrighted. Articles 200-800 wds (3/yr); fiction 200-1,600 wds (1-2/yr). Responds in 4-8 wks. Seasonal 4 mos ahead. Considers simultaneous submissions & reprints. Guidelines; copy for 9x12 SAE/2 stamps.

> **Tips:** "Our publication provides church news, missions information, and spiritual reading for members and friends of the Missionary Church denomination. We seek material that is compatible with our Wesleyan-Armenian church doctrine."

+ENCOURAGER PROVIDER, 4102 NW Dondee, Topeka KS 66618. (913)286-0388. Interdenominational. Charles White, sr ed. Serves home, day-care providers for 2-5 year olds. Biweekly newsletter; 6 pgs; circ 1,600. Estab 1994. 5% freelance. Complete ms. Pays $5-30, on acceptance, for one-time rts. Articles 50-300 wds (5/yr). Seasonal 1 yr ahead. Considers simultaneous submissions & reprints. Sidebars ok.

> **Columns/Departments:** Buys 5/yr. Pays $5.

+END TIMES BULLETIN, P.O. Box 387, Lice Oak FL 32060. (904)364-7318. Interdenominational. Submit to Editor. Focuses on committed Christian living and end-times. Quarterly newsletter. Free subscription. Estab 1992. 50% freelance. **NO PAYMENT.** Not copyrighted. Considers simultaneous submissions & reprints. Sidebars ok. Not in topical listings.

> **Columns/Departments:** Format (hard-hitting preaching/teaching articles; Christian testimonials; Bible prophecy; end-times events).

+ENLACE INFORMATIVO, 7891 W. Flagler St., Ste. 248, Miami FL 33144. (305)559-0084. Fax: (305)559-2735. Maria Isabel Garcia, ed. To spread the Gospel; to unite, inform, and involve the Hispanic Christian community. Monthly newspaper; circ 15,000. Open to freelance.

#EPISCOPAL LIFE, 815 2nd Ave., New York NY 10017. (212)922-5398. Episcopal Church. Jerrold F. Hames, ed; Edward P. Stannard, mng. ed. Denominational. Monthly newspaper; 32 pgs; circ 180,000. Estab 1990. 35% freelance. Query/clips or complete ms/cover letter; phone query on breaking news only. Pays $50-300, on publication, for 1st, one-time or simultaneous rts. Articles 250-1,200 wds (12/yr); assigned book reviews 400 wds ($35). Responds in 1 mo. Seasonal 4 mos ahead. Considers simultaneous submissions & reprints. Kill fee 50%. No guidelines; free copy.

> **Columns/Departments:** Nan Cobbey. Buys 36/yr. Commentary on political/religious topics; 300-600 wds; $35-75. Query.

Tips: "All articles must have Episcopal Church slant or specifics. We need topical/issues, not devotional stuff. Most open to feature stories about Episcopalians—clergy, lay, churches, involvement in local efforts, movements, ministries."

EVANGEL, Box 535002, Indianapolis IN 46253-5002. (317)244-3660. Fax: (317)244-1247. Free Methodist. Carolyn Smith, ed. For young adults and over 50s. Weekly take-home paper; 8 pgs; circ 25,000. Subscription $6.50. 100% freelance. Complete ms/cover letter; no phone query. Pays .04/wd (.03/wd for reprints); on publication; for 1st, one-time & reprint rts. Articles to 1,200 wds; fiction to 1,200 wds. Responds in 4-10 wks. Seasonal 9-12 mos ahead. Accepts reprints (prefers 1st rts). Sidebars ok. Guidelines; copy for #10 SAE/1 stamp.

Poetry: Buys 15/yr. Free verse, haiku, light verse, traditional; 3-16 lines; $10. Submit max. 6 poems.

Fillers: Buys few. Anecdotes, cartoons, games, ideas, prose, quizzes, short humor; 200-400 wds; $10.

Special Needs: Holiday themes other than Christmas.

Tips: "Try fresh approaches—don't be predictable."

THE EVANGELICAL BAPTIST, 679 Southgate Dr., Guelph ON N1G 4S2 Canada. (519)821-4830. Fax: (519)821-9829. The Fellowship of Evangelical Baptist Churches in Canada. Tom Scura, mng ed. Denominational; conservative evangelical. Monthly mag; 32 pgs; circ 4,000. Subscription $13.95. 50% freelance. Complete ms/cover letter; phone/fax query ok. Negotiable payment (or none), for one-time rts. Articles 750-1,500 wds. Responds in 4 wks. Seasonal 2 mos ahead. Considers simultaneous submissions & reprints. Rarely uses sidebars. Guidelines; copy for 9x12 SAE/Canadian postage.

Tips: If you expect payment for your submission, you must say so when submitting.

#THE EVANGELICAL BEACON, 901 E. 78th St., Minneapolis MN 55420-1360. (612)854-1300. Fax: (612)853-8488. Evangelical Free Church of America. Susan Brill, asst. ed. Denominational; informational, inspirational, and evangelistic. Monthly (8x) mag; 40 pgs; circ 33,000. Subscription $12. 30% freelance. Complete ms; no phone query. Pays .07/wd (reprints .03/wd), on publication, for one-time or reprint rts. Articles 600-2,000 wds (20/yr). Responds in 6 wks. Seasonal 4 mos ahead. Considers simultaneous submissions & reprints. Kill fee. Guidelines/theme list; copy for 9x12 SAE/4 stamps.

Tips: "Indicate which issue/theme article relates to; articles are all theme related. We prefer to publish members of the denomination."

***EVANGELICAL FRIEND,** Box 232, Newberg OR 97132. (503)538-7345. Evangelical Friends Intl. Paul Anderson, ed. Denominational organ. Bimonthly mag; 27 pgs; circ 10,500. 5% freelance. Query. **NO PAYMENT.** Not copyrighted. Articles 500-1,800 wds (6/yr). Responds in 4 wks. Seasonal 4 mos ahead. Considers simultaneous submissions. Guidelines; copy for 9x12 SASE.

#EVANGELICAL VISITOR, Box 166, Nappanee IN 46550-0166. (219)773-3164. Fax: (219)773-5934. Brethren in Christ. Glen Pierce, ed. Denominational. Monthly mag; circ 4,800. Subscription $12. 10% freelance. Complete ms. Pays $15-39, on publication, for reprint rts. Articles 750-1,200 wds (3-5 pgs); fiction or true stories 900 wds. Responds in 10 wks. Seasonal 3-4 mos ahead. Considers simultaneous submissions. Guidelines; copy $1.

EXPLORER MAGAZINE, Box 210, Notre Dame IN 46556. (219)277-3465. Raymond Flory, ed. Short, inspirational material. Semiannual mag; 32-44 pgs; circ 200+. Subscription $6. 95% freelance. Complete ms/with or without cover letter; phone query ok. **PAYS COPY OR SMALL CASH PRIZES** (winners determined by readers), for one-time rts. Not copyrighted. Articles 100-400 wds (10/yr); fiction to 400-800 wds (8/yr). Responds in 1 wk. Seasonal 1 yr ahead. No disks. No sidebars. Guidelines; copy $3.

> **Poetry:** Accepts 100+/yr. Any type; 3-24 lines. Submit max. 4 poems.
>
> **Fillers:** Accepts 10/yr. Prose, prayers; 100-300 wds.
>
> **Tips:** "Send one poem per page and camera-ready, if possible. Poems should have an inspirational slant, nature or love theme."

*EXPRESSION CHRISTIAN NEWSPAPER, P.O. Box 44148, Pittsburgh PA 15205. (412)921-1300. Fax: (412)921-1537. Barbara Wilson, dir. of operations; Cathy Hinkling, articles ed. Geared toward bringing unity among the churches in the Pittsburgh and west PA area. Monthly newspaper; circ 15,000. Free subscription/donations accepted. 25-35% freelance. Complete ms/cover letter; no phone query. Pays $25, on publication. Articles 300-500 or 750-1,000 wds; no payment for book or music reviews. Seasonal 2 mos ahead. Considers simultaneous submissions. Guidelines; copy for 9x12 SAE/3 stamps.

> **Columns/Departments:** Editorial and news summary.
>
> **Tips:** "Send local/state stories, for example: Interview with local guy, Mel Blount (ex-Steeler), who has a half-way house for boys. Most open to editorials; PA stories of interest."

FAITH TODAY, Box 8800, Sta. B, Willowdale ON M2K 2R6 Canada. (905)479-5885. Fax: (905)479-4749. Evangelical Fellowship of Canada. Submit to Managing Editor. Canadian news and current issues from an evangelical perspective. Bimonthly mag; 80 pgs; circ 18,000. Subscription $17.99 Canadian. 75% freelance. Query/clips; no phone query; fax query ok. Pays $125-600, on publication, for 1st rts. Articles 1,200-2,500 wds (100/yr). Responds in 6-8 wks. Prefers disk copy. Kill fee 30-50%. Sidebars ok. Guidelines/theme list; copy for 9x12 SAE/$1.35 Canadian postage.

> **Columns/Departments:** Buys 6/yr. Guest Column (current social/political/religious issues of concern to Canadian church); 900 wds; $75-85.
>
> **Special Needs:** "All topics to be approached in a journalistic—not personal viewpoint—style."
>
> **Tips:** "Ask, what does your article say about the church in Canada? We do not need material about Christian faith in general. Most open to news. Learn the difference between a news story and a press release."

** This periodical was #43 on the 1994 Top 50 Plus Christian Publishers list.

THE FAMILY, 50 St. Paul's Ave., Boston MA 02130. (617)522-8911. Fax: (617)541-9805. Catholic. Submit to Submissions Editor. Stresses the special place of the family within society as an irreplaceable center of life, love and faith. Monthly mag; 40 pgs; circ 8,500. Subscription $12. 60% freelance. Complete ms/cover letter; no phone/fax queries. Pays $35-150 ($75 for fiction) or .07/wd, on publication (on acceptance for less than 100 wds), for 1st or reprint rts. Articles 800-2,000 wds (24/yr) & fiction 900-1,200 wds (7/yr). Responds in 3-6 wks. Seasonal 8 mos ahead. Accepts reprints. Kill fee 20%. No disk. Sidebars ok. Guidelines; copy $1.75/9x12 SAE/4 stamps.

> **Fillers:** Buys 10/yr. Anecdotes, prayers, prose, short humor; 50-300 wds; $10-25.
>
> **Special Needs:** Family relationships.
>
> **Tips:** "Need stories portraying family life, either dealing with crisis issues with a faith perspective or humorous. No preaching. Also helpful articles for families."

THE FAMILY DIGEST, P.O. Box 40137, Fort Wayne IN 46804. Our Sunday Visitor/Catholic. Corine B. Erlandson, ed. Geared to young Catholic families. Bimonthly mag; 48 pgs; circ 150,000. Distributed through parishes. 95% freelance. Complete ms; no phone/fax query. Pays .05/wd, on acceptance, for 1st

NASR. Articles 600-1,200 wds (60/yr). Responds in 6-7 wks. Seasonal 7 mos ahead. Accepts some reprints. No disk copy. No sidebars. Guidelines; copy for 6x9 SAE/2 stamps.

Fillers: Buys 20/yr. Anecdotes, cartoons; 25-100 wds; $5-10.

Tips: "Reading and getting to know the publication (and guidelines) is the best way to break in."

** This periodical was #57 on the 1994 Top 50 Plus Christian Publishers list. (#37 in 1993)

+THE FAMILY JOURNAL, P.O. Box 506, Bath NY 14810-0506. (607)776-4151. Fax: (607)776-6929. Interdenominational. Jack Hager, ed. A ministry center and 7 radio stations in Northern PA and southern NY. Bimonthly newspaper; circ 18,000. Free to donors. 10% freelance. Complete ms/cover letter; no phone/fax query. **NO PAYMENT.** Not copyrighted. Articles 250-500 wds (6/yr). Responds in 1 wk. Seasonal 3 mos ahead. Considers simultaneous submissions & reprints. Prefers disk copy. No sidebars. No guidelines; copy for 10x13 SAE/2 stamps.

Poetry: Accepts 4/yr. Free verse, light verse, traditional; 32-40 lines. Submit max. 3 poems.

Tips: "We lean, but not exclusively, on stories/writers from NY and PA."

#FELLOWSHIP TODAY, Fellowship Press, 4909 E. Buckeye Rd., Madison WI 53716. (608)221-1528. Fax: (608)221-4934. Fellowship of Christian Assemblies. Kim Cortez, ed. Inspirational and teaching, informational. Monthly mag; circ 4,000. Subscription $10.60. 15% freelance. Complete ms. Pays $7-20, on publication, for 1st or reprint rts. Articles 500-1,800 wds (12/yr). Responds in 8 wks. Seasonal 3-4 mos ahead. Considers simultaneous submissions. Guidelines; copy for 9x12 SAE/3 stamps.

+FIRST THINGS: A Monthly Journal of Religion and Public Life, 156 Fifth Ave., #400, New York NY 10010. (212)627-1985. Fax: (212)627-2184. Nondenominational/interreligious. James Nuechterlein, ed. Shows relation of religion and religious insights to contemporary issues of public life. Monthly (10X) jour; 64-84 pgs; circ 26,000. 80% freelance. Complete ms/cover letter. Pays $125-450, on publication, for all rts. Articles 800-7,000 wds (800-1,600 or 4,000-6,000), (50-70/yr); book reviews, 800-1,600 wds, $125. Responds in 1-4 wks. Seasonal 4-6 mos ahead. Kill fee. No sidebars. Guidelines; copy for 10x13 SAE/9 stamps.

Poetry: Prof. Jill Baumgaertner. Buys 25-50/yr. Free verse, traditional; $50.

Columns/Departments: Opinion, 800-1,600 wds.

FOCUS ON THE FAMILY MAGAZINE, 8605 Explorer Dr., Colorado Springs CO 80920. (719)531-3400. Fax: (719)531-3499. Focus on the Family. Mike Yorkey, ed. To help families utilize Christian principles in the problems and situations of everyday living. Monthly mag; 16 pgs; circ 2 million. Free to donors. 20% freelance. Complete ms/cover letter; no phone/fax query. Pays $50-500, on acceptance, for 1st rts. Articles 500-1,500 wds (15-20/yr). Responds in 1-3 wks. Seasonal 4-6 mos ahead. Kill fee. Sidebars ok. Guidelines; copy for 9x12 SAE/3 stamps.

Tips: "We are always on the lookout for interesting, first-person accounts and helpful how-tos for our 'Family News' pages."

** This periodical was #54 on the 1994 Top 50 Plus Christian Publishers list. (#11 in 1993)

FOURSQUARE WORLD ADVANCE, 1910 W. Sunset Blvd., Ste. 200, Los Angeles CA 90026-3282. (213)484-2400. Fax: (213)413-3824. International Church of the Foursquare Gospel. Dr. Ronald Williams, ed. Denominational. Bimonthly magazine; 24 pgs; circ 100,000. Free subscription. 10% freelance. Complete ms/cover letter; no phone/fax query. Pays $75; on publication; for all, 1st, one-time or reprint rts. Not copyrighted. Articles 800-1,200 wds (1-2/yr). Responds in 2 wks. Seasonal 6 mos ahead. Considers simultaneous submissions & reprints. Free guidelines/copy.

Poetry: Buys 1-2/yr. Pays $50.

Fillers: Buys 1-2/yr. Anecdotes, cartoons; 250-300 wds; $50.

FRIENDS JOURNAL, 1501 Cherry St., Philadelphia PA 19102-1497. (215)241-7277. Fax: (215)568-1377. Religious Society of Friends (Quaker). Vinton Deming, ed. Denominational. Monthly mag; 32-48 pgs; circ 9,750. Subscription $21. 100% freelance. Query or complete ms/cover letter; phone/fax query ok. **PAYS IN COPIES,** for 1st rts. Articles 2,000-2,500 wds (70/yr); fiction 2,000-2,500 wds (2/yr); book reviews 500 wds. Responds in 2-15 wks. Seasonal 3 mos ahead. Considers simultaneous submissions & reprints (rarely). Sidebars ok. Guidelines; free copy.

> **Poetry:** Accepts 18/yr. Any type or length. Submit any number. Only on Quaker themes: meditation, peace concerns.
>
> **Fillers:** Quaker-related humor and crossword puzzles.
>
> **Columns/Departments:** Accepts 30/yr.

*THE GEM, 700 E. Melrose Ave., Box 926, Findlay OH 45839. (419)424-1961. Fax: (419)424-3433. Churches of God, General Conference. Evelyn Sloat, ed. Weekly take-home paper for youth and adults; circ 8,000. Subscription $7. 98% freelance. Complete ms; no phone query. Pays $7.50-15, on publication, for reprint rts. Not copyrighted. Articles 200-1,700 wds (125/yr). Responds in several months. Seasonal 4 mos ahead. Considers simultaneous submissions & reprints. Guidelines/copy for #10 SAE/1 stamp.

> **Tips:** "We are accepting more material that is 400 wds or less as fillers. Holiday material always welcome, although often we don't use it the first year we have it."

GOD'S REVIVALIST, 1810 Young St., Cincinnati OH 45210. (513)721-7944x296. Ronald E. Shew, ed. Salvation theme; Wesleyan persuasion. Monthly mag; 24 pgs; circ 20,000. Subscription $8. 75% freelance. Complete ms/cover letter. **NO PAYMENT** for one-time rts. Articles 600-1,400 wds (3/yr). Responds in 2 mos. Seasonal 2 mos ahead. Considers simultaneous submissions. Guidelines; copy $1/9x12 SAE.

> **Poetry:** Accepts 5/yr. Free verse, light verse, traditional; 8-20 lines. Submit max. 10 poems.
>
> **Fillers:** Accepts 5/yr. Facts, ideas, prose, short humor; 50-90 wds.
>
> **Tips:** "We need some information about the author."

#GOOD NEWS, Box 150, Wilmore KY 40390. (606)858-4661. Fax: (606)858-4972. United Methodist. James V. Heidinger II, ed. Focus is church renewal—a return to Scriptural Christianity. Bimonthly mag; circ 60,000. Subscription $15. 20% freelance. Query only. Pays .05-.07/wd; on acceptance; for 1st, simultaneous or reprint rts. Articles 1,500-1,800 wds (25/yr). Responds in 3 mos. Seasonal 6 mos ahead. Kill fee. Guidelines; copy $2.75.

GOOD NEWS, ETC., P.O. Box 2660, Vista CA 92085. (619)724-3075. Fax: (619)724-8311. Good News Publishers, Inc. of California. Rick Monroe, ed. Feature stories and local news of interest to Christians in San Diego County. Monthly tabloid; 28-32 pgs; circ 44,000. Subscription $15. 10% freelance. Query/clips. Pays $20, on publication, for 1st rts. Articles 400-700 wds (15/yr). Responds in 2 wks. Seasonal 2 mos ahead. Considers simultaneous submissions & reprints. Prefers disk copy. Sidebars ok. Guidelines/theme list; copy for 9x12 SAE/6 stamps.

> **Special Needs:** Short, local articles in newspaper style.
>
> **Tips:** "Most open to material for youth and family sections."
>
> ** 1994 EPA Award of Merit - Newspaper.

GOOD NEWS JOURNAL, Box 1882, 10900 E Hwy WW, Columbia MO 65205. (314)875-8755. Fax: (314)874-4964. Teresa Shields Parker, ed. Christian newspaper for mid-Missouri area. Monthly tabloid; 16 pgs; circ 50,000. Subscription $20. 25% freelance. Query/clips; phone/fax query ok. **NO PAYMENT,**

for one-time rts. Not copyrighted. Articles 250-1,000 wds (12-24/yr); kid's fiction 500-1,000 wds (6-12/yr); book/music reviews, 50-100 wds. Responds in 2 mos. Seasonal 2 mos ahead. Considers simultaneous submissions & reprints. Prefers disk copy. Sidebars ok. No guidelines; copy $1/ 9x12 SAE.

Fillers: Accepts 12/yr. Cartoons, games, quizzes, quotes, word puzzles.

Columns/Departments: Accepts 12/yr. Good News Kids (fiction for kids up to 12 yrs), 500-750 wds; Golden Digest (testimonies or devotionals for those over 55), 1,000 wds.

Special Needs: Testimonies of healing with verification of physician.

Tips: "Interested in testimonies and personal experience stories that illustrate Christian growth or Christian principles."

+THE GOOD NEWS REPORTER, P.O. Box 8504, Little Rock AR 72215. (501)224-7508. Fax: (501)224-5502. James Strand, ed. News and information from an evangelical Christian perspective. Monthly tabloid; circ 10,000. Subscription $15. 50% freelance. Query; no phone/fax query. **PAYS IN COPIES** ,for one-time rts. Articles 150-500 wds; book/music reviews, 250 wds. Responds in 4 wks. Seasonal 2 mos ahead. Considers simultaneous submissions & reprints. No disk. Sidebars ok. No guidelines; copy for 3 stamps.

Poetry: Accepts 3/yr.

Fillers: Accepts 50/yr. Anecdotes, cartoons, facts, games, ideas, jokes, newsbreaks, prayers, short humor; 10-100 wds.

Columns/Departments: Accepts 15/yr. Current Events (Christian perspective), 250 wds; Features (people/Christian testimony/business/living, 500 wds; Editorial (opinion), 200 wds.

Special Needs: Stories of people sharing their faith with others.

GOSPEL TIDINGS, 5800 S. 14th St., Omaha NE 68107. (402)731-4780. Fax: (402)731-1173. Fellowship of Evangelical Bible Churches. Robert L. Frey, ed. To inform, educate and edify members of affiliate churches. Bimonthly mag; 16-20 pgs; circ 2,200. Subscription $8. 2% freelance. Complete ms/cover letter; no phone query. **NO PAYMENT** to $35. Articles 400-2,500 wds (3/yr); fiction 500-1,000 wds (1-2/yr). Responds in 4 wks. Seasonal 2 mos ahead. Considers simultaneous submissions & reprints. Copy for 9x12 SAE/2 stamps.

Poetry: Light verse, traditional.

GUIDEPOSTS, 16 E 34th St., New York NY 10016. (212)251-8100. Interfaith. Fulton Oursler, Jr., ed-in-chief; submit to The Editors. Personal faith stories showing how faith in God helps each person cope with life in some particular way. Monthly mag; 48 pgs; circ 3.9 million. 30% freelance. Complete ms; phone query ok. Pays $200-400 (sometimes more for repeat sales), on acceptance, for all rts. Articles 750-1,500 wds (50/yr). Responds in 2-4 wks. Seasonal 6 mos ahead. Kill fee 25%. Free guidelines/copy.

Poetry: Colleen Hughes. Buys 2-3/yr. Free verse, light verse, traditional; 2-20 lines; $10-25.

Fillers: Colleen Hughes. Buys 10-12/yr. Anecdotes; quotes, short humor; 10-200 wds; $15-200. "This is new for us."

Columns/Departments: Colleen Hughes. Buys 30-40/yr. His Mysterious Ways, 250 wds; This Thing Called Prayer, 250 wds; The Quiet People, 300 wds ("This is our most open area. Write in 3rd person."); $50-200.

Tips: "Be able to tell a good story, with drama, suspense, description and dialogue. The point of the story should be some practical spiritual help the reader receives from what the author learned through his experience." First person only.

** This periodical was #44 on the 1994 Top 50 Plus Christian Publishers list.

HALLELUJAH!, P.O. Box 223, Stn. A, Vancouver BC V6C 2M3 Canada. (604)498-3895. Bible Holiness Movement. Wesley H. Wakefield, ed. For evangelism and promotion of holiness revivals; readership mostly ethnic, non-white minorities. Bimonthly mag; 40 pgs; circ 5,000. Subscription $5. 5% freelance. Query; no phone/fax query. Pays $15-50, on acceptance, for one-time, reprint or simultaneous rts. Articles 300-2,500 wds (4/yr). Responds in 3-6 wks. Considers simultaneous submissions & reprints. No sidebars. Guidelines; copy for 7x10 SAE.

> **Poetry:** Buys 1-3 poems/yr. Traditional, hymn length. Variable pay rate. Submit max. 2 poems. Prefers poetry of hymn or song quality with identifiable meter.

> **Special Needs:** Heart-holiness; non-conformity; anti-racism; anti-slavery. Against divorce and re-marriage. Use authorized KJV only.

> **Ethnic:** Distributes to Nigeria, Canada and U.S.

> **Tips:** "Avoid Americanisms. No Calvinistic articles or premillenialism."

+HAYDEN HERALD, P.O. Box 1254, Rathdrum ID 83858. Voice mail: (208)769-0863. Kay Younkin, ed. For a small-town audience—professional and blue-collar. Monthly tabloid; 8-16 pgs; circ 4,000. Subscription $18. 50% freelance. Query/clips (or complete ms for fiction & columns); phone query ok. Pays $5-20, on publication, for any rts. Articles 200-1,000 (50/yr); fiction 400-1,000 (6-12/yr—**NO PAYMENT**); music reviews, 250-400 wds, $5-10. Responds in 8-12 wks. Seasonal 3 mos ahead. Accepts reprints. No disks. No sidebars. Copy $2.

> **Poetry:** Accepts 12-24/yr. Free verse, haiku, light verse, traditional; 20-60 wds.

> **Fillers:** Anecdotes, cartoons, jokes, party ideas, short humor, word puzzles.

> **Columns/Departments:** Buys 36-100/yr; Pioneer Journal (historical - pioneers of Idaho - serials), to 2,000 wds; Fishin' Tips, 250-450 wds; Women's Page, 200-500 wds; to $20.

> **Tips:** "Indicate payment expected. Most open to Women's Page—light-hearted, upbeat, positive—no sermons."

+HEAD TO HEAD, P.O. Box 711, Saint Johnsbury VT 05819-0711. (802)748-5708 (& fax). Nondenominational. Paul A. Webb, ed-in-chief. Shows Christ as the greatest hope for brain-injury survivors and caretakers. Bimonthly mag; 24+ pgs; circ 500+. Subscription $12. Estab 1994. 50% freelance. Complete ms/cover letter; fax query ok. **PAYS IN COPIES**, for 1st rts. Articles 250-1,200 wds (to 36/yr); fiction for all ages; book/music/video reviews, 500 wds. Responds in 4 wks. Seasonal 6 mos ahead. Accepts reprints. Prefers disk copy. Guidelines/theme list; copy for 6x9 SAE/2 stamps.

> **Poetry:** Accepts 12/yr. All types, 4-60 lines. Submit max. 5 poems.

> **Fillers:** Most types; 50-250 wds.

> **Columns/Departments:** Tips & Hints; Caregiver Concerns & Family Matters, 250 wds.

> **Special Needs:** All topics should relate to brain injury, traumatic or congenital brain injury, cerebral palsy, encephalitis, multiple sclerosis, strokes, or alcohol/drug induced brain injury.

> **Tips:** "Need how-tos on survival, coping skills, cognitive strategies, social skills, job skills, and communication."

+HEARING HEARTS, 4 Silo Mill Ct., Sterling VA 20164. Tel/Fax (703)430-7387. American Ministries to the Deaf. Beverly Cox, ed. For deaf adults and those with whom they live, work and worship. Quarterly mag; circ 1,000. Subscription $12. 70-80% freelance. Complete ms/cover letter; phone/fax query ok. **PAYS IN COPIES**. Articles 100-1,000 wds (50-100/yr); fiction (new). Responds in 2-4 wks. Seasonal 3-4 mos ahead. Considers simultaneous submissions & some reprints. Accepts hard copy or disk. Sidebars ok. Guidelines/theme list; copy for 9x12 SAE/4 stamps.

Poetry: Accepts 100-200/yr. Free verse,haiku, light verse, traditional; 5-30 lines. Submit max. 5 poems.

Fillers: Cartoons, games, ideas, party ideas, quizzes, word puzzles.

Special Needs: Biblical and modern deaf Christian heroes.

Tips: "We're open to articles proposing more questions than answers. We need more deaf writers, not those who write about them."

*HERALD OF HOLINESS, 6401 The Paseo, Kansas City MO 64131. (816)333-7000 x2302. (816)333-1748. Church of the Nazarene. Dr. Wesley D. Tracy, ed. Denominational. Monthly mag; 64 pgs; circ 81,000. Subscription $10. 20% freelance. Complete ms/cover letter; no phone query. Pays .05/wd (.04/wd for reprints), on acceptance, for one-time rts. Not copyrighted. Articles 350-1,500 wds. Responds in 6-8 wks. Seasonal 6 mos ahead. Accepts reprints. Kill fee 50%. Guidelines/theme list; no copy.

Poetry: Buys 30/yr. Free verse & traditional. Pays .75/line. Submit max. 3 poems.

Fillers: Buys 30 cartoons/yr. Pay negotiable.

Tips: "Need personality pieces about Nazarenes who are making a difference in their world (need not be celebrities); plus personal experiences of God at work in a person's life."

** This periodical was #16 on the Top 50 Plus Christian Publishers list.

+HIGHWAY NEWS AND GOOD NEWS, P.O. Box 303, Denver PA 17517. (717)721-9800. Fax: (717)721-9351. Craig Hartrauft, ed. For truck drivers and related people associated with trucking industry; evangelistic, with articles for Christian growth. Monthly mag; 16 pgs; circ 35,000. To donors of $25 or more. 50% freelance. Query/clips. **NO PAYMENT OR CHARITABLE DONATION.** Articles 800-1,000 wds (4-6/yr); fiction 400-800 wds (1/yr). Responds in 1 wk. Seasonal 4 mos ahead. Considers simultaneous submissions & reprints. Uses some sidebars. Guidelines/theme list; free copy.

Tips: All articles must relate to truckers; need pieces on marriage, parenting and fatherhood.

HOME LIFE, 127 9th Ave. N., Nashville TN 37234. (615)251-2271. Southern Baptist. Leigh Neely, mng. ed. Christian family leisure reading. Monthly mag; 68 pgs; circ 610,000. Subscription $19.95. 60% freelance. Query; no phone/fax query. Pays $75-500 ($150-200 for fiction); on acceptance; for 1st rts. Articles 200-1,800 wds (60-70/yr); fiction 1,500-2,000 wds (12/yr). Responds in 4-12 wks. Seasonal 8 mos ahead. Sidebars ok. Guidelines; copy $1/9x12 SAE/2 stamps.

Poetry: Buys 12-15/yr. Free verse, light verse, traditional; 4-24 lines; $13-35. Submit max. 4 poems.

Special Needs: Fiction on family relationships.

Tips: "Our new Familytime column is a good way to break in (description in guidelines). Also open to fiction."

** This periodical was #24 on the 1994 Top 50 Plus Christian Publishers list. (#17 in 1993)

+HOMESCHOOLING TODAY, P.O. Box 1425, Melrose FL 32666. (904)475-3088 (& fax). S. Squared Productions. Debbie Strayer, ed. To equip homeschooling families. Bimonthly; circ 20,000. Subscription $16. Open to freelance. Query.

HOME TIMES, Box 16096, West Palm Beach FL 33416. (407)439-3509. Dennis Lombard, ed. Conservative, pro-Christian community newspaper. Monthly tabloid; 20 pgs; circ 8,000. Subscription $10. 60% freelance. Complete ms/cover letter; no phone/fax query. Pays to $25, on publication, for one-time rts. Articles 300-900 wds (35/yr); fiction 200-1,200 wds (5/yr); book/music reviews 500 wds, $5-10. Responds in 4 wks. Seasonal 2 mos ahead. Considers simultaneous submissions & reprints. No disks. Sidebars ok. Guidelines; copy for $1/9x12 SAE/4 stamps.

Poetry: Buys 4/yr. Light verse, traditional; 2-36 lines; $5-10. Submit max. 3 poems.

Fillers: Accepts 15-20/yr. Anecdotes, cartoons, ideas, jokes, newsbreaks, quotes, short humor; 25-100 wds; $5 for cartoons only.

Columns/Departments: Buys 20/yr. New column ideas considered, to 600 wds; $10.

Special Needs: Op-eds and current affairs.

Tips: "Very open to new writers, but study guidelines and sample *first*; we are different."

*HOMEWORK, The Home Business Newsletter with a Christian Perspective, 20 Whitcomb Dr., P.O. Box 394, Simsbury CT 06070. (203)651-5503. Christian. Posy Lough, ed. For people who work at home, or plan to. Bimonthly newsletter; 8 pgs. Subscription $20. Open to freelance. Complete ms. Short articles relating to home business. No additional information. Not included in topical listings.

#IDEALS, Ideals Publishing, Box 48000, Nashville TN 37214. (615)231-6740. Lisa Thompson, ed. Seasonal, inspirational, nostalgic magazine for mature men and women of traditional values. Mag published 8 times/yr; 80 pgs; circ 180,000+. 95% freelance. Query (for fiction) or complete ms (copies only, doesn't return). Pays .10/wd, on publication, for one-time rts. Articles 800-1,000 wds (20/yr); fiction 800-1,000 wds (10/yr). Responds in 3 mos. Seasonal 8 mos ahead. Considers simultaneous submissions & reprints. Kill fee. Guidelines/theme list; copy $4.

Poetry: Buys 250/yr. Light verse & traditional; 20-30 lines; $10. Submit max. 15 poems.

Tips: "Most open to optimistic poetry oriented around a season or theme."

*IMPACT MAGAZINE, 12 B East Coast Rd., 1542 Singapore. 65-345-0444. Fax: 65-345-3045. Evangelical Fellowship of Singapore. Andrew Goh, ed. To help young working adults apply Christian principles to contemporary issues. Bimonthly mag; circ 6,000. Subscription $22. 10-15% freelance. Complete ms/cover letter; phone query ok. **NO PAYMENT** up to $20/pg, for all rts. Articles (12/yr) & fiction (6/yr); 1,000-2,000 wds. Seasonal 2 mos ahead. Accepts reprints. No guidelines; copy for $3 & $1.70 postage (surface mail).

Poetry: Accepts 2-3 poems/yr. Free verse, 20-40 lines. Submit max. 3 poems.

Fillers: Accepts 6/yr. Anecdotes, cartoons, jokes, quizzes, short humor, and word puzzles.

Columns/Departments: Closing Thoughts (current social issues), 600-800 wds; Testimony (personal experience), 1,500-2,000 wds; Parenting (Asian context), 1,000-1,500 wds.

Tips: "We're most open to fillers."

#INDIAN LIFE, Box 3765, Sta. B, Winnipeg MB R2W 3R6 Canada. U.S. address: Box 32, Pembina ND 58271. (204)661-9333. Fax: (204)661-3982. Intertribal Christian Communications. Submit to The Editor. Speaking to the social, cultural, and spiritual needs of the North American Indians. Bimonthly mag; 24 pgs; circ 62,000. Subscription $7. 20% freelance. Query; phone query ok. **NO PAYMENT**, for one-time rts. Articles 800-2,500 wds (10/yr); fiction, 500-1,500 wds; book reviews, 500 wds. Responds in 3 wks. Seasonal 6 mos ahead. Considers simultaneous submissions & reprints. Guidelines/copy $1/IRC.

Fillers: Accepts 6/yr. News items; 100-400 wds.

Special Needs: News items of positive achievements by native groups or individuals.

Tips: "Know the Indian people well and write from their perspective. No talking down. Native authors preferred."

+INLAND NORTHWEST CHRISTIAN NEWS, 222 W. Mission #118, Spokane WA 99201. (509)328-0820. Fax: (509)325-2025. Zeda Leonard, ed. To inform, motivate and encourage evangelical Christians in

Spokane and the inland Northwest. Newspaper published 18X/yr; circ 3,500. Subscription $17.95. Open to freelance. Query.

+INSIDE JOURNAL, P.O. Box 16429, Washington DC 20041-6429. (703)478-0100. Fax: (703)318-0235. Prison Fellowship. Tamela Baker, mng ed. To proclaim the Gospel to non-Christian prisoners within the context of a prison newspaper. Bimonthly (8X) newspaper; circ 370,000. Free subscription. Open to freelance. Query. Modest payment, depending on situation. Articles 1,000-1,200 wds or 800 wds. Responds in 2 wks. Sidebars ok.

Fillers: Cartoons.

THE INSPIRER, 737 Kimsey Ln. #620, Henderson KY 42420-4917. (502)826-5720. Billy Edwards, ed. To encourage believers in their Christian life. (Especially open to writers who are physically disabled.) Quarterly newsletter; 8 pgs; circ 1,500. Free subscription. 50% freelance. Complete ms/cover letter; no phone query. Articles 500 wds (10/yr). **PAYS IN COPIES.** Not copyrighted. Responds in 2 wks. Seasonal 2 mos ahead. Considers simultaneous submissions & reprints. No guidelines; copy for #10 SASE/1 stamp.

Poetry: Accepts 8-10/yr. Free verse, to 25 lines. Submit max. 3 poems.

Fillers: Accepts 8-10/yr. Anecdotes, facts, games, prose, quizzes, prayers, word puzzles, to 75 wds.

Columns/Departments: Accepts 10/yr. Food for Thought (Christian living); The Lighter Side; Prayer Works Wonders; all 300 wds.

Special Needs: Issues of interest to (and from) the physically disabled.

*INTERCHANGE, 412 Sycamore St., Cincinnati OH 45202. (513)421-0311. Episcopal. Michael Barwell, ed. Regional paper for the Episcopal and Anglican Church in southern Ohio. Newspaper published 8X/yr; 28 pgs; circ 12,800. 10% freelance. Query/clips. Pays $35-50, on publication, for all rts. Articles 500-2,000 wds. Responds in 2 mos. Considers simultaneous submissions. No guidelines; copy for 9x12 SASE.

#THE INTERIM, 53 Dundas St. E. #306, Toronto ON M5B 1C6 Canada. (416)368-0250. Fax: (416)368-8575. Catholic. Peter Muggeridge, ed. Abortion, euthanasia, pornography, feminism and religion for a pro-life perspective. Monthly newspaper; circ 25,000. 50% freelance. Query; phone query ok. Pays $100-150 (Canadian), on publication. Articles 700-1,000 wds. Responds in 2 wks. Seasonal 2 mos ahead. Considers simultaneous submissions & reprints. No disks. No guidelines.

#INTERVARSITY, Box 7895, Madison WI 53707-7895. (608)274-9001. Fax: (608)274-7882. InterVarsity Christian Fellowship. Neal Kunde, ed. To inform donors and other interested readers of InterVarsity's work on campus. Quarterly mag; circ 50,000. Subscription for donation. 5% freelance. Query. Pays $250, on publication, for 1st rts. Articles 750 wds (21/yr). Seasonal 6 mos ahead. Guidelines; free copy.

Columns/Departments: Buys 4/yr. Campus Datelines (news about life on college campuses); 100 wds; $50.

Tips: "Most open to nonfiction features. Call the editor and ask specific questions."

+IT'S YOUR CHOICE MAGAZINE, P.O. Box 7135, Richmond VA 23221-0135. (804)662-9596. Voice mail: (804)254-9940. FutureWend Publications. Dr. James Rogers, ed. For people seeking fresh and effective approaches to domestic and international crime and violence. Monthly newsletter; to 24 pgs; circ. 2,000. Subscription $7.29. Estab 1993. Complete ms only; no phone/fax query. Pays from copies to $1/wd ($1,000 max.), for all (contest winner), one-time, reprint or simultaneous rts. Articles (40/yr) & fiction (4/yr), to 1,000 wds; book reviews, to 1,000 wds. Responds in 4 wks. Seasonal 6 mos ahead. No disks. No sidebars. Considers simultaneous submissions & reprints. Guidelines; copy for $2/#10 SAE/2 stamps.

Columns/Departments: Op-Ed (ethical issues), to 1,000 wds; Personal Experience (ethical issues), 1,000 wds; Bottom Line (fillers - ethical principles); 50 wds max; $5.

Special Needs: Ethical reviews/critiques of articles in other publications; educational system failure; criminal justice system failure.

Tips: "All fiction related to ethical issues in some way. 'Bottom Line' fillers best place to break in."

Contest: Two divisions, one for public, one for school children. March 31, 1995 deadline. Send SASE for guidelines and a submission form.

JOHN MILTON MAGAZINE, 475 Riverside Dr., Rm. 455, New York NY 10115. (212)870-3335. John Milton Society for the Blind/nonsectarian. Darcy Quigley, ed. For visually impaired church members, some blind. Monthly mag; bimonthly record (talking book); circ 16,400. 0.1% freelance. Complete ms/cover letter; phone query ok. **NO PAYMENT,** for one-time or simultaneous rts. Articles 200-2,500 (5-6/yr); fiction 200-3,000 (1-2/yr); book reviews 200-500 wds. Responds in 8-10 wks. Seasonal 6 mos ahead. Accepts reprints. Free copy.

Poetry: Accepts 20-25/yr. Free verse, haiku, light verse, traditional; to 40 lines. Submit max. 5 poems.

Fillers: Accepts 4-5/yr. Various; 100-200 wds.

Special Needs: Archaeology; children's stories.

Tips: "Well-researched articles on any subject; concise writing."

JOURNAL OF CHRISTIAN NURSING, Box 1650, Downers Grove IL 60515-0780. (708)964-5700. Fax: (708)964-1251. Nurses Christian Fellowship of InterVarsity Christian Fellowship. Melodee Yohe, mng. ed. Personal, professional, practical articles that help nurses integrate Christian faith with nursing profession. Quarterly mag; 48 pgs; circ 10,000. Subscription $17.95. 30% freelance. Complete ms/cover letter; phone/fax query ok. Pays $25-80; on publication; for all (on case studies), one-time (on others) rts. Articles 6-12 pgs (30-40/yr). Responds in 2-4 wks. Seasonal 6-9 mos ahead. Accepts reprints. Kill fee rarely. Sidebars ok. Guidelines/theme list; copy for $4/9x12 SAE/5 stamps.

Columns/Departments: Buys 4/yr. The Last Word (opinion related to nursing), 750-900 wds; $25-50.

Special Needs: All topics must relate to nursing, or contain illustrations using nurses. Spiritual care of children (spring '95); Walking in the truth (summer '95); and encouraging one another (fall '95).

Tips: "Learn our style from our publication. Only submit articles appropriate for our audience. Most open to first person (nurses) experiences—interviewed and written by a freelancer."

** 1994 EPA Award of Merit - Christian Ministry.

JOURNAL OF CHURCH & STATE, P.O. Box 97308, Baylor University, Waco TX 76798. (817)755-1510. Fax: (817)755-1571. Interdenominational. Derek H. Davis, mng ed. Provides a forum for the critical examination of the interaction of religion and government worldwide. Quarterly jour; 200+ pgs; circ 1,700. Subscription $20. 100% freelance. Complete ms (3 copies)/cover letter; no phone query. **NO PAYMENT,** for all rights. Articles 30-35 pgs/footnotes. Responds in 6-8 wks. Prefers disk copy. Guidelines; copy $8 + $1.50 postage.

Special Needs: Church-state issues.

*****JOYFUL NOISE,** 4259 Elkcam Blvd. SE, St. Petersburg FL 33705-4216. Nondenominational. William W. Maxwell, ed. Deals with African-American life and religious culture. Bimonthly mag. Estab 1993. Complete ms/cover letter or query/clips. Pays $50-250, on acceptance, for 1st rts. Articles 700-3,000 wds. Guidelines; no copy.

*KANSAS CITY CHRISTIAN NEWSPAPER, P.O. Box 1114, Lee's Summit MO 64063. (816)524-4522. Fax: (816)525-3444. Non-denominational. Dwight Widaman, pub; Alecia Chai, ed. To promote Christian business, ministries and organizations; provide thought-provoking commentary for edification of the body of Christ. Monthly newspaper; circ 35,000. Subscription $14. 50% freelance. Complete ms/cover letter; short phone query ok. **PAYS IN COPIES** or limited amount for well-researched pieces, for one-time or reprint rts. Not copyrighted. Articles to 1,200 wds (100/yr). Responds in 6 wks. Seasonal 6 mos ahead. Accepts reprints. Guidelines; copy for 9x12 SAE/$1 postage.

> **Fillers:** Accepts 12/yr. Anecdotes, cartoons, ideas, newsbreaks, quotes, short humor; to 500 wds.

> **Tips:** "We look for up-to-date information. Willing to work with new writers who want to learn."

+KOOTENAI COURIER, P.O. Box 1254, Rathdrum ID 83858. Voice mail: (208)769-0863. Kay Younkin, ed. For a small-town audience—historical, folksy and conservative. Monthly tabloid; 8-16 pgs; circ 4,000. Subscription $18. 50% freelance. Query/clips (or complete ms for fiction & columns); phone query ok. Pays $5-20, on publication, for any rts. Articles 200-1,000 (50/yr); fiction 400-1,000 (6-12/yr—**NO PAYMENT**); music reviews, 250-400 wds, $5-10. Responds in 8-12 wks. Seasonal 3 mos ahead. Accepts reprints. No disks. No sidebars. Copy $2.

> **Poetry:** Accepts 12-24/yr. Free verse, haiku, light verse, traditional; 20-60 wds.

> **Fillers:** Anecdotes, cartoons, jokes, party ideas, short humor, word puzzles.

> **Columns/Departments:** Buys 36-100/yr; Pioneer Journal (historical pioneers of Idaho - serials), to 2,000 wds; Fishin' Tips, 250-450 wds; Women's Page, 200-500 wds; to $20.

> **Tips:** "Indicate payment expected. Most open to Women's Page—light-hearted, upbeat, positive— no sermons."

*LIBERTY, Religious Liberty Dept., 12501 Old Columbia Pike, Silver Springs MD 20904. (310)680-6691. Fax: (310)680-6695. Seventh-day Adventist. Roland R. Hegstad, ed. Deals with religious liberty issues for government officials, civic leaders, and laymen. Bimonthly mag; 32 pgs; circ 250,000. 90% freelance. Query. Pays .06-.08/wd, on acceptance, for 1st or reprint rts. Articles & essays 2,000-3,000 wds. Responds in 4 wks. Guidelines; copy $1.

LIFEGLOW, Box 6097, Lincoln NE 68506. (402)489-5922. Christian Record Services. Richard J. Kaiser, ed-in-chief. For sight-impaired adults over 25; interdenominational Christian audience. Quarterly mag; 65-70 pgs (lg. print); circ 30,000. Free to sight-impaired. 95% freelance. Query; phone query ok. Pays .04-.05/wd, on acceptance, for one-time rts. Articles & true stories 750-1,400 wds. Responds in 1-4 wks. Seasonal 18 mos ahead. Considers simultaneous query & reprints. Guidelines; copy for 9x12 SAE/5 stamps.

> **Special Needs:** Nostalgia. Overstocked on historical.

> **Tips:** "Remember the readers are sight impaired or physically handicapped. Would the topics be relevant to them?"

LIGHT AND LIFE, Box 535002, Indianapolis IN 46253. (317)244-3660. Fax: (317)244-1247. Free Methodist Church of North America. Robert B. Haslam, ed. Christian growth, ministry to saved and unsaved, denominational news. Monthly mag; 32 pgs; circ 27,500. Subscription $15. 40% freelance. Complete ms/cover letter; phone query ok/no fax query. Pays .04/wd; on publication; for 1st, one-time, or simultaneous rts. Articles 500-600 or 1,000-1,200 wds (60/yr). Responds in 4-6 wks. Seasonal 8 mos ahead. Considers simultaneous submissions. Kill fee 50%. Sidebars ok. Guidelines; copy $1.50.

Poetry: Buys 6-10/yr. Free verse, traditional; 4-16 lines; $10. Send max. 5 poems.

Tips: "Most open to feature articles. Write to the readers'interest. Our age groupings are approximately: 25% over 65, 30% between boomers and retired; 20% younger than boomers."

** 1994 EPA Award of Excellence - Denominational.

LIGHTHOUSE FICTION COLLECTION, Box 1377, Auburn WA 98071-1377. Tim Clinton, ed/pub. Timeless fiction for the whole family. Quarterly mag; circ 300+. Subscription $7.95. 100% freelance. Complete ms/cover letter. Pays to $5-50, on publication, for 1st NASR. Fiction for all ages 250-5,000 wds (50/yr). Responds in 2-4 mos. Seasonal any time. No disk. Guidelines; copy $3.

Poetry: Buys 25-50/yr. Free-verse, light verse, traditional; 4-50 lines; $1-5. Submit max. 5 poems.

Tips: "Read and follow guidelines. Basic need is for good stories and poems—well-written, interesting, new plot."

LIGUORIAN, One Liguori Dr., Liguori MO 63057. (314)464-2500. Fax: (314)464-8449. Catholic. Allan Weinert, CSSR, ed-in-chief. To help readers lead a fuller Christian life through the sharing of experiences, scriptural knowledge, and a better understanding of the church. Monthly mag; 72 pgs; circ 365,000. Subscription $15. 40% freelance. Complete ms/cover letter; phone/fax query ok. Pays .10-.12/wd, on acceptance, for all rts. Articles 750-2,000 wds (48/yr); fiction to 2,000 wds (12/yr). Responds in 2-8 wks. Seasonal 6 mos ahead. Kill fee 50%. Occasional sidebars. Guidelines; copy for 6x9 SAE/3 stamps.

Poetry: Buys 10/yr. Traditional; 8-24 lines. Submit max. 4 poems; $25-35.

Fillers: Cartoons, jokes, short humor; $2.50-35.

Columns/Departments: Buys 12/yr. Five-Minute Meditation (reflective essay), 750-825 wds. Complete ms.

Tips: "Polish your own ms. Need marriage and parenting articles, articles that touch a reader's life in a personal way. If writing a personal experience piece, beware of limited subjectivity. Most open to human-interest and personal essays with a spiritual theme."

#LIVE, 1445 Boonville Ave., Springfield MO 65802-1894. (417)862-2781. Fax: (417)862-8558. Assemblies of God. Paul W. Smith, ed For adults in Sunday school. Weekly take-home paper; 8 pgs; circ 160,000. Subscription $5.80. 100% freelance. Complete ms (a copy only). Pays .03/wd (.02/wd for reprints & simultaneous), on acceptance, for 1st, one-time or reprint rts. Not copyrighted. Articles 500-2,000 wds (120-150/yr); fiction 1,000-1,500 wds (100/yr). Responds in 4-6 wks. Seasonal 12-18 mos ahead. Considers simultaneous submissions & reprints. Guidelines/copy for 7x9 SAE/2 stamps.

Poetry: Buys 50+/yr. Free verse, light verse, traditional; 12-25 lines; $10-15. Submit max. 4 poems.

Fillers: Anecdotes, cartoons, prose, short humor; 200-700 wds; .02-.03/wd.

Columns/Departments: Reflections (pithy sayings/anecdotes); 50-100 wds; no payment.

Special Needs: Holiday stories—Christmas, July 4th, Easter, Thanksgiving, Mothers/Fathers Day. "No Santa Claus, Halloween or Easter Bunnies."

Tips: "Send scanable copy. Do not send original/only copy. Send SAS postcard for reply. Be patient; staff is limited. Proofread your ms. Be concise."

** This periodical was #20 on the 1994 Top 50 Plus Christian Publishers list. (#26 in 1993)

***LIVING,** Rt. 2 Box 656, Grottoes VA 24441. (703)249-3177. Eugene K. Souder, mng. ed. A positive, practical and uplifting publication for the whole family; mass distribution. Quarterly tabloid; circ 100,000. Estab 1991. 60% freelance. Complete ms; no cover letter or phone query. Pays $25-100, on publication, for all rts. Articles 500-1,200 wds (25/yr). Responds in 4 wks. Seasonal 4-6 mos ahead. Considers simultaneous submissions & reprints. Guidelines; copy for 9x12 SAE/4 stamps.

Fillers: Buys 15/yr. Various; 30-100 wds; $10-25.

Columns/Departments: Open to new family-related columns.

Tips: "Most open to first-person stories on family relationships—spouse and parent-child. Strong on anecdotes, short on moralism. Touch family needs in a practical way with a Christian slant, without being overly religious."

THE LIVING CHURCH, P.O. Box 92936, Milwaukee WI 53202-0936. (414)276-5420. Fax: (414)276-7483. Episcopal. John Schuessler, mng ed. For members of the denomination, many theologically conservative. Weekly mag; 16+ pgs; circ 9,000. Subscription $39.50. 10% freelance. Complete ms/cover letter; phone/fax query ok. **NO PAYMENT FOR UNSOLICITED MSS.** Articles to 1,000 wds (150/yr). Responds in 3-4 wks. Seasonal 2 mos ahead. Prefers disk. Copy for 9x12 SAE.

Poetry: John Schuessler, poetry ed. Accepts 25/yr. Free verse, light verse, traditional; 3-15 lines. Submit max. 3 poems.

Columns/Departments: Buys 5-10/yr. Benediction (devotional/inspirational), 200 wds.

Tips: "Most open to Benediction column."

#THE LOOKOUT, 8121 Hamilton Ave., Cincinnati OH 45231-9981. (513)931-4050. Fax: (513)931-0904. Standard Publishing. Simon J. Dahlman, ed. For adults in Sunday school who are interested in learning more about applying the gospel to their lives. Weekly take-home paper; 16 pgs; circ 118,000. Subscription $19. 50-60% freelance. Complete ms/cover letter; no phone query. Pays .04-.08/wd; on acceptance; for 1st, one-time, simultaneous rts. Articles 500-2,000 wds or 400-700 wds (160/yr); fiction 1,000-2,000 wds (40/yr). Responds in 4 mos. Seasonal 6 mos ahead. Considers simultaneous submissions & reprints. Kill fee 33%. Guidelines/theme list; copy for .50.

Columns/Departments: Buys 45/yr. Outlook (personal opinion), 500-900 wds; Growing in Groups (small group tips), 50-250; $25-50.

Tips: "Show evidence of solid research. In feature articles on hot issues, present accurate information and measured judgments and let the reader decide. Most open to Outlook column."

** This periodical was #3 on the 1994 Top 50 Plus Christian Publishers list. (#2 in 1993) Also EPA 1994 Award of Merit - Sunday School Take-Home.

THE LUTHERAN, 8765 W. Higgins Rd., Chicago IL 60631-4183. (312)380-2540. Fax: (312)380-2751. Evangelical Lutheran Church in America. Edgar R. Trexler, ed.; David L. Miller, articles ed. Addresses broad constituency of the church. Monthly mag; 68 pgs; circ 800,000. 25-50% freelance. Query. Pays $400-1,000 (assigned), $50-400 (unsolicited); on acceptance, for 1st rts. Articles 300-2,000 wds (40/yr). Responds in 3-6 wks. Seasonal 4 mos ahead. Kill fee 50%. Guidelines/theme list; free copy.

Fillers: Roger Kahle. Buys 50/yr. Cartoons, jokes, short humor.

Columns/Departments: Roger Kahle. Lite Side (church and religious humor) and Reader's Viewpoint, 25-100 wds; $10.

Tips: "Most open to feature articles."

** This periodical was #9 on the 1994 Top 50 Plus Christian Publishers list. (#14 in 1993)

THE LUTHERAN DIGEST, Box 4250, Hopkins MN 55343. (612)933-2820. Lutheran. David L. Tank, ed. Blend of secular and light theological material used to win non-believers to the Lutheran faith. Quarterly mag; 72 pgs; circ 150,000. Subscription $20/2 yrs (min). 30% original freelance/70% reprints. Complete ms/cover letter; no phone query. Pays $15-25, on acceptance, for 1st, one-time or reprint rts.

Articles to 1,000 wds (25-30/yr). Responds in 4-6 wks. Seasonal 6-9 mos ahead. Accepts reprints. Guidelines; copy $1.75/6x9 SAE/3 stamps.

Poetry: Accepts 45-50/yr. Light verse, traditional; 4-30 lines; no payment. Submit max. 3 poems.

Fillers: Anecdotes, cartoons, facts, jokes, short humor; no payment.

Tips: "We would like more short articles, 1 page or less. We also look for good-quality nature articles."

** This periodical was #50 on the 1994 Top 50 Plus Christian Publishers list.

#THE LUTHERAN JOURNAL, 7317 Cahill Rd., Edina MN 55439-2081. (612)941-6830. Lutheran. Rev. Armin U. Deye, ed. Family magazine for church members, middle age and older. Quarterly mag; 32 pgs; circ 136,000. 60% freelance. Complete ms/cover letter or query. Pays .01-.04/wd (.01-.02/wd for fiction); on publication; for all, 1st, or one-time rts. Articles 1,500/some to 2,000 (25-30/yr), fiction to 2,000 wds (2/yr). Responds in 3-4 mos. Seasonal 6 mos ahead. Considers simultaneous submissions & reprints (occasionally). No guidelines; copy for 9x12 SAE/2 stamps.

Poetry: Buys 6/yr. Free verse, traditional; to 20 lines. Submit max. 3 poems.

*THE LUTHERAN LAYMAN, 2185 Hampton Ave., St. Louis MO 63139-2983. (314)647-4900x18 or (800)944-3450. Lutheran Laymen's League/Lutheran Church-Missouri Synod. Gerald Perschbacher, ed. Lutheran news for lay adults. Monthly tabloid; 16 pgs; circ 80,000. 10% freelance. Query. Pays negotiable fees (about $110/tabloid pg), on acceptance, for all rts. Not copyrighted. Articles 600-1,500 wds (10+/yr). Responds in 2 wks. Seasonal 3 mos ahead. Guidelines; free copy.

Columns/Departments: Buys 5/yr. Celebrities or Personalities (L.L.L. related, when possible—members, supporters); 600-1,500 wds.

Tips: "No opinion pieces or heavy doctrine. Be in Lutheran Church-Missouri Synod and know about Intl. L.L.L."

*LUTHERAN WITNESS, 1333 S. Kirkwood Rd., St. Louis MO 63122-7295. (314)965-9917. Lutheran Church-Missouri Synod. David L. Strand, mng ed. Denominational. Monthly mag; 26 pgs; circ 350,000. 75% freelance. Complete ms/cover letter. Pays $100-300, on acceptance, for 1st rts. Articles 500-1,500 wds (25+/yr); fiction 500-1,500 wds. Responds in 6-8 wks. Seasonal 6 mos ahead. Considers simultaneous submissions (non-competitive). Kill fee 50%. Guidelines; free copy.

Fillers: Accepts 60+/yr. Cartoons ($50), short humor; no payment.

*MANNA, 7041 Angelsea Dr., West Jordan UT 84084-2602. Christian. Roger A. Ball, ed. Features short, unrhymed poetry by beginning and intermediate writers. Biannual mag; 40 pgs; circ 250. 100% freelance. Complete ms. **NO PAYMENT** but gives cash prizes of $3-7 for best poems in each issue; for 1st rts. Reports in 1 mo. Guidelines; copy $3.50.

Poetry: Free verse. Submit max. 5 poems.

*MARANATHA, P.O. Box 936, Newark NJ 07101. (201)589-3166. Fax: 589-6212. Assemblies of God. Waldir DeOliveira, ed. General publication in Portuguese/English. Bimonthly newspaper; circ 5,000. Free subscription. 100% freelance. Complete ms/cover letter; no phone query. **NO PAYMENT.** Not copyrighted. Articles one page (20/yr); fiction (5/yr). Accepts reprints. Guidelines/theme list; free copy.

Fillers: Accepts 25/yr. Anecdotes, cartoons, facts, games, ideas, jokes, newsbreaks, quizzes, quotes, short humor, and word puzzles.

Columns/Departments: This World, Happening This Way, Conflict, Evangelism; all 1/4 pg.

Tips: "Our publication is 90% in Portuguese language. All the material (English) suitable will be translated into Portuguese."

*MARIAN HELPERS BULLETIN, Eden Hill, Stockbridge MA 01263. (413)298-3691. Catholic. Vincent Flynn, ed. Quarterly mag; circ 500,000. 20% freelance. Query/clips or complete ms/cover letter. Pays .10/wd, on acceptance, for all, 1st, or reprint rts. Articles 500-900 wds; book reviews. Responds in 3 wks. Seasonal 6 mos ahead. Accepts reprints. Kill fee 30%. Free guidelines/copy.

Tips: "Also needs articles on mercy in action or devotion to Blessed Virgin Mary."

#MATURE LIVING, 127 9th Ave. N., Nashville TN 37234. (615)251-2274. Southern Baptist. Al Shackleford, ed. Christian leisure-reading for senior adults (60+) characterized by human interest and Christian warmth. Monthly mag; circ 350,000. 70% freelance. Complete ms. Pays .055/wd, on acceptance, for all or one-time rts. Articles 950-1,475 (100/yr) & fiction 900-1,475 (12/yr). Responds in 3 mos. Seasonal 18 mos ahead. Serials. Guidelines; copy for 9x12 SAE/4 stamps.

Poetry: Buys 50/yr. Light verse, traditional; senior adult themes; any length; $5-24. Submit max. 5 poems.

Fillers: Buys 15/yr. Anecdotes, facts, short humor; to 50 wds; $5.

Tips: "Most open to human-interest stories. All articles and fiction must relate to senior adults."

MATURE YEARS, Box 801, Nashville TN 37202. (615)749-6292. Fax: (615)749-6512. United Methodist. Marvin W. Cropsey, ed. Inspiration, information, and leisure reading for persons of retirement age. Quarterly mag; 112 pgs; circ 77,000. Subscription $12. 40% freelance. Complete ms/cover letter; no phone query. Pays .04/wd; on acceptance; for one-time rts. Articles 400-2,000 wds (40/yr); fiction 1,500-1,800 wds (4/yr). Responds in 3-8 wks. Seasonal 14 mos ahead. Accepts reprints. Guidelines; copy $2.50.

Poetry: Buys 8/yr. Free verse, haiku, light verse, traditional; to 16 lines; .50-$1/line. Submit max. 6 poems.

Fillers: Buys 12/yr. Cartoons, facts, jokes, quizzes, short humor, word puzzles (religious only); $2-5.

Columns/Departments: Buys 16/yr. Health Hints, 1,000-1,800 wds; Modern Revelations (inspirational), 900-1,500 wds; Fragments of Life (true life inspirational), 400-800 wds.

Special Needs: Articles on crafts and pets. Fiction on older adult situation.

** This periodical was #51 on the 1994 Top 50 Plus Christian Publishers list. (#40 in 1993)

THE MENNONITE, Box 347, Newton KS 67114. (316)283-5100. Fax: (316)283-0454. General conference Mennonite Church. Gordon Houser, ed. Practical articles on aspects of Christian living. Biweekly magazine; 24 pgs; circ 8,000. Subscription $25. 5% freelance. Complete ms/cover letter; phone/fax query ok. Pays .05/wd, on publication, for one-time rts. Articles 650-1,200 wds (10/yr); book reviews, 300 wds, $10. Responds in 1 wk. Seasonal 5 mos ahead. Considers simultaneous submissions & reprints. No disk. Sidebars ok. Guidelines/theme list; copy for 9x12 SAE/4 stamps.

Poetry: Buys 5/yr. Free verse; $10-30. Submit max. 4 poems.

Fillers: Cartoons, facts; 100-300 wds; .05/wd.

Columns/Departments: Buys 8/yr. Bible (Anabaptist, practical Bible studies), 650 wds; Speaking Out (opinion), 650 wds; $30-35.

Special Needs: Christmas-related articles that are different.

Tips: "Most open to Bible studies with clear/practical explanation/application. Include a one-sentence blurb summarizing the article, and include 3 possible titles."

MENNONITE BRETHREN HERALD, 169 Riverton Ave., Winnipeg MB R2L 2E5 Canada. (204)669-6575. Fax: (204)654-1865. Mennonite Brethren Conference of Canada. Ron Geddert, ed. Denominational; for spiritual nurture and awareness of our conference and the world around us. Biweekly mag; 32 pgs; circ 15,000. Subscription $24 Canadian/$30 U.S. 15-20% freelance. Complete ms/cover letter; no phone query. Pays .07/wd, on publication, for one-time & reprint rts. Not copyrighted. Articles 250-1,500 wds (15/yr); fiction 300-900 wds (4/yr). Responds in 26 wks. Seasonal 3 mos ahead. Considers simultaneous submissions & reprints. Guidelines; copy for 9x12 SAE/.86 Canadian postage.

> **Poetry:** Buys 10/yr. Avant-garde, free verse; any length; pays to $10.

#MENNONITE REPORTER, 3-312 Marsland Dr., Waterloo ON N2J 3Z1 Canada. (519)884-3810. Fax: (519)884-3331. Mennonite. Ron Rempel, ed. Denominational. Biweekly newspaper; 20 pgs; circ 10,500. 20% freelance. Query; fax query ok. Pays .07/wd, on publication, for 1st rts. Articles 500-1,500 wds; news 400-600 wds. Responds in 4 wks. Considers simultaneous submissions. No disk. Guidelines; free copy.

> **Tips:** "Most of our readers are Canadians; give us a Canadian perspective."

*MENNONITE WEEKLY REVIEW, Box 568, Newton KS 67114-0568. (316)283-3670. Mennonite. Robert Schrag, ed. Features religious and Mennonite news. Weekly newspaper; 12-16 pgs; circ 11,000. 5% freelance. Complete ms/cover letter. Pays .05/wd, on publication, for one-time rts. Articles 400-500 wds. Responds in 1 mo. Accepts simultaneous submissions. No guidelines; copy $1/SAE/2 stamps.

MESSAGE, Review and Herald Pub. Assn., 55 W. Oak Ridge Dr., Hagerstown MD 21740. (301)791-7000 x 2614, 2565. Fax: (301)714-1753. Seventh-day Adventist. Stephen P. Ruff, ed. Blacks and other minorities who have an interest in current issues and are seeking a better lifestyle. Bimonthly mag; 32 pgs; circ 74,000. Subscription $11.95. 25% freelance. Complete ms/no cover letter or phone query. Pays $75-150, on acceptance, for 1st rts. Articles 400-1,600 wds (150/yr); parables; fiction for children, 400 wds. Responds in 2-8 wks. Seasonal 6 mos ahead. Guidelines; free copy for 9x12 SAE.

> **Fillers:** Quizzes; $25.

> **Tips:** "Review past issues to understand audience and focus. Make articles readable; avoid scholarly and technical jargon. Quote experts, use sound logic, make your case with evidence and credibility."

MESSAGE OF THE OPEN BIBLE, 2020 Bell Ave., Des Moines IA 50315. (515)288-6761. Fax: (515)288-2510. Open Bible Standard Churches. Delores Winegar, ed. To inspire, inform and educate the Open Bible family. Monthly (10x) mag; 20 pgs; circ 4,000. Subscription $6. 10% freelance. Complete ms/cover letter; phone/fax query ok. **NO PAYMENT**. Not copyrighted. Articles 700-800 or 1,400-1,600 wds (10-15/yr). Responds in 2 wks. Seasonal 2-3 mos ahead. Some sidebars. Guidelines/theme list; copy for 9x12 SAE/3 stamps.

> **Special Needs:** 1995 - Year of International Ministries.

> **Tips:** "We prefer concise testimony articles (as compared to instructional, sermon-type). We do give preference to Open Bible writers."

#MESSENGER, Box 18068, Covington KY 41018-0068. (606)283-6270. Catholic. Jean Bach, news ed. Diocese paper of Covington KY. Weekly (45X) newspaper; 24 pgs; circ 16,000. Subscription $18. 40% freelance. Query/clips. Pays $1.25/column inch, on publication, for 1st rts. Articles 500-800 wds. Responds in 1 wk. Seasonal 1 mo ahead. Considers simultaneous submissions. Guidelines; free copy.

#THE MESSENGER, Box 1268, Steinbach MB R0A 2A0 Canada. (204)326-6401. Fax: (204)326-1613. Evangelical Mennonite Conference. Menno Hamm, ed. Denominational; informational and devotional. Biweekly (22X) mag; 16 pgs; circ 3,700. Subscription $6. 20% freelance. Complete ms; no phone/fax query. Pays $5-20, on publication, for one-time rts. Not copyrighted. Articles 300-1,500 wds (5/yr).

Responds in 16 wks. Seasonal 6 wks ahead. Considers simultaneous submissions & reprints. No disk. No guidelines; copy for 9x12 SAE/$1.10 Canadian postage.

Poetry: Buys 5/yr. Light verse, traditional; $5-10. Submit max. 2 poems.

#THE MESSENGER, Box 1568, Dunn NC 28335-1568. (919)892-4161. Fax: (919)892-6876. Pentecostal Free Will Baptist. Rev. Don Sauls, ed. Denominational. Monthly (10X) mag; 16 pgs; circ 2,500. Subscription $6.50. 15% freelance. Query or complete ms. Pays $2.50-10, on publication, for simultaneous rts. Not copyrighted. Articles 2-6 pgs (12/yr); fiction to 5.5 pgs (1-2/yr). Responds in 4 wks. Seasonal 6 mos ahead. Accepts reprints. Guidelines; copy .65.

Tips: "Accepting material only from members of local congregations."

#MESSENGER OF THE SACRED HEART, 661 Greenwood Ave., Toronto ON M4J 4B3 Canada. (416)466-1195. Catholic/Apostleship of Prayer. Rev. F.J. Power, S.J., ed. Help for daily living on a spiritual level. Monthly (11X) mag; 32 pgs; circ 18,000. 20% freelance. Complete ms/cover letter; no phone query. Pays .04/wd, on acceptance, for 1st rts. Articles 750-1,500 wds (30/yr); fiction 800-1,500 wds (12/yr). Responds in 1 mo. Seasonal 5 mos ahead. Guidelines; copy $1/9x12 SAE.

Tips: "Most open to inspirational stories and articles."

THE MESSENGER OF ST. ANTHONY, Mater Dei College, RR 2 Box 45, Ogdensburg NY 13669. (315)393-5930. Fax: (315)393-5931. Catholic. Rev. Ronald Mrozinski, pres. For middle-age and older Catholics in English-speaking world; articles that address current issues. Monthly mag. Subscription $15. 65% freelance. Complete ms/cover letter; no phone/fax query. Pays $50-150, on publication, for 1st rts. Articles 700-2,000 wds (95/yr); fiction 700-2,000 wds (6/yr). Responds in 2-3 wks. Seasonal 9 mos ahead. No sidebars. Guidelines.

Special Needs: Family issues.

*METHODIST HISTORY, Box 127, Madison NJ 07940. (201)822-2787. Fax: (201)408-3909. United Methodist. Charles Yrigoyen Jr., ed. History of the United Methodism and Methodist/Wesleyan churches. Quarterly journal; 64 pgs; circ 1,200. 100% freelance. Complete ms/with cover letter; phone query ok. **PAYS IN COPIES** for 1st rts. Historical articles to 5,000 wds (20/yr). Responds in 3 mos. Guidelines; no copy.

*MINISTRY TODAY, Box 9127, Fort Wayne IN 46899. (219)747-2027. Fax: (219)747-5331. Missionary Church. Robert Ransom, mng ed. Denominational; for young adults, 20-45 years old. Bimonthly tabloid; 4 pgs; circ 5,000. Estab 1992. 15% freelance. Complete ms/cover letter; no phone query. Pays .03-.04/wd; on publication; for 1st, one-time, reprint or simultaneous rts. Not copyrighted. Articles 200-800 wds (3-4/yr); fiction 200-1,600 wds (1-2/yr). Responds in 4-8 wks. Seasonal 4 mos ahead. Considers simultaneous submissions & reprints. Guidelines; copy for 9x12 SAE/2 stamps.

Tips: "Limited due to being only 4 tabloid pages with six issues/yr. Family and parenting material is most selected category."

#MINNESOTA CHRISTIAN CHRONICLE, 1619 Portland Ave. S., Minneapolis MN 55404. (612)339-9579. Fax: (612)339-6973. Doug Trouten, ed. Local news and features of interest to the Christian community. Biweekly newspaper; 36 pgs; circ 7,000. Subscription $19.95. 10% freelance. Query; phone query ok. Pays .05/wd, after publication, for one-time rts. Articles 500-1,000 wds (50/yr); book reviews 500 wds. Responds in 3 mos. Seasonal 2 mos ahead. Considers simultaneous query & reprints. Guidelines; copy $2.

Tips: "Not interested in anything without a Minnesota 'hook.' Inspiration section has room for two general personality features each issue; tell us about people and ministries we're not aware of."

** 1994 EPA Award of Excellence - Newspaper.

THE MIRACULOUS MEDAL, 475 E. Chelten Ave., Philadelphia PA 19144-5785. (215)848-1010. Catholic. Rev. John W. Gouldrick, ed. For Catholic adult readers. Quarterly mag; 30 pgs; circ 340,000. 40% freelance. Complete ms/cover letter. Pays .02/wd & up, on acceptance, for 1st rts. Religious fiction 1,600-2,400 wds (5/yr). Responds in 12 wks. Seasonal 1 yr ahead. Guidelines; copy for 6x9 SAE/2 stamps.

> **Poetry:** Buys 5/yr. Free verse, traditional; to 20 lines; .50/line. Send any number. "Must have religious theme, preferably about the Blessed Virgin Mary."

MONTANA CATHOLIC, P.O. Box 1729, Helena MT 59624-1729. (406)442-5820. Fax: (406)442-5191. Catholic. Gerald M. Korson, ed. Diocese paper for Helena, Montana. Tabloid published 16X/yr; 20-24 pgs; circ 8,100. Subscription $10 (MT), $14 (outside). 3% freelance. Complete ms/cover letter; fax query ok. Pays negotiable rates, on publication, for negotiable rts. Articles 500-1,500 wds (8/yr); book reviews, 200-600 wds. Responds in 2-3 wks. Seasonal 2 mos ahead. Considers simultaneous submissions & reprints. Kill fee negotiable. Sidebars ok. Guidelines/theme list; copy for 9x12 SAE/4 stamps.

> **Poetry:** Buys 2-3/yr. Free verse, light verse, traditional; 8-25 lines; $5.

> **Fillers:** Buys 2/yr. Cartoons, quotes.

> **Columns/Departments:** Buys 3-4/yr. Guest Commentary, 600-1,000 wds; $10-25.

> **Special Needs:** Commentaries (usually 600-1,000 wds) can touch on almost any subject; news or features on any subject considered. Publishes annual or occasional special supplements on health, holiday themes, marriage, death, colleges, vocations, weddings, or senior adult issues.

MOODY MAGAZINE, 820 N. LaSalle Blvd., Chicago IL 60610. (312)329-2164. Fax: (312)329-2149. Moody Bible Institute. Andrew Scheer, mng. ed. To encourage and equip evangelical Christians to think and live biblically. Monthly (11X) mag; 68-96 pgs; circ 135,000. Subscription $23.95. 75% freelance. Query only; no phone query; fax only if urgent. Pays $180-500 ($210-375 for fiction), or .15/wd (.20 for assigned); on acceptance; for 1st rts; reserves electronic rts. Articles 1,200-2,500 wds (80/yr); fiction 1,400-2,500 wds (2-3/yr). Responds in 4-8 wks. Seasonal 9 mos ahead. Kill fee. Requires 3.5" disk. Guidelines; copy for 9x12 SASE/3 stamps.

> **Columns/Departments:** Buys 22/yr. Just For Parents (practical), 1,600 wds; First Person (salvation testimonies—may be "as-told-to"), 800-1,000 wds; $150-225.

> **Special Needs:** Focus on "how-I" or "how-we," rather than "how-to."

> **Tips:** "In your query, don't simply say what the article is about; tell us what it is for—intended reader application. We want narratives with well-developed scenes and specifics, not generalizations."

> ** This periodical was #4 on the 1994 Top 50 Plus Christian Publishers list. (#19 in 1993)

***MORNING GLORY**, 314 Spruce St., Fergus Falls MN 56537. Lutheran. Rev. Arnold E. Windahl, ed. Godly living in light of the return of Christ. Quarterly mag; 12 pgs; circ 800. 100% freelance. Query or complete ms/cover letter: no phone query. **NO PAYMENT**. Accepts reprints. Articles to 300 wds. Responds in 4-6 wks. Seasonal 6 mos ahead. Considers simultaneous submissions & reprints. Guidelines; copy for 9x12 SAE/3 stamps.

> **Poetry:** Accepts 10/yr. Free verse, traditional; to 20 lines. Submit max. 2 poems.

> **Fillers:** Accepts 40/yr. Anecdotes, facts, newsbreaks, prayers, quotes, short humor; to 50 wds.

> **Tips:** "No liberal theology or photography."

***NATIONAL CATHOLIC REPORTER**, 115 E. Armour Blvd., Kansas City MO 64141. (816)531-0538. Catholic. Thomas Fox, ed. Independent. Weekly (44X) newspaper; 44-48 pgs; circ 48,000. Query/clips.

Pays varying rates, on publication. Articles any length. Responds in 2 mos. Accepts simultaneous submissions.

Columns/Departments: Query with ideas for columns.

NETWORK, Box 320627, Birmingham AL 35232-0637. (205)328-7112. Interdenominational. Dolores Milazzo Hicks, ed/pub. To encourage and nurture dialog, understanding and unity in Jewish and Christian communities. Monthly tabloid; 12-16 pgs; circ 15,000. 50% freelance. Negotiable payment. Not copyrighted. Considers simultaneous submissions. Articles and news.

#NEW COVENANT, 200 Noll Plaza, Huntington IN 46750. (219)356-8400. Fax: (219)356-8472. Catholic/Our Sunday Visitor. Jim Manney, ed. Serves readers involved in Catholic Charismatic renewal. Monthly mag; 36 pgs; circ 40,200. Subscription $18. 85% freelance. Query/clips or complete ms/cover letter; phone query ok. Pays .10/wd ($100-400); on acceptance; for 1st or one-time rts. Articles 750-3,000 wds (40/yr). Responds in 1 mo. Seasonal 5 mos ahead. Kill fee 50%. Considers simultaneous submissions & reprints. Guidelines; copy for 9x12 SAE/5 stamps.

> **Tips:** "Most open to testimonies. Speak from experience, not teaching. Be familiar with New Covenant's style so you can speak to our audience."

> ** This periodical was #46 on the 1994 Top 50 Plus Christian Publishers list. (#28 in 1993)

A NEW HEART, Box 4004, San Clemente CA 92674-4004. (714)496-7655. Fax: (714)496-8465. Aubrey Beauchamp, ed. For Christian healthcare-givers; info regarding medical/Christian issues. Quarterly mag; 16 pgs; circ 5,000. Subscription $20. 20% freelance. Complete ms/cover letter; phone/fax query ok. **PAYS 2 COPIES** for one-time rts. Not copyrighted. Articles 600-1,800 wds (20-25/yr). Responds in 2-3 wks. Considers simultaneous submissions & reprints. No disk. No sidebars. Guidelines; copy for 9x12 SAE/ 3 stamps.

> **Poetry:** Accepts 1-2/yr. Submit max. 1-3 poems.

> **Fillers:** Accepts 3-4/yr. Anecdotes, cartoons, facts, jokes, short humor; 100-120 wds.

> **Columns/Departments:** Accepts 20-25/yr. Chaplain's Corner, 200-250 wds; Physician's Corner, 200-250 wds.

> **Tips:** "Most open to true stories, short, medically related, including caregivers."

#NEW OXFORD REVIEW, 1069 Kains Ave., Berkeley CA 94706. (510)526-5374. Catholic. Dale Vree, ed. Orthodox Catholic, but open to compatible evangelical views; highly educated audience. Monthly (10X) mag; circ 14,000. Subscription $19. 50% freelance. Query or complete ms; phone query ok. **PAYS IN COPIES**, for all rts. Articles 750-3,750 wds (15/yr). Responds in 3-6 wks. Seasonal 4 mos ahead. No guidelines: copy for $3.50.

> **Tips:** "Manuscripts must have intellectual depth."

NEWS NETWORK INTERNATIONAL NEWS SERVICE, Box 28001, Santa Ana CA 92799. (714)775-4900. Fax: (714)775-7315. CNNI Intl. Kim Lawton, news ed. A religious freedom news and information agency; provides wholesale news to retail news outlets. Biweekly news service; 40-60 pgs. Subscription $75-110. 35% freelance. Query; phone/fax query ok. Call for quote on payment. Pays on publication, for all rts (on-spot news) or one-time rts (for features). Articles 600-1,500 wds. Responds in 2 wks. Seasonal 2 mos ahead. Prefers disk copy. Kill fee 50%. Sidebars ok. No guidelines; free copy.

> **Columns/Departments:** Buys 24/yr. World Perspectives (world affairs and religious liberty issues); 750 wds.

> **Tips:** "Most open to news (spot news/analysis) and features. Focus very specifically on issues/news along the topic of religious freedom. Not interested in reflective, how-to reports. We work with

straight, hard news. We welcome internationally-based correspondents with access to developing trends and issues facing the church."

NEW THOUGHT JOURNAL, Box 700754, Tulsa OK 74170. (918)299-7330. Fax: (918)492-6237. Edward Wincentsen, ed. An inspirational magazine to stimulate thought; goes to general public. Quarterly mag; 20+ pgs; circ 2,000+. Subscription $15. 80% freelance. Query or complete ms/cover letter. PAYS IN COPIES (may pay soon), for one-time rts. Articles & fiction 3 pgs. Responds in 3-4 wks. Considers simultaneous submissions & reprints. No disks. No sidebars. Guidelines/theme list; copy $3.

    Poetry: Avant-garde, free verse, haiku; to 30 lines. Submit max. 4-5 poems.

    Tips: "Our direction is very different than 'Christian' publications; very non-dogmatic and mainly open to make the reader think on positions, etc. Most open to articles, essays and poetry."

+THE NEW TRUMPET, TH130 590 Lower Landing Rd., Blackwood NJ 08012. (609)228-4243. Mae Hart Lovett, ed. To help Christians in their walk and to prepare them for the return of Christ. Quarterly (3X) newsletter; 16 pgs; circ 800. Estab 1993. 100% freelance. Complete ms/cover letter; phone query ok. PAYS IN COPIES. Articles 600-1,500 wds (3/yr); fiction 1,500-2,000 wds (3/yr); book reviews, 400 wds. Considers simultaneous submissions & reprints. Responds in 1-2 wks. No disks. Sidebars ok. Free guidelines/theme list/copy.

    Poetry: Accepts 3-6/yr. Free verse, light verse, traditional; 4-24 lines.

    Fillers: Accepts 3-4/yr. Anecdotes, cartoons, facts, ideas, prose, quotes, short humor; 15-30 wds.

    Columns/Departments: Accepts 3/yr. For Men; For Women; 500-800 wds.

    Special Needs: Interviews with unknown Christians. Slices of life in fiction.

    Tips: Call to discuss your idea.

+NO-DEBT LIVING, P.O. Box 282, Veradale WA 99037. (509)927-1322 or (800)560-3328. Robert Frank, ed. Financial and home-management information from a Christian perspective. Monthly (11X) newsletter. Query or complete ms; phone query ok (5-6:30 a.m. or 8-9:30 p.m. are best). Pays $20-40, within 15 days of publication, for multi-use rights (you may sell reprints). Articles 750-1,000 wds (major features); 400-600 wds (vignettes). Reports in 2-3 wks. Prefers disk copy.

    Tips: "Articles may include references to Christian principles or Bible verses if directly related to topic, but not necessary if it doesn't fit." Writers with journalism training or experience are preferred.

*THE NORTH AMERICAN VOICE OF FATIMA, 1023 Swan Rd., Youngstown NY 14174. (716)754-7489. Catholic. Rev. Stephen McGee, C.R.S.P., ed. To foster Christian ideals with emphasis on Mary, Mother of God, and Mother of the Church. Bimonthly mag; 20 pgs; circ 3,000. 40% freelance. Query or complete ms. Pays .02/wd, on publication, for 1st rts. Not copyrighted. Articles & fiction 700 wds. Responds in 6 wks. Seasonal 6 mos ahead. Considers simultaneous submissions. Free copy.

NORTHWEST CHRISTIAN JOURNAL, Box 59014, Renton WA 98058. (206)255-3552. Fax: (206)228-8749. Tami Tedrow, ed. News with an evangelical perspective for NW Christians; local features & news stories. Monthly tabloid; 12-14 pgs; circ 27,000. Subscription $15. 0-10% freelance. Query/clips; no phone/fax query. Pays $5-35, on publication, for one-time rts. Articles 200-800 wds (1-2/yr). Responds in 6-8+ wks. Accepts some simultaneous submissions & reprints. Prefers disk. Guidelines; copy $1.50.

    Fillers: Cartoons; $5.

    Tips: "This is a news publication, which means we look for stories that are timely and reflect what's happening in the Northwest. No devotional material; we have a news focus/news style and don't want the kind of articles a magazine would publish. Most open to news/interviews assigned by the editor."

+NORTHWESTERN LUTHERAN, 2929 N Mayfair Rd., Milwaukee WI 53222.(414)256-3888. Fax: (414)256-3899. Wisconsin Evangelical Lutheran Synod. Gary Baumler, ed. Denominational. Monthly mag; 36 pgs; circ 61,000. Subscription $9. 20% freelance. Complete ms/cover letter; phone/fax query ok. Pays $50-100, on publication, for one-time & reprint rts. Articles 500-1,000 wds (50/yr). Responds in 4 wks. Seasonal 6 mos ahead. Accepts reprints (if they know where published). Guidelines; copy for 9x12 SAE/2 stamps.

   Tips: "Most of our writers belong to the denomination and write about our members, organizations or institutions."

OBLATES, 15 S. 59th St., Belleville IL 62223-4694. (618)233-2238. Fax: (618)233-8648. Catholic. Mary Mohrman, mss ed. To inspire, comfort, uplift, and motivate an older Catholic/Christian audience. Bimonthly mag; 20 pgs; circ 500,000. 25% freelance. Complete ms/cover letter. Pays $80, on acceptance, for 1st rts. Articles 450-550 wds (12/yr); fiction 450-550 wds. Responds in 8 wks. Seasonal 6-8 mos ahead. No disk. Guidelines; copy for 6x9 SAE/2 stamps.

   Poetry: Buys 12-15/yr. Traditional; 12-20 lines; $30. Submit max. 2 poems.

   Tips: "Need personal, inspirational articles with a strong spiritual theme firmly grounded to a particular incident and poetry."

OUR FAMILY, Box 249, Battleford SK S0M 0E0 Canada. (306)937-7771. Fax: (306)937-7644. Catholic. Fr. Nestor Gregoire, ed. All aspects of family life in the light of Christian Faith. Monthly mag; 40 pgs; circ 10,000. Subscription $15.98. 50% freelance. Complete ms/no cover letter. Pays .07-.12/wd, on acceptance, for 1st rts. Articles 500-2,000 wds (75/yr). Responds in 4 wks. Seasonal 4 mos ahead. Considers simultaneous submissions & reprints. Guidelines/theme list; copy $2.50.

   Poetry: Buys 44/yr. Free verse, haiku, light verse, traditional; 2-25 lines; $1/line.

   Fillers: Buys 40/yr. Anecdotes, cartoons, jokes, short humor; to 150 wds.

   Tips: "Your SASE must have Canadian postage. We aim at the average reader. Our goal is to strengthen, encourage families as they strive to live their faith today. Articles need an experiential point of view with practical guidelines."

   ** This periodical was #29 on the 1994 Top 50 Plus Christian Publishers list. (#42 in 1993)

#OUR SUNDAY VISITOR, 200 Noll Plaza, Huntington IN 46750. (219)356-8400. Fax: (219)356-8472. Catholic. David Scott, ed. Vital news, spirituality for today's Catholic. Weekly newspaper; 24 pgs; circ 120,000. Subscription $36. 5% freelance. Query; no phone query. Pays $100, on acceptance, for 1st rts. Articles 1,000-1,200 wds (25/yr). Responds in 1 mo. Seasonal 2 mos ahead. Kill fee. Guidelines; Copy for #10 SASE.

   Columns/Departments: Buys 50/yr. Viewpoint (editorial/op-ed), 750 wds, $100.

   Tips: "Need familiarity with Catholic Church issues and with Catholic Press—newspapers and magazines."

   ** This periodical was #1 on the 1994 Top 50 Plus Christian Publishers list. (#43 in 1993)

PARENTING TREASURES, 400 West Blvd. S., Elkhart IN 46514. (219)522-1491. Fax: (219)522-0114. Lutheran-Missouri Synod. Deb Graf, administrative ed. Encouraging parents of newborns through college age to apply Christian faith to parenting actions and attitudes. Quarterly mag; 24 pgs; circ 300. Subscription $10. 100% freelance. Complete ms/cover letter; phone/fax query ok. **PAYS 4 COPIES**, for one-time rts. Articles 500-1,500 wds (40/yr); fiction 250-1,000 wds (3-4/yr); book reviews 500 wds.

Responds in 6-8 wks. Seasonal 4 mos ahead. Considers simultaneous submissions & reprints. Prefers disk. Some sidebars. Guidelines/theme list; copy for 9x12 SAE/4 stamps or $1.

>**Poetry:** Accepts 8/yr. Free verse, haiku, light verse, traditional; 4-20 lines. Submit max. 4 poems.
>
>**Fillers:** Accepts 16/yr. Anecdotes, cartoons, facts, quotes, short humor; 50-500 wds.
>
>**Columns/Departments:** Accepts 8/yr. A Time to Laugh (funny things kids say or do), 50-150 wds.
>
>**Special Needs:** Media, gender roles, rights of passage, peer pressure, and dealing with grief.
>
>**Tips:** "As long as an article fits topic, there is a good chance we'll publish it (if well written). Avoid use of Christian jargon and judgmental attitudes. We address both the joys and frustrations of parenting."

+PARENTLIFE, MSN 140, 127 Ninth Ave. N., Nashville TN 37234. (615)251-2229. Fax: (615)251-5008. Southern Baptist. Michelle Hicks, mng. ed. For parents of children—birth to 12 years. Monthly mag; 50 pgs; circ 125,000. Subscription $19.95. Estab 1994. 10% freelance. Query; fax query ok. Pays, on acceptance, for all, first, one-time, or reprint rts. Articles 400-1,500 wds (12/yr); fiction (5/yr). Responds in 6 wks. Seasonal 6 mos ahead. Occasionally takes reprints. Prefers disk. Sidebars ok. Guidelines; copy for 9x12 SAE/4 stamps.

>**Fillers:** Anecdotes, cartoons, games, ideas, party ideas, short humor; to 100 wds; $20.
>
>**Tips:** "Query with resume."

PARENTS OF TEENAGERS, P.O. Box 36630, Colorado Springs CO 80936-3663. (719)531-7776. Fax: (719)535-0172. Good Family Magazines/Cook Communications Ministries. Gloria Chisholm, mng. ed. For parents of teenagers and youth workers. Bimonthly mag; 40 pgs; circ 50,000. Subscription $21.98. 80% freelance. Query. Pays .10-.15/wd, on acceptance, for 1st rts. Articles 1,000-2,500 wds (24/yr); book/music/video reviews, 150 wds, $25. Responds in 8 wks. Seasonal 8 mos ahead. Considers simultaneous submissions & reprints. Kill fee. Prefers disk. Sidebars ok. Guidelines/theme list; copy for 9x12 SAE/4 stamps.

>**Columns/Departments:** John Schinkel. Buys 18/yr. As Your Teen Grows (3 age divisions, practical how-tos), 500-900 wds, $50-75.
>
>**Tips:** "Writer must be in touch with both parents and teenagers' needs and hurts and be able to write in a non-preachy, compassionate tone. Most open to 'As Your Teen Grows' and feature articles."
>
>****** This periodical was #32 on the 1994 Top 50 Plus Christian Publishers list. (#13 in 1993)

+PAX CHRISTI USA, 348 E. 10th, Erie PA 16503-1110.(814)453-4955. Fax: (814)452-4784. Catholic. S. Marlene Bertke, assoc. ed. For adult members of U.S. Catholic Peace Movement. Quarterly mag; 20 pgs; circ 12,000. Distributed free. 5% freelance. Query. Pays, on publication, for one-time rts. Considers simultaneous submissions & reprints. Prefers disk. Guidelines; copy for 9x12 SAE/2 stamps. Not in topical listings.

>**Tips:** "No sexist language."

THE PEGASUS REVIEW, P.O. Box 88, Henderson MD 21640-0088. (410)482-6736. Art Bounds, ed. Theme oriented poetry/prose. Bimonthly mag; 8-10 pgs; circ 200. Subscription $10. 100% freelance. Complete ms/cover letter or query. **PAYS IN COPIES** or occasional book awards, for one-time rts. Fiction 1-3 pgs (25/yr). Responds in 1-3 wks. Seasonal 3 mos ahead. Considers simultaneous submissions & reprints. Guidelines/theme list; copy $2.50/#10 SAE.

>**Poetry:** Accepts over 100/yr. Free verse, haiku, light verse, traditional; 4-24 lines. Theme oriented, to 24 lines. Submit max. 3 poems.

Tips: "We are open to beginners as well as professional writers, with the emphasis on beginner writers."

#PENTECOSTAL EVANGEL, 1445 Boonville, Springfield MO 65802-1894. (417)862-2781. Fax: (417)862-0416. Assemblies of God. John Maempa, ed. Denominational; pentecostal. Weekly mag; 32 pgs; circ 255,000. Subscription $15.95. 33% freelance. Complete ms/cover letter; no phone query. Pays .06-.08/wd (1/2 for reprints), on acceptance, for 1st, one-time, or reprint rts. Articles 500-1,200 wds (260/yr). Responds in 3 mos. Seasonal 6 mos ahead. Accepts reprints. Kill fee. Free guidelines/theme list/copy.

Tips: A writer needs to know the doctrines and traditions of the Assemblies of God, tie into those, and have something significant to say. We need short, nonpreachy articles directed to the unconverted."

** This periodical was #23 on the 1994 Top 50 Plus Christian Publishers list.

*PENTECOSTAL HOMELIFE, 8855 Dunn Rd., Hazelwood MO 63042-2299. (314)837-7300. United Pentecostal Church. Mark Christian, ed. To help couples and parents in everyday living. Monthly (7X) mag; circ 6,000. 90% freelance. Complete ms; no phone query. Pays $15-30, on publication, for reprint rts. Articles 400-800 wds or 1,000-1,500 wds (48/yr); fiction 1,000-1,500 wds. Responds in 1-2 mos. Seasonal 1 yr ahead. Considers simultaneous submissions & reprints. Guidelines/theme list; copy for 9x12 SAE/2 stamps.

Tips: Prefers use of King James Version of the Bible.

THE PENTECOSTAL MESSENGER, Box 850, Joplin MO 64802. (417)624-7050. Fax: (417)624-7102. Pentecostal Church of God. Peggy Allen, mng. ed. Denominational. Monthly (11X) mag; 32 pgs; circ 7,500. Subscription $11. 30-40% freelance. Complete ms. Pays .015/wd; on publication; for one-time, simultaneous or reprint rts. Articles 900-2,400 wds (35-40/yr). Responds in 4 wks. Seasonal 4 mos ahead. Considers simultaneous submissions & reprints. Sidebars ok. Guidelines; copy for 9x12 SAE/$1.05 postage.

Poetry: Buys 4-6/yr. Free verse, traditional; .25/line. Submit max. 3 poems.

Columns/Departments: Buys 2-3/yr. Ladies column (Diana Gee, ed), 900 wds; youth column (Eddie Vansell, ed), 900 wds.

Tips: "We are interested in articles that present the deeper Christian life; particularly those coming from personal experiences."

THE PENTECOSTAL TESTIMONY. 6745 Century Ave., Mississauga ON L5N 6P7 Canada. (905)542-7400. Fax: (905)542-7313. The Pentecostal Assemblies of Canada. Rick Hiebert, ed. Focus is inspirational and Christian living; Pentecostal holiness slant. Monthly mag; 36 pgs; circ 25,000. Subscription $24 US. 30-40% freelance. Query; phone query ok; no fax. Pays $20-75 ($75-100 for fiction), on publication, for 1st rts. Articles 400-1,200 wds (30/yr); fiction 1,200-1,800 wds (6/yr). Responds in 4-6 wks (20-30 wks on mss). Seasonal 3 mos ahead. Accepts reprints. Prefers disk copy (WP 5.1 or 6.0). Sidebars ok. Guidelines in 1995; copy $2/9x12 SAE/$2 Canadian postage.

Poetry: Buys 6-8/yr. Avant-garde, free verse; 8-20 lines; $20-30. Submit max. 3 poems.

Fillers: Buys 8-15/yr. Anecdotes, cartoons, short humor; 100-200 wds; $10-20.

Special Needs: More Canadian content.

Tips: "Sell your idea with a concise, yet detailed, query with some humor. Don't make references to US locations or events."

#PERSPECTIVES ON SCIENCE AND CHRISTIAN FAITH, Box 668, Ipswich MA 01938. (508)356-5656. Fax: (508)356-4375. American Scientific Affiliation. Dr. J.W. Haas, Jr., ed. Scholarly articles and essays dealing with the interaction between the sciences and Christian faith. Quarterly journal; 72 pgs; circ 3,300. Subscription $25. Little freelance. Complete ms (3 copies). **PAYS 2 COPIES** for 1st or all rts. Articles to 9 pgs; book reviews 2-4 pgs. Reports within 1 month. Seasonal 3 mos ahead. Accepts serials. Guidelines; copy for 9x12 SAE/$1.05 postage.

*PLENTY GOOD ROOM, 1800 N. Hermitage Ave., Chicago IL 60622-1101. (312)486-8970. Catholic. J. Glen Murray, ed. Focuses on African-American worship within the church. Bimonthly mag; 12 pgs. Estab 1993. Query. Pays $25/pg, for all rts. Articles. Responds in 3 mos. Guidelines; free copy.

THE PLOWMAN, Box 414, Whitby ON L1N 5S4 Canada. (905)668-7803. Christian. Tony Scavetta, pub. Poetry and prose of social commentary; any topics. Quarterly jour; 56 pgs; circ 15,000. 95% freelance. Complete ms/cover letter; no phone/fax query. **PAYS A SUBSCRIPTION**, but writers eligible for cash prizes. Buys one-time, reprint or simultaneous rts. Articles (1,000/yr) & fiction (500/yr), 1,000-2,000 wds. Responds in 1 wk. Seasonal 3 mos ahead. Considers simultaneous submissions & reprints. Guidelines; free copy.

> **Poetry:** Accepts 100/yr. All types. Submit max. 24 poems.
>
> **Special Needs:** Drama, plays and novellas. Also publishes chapbooks; 20% royalties. Open to all topics.

+PLUS, 66 E. Main St., Pawling NY 12564. (814)855-5000. Fax: (914)855-1462. Peale Center for Christian Living. Bob Chuvala, mng ed. Provides evangelical Christians with inspiring, informative, and practical stories and articles. Monthly (10X) mag; 36 pgs; circ 650,000. Subscription $10. 33% freelance. Complete ms/cover letter; phone/fax query ok. Pays $750, on acceptance, for 1st rts. Articles 2,000-2,500 wds (10/yr). Responds in 3-4 wks. Seasonal 8 mos ahead. Accepts reprints. Kill fee #250. Some sidebars. Guidelines; copy for #10 SAE/1 stamp.

> **Tips:** "Have a deep, living knowledge of evangelical Christianity."

POETRY FORUM SHORT STORIES, 5713 Larchmont Dr., Erie PA 16509. (819)866-2543. Fax: (819)866-2543. Interdenominational. Gunvor Skogsholm, ed. Poetry and prose that takes an honest look at the human condition. Quarterly journal; 24 pgs; circ 500. 90% freelance. Complete ms/cover letter. **NO PAYMENT** for one-time rts. Articles 100-800 wds; fiction 800-3,000 wds. Responds in 1-3 mos. Considers simultaneous submissions. Guidelines; copy $3.

> **Poetry:** Inspirational; any type.

A POSITIVE APPROACH, A National Magazine for the Physically Challenged, Box 910, Millville NJ 08332. (609)451-4777. Fax: (609)451-6678. Pat Swart, ed. asst. For the physically and mentally disabled and churches serving their needs. Quarterly mag; 64 pgs; circ 40,000. Subscription $15. 90% freelance. Query or complete ms/cover letter; phone/fax query ok. **PAYS 10 COPIES**; for one-time, reprint or simultaneous rts. Articles 500-1,000 wds (60-80/yr). Responds in 2 wks. Seasonal 4 mos ahead. Considers simultaneous submissions & reprints. Guidelines; copy $2.50/9x12 SAE.

> **Tips:** "We stress person first/disability last. We encourage people with newly incurred disabilities. Articles must pertain to a person with a disability or a church working with the problems of the disabled."

+POSITIVE LIVING, 66 E. Main St., Pawling NY 12564. (914)855-5000. Fax: (914)855-1462. Peale Center for Christian Living. Bob Chuvala, ed. A spiritual, motivational, self-improvement magazine for the 40 year old. Monthly (10X) mag; 40 pgs. Estab. 1995. Query or complete ms/cover letter. Pays $125- $500, on acceptance. Articles 1,500-2,500 wds. Responds in 4 wks. Seasonal 4 mos ahead. Accepts reprints ($50/pg). Guidelines.

+POURASTAN, 615 Stuart Ave., Outremont QB H2V 3H2 Canada. (514)279-3066. Fax: (514)276-9960. Canadian Diosese of the Armenian Holy Apostolic Church. Mr. N. Ouzounian, ed. Denominational; religious, social and community oriented. Bimonthly mag; 20-24 pgs; circ 1,000. Free for donations. 100% freelance. Complete ms/cover letter. **NO PAYMENT.** Not copyrighted. Articles (10/yr); book reviews, 300 wds. Seasonal 1 mo ahead. Considers simultaneous submissions & reprints. No disks. No sidebars. Free copy.

> **Poetry:** Accepts few. Traditional, to 25 lines. Submit max. 2 poems.
>
> **Fillers:** Facts, ideas, prayers, quotes, short humor, 50-60 wds.

POWER FOR LIVING, Box 632, Glen Ellyn IL 60138. (708)668-6000. Fax: (708)668-3806. Submit to Power for Living. To help adults relate the Power of God and His Word to their everyday lives. Weekly take-home paper; 8 pgs; circ 250,000. Subscription $9.95. 100% freelance. Complete ms/no cover letter; phone query ok. Pays up to .15/wd (reprints up to .10/wd), on acceptance, for one-time, reprint, or simultaneous rts. Articles 300-1,500 wds (120/yr). Responds in 2-10 wks. Seasonal 1 yr ahead. Considers simultaneous submissions & reprints. No disk. Guidelines/theme list; copy for #10 SAE/1 stamp.

> **Poetry:** Buys 10/yr. Free verse, light verse, traditional; 2-80 lines; $25-50. Submit max. 6 poems.
>
> **Fillers:** Buys 12/yr. Anecdotes, quizzes, short humor, word puzzles; 75-250 wds; $25-50.
>
> **Tips:** "Most open to vignettes, 450-1,000 wds; personal experiences, 400-1,500 wds. Writing must clearly demonstrate the Lord's work in individuals' lives. Signed releases required."
>
> ** This periodical was #21 on the 1994 Top 50 Plus Christian Publishers list.

#PRAIRIE MESSENGER, Box 190, Muenster SK S0K 2Y0 Canada. (306)682-1772. Fax: (306)682-5285. Catholic. Rev. Andrew Britz, OSB, ed. Focuses on justice/family/native/women's/church (in the broad sense) issues. Weekly (46X) tabloid; circ 9,000. Subscription $21.50. 10% freelance. Complete ms/cover letter; no phone query. Pays to $40-60 ($2/column inch for news items), on publication, for 1st, one-time or simultaneous rts. Not copyrighted. Articles to 250-600 wds (15/yr). Responds in 2 mos. Seasonal 3 mos ahead. Kill fee 70%. Guidelines; copy for 9x12 SAE/.80 Canadian/$1.05 U.S.

> **Special Needs:** Ecumenism; social justice; native concerns.
>
> **Tips:** "Comment/feature section is most open. Send topic of concern or interest to Prairie readership. It's difficult to break into our publication."

+PRAYERWORKS, P.O. Box 301363, Portland OR 97230. (503)761-2072. Fax: (503)760-1184. V. Ann Mandeville, ed. For prayer warriors in retirement centers; focuses on prayer. Weekly newspaper; 4 pgs; circ 500. Free subscription. 100% freelance. Complete ms/no cover letter; phone/fax query ok. **PAYS IN COPIES,** for one-time rts. Articles (32/yr) & fiction (30/yr); 300-500 wds. Seasonal 2 mos ahead. Considers simultaneous submissions & reprints. Responds in 3 wks. No sidebars. Guidelines; copy for #10 SAE/1 stamp.

> **Poetry:** Free verse, haiku, light verse, traditional. Submit max. 10 poems.
>
> **Tips:** "Write tight. Half our audience is over 70, but 30% is young families. Write about anything that will encourage prayer."

+PRAYING, P.O. Box 419335, Kansas City MO 64141. (816)968-2258. Fax: (816)968-2280. Mostly Catholic readership. Art Winter, ed. To provide Christian spirituality for everyday life. Bimonthly mag; 48 pgs; circ 14,000. Subscription $18. 10% freelance. Complete ms/cover letter. Pays $50-200 ($200 min. for fiction), on acceptance, for one-time rts. Articles 750-2,500 wds (6/yr); fiction to 2,500 wds (2-3/yr).

Responds in 2-3 wks. Seasonal 6 mos ahead. Kill fee. Prefers disk. Guidelines; copy for 9x12 SAE/6 stamps.

Columns/Departments: Buys 6/yr. Our Way (reports on people involved in Christian activities), 750 wds; $50.

Tips: "Write out of experience and share tradition as if for the first time. Most open to column. Tell little stories within big story."

THE PRESBYTERIAN OUTLOOK, Box 85623, Richmond VA 23285-5623. (804)359-8442. Fax: (804)353-6369. Presbyterian Church (USA)/Independent. Robert H. Bullock Jr., ed. For ministers, members and staff of the denomination. Weekly (43X) mag; 16 pgs (up to 40); circ 11,500. Subscription $24.95. 5% freelance. Query or complete ms/cover letter; phone/fax query ok. **NO PAYMENT.** Not copyrighted. Articles to 1,000 wds; book reviews 300 wds. Responds in 1-2 wks. Seasonal 2 mos ahead. Prefers disk. Guidelines; copy for #10 SAE/2 stamps.

Columns/Departments: Forum (current issues before the church); 400 wds.

Tips: "Correspond with editor regarding current needs. Most material is commissioned; anything submitted should be of interest to Presbyterians."

PRESBYTERIAN RECORD, 50 Wynford Dr., North York ON M3C 1J7 Canada. (416)444-1111. Fax: (416)441-2825. Presbyterian Church in Canada. Rev. John Congram, ed. Denominational. Monthly (11X) mag; 52 pgs; circ 60,000. 50% freelance. Query or complete ms/cover letter; fax query ok. Pays $25-75; on publication; for 1st, one-time, reprint or simultaneous rts. Articles (50/yr) & fiction (2/yr-query), 1,500 wds; book reviews, 200 wds/no pay. Responds in 4-6 wks. Seasonal 6 mos ahead. Considers simultaneous submissions & reprints. Sidebars ok. Guidelines; copy for 9x12 SAE/$1.40 Canadian postage or 3 IRCs from U.S. writers.

Poetry: Thomas Dickey. Buys 8-15/yr. Free verse, haiku, light verse traditional; 10-40 lines; $30-50. Send any number.

Fillers: Buys 6/yr. Anecdotes, cartoons, facts, ideas, prose, prayers, short humor; to 200 wds; $15-25.

Columns/Departments: Buys 12/yr. Full Count (controversial issues), 750 wds; $35-50.

Tips: "It helps if submissions have some connection to Canada and/or the Presbyterian Church."

*PRESBYTERIAN SURVEY, 100 Witherspoon St., Louisville KY 40202. (502)569-5637. Presbyterian Church (USA). Catherine Cottingham, mng. ed. Denominational; not as conservative or evangelical as some. Monthly (10X) mag; 44 pgs; circ 105,000. Subscription $11. 70% freelance. Query or complete ms/cover letter; phone query ok. Pays to $50-200, on acceptance, for 1st or (some) reprint rts. Articles 800-1,800 wds/1,200-1,500 preferred (50/yr). Responds in 2-5 wks. Seasonal 4 mos ahead. Kill fee. Guidelines; free copy.

Poetry: Buys 8-10/yr. Free verse, light verse, traditional (if religious); 4-100 lines, prefers 25-30; $50. Submit max. 2 poems.

Fillers: Buys 5-6/yr. Anecdotes, cartoons, prose, short humor; to 100 wds; $10-50.

Tips: "Most open to feature articles or news articles about Presbyterian people and programs (600-800 wds, $50-75). Do not often use inspirational or testimony-type articles."

** #21 on the 1993 Top 50.

#PRISM, 10 Lancaster Ave., Wynnewood PA 19096-3495. (215)645-9391. Fax: (215)645-9395. Evangelicals for Social Action. Gordon Aeschliman, ed. For Christians who are interested in the social and political dimensions of the gospel. Monthly (10X) newsletter; circ 1,700. Subscription $30. 10-25% freelance.

Query; phone query ok. Pays to $25 for one-time rts. Articles 600-2,300 wds (2-3/yr). Responds in 1-2 wks. Seasonal 2-3 mos ahead. Considers simultaneous query & reprints. Free guidelines/copy.

Fillers: Buys 5-7/yr. Cartoons; $20.

Columns/Departments: Buys 2-3/yr. Perspective (analysis of public policy issue), 2,300 wds; Global Intercessors (Christian community outside U.S.), 1,400 wds; Here I Stand (editorial), 600 wds; $25.

Tips: "Contact us and present your idea. Most open to editorials for Here I Stand—speak concisely, with passion, make your case."

+PROFESSIONAL PARENT'S ADVOCATE, P.O. Box 28042-16, Lakewood CO 80228. (303)914-0883. Fax: (the same). Gail Corte, pub/ed. For parents who quit or downscale employment to spend time raising their children at home; not about parenting, but addressing financial/personal needs of such parents. Newsletter (8X/yr); 8 pgs; circ 115. Subscription $12. Estab 1993. 63% freelance. Complete ms/no cover letter; phone/fax query ok. Pays .02/wd, on publication, for one-time rts. Not copyrighted. Articles 400-500 wds (45/yr); book reviews, 100 wds. Responds in 2-3 wks. Considers simultaneous submissions & reprints. No disk. Sidebars ok. Guidelines; copy for #10 SAE/2 stamps.

Fillers: Facts, newsbreaks; .50 ea. for news.

Columns/Departments: Buys 45/yr. Family Journals; alternative Work Options; Single Income Survival; Home Business Development; Nurturing the Parent; 400-500 wds.

Special Needs: Home business; alternative work options, employment, career, and family finances.

Tips: "Writer needs personal experience and interest in balancing career and family or full-time parenting. No parenting articles—we're not about the how-tos of parenting."

PROGRESS, Box 9609, Kansas City MO 64134. (816)763-7800. Fax: (816)765-2522. Stonecroft Ministries. Susan Collard, mng. ed. For women and their families who are involved in some aspect of Stonecroft Ministries. Bimonthly mag; 64 pgs; circ 30,000. Subscription $6.95. 30% freelance. Complete ms/cover letter; fax query ok. **PAYS IN COPIES**, for 1st rts. Not copyrighted. Articles 300-1,500 wds (25/yr). Responds in 2-3 wks. Seasonal 5-6 mos ahead. Accepts reprints. Guidelines; copy for 6x9 SAE/3 stamps.

Columns/Departments: Buys 12-15/yr. Coping Series (how God helped through crisis or stress (prefers other than illness); Family Builders (help for families); 1,000-1,500 wds.

Tips: "We do not include controversial or doctrinal issues about which Christians disagree. Material should be Christ-centered and biblically based. Most open to columns."

*PSYCHOLOGY FOR LIVING, Narramore Christian Foundation, Box 5000, Rosemead CA 91770. (818)288-7000. Fax: (818)288-5333. Ruth E. Narramore, ed. A faith ministry devoted to preventing and solving human problems. Bimonthly mag; 20 pgs; circ 14,000. 40% freelance. Complete ms or query. **NO PAYMENT.** Accepts reprints. Articles 1,000-1,500 wds. Responds in 3 mos. Seasonal 6 mos ahead. Guidelines; free copy.

PURPOSE, 616 Walnut Ave., Scottdale PA 15683. (412)887-8500. Fax: (412)887-3111. Mennonite Church. James E. Horsch, ed. Denominational. Weekly mag; 8 pgs; circ 16,000. Subscription $13.90. 90% freelance. Complete ms/cover letter; phone query ok. Pays .04-.05/wd, on acceptance, for one-time rts. Articles & fiction 200-750 wds (175-200/yr). Responds in 10 wks. Seasonal 6 mos ahead. Considers simultaneous submissions & reprints. No disks. Sidebars ok. Guidelines; copy for 6x9 SAE/2 stamps.

Poetry: Buys 120/yr. Free verse, light verse, traditional; 3-12 lines; $5-15. Submit max. 10 poems.

Fillers: Buys 15/yr. Anecdotes, cartoons, short humor; 200-400 wds; .04/wd.

Tips: "Articles must carry a strong story line. First person is preferred. Don't exceed maximum word length."

** This periodical was #22 on the 1994 Top 50 Plus Christian Publishers list. (#6 in 1993)

PURSUIT, 901 E. 78th St., Minneapolis MN 55420. (612)853-1750. Evangelical Free Church. Carol Madison, ed; submit to Joyce Ellis, asst. ed. An evangelistic mag. written for the unchurched. Quarterly mag; 32 pgs; circ 35,000. Subscription $8. 100% freelance. Complete ms/no cover letter; no phone/fax query. Pays .10/wd, on publication, for one-time rts. Articles 800-2,000 wds (20/yr). Responds in 4-6 wks. Seasonal 6 months ahead. Considers simultaneous submissions & reprints. Kill fee 25%. Guidelines; copy $1/9x12 SAE/2 stamps.

Tips: "Submit article with theme suggested for issue, along with companion article ideas."

+PUZZLER'S DIGEST, Box 394, Society Hill SC 29593. Gene Boone, ed. For people who enjoy word-search puzzles, human interest articles, recipes and other features. Bimonthly digest; 24 pgs. Subscription $10. Estab 1994. 75% freelance. Complete ms/cover letter; no phone/fax query. Pays .01/wd, on acceptance, for 1st rts. Articles 500-6,000 wds (10-25/yr); book reviews, 500-1,000 wds. Responds in 2-4 wks. Seasonal 6-12 mos ahead. Accepts reprints. No disks. Rarely uses sidebars. Guidelines; copy for 6x9 SAE/2 stamps.

Fillers: Buys 20-80/yr. Anecdotes, cartoons, facts, ideas, jokes, newsbreaks, party ideas, prose, quizzes, quotes, short humor; 10-1,000 wds; $5-25.

Special Needs: Human interest articles on various subjects.

QUEEN OF ALL HEARTS, 26 S. Saxon Ave., Bay Shore NY 11706. (516)665-0726. Fax: (516)665-4349. Catholic. Rev. Roger M. Charest, SMM, mng. ed. Focus is Mary, the Mother of Jesus. Bimonthly mag; 48 pgs; circ 5,000. Subscription $15. 50% freelance. Complete ms/cover letter. Pays $40-60, on acceptance, for 1st rts. Not copyrighted. Articles 750-2,500 wds (25/yr); fiction 1,500-2,500 wds (6/yr). Responds in 2-6 wks. Seasonal 6 mos ahead. Guidelines; copy for 9x12 SAE/$2.

Poetry: Dr. Joseph Tusiani. Buys 10/yr. Free verse. Pays 2 year subscription and 6 copies. Submit max. 2 poems.

Special Needs: Articles on Shrines of Our Lady and Saints devoted to Our Lady.

*THE QUIET REVOLUTION, 1655 St. Charles St., Jackson MS 39209. (601)353-1635. Voice of Calvary Ministries. Cornelius J. Jones, ed. Interracial ministry to the poor; conservative/evangelical. Quarterly mag; 7 pgs; circ 3,000. 10% freelance. Query or complete ms/cover letter. **NO PAYMENT** for one-time rts. Articles 3-4 pgs. Responds in 1 mo. Accepts reprints. No guidelines; free copy.

Tips: "Most open to articles about ministering to the poor."

*RATIO: Essays in Christian Thought, 350 Canner St. #405, New Haven CT 06511-2254. Jeff Bearce, ed. For an academic/intellectual audience anchored in the humanities; deals with theology, biblical studies, psychology, science, etc. Semiannual journal; circ 100. Estab 1992. 15-20% freelance. Query. **NO PAYMENT**. Not copyrighted. Articles, fiction & book reviews.

RELIGIOUS BROADCASTING, National Religious Broadcasters, 7839 Ashton Ave., Manassas VA 22110. (703)330-7000. Fax: (703)330-7100. Christine Pryc.r, asst. ed. Topics relate to Christian radio, television and satellite; promoting access excellence in religious broadcasting. Monthly (11X) mag; 56 pgs; circ 8,500. Subscription $24. 35% freelance. Query; phone/fax query ok. **PAYS IN COPIES**. Articles 1,500-2,000+ wds (55-60/yr); book reviews 300 wds. Responds in 4 wks. Seasonal 3 mos ahead. Prefers disk copy. Sidebars ok. Guidelines/theme list; copy for 9x12 SAE/8 stamps.

Columns/Departments: Sarah E. Smith. Accepts 100/yr. Trade Talk or Media Focus (news items/events in religious broadcasting), 300 wds; Socially Speaking (social issues), 1,000 wds.

Special Needs: Electronic media; education. All articles must relate in some way to broadcasting; radio, TV, programs on radio/TV.

Tips: "Our features dept. depends on freelance contributions. Must show clear tie to religious broadcasting—strong, well-written and well-researched pieces."

*RELIGIOUS EDUCATION, 15600 Mulholland Dr., Los Angeles CA 90077. (310)476-9777x326. Fax: (310)471-1278. Religious Education Assn. Hanan A. Alexander, ed-in-chief. A forum for interreligious dialogue for people concerned with issues surrounding religious education. Quarterly journal; circ 3,000. Subscription/membership $40. 95% freelance. Complete ms/cover letter; no phone query. **PAYS 3 COP-IES,** for all rts. Articles to 6,500 wds; book reviews, 250 wds. Responds in 2-3 wks. Guidelines; copy $2.

Columns/Departments: Insights from Scholarship; Insights from Practice; Forum (diverse points of view on topics of interest); and Critique (reviews of books, media and curricula).

Special Needs: Religious, theological, values, moral education, spiritual formation or development, character development.

+RURAL LANDSCAPES, 11625 Beaver Ave., Des Moines IA 50310. (515)270-2634. Fax: (515)270-9447. Catholic. Sandra A. LaBlanc, assoc. ed. Monthly (10X) newsletter; 6 pgs; circ 3,000. Subscription $25. 25% freelance. Query/clips. Pays .10/wd, on publication, for 1st rts. Not copyrighted. Articles 100-500 wds. Responds in 6 wks. Seasonal 6 mos ahead. Considers simultaneous submissions. Sidebars ok. Guidelines/theme list; copy for 9x12 SAE/2 stamps.

Columns/Departments: Building Community, 350 wds; Closer Look (think piece), 750-1,000 wds; no payment.

Special Needs: 1995 Farm Bill material.

#ST. ANTHONY MESSENGER, 1615 Republic St., Cincinnati OH 45210-1298. (513)241-5615. Fax: (513)241-0399. Catholic. Norman Perry, O.F.M., ed-in-chief. National Catholic family magazine. Monthly mag; 59 pgs; circ 320,000. 55% freelance. Prefers query; complete ms/cover letter ok; phone query ok. Pays .14/wd, on acceptance, for 1st rts. Articles to 1,500-3,500 wds (35-50/yr); fiction 2,000-3,000 wds (12/yr); book reviews 500 wds/$25. Responds in 2 mos. Seasonal 6 mos ahead. Guidelines; copy for 9x12 SAE/4 stamps.

Poetry: Catherine Walsh. Buys 50/yr. All types; 3-25 lines; $2/line ($10 min.) Submit max. 5 poems.

Tips: "Any article accepted will employ a Catholic perspective and vocabulary and be in accord with Catholic teaching."

** This periodical was #40 on the 1994 Top 50 Plus Christian Publishers list.

ST. JOSEPH'S MESSENGER AND ADVOCATE OF THE BLIND, Box 288, Jersey City NJ 07303-0288. (201)798-4141. Catholic. Sister Ursula Maphet, CSJP, ed. For older Catholics interested in supporting ministry to the aged, young blind, and needy. Quarterly mag; 16 pgs; circ 20,000. Subscription $5. 80% freelance. Complete ms; no phone query. Pays $10-50, on acceptance, for 1st rts. Articles 800-1,600 wds (20/yr); fiction 800-1,800 wds (25/yr). Responds in 1 mo. Seasonal 3 mos ahead. Considers simultaneous submissions & reprints. No sidebars. Guidelines; copy for 9x12 SAE/2 stamps.

Poetry: Buys 25/yr. Light verse, traditional; 10-30 lines; $5-20, on publication. Submit max. 10 poems.

Fillers: Buys 20/yr. Ideas, 50-100 wds; $5-10.

Tips: "Most open to fiction."

*ST. WILLIBRORD JOURNAL, Box 271751, Houston TX 77277-1751. Christ Catholic Church. Charles E. Harrison, ed. Strictly Catholic; concentrating on the unchurched. Quarterly journal; 40 pgs; circ 500. 5% freelance. Complete ms/cover letter. **NO PAYMENT** for one-time rts. Not copyrighted. Articles to 1,000 wds. Responds in 2 mos. Seasonal 6 mos ahead. No guidelines; copy $2.

Columns/Departments: Question Box; Q & A column on doctrinal and biblical questions.

Tips: "We will read anything if it is sincere and orthodox. Most open to what's happening in the Christian church: doctrinal changes, attitude adjustments, moral attitudes."

*SALT, 205 W. Monroe St., Chicago IL 60606. (312)236-7782. Christian. Mary Lynn Hendrickson, mng ed. Focus is on social justice and prayer. Monthly (10X) mag; 32 pgs; circ 11,000. 50% freelance. Query/clips or complete ms/cover letter. Pays $200-400, on acceptance, for 1st rts. Articles 1,000-3,500 wds. Responds in 1-2 mos. Kill fee. Guidelines; free copy.

+SALT SHAKER, 4609 - 36 Ave., Edmonton AB T6L 3S2 Canada. (403)461-2926. Fax: (403)425-9039. Greg Supina, ed-in-chief. An evangelical family publication which seeks to edify the Body of Christ and promote a biblical walk of faith. Quarterly tabloid; 24-32 pgs; circ 7,000. Subscription $13. 50% freelance. Complete ms/cover letter; phone/fax query ok. Does not return mss. Pays .02/wd (if requested), after publication, for one-time, reprint or simultaneous rts. Articles & fiction 300-900 wds. Seasonal 2 mos ahead. Considers simultaneous submissions & reprints. Prefers disk copy. Guidelines; copy for 9x12 SAE/.86 Canadian postage.

Poetry: Free verse, haiku, light verse, traditional.

Fillers: Anecdotes, cartoons, facts, jokes, prose, prayers.

Tips: "We look for strong, compassionate material. We see the Bible as the authoritative Word of God in all matters. We do not like articles which compromise the gospel, such as psychology, feminism, etc."

#SCP JOURNAL/SCP NEWSLETTER, (Spiritual Counterfeits Project), P.O. Box 4308, Berkeley CA 94704-4308. (510)540-0300. Fax: (510)540-1107. Tal Brooke, ed. Christian apologetics for the college educated. Quarterly; 55 pgs; circ 20,000. Subscription $25. 5% freelance. Query/clips; phone query encouraged. Pays $20-35/typeset pg, on publication, for negotiable rts. Articles 2,500-3,500 wds (5/yr); book reviews 1,500 wds. Responds in 1-3 mos. Considers simultaneous query & reprints. Guidelines; copy $5.

Tips: "Talk to us first."

#SEEK, 8121 Hamilton Ave., Cincinnati OH 45231. (513)931-4050 x365. Standard Publishing. Eileen H. Wilmoth, ed. For young and middle-age adults. Weekly take-home paper; 8 pgs; circ 45,000. 98% freelance. Complete ms/cover letter; no phone query. Pays .05/wd; on acceptance; for 1st rts, .025/wd for reprint rts. Articles 400-1,200 wds (150-200/yr); fiction 400-1,200 wds. Responds in 2-3 mos. Seasonal 1 yr ahead. Accepts reprints. Guidelines; copy for 6x9 SAE/2 stamps.

Fillers: Buys 50/yr. Ideas, jokes, short humor; $15.

** This periodical was #36 on the 1994 Top 50 Plus Christian Publishers list. (#48 in 1993)

#THE SHANTYMAN, 6981 Millcreek Dr., Unit 17, Mississauga ON L5N 6B8 Canada. (905)821-1175. Fax: (905)821-8400. Shantymen's Christian Assn. Margaret Sharpe, ed. Distributed by their missionaries in remote areas of Canada and northern U.S. as an evangelism tool. Bimonthly mag; 16 pgs; circ 17,000. Subscription $6. 80-90% freelance. Complete ms only/cover letter; no phone query; fax query ok. Pays $20-50 ($20-25 for fiction), on publication, for one-time or simultaneous rts. Articles 800-2,000 wds (24/yr); fiction 500-800 (3/yr); book reviews, 500 wds, pays in copies. Responds in 3-4 wks. Seasonal 6 mos ahead. Considers simultaneous submissions & reprints. Prefers disk copy. Guidelines; copy for #10 SAE/2 IRC's.

Poetry: Accepts 6/yr. Free verse, light verse, traditional; any length; no payment. Submit max. 2 poems.

Fillers: Accepts 3-4 cartoons/yr; no payment.

Special Needs: Testimonies and poetry in French. Children's fiction for 8-14 yr. olds.

Tips: "Write in a clear, concise, down-to-earth manner; avoid preachiness and the temptation to moralize. Let your story speak for itself. Keep scripture references to a minimum. Most open to salvation testimonies. We prefer stories of less than 1,200 wds."

*SHARING, A Journal of Christian Healing, Box 1974, Snoqualmie WA 98065. (206)391-9510x512. Fax: (206)391-9512. Order of St. Luke the Physician. Rusty Rae, ed. For Christians interested in spiritual and physical healing. Monthly (10X) journal; 32 pgs; circ 10,000. 100% freelance. Complete ms/cover letter; phone query ok. **NO PAYMENT.** Not copyrighted. Articles 300-2,000 wds (100-150/yr); fiction 300-2,000 wds (few). Responds in 6 wks. Seasonal 2 mos ahead. Considers simultaneous submissions & reprints. Guidelines; free copy.

Poetry: Accepts 20-30/yr. Any type or length.

Tips: "Most open to stories of personal healing."

SIGNS OF THE TIMES, Box 7000, Boise ID 83707. (208)465-2577. Seventh-day Adventist. Marvin Moore, ed. Biblical principles relevant to all of life; for general public. Monthly mag; 32 pgs; circ 270,000. 60% freelance. Complete ms/no cover letter or phone query. Pays $150-450; on acceptance; for 1st, or reprint rts. Articles 750-2,500 wds (20/yr). Responds in 1-5 wks. Seasonal 8-9 mos ahead. Accepts reprints. Kill fee 50%. Free guidelines/copy.

Tips: "Looking for personality profiles."

** This periodical was #33 on the 1994 Top 50 Plus Christian Publishers list. (#22 in 1993)

+SILVER WINGS, P.O. Box 1000, Pearblossom CA 93553. (805)264-3726. Jackson Wilcox, ed. Christian understanding and uplift through poetry. Quarterly mag; 32 pgs; circ 430. Subscription $7. 100% freelance. Complete ms/no cover letter. **PAYS A SUBSCRIPTION,** for 1st rts. Not copyrighted. Responds in 3 wks. Seasonal anytime. Considers simultaneous submissions & some reprints. Guidelines; copy $2.

Poetry: Accepts 250/yr. Free verse, haiku, light verse, traditional; 2-20 lines. Submit max. 5 poems.

+SINGLE-PARENT FAMILY, 8605 Explorer Dr., Colorado Springs CO 80920. Focus on the Family. Dr. Lynda Hunter, ed. To encourage and equip single parents to do the best job they can at creating stable, godly homes for themselves and their children. Monthly mag; 32 pgs. Open to freelance. Query or complete ms.

SMART DADS NEWSLETTER, Box 270616, San Diego CA 92198-2616. (619)487-7099. Fax: (619)487-7356. Paul Lewis, ed. Christian fathering/parenting, with strong crossover to secular dads. Bimonthly newsletter; 8 pgs; circ 10,000. Subscription $24 (includes 2 tapes). Little freelance. Complete ms/no cover letter; fax query ok. Pays negotiable rates, on publication, for 1st rts. Articles 350-900 wds (5/yr). Responds in 2-4 wks. Seasonal 4 mos ahead. Considers simultaneous submissions. Prefers disk copy. Some sidebars. No guidelines; copy for 6x9 SAE/3 stamps.

Fillers: Buys 10/yr. Games, ideas, quotes.

Columns/Departments: Buys 5/yr. Making Your Marriage Better; The Single Parent; To Better Love Her; Good Advice; 325-600+ wds.

Tips: "We are not a magazine and have tight length requirements. Because of cross-over audience, we do not regularly print scripture references or use traditional God-word language."

SOCIAL JUSTICE REVIEW, 3835 Westminster Pl., St. Louis MO 63108. (314)371-3653. Catholic. Rev. John H. Miller, C.S.C., ed. For those interested in the social teaching of the Catholic Church. Bimonthly journal; 32 pgs; circ 3,177. Subscription $15. 80% freelance. Complete ms/cover letter. Pays .02/wd, on publication, for 1st rts. Not copyrighted. Articles 800-3,000 wds (80/yr); book reviews 750 wds. Responds in 1 wk. Seasonal 3 mos ahead. Accepts reprints. No disks. No sidebars. Guidelines; copy for 9x12 SAE/3 stamps.

Tips: "Fidelity to papal teaching and clarity and simplicity of style; thoughtful and thought-provoking writing."

+SOUTHWESTERN NEWS, P.O. Box 22000, Fort Worth TX 76115-9983. (817)923-1921 x7220. Fax: (817)923-1921 x2399. Southern Baptist. Bob Murdaugh, office mngr. For students, faculty, staff, administrators and parents of Southwestern Baptist Theological Seminary. Bimonthly mag; 20 pgs; circ 50,000. 10% freelance. Query/clips or complete ms/cover letter; phone/fax query ok. **NO PAYMENT.** Articles 250-350 wds (12/yr). Seasonal 3 mos ahead. Considers simultaneous submissions & reprints. Prefers disk copy. Sidebars ok. Guidelines; free copy.

Fillers: Facts, newsbreaks, prayers, quotes, short humor.

Special Needs: Open to any topics as long as they tie in some way to at least one student, faculty, staff, or administrator at Southwestern.

Tips: "Most open to news articles pertaining to events or programs involving Southwesterners. No fluff; no editorializing."

SPIRITUAL LIFE, 2131 Lincoln Rd. NE, Washington DC 20002-1199. (202)832-8489. Fax: (202)832-8967. Catholic. Bro. Edward O'Donnell, O.C.D., ed. The contemporary experience of God (with special attention to the Carmelite tradition). Quarterly mag; 64 pgs; circ 10,000. Subscription $14. 85% freelance. Complete ms/cover letter; phone/fax query ok. Pays $50 min. ($10/ms pg), on acceptance, for 1st rts. Articles 3,000-5,000 wds (18/yr); book reviews 1,500 wds, $15. Responds in 3-8 wks. Seasonal 6 mos ahead. Considers simultaneous submissions. Prefers disk copy. No sidebars. Guidelines; copy $1/7x10 SAE/5 stamps.

Tips: "No stories of personal healing, conversion, miracles, etc."

#SPORTS SPECTRUM, Box 3566, Grand Rapids MI 49501-3566. (616)954-1276. Fax: (616)957-5741. Radio Bible Class. Dave Branon, mng. ed. An evangelistic tool that sports fans can use to witness to non-Christian friends. Monthly mag; 32 pgs; circ 48,000. Subscription $18.97. 40% freelance. Query/clips. Pays .15/wd, on acceptance, for 1st rts; no phone query. Articles 500-2,000 wds (25/yr). Responds in 3 wks. Kill fee. Guidelines; free copy.

Columns/Departments: Buys 10/yr. Leaderboard (Christian athletes serving others), 500 wds, $20-40.

Tips: "Show an ability to interview professional athletes and create a well-written article from that interview. We also like ideas from freelancers."

** This periodical was #69 on the 1994 Top 50 Plus Christian Publishers list.

STANDARD, 6401 The Paseo, Kansas City MO 64131. (816)333-7000 x2555. Fax: (816)333-4439. Nazarene. Rev. Everett Leadingham, ed. Examples of Christianity in everyday life for adults college-age through retirement. Weekly take-home paper; 8 pgs; circ 160,000. Subscription $8. 95% freelance. Complete ms/cover letter; no phone/fax query. Pays .035/wd (.02/wd for reprints), on acceptance, for 1st or reprint rts. Not copyrighted. Articles & fiction (200/yr); to 1,700 wds. Responds in 8-12 wks. Seasonal 6 mos ahead. Considers simultaneous submissions & reprints. No disks. Seldom uses sidebars. Guidelines/copy for #10 SAE/2 stamps.

Poetry: Buys 100/yr. Free verse, haiku, traditional; to 30 lines; $5. Submit max. 5 poems.

Fillers: Buys 50/yr. Cartoons, facts, games, prose, quizzes, word puzzles; to 350 wds; $5.

Tips: "Fiction or true-experience stories must demonstrate Christianity in action. Show us, don't tell us. Action in stories must conform to Wesleyan-Armenian theology and practices."

** This periodical was #2 on the 1994 Top 50 Plus Christian Publishers list. (#3 in 1993)

THE STAR OF ZION, 401 E. 2nd St., Charlotte NC 28231. (704)377-4329 Fax: (704)333-1769. African Methodist Episcopal Zion Church. Dr. Morgan W. Tann, ed. Ethnic publication; moderate; conservative. Weekly tabloid; 12-16 pgs; circ 8,000. Subscription $22. 90% freelance. Query or complete ms. **PAYS 5 COPIES.** Not copyrighted. Articles & fiction to 600 wds. Responds in 2 mos. Seasonal 2 mos ahead. Accepts simultaneous submissions.Guidelines; copy $1/10x14 SAE/3 stamps.

Poetry: African-American themes.

Fillers: Cartoons and short humor.

SUNDAY DIGEST, 850 N. Grove, Elgin IL 60120-2892. (708)741-2400. Fax: (708)741-0595. Cook Communications. Sharon Stultz, ed. To encourage Christian adults (mostly women 30-55) of various denominations in their faith. Weekly take-home paper; 8 pgs; circ 100,000. Subscription $9.95. 65% freelance. Complete ms/brief cover letter; no phone/fax query. Pays $50-225, on acceptance, for 1st, one-time, or reprint rts. Articles 400-1,700 wds (100/yr) & fiction 1,200-1,800 wds (10/yr). Responds in 3-9 wks. Seasonal 6 mos ahead. Accepts reprints (less payment). Kill fee 25-50%. Sidebars ok. Guidelines/theme list; copy for #10 SAE/1 stamp.

Poetry: Buys 10/yr. Free verse, light verse, traditional; 5-20 lines; $50-60. Submit max. 3 poems.

Fillers: Buys 5/yr. Prose; 100-300 wds; $30-50.

Columns/Departments: Buys 50/yr. Thinking Out Loud (anecdotal—from life—teaches a truth or lesson with a fresh slant), 350-450 wds, $5-60.

Special Needs: Articles on senior adult issues.

Tips: "Avoid preachy tone, controversial or sensitive topics, or denominational differences. Include a cover letter and briefly introduce yourself. Keep trying; don't give up. We're most open to inspirational/personal experience stories."

** This periodical was #10 on the 1994 Top 50 Plus Christian Publishers list (#10 in 1993). Also 1994 EPA Award of Excellence—Sunday School Take-Home.

TABLE TALK, 6401 The Paseo, Kansas City MO 64131. (816)333-7000 x2359. Nazarene. Bruce Nuffer, ed. A devotional guide for parents to use with their elementary age children. Quarterly mag; circ 16,000. Subscription $6.75. 25% freelance. Query or complete ms/cover letter; phone query ok. Pays .05/wd, on publication, for all rts. Articles 750-1,500 wds (20/yr). Responds in 4-12 wks. Seasonal 10 mos ahead. Rarely accepts reprints. Guidelines; copy for 6x9 SAE/4 stamps.

Poetry: Free verse, light verse, traditional; $10 or .05/wd.

Fillers: Buys 12-15/yr. Anecdotes, cartoons, ideas, short humor; 25-300 wds; $10 or .05/wd.

Tips: "Our main need is parenting articles of all types, activity ideas for families, and occasional craft ideas." Margins should be 1.5" all around.

THE TEACHING HOME, P.O. Box 20219, Portland OR 97220-0219. (503)253-9633. Fax: (503)253-7345. Christian. Sue Welch, ed. Help for parents involved in home schooling. Bimonthly mag; circ 42,000. Subscription $15. Accepts freelance. Query. Not included in topical listings.

> **Note:** This magazine publishes material only from its readers or from those who can speak from first-hand experience in home schooling.

THEMA LITERARY JOURNAL, Box 74109, Metairie LA 70033-4109. (504)887-1263. Virginia Howard, ed. Theme-oriented publication for those who like poetry and short stories. Triannual jour; 200 pgs; circ 300. Subscription $16. 100% freelance. Complete ms/cover letter specifying theme. Pays $10-25, on acceptance, for one-time rts. Articles (only if applies to theme), fiction 500-6,000 wds (40/yr). Responds in 1 week to 6 mos. Considers simultaneous submissions & reprints. Guidelines/theme list; copy $8/9x12 SAE/$1.05 postage.

> **Poetry:** Gail Howard. Buys 40/yr. Any type, including experimental; 3-50 lines; $10. Submit max. 3 poems.

> **Tips:** "Let the theme roll around in your head until it haunts you and a story forms around it. Most open to fiction and poetry; specify theme."

> ** This periodical was #60 on the 1994 Top 50 Plus Christian Publishers list.

+THIS ROCK, P.O. Box 17490, San Diego CA 92177. (619)541-1131. Fax: (619)541-1154. Catholic. Karl Keating, ed. Deals with doctrine, evangelization and apologetics. Monthly mag; circ 10,000. 50% freelance. Query; no phone/fax query. Pays $25-200, on publication, for all rts. Articles 1,500-3,000 wds. Guidelines.

#TIME OF SINGING, A Magazine of Christian Poetry, Box 211, Cambridge Springs PA 16403. (814)382-5911. High Street Community Church. Charles A. Waugaman, ed. We try to appeal to all poets and lovers of poetry. Triannual journal; 40 pgs; circ 300. Subscription $12. 95% freelance. Complete ms/no cover letter. **PAYS 1 COPY** for 1st rts (may reprint). Poetry only. Responds in 4-8 wks. Seasonal 4 mos ahead. Considers simultaneous submissions & reprints. Guidelines/theme list; copy $6 (current) or $3 (back issue).

> **Poetry:** Buys 150-200/yr. Free verse, haiku, light verse (rarely), traditional; any length (prefers short). Submit max. 5 poems.

> **Contest:** Sponsors an annual poetry contest (send SASE for rules).

> **Tips:** "We only review books by our poets. Send SASE and put name and address on every poem."

*TODAY'S BETTER LIFE, P.O. Box 141000, Nashville TN 37214-1000. Fax: (202)364-8910. Nondenominational. Laura Barker, mng ed. For Christian adults seeking spiritual, physical and emotional health. Quarterly mag; 112 pgs; circ 100,000. Subscription $19.80. Estab 1991. 25% freelance. Query; no phone query. Pays .10/wd, on acceptance, for 1st rts. Articles 1,500-2,000 wds. Responds in 8-10 wks. Seasonal 8-10 mos ahead. Guidelines; no copy.

> **Tips:** "Read back issues."

*TODAY'S SINGLE, 1933 W. Wisconsin Ave., Milwaukee WI 53233. (414)344-7300. National Association of Christian Singles. John M. Fisco, Jr., pub.; submit to Rita Bertolas, ed. For Christian single adults: never married, divorced, widowed, or separated. Quarterly newspaper; circ 10,000. 85% freelance. Complete ms. **PAYS IN COPIES**, for one-time or reprint rts. Not copyrighted. Articles 300-2,000 wds (12-15/yr). Responds in 2-4 wks. Seasonal 4-5 mos ahead. Guidelines; free copy.

> **Poetry:** Buys 15-20/yr. Free verse, haiku; 4-30 lines. Submit max. 5 poems.

> **Tips:** Deadlines: January 1, April 1, July 1, and October 1.

*TOGETHER, Rt 2 Box 656, Grottoes VA 24441. (703)249-3900. Fax: (703)249-3177. Shalom Foundation, Inc. Eugene K. Souder, ed. Sent in a mass mailing to every home in a community by a sponsoring congregation. Bimonthly tabloid; 8 pgs; circ 200,000. 50% freelance. Complete ms; no cover letter or phone query. Pays $25-50, on publication, for all, 1st, one-time, reprint or simultaneous rts. Articles 200-1,000 wds (20/yr). Responds in 1 mo. Seasonal 4-6 mos ahead. Considers simultaneous submissions & reprints. Guidelines; copy for 9x12 SAE/2 stamps.

> **Fillers:** Buys 5/yr. Cartoons, quizzes, quotes, word puzzles, word-search puzzles; 25-100 wds; $10-25.
>
> **Tips:** "Need first-person stories of faith in Christ—how I became a believer."

TOTAL HEALTH, 6001 Topanga Canyon Blvd. #300, Woodland Hills CA 91367. (818)887-6484. Fax: (818)887-7960. Submit to Arpi Coliglow, asst. ed. A family health magazine. Bimonthly mag; 70 pgs; circ 90,000. Subscription $16. 75% freelance. Pays $50-75, on publication, for all and reprint rts. Articles 1,400-1,800 wds (48/yr). Reports in 4 wks. Seasonal 4 mos ahead. Considers simultaneous submissions. Query or complete ms/cover letter; no phone query. Sidebars ok. Requires small disk (Mac.) Guidelines; copy $1/9x12 SAE/5 stamps.

> **Columns/Departments:** Contemporary Herbal, 1,000 wds, $50.
>
> **Tips:** "Most open to self-help and prevention articles."

*TOUCHSTONE, A Journal of Ecumenical Orthodoxy, 3300 W. Cullom Ave., Chicago IL 60618. (312)267-1440. Fellowship of St. James. James Kushiner, ed. News and opinion devoted to a thoughtful appreciation of orthodox Christian faith. Quarterly journal; 44 pgs; circ 1,500. 25% freelance. Query/clips or complete ms/cover letter. **PAYS IN COPIES** for one-time rts. Articles 2,500 wds; little fiction 3,000 wds. Responds in 3 mos. Considers simultaneous submissions. Guidelines; copy for 10x13 SAE/7 stamps.

> **Poetry:** Accepts.
>
> **Fillers:** Cartoons.

#THE UNITED CHURCH OBSERVER, 84 Pleasant Blvd., Toronto ON M4T 2Z8 Canada. (416)960-8500. Fax: (416)960-8477. United Church of Canada. Muriel Duncan, ed. Denominational news. Monthly newsmag; 52 pgs; circ 155,000. 20% freelance. Query or complete ms/cover letter; no phone query; fax query ok. Pays varying rates, on publication, for 1st or all rts. News articles to 1,200 wds (8/yr). Responds in 12-16 wks. Seasonal 3 mos ahead. Kill fee. Guidelines; copy $2.

> **Fillers:** Buys 24 cartoons/yr; $20.
>
> **Columns/Departments:** Buys 12/yr. Front Page (church-related opinion pc.), 800 wds.

+UPSOUTH, 3627 Hammett Hill Rd., Bowling Green KY 42101. (502)843-8018. Catholic. Galen Smith, ed/pub. By freelance poets and writers interested in spiritual and Southern life and issues. Quarterly newsletter; circ 75-100. Subscription $5. Query or complete ms/cover letter. **PAYS FREE COPY.** Articles, 100-500 wds; rarely uses fiction; book/music reviews 100-500 wds. Responds in 2 wks. Considers simultaneous submissions & reprints. No disks. No sidebars. Guidelines/copy $1/#10 SAE/1 stamp.

> **Poetry:** Buys large number. Any type, to 21 lines.
>
> **Fillers:** Buys few. Prose, prayers, and short humor.
>
> **Tips:** "It's rare we turn pieces down unless too long or anti-spiritual/religious. Most open to good poems, short articles—concise and to the point."

+URBAN FAMILY, P.O. Box 32, Jackson MS 39205. (601)354-1563. Fax: (601)352-6882. Non-denominational. Jennifer Parker, asst. ed. For the Black family, inner-city community, and liberal evangelical community; with an interest in racial justice and community development. Quarterly mag; variable length. Subscription $12. Complete ms/cover letter; fax query ok. Pays (negotiable) for certain features & assigned articles only, on publication, for all rts. Articles 400-1,200 wds (30/yr); book/music reviews, 250 wds, $25. Responds in 6-12 wks. Seasonal 6-8 mos ahead. Considers simultaneous submissions. Disks ok. Sidebars ok. Guidelines; copy $5/9x12 SAE/6 stamps.

Columns/Departments: Let's Be Honest (first-person opinion); Entertainment Beat (interviews, reviews, opinions on media); The Bright Side (upbeat "Why I like My City"stories); 400-600 wds; $25-100.

Special Needs: More humor; more positive stories from inner-city dwellers.

Tips: "Our columns are wide open. Our pet themes are racial justice and reconciliation, community development, and Black self-reliance and responsibility."

U.S. CATHOLIC, 205 W. Monroe St., Chicago IL 60606. (312)236-7782. Fax: (312)236-7230. Catholic/Claretian. Tom McGrath, exec. ed. Devoted to starting and continuing a dialogue with Catholics of diverse lifestyles and opinions about the way they live their faith. Monthly mag; 52 pgs; circ 35,000. Subscription $18. 95% freelance. Complete ms/cover letter; phone/fax query ok. Pays $250-500 (fiction $300-400), on acceptance, for all rts. Articles 2,500-4,000 wds; fiction 2,500-3,500 wds. Responds in 2 wks. Seasonal 2 mos ahead. Sidebars ok. Guidelines; free copy.

Columns/Departments: (See guidelines first.) Sounding Board, 1,100-1,300 wds, $250; Gray Matter and A Modest Proposal, 1,100-1,800 wds, $250; Actual Grace (humor), to 1,300 wds, $250.

Tips: "All articles should have an explicit religious dimension, enabling readers to see the interaction between their faith and the issue at hand."

#VIBRANT LIFE, 55 W. Oak Ridge Dr., Hagerstown MD 21740-7390. (301)791-7000. Fax: (301)791-7012. Seventh-day Adventist. Barbara Jackson-Hall, ed-in-chief. Total health publication (physical, mental and spiritual); plus articles on family and marriage improvement; ages 25-45. Bimonthly mag; 32 pgs; circ 50,000. Subscription $12.97. 20% freelance. Complete ms; no phone query. Pays $125-250, on acceptance, for 1st, reprint or world rts. Articles 750-1,800 wds (20-25/yr). Responds in 2 mos. Seasonal 6 mos ahead. Accepts reprints. Guidelines; copy $1.

Special Needs: Cancer prevention, alcoholism, men's health issues, and mental health (fear, depression, and how the brain works).

Tips: "Health articles should be current, include quotes from experts in the field, medically accurate, and written for the lay public. They should not have a heavy Christian slant, but where appropriate mention God and prayer."Most open to feature articles.

VISION, 3150 Bear St., Costa Mesa CA 92626. (714)754-1400. Full Gospel Business Men's Fellowship. Dr. Jerry Jensen, ed.; submit to Kay Mangio. For members only (men). Quarterly mag; 32-40 pgs; circ 70,000. Query. Pays .10/wd, on acceptance, for various rts. Articles. Responds in 6 wks. Seasonal 6 mos ahead. Kill fee. Accepts reprints. Free guidelines/copy.

Columns/Departments: 1st Person Male Testimonies (spirit-filled); 2,200 wds.

Tips: "We accept material on an assignment basis, which we delegate."

VISION, 8855 Dunn Rd., Hazelwood MO 63042. (314)837-7304. United Pentecostal Church. R.M. Davis, ed. Denominational. Weekly take-home paper. 90% freelance. Complete ms. Pays $8-25, on publication, for all rts. Articles 800-1,800 wds (to 120/yr); fiction 1,200-1,800 wds (to 120/yr). Seasonal 9 months ahead. Considers simultaneous submissions & reprints. Guidelines; free copy.

Poetry: Buys 30/yr. Pays $3-12.

Tips: "Most open to good stories and articles for a traditional, fundamental, conservative church." Accepts material primarily from members of the denomination.

*VISTA, Box 50434, Indianapolis IN 46250. (317)576-8144. Fax: (317)595-4144. Wesleyan. Kelly Trennepohl, ed. Reinforces Sunday school lessons; addresses family concerns and current issues. Weekly take-home paper; 8 pgs; circ 80,000. Subscription $7.80. 60% freelance. Complete ms/cover letter; no phone query. Pays .02-.04/wd; on acceptance; for 1st, simultaneous or reprint rts. Articles 500-700 wds (175/yr); fiction (for senior adults only) 1,000-1,200 wds (15/yr). Responds in 4-10 wks. Seasonal 10 mos ahead. Considers simultaneous submissions & reprints. Guidelines; copy for 9x12 SAE/2 stamps.

Fillers: Buys 25/yr. Cartoons, $25-50; facts, $5-25.

Columns/Departments: Family, 500-625 wds; Prime Time (fiction/testimonials for seniors), 1,000-1,200 wds; Perspective (insights, opinions, editorials), 500-625 wds; Discipleship (help for discipleship groups), 500-625 wds; Commitment (help for individuals in Christian walk), 500-625 wds.

Special Needs: Articles on Sunday school and small groups; discipleship, commitment and family. Nothing on AIDS, abortion, or homosexuality.

Tips: "Request guidelines and follow them closely. All departments are open."

** This periodical was #7 on the 1994 Top 50 Plus Christian Publishers List.

VITAL CHRISTIANITY, Box 2499, Anderson IN 46018. (317)644-7721. (317)622-9511. Church of God. Steven A. Beverly, mng. ed. Denominational; adults 55 and older. Monthly mag; 48 pgs; circ 19,000. Subscription $19.95. 20% freelance. Complete ms/cover letter. Pays $70-280, on acceptance, for one-time rts. Articles 400-850 wds (36/yr). Responds in 1-6 wks. Seasonal 6 mos ahead. Considers simultaneous submissions & reprints. Kill fee 50%. Prefers disk copy. Sidebars ok. Guidelines/theme list; copy for 9x12 SAE/6 stamps.

Poetry: Buys 4/yr.

Fillers: Buys 2/yr. Prose; 75-100 wds.

Columns/Departments: Buys 36/yr. Journeys (personal, spiritual development), 500 wds; Snapshots (missions), 850 wds; Portraits of Faith (first-person testimonies), 500 wds; Family Ties (family issues), 850 wds; $70/printed pg.

Tips: "Relate or slant all issues toward age 55 plus. Most open to personal testimonies."

VOICE, 3150 Bear St., Costa Mesa CA 92626. (714)754-1400. Fax: (714)557-9916. Full Gospel Business Men's Fellowship Intl. Submit to The Editor. An evangelistic outreach to the business men in the marketplace. Monthly mag; 40 pgs; circ 80,000. Subscription $7.95. 20% freelance. Complete ms/cover letter; fax query ok. **NO PAYMENT.** First Person Male Testimonies (spirit-filled) 600-2,500 wds (200/yr). Responds in 2 wks. Seasonal 2 mos ahead. Considers simultaneous submissions & reprints. No disk. Guidelines; copy for 6x9 SAE/2 stamps.

*THE VOICE, 2917 S. Holly St., Seattle WA 98108. A & A Evangelistic Assn. Rev. Daniel Ashcraft, ed. Christ-honoring poetry and devotionals for street people and everyday folks. Weekly newsletter. 100% freelance. Complete ms/cover letter; no phone query. **PAYS IN COPIES** for all rts. Devotionals 25-50 wds. Responds in 4 wks. Seasonal 6 mos ahead. Considers simultaneous submissions & reprints. Guidelines/theme list; copy for $1/#10 SAE/1 stamp.

Poetry: Accepts 50/yr. Free verse, traditional; 5-10 lines. Submit max. 5 poems.

Tips: "Poetry and devotionals only. Avoid preaching."

WAR CRY, 615 Slaters Ln., Alexandria VA 22313. (703)684-5500. The Salvation Army. Colonel Henry Gariepy, ed-in-chief. Pluralistic readership reaching all socioeconomic strata and including distribution in institutions. Biweekly mag; 24 pgs; circ 505,000. Subscription $7.50. 5% freelance. Complete ms/brief cover letter. Pays .20/wd, on acceptance, for 1st rts. Articles 700-1,000 wds (25/yr). Responds in 6 wks. Seasonal 6 mos ahead. No sidebars. Guidelines; free copy.

Tips: "Most open to current issues, devotional, personality profiles, holiday, and issue-related material."

** This periodical was #70 on the 1994 Top 50 Plus Christian Publishers list. (#50 in 1993)

#WESLEYAN ADVOCATE, Box 50434, Indianapolis IN 46250-0434. (317)576-8156. Fax: (317)577-4397. The Wesleyan Church. Jerry Brecheisen, mng ed. A full salvation family mag; denominational. Monthly mag; 36 pgs; circ 20,000. Subscription $12.50. 50% freelance. Complete ms/cover letter; phone query ok. Pays $10-40 for assigned, $5-25 for unsolicited, .01-.02/wd for reprints; on publication; for 1st or simultaneous rts. Not copyrighted. Articles 250-650 wds (50/yr). Responds in 2 wks. Seasonal 6 mos ahead. Considers simultaneous submissions & reprints. Guidelines; copy $2.

Poetry: Buys 30/yr. Free verse or traditional; $5-10. Send max. 6 poems.

Fillers: Prose, 100-300 wds. Pays $2-6.

Columns/Departments: Personal Experiences, 700 wds; Ministry Tips, 600 wds; $10.

+WHISPER, 509 Enterprise Dr., Rohnert Park CA 94928. (707)585-1436. Anthony Boyd, ed. Poetry and stories for people from all walks of life (not just Christians). Quarterly mag; 20 pgs; circ 1,000. Subscription $10. 90% freelance. Complete ms/cover letter. **PAYS IN COPIES,** for 1st or one-time rts. Articles 1,200-1,700 wds (4/yr); fiction, 1,200-1,700 wds (4/yr). Responds in 2-3 wks. No seasonal. Accepts reprints. Prefers disk copy. No sidebars. Guidelines; copy $2.50.

Poetry: Accepts 100/yr. Any type, 1-45 lines. Submit max. 5 poems.

Fillers: Accepts 4 cartoons/yr.

Tips: "Read guidelines; don't preach. Poetry, stories and interviews are open to freelancers."

+WINE CASTLES, P.O. Box 7265, Duluth MN 55807. (218)727-4025. Christian. Penny Ballantine, ed. To guide readers through adversity. Bimonthly mag; 16 pgs; new. Subscription $14. Estab 1994. 100% freelance. Complete ms/cover letter; phone query ok. Pays $20-25, on publication, for one-time rts. Not copyrighted. Articles 1,000-1,500 wds (50/yr). Responds in 4 wks. Seasonal 6 mos ahead. No disks for now. No sidebars. Guidelines; copy $3.50.

Poetry: Buys 75/yr. Free verse, traditional, prayer poems; 7-10 lines; .50/line. Send any number.

Fillers: Buys 100/yr. Anecdotes, prose, quotes; 300-500 wds.; $5-10.

Columns/Departments: Buys 50-75/yr.

Tips: "I'm still waiting to see 'God's muscle' in your writing."

*THE WITNESS, 1249 Washington Blvd., Detroit MI 48226-1868. (313)962-2650. Fax: (313)962-1012. Episcopal Church Publishing Co. Jeanie Wylie-Kellermann, ed. Seeks to examine society in light of faith and conscience, with clear advocacy for the poor, women, people of color, and other minority groups. Monthly (10X) mag; 28 pgs; circ 3,000. Subscription $20. 10% freelance. Complete ms/cover letter (on first submission). Pays $50-150, on publication, for all rts. Articles to 1,500 wds (10/yr). Responds in 6 wks on accepted mss, no response to unaccepted. Considers simultaneous submissions. Kill fee. Guidelines; copy for 10x13 SAE/4 stamps.

Poetry: Buys 4/yr. Pays $30.

Tips: "We like brevity, wit and humor. Anything long-winded gets dismissed quickly—so it's worth editing your material ruthlessly before you send it."

#WORLD, Box 2330, Asheville NC 28802. (704)253-8063. Fax: (704)253-1556. God's World Publications Inc. Joel Belz, ed. Current news from a Christian perspective. Weekly newspaper; circ 35,000. Subscription $27.95. 20% freelance. Query; phone query ok. Pays .15/wd, on publication, for 1st rts. Articles 400-1,000 wds. Responds in 1 month. Guidelines/copy.

CHILDREN'S MARKETS

+ATTENTION PLEASE! the mini magazine, Rt 1 Box 1913, Lopez Island WA 98261. (206)468-2104. Lois Ludwig, ed. For children 6-18 with Attention Deficit Disorder; shows them how to work positively with their problems and use Christian answers to cope with their difficulties. Bimonthly booklet; 15 pgs; circ 400. Subscription $10. 60% freelance. Complete ms/cover letter; no phone query. Pays $10, on acceptance, for one-time & reprint rts. Articles 50-500 wds (3/yr); fiction (for 6-8 yrs/250-300 wds & 8-12 yrs/350-450 wds), buys 8/yr. Responds in 2 wks. Seasonal 3-4 mos ahead. Accepts reprints. Open to sidebars. Guidelines/theme list; copy for 6x9 SAE/2 stamps.

    Poetry: Accepts 6/yr. From ADD children only.

    Columns/Departments: Buys 15/yr. Games (puzzles—fit 5.5" x 4.5" space); TeenSpace (coping skills for ADD teens), 50-500 wds.

    Special Needs: All articles must relate to Attention Deficit Disorder and how to cope, for the 13-18 year old. Needs good teaching puzzles for themes; ethnic ADD characters.

    Tips: "Show that you know the ADD child and give him/her a lift in addition to sharing an exciting and positive takeaway on how to cope."

BREAD FOR GOD'S CHILDREN, Box 1017, Arcadia FL 33821. (813)494-6214. Fax: (813)993-0154. Interdenominational. Judith M. Gibbs, ed. A family magazine for serious Christians who are concerned about their children or grandchildren (ages 6-18). Monthly mag; 28 pgs; circ 10,000. Free subscription. 80% freelance. Complete ms/no cover letter; phone query ok. Pays $10-20 ($30-40 for fiction); on publication; for 1st, one-time or reprint rts. Not copyrighted. Articles 400-800 wds (10/yr); fiction & true stories 500-800 wds for 4-10 yrs, 700-1,500 wds for youth (10/yr). Responds in 2-12 wks. Seasonal 10 mos ahead. Accepts reprints (depends on where published). Guidelines; 3 copies for 9x12 SAE/5 stamps.

    Tips: "Read the sample copies. We want stories that teach without being overly sweet and without preaching or moralizing. Must be true to life with believable characters."

CLUBHOUSE, c/o Your Story Hour, Box 15, Berrien Springs MI 49103. (616)471-3701. Fax: (616)471-4661. Non-denominational. Krista Phillips, ed. To help young people (9-14) feel good about themselves. Monthly newsletter; 4 pgs; circ 8,000. Subscription $5-8. 75% freelance. Complete ms/no cover letter. Pays $12-35, on publication (or at end of calendar yr), for one-time or simultaneous rts. Articles 25-1,200 wds (3/yr); fiction 100-1,200 wds (30/yr). Responds in 8 wks. Seasonal 6 mos ahead. Considers simultaneous submissions & reprints. No disks. Guidelines; copy for 9x12 SAE/2 stamps.

    Poetry: Buys 5/yr. Free verse, light verse, traditional; to 12 lines; $12. Submit max. 3 poems.

    Fillers: Buys 8-12/yr. Cartoons, facts, games, jokes, prose, quizzes, word puzzles; 50-100 wds; $12.

    Tips: "Send all material once a year in March."

COUNSELOR, Box 632, Glen Ellyn IL 60138. (708)668-6000. Scripture Press. Janice K. Burton, ed. Presents the way spiritual truths in the weekly lesson can be worked out in everyday life—a correlated teaching tool for 8-11 yr olds. Weekly take-home paper; 4 pgs. Subscription $9.95. 95% freelance.

Complete ms/cover letter; phone query ok. Pays .07-.10/wd; on acceptance; for all, one-time, simultaneous or reprint rts. Articles 300-600 wds (10-15/yr); fiction/true stories 900-1,100 wds (10-15/yr). Responds in 4-6 wks. Seasonal 1 yr ahead. Considers simultaneous submissions & reprints (pays .05-.07/wd). Guidelines/theme list; copy for #10 SAE/1 stamp.

Fillers: Buys 15-20/yr. Cartoons, facts, games, jokes, quizzes, word puzzles; 100-200 wds; $8-20.

Tips: "No topic is of interest unless it is addressed to the needs of 8-12 yr. olds, and primarily dealt with in story form. Prefer true stories (always indicate if story is true)."

** This periodical was #67 on the 1994 Top 50 Plus Christian Publishers list. (#35 in 1993)

CRUSADER, Box 7259, Grand Rapids MI 49510. (616)241-5616. Fax: (616)241-5558. Calvinist Cadet Corp. G. Richard Broene, ed. To show cadets and their friends, boys 9-14, how God is at work in their lives and in the world around them. Mag published 7X/yr; 24 pgs; circ 13,000. Subscription $7.70. 50% freelance. Complete ms/cover letter; no phone query. Pays .02-.05/wd; on acceptance; for 1st, one-time, or reprint rts. Articles (6/yr) & fiction (12/yr), 800-1,500 wds. Responds in 4-6 wks. Seasonal 10 mos ahead. Considers simultaneous submissions & reprints. Guidelines/theme list; copy for 9x12 SAE/3 stamps.

Fillers: Robert DeJonge. Buys 7-10/yr. Cartoons, games, word puzzles; 20-200 wds; $5-20.

Tips: "Fiction tied to themes; request new theme list after January of each year."

#DISCOVERIES, 6401 The Paseo, Kansas City MO 64131. (816)333-7000 x2250. Fax: (816)333-4439. Nazarene/Wesleyan Churches. Latta Jo Knapp, ed. For 8-9 yr olds, emphasizing Christian values and holy living. Weekly take-home paper; 4 pgs; circ 30,000. 100% freelance. Complete ms/cover letter; phone query ok. Pays .05/wd, on production, for all rts. Articles (2/yr) & fiction (52/yr), 500-700 wds. Responds in 3 mos. Seasonal 5 mos ahead. Accepts reprints. Guidelines/theme list/copy for #10 SAE/1 stamp.

Fillers: Buys 52 word puzzles/yr; $15.

Tips: "Follow guidelines and theme list. Most open to stories and puzzles; tips with age-level appropriateness."

FAITH 'N' STUFF - See GUIDEPOSTS FOR KIDS.

FOCUS ON THE FAMILY CLUBHOUSE, 8605 Explorer Dr., Colorado Springs CO 80920. (719)531-4579. Fax: (719)531-3499. Focus on the Family. Marianne Hering, ed. For children 8-12 yrs in Christian homes. Monthly mag; 16 pgs; circ 95,000. Subscription $12. 40% freelance. Query or complete ms/cover letter; fax query ok. Pays $120-360 for assigned (less for unsolicited), on acceptance, for 1st rts. Articles 400-1,200 wds (7/yr); fiction 400-1,500 wds (16/yr). Responds in 4-6 wks. Seasonal 6-9 mos ahead. Accepts simultaneous submissions. Sidebars ok. Guidelines; copy for 9x12 SAE/2 stamps.

Fillers: Buys 6/yr. Anecdotes, ideas, party ideas, short humor; to 400 wds; .10-.20/wd.

Tips: "Most open to fiction in a non-contemporary setting and humor."

** This periodical was #15 on the 1994 Top 50 Plus Christian Publishers list. Also 1994 EPA Award of Merit - Youth.

FOCUS ON THE FAMILY CLUBHOUSE JR., 8605 Explorer Dr., Colorado Springs CO 80920. (719)531-3400. Fax: (719)531-3499. Focus on the Family. Lisa Brock, ed. For ages 4-8 yrs. Monthly mag; 16 pgs; circ 95,000. Subscription $12. 25% freelance. Complete ms/cover letter; fax query ok. Pays $100 ($100-200 for fiction), on acceptance, for 1st rts. Articles 300-750 wds (1-2/yr); fiction 300-1,000 wds (10/yr). Responds in 4 wks. Seasonal 5-6 mos ahead. Kill fee. No sidebars. Guidelines; copy for 9x12 SAE/2 stamps.

Poetry: Buys 3/yr. Free verse, light verse, traditional; 10-25 lines; $25-100.

Fillers: Buys 1-2/yr. Cartoons, games, word puzzles; $15-30.

Special Needs: Bible stories.

Tips: "Most open to short, non-preachy fiction, beginning reader stories, and read-to-me."

** This periodical was #15 on the 1994 Top 50 Plus Christian Publishers list. Also 1994 EPA Award of Excellence - Youth.

*GOD'S WORLD TODAY, P.O. Box 2330, Asheville NC 28803. (704)253-8063. Christian. Norman W. Bomer, ed. Current events, published in 5 editions, for kindergarten through jr. high students, mostly in Christian and home schools. Weekly newsletter (during school yr); 8 pgs; circ 260,000. 15-20% freelance. Complete ms/cover letter. Pays $75, on acceptance, for one-time rts. Articles 600-900 wds. Responds in 2 mos. Guidelines; free copy.

Tips: "Keep vocabulary simple. Must present a distinctly Christian world view without being moralistic."

#GOOD NEWS FOR CHILDREN, 330 Progress Rd., Dayton OH 45449. (513)847-5900. Fax: (513)847-5910. Catholic. Joan Mitchell CSJ, ed. For 2nd & 3rd graders. Weekly take-home paper. Not in topical listings.

GUIDE MAGAZINE, 55 W. Oak Ridge Dr., Hagerstown MD 21740. (301)791-7000. Fax: (301)790-9734. Seventh-day Adventist. Randy Fishell assoc. ed. A Christian journal for 10-14 yr olds, presenting true stories relevant to their needs. Weekly mag; 32 pgs; circ 36,000. Subscription $34.97/yr. 25% freelance. Complete ms/cover letter; fax query ok. Pays $25-125, on acceptance, for 1st rts. Articles (75-100/yr) or true stories (50-75/yr); 500-1,200 wds. Responds in 2 wks. Seasonal 6-7 mos ahead. Considers simultaneous submissions & reprints. No disks. Sidebars ok. Guidelines; copy for 6x9 SAE/2 stamps.

Fillers: Buys 40/yr. Games, word puzzles; 20-50 wds; $15-30.

Special Needs: "Most open to true action/adventure and Christian humor. Kids want that—put it together with dialogue and a spiritual slant, and you're on the 'write' track for our readers."

** This periodical was #38 on the 1994 Top 50 Plus Christian Publishers list. (#29 in 1993)

GUIDEPOSTS FOR KIDS (formerly **Faith 'N Stuff**), 16 E 34th St., New York NY 10016. (219)929-4429. Fax: (219)926-3839. Guideposts Inc. Mary Lou Carney, ed; Wallis Metts, articles/columns editor; Lurlene McDaniel, fiction editor. For kids 7-12 yrs. Bimonthly mag; 32 pgs; circ 160,000. Subscription $15.95. 25% freelance. Complete ms/cover letter; fax query ok. Pays $175-350 for fiction; on acceptance; for all rts. Features 1,500 wds., secondary features 1,000 wds., one-pagers 500 wds, kid profiles 200-500 wds (6-10/yr); fiction 700-1,300 wds (8/yr). Responds in 2-8 wks. Seasonal 6 mos ahead. Considers simultaneous submissions. Kill fee 5%. Sidebars ok. Guidelines; copy $3.25/9x12 SAE.

Poetry: Buys 3/yr. Any type, no traditionally religious poetry; $10-50.

Fillers: Buys 6-12/yr. Games, jokes, quizzes; 25-500 wds; $75-150.

Columns/Departments: See guidelines.

Special Needs: Historical fiction, fun trivia, news leads involving kids.

Tips: "Think like a kid. Most open to fiction (no biblical fiction); seasonal pieces. We are more value-centered than we are religious."

#HIGH ADVENTURE, 1445 Boonville Ave., Springfield MO 65802-1894. (417)862-2781 x4178. Fax: (417)862-8558. Assemblies of God. Marshall Bruner, ed. For the Royal Rangers (boys), 5-17 yrs; slanted toward teens. Quarterly mag; 16 pgs; circ 60,000. Subscription $1.75. 75% freelance. Query or complete ms/cover letter; no phone query. Pays .03/wd; on acceptance; for one-time or reprint rts. Articles to 1,000 wds (25-30/yr); fiction 500-1,000 wds (25-50/yr); book reviews 100-200 wds. Responds in 1-2 mos. Seasonal 6 mos ahead. Considers simultaneous submissions & reprints. Guidelines/theme list; copy for 9x12 SAE/3 stamps.

Fillers: Buys 30/yr. Cartoons, jokes, short humor; 50 wds; $2-20.

JUNIOR TRAILS, 1445 Boonville Ave., Springfield MO 65802. (417)862-2781. Assemblies of God. Sinda S. Zinn, ed. Teaching of Christian principles through fiction stories about children (10-12 yrs). Weekly take-home paper; 8 pgs; circ 65,000. 99% freelance. Complete ms. Pays .02-.03/wd, on acceptance, for one-time rts. Not copyrighted. Articles 300-1,000 wds (50/yr); fiction 1,200-1,800 wds (50-75/yr). Responds in 2-4 wks. Seasonal 12-15 mos ahead. Considers simultaneous submissions & reprints. No sidebars. Guidelines/theme lists; copy for #10 SAE/1 stamp.

Poetry: Buys 20-30/yr. Light verse, traditional; $5.

Fillers: Facts, short humor; 300-500 wds; .02-.03/wd.

Tips: "Most open to fiction based on relevant problems for today's kids. Submit well-written, believable stories in which character overcomes real problem based on biblical principles."
** #25 on the 1993 Top 50.

KEYS FOR KIDS, Box 1, Grand Rapids MI 49501. (616)451-2009. Hazel Marett, ed. A daily devotional booklet for children (8-14) or for family devotions. Bimonthly booklet; 96 pgs; circ 40,000. 100% freelance. Complete ms/no cover letter. Pays $12-16; on acceptance; for 1st or simultaneous rts. Not copyrighted. Devotionals (includes short fiction story) 375-425 wds (60-70/yr). Responds in 2-4 wks. Seasonal 4-5 mos ahead. Considers simultaneous submissions & reprints. Guidelines; copy for 6x9 SAE/$1.05 postage.

Tips: "If you are rejected, go back to the sample and study it some more."
** #39 on the 1993 Top 50.

LISTEN, 6401 The Paseo, Kansas City MO 64131. (816)333-7000 x2244. Fax: (816)333-4439. Nazarene/Wesleyan. George Pryor, ed. Weekly activity/story paper for 5 yr olds; 4 pgs; circ 47,500. Subscription $8. 50% freelance. Complete ms/cover letter; no phone query. Pays .05/wd, on publication, for all rts. No articles; contemporary fiction & true stories 300-500 wds (52/yr). Responds in 4 wks. Seasonal 15 mos ahead. Kill fee. Guidelines/theme list in 1996; copy for #10 SAE/1 stamp.

Poetry: Buys 15/yr. Light verse; 4-12 lines; .05/wd.

Fillers: Buys 30/yr. Games, ideas/activities (age-appropriate); $5-15.

Special Needs: Exciting, age-appropriate activities for back page; adventure stories and children's life situation stories.

Tips: "We will not be considering freelance material again until 1996."

MY FRIEND, The Catholic Magazine for Kids. 50 St. Paul's Ave., Boston MA 02130. Sr. Anne Joan Flanagan, mng. ed. Christian values and basic Catholic doctrines for children, ages 7-12. Monthly (10X) mag; 32 pgs; circ 14,000. Subscription $10. 60% freelance. Complete ms/no cover letter; no phone/fax query. Pays $30-150, on acceptance, for all or 1st rts. Articles 200-600 wds (20/yr) & fiction 150-500 wds (15/yr). Responds in 6-8 wks. Seasonal 1 yr ahead. Kill fee. Sidebars ok. Guidelines/theme list; copy $1/9x12 SAE/4 stamps.

Poetry: Accepts 1/yr.

Fillers: Accepts 5/yr. Facts, jokes, party ideas; 10-100 wds; $5-20.

Columns/Departments: Buys up to 20/yr. Wonders of God's Creation, 500 wds; Bible Facts (filler); 100 wds; $20-75.

Special Needs: Media literacy articles and activities.

** This periodical was #39 on the 1994 Top 50 Plus Christian Publishers list.

*NATURE FRIEND MAGAZINE, 22777 State Rd. 119, Goshen IN 46526. (219)534-2245. Pilgrim Publishers/Fundamental creationist. Stanley K. Brubaker, ed. For children's (ages 4-14); about God's wonderful world of nature and wildlife. Monthly mag; 36 pgs; circ 10,000. 40% freelance. Complete ms/cover letter. Pays .05/wd, on publication, for one-time rts. Articles 300-1,500 wds; true stories 300-1200 wds. Responds in 3-6 mos. Seasonal 3 mos ahead. Considers simultaneous submissions & reprints. Guidelines & 2 copies for $5/6x9 SAE.

Poetry: Buys 10-20/yr. Traditional; $8-20. Submit max. 5 poems.

Tips: "Don't bother submitting to us unless you have seen our guidelines and a sample copy. We are very conservative in our approach."

ON THE LINE, 616 Walnut Ave., Scottdale PA 15683. (412)887-8500. Fax: (412)887-3111. Mennonite. Mary Clemens Meyer, ed. Reinforces Christian values in 10-14 yr olds. Weekly take-home paper; 8 pgs; circ 8,000. Subscription $17.10. 90% freelance. Complete ms only/no cover letter; no phone query. Pays .03-.05/wd ($25-45 for fiction), on acceptance, for one-time, reprint, or simultaneous rts. Articles 300-500 wds (52/yr); fiction 1,000-1,800 wds (52/yr). Responds in 4 wks. Seasonal 4 mos ahead. Considers simultaneous submissions & reprints. Guidelines; copy for 7x10 SAE/2 stamps.

Poetry: Buys 20/yr. Free verse, haiku, light verse, traditional; 3-20 lines; $10-25.

Fillers: Buys 20/yr. Cartoons, facts, jokes, quizzes, word puzzles; $10-25.

Ethnic: Targets all ethnic groups involved in the Mennonite religion.

Tips: "Watch kids 10-14. Listen to them talk. Write stories that sound natural—not moralizing, preachy ones that have adults quoting scripture. It has to sound real."

** This periodical was #52 on the 1994 Top 50 Plus Christian Publishers list. (#30 in 1993)

*OUR LITTLE FRIEND, Box 7000, Boise ID 83707. (208)465-2500. Seventh-day Adventist. Aileen Andres Sox, ed. For theme and comments, see **Primary Treasure**. Weekly take-home paper for 1-6 yr olds (through 1st grade); 8 pgs; circ 45,000-50,000. 75% freelance. Complete ms/cover letter. Pays $25-50; on acceptance; for one-time or reprint rts. True stories 650-900 wds. Responds in 3 mos. Seasonal 7 mos ahead. Considers simultaneous submissions & reprints. Guidelines/theme list; copy for 9x12 SAE/2 stamps.

Poetry: 12 lines; $1/line.

Tips: "Stories need to be crafted for this age reader in plot and vocabulary."

PARTNERS, Christian Light Publications, Inc., Box 1212, Harrisonburg VA 22801-1212. (703)434-0768. Fax: (703)433-8896. Mennonite. Crystal Shank, ed. For 9-14 yr olds. Weekly take-home paper; 4 pgs; circ 5,825. Almost 100% freelance. Complete ms. Pays to .02-.05/wd; on acceptance; for all, 1st or reprint rts. Articles 200-800 wds (40-50/yr); fiction & true stories 1,000-1,600 wds (or installments); short fiction to 400 wds (50 fiction/yr). Responds in 6-8 wks. Seasonal 6 mos ahead. Considers simultaneous submissions & reprints; serials 2-13 parts (2-4 parts preferred). No disk. Guidelines/theme list; copy for 9x12 SAE/3 stamps.

Poetry: Buys 40-50/yr. Traditional; 4-24 lines; .50/line. Submit max. 6 poems.

Fillers: Buys 50/yr. Prose, quizzes, word puzzles (Bible related). Payment varies, about $5.

Columns/Departments: Character Corner; Cultures & Customs; Historical Highlights; Maker's Masterpiece; Missionary Mail; Torches of Truth; or Nature Nooks; all 200-800 wds.

Tips: "Personal familiarity with conservative Mennonite applications of biblical truth is very helpful. We do not require that you be Mennonite, but we do send a questionnaire for you to fill out."

POCKETS, Box 189, Nashville TN 37202-0189. (615)340-7333. Fax: (615)340-7006. United Methodist. Janet Knight, ed; submit to Lynn W. Gilliam, assoc. ed. Devotional magazine for children (6-11 yrs). Monthly (11X) mag; 48 pgs; circ 95,000. Subscription $16.95. 60% freelance. Complete ms/no cover letter; phone query ok. Pays .12/wd, on acceptance, for 1st rts. (Will start buying software application rts if commissioned.) Articles 200-1,600 wds (1/yr) & fiction to 1,600 wds (44/yr). Responds in 1-3 wks. Seasonal 1 yr ahead. Considers simultaneous submissions & few reprints. Kill fee 50%. No disk. Guidelines/theme list (new each Dec.); copy for 8x10 SAE/$1.05 postage.

> **Poetry:** Buys 26/yr. Free verse, haiku, light verse, traditional; to 24 lines; $25 & up. Submit max. 5 poems.

> **Fillers:** Could use up to 70-80/yr. Games, quizzes, prayers, riddles, word puzzles; $10.

> **Columns/Departments:** Buys 20/yr. Kids Cook; Pocketsful of Love (ways to show love), 250 wds.

> **Special Needs:** "Stories about real children involved in peace/justice/environmental issues out of a faith basis. Good retelling of Scripture; not overly fictionalized. Role models of people who are or have acted out of a faith perspective. We are including 4 pgs. for younger readers (5-7 yrs). We need stories to 750 wds, simple poems, prayers and activities. Please mark these 'For Wendell's Pages.'"

> **Contest:** Fiction-writing contest; submit between 3/1 & 9/1 every yr. Prize $1,000. Length 1,000-1,700 wds. Send to Pockets Fiction Contest at above address.

> **Tips:** "Get our theme list first. Most open to fiction, Someone You'd Like to Know and Pocketsful of Love."

> ** This periodical was #18 on the 1994 Top 50 Plus Christian Publishers list. (#20 in 1993)

POWER AND LIGHT, 6401 The Paseo, Kansas City MO 64131. (816)333-7000. Fax: (816)333-4439. Nazarene. Beula Postelwait, ed. For pre-teens, 11-12 year olds. Weekly take-home paper; 8 pgs; circ 40,000. Subscription $8. Estab 1993. 50% freelance. Query or complete ms; phone/fax query ok. Pays .05/wd, on publication, for multiple use rts (writer retains right to reuse). Articles 500-800 wds (26/yr); fiction 500-800 wds (26/yr). Responds in 6-15 wks. Seasonal 9 mos ahead. Considers simultaneous submissions & reprints (.035/wd). Kill fee 5%. Disk ok. Guidelines/theme list; copy for 5x7 SAE/2 stamps.

> **Fillers:** Buys 52/yr. Cartoons, games, word puzzles; to 200 wds; $15.

> **Tips:** "Most open to fiction, puzzles and cartoons. Request a theme list. Write about preteens from a preteen perspective."

PRIMARY DAYS, Box 632, Glen Ellyn IL 60138. (708)668-6000. Scripture Press. Janice K. Burton, ed. To show children, 6-8, how Bible truths can work out in everyday life. Weekly take-home paper; 4 pgs. Subscription $9.95. 100% freelance. Complete ms/cover letter; no phone query. Pays .05-.10/wd; on acceptance; for all, one-time, simultaneous or reprint rts. Articles 300-600 wds (10-15/yr); fiction 900-1100 wds (10-15/yr). Responds in 4-6 wks. Seasonal 1 yr ahead. Considers simultaneous submissions & reprints. No disk. Guidelines/theme list/copy for #10 SAE/1 stamp.

> **Fillers:** Buys 15-20/yr. Quizzes, word puzzles; 30-100 wds; $7-10.

*PRIMARY PAL, 1300 N. Meacham, Schaumburg IL 60173. Regular Baptist. Joan Alexander, ed. For ages 6-8; fundamental, conservative. Weekly take-home paper. Query. Pays on acceptance, for all or 1st rts. Articles 100-500 wds; fiction 500-1,000 wds. Responds in 2-8 wks. Seasonal 1 yr ahead. Guidelines; copy for #10 SAE/2 stamps.

Fillers: Games, word puzzles.

Tips: "Most open to fiction, features, puzzles, activities, and devotionals."

*PRIMARY TREASURE, Box 7000, Boise ID 83707. (208)465-2500. Seventh-day Adventist. Aileen Andres Sox, ed. To teach children Christian belief, values, and practice. God's loving us and our loving Him makes a difference in every facet of life, from how we think and act to how we feel. Weekly take-home paper for 7-9 yr olds (2nd-4th grades); 16 pgs; circ 35,000. 75% freelance. Complete ms/cover letter. Pays $25-50; on acceptance; for one-time or reprint rts. True stories to 1,200 wds; articles used rarely (query). Responds in 3 mos. Seasonal 7 mos ahead. Considers simultaneous submissions; serials to 10 parts (query). Guidelines; copy for 9x12 SAE/2 stamps.

Poetry: 12 lines; $1/line.

Tips: "We need positive, lively stories about children facing modern problems and making good choices. We always need strong stories about boys. We need a spiritual element that frequently is missing from submissions. We're changing; refer to guidelines."

#PROMISE, 330 Progress Rd., Dayton OH 45449. (513)847-5900. Fax: (513)847-5910. Catholic. Joan Mitchell CSJ, ed. For preschoolers. Weekly (32X) take-home paper. Not in topical listings.

R-A-D-A-R, 8121 Hamilton Ave., Cincinnati OH 45231. (513)931-4050. Fax: (513)931-0904. Standard Publishing. Elaina Meyers, ed. For 8-11 yr olds; correlates with Sunday-school lesson themes. Weekly take-home paper; 12 pgs; circ 110,000. Subscription $9.50. 90-95% freelance. Complete ms/no cover letter; no phone/fax query. Pays .03-.07/wd, on acceptance, for 1st or one-time rts. Articles 400-500 wds (10/yr) & fiction 900-1,000 wds (2,000 for 2-part). Responds in 6-8 wks. Seasonal 1 yr ahead. Accepts reprints. No disk. Some sidebars. Guidelines/theme list/copy for #10 SAE/1 stamp.

Poetry: Buys 5-10/yr. Traditional; .50/line.

Fillers: Buys 10-15/yr. Cartoons ($17.50), games, ideas, jokes, word puzzles; $15.

Tips: "We mail theme list automatically if you request to be put on list. Keep abreast with the times and where kids are. The issues they are dealing with in personal lives should be a part of their reading."

** This periodical was #13 on the 1994 Top 50 Plus Christian Publishers list. (#8 in 1993)

SKIPPING STONES, A Multicultural Children's Quarterly, P.O. Box 3939, Eugene OR 97403. (503)342-4956. Not specifically Christian. Arun Narayan Toke', ed. Multi-cultural and multi-ethnic writings for children 7-14. Bimonthly (5X) mag; 36 pgs; circ 2,500. Subscription $18. 75% freelance. Complete ms/cover letter; no phone or fax query. **PAYS 2 COPIES** for 1st rts. Articles (15-20/yr) & fiction (20/yr—usually by children), 500-800 wds. Responds in 5-10 wks. Seasonal 3 months ahead. Considers simultaneous submissions & reprints. Sidebars ok. Guidelines/theme list; copy $5/9x12 SAE.

Poetry: Only from kids under 18. Accepts 25-50/yr. Any type; 3-20 lines. Submit max. 3 poems.

Fillers: Accepts 10-20/yr. Cartoons, facts, games, jokes, quizzes, quotes, short humor, word puzzles; 50-100 wds.

Columns/Departments: Accepts 10/yr. Cultural Collage (multicultural), 100-250 wds; Want to Fiddle with These Riddles?, one page; Taking Action (for youth), to 200 wds; Noteworthy News (for youth), to 100 wds.

Special Needs: Multicultural, international experiences, ecological awareness, and social issues. Accepts fiction from adults only if it illustrates multicultural or social issues.

Tips: "We're seeking submissions by minority, multicultural, international, and/or youth writers. Do not be judgmental or preachy; be open or receptive to diverse opinions."

STORY FRIENDS, 616 Walnut St., Scottdale PA 15683. (412)887-5181. Fax: (412)887-3111. Mennonite. Marjorie Waybill, ed. For children 4-9 yrs. Weekly take-home paper; 4 pgs; circ 9,000. Subscription $12.35. 50% freelance. Complete ms only; no cover letter or phone query. Pays .03-.05/wd, on acceptance, for one-time rts. Not copyrighted. Articles (5/yr) & fiction (25/yr), 300-800 wds. Responds in 3 wks. Seasonal 6 mos ahead. Considers simultaneous submissions & reprints. Guidelines; copy for 9x12 SAE/2 stamps.

> **Poetry:** Buys 10/yr. Traditional; to 8 lines (unless story poem); $10.
>
> **Ethnic:** Targets all ethnic groups involved in the Mennonite religion.
>
> **Tips:** "I like stories that relate to kids and everyday joys and sorrows. No stories about children needing money, or not having enough money for toys, etc. Write about things kids experience in real life."
>
> ** #49 on the 1993 Top 50.

STORY MATES, Christian Light Publications, Inc., Box 1212, Harrisonburg VA 22801-1212. (703)434-0768. Mennonite. Miriam Shank, ed. For 4-8 yr olds. Weekly take-home paper; 4 pgs; circ 5,200. 95% freelance. Complete ms/cover letter. Pays .02-.05/wd; on acceptance; for all, 1st, & reprint rts. Realistic or true stories to 800 wds. Responds in 2 mos. Seasonal 7 mos ahead. Guidelines/theme list; copy for 6x9 SAE/2 stamps.

> **Poetry:** Traditional, any length.
>
> **Fillers:** Quizzes, word puzzles. "Need fillers that correlate with theme list."
>
> **Tips:** "No fantasy, child evangelism, Valentine's Day, Halloween, secular Christmas or Easter material." Very conservative.

*TOGETHER TIME, 6401 The Paseo, Kansas City MO 64131. (816)333-7000. Fax: (816)333-4439. Church of the Nazarene. Lynda Boardman, ed. For 3-4 yr olds and parents. Weekly take-home paper; 4 pgs; circ 7,500. 50% freelance. Complete ms; no cover letter; phone query ok. Pays .05/wd, on production, for all rts. Responds in 10-12 wks. Seasonal 6 mos ahead. Considers simultaneous submissions & reprints. Kill fee. Guidelines/theme list; free copy.

> **Poetry:** Buys 52/yr. Traditional; 4-8 lines; .25/line, $2 minimum. Submit max. 5 poems.
>
> **Fillers:** Buys 52/yr. Activities; 25-100 wds; $10.
>
> **Tips:** "We accept freelance for poems and activities only. Keep poems simple and activities easy—3-4-year-old level."

TOUCH, Box 7259, Grand Rapids MI 49510. (616)241-5616. Fax: (616)241-5558. Calvinettes/Para-church (Christian Reformed, Reformed, and Presbyterian). Carol Smith, mng ed. To show girls, ages 7-14, that God is at work in their lives and the world around them. Monthly (10X) mag; 24 pgs; circ 15,200. Subscription $8. 75% freelance. Complete ms/cover letter; no phone/fax query. Pays .025/wd; on acceptance; for 1st, simultaneous & reprint rts. Articles (10/yr) & fiction (20/yr), 250-900 wds. Responds in 4 wks. Seasonal 10 mos ahead. Considers simultaneous submissions & reprints. No disk. Sidebars ok. Guidelines/theme list; copy $1/9x12 SAE/3 stamps.

> **Poetry:** Buys 30/yr. Light verse, traditional; 4-20 lines; $10-20. Poetry fits themes.
>
> **Fillers:** Buys 10/yr. Cartoons, party ideas, short humor; 50-300 wds; .025/wd.
>
> **Columns/Departments:** Buys 6/yr. Tips & Twaddle (some good/some goofy stuff for girls), 50-100 wds; How-To (how to do things), 400-600 wds; $10-20.
>
> **Special Needs:** Focus is on witnessing for 1995-96.
>
> **Tips:** "Most open to fiction. Ask for theme list and send your best manuscript."

VENTURE, Box 150, Wheaton IL 60189. (708)665-0630. Fax: (708)665-0372. Christian Service Brigade. Deborah Christensen, ed. Slanted to boys (8-11) involved in Brigade programs in their churches. Bimonthly mag; 16 pgs; circ 20,000. Subscription $10. 50% freelance. Complete ms/cover letter; no phone/fax query. Pays .05-.10/wd; on publication; for 1st & reprint rts. Articles (6/yr) & fiction (6/yr), 500-1,000 wds. Responds in 1 wk. Seasonal 4 mos ahead. Accepts reprints. Kill fee $35. No disk. Sidebars ok. Guidelines; copy $1.85/10x13 SAE/4 stamps.

> **Fillers:** Buys 12/yr. Cartoons, quizzes, short humor, word puzzles; to 500 wds; $35-45.

> **Tips:** "Need humor for younger boys. Write for the target age group and weave Christianity naturally through the story. Most open to fiction."

VENTURE, 1884 Randolph Ave., St. Paul MN 55105. (612)690-7010. Editorial Development Associates. Sr. Joan Mitchell, ed. Connects young people's real life experiences—successes and conflicts in family, neighborhood, classroom, playground—with the Sunday gospels; for intermediate-age children. Weekly take-home paper; 8 pgs; circ 140,000. 40% freelance. Query. Pays $75-125, on publication, for all rts. Articles (6-8/yr) & fiction (8-10/yr), 800-900 wds. Responds in 2-8 wks. Seasonal 4-6 mos ahead. Considers simultaneous query. Guidelines; copy $1.85.

> **Tips:** "We want realistic fiction and nonfiction that raises current ethical religious questions and conflicts in multi-racial settings, believable and detailed, to which intermediate-age children can relate."

#WONDER TIME, 6401 The Paseo, Kansas City MO 64131. (816)333-7000. Fax: (816)333-4439. Church of the Nazarene. Teresa Gillihan, ed. asst. For 6-8 yr olds (1st & 2nd graders); emphasis on principles, character-building, and brotherhood. Weekly take-home paper; 4 pgs; circ 45,000. 100% freelance. Complete ms/cover letter; phone query ok. Pays $25, on publication, for multi-use rts. Articles 250-350 wds (52/yr); fiction 250-350 wds (52/yr). Responds in 1 mo. Seasonal 6 mos ahead. Kill fee. Guidelines/theme list; copy for 9x12 SAE/2 stamps.

> **Poetry:** Light verse; 4-8 lines; .25/line, $3 minimum.

> **Fillers:** Buys 52/yr. Games, word puzzles; $3-15.

> **Tips:** "Our stories relate to our Sunday school lessons. We try to use it as a Bible-in-action story."

*THE YOUNG CRUSADER, 1730 Chicago Ave., Evanston IL 60201. (708)864-1396. National Woman's Christian Temperance Union. Michael C. Vitucci, mng. ed. Stresses high morals, good character, high values, and abstinence from alcohol, drugs, and tobacco, for 6-12 yr olds. Monthly mag; 12 pgs; circ 3,000. 100% freelance. Complete ms. Pays .005/wd, on publication, for one-time, simultaneous or reprint rts. Not copyrighted. Articles (60/yr) & fiction, 600-700 wds. Responds in 6 wks. Seasonal 6 mos ahead. Guidelines; copy for 6x9 SAE/2 stamps.

> **Poetry:** Buys 30/yr. Light verse; 6-10 lines; .10/line.

> **Fillers:** Facts, games, ideas, quizzes, short humor, word puzzles.

> **Tips:** "We do not want to see any articles that do not build solid character. Send only copies of your stories as they will be destroyed if not accepted."

CHRISTIAN EDUCATION/LIBRARY MARKETS

BAPTIST LEADER, Box 851, Valley Forge PA 19482-0851. (610)768-2143. Fax: (610)768-2056. American Baptist. Linda Isham, ed. Practical "how-to" or thought provoking articles for local church Christian education lay leaders and teachers. Quarterly mag; 32 pgs; circ 6,000. Subscription $8. 5% freelance.

Complete ms/cover letter; no phone/fax query. Pays $10-50, on acceptance, for 1st rts. Articles 1,300-2,000 wds (4/yr). Responds in 2-12 wks. Seasonal 1 yr ahead. Considers simultaneous submissions & reprints. No disks. No sidebars. Guidelines; copy $1.50.

> **Poetry:** Accepts 2-3/yr. Light verse, traditional; $10-15.

> **Fillers:** Buys 4-8/yr. Cartoons, prayers; 25-100 wds; $10-15.

> **Tips:** "Read the magazine. Most open to features—watch the length, make it practical, meet our specs."

BRIGADE LEADER, Box 150, Wheaton IL 60189. (708)665-0630. Fax: (708)665-0372. Christian Service Brigade. Deborah Christensen, mng. ed. For men leading boy's clubs; emphasis on fathering issues. Quarterly mag; 16 pgs; circ 8,000. Subscription $6. 10% freelance. Complete ms/cover letter; no phone/fax query. Pays .05-.10/wd; on publication; for 1st rts. Articles 500-1,500 wds (12/yr). Responds in 1 wk. Seasonal 4 mos ahead. Accepts reprints. Kill fee $35. Sidebars ok. Guidelines; copy $1.50/10x13 SAE/4 stamps.

> **Tips:** "Be familiar with Christian Service Brigade and the issues men are dealing with. We rarely accept freelance mss. We do theme issues and assign specific articles."

#CATECHIST, 330 Progress Rd., Dayton OH 45449. (513)847-5900. Fax: (513)847-5910. Catholic. Patricia Fischer, ed. For Catholic school teachers. Mag. published 8x/yr; 52 pgs; circ 45,700. Query (preferred) or complete ms. Pays $25-75, on publication, for all rts. Articles 1,200-1,800 wds. Not in topical listings. Responds in 2-4 mos. Guidelines; copy $2.50.

*CE CONNECTION, Box 12609, Oklahoma City OK 73157. (405)787-7110. General Christian Education Dept./IPHC. Talmage Garoner, asst to dir. Targets pastors, local Christian education workers/leader for training/how-to. Quarterly mag/newsletter; circ 6,600. 100% freelance. Cover letter; no phone query. **NO PAYMENT.** Not copyrighted. Articles. Seasonal 4 mos ahead. Accepts reprints. No guidelines; free copy.

*CHANGING LIVES & CALLING LEADERS (CLCL), Box 50434, Indianapolis IN 46250. (317)595-4187. Fax: (317)577-4397. The Wesleyan Church. Russ Gunsalus, ed. For church leadership (children, youth, young adult leaders). Quarterly mag; circ 1,800. Estab 1992. 1% freelance. Complete ms/cover letter; no phone query. Pays to $50, on publication, for one-time rts. Not copyrighted. Articles 500-700 wds (6-12/yr). Responds in 4-6 wks. Seasonal 4 mos ahead. Guidelines/theme list; no copy.

*CHILDREN'S MINISTRY, 2890 N. Monroe Ave., Loveland CO 80526. (303)669-3836. Fax: (303)669-3269. Group Publishing. Barbara Beach, dept. ed. For those who work with kids from birth to 6th grade. Bimonthly mag; 48-52 pgs; circ 30,000. Estab 1991. Subscription $24.95. 90% freelance. Query/clips; no phone query. Pays $25-100, on acceptance, for all rts. Articles 150-1,200 wds (30/yr). Responds in 4 wks. Seasonal 6 mos ahead. Kill fee. Guidelines; copy for 9x12 SAE/4 stamps.

> **Columns/Departments:** Buys 30/yr. Teacher Telegram (practical teacher tips); For Parents Only (practical parenting tips); 150 wds; $25-100.

> **Special Needs:** Working with volunteers, discipling children, morals, money, friends, grades, and Sunday school programming that works.

> **Tips:** "Most open to departments. Need 'ah-ha' ideas—practical. Lots of ideas for teachers of children."

CHRISTIAN EDUCATION COUNSELOR, 1445 Boonville Ave., Springfield MO 65802-1894. (417)862-2781. Fax: (417)862-0503. Assemblies of God. Sylvia Lee, ed. Presents teaching and administrative helps to lay leaders in local churches. Monthly mag; 28 pgs; circ 25,000. Subscription $8/leader $12. 40% freelance. Complete ms/cover letter; no phone query. Pays .05-.10/wd; on acceptance; for 1st, one-time, simultaneous & reprint rts. Articles 350-1,500 wds (50/yr); book/music reviews, 400-500 wds, $35. Responds in 2-4 wks. Seasonal 8 mos ahead. Considers simultaneous submissions & reprints. Guidelines/theme list; copy for 9x12 SAE/3 stamps.

Fillers: Buys cartoons 10/yr; $35-85.

Tips: "Most open to general articles. You need to know Christian education from first-hand experience."

** This periodical was #64 on the 1994 Top 50 Plus Christian Publishers list. (#45 in 1993)

#CHRISTIAN EDUCATORS JOURNAL, 1828 Mayfair NE, Grand Rapids MI 49503. (712)722-6252. Fax: (712)722-1198. Lorna Van Gilst, mng. ed. For educators in Christian day schools at the elementary, secondary, and college levels. Quarterly journal; 36 pgs; circ 4,200. Subscription $7.50. 50% freelance. Complete ms/cover letter; phone query ok. Pays $30, on publication, for one-time rts. Articles 600-1,200 wds (20/yr); fiction 600-1,200 wds. Responds in 1 mo. Seasonal 4 mos ahead. Considers simultaneous submissions & reprints. Guidelines/theme list; copy $1 or 9x12 SAE/4 stamps.

Poetry: Buys 6/yr. On teaching day school; 4-30 lines; $10. Submit max. 5 poems.

Tips: "No articles on Sunday school, only Christian day school. Most open to theme topics and features."

THE CHRISTIAN LIBRARIAN, Box 4000, Three Hills AB T0M 2N0 Canada. U.S. address: Box 4, Cedarville OH 45314. (403)443-5511 x3343. Fax: (403)443-5540. Assn. of Christian Librarians. Ron Jordahl, ed. Christian librarianship. Quarterly (3X) jour; 36 pgs; circ 500. Subscription $20. 25% freelance. Query; phone/fax query ok. **NO PAYMENT,** for 1st, one-time, reprint or simultaneous rts. Not copyrighted. Articles to 1,000-5,000 wds (6/yr). Responds in 2-6 wks. Considers simultaneous query & reprints. Prefers disk copy. Sidebars ok. Guidelines; copy $5.

Fillers: Anecdotes, cartoons, newsbreaks, short humor; 25-300 wds.

Special Needs: Articles on libraries, books and reading.

*CHRISTIAN SCHOOL, 1308 Santa Rosa, Wheaton IL 60187. (708)653-4588. Phil Landrum, pub. A publication for Christian school educators and parents. Quarterly mag; 48 pgs; circ 3,000 schools. 2% freelance. Query; phone query ok. **NO PAYMENT.** Articles 500-1,500 wds (1/yr); fiction 1,000-1,500 (1/yr). Responds in 2-4 wks. Free guidelines/copy.

Poetry: Accepts 1/yr. Traditional. Submit max. 5 poems.

Fillers: Accepts 1/yr. Anecdotes.

Special Needs: Education how-to; youth trends; training techniques; children's books.

CHURCH EDUCATOR, 165 Plaza Dr., Prescott AZ 86303. (602)771-8601. Fax: (602)771-8621. Linda Davidson, ed. For mainline Protestant Christian educators. Monthly jour; 36 pgs; circ 5,500. Subscription $24. 80% freelance. Complete ms/cover letter; phone/fax query ok. Pays .03/wd, 60 days after publication, for 1st rts. Articles (75/yr) & fiction (15/yr), 300-1,500 wds. Responds in 1-8 wks. Seasonal 4 mos ahead. Considers simultaneous submissions & reprints. Sidebars ok. Guidelines/theme list; copy for 9x12 SAE/4 stamps.

Fillers: Bible games and Bible puzzles.

Columns/Departments: Buys 20/yr. Noah's Ark (crafts for children); Youth Notebook (tips for working with teens); 200-500 wds.

Tips: "Talk to the educator at your church. What would they find useful? Most open to seasonal articles dealing with the liturgical year. Write up church programs with specific how-tos of putting the program together."

*CHURCH MEDIA LIBRARY MAGAZINE, 127 9th Ave. N., Nashville TN 37234. (615)251-2752. Southern Baptist. Floyd B. Simpson, ed. Supports the establishment and development of church media libraries; provides how-to articles and articles of inspiration and encouragement to media library workers. Quarterly mag; 52 pgs; circ 36,000. Query. Pays .055/wd; on publication; for all, 1st, or reprint rts. Articles 600-1,500 wds (10-15/issue). Responds in 1 month. Seasonal 14 mos ahead. Free guidelines/copy.

*CHURCH WORSHIP, 165 Plaza Dr., Prescott AZ 86303. (602)771-8601. Fax: (602)771-8621. Henry R. Rust, ed. Supplementary resources for Church worship leaders. Monthly journal; 24 pgs; circ 1,000. Subscription $20. Estab 1990. 85% freelance. Complete ms/cover letter; phone query ok. Pays .03/wd, on publication, for 1st rts. Articles to 100-1,500 wds; fiction 100-1,500 wds. Responds in 2-6 wks. Seasonal 4 mos ahead. Guidelines/theme list; copy for 9x12 SAE/3 stamps.

> **Poetry:** Submit max. 5 poems.
>
> **Special Needs:** Complete worship services.
>
> **Tips:** "Call editor any Wednesday and discuss any topic. Most open to creative worship services."

*CORNERSTONE CONNECTIONS, 55 W. Oak Ridge Dr., Hagerstown MD 21740. (301)791-7000 x2547. Seventh-day Adventist. Mark Ford, ed. Resources for leaders of youth groups. Quarterly mag; 48 pgs; circ 2,400. 20% freelance. Complete ms/cover letter; no phone query. Pays $35-100, on acceptance, for one-time rts. Articles 600-800 wds (30/yr); plays/skits 800 wds; book reports $15/pg. Responds in 4 wks. Seasonal 6 mos ahead. Considers simultaneous submissions & reprints. Guidelines; free copy.

> **Columns/Departments:** Buys 30/yr. Outreach Activities (witnessing, caring) 200 wds; Social Activities (games) 200 wds; AY Programs (programs teens can put on) 800 wds.
>
> **Tips:** "Most open to plays or programs for use with Adventist youth."
>
> ****** #44 on the 1993 Top 50.

EVANGELIZING TODAY'S CHILD, Box 348, Warrenton MO 63383-0348. (314)456-4321. Child Evangelism Fellowship. Elsie C. Lippy, ed. To equip Christians to win the world's children (4-12) to Christ and disciple them. Bimonthly mag; 64 pgs; circ 22,000. Subscription $17.95. 40% freelance. Query/clips, or complete ms/no cover letter; no phone query. Pays .10-.12/wd (.07/wd for fiction), on acceptance, for all & 1st rts, some reprints. Articles 1,200-1,500 wds (20-25/yr); fiction 800-1,000 wds (6/yr). Responds in 2-6 wks. Seasonal 1 yr ahead. Reluctantly considers simultaneous submissions. Kill fee. Guidelines; copy for $1/9x12 SAE/2 stamps.

> **Resource Center:** Buys 40-60/yr. Complete ms, 200-250 wds. Pays .06-.08/wd for teaching hints, bulletin board ideas, object lessons, missions incentives, etc.
>
> **Columns/Departments:** Buys 60/yr. Impact (see guidelines); Teacher's Devotional (focusing on a verse/slanted toward teacher of children), 200-300 wds.
>
> **Special Needs:** Salvation testimonies of adults saved before age 12, 700-900 wds; 6/yr. Creative ideas for involving children in ministry.
>
> **Tips:** "Study the publication. Know children and/or children's workers."
>
> ****** This periodical was #49 on the 1994 Top 50 Plus Christian Publishers list. (#33 in 1993)

#GROUP MAGAZINE, Box 481, Loveland CO 80539. (303)669-3836. Fax: (303)669-3269. Rick Lawrence, ed; Cindy Parolini, mng. ed. Aimed at leaders of high-school-age, Christian youth groups. Mag published 8X/yr; 56 pgs; circ 57,000. Subscription $25.95. 60% freelance. Query; no phone query. Pays $75-200, on acceptance, for all rts. Articles 500-1,800 wds (50-60/yr). Responds in 1-2 mos. Seasonal 7 mos ahead. Kill fee $20. Guidelines; copy for 9x12 SAE/3 stamps.

Columns/Departments: Buys 160/yr. Try This One (youth group activities), 125 wds; Strange But True (strange youth-ministry stories), 600 wds; Hands-on Help (tips for leaders), 125 wds; $15-25. Complete ms.

Special Needs: Time management; successful youth group stories.

Tips: "All areas open; new slant; not preachy."

*INSIGHT INTO CHRISTIAN EDUCATION, Box 23152, Charlotte NC 28212. (704)545-6161. Fax: (704)573-0712. Advent Christian. Millie Griswold, ed. For local church Christian education volunteers. Quarterly mag; 8-12 pgs; circ 2,200. Subscription $3.50. 20% freelance. Query or complete ms. Pays $25, on publication. Articles 600-1,500 wds. Responds in 4 wks. Accepts reprints. Seasonal 6 mos ahead. Free copy.

*THE JOURNAL OF ADVENTIST EDUCATION, 12501 Old Columbia Pike, Silver Springs MD 20904-6600. (301)680-5075. Fax: (301)622-9627. Seventh-day Adventist. Beverly J. Rumble, ed. For Seventh-day teachers teaching in the church's school system, K-University. Bimonthly journal; circ 10,000. Subscription $15.75. Variable freelance. Query; phone query ok. Pays $50-100, on publication, for 1st rts. Articles 2-8 ms pgs. Responds in 2-6 wks. Seasonal 4-6 mos ahead. Kill fee. Accepts reprints. Guidelines; copy $1.

Fillers: Pays $20 for cartoons only.

Special Needs: "All articles in the context of denominational schools (*not* Sunday school tips); professional enrichment and teaching tips for Christian teachers. Need feature articles."

KEY TO CHRISTIAN EDUCATION, 8121 Hamilton Ave., Cincinnati OH 45231. (513)931-4050. Fax: (513)931-0940. Standard Publishing. Lowellette Lauderdale, ed. For teachers and Christian education leaders. Quarterly mag; 16 pgs; circ 67,000. Subscription $7.99. 87% freelance. Complete ms/cover letter; no phone/fax query. Pays .03-.05/wd, on acceptance, for 1st, one-time & reprint rts. Articles 700-1,200 wds (44/yr). Responds in 6-8 wks. Seasonal 3 mos ahead. Accepts reprints. Pays .05-.07/wd for disk copy (must be Microsoft Word). Some sidebars. Guidelines/theme list; copy for 9x12 SAE/3 stamps.

Tips: "Request theme list; if it doesn't fit theme we'll reject it. Write what you know about. Include Social Security number."

** This periodical was #65 on the 1994 Top 50 Plus Christian Publishers list.

*LEAD, CYC, Box 50434, Indianapolis IN 46280. Christian Youth Crusaders of the Wesleyan Church. Tom Arminger, ed. To supply ideas, inspiration, and information to CYC leaders, parents, pastors, and persons interested in children's ministries. Bimonthly newspaper; circ 3,600. Query. Pays .02/wd, on publication. Short articles, feature articles, and short ideas that relate to children's ministries; 500 wds. Not in topical listings.

LEADER, Box 2458, Anderson IN 46018. (317)642-0255. Fax: (317)642-0255x299. Church of God (Anderson, IN). Joseph L. Cookston, ed. For teachers, leaders, volunteer workers in local congregations. Bimonthly mag; 16 pgs; circ 3,500. 85% freelance. Complete ms/cover letter. Pays $10-30, on publication, for one-time rts. Articles 100-800 wds or 5,000-8,000 wds (50/yr); book reviews, 100-300 wds, $10. Responds in 8 wks. Seasonal 3 mos ahead. Considers simultaneous submissions & reprints. Some sidebars. Guidelines; free copy.

Poetry: Buys 10/yr. Free verse, haiku, light verse, traditional; to 30 lines.

Fillers: Buys 12/yr. Anecdotes, cartoons, facts, games, ideas, party ideas, quizzes, prayers, quotes, short humor, word puzzles; 50-300 wds; $10.

Columns/Departments: Youth Ministry; Family; Adult; Children; Recreation; Senior Adult; Pastors; Leadership; and Administration; 100-800 wds.

Tips: "Be sure your article appeals to one of the specific groups listed under columns. Brief and to the point. Include practical information—not major think pieces."

LEADER IN THE CHURCH SCHOOL TODAY, 201 Eighth Ave. N, Nashville TN 37202. (615)749-6292. Fax: (615)749-6512. United Methodist. Marvin W. Cropsey, ed. For pastors and Christian education leaders in the church. Quarterly mag; 64 pgs; circ 10,000. Subscription $14. 25% freelance. Complete ms/cover letter; no phone query. Pays .05/wd, on acceptance, for all or 1st rts. Articles to 1,225 wds (20/yr). Responds in 10-12 wks. Seasonal 14 mos ahead. Guidelines; copy for 9x12 SAE/3 stamps.

Fillers: Buys 4/yr. Cartoons, facts, games, ideas; to 250 wds; $20.

Columns/Departments: Buys 20/yr. Idea Exchange (new reports on specific programs and events that are working on local churches), 300 wds, $20.

*LEVEL C TEACHER - EARLY CHILDHOOD, 6401 The Paseo, Kansas City MO 64131. (816)333-7000. Nazarene. Lynda T. Boardman, ed. Lessons and guidelines for Sunday school teachers of 3-4 yr. olds. Quarterly; 64 pgs; circ 1,800. 5% freelance. Complete ms/cover letter; phone query ok. Pays .035/wd, on publication, for all rts. Considers simultaneous submissions & reprints. Kill fee. No guidelines; copy for 6x9 SAE/2 stamps.

Poetry: Traditional; 4-8 lines; .25/line ($2 min.). Submit max. 5 poems.

Tips: "Mostly assigned. If interested in writing for us, give editor a call. We do accept poems periodically."

LEVEL D TEACHER, 6401 The Paseo, Kansas City MO 64131. (816)333-7000 x2359. Nazarene. Janet R. Reeves, ed. Kindergarten Sunday school teacher's manual. No freelance for now.

LIBRARIAN'S WORLD, 9731 Fox Glen Dr. #6F, Niles IL 60714. (708)296-3964. Fax: (708)296-0754. Evangelical Church Library Assn. Lin Johnson, ed. To assist church librarians in setting up, maintaining, and promoting church libraries and media centers. Quarterly mag; 36-48 pgs; circ 800. Subscription $15. 95% freelance. Complete ms/no cover letter; fax query ok. Pays $20-25/pg, on acceptance, for 1st, one-time or reprint rts. Not copyrighted. Articles 250-1,000 wds (12/yr); book/video/cassette reviews by assignment (send SASE for application form), 75-150 wds, free book. Responds in 4-8 wks. Seasonal 6 mos ahead. Accepts reprints. Prefers disk copy. Sidebars ok. Guidelines; copy for 9x12 SAE/5 stamps (to Box 353, Glen Ellyn IL 60138).

Columns/Departments: Buys 36/yr. Idea Cards (3x5 card ideas on any aspect of running a library), 100 wds; Promoting Your Library (sketch or photo/brief description), to 75 wds; $5.

Special Needs: Church profiles; round-up on best books (in print) on a subject; promotional events and ideas; profiles of church libraries; how-to articles related to running and promoting a church library.

Tips: "Talk to church librarians or get involved in library or reading programs. Most open to articles, card ideas, and promotional ideas."

*LOLLIPOPS, The Magazine for Early Childhood Educators, Good Apple, Inc., Box 299, Carthage IL 62321-0299. (217)357-3981. Fax: (217)357-3987. Donna Borst, ed. Easy-to-use, hands-on, practical teaching ideas and suggestions for early childhood educators. Mag published 5 times/yr; circ 20,000. 20% freelance. Query or complete ms. Pays $10-100, on publication, for all rts. Articles 200-1,000 wds; fiction (for young children) 500-1,200 wds. Seasonal 6 mos ahead. Guidelines (2 stamps); copy for 9x12 SAE/3 stamps.

Poetry: Light verse.

Tips: "Looking for something new and different for teachers of young children; seasonal material."

*LUTHERAN EDUCATION, Concordia University, 7400 Augusta, River Forest IL 60305. (708)209-3073. Lutheran Church-Missouri Synod. Wayne Lucht, ed. For Lutheran educators, many who teach on elementary level in Lutheran parochial schools. Bimonthly journal; 64 pgs; circ 4,000. Query. **PAYS IN COPIES.** Not copyrighted. Articles 1,500-3,000 wds (6/yr). Responds in 4 wks. Seasonal 4 mos ahead. Free guidelines/copy.

Fillers: Anecdotes, facts, ideas, jokes, short humor; 50-100 wds.

#MEMOS, 1445 Boonville Ave., Springfield MO 65802-1894. (417)862-2781. Assemblies of God. Linda Upton, ed. Leadership magazine for girl's program (ages 3-teens), called Missionettes. Quarterly mag; 24 pgs; circ 15,000. Subscription $5.50. 30% freelance. Query or complete ms/cover letter; phone query ok. Pays $10-50, on acceptance, for 1st rts. Articles to 1,200 wds; book reviews 50-75 wds. Responds in 4 wks. Seasonal 1 yr ahead. Accepts reprints. Free guidelines/copy.

Special Needs: Children and divorce; children and self image.

Tips: "Most writers are involved as a coordinator/sponsor in Missionettes. Most open to articles on how to work with children; age-level crafts and projects."

PARISH TEACHER, 426 S. 5th St., Box 1209, Minneapolis MN 55440-1209. (612)330-3423. Fax: (612)330-3455. ELCA/Augsburg Fortress Publishers. Carol A. Burk, ed. Articles and ideas for Lutheran church school teachers. Monthly (11X) newsletter; 16 pgs; circ 50,000. 25% freelance. Complete ms/cover letter; fax query ok. Pays $40-50, on publication, for 1st rts. Not copyrighted. Articles 500-650 wds (24-30/yr); plays 400-800 wds (3-4/yr). Responds in 6-8 wks. Seasonal 3-4 mos ahead. Considers simultaneous submissions & reprints. Prefers disk copy. Guidelines; copy for 9x12 SAE/3 stamps.

Fillers: Buys 80-100 ideas/yr.; 100-200 wds; $15.

Special Needs: Ideas for classroom activities.

Tips: "Most open to ideas or general articles; need to be biblical/theological and very practical."

#PERSPECTIVE, Box 788, Wheaton IL 60189-0788. (708)293-1600 x340. Fax: (708)293-3053. Pioneer Clubs. Rebecca Powell Parat, ed. To help and encourage Pioneer Club leaders (for children ages 2-18). Triannual mag; circ 24,000. Subscription $5. 15% freelance. Query; no phone query. Pays $25-90; on acceptance; for 1st or reprint rts. Articles 500-1,500 wds (8-12/yr). Responds in 6 wks. Seasonal 9 mos ahead. Considers simultaneous query & reprints. Guidelines; copy $1.75/9x12 SAE/6 stamps.

Fillers: Buys 1-2/yr. Games, party ideas.

Columns/Departments: Buys 4-6/yr. Storehouse (ideas for crafts, games, service projects, tips for leaders, etc.); 100-200 wds; $8-15. Complete ms.

Tips: "Most articles done on assignment. We'd like to hear from freelancers who have experience with, or access to, a Pioneer Clubs program or Camp Cherith. They should send samples of their work along with a letter introducing themselves."

#RELIGION TEACHER'S JOURNAL, Box 180, Mystic CT 06355. (203)536-2611. Fax: (203)572-0788. Catholic. Gwen Costello, ed. For volunteer religion teachers who need practical, hands-on information as well as theological background for teaching religion to K through high school. 7X yearly mag; 40 pgs; circ 36,000. Subscription $17.95. 100% freelance. Query or complete ms/cover letter; phone query ok. Pays $5-100, on publication, for 1st rts. Not copyrighted. Articles to 6 pgs (40/yr). Responds in 2-4 wks. Seasonal 3 mos ahead. Guidelines; copy for 9x12 SAE/4 stamps.

Fillers: Buys 20-30/yr. Anecdotes (about teaching), games, ideas, prayers; to 2 pgs; $5-25.

Tips: "Write about projects for children that you have tried."

RESOURCE, 6401 The Paseo, Kansas City MO 64131. (816)333-7000 x2581. Fax: (816)333-1683. Church of the Nazarene. Jeanette D. Gardner, ed. To provide information, training, and inspiration to those who are involved in ministering within the Christian Life and Sunday school department of the local church. Quarterly mag.; circ 12,000. Subscription $6.95. 90% freelance. Complete ms/cover letter; phone/fax query ok. Pays .03-.05/wd; on acceptance; for 1st, one-time, or reprint rts. Not copyrighted. Articles 200-1,000 wds (150/yr); book reviews 300 wds. Responds in 2-10 wks. Seasonal 8 mos ahead. Considers simultaneous query and reprints. Kill fee 3%. Encourages sidebars. Guidelines/theme list; copy for 9x12 SAE/2 stamps.

> **Poetry:** Buys 4/yr. Seasonal or on outreach/Sunday school; to 30 lines; .25/line, $5 minimum. Submit max. 1 poem.

> **Fillers:** Buys 4 cartoons/yr; $10-25.

> **Tips:** "I am very open to short, practical how-tos dealing with any aspect of the Sunday school teacher's job—including communication tips. Articles should be focused, not broad."

SHINING STAR MAGAZINE, Box 399, Carthage IL 62321. (800)435-7234. Mary Tucker, ed. Reproducible Bible activities, games, etc. for K-7th grades. Quarterly mag; 80 pgs; circ 22,000. Subscription $16.95. 100% freelance. Query; phone/fax query ok. Pays $10-50; on publication; for all rts. Articles 120-600 wds (20/yr); fiction 120-600 wds (10/yr). Responds in 4-12 wks. Seasonal 9 mos ahead. Considers simultaneous submissions; serials 4 parts. No disk. No sidebars. Guidelines/theme list; copy for 9x12 SAE/3 stamps.

> **Poetry:** Buys 10/yr. Traditional; 8-36 lines; $10-30. Submit max. 4 poems.

> **Fillers:** Buys 25/yr. Anecdotes, facts, games, ideas, quotes, word puzzles; 100-300 wds; $10-40.

> **Special Needs:** Puzzles, games, crafts for kids.

> **Tips:** "Try out material on children before you consider it ready to submit."

TEACHERS IN FOCUS, 8605 Explorer Dr., Colorado Springs CO 80920. (719)548-4578. Fax: (719)531-3499. Focus on the Family. Charles W. Johnson, ed. To encourage, inform and support Christian teachers in public and private education (K-12). Monthly mag; 16 pgs; circ 34,000. Subscription $20 donation. Estab 1992. 60% freelance. Complete ms/cover letter; phone query ok. Pays $150-300, on acceptance, for 1st rts. Articles 1,200-1,800 wds (20/yr); book reviews (educational resources), $25-50. Responds in 3-4 wks. Seasonal 4 mos ahead. Considers simultaneous submissions & reprints (if no overlap). Kill fee 50%. Guidelines; copy for 9x12 SAE/2 stamps.

> **Fillers:** Buys 50/yr. Humorous classroom anecdotes; 50-150 wds; $25.

> **Tips:** Uses articles of interest to teachers trying to cope in the classroom situation. Education issues.

> ** This periodical was #55 on the 1994 Top 50 Plus Christian Publishers list (#34 in 1993). Also 1994 EPA Award of Merit - Christian Ministry.

#TEACHERS INTERACTION, 3558 S. Jefferson Ave., St. Louis MO 63118-3968. (314)268-1000. Concordia Publishing House/Lutheran Church-Missouri Synod. Jane Haas, ed. A magazine church-school workers grow by. Quarterly mag (newsletter 7X/yr); 32 pgs; circ 20,400. 20% freelance. Complete ms/cover letter. Pays $10-75/printed pg, on publication, for 1st rts. Articles 750-1,500 wds (6/yr); fiction 750-1,200 wds. Responds in 3-6 mos. Seasonal 1 yr ahead. Guidelines; copy $1.

> **Poetry:** 12 lines.

Fillers: Cartoons (14/yr); puzzles; teacher tips, 100 wds (60/yr); $20.

*TEAM, Box 7259, Grand Rapids MI 49510. (616)241-5616. Young Calvinist Federation. Dale Dieleman, ed. Geared to leaders of youth programs, not Sunday school. Quarterly mag; circ 2,000. 10% freelance. Complete ms. Pays $30, on publication, for 1st, simultaneous or reprint rts. Articles 700-2,000 wds (6/yr). Responds in 1 month. Seasonal 6 mos ahead. Kill fee 50%. Considers simultaneous submissions & reprints. Guidelines; copy $1/9x12 SAE/2 stamps.

Fillers: Cartoons, ideas, party ideas, short humor.

Columns/Departments: Street Beat (issues in urban youth ministry).

TODAY'S CATHOLIC TEACHER, 330 Progress Rd., Dayton OH 45449. (513)847-5900. Fax: (513)847-5910. Catholic. Stephen Brittan, ed. Directed to personal and professional concerns of teachers and administrators in K-12 Catholic schools. Monthly mag (8X during school yr); 40-112 pgs; circ 60,000. Subscription $14.99. 80% freelance. Query. Pays $75-275, on publication, for all rts. Articles 600-2,500 wds (30-35/yr). Responds in 3-6 wks. Seasonal 4 mos ahead. Considers simultaneous submissions & some reprints. Kill fee. Prefers disk copy. Sidebars ok. Guidelines; copy $3.

Poetry: Buys 1-2/yr. For teachers or includes material they can use to teach it.

Fillers: Buys 9+/yr. Cartoons, facts; $5-35.

Special Needs: Activity pages teachers can copy and pass out to students to work on. Try to provide classroom-ready material teachers can use to supplement curriculum.

Tips: "Looking for material teachers in grades 3-9 can use to supplement curriculum material. Most open to articles or lesson plans."

VISION MAGAZINE, Box 50025, Pasadena CA 91115. (818)798-1124. Fax: (818)798-2346. Christian Educators Assn., Intl. Judy Turpen, ed. asst. To encourage and equip Christian educators and parents in public education; inserted in Teachers in Focus. Monthly newsletter; 4-8 pgs; circ 5,000. Subscription $25. 70% freelance. Complete ms/cover letter; no phone query; fax query ok. Pays $25, on publication, for 1st rts. Articles 50-1,000 wds (1-3/yr); book reviews, 75-100 wds. Responds in 3-6 wks. Seasonal 3-6 mos ahead. Considers simultaneous submissions & reprints. Sidebars ok. Guidelines/theme list; copy for 9x12 SAE/3-4 stamps.

Poetry: Accepts 2-6/yr. Free verse, haiku, light verse, traditional; 4-40 lines; no payment.

Fillers: Accepts 2-6/yr. Anecdotes, cartoons, facts, ideas, newsbreaks, prose, prayers, quotes; 100 wds; no payment.

Tips: "Sharp, crisp writing, to the point; most articles are preferred written by those either in the field of education or very knowledgeable about issues of education."

YOUTH AND CHRISTIAN EDUCATION LEADERSHIP, 1080 Montgomery Ave., Cleveland TN 37311. (615)478-7599. Fax: (615)478-7521. Pentecostal Church of God/Pathway Press. Lance Colkmire, ed. For church workers. Quarterly mag; 32 pgs; circ 9,325. Subscription $7. 15% freelance. Complete ms/cover letter; no phone query. Pays $25-50; on acceptance; for 1st, one-time, simultaneous or reprint rts. Articles 350-1,200 wds (10/yr). Responds in 4 wks. Seasonal 6 mos ahead. Considers simultaneous submissions & reprints. Guidelines; copy $1/9x12 SAE.

Columns/Departments: Sunday school columns for teachers of various age groups; Reaching Out; Music Ministry; The Pastor and C.E.; $25-50.

Special Needs: Articles on children's ministry and Sunday school.

THE YOUTH LEADER, 1445 Boonville Ave., Springfield MO 65802. (417)862-2781 x4041. Fax: (417)862-1693. Assemblies of God. Rich Percifield, ed.; submit to Chuck Goldberg, mng ed. To provide help for people working with teenagers. Mag published 8 times/yr; 24 pgs; circ 2,800. Subscription $14.95. 75% freelance. Query or complete ms/cover letter; no phone query. Pays .04/wd, on publication, for 1st rts. Articles 1,000-2,500 wds. Responds in 8 wks. Seasonal 3 mos ahead. Considers simultaneous submissions & reprints. Guidelines/theme list; copy for 9x12 SAE/3 stamps.

Fillers: Youth facts, newsbreaks, quotes; sermon outlines, 25-250 wds.

Columns/Departments: Brainstorms (ideas for games, fund-raisers, crowd breakers, etc.), 100-250 wds; For Starters (anecdotes, sermon starters, etc.), 100-250 wds; Program Plans, 500-750 wds; Spotlight (interview/profile of successful youth leader), 1,000-2,000 wds.

Tips: "Keep material focused on practice of youth ministry—not theoretical but something they can actually use and/or apply."

DAILY DEVOTIONAL MARKETS

Due to the nature of the daily devotional market, the following market listings will include only the name, address, phone number (if available) and editor's name. Because most of these markets assign all material, they do not wish to be listed in the usual way, if at all.

If you are interested in writing daily devotionals, send to the following markets for guidelines and sample copies, write up sample devotionals to fit each one's particular format, and send to the editor with a request for an assignment. **DO NOT** submit any other type of material to these markets unless indicated.

CHRIST IN OUR HOME, 426 S. 5th St., Box 1209, Minneapolis MN 55440-1209. (612)330-3423. Carol A. Burk, ed. Pays $15/devotion.

*COME YE APART, Box 419527, Kansas City MO 64131. Paul Martin, ed.

DAILY DEVOTIONS FOR THE DEAF, RR 2 Box 26, Council Bluffs IA 51503-9500. (712)322-5493. Duane King, ed. Photos. **NO PAYMENT.**

*DEVOTIONS, 8121 Hamilton Ave., Cincinnati OH 45231. (513)931-4050. Eileen Wilmoth, ed. No devotions. Buys photos.

*FORWARD DAY BY DAY, 412 Sycamore St., Cincinnati OH 45202. (513)721-6659. Charles H. Long, ed. Pays honorarium.

THE HOME ALTAR, Meditations for Families with Young Children, 426 S. 5th St., Box 1209, Minneapolis MN 55440-1209. (612)330-3423. Carol A. Burk, ed. 64 pgs. Pays $15/devotion.

*LIGHT FROM THE WORD, Box 50434, Indianapolis IN 46250-0434. (317)595-4144. Carl W. Pierce, sr. ed.

#LIVING FAITH, 10300 Watson Rd., St. Louis MO 63127. (314)821-1363. Fax: (314)821-9031. Catholic. Circ 410,000. James E. Adams, ed.

MOMENTS WITH GOD, 1 S. 210 Summit Ave., Oakbrook Terrace IL 60181-3994. (708)495-2000. Fax: (708)495-3301. Dorothy Ganoung, ed. Suitable for family devotions. **NO PAYMENT.**

PATHWAYS TO GOD, Box 2499, Anderson IN 46018-2499. (317)644-7721x245. Kathleen Buehler, mng. ed. Pays $15/devotion.

*THE QUIET HOUR, 850 N. Grove Ave., Elgin IL 60120. (708)741-0800. Gary Wilde, ed. Pays $15. Send resume and list of credits, rather than a sample.

REJOICE!, 836 Amidon, Wichita KS 67203. Mennonite. Changing editors. Pays $110 for 7-day assigned meditations. Doesn't send samples. Don't apply for assignment unless you are familiar with the publication and Anabaptist theology.

THE SECRET PLACE, Box 851, Valley Forge PA 19482-0851. (610)768-2240. Kathleen Hayes, ed. Prefers to see completed devotionals. Uses poetry and photos. 64 pgs. Pays $15.

THE UPPER ROOM, P.O. Box 189, Nashville TN 38202-0189. (615)340-7252. Mary Lou Redding, mng. ed. Pays $15 per 250-word devotional. 72 pgs. Note: This publication DOES accept freelance submissions and does not make assignments. Send devotionals up to 250 wds. Buys photos only of art work. Guidelines; copy for 4x6 SAE/2 stamps.

THE WORD IN SEASON, 426 S. 5th St., Box 1209, Minneapolis MN 55440-1209. (612)330-3423. Carol A. Burk, ed. 96 pgs. Pays $15/devotion.

MISSIONS MARKETS

#AMERICAN HORIZON, 1445 Boonville Ave., Springfield MO 65802-1894. (417)862-2781. Fax: (417)863-7276. Assemblies of God. Traci L. Countryman, ed. Denominational magazine of home missions/mostly on assignment. Bimonthly mag; 20 pgs; circ 29,000. Free to contributors. 50% freelance. Estab 1992. Query; phone query ok. Pay .03/wd, on publication, for 1st rts. Articles 700-1,200 wds (17/yr). Responds in 2-3 wks. Seasonal 5 mos ahead. Considers simultaneous submissions & reprints. Free guidelines/copy.

AREOPAGUS MAGAZINE, P.O. Box 33, Shatin, New Territories, Hong Kong. (852)691-1904. Fax: (852)695-9885. Tao Fong Shan Christian Centre. John G. LeMond, ed. Provides a forum for dialogue between the good news of Jesus Christ and people of faith both in major world religions and new religious movements. Quarterly mag; 50 pgs; circ 1,000. Subscription $24/US. 75% freelance. Query; phone query ok. Pays $25-50, on publication, for 1st rts. Articles 1,000-5,000 wds (20/yr); book reviews, 500-750 wds, $25. Responds in 6-12 wks. Seasonal 3 mos ahead. Considers simultaneous submissions & reprints. Kill fee 50%. Guidelines; copy $4.

> **Columns/Departments:** Query.
>
> **Special Needs:** Interreligious dialogue.
>
> **Tips:** "We look for compassionate, direct, and unselfconscious prose that reflects a writer who is firmly rooted in his/her own tradition but is unafraid to encounter other religions."

CATHOLIC NEAR EAST, 1011 First Ave., New York NY 10022-4195. (212)826-1480. Fax: (212)838-1344. Catholic. Michael La Civita, ed. Interest in cultural, religious, human rights development in Middle East, NE Africa, India and Eastern Europe. Bimonthly mag; 32 pgs; circ 100,000. Subscription $10. 60% freelance. Query/clips; phone query ok. Pays .20/wd, on publication, for 1st rts. Articles 1,000-2,500 wds (15/yr). Responds in 4 wks. Seasonal 4 mos ahead. Kill fee. Sidebars ok. Guidelines; copy for 7x10 SAE/2 stamps.

> **Tips:** "We strive to educate our readers about the culture, faith, history, issues and people who form the Eastern Christian churches. Material should not be academic."

CHILDLIFE, 919 W. Huntington Dr., Monrovia CA 91016. (818)357-7979. Fax: (818)357-0915. World Vision, Inc. Rebecca Russell, mng. ed. Child/family life in poverty areas, disaster areas of the Third World; success stories of sponsored children. Quarterly mag; 16 pgs; circ 250,765. 0% freelance. Query only. Pays $100-350 for assigned (otherwise **PAYS IN COPIES**), on acceptance, for 1st rts. Articles 800-2,800 wds (50/yr). Seasonal 6-7 mos ahead. Kill fee. Guidelines; copy for 9x12 SAE/2 stamps.

> **Tips:** "Send a letter with resume of past work experience. Most open to personality profiles, testimonies of children, families whose lives have been enriched through World Vision child spon-

sorship. Third World 'issue' pieces dealing with children and families, i.e., hunger, poverty, child exploitation, etc."

COMPASSION MAGAZINE, Box 7000, Colorado Springs CO 80933. (719)594-9900. Fax: (719)536-9618. Compassion Intl. Jennifer L. Ball, pub. mng. Covering Compassion's worldwide Christian child development activities. Quarterly mag; 24 pgs; circ 140,000. Subscription free to donors. 0% freelance, but open. Complete ms/cover letter; phone query ok. Pay negotiable, on publication, for all rts (releases reprint rts). Articles 800-3,000 wds. Responds in 2-4 wks. Seasonal 3 mos ahead. Prefers disk copy. Sidebars ok. No guidelines; theme list; copy for 9x12 SAE/3 stamps. Not in topical listings.

> **Tips:** "Articles for consideration would need to incorporate our work around the world. Interested writers should call for specific details."

#HEARTBEAT, Box 5002, Antioch TN 37011-5002. (615)731-6812. Fax: (615)731-5345. Free Will Baptist. Don Robirds, ed. To inform and challenge church members with mission needs. Bimonthly mag; 16 pgs; circ 43,700. Subscription free. 3% freelance. Query. Pays .03/wd, on publication, for one-time rts. Articles 1,000 wds (2/yr). Responds in 4-8 wks. Accepts reprints. Guidelines; free copy.

#IMPACT, Box 5, Wheaton IL 60189. (708)260-3800. Fax: (708)665-1418. Conservative Baptist Foreign Mission Society. Art Heerwagen, ed. To inform, stimulate, and educate individuals and churches concerning activities of CBMFS missionaries and Christian nationals. Quarterly mag; circ 42,000. Subscription $4.50. 10% freelance. Query. Pays $50-150, by arrangement, for all rts. Articles 650-1,500 wds. Responds in 2-4 wks. Seasonal 6 mos ahead. Free guidelines/copy.

INTERNATIONAL JOURNAL OF FRONTIER MISSIONS, 7665 Wenda Way, El Paso TX 79915. (915)779-5655. Fax: (915)778-6440. Hans Weerstra, ed. Dedicated to frontier missions in places where there are no missionaries. Quarterly journal; circ 600. Subscription $15. 100% freelance. Complete ms/cover letter; phone query ok. **NO PAYMENT**, for one-time rts. Articles 6-7 pgs. Seasonal 3 mos ahead. Considers simultaneous submissions & reprints. Guidelines/theme list; copy $1/ 9x12 SAE/$1.05 postage.

> **Special Needs:** Contextualization, church in missions, comparative religions, training for missions, trends for missions, biblical basis for missions.

#LATIN AMERICA EVANGELIST, Box 52-7900, Miami FL 33152. (305)884-8400. Fax: (305)885-8649. Latin America Mission. John D. Maust, ed. To present God's work through the churches and missionaries in Latin America. Quarterly mag; 22 pgs; circ 22,000. Subscription $6. 10% freelance. Query only. Pays variable rates, on publication, for 1st rts. Articles 1,000 wds. Reporting time varies. Considers simultaneous submissions. Not in topical listings. No guidelines; free copy.

> **Tips:** "Looking for news and analysis of the religious climate and social conditions in Latin America."

*THE MAP INTERNATIONAL REPORT, MAP International, Box 50, Brunswick GA 31521-5000. (912)265-6010. Phil Craven, ed. Deals with health care in developing countries. Bimonthly newsletter; 8-12 pgs; circ 13,500. 5% freelance. Prefers query. **NO MENTION OF PAYMENT.** Articles 500 wds. Seasonal 4 mos ahead. Not in topical listings. Free guidelines/theme list/copy.

+MESSAGE OF THE CROSS, 6820 Auto Club Rd., Minneapolis MN 55478. (612)829-2492. Fax: (612)829-2953. Bethany Fellowship, Inc. George Foster, ed. Deeper life and Christian missions for a general Christian public. Quarterly mag; 32 pgs; circ 9,000. 20% freelance. Complete ms/cover letter; fax query ok. Pays $20-35, on publication, for first or reprint rts. Articles (8/yr). Responds in 4 wks. Seasonal 6 mos ahead. Accepts reprints. No sidebars. No guidelines; copy for 6x9 SAE.

MISSIOLOGY, Asbury Theological Seminary, Wilmore KY 40390. (606)858-2215. Fax: (606)858-2375. American Society of Missiology. Darrell L. Whiteman, ed. A professional organization for mission studies. Quarterly journal; 128 pgs; circ 2,000. Subscription $18. 80% freelance. Complete ms/cover letter; phone/fax query ok. **PAYS 20 COPIES**, for all & reprint rts. Articles to 20 typed pgs (20-25/yr); book reviews, 200 wds. Responds in 2-6 wks. Guidelines; copy for 7x10 SAE.

>   **Tips:** "Whole journal is open to freelancers as long as they write from a missiological perspective and have adequate documentation."

*NEW WORLD OUTLOOK, 475 Riverside Dr., Room 1351, New York NY 10115. (212)870-3765. Fax: (212)870-3940. United Methodist. Alma Graham, ed. or Christie House, assoc. ed. Denominational missions. Bimonthly mag; 48 pgs; circ 33,000. Subscription $12. 1% freelance. Query; phone query ok. Pays $150-250, on publication, for all rts. Articles 500-2,000 wds; book reviews 200-500 wds. No guaranteed response time. Seasonal 5 mos ahead. Kill fee 50%. Guidelines; copy $2.50/9x12 SASE.

>   **Poetry:** Buys 1-2/yr. Free verse; no more than a pg. Pay varies. Submit max. 3 poems.
>
>   **Special Needs:** Ecumenical mission study issues.
>
>   **Tips:** "Ask for a list of United Methodist mission workers and projects in your area. Investigate them, propose a story, and consult with the editors before writing. Most open to articles and/or photos of U.S. or foreign mission sites visited as a stringer, after consultation with the editor."

#THE OBLATE WORLD AND VOICE OF HOPE, Box 680, 486 Chandler St., Tewksbury MA 01876. (508)851-7258. Missionary Society of the Oblate Fathers of Texas. Rev. Thomas J. Reddy, OMI, ed. Missions publication for Catholic clergy and laity. Bimonthly newspaper; circ 25,000. Pays .01-.02/wd, on acceptance. Missions stories 1,000-1,600 wds. Responds in 3 wks. Not in topical listings. Copy.

+PARTNERS, 919 W. Huntington Dr., Monrovia CA 91016. (818)357-1111 x3420. Fax: (818)357-0915. World Vision. Rebecca Russell, mng. ed.; submit to Jane Sutton, asst. ed. To educate and affirm donors to World Vision. Quarterly mag; 16 pgs; circ 161,000. Free to donors. 0-1% freelance. Query; phone/fax query ok. Pays $100-500 or .20/wd, on acceptance, for 1st rts. Articles 600-1,400 wds (3/yr). Responds in 6-8 wks. Seasonal 10 mos ahead. Prefers disk copy. Kill fee 70%. Sidebars ok. Guidelines; copy for 9x12 SAE/$1 postage.

>   **Tips:** Call or query editors.

P.I.M.E. WORLD, 17330 Quincy St., Detroit MI 48221-2765. (313)342-4066. Fax: (313)342-6816. Pontifical Inst. for Foreign Missions/Catholic. Paul Witte, mng. ed. For those interested in and supportive of foreign missions. Monthly (10X) mag; 16 pgs; circ 30,000. Subscription $5. 15% freelance. Complete ms/cover letter; no phone query. Pays .06/wd, on publication, for one-time rts. Photos $5-10. Not copyrighted. Articles 800-1,200 wds (10/yr). Responds in 2-4 wks. Considers simultaneous submissions & reprints. Sidebars ok. Guidelines; copy for 9x12 SAE/2 stamps.

>   **Tips:** "Most open to popular-style writing about missionaries, their work, the countries they work in. Concentrate on interesting details of mission life and what motivates missionaries, lay and clerical. Send feature articles about missionaries."

*THE RAILROAD EVANGELIST, P.O. Box 3846, Vancouver WA 98662. (206)699-7208. Joe Spooner, ed. For railroad and transportation employees and their families. Quarterly mag; circ 2,500. Subscription $6. 100% freelance. Complete ms/no cover letter; phone query ok. **NO PAYMENT**. Articles 100-700 wds (10-15/yr). Seasonal 4 months ahead. Considers simultaneous submissions & reprints. Guidelines; copy for 9x12 SAE/2 stamps.

>   **Poetry:** Accepts 4-8/yr. Traditional, any length. Send any number.

Fillers: Accepts many. Anecdotes, cartoons, quotes; to 100 wds.

Tips: "We need 400-700 word salvation testimonies."

*URBAN MISSION, Box 27009, Philadelphia PA 19118. (215)887-5511. Fax: (215)884-5404. Westminster Theological Seminary. H.M. Conn, ed. Dedicated to advancement of Christ in cities throughout the world. Quarterly journal; circ 1,300. Subscription $16. 100% freelance. Complete ms/cover letter; no phone query. **PAYS 3 COPIES.** Articles 2,100-6,000 wds (40/yr). Responds in 1-2 wks. Accepts reprints. No guidelines/copy.

WHEREVER, Box 969, Wheaton IL 60189. (708)653-5300. Fax: (708)653-1826. The Evangelical Alliance Mission/interdenominational. Dana Felmly, ed. coord. For yg. adults interested in overseas missions, short or long term. Mag. published 3X/yr; 16 pgs; circ 7,000. Free subscription. 80% freelance. Query; no phone query. Pays $75-150, on publication, for all or one-time rts. Articles 500-1,500 wds (24/yr). Responds in 2-4 wks. Sidebars ok. Guidelines/theme list; copy for 9x12 SAE/3 stamps.

> **Tips:** "Write and ask to be put on mailing list for themes, then query. No first-mission-trip stories unless it has dramatic conflict. You need some kind of experience with overseas missions."

*WORLD CHRISTIAN, Box 25, Colfax WA 99111. Independent. Submit to Gordon Aeschliman, ed.; June Mears, mng. ed. Missions slant. Monthly mag; circ 40,000. Query. **NO PAYMENT FOR NOW.** Responds in 6-8 wks. Accepts reprints. Articles 1,500-4,500 wds. Considers simultaneous query. Guidelines/theme list; copy for SASE.

WORLD VISION MAGAZINE, 919 W. Huntington Dr., Monrovia CA 91016. (818)357-7979. Fax: (818)357-0915. World Vision Inc. Terry Madison, ed. Relevant issues pertaining to the U.S. and the Third World, as well as poverty. Bimonthly mag; 24 pgs; circ 76,770. Subscription free. 10% freelance. Query; phone/fax query ok. Pays $100-500 or .20/wd, on acceptance, for 1st rts. Articles 1,200-2,000 wds (10-15/yr). Responds in 6-8 wks. Seasonal 6-7 mos ahead. Accepts reprints. Kill fee 2%. Sidebars ok. Guidelines/theme list; copy for 9x12 SAE/2 stamps.

> **Columns/Departments:** Buys 6/yr. Turning Points (personal experience relating to poor), 450-700 wds; .20/wd.

> **Tips:** "Send us copies of anything written previously. Have experience in nonfiction writing for publications. Be fairly knowledgeable about the Third World. To break in call an editor—Terry Madison, Bruce Brander or Larry Wilson."

> ****** This periodical was #61 on the 1994 Top 50 Plus Christian Publishers list (#23 in 1993). Also 1994 EPA Award of Merit - Missionary.

#WORLDWIDE CHALLENGE, 100 Sunport Ln., Dept. 1600, Orlando FL 32809. (407)826-2390. Fax: (407)826-2374. Campus Crusade for Christ. Diane McDougall, ed; submit to Tisha Gentry, asst. ed. For financial supporters of Campus Crusade. Bimonthly mag; 52 pgs; circ 91,500. Subscription $12.95. 10% freelance. Query/clips; no phone query. Pays $25-50 (.10/wd + $100 for assigned), on acceptance, for 1st rts. Articles 300-1,200 wds. Responds in 2-4 wks. Seasonal 4-5 mos ahead. Accepts reprints. Kill fee. Guidelines; copy $2/9x12 SAE/5 stamps.

> **Columns/Departments:** Buys 2-5/yr. Upfront (personal experience/commentary); 300-1,000 wds. Most open area. People (with unique ministry of evangelism or discipleship), 1,900 wds; History's Hero, 1,350 wds. Complete ms.

> **Special Needs:** News reports.

> **Tips:** "Give the human face behind a topic or story. Show how the topic relates to evangelism and/or discipleship."

** This periodical was #35 on the 1994 Top 50 Plus Christian Publishers list. Also 1994 EPA Award of Merit - Organizational.

MUSIC MARKETS

*THE CHURCH MUSICIAN, 127 9th Ave. N., Nashville TN 37234. (615)251-2961. Southern Baptist. William M. Anderson, ed. For church music leaders. Quarterly; 16 pages (music), 98 pgs total; circ 16,000. 20% freelance. Complete ms. Pays to .055/wd, on acceptance, for all rts. Articles & fiction (related to church music), to 1,300 wds. Responds in 2 mos. Accepts reprints (pays 50%). Copy for 9x12 SAE/3 stamps.

> **Poetry:** Church music slant/inspirational, 8-24 lines; $5-15.
> **Fillers:** Short humor (with a musical slant); $5-15.
> **Note:** Planning to change format.

*THE CHURCH MUSIC REPORT/CHURCH MUSIC WORLD, Box 1179, Grapevine TX 76099. (817)488-0141. Bill Rayborn, ed. For church music leaders. Monthly newsletter; 8-12 pgs. Ideas, tips, how-tos, and the like. Articles; interviews.

CHURCH PIANIST/SAB CHOIR/THE CHOIR HERALD, Box 268, Alcoa TN 37701. (615)982-5669. Now a division of The Lorenz Corp. Hugh S. Livingston Jr., ed. Each of these music magazines has one page devoted to articles that deal with problems/solutions of choirs and accompanists. Bimonthly mags; 36-52 pgs; circ 25,000. 45% freelance. Complete ms/cover letter; no phone query. Pay $15-150, on publication, for all rts. Articles 250-1,250 wds (10-20/yr). Seasonal 1 yr ahead. Responds in 3-6 wks. Guidelines; copy for 9x12 SAE/3 stamps.

> **Poetry:** Accepts 25/yr. Free verse, light verse, traditional, or poetry suitable for song lyrics; $10. Submit max. 5 poems.
> **Fillers:** Accepts 5-10/yr. Anecdotes, cartoons.
> **Special Needs:** Choir experiences; pianist/organist articles.
> **Tips:** "Best approach is from direct experience in music with the small church."

*CREATOR MAGAZINE, 4631 Cutwater Ln., Hilliard OH 43026. (614)777-7774. Marshall Sanders, pub. For interdenominational music ministry; promoting quality, diverse music programs in the church. Bimonthly mag; 52 pgs; circ 5,500. 20% freelance. Query or complete ms/cover letter. Pays $35-60, on publication, for negotiable rts. Articles 1,000-4,000 wds (6-8/yr). Responds in 3-5 mos. Seasonal 6 mos ahead. Considers simultaneous submissions. Guidelines; copy for 9x12 SAE/6 stamps.

> **Fillers:** Buys 12-15/yr. Cartoons, short humor; 200-800 wds; $10-30.
> **Special Needs:** Music; the arts in church.

*GLORY SONGS, 127 9th Ave. N, Nashville TN 37234. (615)251-2913. Southern Baptist. Jere V. Adams, ed. Easy choral music for church choirs; practical how-to articles for small church music programs. Quarterly mag; 26 pgs; circ 85,000. 100% freelance. Complete ms. Pays .055/wd, on acceptance, for 1st rts. Articles 550-1,000 wds (6-7/yr). Responds in 2-4 wks. Seasonal 1 yr ahead. Considers simultaneous submissions & reprints. Guidelines; free copy.

> **Poetry:** Buys 2-3/yr. Free verse, traditional.
> **Fillers:** Cartoons, ideas, party ideas, musical quizzes, short humor.
> **Special Needs:** Vocal techniques, choir etiquette, mission/outreach ideas, music training, etc.

THE HYMN, Box 30854, Texas Christian University, Ft. Worth TX 76129. (817)921-7608. Fax: (817)921-7333. Hymn Society in the U.S. & Canada. W. Thomas Smith, exec. dir.; articles to David W. Music. For church musicians, hymnologists, scholars; articles related to hymnology. Quarterly journal; 60 pgs; circ 3,500. Subscription $40. 100% freelance. Complete ms/cover letter; phone or fax query ok. **NO PAYMENT** for all rts. Articles to 1,000 wds (10/yr); book & music reviews to 500 wds. Responds in 3 wks. Seasonal 3 mos ahead. Considers simultaneous submissions & reprints. Guidelines; free copy.

> **Poetry:** Hymn poetry.

> **Special Needs:** Hymns and articles on history of hymns.

*THE MUSIC LEADER, 127 9th Ave. N., Nashville TN 37234. (615)251-2513. Southern Baptist. Anne Trudel, coordinating ed. How-to material for leaders of preschool and children's choirs. Quarterly mag; 92 pgs; circ 35,000. 5% freelance. Query or complete ms/cover letter. Pays .055/wd, on acceptance, for all or one-time rts. Articles 75-80 lines, or 150-170 lines typed 40 characters/line; 250 lines max. Seasonal dramas, 7-8 pgs. Responds in 1-2 mos. Guidelines; copy for 9x12 SASE.

> **Poetry:** For choir leaders.

*MUSIC MAKERS, 127 9th Ave. N., Nashville TN 37234. (615)251-2961. Southern Baptist. Darrell Billingsley, ed. For children ages 6-11. Quarterly mag; circ 105,000. Pays .06/wd, on acceptance, for all rts. Articles & fiction 250-500 wds. Responds in 4 wks. Not in topical listings. Guidelines/copy.

*MUSIC TIME, 127 9th Ave. N., Nashville TN 37234. (615)251-2000. Southern Baptist. Derrell Billingsley, literary design ed. For 4 & 5 yr olds; directly related to unit material found in **The Music Leader.** Quarterly mag; circ 60,000. Complete ms. Pays .05/wd for stories. Pays $9-12, on acceptance, for all rts. Stories for 4 & 5 yr olds. Responds in 15-30 days. Not in topical listings. Guidelines; free copy.

> **Poetry:** 1-7 lines; $5-9.

+QUEST, P.O. Box 14804, Columbus OH 43214. Rick Welke, ed. Geared to 16-30 year olds and radio personnel. Monthly newsletter. Estab 1995. Query; fax query ok. **PAYS A SUBSCRIPTION.** Articles 100-500 wds (4/yr); fiction, 150-750 wds (4/yr); book/music reviews, 30-75 wds. Seasonal 3 mos ahead. Considers simultaneous submissions & reprints. No disks. No guidelines but has theme list; copy for #10 SAE/2 stamps.

> **Poetry:** Accepts 12/yr. Any type, 4-24 lines. Submit max. 4 poems.

> **Fillers:** Accepts 36/yr. Cartoons, facts, jokes, quizzes, quotes, short humor, word puzzles.

> **Columns/Departments:** Artist Action (any specific artist information).

> **Special Needs:** Organizational pieces; new music releases/photos; artist's concert schedules; radio station playlists.

> **Tips:** "Submit between the 10th and 20th of each month for best review."

*RENAISSANCE, The Resource Publication for the Christian Musician, Box 2134, Lynnwood WA 98036. Renaissance Artists Group/Christian Artists International. Nathan L. Csakany, ed. Issues of interest to Christian musicians. Not in topical listings. Copy.

+SCORE, 2201 Murfreesboro Rd. #C-206, Nashville TN 37229. (615)360-9444. Fax: (615)361-1274. America's Leading Gospel News Publication. Teresa Hairston, pub. All about Gospel music and news of the African-American church community. Bimonthly mag; 68+ pgs; circ 30,000. Subscription $20. 50% freelance. Query/clips. Negotiable payment, for all rts. Seasonal 2.5 mos ahead. Considers simultaneous submissions & reprints. Prefers disk copy. Sidebars ok. No guidelines; copy $3.50/9x12 SAE/8 stamps.

> **Poetry:** Accepts.

> **Tips:** "Most open to specific articles of interest that fall in line with the direct target audience."

*THE SENIOR MUSICIAN, 127 9th Ave. N, Nashville TN 37234. (615)251-2913. Southern Baptist. Jere V. Adams, ed. For music directors and choir members of senior adult choirs. Quarterly mag; 26 pgs; circ 32,000. 100% freelance. Complete ms. Pays .055/wd, on acceptance, for 1st rts. Articles 500-900 wds (6-7/yr). Responds in 2-4 wks. Seasonal 1 yr ahead. Some simultaneous submissions; reprints. Guidelines; free copy.

> **Poetry:** Buys 2-3/yr. Traditional.
>
> **Fillers:** Buys 3-4/yr. Cartoons, ideas, party ideas, musical quizzes, short humor.
>
> **Special Needs:** Senior adult's testimonials, inspirational stories, personal growth and development, music training, and choir projects.
>
> **Tips:** "All topics must relate to senior adult musicians and senior choirs—anything else will be returned."

#TRADITION, Box 438, Walnut IA 51577. (712)366-1136. Prairie Press Ltd. Robert Everhart, ed. Devoted to acoustic traditional music with an over-35 audience. Bimonthly mag; circ 2,500. 20% freelance. Query. Pays $10-15, on publication, for one-time rts. Not copyrighted. Articles 800-1,200 wds (2/yr). Responds in 1 month. Seasonal 6 mos ahead. Considers simultaneous query & reprints. Copy $1.

> **Poetry:** Buys 4/yr. Free verse, traditional; 5-20 lines; $2-5. Submit max. 2 poems.
>
> **Fillers:** Buys 5/yr. Anecdotes, clippings, jokes; 15-50 wds; $5-10.
>
> **Special Needs:** Articles on gospel music.

*YOUNG MUSICIANS, 127 9th Ave. N., Nashville TN 37234. (615)251-2944. Southern Baptist. Clinton Flowers, ed. For children 9-11 yrs. Quarterly mag.; 52 pgs; circ 85,000. Query. Pays .05/wd, on acceptance, for 1st rts. Music and music-related articles, stories 400-800 wds. Responds in 1 mo. Free guidelines/copy.

> **Fillers:** Prose, word puzzles (music-related).

PASTOR/LEADERSHIP MARKETS

#ADVANCE, 1445 Boonville Ave., Springfield MO 65802. (417)862-2781 x4095. Fax: (417)862-0416. Assemblies of God. Harris Jansen, ed. Directed to denominational ministers and church leaders. Monthly mag; 40-44 pgs; circ 30,250. Subscription $14.75. 5% freelance. Complete ms/cover letter. Pays to .06/wd, on acceptance, for 1st or reprint rts. Articles 1,000-1,500 wds. Responds in 2 mos. Seasonal 6-8 mos ahead. Accepts reprints. Guidelines; copy for SAE/1 stamp.

> **Special Needs:** Accepts sermon ideas; sermon illustrations; articles on preaching, doctrine, practice, etc.; and how-to-do-it features (for ministers and leaders).

ARTPLUS (formerly ART+ REPRO RESOURCE), For Christian Communicators, Box 4710, Sarasota FL 34230-4710. (813)955-2950. Fax: (813)955-5723. Mission Media Inc. Wayne Hepburn, pub. Reproducible illustrations and verse for church bulletins and newsletters. Quarterly mag; 26 pgs; circ 3,000. Subscription $49. 100% freelance. Complete ms/no cover letter; phone/fax query ok. Pays $5-50, on acceptance, for all rts only. Responds in 6-8 wks. Seasonal 6 mos ahead. Considers simultaneous submissions. Prefers disk copy in ASCII only (pays 20% extra). Guidelines/theme list; copy for 9x12 SAE/4 stamps.

> **Poetry:** Buys 12-20/yr. Traditional (no unrhymed); to 16 lines; $5-15. Submit max. 10 poems.
>
> **Fillers:** Buys 150+/yr. Anecdotes, cartoons, facts, jokes, prayers, quotes, short humor; 5-50 wds; $5-25.

Tips: "We are seasonally oriented; more open to art than writing. Target our audience—churched adults and kids."

#THE BETHANY CHOICE, 901 Eastern Ave. NE, Grand Rapids MI 49503-1295. (616)459-6273. Fax: (616)459-0215. Bethany Christian Services. Kathy Adams, mng ed. For professionals in medicine, law, and counseling who deal with pregnancy and adoption issues, including infertility. Triannual newsletter; circ 7,300. Subscription free. 20% freelance. Query; no phone query. Pays $15-60, on acceptance, for one-time rts. Articles 250-1,250 wds (4-6/yr); book reviews, $15. Responds in 2-4 wks. Accepts reprints. Guidelines/theme list; copy $1/6x9 SAE.

Tips: Keep professional audience in mind. Most open to personal experience with out-of-wedlock pregnancy, abortion, adoption (as birth parent); infertility and adoption (as adoptive parent).

+CATECHUMENATE: A JOURNAL OF CHRISTIAN INITIATION, 1800 N. Hermitage Ave., Chicago IL 60622-1101. (312)486-8970. Fax: (800)933-7094. Catholic. Victoria M. Tufano, ed. For clergy and laity who work with those who are planning to become Catholic. Bimonthly jour; 48 pgs; circ 5,600. Subscription $20. Complete ms/cover letter; phone/fax query ok. Pays $100-250, on publication, for all rts (poetry, one-time rts). Articles 1,500-3,000 wds (10/yr). Responds in 2-6 wks. Considers simultaneous submissions. Kill fee. No sidebars. Guidelines; copy for 6x9 SAE/4 stamps.

Poetry: Buys 6/yr. Free verse, traditional; 5-20 lines; $75. Submit max. 5 poems.

Columns/Departments: Buys 12/yr. Sunday Word (scripture reflection on Sunday readings, aimed at catechumers); 450 wds; $200-250. Query for assignment.

Special Needs: Christian initiation; reconciliation.

Tips: "It helps if the writer has experience working with Christian initiation. Approach is that this is something we are all learning together through experience and scholarship."

#CHICAGO STUDIES, Box 665, Mundelein IL 60060. (708)566-1462. Catholic. Rev. George J. Dyer, ed. For the continuing theological development of priests and other religious educators. Triannual journal; circ 6,100. Subscription $17.50. 50% freelance. Complete ms. Pays $35-100, on acceptance, for all rts. Articles 3,000-4,000 wds (30/yr). Responds in 2 mos. Seasonal 6 mos ahead. Guidelines; copy $5.

Tips: "Include cover letter with information about yourself."

CHRISTIAN CENTURY, 407 S. Dearborn St., Chicago IL 60605. (312)427-5380. Fax: (312)427-1302. Nondenominational. David Heim, mng. ed. For ministers, educators and church leaders interested in events and theological issues of concern to the ecumenical church. Magazine published 38X/yr; 32 pgs; circ 30,000. Subscription $35. 90% freelance. Query; phone/fax query ok. Pays $75-150 (to $200 for fiction), on publication, for all rts. Articles 1,500-3,000 wds (90/yr); fiction 2,000-3,000 wds (3/yr); book/music reviews, $75. Responds in 1-4 wks. Seasonal 6 mos ahead. Kill fee. Rarely uses sidebars. Guidelines; copy $2.

Poetry: Dean Peerman. Buys 50/yr. Any type (religious but not sentimental); 3-25 lines; $20. Submit max. 10 poems.

Fillers: Buys 20 cartoons/yr.

Tips: Looking for more fiction. "Know our audience—sophisticated, not scholarly, interested in social justice, developments in the world church, not inclined to easy piety."

CHRISTIAN MANAGEMENT REPORT, P.O. Box 4638, Diamond Bar CA 91765. (909)861-8861. Fax: (909)860-8247. Church Management Association. Sandy Scruggs, dir. For Christian managers of non-profit organizations and people from ministries in general. Bimonthly journal; 24 pgs; circ 3,000. Subscription $49. 60% freelance. Complete ms/cover letter; fax query ok. **NO PAYMENT,** for 1st rts.

Articles 500-900 wds (20/yr); book reviews 200-500 wds. Responds in 3-6 wks. Seasonal 6 mos ahead. Considers simultaneous submissions & reprints. Guidelines; copy for 9x12 SAE/8 stamps.

Fillers: Anecdotes, cartoons, facts, newsbreaks, prose, prayers, quotes, short humor; 50-100 wds.

Columns/Departments: Management Q & A; Hiring Insights; both 500-700 wds. Query.

Special Needs: Non-profit management; fund-raising; marketing; and hiring issues.

CHRISTIAN MINISTRY, 407 S. Dearborn St., Ste. 1405, Chicago IL 60605-1150. (312)427-5380. Fax: (312)427-1302. The Christian Century Foundation. Victoria Rebeck, mng. ed. For clergy seeking thoughtful, practical advice for parish ministry challenges. Bimonthly mag; 48 pgs; circ 12,000. Subscription $14. 90% freelance. Complete ms/cover letter; fax query ok. Pays $50-75, on publication, for all rts. Articles 1,000-3,000 wds (100/yr); book reviews, 500 wds, keep book. Responds in 6 wks. Seasonal 3 mos ahead. Kill fee 50%. Prefers disk copy. Sidebars ok. Guidelines/theme list; copy for 9x12 SAE/4 stamps.

> **Columns/Departments:** Buys 3/yr. Tricks of the Trade (1-pg explanation of an efficiency technique), 250 wds; Women of the Word (women clergy's reflections on their work), 2,000 wds; $25-60.

> **Tips:** "Articles should be theologically thoughtful (to a mainline Protestant, seminary-educated audience), while offering practical application."

THE CHRISTIAN SENTINEL, Box 11322, Philadelphia PA 19137. (215)289-7885. Fax: (215)289-8808. Calvary Chapel. Jackie Alnor, ed. Leaders-oriented publication exploring Christian apologetics issues; cults; issues affecting the church. Quarterly mag; 36 pgs; circ 10,000. Estab 1992. 10% freelance. Query/clips; no phone query. **NO PAYMENT,** for 1st rts. Articles 100-700 wds; book reviews 500 wds. Responds in 2 wks. No disk. Sidebars ok. No guidelines; copy for 9x12 SAE/2 stamps.

> **Fillers:** Accepts 10/yr. Cartoons.

> **Special Needs:** Heresy in the church; defense of the faith; signs of the times; eye-witness accounts of the introduction of lying signs and wonders in the church.

> **Tips:** "Be called to a discernment ministry; be provoked by evil and false teachings. Most open to news. Be big on fact, short on opinion."

*CHURCH ADMINISTRATION, MSN 157, 127 9th Ave. N., Nashville TN 37234. (615)251-2062. Fax: (615)251-3866. Southern Baptist. George Clark, ed. Practical pastoral ministry/church administration ideas for pastors and staff. Monthly mag; 50 pgs; circ 12,000. 15% freelance. Query. Pays .055-.065/wd, on acceptance, for all rts. Articles 1,800-2,000 wds (60/yr). Responds in 8 wks. Guidelines/copy for #10 SAE/2 stamps.

> **Columns/Departments:** Buys 60/yr. Weekday Dialogue; Minister's Mate; Secretary's File; all 2,000 wds.

CHURCH BYTES, 562 Brightleaf Sq. #9, 905 W. Main St., Durham NC 27701. (919)490-8927. Fax: (919)490-8927. Neil B. Houk, ed. Everything about church computing. Bimonthly newsletter; 24 pgs; circ 1,000. Subscription $14.95. 10% freelance. Query; phone/fax query ok. Pays $35; on publication; for one-time or reprint rts. Articles 1,000-1,200 wds (6-8/yr). Responds in 2 wks. Accepts reprints. Prefers disk copy. Copy for 9x12 SAE/3 stamps. Not in topical listings.

> **Tips:** "Write about personal experience in church computing, rather than reviews of software; tips for church staff; computer-related Christian education."

CHURCH GROWTH NETWORK, 3630 Camellia Dr., San Bernardino CA 92404. (909)882-5386. Fax: (909)882-5386. Independent. Dr. Gary L. McIntosh, ed. For pastors and church leaders interested in church growth. Monthly newsletter; 2 pgs; circ 7,000. Subscription $12. 20% freelance. Query; fax query ok. **PAYS A SUBSCRIPTION**, for 1st rts. Articles 1,000-1,250 wds (2/yr). Responds in 4-8 wks. Accepts reprints. Prefers disk copy. Copy for #10 SAE/1 stamp.

> **Tips:** "All articles must have a church growth slant. Should be very practical, how-to material; very tightly written with bullets, etc."

*THE CLERGY JOURNAL, 6160 Carmen Ave. E., Inver Grove Heights MN 55076-4420. Manfred Holck, Jr., pub. "How-to"articles on church administration for protestant ministers. Monthly (10X) mag; 48 pgs; circ 15,000. 20% freelance. Query. Pays $25-50, on publication, for all rts. Articles 1,000-1,500 wds (15/yr); book reviews 250 wds/no pay. Responds in 2 wks. Seasonal 4 mos ahead. Kill fee 50%. No guidelines; copy $3.50/9x12 SAE/6 stamps.

> **Special Needs:** How to manage churches.

CROSS CURRENTS, College of New Rochelle, New Rochelle NY 10805-2308. (914)654-5425. Fax: (914)654-5925. Association for Religious and Intellectual Life. Nancy Malone, OJU, ed. For thoughtful activists for social justice and church reform. Quarterly jour; 144 pgs; circ 4,500. Subscription $25. 99% freelance. Mostly written by academics. Complete ms/cover letter; phone/fax query ok. **NO PAYMENT**, for all rts. Articles 3,000-5,000 wds. Responds in 2-8 wks. Seasonal 6 mos ahead. Considers simultaneous submissions & reprints. Prefers disk copy. No sidebars. Guidelines; copy for 9x12 SAE/4 stamps.

> **Poetry:** Jonathan Levin. Accepts 8/yr. Any type or length; no payment. Submit max. 5 poems.

> **Tips:** "Send 3 double-spaced copies; SASE; use Chicago Manual of Style; non-sexist language."

*DIACONALOGUE, 1304 LaPorte Ave., Valparaiso IN 46383. (219)464-0909. Lutheran Deaconess Assn. Dot Nuechterlein, ed. Focus on ministries of Christian service in everyday life. Semiannual (2-3X) newsletter; 4-6 pgs; circ 1,000. 50% freelance. Complete ms/cover letter. Pays $25, on publication, for one-time rts. Not copyrighted. Articles 1,000 wds (3/yr). Responds in 2-4 wks. Seasonal 6 mos ahead. Accepts reprints. Guidelines/copy for #10 SAE/1 stamp.

> **Poetry:** Free verse.

> **Tips:** "Most open to articles or poems that advocate or illustrate service and caregiving."

*DISCIPLESHIP TRAINING, 127 9th Ave. N., Nashville TN 37234. (615)251-2831. Southern Baptist. Richard Ryan, sr. ed. Training Christians for discipleship. Quarterly mag; 64 pgs; circ 30,000. 10% freelance. Query. Pays .05/wd, 30 days after acceptance, for all or 1st rts. Articles 500-1,500 wds (15/yr). Responds in 6 wks. Seasonal 1 yr ahead. Free guidelines/copy.

> **Tips:** "Most open to testimonies regarding discipleship in the lives of growing Christians."

+ECUMENICAL TRENDS, Box 16136, Ludlow KY 41016. (606)581-6216. Fax: (216)449-3862. Catholic. William D. Carpe, ed. For ecumenical officers, pastors, academics; ecumenical news and articles on ecumenical topics. Monthly jour; circ 9,000. Subscription $10. 100% freelance. Complete ms. Pays $50 & up, on publication. Not copyrighted. Articles 3,000-6,000 wds (40/yr); book reviews, $50. Accepts simultaneous submissions & reprints. No sidebars.

> **Poetry:** 2-3 pgs maximum; $35.

> **Tips:** Also uses meditations, 1,000-1,250 wds. Pays $50.

+EMMANUEL, 5384 Wilson Mills, Cleveland OH 44143. (216)449-2103. Fax: (216)449-3862. Catholic. Rev. Anthony Schueller, ed. Eucharistic spirituality for priests and others in church ministry. Monthly (10X) mag; 62 pgs; circ 4,500. Subscription $19.95. 50% freelance. Query or complete ms. Pays $100, on publication, for all rts. Articles 2,000-3,000 wds. Not in topical listings.

+ENVIRONMENT & ART LETTER, 1800 N. Hermitage Ave., Chicago IL 60622-1101. (312)486-8970 x64. Fax: (312)486-7094. Catholic. David Philippart, ed. For artists, architects, building professionals, pastors, parish committees interested in church architecture, art and decoration. Monthly newsletter; 12 pgs; circ 2,500. Subscription $20. 80% freelance. Query/clips; phone/fax query ok. Pays, on publication, for all rts. Responds in 2-8 wks. Seasonal 2 mos ahead. Considers simultaneous submissions. Theme list; copy for 9x12 SAE/3 stamps.

> **Tips:** "Need a thorough knowledge of the liturgical documents pertaining to architecture and art, especially environment and art for Catholic worship."

#EUCHARISTIC MINISTER, 115 E. Armour Blvd., Box 419493, Kansas City MO 64141. (816)531-0538. Catholic. Rich Heffern, ed. For eucharistic ministers. Monthly newsletter; 4-8 pgs; circ 50,000. 90% freelance. Complete ms. Pays $20-200, on acceptance, for one-time rts. Articles 200-2,000 wds (30+/yr). Responds in 1-2 wks. Seasonal 4-6 mos ahead. Considers simultaneous submissions & reprints. Guidelines; free copy.

> **Fillers:** Buys 10-12/yr. Anecdotes, cartoons, short humor.

> **Tips:** "We want articles to be practical, inspirational, or motivational. They need to be simple and direct enough for the average person to read easily—no heavy theology, pious inspiration, or excess verbiage."

#EVANGELISM, 12800 N. Lake Shore Dr., Mequon WI 53097-2402. (414)243-4207. Fax: (414)243-4409. Dr. Joel Heck, ed. For pastors and lay people concerned about personal evangelism. Quarterly journal; 48 pgs; circ 1,000. Subscription $12. 50% freelance. Query or complete ms/cover letter; no phone query. Sometimes pays for first or reprint rts. Articles 1,000-5,000 wds (8/yr). Responds in 4-8 wks. Seasonal 3 mos ahead. Considers simultaneous submissions & reprints. Guidelines/theme list; copy for 6x9 SAE.

> **Columns/Departments:** Accepts 10/yr. Idea Bank (evangelism ideas), 50-500 wds; News Bank (evangelism news), 50-500 wds; Conference Bank (evangelism conferences), 50-500 wds; Introducing... (info on outreach organizations), 1,000-5,000 wds.

> **Special Needs:** Assimilation and church growth.

> **Tips:** "We need articles on evangelism programs, witnessing, and profiles of outreach organizations."

*THE FIVE STONES, Box D-2, Block Island RI 02807. (401)466-5940. Ecumenical-American Baptist. Anthony G. Pappas, ed. Primarily to small church pastors and laity, denominational staff, and seminaries; to equip for service. Quarterly newsletter/journal; circ 550. Query or complete ms. Pays $5, on publication, for one-time rights. Not copyrighted. Articles (16/yr) & fiction, 500-2,500 wds. Responds in 4-12 wks. Seasonal 6 mos ahead. Considers simultaneous submissions & reprints. Guidelines/theme list; free copy.

> **Columns/Departments:** Buys 4/yr. Seminary Programs for Small Church Pastors, 500-1,000 wds, $5. Complete ms.

> **Tips:** "Good place for unpublished to break in. Best to call and talk."

*GROUP'S JR. HIGH MINISTRY, Box 481, Loveland CO 80539. (303)669-3836. Rick Lawrence (articles); Barbara Beach (columns). For youth ministers who work with the junior-high age group. Mag published 5 times/yr; 40 pgs; circ 30,000. 50% freelance. Query/clips or complete ms/cover letter; no phone query. Pays $75-150, on acceptance, for all rts. Articles 500-2,200 wds (50/yr). Responds in 1 mo. Seasonal 5 mos ahead. Considers simultaneous submissions. Kill fee $25. Guidelines; copy $1/9x12 SAE/4 stamps.

> **Columns/Departments:** Buys 30/yr. Parents Page (tips for parents of jr. highers); 150 wds; $25.

Tips: "Most open to features and creative programming; practical articles on issues that really mean something to jr. high leaders. Get a copy of the magazine so you can conform to our style."

#HOMILETIC AND PASTORAL REVIEW, 86 Riverside Dr., New York NY 10024. (212)799-2600. Catholic. Kenneth Baker S.J., ed. Promotion of Catholic faith, primarily for priests. Monthly journal; 80 pgs; circ 15,000. 90% freelance. Complete ms/cover letter. Pays $100, after publication, for all rts. Articles to 6,000 wds. Responds in 1 mo. No guidelines; free copy.

*THE IVY JUNGLE REPORT, 2639 Iron St., Bellingham WA 98225. (206)733-6212. Fax: (206)734-6228. Mike Woodruff, ed. For people who minister to collegians. Quarterly journal; circ 150. Subscription $24.50. Estab 1992. 80% freelance. Query; phone query ok. NO PAYMENT for one-time rts. Not copyrighted. Articles 500-1,500 wds; book reviews. Responds in 2 wks. Considers simultaneous submissions & reprints. Guidelines/theme list; copy for 6x9 SAE/3 stamps.

Fillers: Accepts 10/yr. Anecdotes, cartoons, facts, ideas, jokes, newsbreaks, party ideas, quizzes, quotes, short humor; 15-100 wds.

Tips: "We are looking for writers who understand the unique demands and challenges of college ministry, both church and parachurch."

+JOURNAL OF BIBLICAL ETHICS IN MEDICINE, P.O. Box 13231, Florence SC 29504. (803)665-6853. Dr. Hilton Terrell, ed. Ethical issues in medicine for physicians, pastors, health professionals, and concerned citizens. Quarterly jour; circ 1,200. Subscription $18. 90% freelance. Complete ms/cover letter. Pays variable rates, on publication, for all rts. Articles to 5,000 wds; book reviews, no pmt. Responds in 2-4 wks. Considers simultaneous submissions & reprints. Guidelines; copy for 9x12 SAE/4 stamps.

JOURNAL OF CHRISTIAN CAMPING, 405 W. Rockrimmon Blvd., Colorado Springs CO 80919. (719)260-9400. Fax: (719)260-6398. Christian Camping Intl. Dean Ridings, ed. For those involved in organized camps and conference centers. Bimonthly mag; 32 pgs; circ 7,000. Subscription $24.95. 75% freelance. Query; fax query ok. Pays .06/wd, on publication, for all rts. Articles 250-1,000 wds (5-8/yr). Responds in 4-6 wks. Seasonal 4 mos ahead. Considers simultaneous submissions & reprints. Prefers disk copy. Sidebars ok. Guidelines; copy $2.50/9x12 SAE/6 stamps.

Fillers: Buys 3-5 cartoons/yr; $25-50.

Special Needs: Outdoor setting; purpose and objectives; administration and organization; personnel development; camper/guest needs; programming; health and safety; food service; site/facilities maintenance; business/operations; marketing and PR; and fund raising. Also prominent Christian making a difference because of Christian camping experience and/or in Christian camping.

JOURNAL OF CHRISTIAN HEALING, 3661 S. Kinnickinnie Ave., St. Francis WI 53235. (414)481-3696. Assoc. of Christian Therapists. Father Louis Lussier, OSCAS, ed. Focuses on the healing power and presence of Jesus Christ, for health and mental health professionals and healing ministries. Quarterly journal; 40 pgs; circ 1,200. 100% freelance. Complete ms/cover letter; phone query ok. PAYS IN COPIES, for all rts. Articles 10-20 pgs (12/yr); fiction 2-5 pgs; book reviews, 2-5 pgs. Accepts reprints. Responds in 8 wks. Guidelines; copy $8.

Poetry: Charles Zeiders. Accepts 12/yr. Free verse, haiku, light verse or traditional; to 40 lines. Submit max. 10 poems.

Fillers: Accepts 10/yr. Various; to 250 wds.

Columns/Departments: Accepts 12/yr. Resources, Medical practices, Nursing, Pastoral Ministry, Psychiatry, Prayer Ministry, Sexuality, Dreams; 2-5 pgs.

Tips: "All articles or short stories must relate to healing."

LEADERSHIP JOURNAL, 465 Gundersen Dr., Carol Stream IL 60188. (708)260-6200. Fax: (708)260-0114. Christianity Today, Inc. Kevin A. Miller, ed. For pastors; provides encouragement and practical tools for ministry. Quarterly journal; 145 pgs; circ 65,000. Subscription $24. 75% freelance. Complete ms/cover letter; fax query ok. Pays .10/wd, on acceptance, for 1st & some reprint rts. Articles 1,000-3,000 wds (60/yr). Responds in 4-6 wks. Seasonal 6 mos ahead. Kill fee 50%. Sidebars ok. Guidelines/theme list; copy $5/10x13 SAE/4 stamps.

> **Fillers:** Cartoons, facts, ideas, quotes.
>
> **Columns/Departments:** Buys 40/yr. Ideas That Work, 250-500 wds; To Illustrate (sermon illustrations), 100-250 wds; Trend Watch (what's new in church life), 1,000 wds; Back Page (opinion), 1,200 wds; $15-100. Complete ms.
>
> ** This periodical was #16 on the 1994 Top 50 Plus Christian Publishers list. (#18 in 1993)

LITURGY, 8750 Georgia Ave., Ste. 123, Silver Spring MD 20910. (301)495-0885. Fax: (301)495-5945. The Liturgical Conference. Blair Gilmer Meeks, ed. For clergy, liturgy planners, musicians, and religious educators. Bimonthly jour; 100 pgs; circ 2,300. Subscription $42. 10% freelance. Query; phone query ok. Pays $35-75, on publication, for all rts. Articles 600-1,500 wds (3/yr). Responds in 2-6 wks. Seasonal 10 mos ahead. Accepts simultaneous submissions & reprints. Prefers disk copy. No sidebars. Guidelines/theme list; copy for 9x12 SAE/3 stamps.

#LUTHERAN FORUM, P.O. Box 327, Delhi NY 13753-0327. (607)746-7511. Fax: (607)829-2158. Evangelical Catholic Lutherans. Dr. Leonard R. Klein, ed. For church leadership, clerical and lay. Quarterly journal; 56 pgs; circ 3,500. 90% freelance. Query or complete ms. Pays, on publication, for all, first, one-time, reprint and simultaneous rts. Articles 1,000-3,000 wds (2-3/yr). Responds in 6-8 mos. Considers simultaneous submissions & reprints. Guidelines; copy $2/9x12 SAE/5 stamps.

+LUTHERAN PARTNERS, 8765 W. Higgins Rd., Chicago IL 60631. (312)380-2875. Fax: (312)380-1465. Evangelical Lutheran Church in America. Carl E. Linder, ed. To encourage and challenge rostered leaders in the ELCA, including pastors and lay leaders. Bimonthly mag; 40-48 pgs; circ 22,000. Distributed free. 30-35% freelance. Query or complete ms/cover letter; phone/fax query ok. Pays $100-200, on publication, for 1st rts. Articles 1,200-3,000 wds (10-15/yr); fiction (used rarely, query); book reviews 700 wds (contact book review ed.—Thelma Magill-Cobbler), no pmt. Responds in 4-16 wks. Seasonal 1 yr ahead. Considers simultaneous submissions & reprints. Kill fee. Prefers disk copy. Some sidebars. Guidelines; copy $2/9x12 SAE/5 stamps.

> **Poetry:** Buys 5-6/yr. Free verse, traditional: $75. Submit max. 4 poems.
>
> **Fillers:** Ideas for parish ministry; to 500 wds; $50-75.
>
> **Special Needs:** Seminary education; ecumenical (inter-church cooperation); technological application (computer & video); video reviews (consult video editor).
>
> **Tips:** "Aim at issues and concerns of congregational and parish life. Integrate current issues with biblical and theological foundations."

#MINISTRIES TODAY, 600 Rinehart Rd., Lake Mary FL 32746. (407)333-9753. Fax: (407)333-9753. Strang Communications. Jim Buchan, ed. Helps for pastors and church leaders in charismatic churches. Bimonthly mag; 84 pgs; circ 30,000. Subscription $21.95. 30-40% freelance. Query or complete ms/cover letter; no phone query; fax query ok. Pays $200-500, on publication, for all, 1st, one-time or reprint rts. Articles 1,800-3,000 wds; book reviews, $20. Responds in 3-6 wks. Seasonal 6 mos ahead. Accepts reprints only if published in non-profit newsletters, newspapers or magazines. Kill fee. Guidelines; copy $4/9x12 SAE.

Columns/Departments: Buys 12/yr. Soap Box (opinion pcs); The Next Generation (youth/children's ministry); 800 or 1,050 wds; $100.

Tips: "Most open to columns. Write for guidelines and study the magazine."

NATIONAL & INTERNATIONAL RELIGION REPORT, Box 21433, Roanoke VA 24018. (703)989-7500. Fax: (703)989-0189. Lawrence W. Pierce, sr. ed. Report of religious news around the world. Biweekly newsletter; 8 pgs; circ 7,200. Subscription $39. 5% freelance. Query/clips; fax query ok. Pays $50, on publication, for 1st rts. News articles 250-300 wds. Responds in 1 wk. Kill fee 50%. No disks. No sidebars. Guidelines/theme list/copy for #10 SASE/1 stamp.

Tips: "Looking for interesting news stories of broad significance. We don't need newswire rewrites."

*NETWORKS, Box 685, Cocoa FL 32923. (407)632-0130. Fax: (407)631-8207. Christian Council on Persons with Disabilities. Linda G. Howard, ed. For those with specialized ministry to the mentally retarded. Bimonthly newsletter; 8 pgs; circ 1,700. Estab 1989. 80% freelance. Query or complete ms. **NO PAYMENT** for 1st rts. Articles 250-450 wds (12/yr); book reviews 350 wds. Responds in 6 wks. Seasonal 4 mos ahead. Considers simultaneous submissions & reprints. Guidelines; copy for 9x12 SAE/6 stamps.

Poetry: Accepts 4/yr. Any type; to 66 lines. Submit max. 10 poems.

Columns/Departments: Accepts 8/yr. Program Highlights, 1,000 wds; Teachers' Tips, 750 wds.

Special Needs: Advocacy, normalization/integration, church/state issues. June 15 deadline for annual issue on the Christian Council on Persons with Disabilities.

PASTOR'S TAX & MONEY, P.O. Box 50188, Indianapolis IN 46250. (800)877-3158. Fax: (317)594-8311. Daniel D. Busby, ed. Guidance for pastors in management of church and personal finances. Quarterly newsletter; 8 pgs; circ 6,000. Subscription $59.95. 50% freelance. Complete ms/cover letter. Pays $50, on publication, for 1st rts. Articles 600-800 wds (8/yr). Responds in 3 mos. No sidebars. No guidelines; copy $1/6x9 SAE/2 stamps.

Special Needs: Minister's taxes; computers; personal finances and church finances.

PREACHER'S ILLUSTRATION SERVICE, Box 3102, Margate NJ 08402. (609)822-9401. Fax: (609)822-1638. James Colaianni, pub. Sermon illustration resource for professional clergy. Bimonthly loose-leaf booklet, 16 pgs. 15% freelance. Complete ms. Pays .15/wd, on publication, for any rts. Illustrations/anecdotes 50-250 wds. Responds in 6 wks. Seasonal 4 mos ahead. Accepts reprints. Prefers disk copy. Guidelines/topical index; copy for 9x12 SAE.

Poetry: Light verse, traditional; 50-250 lines; .15/wd. Submit max. 3 poems.

Fillers: Various; sermon illustrations; 50-250 wds; .15/wd.

THE PREACHER'S MAGAZINE, 10814 E. Broadway, Spokane WA 99206. (509)226-3464. Fax: (509)926-8740. Nazarene. Rev. Randal E. Denny, ed. A trade journal for holiness ministers. Quarterly mag; 80 pgs; circ 18,000. 30% freelance. Complete ms/cover letter; phone query ok. Pays .035/wd, on publication, for 1st rts. Articles 700-2,500 wds (32/yr); book reviews 300-400 wds. Responds in 4 wks. Seasonal 6 mos ahead. Considers simultaneous submissions & reprints. Uses some sidebars. Guidelines; no copy.

Fillers: Buys 10/yr. Anecdotes, cartoons, ideas, jokes, prose; 300-500 wds.

Tips: "Material must be relevant to pastor's ministry or personal life."

#PREACHING, P.O. Box 7728, Louisville KY 40257-0728. Fax: (502)899-3119. Dr. Michael Duduit, ed. Professional magazine for evangelical preachers; focus is on pulpit ministry. Bimonthly mag; 64 pgs; circ 9,000. Subscription $24.95. 75% freelance. Query (articles) or complete ms (sermons)/cover letter; no phone query. Pays $35-50, on publication, for 1st rts. Articles 1,000-2,000 wds (18-24/yr). Responds in 4 mos. Seasonal 1 yr ahead. Guidelines; copy $3.50.

Fillers: Buys 10-15/yr. Cartoons only; $25.

Tips: "Need practical feature articles about preaching—written by preachers or college/seminary faculty (nothing written by laity). We use articles that provide practical insights and skills for strengthening the preaching ministry."

#THE PRIEST, 200 Noll Plaza, Huntington IN 46750-4304. (219)356-8400. Fax: (219)356-8472. Catholic. Owen F. Campion, ed. For Catholic priests, deacons and seminarians; to help in all aspects of ministry. Monthly mag; 48 pgs; circ 9,800. Subscription $30. 80% freelance. Complete ms/cover letter; phone query ok. Pays $50-300, on acceptance, for 1st rts. Not copyrighted. Articles 1,500-5,000 wds (96/yr). Responds in 4 wks. Seasonal 4 mos ahead. Free guidelines/copy.

Columns/Departments: Buys 36/yr. Viewpoint (about priests or the church), 1,000 wds, $50-100. Complete ms.

Tips: "Write to the point, with interest, and when you have said your piece, quit. Most open to features. Keep the audience in mind."

** This periodical was #62 on the 1994 Top 50 Plus Christian Publishers list. (#38 in 1993)

PROCLAIM, 127 Ninth Ave. N, Nashville TN 37234. (615)251-2874. Fax: (615)21-3866. Southern Baptist. Billy J. Chitwood, ed. Sermons, illustrations and worship materials for pastors. Quarterly mag; 50 pgs; circ 15,000. Subscription $13.30. 75% freelance. Query; phone query ok. Pays .055/wd, on acceptance, for all, 1st or reprint rts. Articles 600-4200 wds (25-30/yr). Responds in 3-6 wks. Seasonal 1 yr ahead. Accepts reprints. No sidebars. Guidelines; free copy for 9x12 SAE.

Columns/Departments: Features, 2,400 wds; Sermon Workshop (sermon helps), 50-700 wds; Worship Workshop, 2,400 wds; Pulpit Performance, 3,000 wds.

** This periodical was #68 on the 1994 Top 50 Plus Christian Publishers list.

PULPIT HELPS (formerly **PULPIT & BIBLE STUDY HELPS**), 6815 Shallowford Rd., Chattanooga TN 37421. (615)251-6060. Ted Kyle, ed. To help preachers and serious students of the Bible. Monthly newspaper; 28 pgs; circ 105,000. Subscription $15. 10% freelance. Complete ms/cover letter; no phone query. NO PAYMENT. Articles to 1,500 wds (15-25/yr). Seasonal 4 mos ahead. Considers simultaneous submissions & reprints. Seldom uses sidebars. Free copy.

Poetry: Traditional.

Fillers: Anecdotes, prose; 10-300 wds.

Columns/Departments: Family Helps, to 1,000 wds; Illustrations (for sermons), 100-400 wds.

*QUARTERLY REVIEW, A Journal of Theological Resources for Ministry, Box 871, Nashville TN 37202. (615)340-7383. Fax: (615)340-7048. United Methodist. Dr. Sharon J. Hels, ed. A theological approach to subjects of interest to clergy—scripture study, ethics, and practice of ministry in Wesleyan tradition. Quarterly journal; 112 pgs; circ 3,000. 95% freelance. Complete ms/cover letter; no phone query. NO PAYMENT for one-time rts. Articles 15-18 pgs/3,250-5,000 wds (15/yr); book reviews to 1,000 wds. Responds in 3 mos. Seasonal 9 mos ahead. Guidelines; no copy.

Tips: "Emphasis on top-notch scholarship and accessible writing style. Use up-to-date sources and be prepared to rewrite. Most open to theological reflection or pastoral experiences. Hone essay-writing skills."

*REFORMED WORSHIP, 2850 Kalamazoo SE, Grand Rapids MI 49560. (616)246-0752. Christian Reformed Church in North America. Dr. Emily R. Brink, ed. To provide liturgical and musical resources for pastors, church musicians, and other worship leaders. Quarterly journal; 48 pgs; circ 3,000. 75% freelance. Query or complete ms/cover letter. Pays $30/printed pg, on publication, for all or 1st rts. Articles 250-1,500 wds (4/yr); book reviews 250 wds, $15. Responds in 3 mos. Seasonal 1 yr ahead. Accepts reprints. Kill fee 50%. Guidelines; copy $5/9x12 SASE.

Fillers: Buys 4-6 cartoons/yr; $50.

RESOURCE: The National Leadership Magazine, 6745 Century Ave., Mississauga ON L5N 6P7 Canada. (905)542-7400. Fax: (905)542-7313. Pentecostal Assemblies of Canada. Michael Horban, ed. For church leadership and practical how-to's on leadership issues. Bimonthly mag; 48 pgs; circ 10,000. Subscription $20. 20% freelance. Query. Pays $30-100, on publication, for all rts. Articles 500-1,500 wds (8-10/yr); book reviews 250 wds, $20. Responds in 4-6 wks. Seasonal 3 mos ahead. Accepts reprints. Prefers disk copy. Sidebars ok. Guidelines/theme list; copy $2/9x12 SAE.

Fillers: Buys 4-8/yr. Anecdotes, cartoons, short humor; 200-300 wds; $20-30.

Columns/Departments: Kevin Johnson. Buys 6-12/yr. Resources for Youth Workers; Resources for CE Workers; 300 wds; $20-30.

Special Needs: Good missions promotional features.

Tips: "Say something positive to leaders that stretches and enriches them."

REVIEW FOR RELIGIOUS, 3601 Lindell Blvd., Rm. 428, St. Louis MO 63108-3393. (314)535-3048. Fax: (314)535-0601. Catholic. Rev. David L. Fleming, S.J., ed. For Catholic priests, brothers, and sisters, to deal specifically with the requirements of religious life. Bimonthly journal; 160 pgs; circ 11,000. Subscription $20/$24 foreign. 100% freelance. Complete ms/cover letter; phone query ok. Pays $6/printed page, on publication, for all rts. Articles 1,500-5,000 wds (80/yr); book reviews, 300-900 wds (pays 2 copies). Responds in 1-4 wks. Seasonal 6 mos ahead. Guidelines; copy for 24x16.5 SAE/$1.05 postage.

Poetry: Buys 10/yr. Free verse; to 12 lines; $10.

Tips: "Our guidelines give explicit instructions; write for them."

*SEARCH, 127 9th Ave. N., Nashville TN 37234. (615)251-2074. Fax: (615)251-2074. Southern Baptist Sunday School Board. Judith S. Hayes, sr. design ed. Practical theology, Christian education, preaching/worship, and pastoral care for pastors and staff. Quarterly journal; 66 pgs; circ 10,000. 50% freelance. Query. Pays .055-.06/wd, after acceptance, for all rts. Articles 2,500-5,000 wds (20/yr); book reviews 200-800 wds. Responds in 3 mos. Seasonal 15 mos ahead. Guidelines; free copy.

#SINGLE ADULT MINISTRIES JOURNAL, Box 60430, Colorado Springs CO 80960. (719)579-6471. Fax: (719)579-9732. Cook Communications Ministries. Jerry D. Jones, ed. For pastors and lay leaders involved in ministry with single adults. Journal pub. 8X/yr; 24 pgs; circ 5,000. Subscription $24. 5% freelance. Query; phone query ok. USUALLY NO PAYMENT for 1st rts. Articles 200-2,500 wds (0-4/yr); book reviews 50-300 wds/$15-75. Responds in 6-12 wks. Seasonal 4-6 mos ahead. Theme list; copy for 9x12 SAE/4 stamps.

Fillers: Buys 0-5/yr. Facts, newsbreaks, quotes; 25-200 wds; $10-50.

Tips: "Write to the pastor or leader, not to singles themselves. Interview singles or the leaders who work with them."

+SUNDAY SERMONS, P.O. Box 3102, Margate NJ 08402. (609)822-9401. Fax: (609)822-1638. Ecumenical. J. Colaianni, ed-in-chief. Full-text sermon resource for clergy. Bi-monthly bound workbook; 54-60 pgs. 5% freelance. Pays, on publication, for all rts. Responds in 6 wks. Seasonal 6 mos ahead. Accepts reprints. Prefers disk copy. Guidelines/theme list; copy for 9x12 SAE. Not in topical listings.

Tips: "Sermons must include several relevant illustrations."

+THEOLOGY TODAY, P.O. Box 29, Princeton NJ 08542. (609)497-7714. Nondenominational. Explores key issues, current thoughts and trends in the fields of religion and theology. Quarterly jour; circ 13,000. Subscription $21. Little unsolicited accepted. Complete ms. Pays $100-200, on publication. Articles. Sidebars ok. Guidelines. Incomplete topical listings.

+TODAY'S CHRISTIAN PREACHER, 401 E. Main St., Morgantown PA 19543. (215)286-7744. Fax: (215)286-6721. Marketing Partners, Inc. Jerry Thacker, ed. To provide material on current topics to help preachers in their personal life. Quarterly mag; circ 30,000. Free subscription. Open to freelance.

#TODAY'S PARISH, Box 180, Mystic CT 06355. (203)536-2611. Fax: (203)572-0788. Catholic. Daniel Connors, ed. Practical ideas and issues relating to parish life, management and ministry; human interest relevant to parish life. Mag published 7 times/yr; 40-42 pgs; circ 14,800. Subscription $22. 25% freelance. Query or complete ms. Pays $50-100, on publication, for 1st rts. Articles 800-1,800 wds (45/yr). Responds in 3 mos. Seasonal 6 mos ahead. Guidelines; copy for 9x12 SASE.

> **Poetry:** Free verse; to 25 lines.

*WORD & WORLD: Theology for Christian Ministry, 2481 Como Ave., St. Paul MN 55108. (612)641-3482. Fax: (612)641-3354. E.L.C.A./ Luther Northwestern Theological Seminary. Frederick J. Gaiser, ed. Addresses ecclesiastical and secular issues from a theological perspective and addresses pastors and church leaders with the best fruits of theological research. Quarterly journal; 104 pgs; circ 3,100. Subscription $18. 10% freelance. Complete ms/cover letter; phone query ok. Pays $50, on publication, for all rts. Articles 5,000-6,000 wds. Responds in 2-8 wks. Guidelines/theme list; copy $5.

> **Special Needs:** Themes for 1995: Children; Revelation and Apocalyptic; The Ministry of Women; Why do the Nations Rage?
>
> **Tips:** "Most open to general articles. We look for serious theology addressed clearly and interestingly to people in the practice of ministry. Creativity and usefulness in ministry are highly valued."

WORSHIP LEADER, 107 Kenner Ave., Nashville TN 37205. (615)386-3011. Fax: (615)386-3380. CCM Communications. Melissa L. Riddle, mng ed. Intellectual tone with practical advice on leading worship. Bimonthly mag; 40+ pgs; circ 40,000+. 60% freelance. Query; no phone query. Pays .10/wd; on publication; for 1st rts. Articles 400-1,500 wds. Responds in 1 yr. Seasonal 10-12 mos ahead. Kill fee 50%. Sidebars ok. No guidelines; copy for 9x12 SAE/6 stamps.

> **Columns/Departments:** Buys 6/yr. Profile of worship leader or minister of music (Q & A format), 1,200-2,200 wds.
>
> **Special Needs:** Contemporary vs. traditional worship trends.
>
> **Tips:** "We need writers from all parts of the country to do profiles of churches, worship leaders/ministers of music in their home cities. Also, suggest articles on worship applications outside the church."

+YMR TODAY (Youth Ministry Resources), 700 Old Roswell Lakes Pkwy, Roswell GA 30076. (404)993-9177. Fax: (404)594-0014. Interdenominational. Lanny Donoho, pres. For youth leaders in the 10 SE states; general info on camps and conferences. Free newspaper; 113,000. 100% freelance. Query or complete ms/cover letter; phone/fax query ok. **NO PAYMENT.** Not copyrighted. Copy available.

YOUR CHURCH, 465 Gundersen Dr., Carol Stream IL 60188. (708)260-6200. Fax: (708)260-0114. Christianity Today Inc. Richard Doebler, ed. Deals only with the business-administration side of Christian ministry. Monthly mag; 50 pgs; circ 180,000. Subscription $15. 90% freelance. Complete ms/no cover letter. Pays $50-250, on acceptance, for 1st, one-time or reprint rts. Articles 650-2,000 wds (50/yr).

Responds in 2-6 wks. Seasonal 6 mos ahead. Considers simultaneous submissions & reprints. Kill fee. Occasional sidebar. Guidelines; copy for 9x12 SAE/4 stamps.

Fillers: Buys 20 cartoons/yr; $125.

Columns/Departments: Buys 5/yr. Finance & Law, Ministry Tools, Music & Sound, Maintenance & Construction, Church furnishings, Computers & Office Equipment; all 1,100 wds; $100.

Special Needs: Audio/visual equipment; books/curriculum resources; music equipment.

Tips: "Need true experts, or those who have access to experts on church purchasing, needs, business administration."

#YOUTHWORKER, 1224 Greenfield Dr., El Cajon CA 92021. (619)440-2333. Fax: (619)440-4939. Youth Specialties Inc. Wayne Rice, ed. For youth workers/church and parachurch. Quarterly journal; 120 pgs; circ 9,000. Subscription $25.95. 90% freelance. Query; phone query ok. Pays $100-150; on acceptance; for 1st & reprint rts. Articles 2,000-3,500 wds (30/yr). Responds in 5 wks. Seasonal 10 mos ahead. Accepts reprints. Kill fee $50. Guidelines/theme list; copy $3/10x13 SAE.

Columns/Departments: Buys 10/yr. High School Minister; Middle School Minister; Report From the Front Lines (ideas that worked); 2,000-3,000 wds; $100-150.

Special Needs: Upcoming themes include the future, sexuality, resources and results.

Tips: "Read Youthworker; imbibe its tone (professional, though not academic; conversational, though not chatty). Query me with specific, focused ideas that conform to our needs. Writer needs to be a youth minister."

** This periodical was #53 on the 1994 Top 50 Plus Christian Publishers list. Also 1994 EPA Award of Merit - Christian Ministry

TEEN/YOUNG ADULT MARKETS

#BREAKAWAY, 8605 Explorer Dr., Colorado Springs CO 80920. (719)531-3400. Fax: (719)531-3499. Focus on the Family. Michael Ross, ed. The 14-year-old, unchurched teen (boy) in the public school is our target; boys 12-17 yrs. Monthly mag; 24-32 pgs; circ 95,000. Subscription $15. Estab 1990. 60-70% freelance. Complete ms/cover letter; phone query ok. Pays .12-.15/wd, on acceptance, for all, 1st, one-time & reprint rts. Articles 400-1,800 wds (40/yr); fiction 1,200-2,200 wds (15/yr); music reviews, 300 wds, $30-40. Responds in 1 mo. Seasonal 8 mos ahead. Considers simultaneous submissions & reprints. Kill fee 33-50%. Guidelines/theme list; copy for 9x12 SAE/3 stamps.

Fillers: Buys 50/yr. Cartoons ($75), facts, quizzes; 200-600 wds; .20-.25/wd.

Columns/Departments: Buys 12/yr. Plugged In (devotional); 700-900 wds.

Tips: "Need strong lead. Brevity and levity a must. Have a teen guy or two read it. Make sure the language is up-to-date, but not overly hip."

** This periodical was #5 on the 1994 Top 50 Plus Christian Publishers list. (#9 in 1993)

#BRIO, 8605 Explorer Dr., Colorado Springs CO 80920. (719)548-4577. Fax: (719)531-3499. Focus on the Family. Susie Shellenberger, ed. For teen girls, 12-16 yrs. Monthly mag; 32 pgs; circ 158,000. Subscription $15. 30% freelance. Complete ms/cover letter; phone query ok. Pays .08-.15/wd, on acceptance, for 1st rts. Articles 800-1,000 wds (50/yr); fiction 1,000-1,500 wds (40/yr). Responds in 6 wks. Seasonal 6 mos ahead. Sometimes pays kill fee. Guidelines; copy for 9x12 SAE/6 stamps.

Fillers: Buys 10/yr. Cartoons, facts, ideas, quizzes, short humor; 500 wds.

Special Needs: All topics of interest to female teens are welcome: boys, make-up, dating, weight, ordinary girls who have the extra-ordinary, female adjustments to puberty, etc. Also teen-related female fiction.

Tips: "Study at least 3 issues of *Brio* before submitting. We're looking for a certain, fresh, hip-hop conversational style. Most open to fiction, articles and quizzes."

** This periodical was #37 in the 1994 Top 50 Plus Christian Publishers list. Also 1994 EPA Award of Merit - Youth.

CAMPUS LIFE, 465 Gundersen Dr., Carol Stream IL 60188. (708)260-6200. Fax: (708)260-0114. Christianity Today, Inc. Christopher Lutes, mng. ed. Seeks to help high school students and early college students navigate adolescence with their faith intact; not overtly religious. Monthly (8X) mag; 62 pgs; circ 120,000. Subscription $14.95. 25% freelance. Query. Pays .10-.20/wd, on acceptance, for 1st rts. Articles 500-2,500 (1/yr); fiction 1,000-2,500 wds (1-3/yr). Responds in 6 wks. Seasonal 5 mos ahead. Considers simultaneous submissions & occasionally reprints. Kill fee. Sidebars ok. Guidelines; copy $2/9x12 SAE.

   Poetry: Buys 1-5/yr. Free verse; to 25 lines; $25-75. Submit max. 1 poem.

   Fillers: Buys 30 cartoons/yr; $50.

   Columns/Departments: Buys 20/yr. Making the Grade (study tips), 100-250 wds, $25-50.

   Tips: "Most open to as-told-to stories. Interview students and get their stories."

   ** This periodical was #63 on the 1994 Top 50 Plus Christian Publishers list.

CERTAINTY, 1300 N. Meacham Rd., Box 95500, Schaumburg IL 60173-4888. Regular Baptist Press. Joan E. Alexander, ed., Sunday school papers. For senior high youth; conservative/fundamental. Weekly take-home paper; circ 20,000. 30-40% freelance. Complete ms/cover letter (first time). Pays .03-.05/wd, on acceptance, for all, 1st or one-time rts. Articles 250-1,000 wds (10-12/yr); fiction 600-1,200 wds (some multi-part), (15/yr). Responds in 4-8 wks. Seasonal 1 yr ahead. Guidelines; copy for #10 SAE/2 stamps.

   Fillers: Buys 10-15/yr. Anecdotes, cartoons, games, ideas, quizzes, prayers, word puzzles; 200-350 wds.

   Tips: "Not everything that is Christian is suitable in a publication intended for readers in fundamental Baptist churches."

*CHALLENGE (IL), 1300 N. Meacham Rd., Box 95500, Schaumburg IL 60173. Regular Baptist Press. Joan E. Alexander, ed., Sunday school papers. For junior high youth; conservative/fundamental. Weekly take-home paper. Query. Pays .03-.05/wd, on acceptance, for all or 1st rts. Articles 100-1,500 wds; fiction 500-1,500 wds (some multi-part). Responds in 2-8 wks. Seasonal 1 yr ahead. Guidelines; copy for #10 SAE/2 stamps.

   Fillers: Anecdotes, facts, games, newsbreaks, prose, word puzzles; 100-400 wds.

   Tips: "Not everything that is Christian is suitable in a publication intended for readers in fundamental Baptist churches."

CHALLENGE (TN), 1548 Poplar Ave., Memphis TN 38104. (901)272-2461. Fax: (901)726-5540. Southern Baptist. Shelley Smith, asst. ed. Missions interest articles for young men, grades 7-12. Monthly mag; 24 pgs; circ 35,000. Subscription $11.28. 60% freelance. Complete ms/no cover letter; no phone query. Pays .05/wd, on acceptance, for 1st rts. Articles 400-800 wds (36-48/yr). Responds in 4 wks. Seasonal 6 mos ahead. Considers simultaneous submissions. Sidebars ok. Guidelines; copy for 9x12 SAE/3 stamps.

   Fillers: Buys 24/yr. Cartoons, games, word puzzles; 25-50 wds; $10-25.

   Tips: "Most open to current teen issues or articles that focus on male Christian athletes, school, family or relationships."

*THE CONQUEROR, 8855 Dunn Rd., Hazelwood MO 63042. (314)837-7300. United Pentecostal Church, Intl. Darrell Johns, ed. For teenagers in the denomination. Bi-monthly mag; 16 pgs; circ 6,000. Subscription $7.50. 90% freelance. Complete ms/no cover letter or phone query. Pays $30, on publication, for various rts. Articles & fiction (many/yr), 500-3,000 wds. Responds in 10 wks. Seasonal 4 mos ahead. Considers simultaneous submissions & reprints. Guidelines; copy for 11x14 SAE/2 stamps.

> **Fillers:** Various.

> **Tips:** "Articles should be written with the idea of strict morals, standards and ethics in mind."

CROSS WALK (formerly **TEENS TODAY**), 6401 The Paseo, Kansas City MO 64131. (816)333-7000 x2203. Fax: (816)333-4315. Holiness denominations. Becki Privett, ed. Written by teens (and youth leaders) for teens. Weekly take-home paper; circ 50,000. Subscription $9. Estab 1995. By assignment only. Query only. Pays on acceptance, for all rts. Responds in 2 wks. Kill fee 50%. No sidebars. Guidelines; copy available March 1995 for 9x12 SAE/2 stamps.

> **Tips:** "A Cross Walk writer is a youth worker (professional or volunteer) who is looking for an opportunity to write with five teens from his/her youth group."

THE EDGE, 455 N. Service Rd. E., Oakville ON L6H 1A5 Canada. (905)845-9235. Fax: (905)845-1966. The Salvation Army (Canada & Bermuda). Capt. Bruce Power, ed. Official youth publication of the Salvation Army in Canada; contemporary social and moral issues, Christian lifestyle and contemporary Christian music. Monthly mag; 16 pgs; circ 5,000. Subscription $11 (Canada); $14 (outside). 50% freelance. **NO PAYMENT.** Not copyrighted. Articles 500-2,000 wds (50/yr). Responds in 3 wks. Seasonal 3 mos ahead. Considers simultaneous submissions & reprints. Prefers disk copy. Some sidebars. Copy available.

> **Fillers:** Accepts 12 cartoons/yr.

FREEWAY, Box 632, Glen Ellyn IL 60138. (708)668-6000. Fax: (708)668-3806. Scripture Press. Amy J. Cox, ed. To help teens (15-22) make wise, biblical choices in their lives. Weekly take-home paper; 4 pgs. Subscription $9.95. 100% freelance. Complete ms/cover letter; no phone query. Pays .07-.10/wd; on acceptance; for one-time or simultaneous rts. Articles 300-700 wds (40/yr); fiction & true stories 600-1,200 wds (40/yr). Responds in 4-6 wks. Seasonal 1 yr ahead. Considers simultaneous submissions & reprints (pays .05-.07/wd). Guidelines/theme list; copy for #10 SAE/1 stamp.

> **Poetry:** Buys 8/yr. Free verse, light verse, traditional; 4-20 lines; $20-40. Submit max. 5 poems.

> **Fillers:** Buys 5/yr. Cartoons, prose, quizzes, prayers, short humor, word puzzles; 100-500 wds; $10-50.

> **Tips:** "Know the age group: What makes high school and college-age young people tick and what issues they're dealing with. Looking for true stories (profiles, as-told-to's, personal experience). Should show real life struggles, not 'super-Christians'."

> ** This periodical was #30 on the 1994 Top 50 Plus Christian Publishers list. (#15 in 1993)

HICALL - See TEEN LIFE.

HIGH SCHOOL I.D. - See PATHWAY I.D.

#INSIGHT, 55 W. Oak Ridge Dr., Hagerstown MD 21740. (301)791-7000. Fax: (301)791-9734. Seventh-day Adventist. Lori Peckham, ed. For Adventist teenagers, 14-19 yrs. Weekly mag; 16 pgs; circ 23,000. Subscription $35.97. 60% freelance. Complete ms/cover letter; phone query ok. Pays $40-125; on acceptance; for 1st, one-time or reprint rts. Articles 500-1,800 wds (100-150/yr); fiction 500-1,500 wds (50/yr); book and music reviews, 500 wds, $25-50. Responds in 2-4 wks. Seasonal 4-5 mos ahead. Accepts reprints. Guidelines; copy for 9x12 SAE/2 stamps.

> **Poetry:** Buys 60/yr. Avant-garde, free verse, haiku, light verse; to 1 pg; $15-40.

Fillers: Buys 5-10/yr. Anecdotes, cartoons, facts, newsbreaks, party ideas, short humor; to 500 wds; $10-25.

Columns/Departments: Buys 100+/yr. Well-Versed (personal story that demonstrates truth of a Bible verse), 1,000-1,500 wds; On the Edge (Drama in real life), 1,000-2,000 wds; $50-100.

Tips: "Write in a realistic, teen point of view. True stories about teens are most appreciated, especially with photos. Most open to Drama-in-Real-Life stories (told like in Reader's Digest)."

** This periodical was #6 on the 1994 Top 50 Plus Christian Publishers list.

*INSIGHT/OUT, 55 W. Oak Ridge Dr., Hagerstown MD 21740. (301)791-7000. Fax: (301)791-7012. Seventh-day Adventist. Lori Peckham, ed. For teenagers, 15-19 yrs, of all denominations. Monthly mag; 30 pgs; circ 25,000. 60% freelance. Complete ms. Pays $60-100; on acceptance; for 1st, or reprint rts. Articles & fiction (20 ea/yr), 500-1,500 wds. Responds in 4-12 wks. Seasonal 6 mos ahead. Discourages simultaneous submissions. Kill fee. Guidelines/theme list; free copy. ·

Poetry: Buys 10/yr. Avant-garde, free verse, haiku; 2-45 lines; $15-40.

Fillers: Buys 10/yr. Various; $10-40.

*ISSUES & ANSWERS, The Caleb Campaign, Rt. 4 Box 274, West Frankfort IL 62896-9661. (618)937-2348. Fax: (618)937-2405. D. Ivan Rodden IV, ed.; submit to JoAnne Tegtmeyer, mng ed. A newspaper written from a biblical/creationist viewpoint for young people, 12-20 yrs. Monthly (9X) newspaper; 16 pgs; circ 15,000. 20-50% freelance. Query or complete ms. **NO PAYMENT** for all rts. Not copyrighted. Articles 1,000-2,000 wds (25/yr). Responds in 8 wks. Seasonal 3 mos ahead. Considers simultaneous submissions & reprints. Guidelines/theme list; copy $1.

Tips: "We are eager for new writers. Need history (list available) and sports interviews. Make articles interesting and relevant."

*THE KILN, Box 5763, Vancouver WA 98668. Gregory Zschomler, ed. To encourage teens (13-19 yrs) in the Christian faith. Monthly mag; 12-16 pgs. 30% freelance. Query; no phone query. **USUALLY NO PAYMENT**, pays $12-15 for best work in each issue; for 1st or reprint rts. Articles 1,200-3,000 wds (4/yr). Responds in 1 mo. Seasonal 4 mos ahead. Considers simultaneous submissions & reprints. Guidelines/theme list; copy .30.

Fillers: Buys 50/yr. Anecdotes, cartoons, jokes, quotes, short humor; $1-12.

Columns/Departments: Friar Yuk (humor), $1; Whispers of Wisdom (quotes). Open to new column ideas.

Special Needs: Missions, evangelism on campus, values.

Tips: "Most open to articles biblically on target; approach issues that need change; appeal to teens' sense of idealism."

THE MAGAZINE FOR CHRISTIAN YOUTH!, Box 801, Nashville TN 37202. (615)749-6319. Fax: (615)749-6079. United Methodist. Anthony E. Peterson, ed. To help teenagers (11-18 yrs) develop Christian identity and live the Christian faith in their contemporary culture. Monthly mag; 48 pgs; circ 25,000. Subscription $18. 50% freelance. Query; phone/fax query ok. Pays $20-150 (assigned) or .05/wd (unsolicited), on acceptance, for any rts. Articles (15/yr) & fiction (12/yr - from teens only), 500-2,000 wds. Responds in 4-8 wks. Seasonal 8 mos ahead. Considers simultaneous query & reprints. Prefers disk copy; some extra compensation. Guidelines; copy for $2 or 9x12 SAE/5 stamps.

Poetry: Accepts 60/yr. Any type; to 50 lines; no payment. From teens only.

Fillers: Buys 6/yr. Cartoons, ideas, newsbreaks, prose, quizzes, short humor; 50-200 wds; .05/wd.

Tips: "Most open to humor, how-to, social issues, and personal experience that is not preachy. Keep tone personal."

** This periodical was #48 on the 1994 Top 50 Plus Christian Publishers list. (#27 in 1993)

#PATHWAY I.D., Box 2250, Cleveland TN 37320-2250. (615)476-4512. Pathway Press/Church of God. Lance Colkmire, ed. Emphasizing victorious, Spirit-filled living in a secular world for senior highs (15-17 yrs). Weekly take-home paper; 8 pgs; circ 18,000. 5-10% freelance. Complete ms/cover letter. Pays $20-45, on acceptance, for 1st, one-time, reprint & simultaneous rts. Articles 400-800 wds (5/yr). Responds in 1 mo. Seasonal 1 yr ahead. Considers simultaneous submissions & reprints. Guidelines/copy for #10 SASE/1 stamp.

Tips: "Need true stories of how Christ is making a difference in teens' lives." Not accepting fiction for now; query about future issues.

*PIONEER, 1548 Poplar Ave., Memphis TN 38104. (901)272-2461. Fax: (901)726-5540. Southern Baptist/Baptist Brotherhood Commission. Jene C. Smith, ed. For boys 12-14 yrs who are members of Pioneer Royal Ambassadors, a missions education organization. Monthly mag; 24 pgs; circ 25,500. 5% freelance. Complete ms. Pays .045/wd, on publication, for one-time & reprint rts. Articles 100-800 wds. Responds in 1 month. Seasonal 8 mos ahead. Considers simultaneous submissions. Guidelines/theme list; copy for 9x12 SAE/5 stamps or $1.20.

Tips: "Most open to stories of Christians involved in sports; articles about nature and outdoors; special interest stories. Nothing preachy."

*QUEST, 475 Riverside Dr., 10th Floor, New York NY 10115. United Church of Christ, Board for Home Ministries. Submit to Editor. For senior highs (15-18 yrs). Theme list available.

#SHARING THE VICTORY, 8701 Leeds Rd., Kansas City MO 64129. (816)921-0909. Fax: (816)921-8755. Fellowship of Christian Athletes (Protestant and Catholic). John Dodderidge, ed. Equipping and encouraging athletes and coaches to take their faith seriously, in and out of competition. Monthly (Sept-May) mag; 24 pgs; circ 50,000. 60% freelance. Query; no phone query. Pays $100-200, on publication, for 1st rts. Articles 500-1,000 wds (5-20/yr). Responds in 1-2 wks. Seasonal 3 mos ahead. Accepts reprints. Kill fee. Guidelines; copy $1/9x12 SAE/3 stamps.

Poetry: Buys 3/yr. Free verse; $50.

Tips: "Most open to sports personality features including jr. high, high school and college."

#SPIRIT, Lectionary-based Weekly for Catholic Teens, 1884 Randolph Ave., St. Paul MN 55105-1700. (612)690-7005. Catholic. Therese Sherlock, CSJ, mng. ed. For the religious education of high schoolers (14-18 yrs). Biweekly newsletter; 4 pgs; circ 26,000. 50% freelance. Query (complete ms/cover letter for fiction). Pays $75-150, on publication, for all rts. Articles & fiction 1,100-1,200 wds (12 ea/yr). Responds in 2-6 wks. Seasonal 6 mos ahead. Considers simultaneous query. Free guidelines/copy.

STRAIGHT, 8121 Hamilton Ave., Cincinnati OH 45231. (513)931-4050. Fax: (513)931-0904. Standard Publishing. Carla J. Crane, ed. For Christian teens (13-19 yrs). Weekly take-home paper; 12 pgs; circ 35,000. Subscription $9.99. 100% freelance. Complete ms/cover letter; no phone/fax query. Pays .03-.07/wd, on acceptance, for all, 1st or reprint rts. Articles to 500-1,400 wds (50-75/yr); fiction 900-1,500 wds (60-80/yr). Responds in 1-8 wks. Seasonal 9-12 mos ahead. Considers simultaneous submissions & reprints. Kill fee. Prefers disk copy (check with editor first). Sidebars ok. Guidelines/theme list; copy for #10 SAE/2 stamps.

Poetry: Buys 40-60/yr. Free verse, light verse, traditional; from teens only; $10. Submit max. 5 poems.

Fillers: Buys 10-15/yr. Prayers, short humor, 300-700 wds.

Tips: "Request to be put on our theme list. Get to know and work with teenagers."

** This periodical was #17 on the 1994 Top 50 Plus Christian Publishers list. (#12 in 1993)

#THE STUDENT, 127 9th Ave. N, Nashville TN 37234. (615)251-2788. Southern Baptist. Gina Howard, acting ed. Helping college students grow in relationship to Jesus Christ by dealing with needs, problems, current issues, and suggestions for personal growth. Monthly mag; 52 pgs; circ 40,000. 10% freelance. Complete ms. Pays .055/wd; on acceptance, for all rts. Articles to 1,000 wds (20/yr); fiction to 1,000 wds (5-6/yr). Responds in 2 mos. Seasonal 1 yr ahead. Considers simultaneous submissions. Guidelines; copy for 9x12 SAE/3 stamps.

STUDENT LEADERSHIP JOURNAL, Box 7895, Madison WI 53707. (608)274-9001x425/413. Fax: (608)274-7882. InterVarsity Christian Fellowship. Jeff Yourison, ed. Undergraduate college student Christian leaders, single, ages 18-36. Quarterly journal; 32 pgs; circ 10,000. Subscription $16. 20-30% freelance. Query/clips; no phone/fax query. Pays $35-125, on acceptance, for 1st or one-time rts. Articles to 2,000 wds (1/yr); fiction to 1,500 wds (0-1/yr), $25-100; book reviews 150-400 wds, $25-50. Responds in 16 wks. Seasonal 8 mos ahead. Accepts reprints. Guidelines/theme list; copy $3/9x12 SAE/4 stamps.

> **Poetry:** Buys 4-6/yr. Avant-garde, free verse; to 15 lines; $25-50. Submit max. 5 poems.
>
> **Fillers:** Buys 0-5/yr. Facts, games, party ideas, quizzes; to 200 wds; $10-50.
>
> **Columns/Departments:** Buys 6-10/yr. Collegiate Trends, 20-100 wds; Student Leadership Network, 500-800 wds; Chapter Strategy (how-to planning strategy for campus groups), 500-800; $10-75. Query.
>
> **Special Needs:** Campus issues/trends/ministry/spiritual growth/leadership; Kingdom values.
>
> **Tips:** "Most open to main features targeted to college-age students. Be upbeat, interesting and fresh. Use both Scripture and life illustrations."

*TAKE FIVE, 1445 Boonville Ave., Springfield MO 65802. (417)862-2781x4359. Fax: (417)862-8558. Assemblies of God. Tammy Bicket, youth ed. A daily devotional for teens, grades 7-12. Quarterly booklet; 112 pgs; circ 23,000. Subscription $6. 10% freelance. Write for assignment. Pays $15/devotion, on acceptance, for all rts (one-time rts for poetry). Responds in 13 wks. Seasonal 15 mos ahead. Considers simultaneous submissions & reprints on poetry only. Guidelines; no copy.

> **Poetry:** Buys 36/yr. Any type; 8-25 lines; $15. Submit max. 5 poems. "Poetry is held on file unless writer requests its return."
>
> **Special Needs:** Photos; photos of ethnic groups are a plus. Poetry from teens.
>
> **Tips:** "All devotional writing is done on assignment to Assemblies of God writers only. Sample devotional or similar writing can be submitted for editors evaluation and for future consideration when writing assignments are made."

TEENAGE CHRISTIAN MAGAZINE, P.O. Box 111276, Nashville TN 37222-1276. Church of Christ. Marty Dodson, ed. For Christian teens (13-19 yrs). Bimonthly mag; 32 pgs; circ 14,000. Subscription $14.95. 70% freelance. Complete ms/no cover letter; no phone/fax query. Pays $15-50, on publication, for one-time rts. Articles 750-2,000 wds (15-20/yr); fiction 1,000-2,000 wds (6/yr); book/music reviews, 750 wds ($15-25). Responds in 4-8 wks. Seasonal 6 mos ahead. Accepts reprints. Occasional sidebars. Guidelines/theme list; copy for 9x12 SAE/4 stamps.

> **Poetry:** Buys 6/yr. Free verse, traditional; 10-25 lines; $10-15. Submit max. 5 poems.
>
> **Fillers:** Buys 6-10/yr. Various; 150-350 wds; $5-15.

Special Needs: "Would like some Christian celebrity interviews, biographies, etc."

Tips: "Write general-interest articles for Christian teens, 'teen friendly,' not preachy."

TEEN LIFE (formerly **HICALL**), 1445 Boonville Ave., Springfield MO 65802. (417)862-2781. Fax: (417)862-6059. Assemblies of God. Tammy Bicket, ed. To emphasize Christian living through biblical principles for Spirit-filled young people ages 15-17. Weekly take-home paper (newspaper format); 2 pgs; circ 75,000. Subscription $6.20. 50-70% freelance. Complete ms/cover letter; no phone/fax query. Pays $25-50 (.03/wd for fiction), on acceptance, for one-time rts. Articles 500-1,200 wds (30/yr); fiction 800-1,200 wds (30/yr). Responds in 20 wks. Seasonal 1 yr ahead. Considers simultaneous submissions & reprints. Prefers disk copy. Sidebars ok. Guidelines/theme list; copy for 9x12 SAE/2 stamps

   Special Needs: Looking for articles & stories that deal with our themes.

   Tips: "We don't want stories that always have a happy ending or clichéd, trite situations with pat Christian answers. Real life is more complex. Needs Christian slant. Be realistic and interact with reader."

   ** This periodical was #11 on the 1994 Top 50 Plus Christian Publishers list.

*TEEN LIFE, 8855 Dunn Rd., Hazelwood MO 63042. (314)837-7304. United Pentecostal Church. R.M. Davis, ed. For teens 13-15 yrs. Weekly take-home paper. 90% freelance. Complete ms; no cover letter or phone query. Pays $8-25, on publication, for all rts. Articles 800-1,800 wds (up to 120/yr); fiction 1,200-1,800 wds (up to 120/yr). Seasonal 9 mos ahead. Considers simultaneous submissions & reprints. Guidelines; free copy.

   Poetry: Accepts 30/yr; $3-12.

   Tips: "Most open to good stories and articles for a traditional, fundamental audience."

TEEN POWER, Box 632, Glen Ellyn IL 60138. (708)668-6000. Fax: (708)668-3806. Scripture Press. Amy J. Cox, ed. To help young teens (11-15 yrs) explore ways Jesus relates to them in everyday life. Weekly take-home paper; 8 pgs. Subscription $9.95. 100% freelance. Complete ms/cover letter; no phone query. Pays .07-.10/wd, on acceptance, for one-time or simultaneous rts. Articles 300-700 wds (50/yr); fiction & true stories 600-1,200 wds (60/yr). Responds in 8-12 wks. Seasonal 1 yr ahead. Considers simultaneous submissions & reprints (pays .05-.07/wd). Guidelines/theme list/copy for #10 SAE/1 stamp.

   Poetry: From teens only. Free verse, light verse, traditional.

   Fillers: Buys 10/yr. Cartoons, prose, quizzes, prayers, short humor, word puzzles; 200-600 wds; $15-60.

   Tips: "We rely heavily on freelance writers, so this is a good place to break in. Study young teens (jr. high). Know what issues they're dealing with and what makes them click. We're always in need of true stories (profiles, as-told-to, personal experience) and short nonfiction."

   ** This periodical was #41 on the 1994 Top 50 Plus Christian Publishers list. (#31 in 1993)

*TEEN QUEST (TQ), P.O. Box 3512, Irving TX 75015. (214)570-7599. Shepherd Ministries/evangelical. Christopher Lyon, ed. To show teens (13-17 yrs) why a relationship with Christ is important now and how to grow in this relationship. Monthly (10X) mag; 48 pgs; circ 35,000-40,000. 50% freelance. Query; phone query ok. Pays .08-.15/wd (reprints .03/wd), on acceptance, for 1st rts. Articles 1,000-2,500 wds (15-20/yr); fiction 1,500-2,250 wds (20-25/yr). Responds in 6 wks. Seasonal 6 mos ahead. Considers simultaneous submissions. Some kill fees. Guidelines; copy for 9x12 SAE/4 stamps.

   Poetry: Buys 10-20/yr. Devotional/thought-provoking; teen-written only; no payment. Submit max. 3 poems.

Columns/Departments: Buys 5-6/yr. Together (dating/relationships), 1,000-1,200 wds; BreakOut (profiles of outstanding teenagers), 1,000-1,200 wds; .07-.12/wd.

Tips: "Teen language and behavior must be current. Not too preachy in moral—let the story make its own point. Most open to fiction, personal experience. Ask yourself if teens can readily identify with main characters."

+TODAY'S CHRISTIAN TEEN, 401 E. Main St., Morgantown PA 19543. (215)286-7744. Fax: (215)286-6721. Marketing Partners, Inc. Jerry Thacker, ed. To help today's Christian teens by presenting material which applies the Bible to contemporary issues. Triannual mag; circ 100,000. Free subscription. Open to freelance.

#VISIONS, Lectionary-based Weekly for Catholic Junior Highs, 330 Progress Rd., Dayton OH 45449. (513)847-5900. Fax: (513)847-5910. Peter Li, Inc./Catholic. Joan Mitchell, CSJ, mng. ed. Connects young people's real life experiences—successes and conflicts in family, neighborhood, classroom—with the Sunday gospels; for grades 7-9. Weekly (28X during school yr) take-home paper; circ 140,000. 40% freelance. Query. Pays $75-125, on publication, for all rts. Articles (6-8/yr) & fiction (8-10/yr), 900-1,000 wds. Responds in 2-8 wks. Seasonal 4-6 mos ahead. Considers simultaneous query. Guidelines; copy $1.85.

WITH, The Magazine for Radical Christian Youth, Box 347, Newton KS 67114. (316)283-5100. Mennonite, Brethren & Mennonite Brethren. Carol Duerksen (fillers & poetry) & Eddy Hall (articles & fiction), co-eds. For high-school teens (15-18 yrs), Christian and non-Christian. 8 time/yr mag; 32 pgs; circ 6,100. Subscription $18.95. 75% freelance. Query (on first-person and how-to articles); complete ms on everything else/short cover letter; no phone/fax query. Pays .05/wd for 1st rts; .05-.10/wd (.05-.07/wd for fiction) for assignments, .03/wd for reprints; on acceptance; for first, simultaneous or reprint rts. Articles 500-1,600 wds (20/yr); fiction 800-1,900 wds (20-25/yr); music review, 500 wds, $30. Responds in 4 wks. Seasonal 6-8 mos ahead. Considers simultaneous submissions & reprints. Kill fee 25-35%. Sidebars ok. Guidelines/theme list; copy for 9x12 SAE/5 stamps. Separate guidelines for 1st-person and how-to articles sent only when requested.

Poetry: Buys 5/yr. Most types; 4-50 lines; $10-25. Submit max. 5 poems.

Fillers: Buys 10-20 cartoons/yr; $15-35 ($50 for cover).

Special Needs: Stories/articles on divorce, from teens.

Tips: "The how-to article is a good place to break in. Study special guidelines and send a query at least 8 months before appropriate theme issue. Fiction to match upcoming theme also good way to break in."

** This periodical was #12 on the 1994 Top 50 Plus Christian Publishers list. (#24 in 1993)

#YOU! MAGAZINE, 31194 La Baya Dr., Suite 200, West Lake Village CA 91362. (818)991-1813. Fax: (818)991-2024. Catholic. Tom Ehart, mng. ed. An alternative teen magazine (13-18 yrs) aimed at bridging the gap between religion and pop culture. Monthly (10X) tabloid; 28 pgs; circ 35,000. Subscription $19.95. 50% freelance. Query/clips or complete ms/cover letter. Pays .05-.075/wd ($10-105), on publication, for one-time & reprint rts. Articles 250-1,000 wds (25-50/yr); book reviews, 500 wds, .07/wd. Responds in 2 mos. Seasonal 4 mos ahead. Considers simultaneous query & reprints. Guidelines; copy $2.50 for 10x15 SAE/5 stamps.

Fillers: Anecdotes, cartoons, facts, ideas, jokes, short humor; 75-250 wds.

Columns/Departments: Buys 30/yr. School (issues); Family (issues); Friends (issues); all 350 wds; $20-35.

Tips: "Write in the language of teens. Must be 'hip'. Most open to columns."

*YOUNG ADULT TODAY, 1350 W. 103rd St., Chicago IL 60643. (312)233-4499. Urban Ministries, Inc. Dr. Colleen Birchett, ed. Young adult curriculum for ages 18-24 (student and teacher manuals). Quarterly booklet; 72 pgs; circ 7,500. 60% freelance. Complete ms. Pays $35-50, on publication, for all rts. Articles (24/yr) & fiction (12/yr); 2,900-3,500 characters. Responds in 1-2 wks. Seasonal 3 mos ahead. Free guidelines/theme list/copy.

Tips: "Send resume and writing sample. Writer must be able to relate the writing to the outline given and the biblical material.

*YOUNG AND ALIVE, Box 6097, Lincoln NE 68506. (402)488-0981. Christian Record Services. Richard Kaiser, ed. For sight impaired young adults, 16-20 yrs; for interdenominational Christian audience. Quarterly mag; 65-70 pgs; circ 26,000. 90% freelance. Query or complete ms/cover letter; phone query ok. Pays .03-.05/wd, on acceptance, for one-time rts. Articles & true stories 800-1,400 wds (30/yr). Responds in 2-3 mos. Seasonal 1 yr ahead. Considers simultaneous query & reprints. Guidelines; copy for 9-12 SAE/6 stamps.

Special Needs: Adventure and relationships for the handicapped.

Tips: "Although many blind and visually impaired yg. adults have the same interests as their sighted counterparts, the material should meet their needs specifically."

Note: This publication has cut back to fewer issues and is overstocked.

YOUNG SALVATIONIST, Box 269, Alexandria VA 22313. (703)684-5500. Fax: (703)684-5539. The Salvation Army. Lesa Davis, asst. ed. For high-school teens in the Salvation Army. Monthly (10X) mag; 12-16 pgs; circ 50,000. Subscription $4. 80% freelance. Query or complete ms/no cover letter; phone/fax query ok. Pays .10/wd, on acceptance, for 1st, one-time & reprint rts. Articles (10-15/yr) & fiction (5-10/yr); 750-1,200 wds. Responds in 6 wks. Seasonal 6 mos ahead. Considers simultaneous submissions & reprints. Will accept disk. Some sidebars. Guidelines/theme list; copy for 9x12 SAE/3 stamps.

Tips: "We are always looking for articles/interviews about Christian entertainers or athletes. Ask for theme list. Be contemporary—no stories about how it used to be."

** This periodical was #14 on the 1994 Top 50 Plus Christian Publishers list. (#7 in 1993)

*YOUTH FOCUS, Paywoods Communications, 4 Daniels Farm Rd., Ste. 134, Trumbull CT 06611. (203)924-5646. For African-American youth, ages 12-17. Quentin Plair, ed. Monthly newsletter; circ 10,000. 75% freelance. Complete ms. Pays $15-100, on publication, for 1st or one-time rts. Articles 10-3,000 wds (2/yr). Responds in 2 mos. Seasonal 5 mos ahead. Considers simultaneous submissions & reprints. Guidelines; copy $1.

Poetry: Buys 7/yr. Any type; 1-200 lines; $10-30.

YOUTH UPDATE, 1615 Republic St., Cincinnati OH 45210-1289. (513)241-5615. St. Anthony Messenger Press/Catholic. Carol Ann Morrow, ed. For high-school teens, to support their growth in a life of faith. Monthly newsletter; 4 pgs; circ 25,000. 88% freelance. Query; no phone/fax query. Pays $325-400 (.14/wd), on acceptance, for 1st rts. Articles 2,300 wds (12/yr). Responds in 8 wks. Seasonal 6 mos ahead. Prefers final on disk. Sidebars ok. Guidelines; copy for #10 SAE/1 stamp.

*YOUTH WORLD, 8855 Dunn Rd., Hazelwood MO 63042. (314)837-7304. United Pentecostal Church. R.M. Davis, ed. For teens 13-15 yrs. Weekly take-home paper. 90% freelance. Complete ms; no cover letter or phone query. Pays $8-25, on publication, for all rts. Articles 800-1,800 wds (up to 120/yr); fiction 1,200-1,800 wds (up to 120/yr). Seasonal 9 mos ahead. Considers simultaneous submissions & reprints. Guidelines; free copy.

Poetry: Accepts 30/yr; $3-12.

Tips: "Most open to good stories and articles for a traditional, fundamental audience."

WOMEN'S MARKETS

ANNA'S JOURNAL, Rt 8 Box 655, Ellijay GA 30540. (706)276-2307. Catherine Ward-Long, ed. Spiritual support for childless couples who for the most part have decided to stay that way. Quarterly newsletter. Subscription $20. Estab 1995. 90% freelance. Complete ms/cover letter; no phone/fax query. **PAYS IN COPIES,** for 1st, one-time or reprint rts. Not copyrighted. Articles 500-1,500 wds (16/yr). Responds in 4-8 wks. Seasonal 3 months ahead. Accepts reprints. No disks. No sidebars. Guidelines.

> **Poetry:** Accepts 4/yr. Any type. Submit max. 3 poems.
>
> **Fillers:** Anecdotes, ideas (on how church can meet our needs), prose, prayers, letters; 50-250 wds.
>
> **Tips:** "Looking for innovative ways to improve the child-free lifestyle and self-esteem. No articles on adoption or infertility. It helps if writer is childless or knows someone who is."

*THE CHURCH WOMAN, 475 Riverside Dr., Room 812, New York NY 10115. (212)870-2347. Fax: (212)870-2338. Church Women United. Margaret Schiffert, ed. Highlights women's, peace and justice issues. Quarterly mag; 24 pgs; circ 10,000. Little freelance. Query. **PAYS IN COPIES.** Articles to 3 pgs. Guidelines; copy $1.

+CLARITY - At press time, **Clarity** has just been sold to **Guideposts.** After completing additional research, Guideposts Associates hopes to relaunch this publication targeting the same demographic group as the original magazine. Contact Guideposts at 16 E. 34th St., New York NY 10016, for new guidelines.

CO-LABORER, Box 5002, Antioch TN 37011-5002. (615)731-6812. Fax: (615)731-0071. Free Will Baptist/Women Nationally Active for Christ. Submit to The Editor. For members of WNAC; emphasizes missions, Christian issues, and spiritual development resources. Bimonthly mag; 32 pgs; circ 13,000+. Subscription $5.95. 10% freelance. Complete ms/cover letter; no phone/fax query. **PAYS IN COPIES** for 1st rts. Not copyrighted. Articles 300-1,500 wds (20/yr); book reviews, 1,000 wds. Responds in 3-12 wks. Seasonal 6 mos ahead. Considers simultaneous submissions & reprints. Sidebars ok. Guidelines; copy $1.25/ 9x12 SAE/4 stamps.

> **Poetry:** Free verse, haiku, traditional; 1-21 lines; on missions only. Submit max. 6 poems.
>
> **Fillers:** Anecdotes, facts, ideas, prose, prayers, quotes, short humor; 300-500 wds.
>
> **Columns/Departments:** Crosswinds (overcoming obstacles), 500-1,500 wds.
>
> **Fillers:** Anecdotes with missions slant.
>
> **Tips:** "Intelligent queries get attention. Most open to feature columns."

#CONSCIENCE, A Newsjournal of Prochoice Catholic Opinion, 1436 U St. NW, Ste. 301, Washington DC 20009-3997. (202)986-6093. Catholic. Maggie Hume, ed. For laypeople, theologians, policymakers, and clergy. Quarterly newsjournal; 48 pgs; circ 12,000. 80% freelance. Query or complete ms/cover letter; no phone query. Pays $25-150, on publication, for 1st rts. Articles 1,000-3,500 wds (8-12/yr); book reviews 600-1,200 wds, $25-50. Responds in 4 mos. Seasonal 6 mos ahead. Considers simultaneous submissions & reprints. Kill fee. Guidelines; copy for 9x12 SAE/4 stamps.

> **Poetry:** Buys 16/yr. Any type, on subject, to 50 lines; $10 + copies. Submit max. 5 poems.
>
> **Fillers:** Buys 6-10/yr. Newsbreaks; 100-300 wds; $25-35.
>
> **Tips:** "Focus on issues of reproductive choice. Raise serious ethical questions within a generally prochoice framework. Most open to feature articles and book reviews."

*CONTEMPO, P.O. Box 830010, Birmingham AL 35283-0010. (205)991-8100. Southern Baptist. Cindy L. Dake, ed. A young women's (18-34 yrs) publication focusing on missions education and women's/family issues. Monthly mag; 48 pgs; circ 65,000. 95% freelance. Complete ms/cover letter. Pays .055/wd, on publication, for all rts. Articles to 600 wds. Responds in 12-18 mos.

DAUGHTERS OF SARAH, 2121 Sheridan Rd., Evanston IL 60201-2926. (708)866-3882. Ecumenical. Cathi Falsani, asst. ed.; Dulcie Gannett, book review ed. Christian feminism magazine with a biblical emphasis, using inclusive language. Quarterly mag; 64 pgs; circ 4,000. Subscription $18. 50% freelance. Query; no phone/fax query. Pays $15-90, on publication, for one-time rts. Articles (16/yr) & fiction (2/yr), 500-2,000 wds; book reviews 500 wds/pays in copies. Responds in 6-12 wks. Seasonal 6 mos ahead. Accepts reprints. Kill fee. No sidebars. Guidelines/theme list; copy $4/9x12 SAE/5 stamps.

> **Poetry:** Buys 8/yr. Avant-garde, free verse, traditional; $15-45. Submit max. 2 poems.
>
> **Columns/Departments:** Buys 12/yr. Segue (evangelical women), 700-1,000 wds; Bible Interpretation, 500-2,000 wds; Women in Ministry, 500-2,000 wds; $15-75.
>
> **Tips:** "Most open to articles and poetry. Thematic; write for themes."

ESPRIT, Evangelical Lutheran Women, 1512 St. James St., Winnipeg MB R3H 0L2 Canada. (204)775-8591. Fax: (204)783-7548. Evangelical Lutheran Church in Canada. Submit to Anne Beretta, ed. (53 Glenary Ave., Toronto ON M4P 2T9 Canada) For denominational women. Bimonthly mag; 52 pgs; circ 7,200. Subscription $15.50, $25 US. 50% freelance. Complete ms/cover letter; phone query ok. Pays $12.50-50 Canadian (fiction $12.50-37.50), on publication, for 1st rts. Articles 350-1,400 wds (36/yr); fiction 350-1,000 wds (6/yr); book reviews, to 350 wds, $10. Reports immediately. Seasonal 3 mos ahead. Considers simultaneous submissions & reprints. Sidebars ok. Guidelines/theme list; copy for 6x9 SAE/.88 Canadian postage or $1 for non-Canadians.

> **Poetry:** Accepts 10-12/yr. Traditional; 5-100 lines; up to $12.50.
>
> **Fillers:** Buys 20-30/yr. Anecdotes, cartoons, prose, prayers, quotes, word puzzles; 50-350 wds; $3.25-12.50.
>
> **Tips:** "Be a Lutheran living in Canada. Use inclusive language, NRSV as reference Bible, focus on women and spiritual/faith issues. Choose theme from theme calendar."

HELPING HAND, Box 12609, Oklahoma City OK 73157-2609. (405)787-7110. Fax: (405)789-3957. Pentecostal Holiness Church/Women's Ministries. Doris L. Moore, ed. Denominational; for women. Bimonthly mag; 20 pgs; circ 4,000. Subscription $6.50. 70% freelance. Complete ms/cover letter; no phone query. Pays $20, on publication, for 1st, one-time, reprint & simultaneous rts. Articles 500-2,000 wds (24/yr); fiction 500-2,000 wds (24/yr). Responds in 1-3 wks. Seasonal 4 mos ahead. Considers simultaneous submissions & reprints. Guidelines; copy for 9x12 SAE/2 stamps.

> **Poetry:** Buys 5/yr. Traditional; $10-20. Submit max. 4 poems.

*HORIZONS, 100 Witherspoon St., Louisville KY 40202. (502)569-5379. Fax: (502)569-8085. Presbyterian Church (USA). Barbara Roche, ed. Justice issues and spiritual life for Presbyterian women. Bimonthly mag.; 40 pgs; circ 30,000. 10% freelance. Complete ms. Pays $50/pg., on publication, for all rts. Articles & fiction 1,500-2,000 wds. Responds in 4 wks. Seasonal 6 mos ahead. Accepts reprints. Guidelines/theme list; copy $2.

> **Poetry:** Buys 4/yr. All types; $25.
>
> **Tips:** "Know our audience—mostly women in their 40s and up who are interested in social concerns." Most open to fiction and poetry.

*JOURNAL OF WOMEN'S MINISTRIES, 46 Olive St., Methuen MA 01844. (800)334-7626. Episcopal/Council for Women's Ministries. Marcy Darin, ed. Deals with issues of interest to women from a liberal perspective. Biannual mag; 36 pgs; circ 10,000. Query. Pays $50, on publication, for 1st rts. Articles 1,200-1,500 wds. Responds in 1 mo. Seasonal 3 mos ahead. Guidelines; copy for 9x12 SAE/3 stamps.

> **Poetry:** Free verse, traditional. Submit max. 2 poems.

+JOURNEY, 127 Ninth Ave. N., Nashville TN 37234. (615)251-3824. Fax: (615)251-5008. Southern Baptist. Selma Wilson, ed-in-chief. Devotional magazine for women of the 90s. Monthly mag; 80 pgs; circ 35,000. Subscription $18.50. Estab 1994. Query/published clips. Pay is negotiable, on acceptance. Articles 350-700 wds. Responds in 6 wks. Seasonal 6 mos ahead. Accepts reprints. Prefers disk copy (3.5 HD. MAC). Sidebars ok. Guidelines; copy for 9x12 SAE/3 stamps.

> **Columns/Departments:** Buys 12/yr. Prayer Diary. Query.

THE JOYFUL WOMAN, P.O. Box 90028, Chattanooga TN 37412-6028. (615)894-4500. Fax: (615)894-0907. Joy Rice Martin, ed. For and about Bible-believing women who want God's best. Bimonthly mag; 24 pgs; circ 10,000. Subscription $15. 30% freelance. Query; fax query ok. Pays $15-50 (.02/wd & up), on publication, for 1st rts. Articles 1,500 wds (25/yr); music reviews, 200-400 wds, $20. Responds in 2-16 wks. Seasonal 6 mos ahead. Considers simultaneous submissions & reprints. Prefers disk on acceptance. Sidebars ok. Guidelines/theme list; copy $3/9x12 SAE/4 stamps.

> **Poetry:** Buys 6/yr. Free verse, light verse, traditional; 15-40 lines; $15-40. Submit max. 2 poems.
>
> **Fillers:** Buys 10/yr. Cartoons, jokes, newsbreaks, prayers, quotes, short humor; 25-300 wds; $15-25.
>
> **Tips:** "Our biggest need is true-life stories. We prefer 1,000 word or less manuscripts, and would like color pictures of author and/or manuscript subject. Please allow 16 weeks before you call about your manuscript."

*JUST BETWEEN US, Jill Briscoe's Newsletter for Ministry Wives, P.O. Box 7728, Louisville KY 40257. (502)899-3119. Submit to Managing ed. Ideas, encouragement and resources for wives of evangelical ministers. Quarterly mag; 20 pgs; circ 5,000. Estab 1990. 90% freelance. Query. **NO PAYMENT** for one-time rts. Any length. Reporting time varies. Considers simultaneous submissions. Guidelines; copy for 9x12 SAE/3 stamps.

> **Tips:** "Virtually all material is written by ministry wives. Always include bio notes."

#THE LINK & VISITOR, 30 Arlington Ave., Toronto ON M6G 3K8 Canada. (416)651-7192. Fax: (416)651-0438. Baptist Women's Missionary Society of Ontario and Quebec. Esther Barnes, ed. A positive, practical magazine for Canadian Baptist women who want to make a difference in our world. Monthly (9X) mag; 16 pgs; circ 5,500. Subscription $10 Canada, $14 U.S. 30% freelance. Complete ms/cover letter; phone query ok. Pays to $25-100 Canadian, on publication, for 1st, one-time, or simultaneous rts. Articles 750-1,800 wds. Responds in 36 wks. Seasonal 4-6 mos ahead. Considers simultaneous submissions & reprints. Guidelines; copy for 9x12 SAE/.86 Canadian postage.

> **Poetry:** Buys 6/yr. Free verse; 12-32 lines; $25. Submit max. 4 poems.
>
> **Special Needs:** Articles on courage; stories on a single Beatitude.
>
> **Tips:** "Canadian writers preferred. If U.S. writers send U.S. postage for returns, they will be rejected. Too many writers seem too focused on themselves and their own experiences."

*LUTHERAN WOMAN TODAY, 8765 W. Higgins Ave., Chicago IL 60631-4189. (312)380-2743. Evangelical Lutheran Church in America. Nancy J. Stelling, ed. For women in the denomination. Monthly (11X) mag: 48 pgs; circ 250,000. 25% freelance. Complete ms/cover letter or query. Pays $60-280, on publication, for 1st rts. Articles (24/yr) & fiction (5/yr), to 1,250 wds. Responds in 1-2 mos. Seasonal 7 mos ahead. Guidelines; free copy.

> **Poetry:** Buys 5/yr. Free verse, haiku, light verse, traditional; to 60 lines; $15-60. Submit max. 3 poems. Poetry must have a spiritual and women's focus.

> **Columns/Departments:** Buys 5/yr. Devotion, 350 wds; Season's Best (reflection on the church yr), 350-700 wds; About Women; Forum (essay); $50-250.

> **Tips:** "Submit a short, well-written article using inclusive language and offering a women's and spiritual focus."

#PROBE, 529 S. Wabash, Ste. 404, Chicago IL 60605. (312)663-1980. National Assembly of Religious Women/Catholic/Ecumenical. Ann Wetherilt, ed. Networking tool for members with a progressive, social justice and feminist thrust. Quarterly newspaper; 12 pgs; circ 3,000. 90% freelance. Query. **PAYS A SUBSCRIPTION** for one-time rts. Articles to 2,000 wds; fiction to 2,000 wds. Considers simultaneous submissions. No guidelines; copy $1.

> **Poetry:** Must be theme-related.

*RESPONSE, 475 Riverside Dr., Rm. 1344, New York NY 10115. (212)870-3755. United Methodist. Dana E. Jones, ed. Program journal of United Methodist Women. Monthly (11X) mag; 48 pgs; circ 75,000. 50% freelance. Query. Pays variable rates, on publication, for all rts. Articles 1,000 wds; book reviews 1,000 wds. Seasonal 5 mos ahead. Kill fee. No guidelines; free copy.

> **Tips:** "Send us something that focuses on the concerns of women, youth or children."

*ROYAL SERVICE, P.O. Box 830010, Birmingham AL 35283-0010. (205)991-8100. Southern Baptist/Women's Missionary Union. Cindy Lewis Dake, mng ed.; Laura Savage, prod. ed. Focuses on missions; women and family issues. Monthly mag; 48 pgs; circ 290,000. 95% freelance. Complete ms/cover letter. Pays .055/wd, on publication, for all rts. Articles to 600 wds. Responds in 12-18 mos. No guidelines or copy.

SALT AND LIGHT, Christian Career Women, Inc., Box 531152, Indianapolis IN 46253-1152. Mary Reynolds-Williams, ed. For Christian working women (25-60 yrs); conservative. Quarterly newsletter; 6-8 pgs; circ 300. Subscription $15.95. 100% freelance. Complete ms/no cover letter. **PAYS IN COPIES.** Not copyrighted. Articles 800-1,200 wds (10-20/yr). Responds in 6-12 wks. Seasonal 6 mos ahead. Accepts reprints. No disk. Sidebars ok. Guidelines; copy for 9x12 SAE/3 stamps.

> **Poetry:** Accepts 4-6/yr. Light verse, traditional. Submit max. 3 poems.

> **Fillers:** Accepts 5-15/yr. Anecdotes, prose, prayers, quotes, short humor.

> **Tips:** "Be aware of current issues that Christian working women are faced with—especially the corporate setting. We look for uniqueness and top-notch writing."

SISTERS TODAY, The Liturgical Press, St. John's Abbey, P.O. Box 7500, Collegeville MN 56321-7500. (612)363-7065. Fax: (800)445-5899. Catholic. Sr. Mary Anthony Wagner, O.S.B., ed. (St. Benedict's Convent, St. Joseph MN 56374). To explore the role of women and the Church in our time. Bimonthly mag; 80 pgs; circ 4,500. 70% freelance. Complete ms/cover letter; phone/fax query ok. Pays $5/printed page, on publication, for 1st rts. Articles up to 10-12 pgs (40-50/yr). Responds in 4 wks. Seasonal several mos ahead. Guidelines/theme list; copy $3.50.

> **Poetry:** Sr. Mary Virginia Micke, C.S.J. Buys 50-80/yr. Free verse, haiku, light verse, traditional; to 25 lines (prefers 16-20); $10. Submit max. 4 poems.

> **Special Needs:** United Nations anniversary significance.

Tips: "Most open to articles and poems."

TODAY'S CHRISTIAN WOMAN, 465 Gundersen Dr., Carol Stream IL 60188-2498. (708)260-6200. Fax: (708)260-0114. Ramona Cramer Tucker, mng. ed; submit to Camerin Courtney, asst. ed. To help Christian women grow in their relationship to God by providing practical, biblical perspectives on marriage, sex, parenting, work, health, friendship, and self. Bimonthly mag; 100-150 pgs; circ 375,000. Subscription rate changing. 25% freelance. Query; no phone/fax query. Pays .15/wd, on publication, for 1st rts. Articles 1,000-2,000 wds (12/yr); no fiction. Responds in 4-6 wks. Seasonal 6 mos ahead. Sidebars generated in-house. Guidelines; copy $4.

Fillers: Buys 1/yr. Facts, prose; 50-200 wds; $20.

Columns/Departments: Buys 12/yr. One Woman's Story (dramatic story of overcoming a difficult situation), 1,000-1,500 wds, $150; Heart to Heart (true humorous or inspirational anecdotes), 50-200 wds, $20; Issues (first-person perspective on current issues), 1,000-1,500 wds.

Tips: "Most open to One Woman's Story: Should tell how you, through a personal experience, came to a spiritual turning point, solved a problem, or overcame a difficult situation."

** This periodical was #34 on the 1994 Top 50 Plus Christian Publishers list.

+UNIQUE, P.O. Box 2430, Cleveland TN 37320-2430. (615)478-7170. Fax: (615)478-7891. Church of God (Cleveland TN). Denominational magazine for pentecostal women. Bimonthly mag; circ 8,000. Subscription $6.50. Open to freelance.

VIRTUE, P.O. Box 36630, Colorado Springs CO 80936-3663. (719)531-7776. Fax: (719)535-0172. Jeanette Thomason, mng. ed. Bimonthly mag; 80 pgs; circ 135,000. Subscription $16.95. 40% freelance. Query (complete ms for fiction, poetry or departments); no phone/fax query. Pays .15-.25/wd, on publication, for 1st rts (sometimes exclusive rts). Articles 900-1,200 to 2,000 wds (20/yr) & fiction 1,200-2,500 wds (6-8/yr). Responds in 9 wks. Seasonal 6-7 mos ahead. Considers simultaneous query & reprints only from unknown publications. May pay kill fee. Disk for final. Encourages sidebars. Guidelines; copy for 9x12 SAE/5 stamps or $3.

Poetry: Karen Beattie. Buys 6-12/yr. Avant-garde, light verse; any length; .15-.20/wd. Submit max. 3 poems.

Departments: Buys 30/yr. Equipped for Ministry (how-to), 300-500 wds; Working Smarter (household hints), 100 wds; One Woman's Journal, to 1,200 wds; Good for You (health/fitness), 200-400 wds. Pays .15-.20/wd.

Tips: "Send submissions for specific departments after you're familiar with the magazine. Most open to 'One Woman's Journal'(story of how a woman works through a struggle—not necessarily solving it—and where God is in that)."

**This periodical was #42 on the 1994 Top 50 Plus Christian Publishers list. (#1 in 1993)

THE WESLEYAN WOMAN, P.O. Box 50434, Indianapolis IN 46250-0434. (317)595-4164. Fax: (317)594-8309. Wesleyan Church. Martha Blackburn, ed. Inspiration, education and sharing to meet the needs of Wesleyan women. Quarterly mag; circ 3,400. Subscription $10. Complete ms/cover letter. Pays .04/wd (.02/wd for reprints), on publication, for 1st & one-time rts. Articles 700-1,000 wds; fiction. Seasonal 6 mos ahead. Considers simultaneous submissions & reprints. Guidelines/theme list; free copy.

Poetry: Accepts 4-5/yr. Avant-garde, free verse, light verse, traditional.

Fillers: Cartoons, facts, newsbreaks.

Tips: "Most open to personal stories of 'guts' and grace to follow the Lord. Ways you see God at work in your life."

#WOMAN'S TOUCH, 1445 Boonville Ave., Springfield MO 65802-1894. (417)862-2781. Fax: (417)862-0503. Assemblies of God. Peggy Musgrove, ed. A general readership magazine committed to providing help and inspiration for Christian women, strengthening family life, and reaching out in witness to others. Bimonthly mag; 28 pgs; circ 17,000. Subscription $6/leader $7.50. 75-90% freelance. Complete ms/cover letter. Pays $10-35 (.03/wd), on acceptance, for one-time rts. Articles 500-1,200 wds (75/yr). Responds in 3 mos. Seasonal 8 mos ahead. Considers simultaneous submissions & reprints. Guidelines; copy for 9x12 SAE/3 stamps.

> **Poetry:** Buys 10/yr. Free verse, light verse, traditional; 4-50 lines; $5-20. Submit max. 4 poems.
>
> **Fillers:** Buys 5/yr. Facts; 50-200 wds; $5-15.
>
> **Columns/Departments:** Buys 10/yr. An Added Touch (special crafts/decorations/activities); A Personal Touch (personal improvement); A Final Touch (short human interest); 500-800 wds; $20-35. Query/clips.

WOMEN ALIVE!, Box 4683, Overland Park KS 66204. (913)649-8583. Fax: (913)649-8583. Aletha Hinthorn, ed. To encourage Holiness women to apply Scripture to their daily lives. Bimonthly mag; 20 pgs; circ 4,000. Subscription $9.95. 50% freelance. Complete ms/no cover letter; phone query ok. Pays $15-50, on publication, for one-time rts. Articles 900-2,000 wds (25/yr); fiction 900-2,000 wds (0-1/yr). Responds in 2-4 wks. Seasonal 4-6 mos ahead. Considers simultaneous submissions & reprints. Sidebars ok. Guidelines; copy for 9x12 SAE/4 stamps.

> **Poetry:** Buys 0-3/yr. Traditional, $10-40. Submit max. 3.
>
> **Fillers:** Buys 0-1/yr. Cartoons, jokes, short humor.
>
> **Columns/Departments:** Buys 6/yr. Senior Savvy (for older women); 900-1,200 wds; $15-40.

WRITER'S MARKETS

BYLINE MAGAZINE, Box 130596, Edmond OK 73013-0001. (405)348-5591. General publication for freelance writers and poets. Kathryn Fanning, mng. ed. Teaching new writers how to write and sell their work. Monthly (11X) mag; 28 pgs; circ 3,000+. Subscription $20. 80% freelance. Query or complete ms/no cover letter; no phone/fax query. Pays $50 ($100 for fiction), on acceptance, for 1st rts. Articles 1,500-1,800 wds (72/yr); personal experiences 800 wds; fiction 2,000-4,000 wds (11/yr). Responds in 4-6 wks. Seasonal 6-8 mos ahead. Considers simultaneous submissions. Disk for final. Encourages sidebars. Guidelines; copy $3.50/9x12 SAE.

> **Poetry:** Marcia Preston. Buys 110-120/yr. Any type; to 30 lines; $5-10. Writing themes. Submit max. 3 poems.
>
> **Columns/Departments:** End Piece (personal essay on writing theme), 800 wds; First Sale accounts, 300-600 wds; Only When I Laugh (writing humor), 300-800 wds; $15-35. Complete ms.
>
> **Tips:** "Most open to First Sale account; be upbeat about writing."

#CANADIAN WRITER'S JOURNAL, Box 6618, Depot 1, Victoria BC V8P 5N7 Canada. (604)477-8807. Gordon M. Smart, ed. How-to articles for writers. Quarterly mag; circ 350. 75% freelance. Query or complete ms/cover letter; no phone query. Pays $5/published pg (Canadian), on publication, for 1st, one-time or reprint rts. Not copyrighted. Articles 500-1,200 wds (50-55/yr); book reviews 250-500 wds/$5. Responds in 2 mos. Seasonal 3 mos ahead. Accepts reprints. Kill fee. Guidelines; copy $4.

> **Fiction:** "Most fiction requirements filled by annual contest; 500-1,200 wds."
>
> **Poetry:** Traditional, haiku: on writing. Sponsors annual poetry contest.

Fillers: Anecdotes, cartoons, ideas, short humor; 100-250 wds.

*CHIPS OFF THE WRITER'S BLOCK, Box 83371, Los Angeles CA 90083. Secular. Wanda Windham, ed. For beginning writers. Bimonthly newsletter; circ 500+. 100% freelance. Complete ms/cover letter; no phone query. PAYS IN COPIES, for one-time rts. Articles to 1,500 wds (100/yr); fiction to 1,200 wds (50+/yr). Responds in 6 wks. Seasonal 6 mos ahead. Considers simultaneous submissions & reprints. Guidelines; copy $3.

Poetry: All forms (on writing only); 1-40 lines. Submit max. 5 poems.

Fillers: Anything on writing; to 300 wds.

Tips: "Need more one-page, well-researched, how-to articles. Open to new columns and ideas."

+CHRISTIAN AUTHOR NEWSLETTER, 177 E. Crystal Lake Ave., Lake Mary FL 32746. (407)324-5465. Fax: (407)324-0209. Christian Writers Institute. June Eaton, ed. Information for writers; 90% of submissions come from their instructors or students. Bimonthly newsletter; 4 pgs; circ 500. Subscription $12. 10% freelance. NO PAYMENT. Seasonal 3 mos ahead.

Special Needs: Writers'interests.

THE CHRISTIAN COMMUNICATOR, 3133 Puente St., Fullerton CA 92635. (714)990-1532. Fax: (714)493-6552. American Christian Writers/Reg Forder, Box 5168, Phoenix AZ 85010, 800-21-WRITE (for advertising or subscriptions). Susan Titus Osborn, ed. For Christian writers/speakers who want to polish writing skills, develop public-speaking techniques, and sell their mss. Monthly mag; 24 pgs; circ 4,000. Subscription $20. 50% freelance. Complete ms/cover letter; phone/fax query ok. Pays $5-10, on publication, for 1st, one-time or reprint rts. Articles 600-1,200 wds (62/yr). Responds in 4-6 wks. Seasonal 6 mos ahead. Accepts reprints. Free guidelines/copy.

Poetry: Accepts 12/yr. Poems on writing; $5. Submit max. 4 poems.

Fillers: Accepts 12/yr. Cartoons, quotes; $5.

Columns/Departments: Buys 12/yr. Communicator Interview (published author), 800-1,200 wds; Publisher's Profile, 800-1,200 wds; Speaker's Corner (techniques for speakers), 600-1,000 wds; Book Reviews (writing/speaking books), 300-400 wds; $5-10.

Tips: "Most in need of publisher or author profiles or book reviews (see columns above)."

+THE CHRISTIAN RESPONSE, Rt. 2 Box 1, P.O. Box 125, Staples MN 56479. (218)894-1165. Christian Writers of America. Hap Corbett, ed. For Christian writers, mostly, who write letters in defense of Christianity. Bimonthly newsletter; 6 pgs; circ 300. Subscription $15. Estab 1993. 10% freelance. Complete ms/cover letter. Pays $5-20, on acceptance, for 1st or simultaneous rts. Articles 1-300 wds. Responds in 2 wks. Seasonal 6 mos ahead. Considers simultaneous submissions & reprints. No sidebars. Guidelines; copy $1.

Fillers: Anecdotes & tips; 10-100 wds; $5-10.

Special Needs: Tips on writing effective letters to the editor.

Tips: "We are looking for news/articles about anti-Christian bias in the media, and how you, as a writer, responded to such incidents."

CROSS & QUILL, Rt 3 Box 1635, Jefferson Davis Rd., Clinton SC 29325. (803)697-6035. Fax: (803)697-6035. Christian Writers Fellowship Intl. Sandy Brooks, ed. For Christian writers, editors, agents, conference directors. Bimonthly newsletter; 8 pgs; circ 1,000. Subscription $18; CWFI membership $35. 50% freelance. Complete ms/no cover letter; no phone query. PAYS IN COPIES, for 1st, one-time or reprint rts. Articles 300-800 wds (20/yr). Responds in 3 wks. Seasonal 1 yr ahead. Accepts reprints. Prefers disk copy in ASCII. Guidelines; copy $1/9x12 SAE/2 stamps.

Poetry: Accepts 20/yr. Any type; to 12 lines. Submit max. 3 poems. Must pertain to writing/publishing.

Fillers: Accepts 20/yr. Anecdotes, cartoons, facts, prayers; 50-100 wds.

Columns/Departments: Accepts 20/yr. Writing Rainbows! (devotional), 400-500 wds; Writer to Writer (how-to), 200-800 wds; Editor's Roundtable (interview with editor), 500-800 wds.

Special Needs: "More informational articles; less personal experience; more help for pros."

Tips: "Looking for articles that are more informational and less philosophical. Most open to columns."

EXCHANGE, #104-15 Torrance Rd., Scarborough ON M1J 3K2 Canada. 416-439-4320. Audrey Dorsch, ed. A forum for Christian writers to share information and ideas. Quarterly newsletter; 8 pgs; circ 285. Subscription $11 US/$14 Canada. 75% freelance. Complete ms/cover letter; phone query ok. Pays .06-.08/wd, on publication, for one-time rts. Articles 300-500 wds (16/yr). Responds in 4 wks. No sidebars. Guidelines/copy for #10 SAE/1 Canadian stamp.

Columns/Departments: Buys 4/yr. Out on a Limb (opinion), 300 wds, $20.

Fillers: Ideas, quotes; 25-100 wds; no payment.

Tips: "Think about what kind of help you would like as a writer."

+FELICITY, HCR-13, Box 21AA, Artemas PA 17211. (814)458-3102. Ann Weems, ed. Thematic issues from writers for adults of all ages. Quarterly newsletter; 30-40 pgs; circ 200+. Subscription $15. 100% freelance. Complete ms/cover letter; no phone query. **PAYS IN COPIES,** small payment to contest winners, for one-time, reprint & simultaneous rts. Articles 100-250 wds (12/yr); fiction to 2,500 wds (see Contests). Responds in 6-24 wks. Seasonal 3 mos ahead. Accepts simultaneous submissions & reprints. No sidebars. Guidelines/theme list; copy for #10 SAE/2 stamps.

Poetry: Any type, to 36 lines.

Fillers: Anecdotes, cartoons, writing ideas, jokes, quizzes, word puzzles. Pays one copy.

Contests: Sponsors two contests/issue. Send for information.

#GOTTA WRITE NETWORK LITMAG, 612 Cobblestone Cr., Glenview IL 60025. (708)296-7631. Fax: (708)296-7631. Secular. Denise Fleischer, ed. A support system for writers, beginner to well established. Semiannual mag; circ 200. Subscription $12.75. 60-80% freelance. Query or complete ms/cover letter; phone query ok. Pays $5 ($10 for fiction), before publication, for 1st rts. Articles 3-5 pgs (25/yr); fiction to 5-10 pgs (10+/yr) on writing techniques; book reviews 2.5 pgs. Responds in 2-4 mos. Seasonal 6 mos ahead. Guidelines; copy $5.

Poetry: Accepts 75+/yr. Avant-garde, free verse, haiku, experimental; 4 lines to 1 pg. Submit max. 5 poems.

Fillers: Accepts 100/yr. Anecdotes, facts, newsbreaks, tips; 100-250 wds; pays in copies.

Tips: "Most open to articles on writing techniques. Give me something different and in-depth. No I-love-writing, how-I-did-it."

+HEAVEN, HCR-13 Box 21AA, Artemas PA 17211. (814)458-3102. Kay Weems, ed. Published for Easter. New publication. 100% freelance. **NO PAYMENT.**

Poetry: All types of poetry on heaven, to 36 lines.

#HOME OFFICE OPPORTUNITIES, P.O. Box 780, Lyman WY 82937. (307)786-4513. Diane Wolverton, ed. Help and support for people who run offices in their homes. Bimonthly mag; circ 500. Subscription $18. 90% freelance. Query (complete ms for humor & fiction); no phone query. Pays .01/wd, on acceptance, for 1st or reprint rts. Articles 400-2,000 wds (50/yr); fiction to 2,000 wds (6/yr). Responds in 1-3 mos. Seasonal 6 mos ahead. Considers simultaneous submissions & reprints. Guidelines; copy $2.

Fillers: Buys 6-12 facts/yr; 50-250 wds; $1-3.

Special Needs: All articles must be related to running a home office. How-to business tips. Would like to see some good, business-related fiction.

Tips: "Our profiles are designed to show readers how others have become successful or solved problems—lots of nuts and bolts. We are very open to freelancers in all departments."

#HOUSEWIFE-WRITER'S FORUM, Box 780, Lyman WY 82937-0780. (307)786-4513. Secular. Diane Wolverton, ed.; Bob Haynie, fiction ed. Publishes the writings of housewife-writers. Bimonthly magazine; 48 pgs; circ 1,500. 90% freelance. Query (complete ms for fiction/cover letter); no phone query. Pays .01/wd, on acceptance, for 1st rts. Articles (60-100/yr) & fiction to 2,000 wds (12-15/yr, prefers 1,000-1,500). Responds in 1-3 mos. Seasonal 6 mos ahead. Considers simultaneous query & reprints (sometimes). Guidelines; copy $3.

Poetry: Buys 30-60/yr. Free verse, light verse, traditional; to 45 lines; $1-2. Submit max. 5 poems.

Fillers: Buys 24-30/yr. Anecdotes, cartoons, facts, ideas; hints (on writing/running a home); 25-200 wds; $1-4.

Columns/Departments: Buys 30-40/yr. Confessions of a Housewife-Writer, 250-750 wds; or various writing tips, 150-250 wds; $3. Complete ms.

Tips: "Write articles that are specific, vivid, and helpful for housewife/writers. Look for different angles."

+INKLINGS, P.O. Box 12181, Denver CO 80212-0181. (303)861-0911. Fax: (303)861-0911. Brad Hicks, exec. ed.; Nancy Hicks, fiction ed.; Jo Kadlecek, articles ed. For thinking Christians and seekers interested in the arts and literature. Quarterly tabloid; circ 8,000. Subscription $12. Estab 1993. 50-75% freelance. Complete ms/cover letter; no phone query. **PAYS IN COPIES,** for 1st rts. Articles/fiction, 250-10,000 wds. Responds in 3 wks. Seasonal 3 mos ahead. Considers simultaneous submissions & reprints. Guidelines; copy $4.

Poetry: Joy Sawyer. All types, 2-500 lines. Submit max. 10 poems.

Special Needs: Culture, the arts, literature, writing, book/theater/film reviews.

Tips: "Always looking for good children's fiction written by minorities, the oppressed, and writers from developing countries."

*MERLYN'S PEN, The National Magazine of Student Writing, Box 1058, East Greenwich RI 02818. Secular. R. James Stahl, ed. Written by students in grades 7-12 only. Mag. Fiction to 2,500 wds; reviews and travel pieces to 1,000 wds. **PAYS IN COPIES.** Not in topical listings. Students send for guidelines.

Poetry: To 100 lines.

MINNESOTA INK - See WRITER'S JOURNAL.

+MY LEGACY, HCR-13 Box 21AA, Artemas PA 17211. (814)458-3102. Ann Weems, ed. For young adults and up. Quarterly booklet; 70-80 pgs; circ 200+. 100% freelance. **NO PAYMENT.** No articles; fiction to 2,500 wds (100/yr). Responds in 14-16 wks. Accepts simultaneous submissions & reprints. No disk. Guidelines; copy for 6x9 SAE/4 stamps & $3.50.

Poetry: Accepts 200+/yr. Any types; to 36 lines.

+OMNIFIC, HCR-13 Box 21AA, Artemas PA 17211. (814)458-3102. Ann Weems, ed. Family-type publication for writers/adults. Quarterly booklet; 100+ pgs; circ 300+. Subscription $16. 100% freelance.

SMALL AWARDS GIVEN. Accepts simultaneous submissions & reprints. No articles; poetry only. Guidelines; copy for 6x9 SAE/4 stamps & $4.

Poetry: Any type; to 36 lines. Submit max. 4-8 poems.

*TEACHERS & WRITERS, 5 Union Square W, New York NY 10003. (212)691-6590. Ron Padgett, ed. On teaching creative and imaginative writing. Mag published 5 times/yr; circ 1,500-2,000. Query. **PAYS IN COPIES.** Articles 3,000-6,000 wds. Not in topical listings. Copy $2.50.

+TICKLED BY THUNDER, 7385 - 129 St., Surrey BC V3W 7B8 Canada. (604)591-6095. Fax: (604)591-6095. Larry Lindner, ed. Writer's news and roundtable; fiction and poetry need not be about writing. Magazine published 3-4 times/yr; 16-20 pgs.; circ 100. Subscription $12 (or $10 in US postage). 100% freelance. Query/clips; fax query ok. **PAYS IN COPIES** for one-time rts. Articles to 1,200 wds (4-8/yr); fiction to 2,000 wds (4-10/yr); magazine reviews. Responds in 4-12 wks. Seasonal 6 mos ahead. Considers simultaneous submissions. Prefers disk copy. Sidebars ok. Guidelines; copy for #10 SAE/$2 in U.S. postage (unattached).

Poetry: Accepts 12-22/yr. Free verse, haiku, light verse, traditional; to 75 lines. Submit max. 7 poems.

Fillers: Ideas; to 100 wds.

Contest: Send for guidelines.

Tips: "Participate in contests. If writing a religious story, it must do more than push religious buttons. It must stand on its own and not be dragged down by the 'moral' at the end."

+VIRGINIA CHRISTIAN WRITER, CCM Publishing, P.O. Box 12624, Roanoke VA 24027. (703)342-7511. Fax: (703)342-7511. A division of Creative Christian Ministries. Betty Robertson, ed. To inform, encourage and unite writers in Virginia. Quarterly newsletter; 4 pgs. Estab 1994. 50% freelance. Complete ms/no cover letter; phone/fax query ok. **PAYS ONE COPY,** for one-time or simultaneous rts. Not copyrighted. Articles to 500 wds. Responds in 6 wks. Responds in 4-6 wks. Considers simultaneous submissions & reprints. Prefers disk copy. Guidelines; copy for #10 SAE/1 stamp & $1.

Tips: "Short how-to articles needed."

+THE WRITE TOUCH, P.O. Box 695, Selah WA 98942. (509)966-3524. Tim Anderson, ed. For writers trying to get published. Monthly newsletter; 12 pgs; circ 40. Subscription $15/yr. Estab 1994. 100% freelance. Complete ms/cover letter. **PAYS 3 COPIES,** for one-time rts. Essays on various subjects (120/yr) & fiction for all ages (120/yr), 100-500 wds. Responds in 2-4 wks. Seasonal 2 mos ahead. Discourages simultaneous submissions & reprints. Accepts disk copy. Guidelines; copy $1.

Poetry: Any type; 4-30 lines. Submit maximum 3 poems.

Fillers: Anecdotes, facts, ideas, prose, short humor; 15-50 wds.

THE WRITER, 120 Boylston St., Boston MA 02116-4615. Secular. Submit to The Editor. How-to for writers; lists religious markets in December. Monthly mag; 48 pgs; circ 54,000. 20-25% freelance. Query or complete ms; no phone/fax query. Pays $75-100, on acceptance, for 1st rts. Articles to 2,000 wds (96/yr). Responds in 2-3 wks. Not in topical listings. Copy $3.

Poetry: Accepts poetry for critiques in "Poet to Poet" column; to 30 lines; no payment. No religious poetry. Submit max. 3 poems.

Columns/Departments: Buys 24+/yr. Rostrum (shorter pcs. on the craft of writing), 1,000-1,200 wds; Off the Cuff (somewhat more personal tone), 1,000-1,200 wds; $75.

Special Needs: How-to on the craft of writing only.

WRITERSANCHOR, 100 Greenwood Rd., York PA 17404. (717)792-0228. York Writers. Rita Atwell-Holler, ed. Quarterly newsletter; 6-12 pgs; circ 30. Subscription $4. 100% freelance. Complete ms/no cover letter; phone query ok. **PAYS IN COPIES** for any rts. Not copyrighted. Articles 50-400 wds (6/yr); book reviews 250 wds. Responds in 8-12 wks. Seasonal 6 mos ahead. Considers simultaneous submissions & reprints. No disk. No sidebars. Guidelines/copy for #10 SAE/1 stamp.

> **Poetry:** Accepts 6-12/yr. All types; 22-32 lines. Submit max. 6 poems.
>
> **Fillers:** Accepts 6/yr. All types; 35-50 wds.
>
> **Columns/Departments:** Exhilaration, 75 wds; Questions & Answers, 35 wds; Game, 150 wds.

#WRITERS CONNECTION, P.O. Box 24770, San Jose CA 95154-4770. (408)554-2090. Fax: (408)554-2099. Jan Stiles, ed. Nuts and bolts information on writing and publishing in all fields (except poetry). Monthly newsletter; circ 2,500. Subscription/membership $45. 60% freelance. Complete ms; query/clips for profiles; no phone query. Pays $25-75, on acceptance, for 1st or reprint rts. Articles 800-1,800 wds (25-32/yr); book reviews, 200-300 wds (pays 2 copies). Responds in 2 mos. Seasonal 4 mos ahead. Accepts reprints. Guidelines; copy $5.

> **Fillers:** Accepts 4-10/yr. Facts, newsbreaks, tips, resources; 50-350 wds.
>
> **Columns/Departments:** Profiles (useful info/insights from professional editors/agents), 725-800 wds; Business & Technical Writing (hard info on how to write), 750-825 wds; $25-50.
>
> **Special Needs:** In-depth articles on how to write or market your writing (technique). No religious slant or tone.
>
> **Tips:** "Most open to short features or columns; shorter articles that offer specific, in-depth help for writers."

WRITER'S DIGEST, 1507 Dana Ave., Cincinnati OH 45207. (513)531-2222. Fax: (513)531-1843. Secular. Jo Gilbert, assoc. ed. To inform, instruct or inspire the freelancer. Monthly mag; 80 pgs; circ 250,000. Subscription $27. 90% freelance. Query (feature articles) or complete ms (columns)/cover letter; no phone/fax query. Pays .10/wd & up, on acceptance, for 1st rts. Articles 1,500-3,000 wds (200/yr). Responds in 4 wks. Seasonal 4 mos ahead. Kill fee. Sidebars ok. Guidelines/theme list; copy $3.25/9x12 SAE/3 stamps.

> **Poetry:** Buys 24-30/yr. Light verse on writing; 2-20 lines; $10-50. Submit max. 8 poems.
>
> **Fillers:** Buys 48/yr. Anecdotes & short humor on writing; 50-250 wds; .10/wd.
>
> **Columns/Departments:** The Writing Life, 50-500 wds; Tip Sheet, to 1,000 wds; Chronicle, to 1,500 wds.
>
> **Special Needs:** Nonfiction technique.

WRITER'S EXCHANGE, Box 394, Society Hill SC 29593. (803)378-4556. Gene Boone, ed. Uses poetry of all types, including religious material. Quarterly mag; circ 250. Subscription $10. 95% freelance. Complete ms/cover letter; no phone query. **PAYS IN COPIES**, for one-time or reprint rts. Articles 200-1,200 wds (10+/yr). Responds in 3 wks. Seasonal 6 mos ahead. Accepts reprints. Guidelines/theme list; copy $1/9x12 SAE/2 stamps.

> **Poetry:** Accepts 300/yr. Any type; 3-24 lines. Submit max. 6 poems.
>
> **Fillers:** Accepts 300/yr. Various; 10-750 wds.

+WRITER'S FORUM, Writer's Digest School, 1507 Dana Ave., Cincinnati OH 45207. (513)531-2222. Tom Clark, ed. Writing techniques, marketing and inspiration for Writer's Digest correspondence school students. Quarterly newsletter; circ 13,000. 100% freelance. Complete ms; no phone query. Pays $10-25, on acceptance, for 1st or reprint rts. Articles 500-1,000 wds (12/yr). Reports in 4-6 wks. Seasonal 4 mos ahead. Considers simultaneous submissions & reprints. Free copy.

*WRITER'S FORUM, 1420 Arbor Lake Blvd., Hermitage TN 37076-2926. Dr. Bob Mulder, ed. To assist writers in selling. Bimonthly newsletter. 50% freelance. Query. Pays on acceptance for one-time rts. Not copyrighted. Articles to 500 wds (20/yr). Responds in 2 wks. Seasonal 6 mos ahead. Considers simultaneous submissions & reprints. No guidelines/copy.

#WRITER'S GUIDELINES, Box 608, Pittsburg MO 65724. Fax: (417)993-5544. Susan Salaki, ed. A forum for all those involved with writing/publishing. Bimonthly newsletter; 10 pgs; circ 1,000. Subscription $18. 97% freelance. Query or complete ms/cover letter; no phone query. Pays to $25, on publication, for one-time rts. Articles 800-1,000 wds (20/yr); book reviews 100 wds (query). Responds in 1 wk. Seasonal 6 mos ahead. Guidelines; copy $4.

> **Fillers:** Accepts 7/yr. Cartoons, facts, newsbreaks; 50-200 wds; pays copy only.

WRITERS INFORMATION NETWORK (W.I.N.), Box 11337, Bainbridge Island WA 98110. (206)842-9103. Fax: (206)842-0536. Professional Assn. of Christian Writers. Elaine Wright Colvin, ed. Bimonthly newsletter; 20-24 pgs; circ 1,000. Subscription $25. 50% freelance. Complete ms/cover letter; phone query ok. Pays $10-25 (copies or subscription), on acceptance, for 1st rts. Articles 50-350 wds; book reviews, 100 wds, $10. Responds in 4-8 wks. Seasonal 3 mos ahead. Sidebars ok. Guidelines; copy for 9x12 SAE/3 stamps.

> **Poetry:** Any type.
>
> **Fillers:** Anecdotes, cartoons, facts, ideas, newsbreaks, short humor.
>
> **Columns/Departments:** Industry News, Market News, Word from the Warrior Bard, The Bulletin Board, Computer Corner, Speakers Corner, Resources for Writers, and Our Readers Write; $10-25.
>
> **Tips:** "Attend writer's conferences, C.B.A., and E.P.A., and report on what's happening in the industry. Most columns open."

#WRITER'S JOURNAL, Minnesota Ink Inc., 3585 N. Lexington Ave. #328, Arden Hills MN 55126. (612)486-7818. Secular. Valerie Hockert, ed. Bimonthly journal; circ 49,000. 40% freelance. Complete ms. Pays to $50, on publication, for 1st rts. Articles 700-1,000 wds (30-40/yr). Responds in 4-6 wks. Seasonal 6 mos ahead. Considers simultaneous query. Not in topical listings. Guidelines; copy $4.

> **Poetry:** Esther M. Leiper. Buys 20-30/yr. All types; to 25 lines; .25/line. Submit max. 5 poems.
>
> **Contest:** Runs 2 poetry contests each year, spring and fall.

*WRITER'S LIFELINE, Box 1641, Cornwall ON K6H 5V6 Canada. (613)932-2135. Stephen Gill, mng. ed. For professional freelancers and beginning writers. Bimonthly mag; 16-35 pgs; circ 1,500. Needs articles of interest to writers, news items of national and international interest, letters to the editor, poetry, interviews. Needs book reviewers; **PAYS IN BOOK REVIEWED & COPIES**. Not in topical listings.

#THE WRITER'S NOOK NEWS, 38114 3rd St. #181, Willoughby OH 44094-6140. (216)953-9292. Fax: (216)354-6403. Secular. Eugene Ortiz, ed./pub. Dedicated to giving freelance writers specific information for their immediate practical use in getting published and staying published. Quarterly newsletter; circ 2,000. Subscription $18. 100% freelance. Complete ms. Pays .06/wd, on acceptance, for 1st rts. Not copyrighted. Articles 100-400 wds (80/yr); book reviews 50-100 wds (.06/wd). Responds in 6 mos. Guidelines; copy $5.

> **Fillers:** Buys 20/yr. Facts, newsbreaks; 20-100 wds.
>
> **Tips:** "Most open to tips and suggestions about the process of writing and publishing."

*WRITER'S RESOURCE NETWORK, Box 940335, Maitland FL 32794. (407)260-5150. Jeffrey Atwood, ed. News and resources for writers and editors. Bimonthly newsletter; circ 1,500. 30% freelance. Complete ms/cover letter; no phone query. Pays .03/wd, on publication, for all rts. Articles 350 wds (4/yr). Responds in 2-4 wks. Seasonal 6 mos ahead. Considers simultaneous submissions & reprints. Guidelines/theme list; free copy.

 Poetry: Buys 2/yr. Haiku, light verse, traditional; 4-20 lines; .03/wd. Submit max. 5 poems.

 Fillers: Accepts 10-15/yr. Anecdotes, cartoons ($1), facts, newsbreaks; 10-100 wds.

 Tips: "Most open to short techniques/how-tos on how you overcame a specific problem to get published; first-person articles."

*WRITING RIGHT NEWSLETTER, Box 35132, Elmwood Park IL 60635. (708)453-5023. John Biardo, ed. Helping writers and poets with their writing career. Monthly newsletter; circ 500. Estab 1992. 50% freelance. Complete ms (query for fiction). **PAYS IN COPIES,** for one-time rts. Articles 600-1,000 wds (50/yr); fiction 500-700 wds (10/yr); book reviews 600 wds. Responds in 2-4 wks. Accepts reprints. Guidelines; copy $4.

 Fillers: Accepts 10/yr. Ideas, newsbreaks; 200-300 wds.

 Tips: "Most open to writer's tips that have worked for you."

MARKET ANALYSIS

TOP PERIODICALS IN EACH CATEGORY BY LARGEST CIRCULATION

TOP 50 ADULT/GENERAL MARKETS

1. Guideposts 3,900,000
2. Focus on the Family 2,000,000
3. Decision 1,800,000
4. Columbia 1,500,000
5. The Lutheran 960,000
6. Plus 650,000
7. Home Life 610,000
8. Catholic Digest 550,000
9. War Cry 505,000
10. Marion Helpers 500,000
11. Oblates 500,000
12. AFA Journal 400,000
13. Liguorian 365,000
14. Lutheran Witness 350,000
15. Mature Living 350,000
16. Miraculous Medal 340,000
17. St. Anthony Messenger 320,000
18. American Bible Society Record 275,000
19. Anglican Journal 272,000
20. Signs of the Times 270,000
21. Pentecostal Evangel 255,000
22. Christian Reader 250,000
23. Class 250,000
24. Liberty 250,000
25. Power for Living 250,000
26. Christian Parenting Today 225,000
27. Charisma & Christian Life 200,000
28. Together 200,000
29. Christianity Today 180,000
30. Episcopal Life 180,000
31. Ideals 180,000
32. Live 160,000
33. Standard 160,000
34. Unit Church Observer 155,000
35. The Family Digest 150,000
36. Lutheran Digest 150,000
37. Celebrate Life 145,000
38. Lutheran Journal 136,000
39. Moody 135,000
40. ParentLife 125,000
41. Our Sunday Visitor 120,000
42. The Lookout 118,000
43. Church Herald 108,000
44. Presbyterian Survey 105,000
45. Catholic Forester 103,000
46. Discipleship Journal 100,000
47. Foursquare World Advance 100,000
48. Living 100,000
49. Sunday Digest 100,000
50. Today's Better Life 100,000

TOP 18 CHILDREN'S MARKETS

1. God's World Today 260,000
2. Guideposts for Kids 160,000
3. Venture 140,000
4. Focus on Fam/Clubhouse 95,000
5. Focus on Fam/Clubhouse Jr 95,000
6. Pockets 95,000
7. Junior Trails 65,000
8. High Adventure 60,000
9. Our Little Friend 45-50,000
10. Power & Light 39,000
11. GUIDE 36,000
12. Primary Treasure 35,000
13. Venture 20,000
14. Touch 15,200
15. My Friend 14,000

16. Crusader (MI) 13,000
17. BREAD for God's Children 10,000
18. Nature Friend 10,000

TOP 14 CHRISTIAN EDUCATION/LIBRARY MARKETS

1. Today's Catholic Teacher 60,000
2. GROUP 57,000
3. Parish Teacher 50,000
4. Catechist 45,700
5. Religion Teacher's Journal 36,000
6. Teachers in Focus 34,000
7. Children's Ministry 30,000
8. CE Counselor 25,000
9. Perspective 24,000
10. Evangelizing Today's Child 22,000
11. Shining Star 22,000
12. Teachers Interaction 20,400
13. Lollipops 20,000
14. Memos 15,000

TOP 10 MISSIONS MARKETS

1. Childlife 250,765
2. Partners 161,000
3. Compassion 140,000
4. Catholic Near East 100,000
5. Worldwide Challenge 91,500
6. World Vision 79,770
7. Heartbeat 43,700
8. Impact 42,000
9. World Christian 40,000
10. New World Outlook 33,000

TOP 6 MUSIC MARKETS

1. Music Makers 105,000
2. Glory Songs 85,000
3. Young Musicians 85,000
4. Music Time 60,000
5. Church Pianist 35,000
6. Music Leader 35,000

TOP 10 PASTOR/LEADER MARKETS

1. Your Church 180,000
2. YMR Today 113,000
3. Pulpit Helps 105,000
4. Leadership Journal 65,000
5. Eucharistic Minister 50,000
6. Worship Leader 40,000+
7. Christian Century 37,000
8. Advance 30,250
9. Today's Christian Preacher 30,000
10. Lutheran Partners 22,000

TOP 14 TEEN/YOUNG ADULT MARKETS

1. Brio 158,000
2. Visions (MN) 140,000
3. Campus Life 120,000
4. Today's Christian Teen 100,000
5. Breakaway 95,000
6. Teen Life 75,000
7. Cross Walk 50,000
8. Sharing the Victory 50,000
9. Young Salvationist 50,000
10. The Student 40,000
11. Teen Quest 35-40,000
12. Challenge (TN) 35,000
13. Straight 35,000
14. You! 35,000

TOP 8 WOMEN'S MARKETS

1. Today's Christian Woman 375,000
2. Royal Service 290,000
3. Lutheran Woman Today 250,000
4. Virtue 135,000
5. Response 75,000
6. Contempo 65,000
7. Journey 35,000
8. Horizons 30,000

TOP 6 WRITERS' MARKETS

1. Writer's Digest 250,000
2. The Writer 54,000
3. Writer's Journal 49,000
4. Writer's Forum (OH) 13,000
5. Inklings 8,000
6. Christian Communicator 4,000

ALL PERIODICALS IN ORDER OF LARGEST CIRCULATION

Adult/General

Guideposts 3,900,000
Focus on the Family 2,000,000
Decision 1,800,000
Columbia 1,500,000
The Lutheran 960,000
Plus 650,000
Home Life 610,000
Catholic Digest 550,000
War Cry 505,000
Marion Helpers 500,000
Oblates 500,000
AFA Journal 400,000
Liguorian 365,000
Lutheran Witness 350,000
Mature Living 350,000
Miraculous Medal 340,000
St. Anthony Messenger 320,000
American Bible Society Record 275,000
Anglican Journal 272,000
Signs of the Times 270,000
Pentecostal Evangel 255,000
Class 250,000
Christian Reader 250,000
Liberty 250,000
Power for Living 250,000
Christian Parenting Today 225,000
Charisma & Christian Life 200,000
Together 200,000
Christianity Today 180,000
Episcopal Life 180,000
Ideals 180,000
Live 160,000
Standard 160,000
Unit Church Observer 155,000
The Family Digest 150,000
Lutheran Digest 150,000
Celebrate Life 145,000
Lutheran Journal 136,000
Moody 135,000

ParentLife 125,000
Our Sunday Visitor 120,000
The Lookout 118,000
Church Herald 108,000
Presbyterian Survey 105,000
Catholic Forester 103,000
Discipleship Journal 100,000
Foursquare World Advance 100,000
Living 100,000
Sunday Digest 100,000
Today's Better Life 100,000
Total Health 90,000
Herald of Holiness 81,000
Christian History 80,000
Lutheran Layman 80,000
Vista 80,000
Voice (CA) 80,000
Mature Years 77,000
Message 74,000
Christian Single 70,000
Vision (CA) 70,000
alive now! 65,000
Indian Life 62,000
Christian Standard 61,000
Northwestern Lutheran 61,000
Catholic Answer 60,000
Conquest 60,000
Good News 60,000
Presbyterian Record 60,000
Acts 29 55,000
Christian Home & School 52,000
Annals of St. Anne 50,000
A Better Tomorrow 50,000
Christian Event Journal 50,000
Church of God Evangel 50,000
Good News Journal 50,000
InterVarsity 50,000
Parents of Teenagers 50,000
Southwestern News 50,000
Vibrant Life 50,000
Sports Spectrum 48,000
Seek 45,000
The Teaching Home 42,000

New Covenant 40,200
Bible Review 40,000
Christmas 40,000
A Positive Approach 40,000
America 36,000
Cathedral Age 35,000
Highway News 35,000
Pursuit 35,000
U.S. Catholic 35,000
World 35,000
Christian Research Journal 34,000
Church & State 33,000
Evangelical Beacon 33,000
Catholic Parent 30,000
Catholic Twin Circle 30,000
Cornerstone 30,000
Lifeglow 30,000
Progress 30,000
At Ease 28,000
Light and Life 27,500
Common Boundary 26,000
First Things 26,000
African-American Heritage 25,000
Catholic Heritage 25,000
Evangel 25,000
Interim 25,000
Pentecostal Testimony 25,000
Indian Life 24,000
Canada Lutheran 23,000
Covenant Companion 22,000
B.C. Catholic 20,000
Discovery 20,000
God's Revivalist 20,000
Homeschooling Today 20,000
St. Joseph's Messenger 20,000
SCP Journal 20,000
Wesleyan Advocate 20,000
Commonweal 19,000
Vital Christianity 19,000
Faith Today 18,000
The Family Journal 18,000
Messenger/Sacred Heart 18,000
The Shantyman 17,000

John Milton 16,400
Purpose 16,000
Table Talk 16,000
AXIOS 15,670
Mennonite Brethren Herald 15,000
Network 15,000
The Plowman 15,000
New Oxford Review 14,000
Praying 14,000
Psychology for Living 14,000
Emphasis on Faith & Living 13,000
Interchange 12,800
Bible Advocate 12,600
Pax Christi USA 12,000
Canadian Baptist 11,500
Presbyterian Outlook 11,500
The Door 11,000
Review for Religious 11,000
Salt 11,000
Evangelical Friend 10,500
Baptist Informer 10,000
Bookstore Journal 10,000
Good News Reporter 10,000
Journal of Christian Nursing 10,000
Our Family 10,000
Sharing 10,000
Smart Dads 10,000
Spiritual Life 10,000
This Rock 10,000
Today's Single 10,000
Friends Journal 9,750
Christian Retailing 9,500
Celebration 9,000
Living Church 9,000
Prairie Messenger 9,000
The Family 8,500
Religious Broadcasting 8,500
The Bible Today 8,000
Companions 8,000
The Gem 8,000
Home Times 8,000
The Mennonite 8,000
Star of Zion 8,000

Pentecostal Messenger 7,500
MN Christian Chronicle 7,000
Salt Shaker 7,000
Church Advocate 6,300
Alive! 6,000
Christian Courier (Canada) 6,000
Christian Living 6,000
Impact 6,000
Pentecostal Homelife 6,000
Companion 5,000
Hallelujah! 5,000
Maranatha 5,000
Ministry Today 5,000
A New Heart 5,000
Queen of All Hearts 5,000
Evangelical Visitor 4,800
Christian Civic League/ME 4,600
Christian Renewal 4,300
Cresset 4,300
Christian Media 4,000
Evangelical Baptist 4,000
Fellowship Today 4,000
Hayden Herald 4,000
Kootenai Courier 4,000
Message of the Open Bible 4,000
The Witness 4,000
Advent Chr Witness 3,700
ADVOCATE 3,700
Compass 3,700
The Messenger (Canada) 3,700
Cross Currents 3,500
Perspectives on Science 3,300
Social Justice Review 3,177
North American Voice 3,000
Quiet Revolution 3,000
Religious Education 3,000
Rural Landscapes 3,000
The Witness 3,000
Christian Social Action 2,500
Church Herald/Holiness Banner 2,500
The Messenger (NC) 2,500
Railroad Evangelist 2,500
Gospel Tidings 2,200

Answers in Action 2,000
Baptist History & Heritage 2,000
Christian Observer 2,000
The Critic 2,000
It's Your Choice 2,000
New Thought Journal 2,000
Journal/Church & State 1,700
Prism 1,700
Encourager Provider 1,600
Christian Edge 1,500
Comments From the Friends 1,500
The Inspirer 1,500
Touchstone 1,500
Methodist History 1,200
Bible Reflections 1,100
Apocalypse Chronicles 1,000
Canadian Catholic Review 1,000
Connecting Point 1,000
Hearing Hearts 1,000
Pourastan 1,000
Whisper 1,000
Evangelism 900
Dovetail 800
Morning Glory 800
The New Trumpet 800
Head to Head 500+
Broken Streets 500
Poetry Forum Short Stories 500
Prayerworks 500
St. Willibrord Journal 500
Silver Wings 430
God's Special People 400
Lighthouse Fiction Collection 300+
Baptist Beacon 300
Burning Light 300
Christian Drama 300
Parenting Treasures 300
Thema 300
Time of Singing 300
Manna 250
Explorer 200+
Dreams & Visions 200
Pegasus Review 200

Professional Parent's Advocate 115
Ratio 100
Upsouth 75-100

Children
God's World Today 260,000
Guideposts for Kids 160,000
Venture 140,000
Focus on Fam Clubhouse 95,000
FOF Clubhouse Jr 95,000
Pockets 95,000
Junior Trails 65,000
High Adventure 60,000
Our Little Friend 45-50,000
Power & Light 39,000
GUIDE 36,000
Primary Treasure 35,000
Venture 20,000
Touch 15,200
My Friend 14,000
Crusader (MI) 13,000
BREAD for God's Children 10,000
Nature Friend 10,000
Story Friends 9,000
On the Line 8,000
CLUBHOUSE 8,000
Together Time 7,500
Partners 5,825
Story Mates 5,200
Young Crusader 3,000
Skipping Stones 2,500
Attention Please! 400

Christian Education/Library
Today's Catholic Teacher 60,000
GROUP 57,000
Parish Teacher 50,000
Catechist 45,700
Religion Teacher's Journal 36,000
Teachers in Focus 34,000
Children's Ministry 30,000
CE Counselor 25,000
Perspective 24,000

Evangelizing Today's Child 22,000
Shining Star 22,000
Teachers Interaction 20,400
Lollipops 20,000
Memos 15,000
Resource 12,000
Journal/Adventist Ed 10,000
Leader/Church School Today 10,000
Youth & CE Leadership 9,325
CE Connection 6,600
Church Educator 5,500
Vision (CA) 5,000
Christian Educator's Journal 4,200
Lead 3,600
Leader 3,500
The Youth Leader 2,800
Cornerstone Connections 2,400
Insight into CE 2,200
Team 2,000
Changing Lives 1,800
Librarian's World 800
Christian Librarian 500

Missions
Childlife 250,765
Partners 161,000
Compassion 140,000
Catholic Near East 100,000
Worldwide Challenge 91,500
World Vision 79,770
Heartbeat 43,700
Impact 42,000
World Christian 40,000
New World Outlook 33,000
P.I.M.E. World 30,000
American Horizon 29,000
Oblate World 25,000
Latin America Evangelist 22,000
Message of the Cross 9,000
Wherever 7,000
Missiology 2,000
Urban Mission 1,300
Areopagus 1,000

Intl. Journal/Frontier 600

Music
Music Makers 105,000
Glory Songs 85,000
Young Musicians 85,000
Music Time 60,000
Church Pianist 35,000
Music Leader 35,000
Senior Musician 32,000
Score 30,000
Church Musician 16,000
Creation 5,500
The Hymn 3,500
Tradition 2,500

Newspapers
United Methodist Reporter 450,000
Inside Journal 370,000
Christian American 325,000
Anglican Journal 272,000
Episcopal Life 170,000
Catholic New York 130,000
Our Sunday Visitor 125,000
Christian Chronicle 112,000
Pulpit Helps 105,000
Good News Journal 50,000
Catholic Accent 48,000
Catholic Courier 48,000
National Catholic Reporter 48,000
Arlington Catholic Herald 45,000
Good News Etc. 44,000
Spokane/Inland NW Christian 42,000
Catholic Exponent 37,000
Beacon Christian News 35,000
Kansas City Christian 35,000
Catholic Twin Circle 30,000
World 29,000
Catholic Telegraph 27,000
NW Christian Journal 27,000
Christian Crusade 25,000
The Interim 25,000
Discovery 20,000

Catholic Sentinel 15,000
Christian Focus 15,000
Enlace Informativo 15,000
Expression Christian Newspaper 15,000
Issues & Answers (teen) 15,000
Messenger (KY) 15,000
Interchange 12,800
Mennonite Weekly Review 11,000
Mennonite Reporter 10,500
Christian Courier (WI) 10,000
Today's Single 10,000
Montana Catholic 8,100
Home Times 8,000
Minnesota Chronicle 7,500
Arkansas Catholic 7,000
Christian Courier (Canada) 5,000
Maranatha 5,000
Christian Renewal 4,500
Lead 3,600
Inland NW Christian 3,500
Probe 1,800
Christian Edge 1,500

Pastors/Leaders
Your Church 180,000
YMR Today 113,000
Pulpit Helps 105,000
Leadership Journal 65,000
Eucharistic Minister 50,000
Worship Leader 40,000+
Christian Century 37,000
Advance 30,250
Today's Christian Preacher 30,000
Lutheran Partners 22,000
Preacher's Magazine 18,000
Clergy Journal 15,000
Homiletic/Pastoral Review 15,000
Proclaim 15,000
Today's Parish 14,800
Theology Today 13,000
Christian Ministry 12,000
Church Administration 12,000
Review for Religious 11,000

Christian Sentinel 10,000
Resource 10,000
Search 10,000
Celebration 9,000
Ecumenical Trends 9,000
Preaching 9,000
Youthworker 9,000
The Priest 9,800
Brigade Leader 8,000
Faith & Renewal 8,000
Student Leadership Journal 8,000
The Bethany Choice 7,300
National/Intl Religion Report 7,200
Church Growth Network 7,000
Journal/Christian Camping 7,000
Chicago Studies 6,100
Baptist Leader 6,000
Journal/Christian Camping 6,000
Pastor's Tax & Money 6,000
Catechumenate 5,600
Single Adult Min Jour 5,000
Cross Currents 4,500
Emmanuel 4,500
Lutheran Forum 3,500
Word & World 3,100
ArtPlus 3,000
Christian Management Report 3,000
Quarterly Review 3,000
Reformed Worship 3,000
Environment & Art 2,500
Liturgy 2,300
Networks 1,700
Jour/Biblical Ethics 1,200
Jour/Christian Healing 1,200
Church Bytes 1,000
Church Worship 1,000
Diaconalogue 1,000
Evangelism 1,000
Five Stones 550
Ivy Jungle Report 150

Teen/Young Adult
Brio 158,000

Visions 140,000
Campus Life 120,000
Today's Christian Teen 100,000
Breakaway 95,000
Teen Life (formerly HICALL) 75,000
Cross Walk 50,000
Sharing the Victory 50,000
Young Salvationist 50,000
The Student 40,000
Teen Quest 35-40,000
Challenge (TN) 35,000
Straight 35,000
You! 35,000
Spirit 26,000
Young & Alive 26,000
Mag/Christian Youth! 25,000
Pioneer 25,500
Insight/Out 25,000
Youth Update 25,000
Insight 23,000
Take Five 23,000
Certainty 20,000
Pathway I.D. 18,000
Issues & Answers 15,000
Teenage Christian 14,000
Student Leadership 10,000
Youth Focus 10,000
Young Adult Today 7,500
With 6,100
The Conqueror 6,000
The Edge 5,000

Women
Today's Christian Woman 375,000
Royal Service 290,000
Lutheran Woman Today 250,000
Virtue 135,000
Response 75,000
Contempo 65,000
Journey 35,000
Horizons 30,000
Woman's Touch 17,000
Co-Laborer 13,000+

Conscience 12,000
Church Woman 10,000
Journal/Women's Ministries 10,000
Joyful Woman 10,000
Unique 8,000
Esprit 7,200
Link & Visitor 5,500
Just Between Us 5,000
Sisters Today 4,500
Daughters of Sarah 4,000
Helping Hand 4,000
Women Alive! 4,000
Wesleyan Woman 3,400
Probe 3,000
Salt & Light 300

Writers

Writer's Digest 250,000
The Writer 54,000
Writer's Journal 49,000
Writer's Forum (OH) 13,000
Inklings 8,000
Christian Communicator 4,000
Byline 3,000+
Writers Connection 2,500
Teachers & Writers 1,500-2,000
Writer's Nook News 2,000
Housewife-Writers Forum 1,500
Writer's Lifeline 1,500
Writer's Resource Network 1,500
Cross & Quill 1,000
Writer's Guidelines 1,000
Writer's Information Network 1,000
Chips off Writer's Block 500+
Christian Author 500
Home Office Opportunities 500
Writing Right Newsletter 500
Canadian Writer's Journal 350
Omnific 300+
Christian Response 300
Exchange 285
Writer's Exchange 250
Felicity 200+

My Legacy 200+
Gotta Write Network 200
Tickled By Thunder 100
The Write Touch 40
Writer's Anchor 30

PERIODICAL TOPICS IN ORDER OF POPULARITY

NOTE: Following is a list of topics in order by popularity. To find the list of publishers interested in each topic, go to the Topical Listings for periodicals. The numbers indicate how many periodical editors said they were interested in seeing something of that type or topic. (* - new topics this year)

1. Current/Social Issues 251
2. Family Life 233
3. Poetry 226
4. Christian living 225
5. Personal Experience 222
6. Interviews/Profiles 215
7. Inspirational 212
8. Prayer 210
9. Holiday Themes 206
10. Spirituality 176
11. Humor 173
12. Marriage 172
13. True Stories 171
14. Missions 168
15. Christian Education 165
16. Youth Issues 158
17. Worship 154
18. How-To/Self-Help 154
19. Devotions/Meditations 149
20. Evangelistic 148
21. Parenting 147
22. Book Reviews 144
23. Church Outreach 144
24. Women's Issues 143
25. Fillers: Cartoons 138
26. Controversial Issues 136
27. Witnessing 135

28. Theological 134
29. World Issues 125
30. Bible/Biblical Studies 124
31. Discipleship 123
32. Ethics 123
33. Historical 122
34. Think Pieces 120
35. Environmental Issues 116
36. Short Story:Adult 109
37. Health 107
38. Relationships 106
39. Book Excerpts 103
40. Singles Issues 102
41. Leadership 101
42. Religious Freedom 100
43. Senior Adult Issues 100
44. Money Management 98
45. Opinion Pieces 98
46. Salvation Testimonies 98
47. Short Story: Humorous 98
48. Fillers: Anecdotes 97
49. Divorce 96
50. Celebrity Pieces 95
51. Doctrinal 94
52. Fillers: Short Humor 94
53. Essays 88
54. Cults/Occult 86
55. Healing 82
56. Fillers: Facts 80
57. Men's Issues 79
58. Political 76
59. Miracles 75
60. Short Story: Parables 74
61. Short Story: Contemporary 73
62. Sports 71
63. Economics 70
64. Short Story: Historical 69
65. Filler: Ideas 68
66. Liturgical 68
67. Home Schooling 66
68. Christian Business 64
69. Short Story: Adventure 64
70. Short Story: Biblical 64

71. Fillers: Newsbreaks 57
72. Psychology 55
73. Fillers: Word Puzzles 54
74. Ethnic Markets 53
75. Newspapers 51
76. Fillers: Prose 49
77. Short Story:Juvenile 49
78. Sociology 49
79. Fillers: Quizzes 48
80. Nature 48
81. Fillers: Quotes 46
82. How-To Activities (juv.) 46
83. Short Story: Teen/YA 46
84. Prophecy 45
85. Church Management 44
86. Fillers: Games 44
87. Travel 43
88. Social Justice 41
89. Science 42
90. Short Story: Allegory 41
91. Fillers:J okes 40
92. Take-Home Papers 40
93. Short Story: Mystery 39
94. Stewardship 39
95. Short Story: Literary 35
96. Sermons 33
97. Short Story: Fantasy 33
98. Fillers: Prayers 32
99. Food/Recipes 31
100. Short Story: Science Fiction 30
101. Music Reviews 29
102. Short Story: Frontier 26
103. Short Story: Romance 23
104. Short Story: Plays 20
105. Fillers:Party Ideas 18
106. Short Story: Skits 17
107. Short Story: Historical/Rom 11
108. Short Story: Mystery/Rom 11
109. Contests 10
110. Short Story: Frontier/Rom 10
111. Puppet Plays 5

Comments:

If you are a short story writer, the biggest market is for adult fiction (108 markets - 13 more than last year), then juvenile (49 markets - 6 more than last year), then teen (46 markets - 9 more than last year). The most popular genres (in order) are Humorous, Parables, Contemporary, Historical, Adventure, and Biblical. Compared to last year, Parables moved ahead of Contemporary fiction, and Historical and Adventure both moved ahead of Biblical. The least desirable are still the genre romances.

If you are a poet, you should be encouraged by the fact that poetry has moved up two places from 5th to 3rd most popular topic. Not all poetry markets said how many poems they bought per year, but the 176 who did added up to 5,276 poems (1091 more than last year). Although there are more book markets for poetry this year than ever before, the serious poet should pursue the periodical markets and can certainly sell regularly if care is taken to target your poetry to fit the needs of the specific markets.

After two years of the top 12 topics remaining the same, this year shows some change. Spirituality, marriage and humor all moved ahead of true stories; poetry moved ahead of Christian living. This year Christian Education and true stories dropped out of the top 12, and humor and spirituality moved into the top 12. All types of fiction dropped in the ratings, with the exception of Adult and Juvenile which remained the same, and Parables, Historical, and Allegory which went up.

Following is a list of topics that either increased or decreased in demand since last year. The number following the topic indicates how many positions that particular topic moved up or down in the ratings.

Decreased in interest:

Liturgical - down 11
Opinion Pieces - down 8
Theological - down 8
Church Management - down 7
Church Outreach - down 7
Fillers: Word Puzzles - down 7

How-to Activities (juv.) - down 7
Fillers: Games - down 6
Sermons - down 6
Short Story: Frontier - down 6
Short Story: Humorous - down 6
Short Story: Plays - down 6
Christian Business - down 5
Fillers: Jokes - down 5
Fillers: Quizzes - down 5
Missions - down 5
Money Management - down 5
Prophecy - down 5
Science - down 5
Short Story: Biblical - down 5
Sociology - down 5
Doctrinal - down 4
Fillers: Short Humor - down 4
Short Story: Contemporary - down 4
Short Story: Fantasy - down 4
Short Story: Skits - down 4
Short Story: Frontier/Romance - down 4

Increased in interest:

Relationships - up 18
Ethnic Markets - up 17
Men's Issues - up 14
Book Reviews - up 8
Fillers:Facts - up 6
Fillers: Prose - up 5
Fillers: Quotes - up 5
Home Schooling - up 5
Short Story: Historical - up 6
How-to/Self-Help - up 5
Book Excerpts - up 4
Fillers: Anecdotes - up 4
Short Story:Parables - up 4
Spirituality - up 4

SUMMARY OF INFORMATION ON CHRISTIAN PERIODICAL PUBLISHERS FOUND IN THE ALPHABETICAL LISTINGS

NOTE: The following numbers are based on the maximum total estimate for each periodical. For example, if they gave a range of 4-6, the average was based on the higher number, 6. These figures were all calculated from those periodicals that reported information in each category.

WANTS QUERY OR COMPLETE MANUSCRIPT:

Of those periodicals that indicated a preference, 71% will accept a complete manuscript, and 45.5% require or will accept a query. Sixteen percent of the combined group will accept either.

ACCEPTS PHONE QUERY:

Fifty-two percent say no phone queries, with 48% accepting them. Seven percent more publishers are accepting phone queries this year than did last year. It is suggested that you reserve phone queries for timely material that won't wait for the regular mailed query. If you phone in a query, be sure you have your idea well thought out and can present it succinctly and articulately.

ACCEPTS FAX QUERY:

This is the first year we have asked about fax queries. Surprisingly, of those who responded, 67% said they would accept them, with 33% saying no. Since a fax query will not have an SASE, it is suggested that you make fax queries only if you have your own fax machine to accept their response.

PAYS ON ACCEPTANCE OR PUBLICATION:

Forty-six percent of the publishers pay on acceptance (up 2% from last year), while 54% pay on publication.

PERCENTAGE OF FREELANCE:

Most of the publishers responded to the question about how much freelance material they use. The average indicates that 52% of material used is from freelancers. As to the question of whether the amount of freelance used is going up or down, of those who responded this year, 37% are using the same amount of freelance material, 29% are using less, and 34% are using more than last year.

CIRCULATION:

In dividing the list of periodicals into three groups, according to size of circulation, the list comes out as follows: Publications with a circulation of 100,000 or more (up to 3,900,000), 13%; publications with circulations between 51,000 and 99,000, only 7%; the remaining 80% have circulations of 50,000 or less. If we break that last group into three more groups by circulation, we come out with 14% of those from 33,000-50,000; 16% from 17,000-32,000; and the remaining 70% at 16,000 or less. That means that over 56% of all the periodicals that reported their circulation are at a circulation of 16,000 or below.

Looking at just those periodicals that completed questionnaires this year and indicated their circulation, for 34% their circulation went up, for 42% their circulation went down, and for 24% their circulation remained the same.

RESPONSE TIME:

According to the 490 publishers who indicated response time, the average response is $7\frac{1}{2}$ weeks. Those who are writing and submitting regularly will attest to the fact that most publishers are taking longer than they used to to respond to submissions.

REPRINTS:

Over 54% of the periodicals reporting accept reprints. Although in the past it has not been necessary to tell a publisher where a piece has been published previously, that seems to be changing. Most Christian publishers are now wanting a tear sheet of the original publication and a cover letter telling when and where it appeared originally. They are also paying less for reprints than for original material.

PERIODICALS THAT HAVE CHANGED NAMES OR CEASED PUBLICATION

Aglow Magazine (WA)
All About Issues - See Celebrate Life
Anglican Magazine (Canada)
Art+ Repro Resource - See ArtPlus
Beacon Christian News (NY)
Believers News (MI)
Bread (MO)
Calvinist Contact - See Christian Courier
Campus Leaders Fellowscrip (MO)
Canticle of Mary (IA)
Caring Connection (CO)
Cathedral Voice
Cherith (MN)
Choosing (MN)
Choralation (IN)
Christianity & Crisis (NY)
Christian College Handbook (IL)
Christian Education Today (CO)
Christian Herald (NY)
Christian Outdoorsman (TX)
Christian Outlook (ID)
Christian Singles
Christian Vision (Canada)
Church Business (Canada)
Church Ministries WORKER (MD)
Church Recreation (TN)
Church Teachers - See Church Educator
Clarity (CO)
The Communicator (OR)
Companion of St. Francis & St. Anthony - See Companion Magazine
Congregational Journal (CA)
Connection (CA/UT)
Confident Living (NE)
Cottage Cheese (MN)
Creation Social Science (KS)
Crystal Rainbow (FL)
Dads Only - See Smart Dads
ESA Advocate - See Prism
Event (TN)

Faith 'N'Stuff - See Guideposts for Kids
Family Forum (MO)
Family Resources (IL)
Final Draft, The (AZ)
For Parents (NY)
Free Spirit (CA)
Friend (IN)
God's Special People (WA)
Gospel Truth (MA)
Growing Churches (TN)
Happenings (TN)
HiCall - See Teen Life
High School I.D. (TN) - See Pathway I.D.
His Garden (IL)
IDEASheet (IL)
Inner Horizons (MA)
Insights... (GA)
International Report (bad phone)
In Touch (IN)
It's God's World - See God's World Today
Journey (MO)
Journey (TN)
Junebugs Knocking (IL)
Junior Publications (IN)
Life Advocate (bad phone)
Lighted Pathway - See Pathway I.D.
Light...For the Christian Walk (KY)
Light for Today (MN)
Literary Markets (Canada)
Living Words - See Living Faith
Living Streams (IN)
Mountain Laurel (bad phone)
New England Christian (MA)
New Heaven/New Earth (IN)
Newsletter (FL)
Opus One/Opus Two (TN)
The Overcomer (IA)
Parent Care - See Caregiver's Connection
Paraclete (MO)
Parish Family Digest - See The Family Digest
Pastoral Life (OH)
Pavilion/CNF Perspective (CA)
Phoenix Rising (VA)

Pocket Inspirations (CA)
The Prayer Line (WA)
Primary Teacher - See Wonder Time
Progressions (IL)
Scoreboard Publications (UT)
Shoe Tree (NM)
Spirituality Today (MO)
Starlight Magazine (NC)
Sunday School Counselor - See Christian Education
    Counselor
Teens Today - see Cross Walk
Thirteen Poetry Magazine (NY)
Tree of Life (bad phone)
The Trumpet Sounds (TX)
Twin Cities Christian (MN) - See Minnesota Christian
    Chronicle
Tyro Magazine (Canada)
Vision (MI)
Voice of Sarah (KS)
Voices in the Wilderness (MA)
World Mission Journal - See Missions Today
Worship Today (FL)
Writer's Info (ID)
Writers Newsletter (IL)

PERIODICALS NOT INTERESTED IN FREELANCE SUBMISSIONS, OR WHO ASKED NOT TO BE LISTED

Absolute Sound (NY)
Action Tracks
Acorn, The
Action Information (DC)
Adolescence (CA)
Adult Focus (TN)
Adult Teacher (MO)
Alliance Life (CO)
The A.M.E. Church Review (GA)
Anglican Theological Review (IL)
Answers in Action (CA)
Assoc Reformed Presby (SC)
Atlantic Baptist (Canada)
Australian Evangel

The Banner (MI)
Baptist Bulletin (IL)
Baptist Herald (IL)
Baptist World VA)
Berean Statesman (MN)
Bible-in-Life Friends (IL)
Bible-in-Life Pix (IL)
Bible-in-Life Stories (IL)
Bible-Science News (MN)
Bible Time 4s and 5s
Bible World (NJ)
Biblical Illustrator (TN)
Bodywise (AR)
Books & Religion (NC)
Bookviews (WI)
Brethren Evangelist (OH)
Brethren Missionary Herald (IN)
Builder (PA)
Catholic Health World (MO)
Catholic Library World (PA)
CBMC Contact (TN)
Challenge (IL)
Children's Church Exchange (MO)
The Chosen People (NC)
Christ for the Nations (TX)
Christian Conquest (AL)
Christian Education Journal (IL)
Christian Example
Christianity & Crisis (IL)
Christian Info (Canada)
Christian Life (OH)
Christian Living (TN)
Christian Medical Society Journal (TX)
Christian Week (Canada)
Christ in Our Home (MN)
Christopher News Notes (NY)
CHURCHFACTS from Western NY
Church of God MISSIONS (IN)
Church Programs/ Middlers/Jrs (MO)
Church Programs/ Preschoolers (MO)
Church Programs/Primaries (MO)
Circuit Rider (TN)
Columban Mission (NE)

Command (CO)
Compassion Today (Canada)
The Congregationalist (WY)
Contact (TN)
Contemporary Christian Music (TN)
COSMET Newsletter (CA)
Courage (IL)
Covenanter Witness (PA)
Daily Blessing (OK)
Daily Meditation (TX)
Dialog (MN)
Directions in Faith (TN)
The Disciple (MO)
Door of Hope (CA)
Doorways (CO)
Elmbrook (WI)
El Orador
Epiphany Journal (CA)
Eurovision Advance (CA)
Evangelical Missions Quarterly (IL)
Exodus Standard (CA)
Faith & Renewal (MI)
Faith at Work, Inc. (Canada)
FaithQuest (IL)
Family Forum (MO)
Family Therapy (CA)
Family Voice (DC)
Family Walk (GA)
Festivals (CA)
Firm Foundation (TX)
Focus Magazine (TN)
The Forerunner (FL) - no response
Forward Day by Day (OH)
Four and Five (OH)
The Free Methodist Pastor (IN)
Fulness Magazine (TX)
God's Word for Today (MO)
Gospel Herald (PA)
Gospel Message (MO)
Greater Europe Report (IL)
Growing Together (IL)
The Herald (KY)
Heritage Herald (NC)

High School I.D. (IL)
High School Teaching Guide (IL)
The Home Altar (MN)
Image (KS)
IMAGE (VA)
Insight (NC)
Insights (CA)
Interchange (OH)
Interest (IL)
Interlit (IL)
Invitation (TN)
It's Our World (DC)
Jubilee (DC)
Kindred Spirit (TX)
Last Day Messenger (OR)
Light for Today (MN)
Listen Magazine (DC)
Living Light (DC)
Living Values (IL)
Living with Children (TN)
Living with Preschoolers (TN)
Living with Teenagers (TN)
Look and Listen (TN)
The Lookout (NY)
Luke Society News (MS)
Lutheran Libraries (MN)
Maranatha Manna (MD)
Marriage & Family (IN)
Marriage Partnership (IL)
Maryknoll (NY)
Media Update (CA)
Men's Ministries (MO)
Messenger (IL)
Ministry (MD)
Miracle Living (AZ)
Mission (MD)
Missionary Monthly (MI)
Missionary Tidings (IN)
Mission Frontiers (CA)
Missions Today (TN)
Modern Liturgy (CA)
Momentum (DC)
Money Matters (GA)

Musicline (CA)

My Daily Visitor

My Delight (OH)

My Devotions (MO)

My Jewels (OH)

My Pleasure (OH)

Nat Christian Reporter (TX)

Neighborly Good News (Canada - now Relationships)

New Catholic World (NJ)

New Jerusalem Music (NJ)

Nor'Easter (NY)

OC International (CA)

Open Doors News Briefs (CA)

Opening the Word (KS)

Open Windows (TN)

The Other Side (PA)

PCA Messenger (GA)

People of Destiny (MD)

The Plough (PA)

Poet & Writers (NY)

Portals of Prayer (MO)

Preschool Playhouse (assigned)

Preteen Teacher (MO)

Primary St. (assigned)

Quaker Life (IN)

Reflections (MD)

Reformed Journal (MI)

Religion Teacher's Journal (CT)

The Rock (IL)

Sally Ann (Canada)

Servant (Canada)

Single Adult Ministry Information (MO)

Sojourners (DC)

Sower, The (IL)

Spiritual Women's Times (WA)

The Standard (IL)

Student Venture Newsletter (CA)

Sunday School Illustrator (TN)

The Sunday School Times & Gospel Herald (OH)

Tabletalk (FL)

Teacheraid (PA)

Teen Triumph (TN)

These Days (GA)

Today's Better Life (TX)

The Trim Tab (GA)

The United Brethren (IN)

United Evangelical ACTION (IL)

United Methodist Reporter (TX)

U.S. Catholic (IL)

Veritas (CA)- no response

Weavings (TN)

Weekly Bible Reader (OH)

Wee Lambs (PA)

Wesleyan World (IN)

Wheaton Alumni (IL)

The Winner (DC)

The Witness (PA)

Word & Way (MO)

Word in Season (MN)

Word of Faith (OK)

Words of Hope (MI)

World Encounter (IL)

Worldorama (OK)

World Pulse (IL)

Worldwide THRUST (PA)

Young Life (CO)

Young Missionary (IN)

Youth Alive (MO)

YouthGuide (KS)

Youth Illustrated (IL)

Youth Walk (GA)

GREETING CARD/GIFT/SPECIALTY MARKETS

(*) Indicates that publisher did not return questionnaire.

(#) Indicates that listing was updated from guidelines or other sources.

(+) Indicates new listing.

NOTE: See the end of this listing for specialty product lists.

+ALLPORT GREETING CARD CO., 532 NW 12th, Portland OR 97209. Michael & Victoria Allport, eds. General card publisher that does inspirational cards. 10% freelance. Pays on publication. Responds in 3 mos. Seasonal/holiday 6 mos ahead. Submit at least 8 ideas. Guidelines.

ARGUS COMMUNICATIONS, 200 E. Bethany, Allen TX 75002. (214)390-6300. Fax: (214)390-6555. Lori Potter, ed. General card publisher with a religious line. 90% freelance. Query. Outright purchase. Pays $75, on acceptance, for all rts. Royalty 5-8%. Responds in 6-9 wks. Uses unrhymed, traditional, light verse; 1-2 lines. Produces humorous and inspirational (one line of sweet, light bear cards. Needs birthday, congratulations, friendship, get well, keep in touch, love, miss you, sympathy, thank you, and wedding. Submit maximum 20 ideas. Also open to calendars, postcards, posters, and banners appropriate for Christian schools and Sunday school classrooms. Guidelines; catalog for 9x12 SAE/3 stamps.

> **Special Needs:** "We prefer to receive editorial for humorous and inspirational posters and postcards, and Pass It Ons. The material is generally short and to-the-point and offers cheer, encouragement, hope, and inspiration to keep the faith in today's world."
>
> **Tips:** "Our greeting card line is limited. We update our freelance writers as new needs arise."

RUSS BERRIE & CO., Inc., 111 Bauer Dr., Oakland NJ 07436. (201)337-9000. Heather Rockwell, dir. A general card publisher/inspirational and religious lines. 20% freelance; buys 40 ideas/yr. Outright submission. Pays $100, on acceptance, for all rts. Royalty 2%. Responds in 6-8 wks. Uses rhymed, unrhymed, traditional, light verse; various lengths. Produces conventional, humorous, informal, inspirational, juvenile, novelty, religious, sensitivity, soft line. Needs card verse for anniversary, birthday, friendship, get well, keep in touch, love, miss you, new baby, please write, sympathy, thank you, wedding. Needs verses for other products for Christmas, Easter, graduation, Halloween, relatives, mother, St. Patrick's Day, Thanksgiving, Valentine's Day. Holiday/seasonal 18-24 mos. ahead. Open to new card lines. Prefers 10 (long) to 20 (short) ideas/submission. Open to ideas for perpetual and undated calendars, gift books, greeting books, plaques, postcards, novelty products/copy, mugs, magnets, picture frames, gift bags, diaries, address books, stationary and gift items. Guidelines; no catalog.

*THE BRANCHES, INC. (formerly **NEW BOUNDARY DESIGNS, INC**), 1389 Park Rd., Chanhassen MN 55317. (612)474-0924. Ronald Olson, marketing mngr. General card publisher/religious line. 5% freelance; 9 ideas/yr. Pays $240/camera-ready design, on publication. Royalties 2-5%. Responds in 6 mos. Prefers unrhymed. Produces traditional, inspirational, juvenile and sensitivity. Holiday/seasonal 1 yr ahead. Open to ideas for greeting books, plaques, postcards, mugs, coaster magnets, bookmarks. Catalog.

*THE CALLIGRAPHY COLLECTION, 2604 NW 74th Pl., Gainesville FL 32606-1237. (904)375-8530. Fax: ((904)374-9957. Katy Fischer, ed. General card publisher/inspirational cards. Pays $50-100/framed print idea, on publication, for all rts. Responds in 6 months. Uses rhymed and unrhymed (preferred). Produces conventional, humorous, informal, inspirational, sensitivity, and soft line. Holiday/seasonal 6 months ahead. Prefers 3 ideas/submission. Also produces gift books, greeting books and plaques.

Tips: Especially needs friendship greetings.

*CARING CARD COMPANY, Box 90278, Long Beach CA 90809. Shirley Hassell, ed. A specialty card publisher/inspirational and religious cards. 45% freelance. Outright submissions. Pays $10-25, on publication, for all rts. Responds in 8-16 wks. Uses rhymed, unrhymed and traditional; length open. Produces inspirational, religious, sensitivity and soft line. Needs Christmas, friendship, get well, keep in touch, love, miss you, please write, Valentines, significant loss/sympathy (bereavement, hospice environment, life/death transitions). Holiday/seasonal 6-12 months ahead. Prefers 1-12 ideas/submission. Also open to ideas for calendars, posters, plaques, postcards, and T-shirts. Guidelines.

+CEDAR HILL STUDIO, P.O. Box 328, Waynesville NC 28786. (704)456-6344. Fax: (704)456-6303. Mark Clasby, CEO. Christian/religious card publisher. Open to freelance. Prefers outright submission. Pays $100, on publication, for reproduction rts. No royalties. Responds in 4 wks. Buys short humor. Produces humorous, inspirational, and sensitivity. Needs anniversary, birthday, Christmas, congratulations, friendship, get well, keep in touch, love, miss you, please write, relative, sympathy, thank you, and wedding. Seasonal 1 yr ahead. Open to new card lines. Also open to ideas for calendars and plaques. No guidelines; catalog on request.

Tips: "Messages must be uplifting and encouraging."

CELEBRATION GREETINGS (A div. of Leanin' Tree), Box 9500, Boulder CO 80301. (303)530-1442. Fax: (303)581-2512. Verse Submission Committee. Christian/religious card publisher. 30% freelance. Buys 30 ideas/yr. Query. Pays $100/idea, on publication, for exclusive rts. No royalties. Responds in 12 wks. Rhymed/unrhymed (preferred)/light verse; to 4 lines. Produces humorous, informal, inspirational, religious, sensitivity, soft line, studio. Needs anniversary, birthday, Christmas, congratulations, friendship, get well, keep in touch, love, miss you, new baby, please write, sympathy, thank you, wedding, and encouragement. Holiday/seasonal 8 mos ahead. Open to new card lines; also posters, novelty products/copy, mugs and magnets. Prefers 25 or less ideas/submission. Guidelines; no catalog.

Tips: "No special occasion or narrow categories."

+CITY ALIVE, P.O. Box 4952, Chicago IL 60680-4952. (312)433-3838. Fax: (312)433-3839. Videos only.

CREATIVE GRAPHICS, 785 Grant, Eugene OR 97402. (503)484-2726. Submit to Terry Dusseault, corp. sec. General card publisher/religious lines. Open only to photographs/artwork. Query. Pays $50/card.

#CURRENT, INC., Box 2559, Colorado Springs CO 80901-2559. (719)594-4100. Nan Stine, Supervisor, creative writing. General card publisher/religious line. 5-10% freelance. Buys 150 ideas/yr. Outright submissions. Pays $50, on acceptance, for all rights. No royalty. Responds in 2 mos. Prefers rhymed, unrhymed, traditional, light verse, original/tasteful humor; short. Produces announcements, conventional, humorous, informal, inspirational, juvenile, novelty, religious, sensitivity, soft line, studio. Needs anniversary, birthday, Christmas, congratulations, Easter, friendship, get well, graduation, Halloween, keep in touch, love, miss you, new baby, please write, sympathy, Thanksgiving, thank you, Valentines, wedding; also terminal illness and coping. Holiday/seasonal 18 months ahead. 12-15 ideas/submission. Open to new card lines, calendars, coloring books, gift books, greeting books, plaques, postcards, posters, puzzles. Guidelines; catalog (call 1-800-525-7170).

DAYSPRING GREETING CARDS/OUTREACH PUBLICATIONS INC., Box 1010, Hwy. 16 E., Siloam Springs AR 72761. (501)524-9301. Fax: (501)524-8959. Ann Woodruff, ed. coord. Christian/religious card publisher. 20% freelance; buys 750-1,000 ideas/yr. Query or outright submission. Pays from $35-50/idea, on acceptance, for all rts. No royalty. Responds in 4-8 wks. Uses rhymed, unrhymed (preferred), traditional and light verse; various lengths. Produces humorous, inspirational, juvenile, religious. Needs anniversary, birthday, Christmas, congratulations, Easter, friendship, get well, graduation, keep in touch, love, miss you, new baby, please write, relatives, sympathy, Thanksgiving, thank you, Valentines, wedding, and all major sending seasons and everyday occasions. Holiday/seasonal 1 yr ahead. Open to new card lines and calendar ideas. Send any number. Guidelines; no catalog.

*FREEDOM GREETING CARDS, Box 715, Bristol PA 19007. (215)945-3300. J. Levitt, pres. General card publisher/religious and inspirational lines. Currently has all the freelancers they need. Let them know the kind of work you can do and they will put your name in their file.

*GALLANT GREETINGS, 2654 W. Medill, Chicago, IL 60647. (312)489-2000. General card publisher/a few inspirational/religious cards. Carolyn McDilda, ed. coord. 90% freelance; buys 500 ideas/yr. Query. Responds in 1 month. Pays 60-90 days after acceptance, for world greeting card rts. Pays royalties. Uses rhymed, unrhymed, traditional and light verse; 4-6 lines. Produces announcements, conventional, humorous, informal, inspirational, invitations, juvenile, religious, studio. Needs all types of greetings. Holiday/seasonal 6 months ahead. Open to new card lines. Prefers 6-10 ideas/submission. Guidelines/needs list; no catalog.

*THE C.R. GIBSON CO., 32 Knight St., Norwalk CT 06856. (203)847-4543. John Carroll, product mgr. General card publisher that does a few inspirational and religious cards. Open to freelance. Query. Pays variable amounts, on publication, for greeting card rts. Sometimes pays variable royalties. Responds in 8-12 wks. Uses rhymed, unrhymed and traditional. Produces announcements, conventional, humorous, informal, inspirational, invitations, juvenile, novelty, and religious. Needs anniversary, birthday, Christmas, Easter, friendship, get well, keep in touch, love, miss you, please write, and Valentines; 12 months ahead. Open to ideas for new card lines. Also open to ideas for gift books, greeting books and postcards. Guidelines.

+GIFTED LINE, 999 Canal Blvd., Point Richmond CA 94804. Julie Grovhoug, ed. General card publisher that does inspirational cards. 5% freelance. Pays on acceptance. Responds in 1 mo. Holiday/seasonal 6 mos ahead. Submit max. 6-10 ideas. Victorian cards only.

+IMAGE CRAFT, INC., 1245 Franklin Blvd., Box 814, Cambridge ON N1R 5W6 Canada. (519)622-4310. Fax: (519)622-6774. Jeanette Gilmour, ed. General card publisher with a religious line. Open to freelance. Prefers outright submission. Pays on acceptance. No royalties. Produces announcements, conventional, humorous, informal, inspirational, invitations, juvenile, religious and studio cards. Needs anniversary, birthday, Christmas, congratulations, Easter, friendship, get well, graduation, keep in touch, love, miss you, Mother's Day/Father's Day, new baby, relatives/all occasion, sympathy, Thanksgiving, thank you, Valentines, wedding, confirmation, and First Communion. Seasonal 7 mos ahead. Open to new card lines. Also open to ideas for gift books and plaques.

+LATE FOR THE SKY PRODUCTION COMPANY, 561 Reading Rd., Cincinnati OH 45202. Fax: (513)721-5757. Board games.

LIFE GREETINGS, Box 468, Little Compton RI 02837. (401)635-8535. Kathy Brennan, ed. Christian/religious card publisher. Open to freelance. Outright purchases. Pays $10, on acceptance, for all rts. No royalties. Responds in 6 wks. Uses rhymed, unrhymed, traditional; 6-8 lines. Produces announcements, conventional, humorous, inspirational, and religious. Needs congratulations, friendship, get well, new baby, sympathy, thank you and wedding. Also clergy reassignment, ordination, anniversary of ordination, and pro-life Christmas. Seasonal 6 mos ahead. Open to new card lines. Prefers 6 ideas/submission. Guidelines; no catalog.

*MAILAWAYS, P.O. Box 782, Tavares FL 32778. (908)742-8196. Gene Chambers, ed. General card publisher that does a few inspirational and religious cards. 100% freelance. Outright submission. Buys variable rights. Variable payment, on acceptance. No royalties. Responds in 1-2 wks. Uses rhymed, unrhymed, traditional, light verse, fables or anecdotes; the shorter the better. Produces conventional, humorous, inspirational, religious and sensitivity. Poetic or humorous verses only; no cards for holidays or special events. Seasonal 3 mos ahead. Not open to new card lines. Send a handful of ideas at a time. May be open to ideas for gift books. Guidelines; no catalog.

*MANHATTAN GREETING CARD CO., 150 E 52 St. c/o Platzer/Fineberg, New York NY 10022. (718)894-7600. Paula Haley, ed. General card publisher/inspirational line. 100% freelance. Pays $5-250. Responds in 3 wks. Produces announcements, conventional, humorous, informal, inspirational, invitations, juvenile, sensitivity, soft line, studio, Christmas (85% of the line). Holiday/seasonal 18 months ahead. Also open to ideas for bumper stickers, calendars, gift books, greeting books, post cards, and promotions. Free guidelines.

+M.J.N. ENTERPRISES, 1624 McMillan, Memphis TN 38106. (901)946-8185. Board games.

*NOVO CARD PUBLISHERS, INC., 4513 N Lincoln Ave., Chicago IL 60625. (312)769-6000. Fax: (312)769-6769. Julia Chae, gen mgr. General card publisher that does a few inspirational and religious cards. 40% freelance; buys 50-100 ideas/yr. Outright submissions. Pays $15-30, on acceptance, for all rts. No royalties. Responds in 4 wks. Uses rhymed, unrhymed, traditional and light verse. Produces announcements, conventional, humorous, informal, inspirational, invitations, juvenile, novelty, religious, sensitivity, soft line and studio. Needs anniversary, birthday, Christmas, congratulations, Easter, friendship, get well, graduation, Halloween, keep in touch, love, miss you, new baby, relatives (all occasions), sympathy, thank you, Valentines, and wedding. Seasonal 9 mos ahead. No new card lines. Submit 5-10 ideas max. Guidelines; no catalog.

> **Special Needs:** "We would like to do a line of inspirational cards, 24 designs, either with one writer or several writers."

*PACIFIC PAPER GREETINGS, INC, Box 2249, Sidney BC V8L 3S8 Canada. (604)656-0504. Louise Rytter, ed. Inspirational cards. 50% freelance; buys 20 ideas/yr. Pays on acceptance, for all rts. Responds in 3 wks. Produces conventional, inspirational, romantic, sensitivity, soft line. Holiday/seasonal 12 months ahead. Guidelines for SAE/1 IRC.

PAINTED HEARTS & FRIENDS, 1222 N. Fair Oaks Ave., Pasadena CA 91103. (818)798-3633, Fax: (818)798-7385. Susan Kinney, pres. General card publisher that does a few inspirational and religious cards. 10% freelance; buys 20-30 ideas/yr. Outright submission (copies only, no original artwork). Pays $75-100/idea, on publication. Variable royalty. Responds in 1-2 wks. Uses unrhymed, traditional, light verse; 2-3 liners. Produces announcements, humorous, informal, inspirational, invitations, juvenile, novelty religious. Needs most types of greetings (no St. Patrick's Day), plus graduation and Jewish holidays. Holiday 2 mos ahead. Open to ideas for new card lines. Submit 12 art designs max., or as many sentiments as fit on a page. Open to ideas for post cards and posters; growing up books. Guidelines; catalog for 9x12 SAE/5 stamps.

*PAPER MAGIC GROUP, INC, P.O. Box 977, Scranton PA 18501-0977. Anne Leaf, VP/Creative. Secular card company specializing in Christmas cards; also does inspirational cards. 50% freelance. Outright submission on 8½x11 paper. Pays negotiable rates ($20-150), within 30 days, for all rts. Does Christmas, seasonal, inspirational, cute and humorous.

Tip: "MUST be original."

*PARAMOUNT CARDS INC., Box 6546, Providence RI 02940. (401)726-0800. Tammy O'Keefe, ed.; submit to Editorial Freelance. General card publisher that does a few inspirational/religious cards. 10% freelance; humor only (no religious humor). Outright submission. Pays $100, on acceptance, for complete world rts. No royalty. Responds in 3 wks. Prefers 10-15 ideas/submission. Guidelines for SASE; no catalog.

*C.M. PAULA COMPANY, 7773 School Rd., Cincinnati OH 45249. Submit to Editorial Supervisor. General gift-line items with inspirational verse; no greeting cards. 10% freelance. Pays on acceptance, for all rts. Responds in 4-6 wks. Holiday/seasonal 1 yr head. Open to verse and prose for plaques, key rings, magnets, stationary pads, mugs, plates, awards and statues. Guidelines.

*RED FARM STUDIO, Box 347, Pawtucket RI 02862-0347. (401)728-9300. Lisa Harter Saunders, creative dir. General card publisher with a religious line. 100% freelance. Query or outright submission (get guidelines first). Pays $3/line, on acceptance, for exclusive rts. No royalties. Responds in 2 mos. Use traditional and light verse; 1-4 lines. Produces announcements, invitations, religious. Needs anniversary, birthday, Christmas, friendship, get well, new baby, sympathy, wedding. Holiday 6 months ahead. Not open to ideas for new card lines. Submit any number of ideas. Guidelines/needs list for SASE.

+SCANDECOR, 430 Pike Rd., Southampton PA 18966. (215)355-2410. Fax: (215)364-8737. Lauren Harris Karp, product mngr. A general poster publisher that does a few inspirational posters. 50% freelance; buys 20 ideas/yr. Makes outright purchase, for world-wide, exclusive rts. Payment, on publication, depends on size of poster. No royalties. Responds in 8 wks. Uses rhymed, unrhymed and light verse; one line up to 20 lines. Produces humorous, inspirational, juvenile, novelty and soft line. No holiday posters. Submit several ideas. Open to ideas for calendars, posters and novelty products/copy. Guidelines; no catalog.

MARCEL SCHURMAN CO., INC., 2500 N. Watney Way, Fairfield CA 94533-6724. Meg Schutte, ed. General card publisher that does a few religious and inspirational cards. 5-10% freelance; buys 20-25 ideas/yr. Query. Pays $75-125, on acceptance. Responds in 2-3 wks. Uses mostly unrhymed (rhymed ok for juvenile), traditional, light verse, contemporary, whimsical; 2-3 lines. Produces counter cards only; all holidays/all captions. Holiday 6 mos. ahead. Open to new card lines. Prefers 10 ideas/submission. Guidelines.

*SUNRISE PUBLICATIONS, INC, 1145 Sunrise Greeting Ct., Box 4699, Bloomington IN 47402. (812)336-9900. Fax: (812)336-8712. Sheila Gerber, Editorial Coordinator. General card publisher that does inspirational cards. 10% freelance; buys 100 ideas/yr. Outright submission. Pays $50, on acceptance, for exclusive rts in all commercial formats. No royalties. Responds in 6 wks. Prefers unrhymed, traditional, contemporary; 1-4 lines. Produces announcements, conventional, informal, inspirational, invitations. Needs anniversary, birthday, belated birthday, Christmas, congratulations, Easter, friendship, get well, graduation, Halloween, love, miss you, new baby, St. Patrick's Day, sympathy, Thanksgiving, thank you, Valentines, wedding; also baptism, confirmation, bar and bat mitzvah. Holiday/seasonal any time. Not open to ideas for new card lines. Up to 20 ideas/submission. Guidelines; no catalog.

WARNER PRESS INC., 1200 E 5th St, Anderson IN 46018. (317)644-7721. Fax: (317)649-3664. Robin Fogle, product ed. Christian/religious card publisher. 30% freelance; buys 100+ ideas/yr. Query. Pays $20-25, on acceptance, for full rts. No royalties. Responds in 4-6 wks. Uses rhymed, unrhymed, traditional, light verse; 4-8 lines. Produces inspirational, religious. Needs anniversary, birthday, Christmas (needs a good amount for boxed cards), Easter, friendship, get well, graduation, new baby, sympathy, thank you, Valentines, wedding, secret pal, and from the pastor. Holiday/seasonal 6 months ahead. Accepts Christmas material in September for next year. Open to new card lines. Accepts 10 ideas/submission. Also open to ideas for calendars, coloring books, gift books, postcards, posters and Sunday bulletins (devotional material). Guidelines; no catalog.

Special Needs: "We purchase for boxed greeting cards. Verses should be warm and personal, but general enough to be sent by a group."

Tips: "We prefer submissions be typed on 3x5 cards with name, address, telephone #, and freelance identification # on the back."

ADDITIONAL CARD PUBLISHERS

The following greeting card publishers do not use freelance material, or did not complete a questionnaire, but are included for reference or to contact on your own. Do not submit to them before you send for guidelines or ascertain their needs.

ABBEY PRESS, St. Meinrad IN 47577. No freelance.

+ABUNDANT TREASURES, P.O. Box 605, Calimesa CA 92320-0605.

ACT NOW, INC., P.O. Box 294, Mogadore OH 44260. No freelance.

APPALACHIAN BIBLE CO INC., 506 Princeton Rd, Johnson City TN 37601.

+ART BEATS, 33 River Rd., Cos Cob CT 06807-2717.

BARTON-COTTON INC., 1405 Parker Rd., Baltimore MD 21227. No freelance.

B B STUDIOS, 337 Timberhead Ln., Foster City CA 94404-3917.

CAROLYN BEAN PUBLISHING, 1129 N McDowell Blvd., Petaluma CA 94954.

BERG CHRISTIAN ENTERPRISES, 4525 SE 63rd Ave, Portland OR 97206.

BETH HA DAVAR, 10 Brick Row, Athens NY 12015. No freelance.

BLUE MOUNTAIN ARTS, P.O. Box 1007, Boulder CO 80306. Asked to be deleted.

BOB SIEMON DESIGNS INC., 11609 Martens River Cir., Fountain Valley CA 92708.

BRETT-FORER GREETINGS, 5400 W. 35th St., Chicago IL 60650-4400.

+CATHEDRAL ART METAL CO., 250 Esten Ave., Pawtucket RI 02860.

EARTH CARE PAPER, INC., P.O. Box 8507, Ukiah CA 95482.

EISNER ADVERTISING STUDIO (OH) - No freelance.

+KRISTEN ELLIOTT, INC., 6 Opportunity Way, Newburyport MA 01950.

+FAMILY LINE ALLISON GREETINGS, 79 - 5th Ave 4th Fl, New York NY 10003-3034.

FAYE'S SPECIALTY CARDS (NY) - No freelance.

FLAVIA - No freelance.

FULL MOON CREATIONS, 74 S. Hamilton St., Doylestown PA 18901 - Inspirational cards.

+GOSPEL GIGGLES, 6745 SW Scholls Ferry Rd., Apt. 14, Beaverton OR 97005-5450.

GUERNICA EDITIONS (Canada) - No freelance.

THE HERMITAGE ART COMPANY INC., 5151 N. Ravenwood Ave., Chicago IL 60640.

HIGHER HORIZONS, Box 78399, Los Angeles CA 90016.

IT TAKES TWO, INC., 100 Minnesota Ave., Le Sueur MN 56058. No freelance.

J-MAR ASSOCIATES, P.O. Box 23149, Waco TX 76702-3149. Not open to freelance at this time.

JONATHAN & DAVID INC, Box 1194, Grand Rapids MI 49501.

KIMBERLY ENTERPRISES INC., 15029 S. Figueroa St., Gardena CA 90248 - Inspirational cards.

KINKA, 1 Orchard Park, Madison CT 06443. No freelance.

THE LORENZ COMPANY, 1208 Cimmaron Dr., Waco TX 76712-8174.

MAINE LINE CO. - See RUSS BERRIE AND CO.

MALENA PRODUCTIONS INC., Box 14483, Ft. Lauderdale FL 33302 - Inspirational cards.

MANUSCRIPTURES (WI) - No freelance.

MARIAN HEATH GREETING CARDS, 9 Kendrick Rd., Wareham MA 02571 - No freelance.

+MASTERPIECE STUDIO, 5400 w 35th St., Chicago IL 60650. Sandy Klein, ed.

+MERI MERI, 300 Stein AM Rhein Ct.Unit C, Redwood City CA 94063.

+MIRACLE WATERS GREETING CARDS, P.O. Box 1307, New York NY 10028.

.NORTHWESTERN PRODUCTS INC. (MN) - No freelance.

OAKSPRINGS IMPRESSIONS, Box 572, Woodacre CA 94973.

+OATMEAL STUDIOS, P.O. Box 138, Rochester VT 05767. Helene Lehrer, creative dir.

+PALOMA CHRISTIANA, P.O. Box 2605, Rancho Mirage CA 92270.

PRINTERY HOUSE (MO) - No freelance.

QUADRIGA ART (NY) - No freelance.

QUALITY ARTWORKS, 2262 N. Penn Rd., Hatfield PA 19440 - Inspirational cards.

RAINFALL, INC. (MI) - No freelance.

+RAYS OF SUNSHINE, 910 Ave. E Box 775, Wisner NE 68791.

RENAISSANCE GREETING CARDS (ME) - No freelance.

ROSERICH DESIGNS LTD., 79 5th Ave. 4th Fl, New York NY 10003-3034. Moved; no forwarding address.

SANGAMON INC. (IL) - No freelance.

JOSEPH E. SCHULTZ ART STUDIO (IN) - No freelance.

SECOND NATURE LTD. (England) - No freelance.

SEEDS EVANGELICAL GREETING CARDS (NC) - No freelance

+SENDJOY GREETING CARDS, Laurel Park, Wappingers Falls NY 12590.

+THESE THREE, INC., 2103 - 18th St. N. #1035, Arlington VA 22201-3537. Jean Bridgers, ed.

+TLC GREETINGS, 615 McCall Rd., Manhattan KS 66502-8512. Michelle Johnson, dir.

+TRISTOPHER'S GREETINGS, P.O. Box 401, Bloomingdale IL 60108-0401. Trudi M. Smolinski, ed.

+WEST GRAPHICS, 385 Oyster Point Blvd #7, S. San Francisco CA 94080-1934. Carol West, ed.

+WILDEST DREAMS, Fairview Dr Rd 10, Carmel NY 10512.

WIZWORKS, Box 240, Masonville CO 80541 - Overstocked.

PUBLISHERS PRODUCING SPECIALTY PRODUCTS

NOTE: Most of the following publishers are greeting card publishers, but some will be found in the book publisher listings.

ACTIVITY/COLORING BOOKS
Current
Rainbow Books

Regina Press
Shining Star
Standard
Warner Press

BANNERS
Argus Communications

BOARD GAMES
Chariot (Rainfall Inc.)
Late for the Sky
Master Books
Joshua Morris Publishing
M.J.N.Enterprises
Shining Star
Standard Publishing
Tyndale House
Warner Press (maybe)

CALENDARS
Argus Communications
Russ Berrie
Caring Card Co.
Cedar Hill Studio
Current
Dayspring/Outreach
Group Publishing
Manhattan Greeting Card
Neibauer Press
Pilgrim Press
Scandecor
Tyndale House
Warner Press

COLORING BOOKS
Warner Press

COMIC BOOKS
Thomas Nelson

COMPUTER GAMES
Brown-ROA
Master Books
NavPress Software
Wood Lake Books

COMPUTER PROGRAMS
Baker (BakerBytes)
NavPress
Resource Publications

Zondervan

GIFT BOOKS
(See listing under Book Topics)
Russ Berrie
Image Craft
Painted Hearts & Friends
Review and Herald
Warner Press

GIFT/NOVELTY ITEMS
Argus Communications
Russ Berrie
Celebration Greetings
C.M. Paula Co. (key rings)
Manhattan Greeting Card
New Boundary Designs
Scandecor

GREETING BOOKS
Russ Berrie
Calligraphy Collection
Current
C.R. Gibson
Joshua Morris (novelty books)
Manhattan Greeting Card
New Boundary Designs

MAGNETS
Russ Berrie
Celebration Greetings
C.M. Paula Co.
New Boundary Designs

MUGS
Russ Berrie
Celebration Greetings
C.M. Paula Co.
New Boundary Designs

PLAQUES
Russ Berrie

Calligraphy Collection
Caring Card Company
Cedar Hill Studio
Current
C.M. Paula Co.
Image Craft
New Boundary Designs

POSTCARDS
Argus Communications
Russ Berrie
Caring Card Co.
Current
C.R. Gibson
Manhattan Greeting Card
New Boundary Designs
Painted Hearts & Friends
Warner Press

POSTERS
Argus Communications
Caring Card Co.
Celebration Greetings
Current
Painted Hearts & Friends
Scandecor
Warner Press

PUZZLES
Current

SUNDAY BULLETINS
Warner Press

T-SHIRTS
Caring Card Co.
Celebration Greetings

VIDEOS/VIDEO GAMES
Broadman & Holman
Brown-ROA
City Alive

Focus on the Family

Gospel Light

InterVarsity

Moody Press

Tyndale Family Video

Word

Zondervan

SECULAR NEWSPAPERS WITH RELIGION EDITORS

Following is a listing of about 245 secular newspapers or news magazines with the names of their religion editors. If you have broad interest religious pieces appropriate for a secular newspaper, send them to these editors, keeping in mind that most of them will want articles written in a journalistic style and with a news peg. You also might use the addresses of publications in your area to send local op-ed pieces or letters to the editor. In researching this market, I find that few newspapers are open to op-ed pieces from freelancers (particularly those outside their local area) unless they are well known or experts in their field. If you should have an opinion piece (with a religious slant and Scripture quotation) published in a secular publication, remember you may be eligible for one of several Amy Awards, including the $10,000 grand prize. Writing such pieces is also an excellent way to make an impact on society with your Christian principles. Send for rules to: Amy Awards, P.O. Box 16091, Lansing MI 48901.

The names given below are religion editors. The number at the end of some listings indicates circulation. (+) before a listing indicates a new listing this year.

Abilene Reporter-News, Roy Jones, 101 Cypress St, Box 30, Abilene TX 79604. 915-673-4271. 40,000.

Advocate, The, Ed Pratt, 525 Lafayette St, Box 588, Baton Rouge LA 70821. 504-383-1111. 30,000.

Akron Beacon Journal, Laura Haferd, 44 E Exchange St, Box 640, Akron OH 44328. 216-375-8111. 159,000.

Albuquerque Journal, Bruce Daniels, 7777 Jefferson St NE, Drawer J, Albuquerque NM 87103. 505-823-3912. 121,000.

Albuquerque Tribune, Jim Wagner, Drawer T, Albuquerque NM 87103. 505-823-3665. 35,000.

Amarillo Globe-News, Dora Dominguez, Box 2091, Amarillo TX 79166. 806-376-1488.

Anniston Star, Sean Reilly, Box 189, Anniston AL 36202. 205-236-1551.

Arizona Daily Star, Tom Turner, 4850 S Park Ave, Box 26807, Tucson AZ 85726. 602-573-4132. 90,000.

Arizona Republic, Kim Sue Lia Perkes, 120 E Van Buren St., Box 1950, Phoenix AZ 85001. 602-271-8487. 400,000.

+**Arkansas Democrat-Gazette**, Juanita Taylor, 714 N. Walnut, Little Rock AR 72205. 501-378-3400.

Atlanta Journal & Constitution, Gayle White, 72 Marietta St NW, Box 4689, Atlanta GA 30303. 404-526-5151. 282,000.

Augusta Chronicle & Herald, Allison Kennedy, 725 Broad St, Box 1928, Augusta GA 30909. 404-724-0851. 83,000.

Aurora Beacon-News, Mary Fran Fulton, 101 River St., Aurora IL 60504. 708-844-5585.

Austin American-Statesman, Carlos Vidal Greth, 305 S Congress, Box 670, Austin TX 78767. 512-445-3604. 180,000.

Bakersfield Californian, Ed King, 1707 Eye St, Box 440, Bakersfield CA 93302. 805-395-7384. 83,000.

Baltimore Sun, Jay Merwin or Frank Somerville, 501 N Calvert St, Baltimore MD 21278-0001. 410-332-6000. 238,000.

Bay City Times, Bob Carrier, 311 Fifth St, Bay City MI 48708. 517-895-8551. 42,000.

Beacon News, Marcia Nelson, 101 S. River St., Aurora IL 60506. 312-232-7000.

+Beaver County Times, Leigh Ann Eagleston, 400 Fair Ave., Beaver PA 15009. 412-775-3200.

Bergen Record, David Gibson, 150 River St., Hackensack NJ 07602. 201-646-4100.

Berkshire Eagle, William Bell, 75 S. Church St., Pittsfield MA 04005. 413-447-7311.

Billings Gazette, Sue Olt, 401 North Broadway, Billings MT 59101. 406-657-1200. 54,000.

Birmingham News, Greg Garrison, 2200 4th Ave N, Box 2553, Birmingham AL 35202. 205-325-2222. 215,000.

Bismarck Tribune, Julie Fredericksen, Seventh and Front Sts, Box 1498, Bismarck ND 58502. 701-223-2500. 32,000.

Boca Raton News, Mary Lou Simms, 33 SE Third St, Box 580, Boca Raton FL 33429. 407-338-4920. 38,000.

Boston Globe, James L. Franklin, 135 Morrissey Blvd, Box 2378, Boston MA 02107. 617-929-2000. 500,000.

Boston Herald, (no religion editor at this time), One Herald Sq, Box 2096, Boston MA 02106. 617-426-3000. 356,000.

Bozeman Daily Chronicle, Barb Smith, 32 S Rouse St, Box 1188, Bozeman MT 59771. 406-587-4491. 14,000.

Bridgeport Post, Frank M. Szivos, 410 State St., Bridgeport CT 06604. 203-333-0161. 90,000.

Calgary Herald, Gordon Legge, 215 - 16th St SE, Box 2400, Station M, Calgary AB T2P 0W8 Canada. 403-235-7560. 123,000.

Camden Courier-Post, Karen Morgan, 301 Cuthbert Blvd, Box 530, Cherry Hill NJ 08034. 609-663-6000. 101,000.

Canton Repository, Charita Goshay, 500 Market Ave S, Canton OH 44702. 216-454-5611. 84,000.

Casper Star Tribune, G. Thomas Morton, Box 80, Casper WY 82602-0080. 307-266-0592.

Cedar Rapids Gazette, Bev Duffy, 500 Third Ave SE, Cedar Rapids IA 52401. 319-398-8211. 71,000.

Chattanooga News-Free Press, Jim Ashley, 400 East 11th St, Chattanooga TN 37402. 615-756-6900. 104,000.

Chattanooga Times, Ruth Robinson, 117 E Tenth St, Box 951, Chattanooga TN 37401. 615-756-1234. 45,000.

+Chicago Reporter, Roy Larson, 332 S. Michigan Ave., Chicago IL 60604. 312-427-4830.

Chicago Sun-Times, Andrew Hermann, 401 N Wabash, Chicago IL 60611. 312-321-3000. 531,000.

Chicago Tribune, Michael Hirsley or Monique Parsons (Box 57, Carpinteria CA 93013), 435 N Michigan Ave, Chicago IL 60611. 312-222-3405. 723,000.

Cincinnati Inquirer, Ben Kaufman or Christiane Wolff, 312 Elm St, Cincinnati OH 45202. 513-768-8370/369-1925. 348,000.

Cincinnati Post, Carmen Carter, 125 East Court St, Cincinnati OH 45202. 513-352-2000. 114,000.

Cleveland Plain Dealer, Darryl Holland, 1801 Superior Ave NE, Cleveland OH 44114. 216-344-4500. 414,000.

Columbia State, Jennifer Nicholson, Box 1333, Columbia SC 29202. 803-771-8507. 180,000.

Columbus Dispatch, Darris Blackford, 34 S Third St, Columbus OH 43215. 614-461-8521. 263,000.

Commercial Appeal, Thomas Bailey or David Waters, 495 Union, Memphis TN 38103. 901-529-2399.

Contra Costa Times, Diane Weddington, Walnut Creek CA 94596. 100,000.

Courier Journal, Bill Wolfe, 525 W Broadway, Louisville KY 40202. 502-582-4248.

Daily Gleaner, Sterling Kneebone, Box 3370, Fredericton NB E3B 5A2 Canada. 506-452-6671. 31,000.

Daily Intelligencer, Louise Heath, 333 N Broad St., Doylestown PA 18901. 215-345-3000.

Daily Mail, Robert N. Mitchell, Box 484 - 30 Church, Catskill NY 12414. 518-943-2100.

Daily Press, Lisa Daniels, 7505 Warwick, Newport News VA 23601. 804-247-4793. 124,000.

+Daily Times, Julia Duin, Box 450, Farmington NM 87499. 505-325-4545.

Dallas Morning News, Communications Center, Daniel J. Cattau, Box 655237, Dallas TX 75265. 214-977-8222/800-431-0010. 800,000.

Dayton Daily News, Dave Kepple, 45 S Ludlow St, Box 1287, Dayton OH 45402. 513-225-2223. 185,000.

Denver Post, Virginia Culver, Box 1709, Denver CO 80201. 303-820-1223. 262,000.

Detroit Free Press, David M. Crumm, 321 W. Lafayette, Detroit MI 48226. 313-223-4526. 575,000.

Detroit News, Kate DeSmet, 615 W Lafayette Blvd, Detroit MI 48231. 313-222-2245. 434,000.

Duluth News Tribune, Sue Hogan-Albach, 424 W 1st St., Duluth MN 55816. 218-723-5281.

Elkhart Truth, Tom Price, 421 S 2nd, Elkhart IN 46515. 219-294-1661.

Extra News Bureau, Celia Sibley, 6455 Best Friend Rd., Norcross GA 30071. 404-263-3858.

Fayetteville Observer & Times, James Pharr or Earl M. Vaughan, 2702 Huntington Rd., Fayetteville NC 28303. 919-323-4848. 82,000.

Flint Journal, Betty Brenner, 200 E First St, Flint MI 48502. 313-767-0660. 120,000.

Florida Times Union, Barbara White, 1 Riverside Ave, Box 1949, Jacksonville FL 32231. 904-359-4111. 186,000.

Fort Lauderdale News, James Davis or Earl Maucker, 101 N. River Dr. E., Ft. Lauderdale FL 33301. 305-761-4000.

Fort Lauderdale Sun-Sentinel, Damon Adams, 3 SW 129th Ave. Ste. 101, Pembroke Pines FL 33027. 305-436-7157. 240,000.

Fort Worth Star Telegram, Jim W. Jones, 400 W 7th St., Fort Worth TX 76102. 817-390-7707. 255,000.

+Free-Lance Star, 616 Amelia St., Fredericksburg VA 22401. 703-373-5000.

Fremont Argus, Chris O'Connell, 3850 Decoto Road, Fremont CA 94536. 510-794-0111. 33,000.

Fresno Bee, Dee Anne Finken or John G. Taylor, 1626 E. St., Fresno CA 93786. 209-441-6375.

Galveston Daily News, Robert Frelow, Box 628, Galveston TX 77553. 409-744-3611. 409-744-3611.

Gazette Telegraph, Steve Rabey, Box 1779, Colorado Springs CO 80901. 719-636-9276. 107,000.

Grand Forks Herald, Steve Lee, 120 N Fourth St, Box 6008, Grand Forks ND 58203. 701-780-1114. 40,000.

Grand Rapids Press, Ed Golder, 155 Michigan St. NW, Grand Rapids MI 49503. 150,000.

Grass Valley Union, Susan Genovese, Box 1025, Grass Valley CA 95945. 916-273-9561. 20,000.

Greensboro Daily News & Record, Andrew Barron, 200 E. Market St., Greensboro NC 27420. 919-373-7000. 116,000.

Hamilton Spectator, Ray Brown, 44 Frid St, Hamilton ON L8N 3G3 Canada. 416-526-3333. 134,000.

Harrisburg Patriot-News, Judith Patton, 812 Market St, Box 2265, Harrisburg PA 17105. 717-255-8100. 170,000.

Hartford Courant, Gerald Renner, 285 Broad St., Hartford CT 06115. 203-241-6200. 228,000.

Herald, The, Richard Jackson, Box 930, Everett WA 98206. 206-339-3423.

Herald & Review, Theresa Churchill, 601 E. William St., Decatur IL 62525. 217-429-5151.

Herald Sun, Flo Johnston, Box 2092, Durham NC 27702. 919-419-6638.

Hillsdale Daily News, Janet Lee, 4300 W Bacon Rd., Hillsdale MI 49242. 517-431-7351.

Honolulu Star-Bulletin, City Desk (for now), 605 Kapiolani Blvd, Box 3080, Honolulu HI 96802. 808-525-8640. 100,000.

Houston Chronicle, Richard Vara or Cecile Holmes White, 801 Texas St., Houston TX 77002. 713-220-7171. 440,000.

Houston Post, Steve Brunsman, 4747 SW Freeway, Box 4747, Houston TX 77001. 713-840-5600. 297,000.

Huntsville Times, Yvonne T. White, Box 1487 West Station, Huntsville AL 35807. 205-532-4419. 74,000.

Hutchinson News, Joyce Hall, Box 190, Hutchinson KS 67504. 316-662-3311. 42,000.

Imperial Valley Press, Peggy Dale, 205 N 8th St, El Centro CA 92244. 619-352-2211. 19,000.

Independence Examiner, Richard LeComte, Box 458, Independence MO 64051. 816-254-8600.

Indianapolis Star, Carol Elrod or Gregory Weaver, 307 N. Pennsylvania St., Indianapolis IN 46204. 317-663-9471. 229,000.

Inland Valley Daily Bulletin, Nan Cretens, Box 4000, Ontario CA 91761. 909-987-6397. 80,000.

Jackson Sun, Tonya Smith, Box 1059, Jackson TN 38301. 901-427-3333. 36,000.

Jersey Journal, Elizabeth A. Foley, 30 Journal Sq, Jersey City NJ 07306. 201-653-1000. 70,000.

Johnson City Press-Chronicle, Robert Pierce, 204 W Main St, (37601), Box 1717, Johnson City TN 37605. 615-929-3111. 32,000.

Journal Tribune, Donna Landry, Box 627, Biddeford ME 04005. 207-282-1535.

Kansas City Star, Helen Gray, 1729 Grand Ave, Kansas City MO 64108. 816-234-4300. 282,000.

Keene Sentinel, Diane Nix, 60 West St., Keene NH 03431. 603-352-1234.

Kentucky New Era, Tonya Smith, Box 729, Hopkinsville KY 42240. 502-886-4444. 16,000.

Kingston Whig-Standard, Mr. Rosalind Malcolm, 306 King St, Kingston ON K7L 4Z7 Canada. 613-544-5000. 36,000.

Kitchener Waterloo Record, Donna Shea, 225 Fairway Road S, Kitchener ON N2G 4E5 Canada. 519-894-2231. 83,000.

Lacrosse Tribune, Gayda Hollnagel, 401 N. Third St., Lacrosse WI 54601. 608-782-9710.

Lafayette Journal & Courier, Byron Parvis, 217 N Sixth St, Lafayette IN 47901. 317-423-5511. 40,000.

Lake County News Herald, Kathy Baur, 38879 Mentor Road, Willoughby OH 44094. 216-951-0000. 46,000.

Lakeland Ledger, Maryalice Quinn, Lime & Missouri Sts, Box 408, Lakeland FL 33802. 813-687-7000. 50,000.

Lansing State Journal, Sheila Schimpf, 120 E. Lenawee, Lansing MI 48919. 517-377-1000. 92,000.

+Las Cruces Sun-News, Box 1749, Las Cruces NM 88004-1749. 505-523-4581.

Las Vegas Review-Journal, Sandy Varvel, 1111 W Bonanza Road, Box 70, Las Vegas NV 89125. 702-385-4241. 129,000.

Lewiston Daily Sun, Jean Lachance, 104 Park St, Lewiston ME 04240. 207-784-5411. 43,000.

Lewistown Tribune, Jeannie DePaul, 505 C St, Box 957, Lewiston ID 83501. 208-743-9411. 26,000.

Lexington Herald Leader, Paul Prather, 100 Midland Ave., Lexington KY 40508. 606-231-3342. 120,000.

Long Beach Press Telegram, Joy Thompson, 604 Pine Ave, Box 230, Long Beach CA 90844. 310-435-1161. 131,000.

Los Angeles Sentinel, Virgie W. Murray, 1112 E. 43rd, Los Angeles CA 90011. 213-232-3261. 40,000.

Los Angeles Times, John S. Dart, 20000 Prairie, Chatsworth CA 91311. 818-772-3342. 1,177,000.

+Los Angeles Times, Larry Stammer, Times-Mirror Sq., Los Angeles CA 90053.

Lowell Sun, Virginia Kimball, 4 Wayne Rd., Westford MA 01886. 508-458-7100. 57,000.

Lubbock Avalanche Journal, Beth Pratt, P.O. Box 491, Lubbock TX 79408. 806-762-8844. 70,000.

Lufkin Daily News, Beverly Johnson, Box 1089, Lufkin TX 75902. 409-632-6631. 9,000.

Macomb Daily, Bill Fleming, 67 Cass Ave, Mount Clemens MI 48043. 313-469-4510. 48,000.

Macon Telegraph & News, Rosalan Thompson, 120 Broadway, Box 4167, Macon GA 31213. 912-744-4200. 75,000.

Medford Mail Tribune, Gary Nelson, 33 N First St, Box 1108, Medford OR 97501. 503-776-4411. 35,000.

Merced Sun-Star, Jeffery Williams, Box 739, 3033 North C St, Merced CA 95341. 209-722-1511. 23,000.

Meriden Record-Journal, Marjorie Fay, 11 Crown St, Box 915, Meriden CT 06450. 203-235-1661. 31,000.

Mesa Tribune, Lawn R. Griffiths, 120 W 1st Ave., Mesa AZ 85201. 602-898-6514.

Miami Herald, Bea Hines or Adon Taft, One Herald Plaza, Miami FL 33132. 305-376-3470/3463. 433,000.

Milwaukee Journal, Marie Rohde, 333 W State St, Box 661, Milwaukee WI 53201. 414-224-2000. 260,000.

Milwaukee Sentinel, Ernie Franzen, 918 N Fourth St, Box 371, Milwaukee WI 53203. 414-224-2151. 179,000.

Mineral Daily News-Tribune, Ed Bernard, Box 1266, Keyser WV 26726-1266.

Minneapolis Star-Tribune, Neal M. Gendler, 425 Portland Ave., Minneapolis MN 55488. 612-673-4138. 400,000.

Missoulian, The, Lynn Schwanke, religion reporter, Box 8029, Missoula MT 59807. 406-523-5240. 31,000.

Mobile Press-Register, Parker Holmes, 304 Government St, Box 2488, Mobile AL 36630. 205-434-8696. 117,000.

Modesto Bee, Dennis Roberts, 1325 H St, Box 3928, Modesto CA 95354. 209-578-2000. 80,000.

Monterey Herald, Mariann Zambo, Monterey Peninsula Herald Co., Box 271, Monterey CA 93942. 408-372-3311. 39,000.

Montgomery Advertiser, Lynn Williamson, 200 Washington Ave, Box 1000, Montgomery AL 36101-1000. 205-262-1611. 60,000.

Montgomery Journal, Jane Dumont, 11131 Dewey Rd., Kensington MD 20895. 301-942-0103.

Montreal Gazette, Harvey L. Shepherd, 250 St. Antoine St., Montreal QB H2Y 3R7 Canada. 514-987-2847. 276,000.

Morning News Tribune, Steve Maynard, 1950 S State St, Box 11000, Tacoma WA 98411. 206-597-8649. 110,000.

Mt. Carmel Register, Larry Reynolds, 115 E 4th, Mt Carmel IL 62863. 618-262-5144.

Muncie Evening Press, Renee Jennings, 125 S High St, Box 2408, Muncie IN 47302. 317-747-5700. 14,000.

Nashville Banner, Frances Meeker, 1100 Broadway, Nashville TN 37203. 615-259-8270. 67,000.

Nashville Tennessean, Ray Waddle, 1100 Broadway, Nashville TN 37203. 615-259-8077. 130,000.

New Orleans Times-Picayune, Religion Editor, 3800 Howard Ave, New Orleans LA 70140. 504-826-3448. 279,000.

New York Daily News, Bill Bell, 220 East 42nd St, New York NY 10017. 212-210-2100. 800,000.

New York Newsday, Paul Moses, 2 Park Ave, New York NY 10016. 212-251-6850. 271,000.

New York Times, Gustav Niebuhr or Peter Steinfels, 229 W 43rd, New York NY 10036. 212-556-1234. 1,115,000.

Newark Star Ledger, Monica Maske, Star Ledger Plaza, Newark NJ 07101. 201-877-4020/4040. 471,000.

News & Daily Advance, Dave Schleck, 101 Wyndale Dr., Lynchburg VA 24506. 804-385-5543.

News & Observer, Erin Kelly or Donna Seese, 215 S McDowell St., Raleigh NC 27604. 919-829-4860.

News Chronicle, John Mitchell, 2595 Thousand Oaks Blvd, Box 3129, Thousand Oaks CA 91359. 805-496-3211. 22,000.

News Journal, The, Janet Applegren, 901 Sixth St, Box 2831, Daytona Beach FL 32117. 904-252-1511. 100,000.

News Press, The, Glenda Anderson, 2442 Dr Martin Luther King Blvd, Box 10, Fort Myers FL 33902. 813-335-0200. 90,000.

News Tribune, Steven Maynard, P.O. Box 11000, Tacoma WA 98411. 206-597-8738.

Newsweek, Kenneth L. Woodward, 444 Madison Ave., New York NY 10022.

Oceanside Blade-Tribune, Debbie Rosen, 1722 S Hill, Box 90, Oceanside CA 92054. 619-433-7333. 45,000.

Omaha World Herald, Julia McCord, World Herald Sq, Omaha NE 68102. 402-444-1000. 222,000.

Orange County Register, Ms.Tracy Weber, 625 N Grand Ave, Box 11626, Santa Ana CA 92711. 714-664-5029. 348,000.

Oregonian, Sura Rubenstein, 1320 SW Broadway, Portland OR 97201. 503-221-8327. 337,000.

Oregon Statesman, Lewis H. Ahrends, Jr., P.O. Box 13009, Salem OR 97309. 503-399-6611.

Orlando Sentinel, Adelle Banks, 633 N Orange Ave, Box 2833, Orlando FL 32801-1349. 407-420-5459. 273,000.

Ottawa Citizen, Bob Harvey, 1101 Boxter Rd., Ottawa ON K2C 3P4 Canada. 613-596-3689. 500,000.

Palm Beach Post, Lois Kaplan, Box 24700, West Palm Beach FL 33416. 407-820-4100. 182,000.

Patriot Ledger, Ann Doyle or Dot Newell, George W. Prescott Publishing, Quincy MA 02169. 617-786-7000/7026. 189,000.

+Peoria Star Journal, Michael Miller, 1 News Plaza, Peoria IL 61643. 309-686-3106.

Philadelphia Daily News, no religion editor, 400 N Broad St, Box 7788, Philadelphia PA 19101. 215-854-5900. 225,000.

Philadelphia Inquirer, Kristen Holmes or Michael D. Schaffer, 400 N Broad St, Box 8263, Philadelphia PA 19130. 215-854-2000. 500,000.

Phoenix Gazette, Ben Winton, 120 E Van Buren St.,Phoenix AZ 85004. 800-331-9270. 115,000.

Pittsburgh Press, Ann Rogers-Melnick, 34 Blvd of the Allies, Pittsburgh PA 15230. 412-263-1416. 168,000.

Placerville Mountain Democrat, Joy Haessler, Box 1088, Placerville CA 95667. 916-622-1255. 14,000.

+Portland Press Herald, Steve Vegh, 390 Congress St., Portland ME 04101. 800-442-6036.

Post and Courier, Marsha B. Guerard, 134 Columbus St., Charleston SC 29403. 803-745-4151.

Post Herald, William Singleton, Box 2553, Birmingham AL 35202. 205-325-2370.

Post Standard, Alva James, Box 4818, Syracuse NY 13211. 315-470-2166.

Providence Journal & Ledger, Richard Dujardin, 75 Fountain St., Providence RI 02902. 401-277-7000. 202,000.

Publishers Weekly (magazine), Henry William Griffin, 5120 Prytania St., New Orleans LA 70115. 504-899-5889.

Reading Eagle Times, John Smith, Box 582, Reading PA 19603. 215-371-5007. 78,000.

Record, The, David Gibson, Bergen Record Co., 150 River St, Hackensack NJ 07601. 201-646-4182. 700,000.

Religious News Service, David Anderson or Tom Roberts or Carlton Smith or Gustav D. Spohn, 475 Riverside Dr. - 1902, New York NY 10115. 212-870-3311.

+Religious News Service, Joan Connell, 1101 Connecticut Ave. NW, Ste. 350, Washington DC 20036. 202-463-8777.

Reno Gazette Journal, Sharon Genung, 955 Kuenzli, Box 22000, Reno NV 89520. 702-788-6397. 85,000.

Richmond County Journal, Jeffrey D. Holland, P.O. Box 1888, Rockingham NC 28379. 919-997-3111.

Richmond News Leader, Tom Mullen, PO Box C-32333, Richmond VA 23293. 804-649-6000.

Richmond Times Dispatch, Ed Briggs, Box 85333, Richmond VA 23293-0001. 804-649-6754. 220,000.

Riverside Press Enterprise, Cindy Friday, 3512 14th St, Box 792, Riverside CA 92502. 909-684-1200. 160,000.

Roanoke Times & World News, Stephen D. Haner & Cody Lowe, Box 2491, Roanoke VA 24010. 703-981-3100. 125,000.

Rocky Mountain News, Gary Massaro, 400 West Colfax Ave, Box 719, Denver CO 80201. 303-892-5000. 356,000.

Rutland Daily Herald, Charlene Tenney, 27 Wales St, Norwich VT 05701. 802-775-5511. 23,000.

Sacramento Bee, Janet Vitt, 2100 Q St, Box 15779, Sacramento CA 95852. 916-321-1000. 263,000.

+Salt Lake Tribune, Peggy Stack, 143 S. Main, Salt Lake City UT 84111.

San Antonio Express News, Michael Parker, Ave E & 3rd St, Box 2171, San Antonio TX 78297. 210-225-7411. 187,000.

San Bernardino Sun, Rosemary McClure, 399 N D St, San Bernardino CA 92401. 909-889-9666. 94,000.

San Diego Evening Tribune, Bob Diveroli, Box 191, San Diego CA 92112-4106. 619-299-3131. 385,000.

San Diego Union Tribune, Sandi Dolbee, 350 Camino de la Reina, San Diego CA 92112. 619-293-2082. 458,000.

San Francisco Chronicle, Don Lattin, 901 Mission St, San Francisco CA 94103-2988. 415-777-7018. 600,000.

+San Francisco Examiner, Venise Wagner, 110 Fifth St., San Francisco CA 94120. 415-777-2424.

San Jose Mercury News. Jill Wolfson, 450 Ridder Park Dr., San Jose CA 95190. 408-920-5974. 279,000.

San Mateo Times, Tom Krogstad or Steven Shelby, 1080 S. Amphlett Blvd., San Mateo CA 94402. 415-348-4321. 47,000.

Santa Barbara News Press, Mr. Willie Mears, Box 1359, Santa Barbara CA 93102. 805-564-5200. 58,000.

Santa Rosa Press Democrat, Suzanne Boynton, 427 Mendocino Ave, Santa Rosa CA 95401. 707-546-2020. 95,000.

Santa Ynez Valley News, Bart Ortberg, 423 Second St, Box 647, Solvang CA 93463. 805-688-5522. 8,000.

Seattle Times, Lee Mosciwal or Carol M. Ostrom, Box 70, Seattle WA 98111. 206-464-2323. 239,000.

Shreveport Times, David Westerfield, 222 Lake St, Shreveport LA 71101. 318-459-3271. 110,000.

Sioux City Journal, Glenn Olson, Sixth and Pavonia Sts, Sioux City IA 51102. 712-279-5075. 60,000.

Sonora Union Democrat, Lenore Rutherford, 84 S Washington St, Sonora CA 95370. 209-532-7151. 19,000.

St Joseph News Press, Tim Janulewicz, 825 Edmond St, Box 29, Saint Joseph MO 64501. 816-271-8595. 40,000.

St Louis Post-Dispatch, Patricia Rice or Kathy Rogers or Pamela Schaefer, 900 N Tucker Blvd, Saint Louis MO 63101. 314-340-8000. 340,000.

St Paul Pioneer Press Dispatch, Clark Morphew, 345 Cedar St, Saint Paul MN 55101. 612-222-5011. 209,000.

St Petersburg Times, Tom Billitteri or Susan Willey, 490 First Ave S, Box 1121, St Petersburg FL 33704. 813-893-8410. 352,000.

Southern Illinoisan, Sharon A. Gibson, 710 N. Illinois Ave., Carbondale IL 62902. 618-529-5454.

Spartanburg Herald-Journal, Debra Lester, P.O. Box 1657, Spartanburg SC 29304. 803-582-4511.

Star and Tribune, Martha Allen, 425 Portland Ave., Minneapolis MN 55488. 612-372-4141.

Standard Examiner, John DeVilbiss, 455 23rd St, Ogden UT 84302. 801-625-4237.

Staten Island Advance, Julia Martin, 950 Fingerboard Road, Staten Island NY 10305. 718-981-1234. 77,000.

+Sun, The, Jim Campbell, 545 Fifth St., Bremerton WA 98310. 206-792-9219.

Sun-Sentinel, Carol Brzozowski or Ken Swart, 3333 S. Congress Ave., Delray Beach FL 33445.

Syracuse Herald-Journal, Jim Reilly, 1 Clinton Sq, Box 4915, Syracuse NY 13221. 315-470-2265. 89,000.

Syracuse Post Standard, Tom Boll, Clinton Sq, Box 4818, Syracuse NY 13221. 315-470-0011. 90,000.

Tampa Tribune, Karen Long, 202 S Parker St, Box 191, Tampa FL 33601. 813-272-7711. 286,000.

Telegraph Herald, Lyn C. Jerde, Box 688, Dubuque IA 52001. 319-588-5660.

Telegram Tribune, Mike Stover, 1321 Johnson, Box 112, San Luis Obispo CA 93406. 805-781-7800. 33,000.

Time Magazine, Richard N. Ostling, Rm 2344, Time-Life Bldg, New York NY 10020. 212-522-3040.

Times-Advocate, Ann Moss, 207 E Pennsylvania Ave, Escondido CA 92025. 619-745-6611. 45,000.

Times Herald, James Ketchum, 911 Military St., Port Huron MI 48060. 313-985-7171.

+Times-Union, The, Winifred Yu, 645 Albany-Shaker Rd., Albany NY 12212. 518-454-5445.

Toledo Blade, Judy Tarjanyi, 541 Superior St, Toledo OH 43660. 419-245-6153. 147,000.

Topeka Capital-Journal, Jim Baker, Stauffer Communications, 616 Jefferson, Topeka KS 66607. 913-295-1111. 70,000.

Torrence Daily Breeze, Thom Meade, 5215 Torrence Blvd, Torrence CA 90503. 310-540-5511. 131,000.

Trentonian, Chris Billings, Southarn & Perry Sts., Trenton NJ 08602. 609-989-7800.

Trenton Times, Debbie Kovach, 500 Perry St, Box 847, Trenton NJ 08605. 609-396-3232. 79,000.

Tribune-Herald, Sandra Gines, Box 2588, Waco TX 76702. 817-757-5757.

Tribune Star, Madonna Yates, Box 149, Terre Haute IN 47808. 812-231-4200.

Tucson Citizen, Religion Editor, 4850 S Park Ave, Box 26767, Tucson AZ 85726. 602-573-4560. 52,000.

Tulsa World, Carolyn Jenkins, 318 South Main Mall, Box 1770, Tulsa OK 74102. 918-581-8300. 175,000.

Tyler Morning Telegraph, Tom Pratt, P.O. Box 2030, Tyler TX 75710. 214-597-8111.

Union Leader, The, John Tucker, 100 William Loeb Dr, Box 9555, Manchester NH 03108. 603-668-4321. 72,000.

USA Today, Cathy Grossman, 1000 Wilson Blvd, Arlington VA 22229. 703-276-3400. 6,600,000.

US News & World Report, Jeffery Sheler, 2400 North St. NW, Washington DC 20037. 202-955-2383.

Vancouver Sun, Douglas Todd, 2250 Granville St., Vancouver BC V6H 3G2 Canada. 604-732-2159. 491,000.

Virginian Pilot/Ledger-Star, Marjorie M. Mayfield or Mark O'Keefe, 150 W Brambleton Ave, Norfolk VA 23510. 804-446-2332. 750,000.

Waco Tribune Herald, Douglas Wong, 900 Franklin Ave, Box 2588, Waco TX 76702. 817-757-5757. 47,000.

#Wall Street Journal, Mr. R. Gustav Neibhur, 200 Liberty St, New York NY 10281. 212-416-2500 or 404-233-2831. 2,000,000.

Washington Post, Laurie Goodstein or Laura Sessions Stepp, 1150 15th St NW, Washington DC 20071. 202-334-7215. 814,000.

Washington Post Magazine, Yvonne Lamb, 1150 15th St NW, Washington DC 20071. 202-334-6000. 791,000.

+Washington Times, Larry A. Witham, 3600 New York Ave. NE, Washington DC 20002. 202-636-3302.

Wisconsin State Journal, William Wineke, 1901 Fish Hatchery Rd, Box 8058, Madison WI 53708. 608-252-6100. 85,000.

Wichita Eagle Beacon, Tom Schaefer, PO Box 820, Wichita KS 67201. 316-268-6586. 185,000.

Youngstown Vindicator, Marie Shellock, Vindicator Sq, Box 780, Youngstown OH 44501. 216-747-1471. 90,000.

CHRISTIAN WRITERS' CONFERENCES AND WORKSHOPS

(*) Asterisk before a listing means the information was not verified or updated by the group leader.
(+) A plus sign before a listing indicates a new listing.

ALABAMA
*SOUTHERN CHRISTIAN WRITERS CONFERENCE. Samford University/Birmingham, June 1995. Contact: Joanne Sloan, 3230 Mystic Lake Way, Northport AL 35476. (205)333-8603.

ARIZONA
AMERICAN CHRISTIAN WRITERS SEMINARS. Sponsors conferences in various locations around the country (see individual states for dates and places). This year will also sponsor several Impact Days (one-day mini-conferences) in several cities not already offering seminars. Call for dates and locations. Sponsoring a Caribbean cruise, December 2-9, 1995. Contact: Reg Forder, Box 5168, Phoenix AZ 85010. 1-800-21-WRITE.

ARIZONA CHRISTIAN WRITERS CONFERENCE. Phoenix, November 9-11, 1995. Contact: Reg A. Forder, Box 5168, Phoenix AZ 85010. (602)838-4919. Attendance: 200.

CENTRAL ARIZONA CHRISTIAN WRITERS WORKSHOP. Cottonwood, March 11, 1995. Speaker: Jack Cavanaugh. Contact: Mona Gansberg Hodgson, Box 999, Cottonwood AZ 86326-0999. (602)634-0384. Attendance: 70.

MINI WRITING WORKSHOPS. Held in various U.S. locations, throughout the year. Contact and speaker: Donna Goodrich, 648 S. Pima St., Mesa AZ 85210. (602)962-6694. Two-hour to day-long workshops on various topics. Attendance: 10-20. Correspondence course offered.

*PRESCOTT CHRISTIAN WRITERS SEMINAR. Prescott, September 1995 (usually 4th Saturday). Contact: Barbara Spangler, Box 26449, Prescott Valley AZ 86312. (602)772-6263 or Pauline Dunn, 1840 Iron Springs Rd. #A2F, Prescott AZ 86301. (601)778-7342.

CALIFORNIA
+AMERICAN CHRISTIAN WRITERS SAN DIEGO CONFERENCE. March 16-18, 1995; March 14-16, 1996. Contact: Reg Forder, Box 5168, Phoenix AZ 85010. 1-800-21-WRITE. Attendance: 75.

+CASTRO VALLEY CHRISTIAN WRITERS SEMINAR. Castro Valley, February 24-25, 1995. Contact: Pastor Jon Drury, 19300 Redwood Rd.,Castro Valley CA 94546. (818)886-6300/881-5888.

CHRISTIAN COMMUNICATORS CONFERENCE AT THE MASTER'S COLLEGE. Santa Clarita, July 27-30, 1995. Keynote speaker: Liz Curtis Hicks. Offers a track for advanced writers and one unit of college credit. Contact: Susan Titus Osborn, 3133 Puente Blvd., Fullerton CA 92635-1952. (800)-95 WORDS. Attendance: 150.

CHRISTIAN LEADERS AND SPEAKERS SEMINARS (C.L.A.S.S.). Various dates & locations across the country. Speakers: Florence Littauer, Marita Littauer, and Marilyn Heavilin. Contact: Marita Littauer, 1645 S. Rancho Santa Fe #102, San Marcos CA 92069. (619)471-1722. Attendance: 100.

CHRISTIAN WRITERS FELLOWSHIP OF ORANGE COUNTY WRITER'S DAYS. Garden Grove, April 22 (speaker Diana James) and October 21, 1995. Contact: Louis Merryman (310)379-5646, or Carol Fitzpatrick, (714)768-3891, P.O. Box 538, Lake Forest CA 92630. Attendance: 60.

INLAND EMPIRE CHRISTIAN WRITERS SEMINARS. Moreno Valley, February 25 & September 30, 1995. Contact: Bill Page, Unit 112, 23571 Sunnymead Ranch Pkwy, Ste. 103, Moreno Valley CA 92557-2867. (909)924-0610. Attendance: 50-60

LODI ALL-DAY WRITERS SEMINAR. Stockton, no date set for 1995. General writing conference; not just Christian writers. Contact: Walt Merryman, Box 1863, Lodi CA 95241. (209)368-9849. Write and ask to be put on mailing list.

MOUNT HERMON CHRISTIAN WRITERS CONFERENCE. Mount Hermon (near Santa Cruz), April 7-11, 1995. Offers advanced track with Sally Stuart. Contact: David R. Talbott, Box 413, Mount Hermon CA 95041-0413. (408)335-4466. Attendance: 175-250.

*NARRAMORE CHRISTIAN WRITERS CONFERENCE. Narramore Christian Foundation/Rosemead, April 1995. Contact: Dr. Clyde M. Narramore, 1409 N Walnut Grove Ave., Rosemead CA 91770. (818)288-7000. Attendance: 30.

SAN DIEGO CHRISTIAN WRITERS GUILD ONE-DAY SEMINAR. San Diego, September 1995. Contact: Dr. Sherwood Wirt, 14140 Mazatlan Ct., Poway CA 92064. (619)748-0565. Attendance: 115.

SAN DIEGO STATE UNIVERSITY WRITERS CONFERENCE. SDSU Aztec Center, January 21-22, 1995. Keynote speaker: Richard Curtis. To advanced writers offers a read and critique by editors and agents. Contact: Jan Wahl, Gateway Center, College of Extended Studies, 5250 Campanile Dr., San Diego CA 92182. (619)594-2514. Attendance: 350.

*SOUTH BAY CHRISTIAN WRITERS SEMINARS. Hermosa, contact for dates. Contact: Diane Shober, 14100 S. Mariposa, Gardena CA 90247. (310)323-6847. Attendance: 75. Also has critique groups and writing classes.

*VENTURA COUNTY WRITERS SEMINAR. Ventura, February 1995. Speaker: Wes Haystead. Contact: Julie Carobine, 10142 Fallen Leaf Ct., Ventura CA 93004. (805)647-4566.

+WRITERS IN THE REDWOODS WEEKEND RETREAT. Alliance Redwoods, Occidental CA; November 3-5, 1995. Contact: Elaine Wright Colvin, 6250 Bohemian Hwy, Occidental CA 95465. (707)874-3507. Attendance: 125.

WRITE TO BE READ WORKSHOPS. Atlanta GA, March 3, 1995; Hume Lake, July 15, 1995. Speaker & contact: Norman B. Rohrer, 260 Fern Ln., Hume Lake CA 93628. (209)335-2333. Also features 2 other professional writers at each workshop. Attendance: 45.

*YWAM CHRISTIAN WRITERS SEMINARS. Various states, Africa, Middle East, and South America; various dates. Contact: Registrar, YWAM Writer's Seminars, Box 3464, Orange CA 92665. (714)637-1733. Fax: (714)282-0496.

COLORADO

CHRISTIAN ARTISTS' SEMINAR IN THE ROCKIES. Estes Park, July 30-August 5, 1995. For anyone interested in Christian music industry and ministry. Has classes in song writing and sketch writing. Contact: Cam Floria, 425 W 115th Ave., Denver CO 80234. (303)452-1313. Attendance: 1,000-1,300.

CHRISTIAN BOOKSELLERS ASSN. CONVENTION. Denver, June 15-20, 1995. Contact: CBA, Box 200, Colorado Springs CO 80901. (719)576-7880. Entrance badges available through book publishers.

*COLORADO CHRISTIAN COMMUNICATORS RETREAT. Colorado Springs, September 1995. Contact: Scoti Domeij, 5209 Del Paz Dr., Colorado Springs CO 80918-2001. Attendance: 100.

COLORADO CHRISTIAN WRITERS CONFERENCE. Boulder; March 2-4, 1995. Speakers: Marva Dawn & Ron Klug. Offers an advanced track and a beginners' symposium. Contact: Debbie Barker, 67 Seminole Ct., Lyons CO 80540. (303)823-5718. Attendance: 225.

GLEN EYRIE WRITERS' WORKSHOPS. Glen Eyrie Conference Center, Colorado Springs; February 5-10, April 9-14, June 18-23, October 15-20, 1995; advanced August 20-25, 1995. Speaker: Monte Unger. Contact: Grace Saint, Box 6000, Colorado Springs CO 80934. (719)594-2535. Attendance: 20 maximum in each.

OBSERVATION SKILLS WORKSHOP. Denver, April 1995. Contact: Chris Adams, 2573 Benton St., Edgewater CO 80214. (303)232-9470. Attendance: 50.

CONNECTICUT
*WESLEYAN WRITERS CONFERENCE. Middletown, June 1995. Contact: Anne Green, c/o Wesleyan University, Middletown CT 06459. (203)347-9411, ext. 2448. Attendance: 100.

DELAWARE
+DELMARVA CHRISTIAN WRITERS' SEMINAR, Dover, March 1995 (tentative). Contact: Sina McLaughlin, P.O. Box 1111, Dover DE 19903-1111. (302)735-4774. Attendance: 50.

DISTRICT OF COLUMBIA
+AMERICAN CHRISTIAN WRITERS WASHINGTON DC CONFERENCE. August 17-19, 1995. Contact: Reg Forder, Box 5168, Phoenix AZ 85010. 1-800-21-WRITE. Attendance: 75.

EVANGELICAL PRESS ASSOCIATION CONVENTION. May 7-10, 1995; Washington DC. (held in different location each year). Contact: Ron Wilson, dir., Rt 2 Box 83, Earlysville VA 22936. (804)973-5941. Attendance: 300-400. Annual convention; freelance communicators welcome.

FLORIDA
+AMERICAN CHRISTIAN WRITERS MIAMI / FT. LAUDERDALE CONFERENCE. October 5-7, 1995. Contact: Reg Forder, Box 5168, Phoenix AZ 85010. 1-800-21-WRITE. Attendance: 75.

*CATHOLIC PRESS ASSOCIATION ANNUAL CONVENTION. Tampa, 1995. Contact: Owen McGovern, exec. dir., 3555 Veterans Memorial Hwy Ste. O, Ronkonkoma NY 11779-7636. Attendance: 350.

CHRISTIAN WRITERS' INSTITUTE INTL. CONFERENCE. Orlando; February 23-26, 1995. Speakers: Brock & Bodie Thoene. Advanced Track with Janet Thoma; Youth Track for 15-18 year olds; Spanish Track. Contest theme: "My Writing Dreams and Goals." Contact: Dottie McBroom, 177 E. Crystal Lake Ave., Lake Mary FL 32746-4244. (407)324-5465, Fax: (407)324-0209. Attendance: 200.

FLORIDA CHRISTIAN WRITERS CONFERENCE. Park Avenue Retreat Center/Titusville; January 26-30, 1995; Calvin Miller, keynote speaker; January 25-29, 1996. Offers advanced track by application only. Contact: Billie Wilson, 2600 Park Avenue, Titusville FL 32780. (407)269-6702x202. Attendance: 200.

*WRITING STRATEGIES FOR THE CHRISTIAN MARKET. Classes for beginning, intermediate & advanced writers. Also material available for an independent studies program by mail. Contact: Rosemary J. Upton, 1420 N Atlantic Ave. #801, Daytona Beach FL 32118. (904)253-6666. Write to be put on mailing list.

GEORGIA
+AMERICAN CHRISTIAN WRITERS ATLANTA CONFERENCE. October 12-14, 1995. Contact: Reg Forder, Box 5168, Phoenix AZ 85010. 1-800-21-WRITE. Attendance: 75.

NORTHEAST GEORGIA WRITERS CONFERENCE. Gainesville, October 1996 (biennial). Contact: Elouise Whitten, 660 Crestview Terrace, Gainesville GA 30501-3110. (404)532-3007. Attendance: 30-50.

SOUTHEASTERN WRITERS CONFERENCE, St. Simons Island; June 18-42, 1995. Contact: Pay Laye, Rt. 1 Box 102, Cuthbert GA 31740. (912)679-5445. Attendance: 100.

WRITE TO BE READ WORKSHOPS. Atlanta GA, March 3, 1995; Hume Lake, July 15, 1995. Speaker & contact: Norman B. Rohrer, 260 Fern Ln., Hume Lake CA 93628. (209)335-2333. Also features 2 other professional writers at each workshop. Attendance: 45.

HAWAII
*YWAM WRITERS SEMINAR. Kona, July 1995. Speakers: Janice Rogers & Beverly Caruso. Contact: Beverly Caruso, 1621 Baldwin Ave., Orange CA 92665. (714)637-1733. Fax: (714)282-0496. Attendance: 30-40.

IDAHO
NORTHWEST CHRISTIAN WRITERS CONFERENCE. Post Falls; September 21-23, 1995. Keynote speaker: Frank Peretti. Contact: Sheri Stone, Box 1754, Post Falls ID 83854-1754. (208)667-9730. Attendance: 125.

ILLINOIS
*AFRICAN-AMERICAN CHRISTIAN WRITERS' CONFERENCE. Chicago, May 1995. Contact: Dr. Stanley B. Long, c/o American Tract Society, P.O. Box 462008, Garland TX 75046.

CHRISTIAN WRITERS INSTITUTE CONFERENCE. 50th Anniversary Homecoming Conference. Wheaton College, June 1-4, 1995. Advanced track with Susan Titus Osborn. Contact: Dottie McBroom, 177 E Crystal Lake Ave., Lake Mary FL 32746. (407)324-5465. Fax: (407)324-0209. Attendance: 150. Send for information on their fall conference to be held October 1995.

*MISSISSIPPI VALLEY WRITERS CONFERENCE. Augustana College/Rock Island, June 1995. Contact: David R. Collins, 3403 45th St., Moline IL 61265. (309)762-8985. Attendance: 80.

*THE SALVATION ARMY CHRISTIAN WRITERS' CONFERENCE. Des Plaines IL, March or April 1995 (held every other year). Contact: Major Marlene Chase, 10 W. Algonquin Rd., Des Plaines IL 60016-6006. (708)294-2050. Attendance: 60. For S.A. officers, laymen, and employee staff.

WRITE-TO-PUBLISH SEMINARS. Chicago, spring, fall, & summer (dates to be announced). One-day seminars. Contact: Lin Johnson, 9731 Fox Glen Dr. #6F, Niles IL 60714-5829. (708)296-3964. Attendance: 50-75.

WRITE-TO-PUBLISH CONFERENCE. This conference will not be held in 1995. Call Lin Johnson above for future plans.

INDIANA
*CHARLENE FARIS WRITING CLASSES. Indianapolis; June 1995. Contact: Charlene Farris, 9524 Guilford Dr. #A, Indianapolis IN 46240. (317)848-2634. Attendance: 6-10.

MIDWEST WRITERS WORKSHOP. Muncie, July 26-29, 1995. Contact: Dr. Earl Conn, Dept. of Journalism, Ball State University, Muncie IN 47306-0485. (317)285-8200. Attendance: 130.

KANSAS

*BCCC CREATIVE WRITING WORKSHOP. Butler County Community College, El Dorado; Fall 1995. Contact: Vivien Minshull-Ford, 901 S. Haverhill Rd., El Dorado KS 67042. (316)321-5083, ext. 233. Attendance: 200.

+BOONDOCKS RETREAT. Dodge City; possibly June, date not set. Contact: Linda Fergerson, 2216 Thompson, Dodge City KS 67801. (316)225-1126. Attendance: 25-40. Offers a spiritual retreat for writers, rather than a nuts & bolts conference.

+PITTSBURG CHRISTIAN WRITERS' SEMINAR. Pittsburg; April 8, 1995. Keynote speaker: Jeanette Gardner. Contact: LeAnn Campbell, 267 SW 1st Ln., Lamar MO 64759. (417)682-2713.

LOUISIANA

*LOUISIANA BAPTIST CHRISTIAN WRITERS CONFERENCE. Tall Timbers, April 1995. Contact: Louisiana Baptist Convention, Box 311, Alexandria LA 71309.

*LOUISIANA CHRISTIAN WRITERS GUILD WORKSHOP. Shreveport; July 1995. Contact: Dr. Don M. Aycock, 4754 N. Milnor Dr., Memphis TN 38128. (318)855-6280. Attendance: 50+.

MARYLAND

SANDY COVE CHRISTIAN WRITERS CONFERENCE. Sandy Cove/North East, October 1-5, 1995. Speaker: Dr. Harold Ivan Smith. Contact: Gayle Roper, RD 6 Box 112, Coatesville PA 19320. (610)384-8125. Attendance: 125+.

*REVIEW AND HERALD WRITERS' WEEK. Review & Herald Publishing Assn., Hagerstown; July 1995. Contact: Penny E. Wheeler, 55 W. Oak Ridge Dr., Hagerstown MD 21740. (301)790-9731. Attendance: 50.

MASSACHUSETTS

*CAPE COD WRITERS' CONFERENCE. Craigville Conference Center, August 1995. Contact: Marion Vuilleumier, c/o Cape Cod Conservatory, Rt. 132, West Barnstable MA 02668. (508)775-4811 or 362-2772. Attendance: 150. Also offers **CAPE LITERARY ARTS WORKSHOPS**: 6 simultaneous week-long workshops (poetry, romance novels, juvenile writing, children's book illustrating, and play writing), August 1995. Limited to 10 in each workshop.

MICHIGAN

+AMERICAN CHRISTIAN WRITERS DETROIT CONFERENCE. June 8-10, 1995; June 20-22, 1996. Contact: Reg Forder, Box 5168, Phoenix AZ 85010. 1-800-21-WRITE. Attendance: 75.

*ANDREWS UNIVERSITY CHRISTIAN WRITER'S AND COMMUNICATOR'S CONFERENCE. Berrien Springs, June 1995. Contact: Dr. Kermit Netteburg, Communications Dept., Andrews University, Berrien Springs MI 49104. (616)471-3618. Attendance: 85.

MARANATHA CHRISTIAN WRITERS SEMINAR. Maranatha Bible & Missionary Conference/Muskegon, August 21-2595. Speakers: Jack Metzler, Paul Tell, Jr., Nellie Pickard, and Leona Hertel. Contact: Leona Hertel, 4759 Lake Harbor Rd., Muskegon MI 49441-5299. (616)798-2161. Attendance: 50.

*MICHIGAN NORTHWOODS WRITERS CONFERENCE. Glen Arbor, July 1995. Contact: Robert Karner, 1 Old Homestead Rd., Glen Arbor MI 49636. (616)334-3072.

"SPEAK UP WITH CONFIDENCE" SEMINARS. Hillsdale, July 27-29, 1995. Contact: Carol Kent, 4184 Quaker Hill Dr., Port Huron MI 48059. (810)982-0898. Speaking seminar. Attendance: 100.

MINNESOTA

+AMERICAN CHRISTIAN WRITERS MINNEAPOLIS CONFERENCE. August 10-12, 1995. Contact: Reg Forder, Box 5168, Phoenix AZ 85010. 1-800-21-WRITE. Attendance: 75.

MINNESOTA CHRISTIAN WRITERS GUILD SPRING SEMINAR. Minneapolis/St. Paul, April 7-8, 1995. Speaker: Maxine Hancock. Contact: Sue Campbell, 3551 Virginia Ave. N., Minneapolis MN 55427. (612)545-1573. Attendance: 50-100.

MISSOURI

+AMERICAN CHRISTIAN WRITERS ST. LOUIS CONFERENCE. June 15-17, 1995; June 27-29, 1996. Contact: Reg Forder, Box 5168, Phoenix AZ 85010. 1-800-21-WRITE. Attendance: 75.

*CENTRAL MISSOURI WRITER'S RETREAT. Secular. Warrensburg. July 1995. Contact: Central Missouri State University, Office of Extended Campus, 402 Humphreys Bldg., Warrensburg MO 64093. 1-800-SAY-CMSU.

*GREATER ST. LOUIS INSPIRATIONAL WRITERS WORKSHOP. St. Louis metro area. Contact: Lila Wold Shelburne, 23 Blackberry, St. Charles MO 63301. (314)946-8533.

MARK TWAIN WRITERS CONFERENCE. Hannibal-LaGrange College, June 11-13, 1995. Speakers include Gene Perret. Contact: Dr. James C. Hefley, 921 Center St., Hannibal MO 63401. (800)947-0738. Attendance: 125. Note: This is a general conference under the direction of evangelical Christians.

NAZARENE WRITERS CONFERENCE. No date or location set for next conference; not in 1995. Contact: Shona Fisher, 6401 The Paseo, Kansas City MO 64131. (816)233-7000. Attendance: 200.

*RIGHT WRITING CHRISTIAN WRITERS' WORKSHOP. Columbia, October 1995. Contact: Teresa Parker/Linda Ordway/Mike Kateman, 237 E. Clearview Dr., Columbia MO 65202. (314)875-1141/449-2465. Attendance: 100.

NEW JERSEY

*THE CHRISTIAN PERSPECTIVE JOURNALISM & FICTION WRITING WORKSHOPS, 66 Witherspoon St., Ste. 334, Princeton NJ 08542.

+DAYSTAR COMMUNICATIONS WRITING WORKSHOPS. Half-day (3 hour) and Full-day (6 hour) Workshops on a wide variety of writing topics. Send for brochure. Contact: Dr. Mary Ann Diorio, P.O. Box 748, Millville NJ 08332-0748. (609)327-1231. Fax: (609)327-0291.

NEW MEXICO

SOUTHWEST CHRISTIAN WRITERS SEMINAR. Farmington, September 16, 1995. Contact: Kathy Cordell, 91 - Rd. 3450, Flora Vista NM 87415. (505)334-0617. Attendance: 25.

*WRITERS' CONFERENCE AT SANTA FE. Santa Fe, February 1995. Contact: Ruth Crowley, Program Coordinator, Santa Fe Community College, Box 4187, Santa Fe NM 87502-4187. (505)438-1251. Attendance: 150.

NEW YORK
GREATER SYRACUSE CHRISTIAN WRITER'S CONFERENCE. Liverpool, May 1995. Contact: Pat Spencer, 108 Woodpath Rd., Liverpool NY 13090. (315)652-3178. Attendance: 60-75.

OHIO
ANTIOCH WRITERS WORKSHOP. Secular. Antioch College/Yellow Springs; July 22-29, 1995. Keynote speaker: Sue Grafton. Contact: Judy DuPolito, P.O. Box 494, Yellow Springs OH 45387. (513)866-9060. Attendance: 70.

*CINCINNATI BIBLE COLLEGE CHRISTIAN WRITERS WORKSHOP. Cincinnati, September 1995. Contact: Dana Eynon, 2700 Glenway Ave., Cincinnati OH 45204. (513)244-8181. Attendance: 100.

COLUMBUS CHRISTIAN WRITERS FALL CONFERENCE. Salt Fork Lodge/Cambridge, October 5-7, 1995. Speaker: Sally E. Stuart. Contact: Brenda Custodio, 3069 Bocastle Ct., Reynoldsburg OH 43068. (614)861-1011. Attendance: 120.

*MARION AREA CHRISTIAN WRITERS SEMINAR. Marion; April 1995 (tentative). Contact: Irene M. Sprague, 603 Henry St., Marion OH 43302

NORTHWEST OHIO CHRISTIAN WRITERS SEMINAR. Bowling Green; September 30, 1995; September 28, 1996. Speaker: Dr. Dennis Hensley. Contact: Nancy Kintner, 4235 Lyman Ave., Toledo OH 43612-1584. (419)478-1055. Attendance: 75-100.

THE PRESBYTERIAN WRITERS GUILD SEMINAR. Cincinnati, July 18, 1995. Contact: Ann Barr Weems, 6900 Kingsbury Blvd., St. Louis MO 63130. (314)725-6290. Attendance: 70.

*WRITER'S WORLD CONFERENCE. Akron, May 1995. Contact: Tom Raber, Box 966, Cuyahoga Falls OH 44223. Attendance: 100-200.

OKLAHOMA
*WRITING WORKSHOPS. Various locations and dates. Contact: Kathryn Fanning, 1016 NW 39th, Oklahoma City OK 73118.

PROFESSIONALISM IN WRITING SCHOOL. Tulsa, March 31-April 1, 1995. Keynote speaker: Harold Ivan Smith. Contact: Norma Jean Lutz, 4308 S. Peoria, Ste. 701, Tulsa OK 74105. (918)749-5588. Attendance: 180-200.

OREGON
OREGON CHRISTIAN WRITERS COACHING CONFERENCE. Aldersgate (near Salem), July 31-August 3, 1995. Contact: Kris Ingram, 955 S. 59th St, Springfield OR 97478-5452. (503)726-8320. Attendance: 150.

PENNSYLVANIA
*CHRISTIAN WRITERS WORKSHOP. Northeastern Christian Junior College, Villanova; mid-October 1995. Contact: Eva Walker Myer, 1860 Montgomery Ave., Villanova PA 19085. (215)525-6780. Attendance: 100.

GREATER PHILADELPHIA CHRISTIAN WRITERS' CONFERENCE. Downingtown, April 27-29, 1995. Pre-conference day for beginners with Lin Johnson, April 27. Contact: Marlene Bagnull, 316 Blanchard Rd., Drexel Hill PA 19026-3507. (610)626-6833. Attendance: 250.

+KHS MEMORIAL WRITERS CONFERENCE. York, July 1995. Contact: Rita Atwell-Holler, 100 Greenwood Rd., York PA 17404-5766. (717)792-0228. One-day seminar. Attendance: 50.

MONTROSE BIBLE CONFERENCE CHRISTIAN WRITERS CONFERENCE. Montrose, July 10-14, 1995. Speaker: Les Stobbe. Contact: Jill Renich Meyers, 204 Asbury Dr., Mechanicsburg PA 17055-4303. (712)766-1100. Attendance: 50-60.

ST. DAVIDS CHRISTIAN WRITERS' CONFERENCE. St. Davids, June 25-30, 1995. Speaker: Michael King, Herald Press. Contact: Carol Wedeven, 1 Old Covered Bridge Rd., Newtown Square PA 19073. (610)356-8208. Attendance: 60-100.

*"WRITE HIS ANSWER" SEMINARS. Various locations around U.S.; dates throughout the year. Contact: Marlene Bagnull, 316 Blanchard Rd., Drexel Hill PA 19026. (215)626-6833. Attendance: 40-100. Day or day-and-a-half seminars by the author of *Write His Answer—Encouragement for Christian Writers.*

WRITING FOR PUBLICATION. Pittsburgh Theological Seminary, April 26-27, 1995. Speaker: Dr. Roland Tapp. Contact: Mary Lee Talbot, 616 N. Highland Ave., Pittsburgh PA 15206. (412)362-5610. Attendance: 25.

TENNESSEE

*RELIGIOUS COMMUNICATIONS CONGRESS. Nashville, April 1995. Contact: RCC, Mail Stop 192, 127 Ninth Ave. N., Nashville TN 37234.

SOUTHERN BAPTIST WRITERS WORKSHOP. Nashville, July 1995 (if new director found). Contact: Director, 127 Ninth Ave. N., Nashville TN 37234. (615)251-2939. Attendance: 50.

THE WRITING ACADEMY SEMINAR. Nashville; August 6-11, 1995. Contact: Ann Poppen, 6512 Colby, Des Moines IA 50311-1713. (515)274-5026. Attendance: 50.

TEXAS

+AMERICAN CHRISTIAN WRITERS DALLAS/FORT WORTH CONFERENCE. May 18-20, 1995; May 16-18, 1996. Contact: Reg Forder, Box 5168, Phoenix AZ 85010. 1-800-21-WRITE. Attendance: 75.

+AMERICAN CHRISTIAN WRITERS HOUSTON CONFERENCE. January 19-21, 1995; January 18-20, 1996. Contact: Reg Forder, Box 5168, Phoenix AZ 85010. 1-800-21-WRITE. Attendance: 75.

+AMERICAN CHRISTIAN WRITERS CONFERENCE DIRECTORS CONFERENCE. Houston, January 21-22, 1995. Contact: Reg Forder, Box 5168, Phoenix AZ 85010. 1-800-21-WRITE.

*THE ART OF WRITING, THE ACT OF WRITING. Longview, March 1995. Contact: Ernestine Finigan, Box 8513, Marshall TX 75670. (214)935-3047 or 938-0756 (days). Attendance: 50+.

FRONTIERS IN WRITING. Amarillo College, August 5-6, 1995. Sponsored by Panhandle Professional Writers. Contact: Doris R. Meredith, Box 19303, Amarillo TX 79114. (806)352-3889. Attendance: 100. Write for contest information.

+INSPIRATIONAL WRITERS ALIVE!/AMARILLO SEMINAR. April 8, 1995. Contact: Helen Luecke, 2921 S. Dallas, Amarillo TX 79103-6713. (806)376-9671.

*SOUTHWEST CHRISTIAN WRITERS GUILD CONFERENCE. Dallas, early October 1995. Contact: Debra Frazier, 1809 Waterford Ln., Richardson TX 75082. (214)783-6319.

TEXAS CHRISTIAN WRITERS FORUM. Houston; August 1995. Speakers: Bea Carlton, Charlie Warren, Vicki Crumpton. Contact: Maxine E. Holder, 3606 Longwood Dr., Pasadena TX 77503-2221. (713)477-3716. Attendance: 60.

VIRGINIA

VIRGINIA CHRISTIAN WRITERS CONFERENCE. Roanoke, April 22, 1995. Speakers: Nancy Hoag & Leona Choy. Contact: Betty B. Robertson, P.O. Box 12624, Roanoke VA 24027-2624. (703)342-7511. Fax: 989-1615. Attendance: 75.

*WRITING FOR CHRISTIAN PUBLISHERS. Regent University/Virginia Beach; August 1995. Contact: Dr. Doug Tarpley, chairman, School of Journalism, Regent University, Virginia Beach VA 23464. (804)532-7091/436-2926. New—projected attendance: 100-200.

*WRITING FOR THE LOCAL CHURCH . . . AND SOMETIMES BEYOND. Held in various locations by invitation. Contact: Betty B. Robertson, P.O. Box 12624, Roanoke VA 24027-2624. (703)342-4003.

WASHINGTON

+AMERICAN CHRISTIAN WRITERS SEATTLE CONFERENCE. March 9-11, 1995; March 21-23, 1996. Contact: Reg Forder, Box 5168, Phoenix AZ 85010. 1-800-21-WRITE. Attendance: 75.

*SDA CAMP MEETING WRITING CLASS. Auburn, June 1995. Open to non-Adventists. Contact: Marion Forschler, 18115 - 116th Ave. SE, Renton WA 98058-6562. (206)235-1435. Attendance: 65.

*NORTHWEST CHRISTIAN WRITERS ASSN. SEMINARS. Seattle area, date to announced. Contact: Margaret Sampson, 8227 NE 115th Way, Kirkland WA 98034.

+PACIFIC NORTHWEST WRITERS CONFERENCE. Tukwilla (Seattle); no date given. Contact: Don Clark, 2033 - 6th Ave. #804, Seattle WA 98121. (206)443-3807. This is a secular conference that includes classes in Christian writing. Also sponsors a contest and conference for high school students. Attendance: 700.

SEATTLE PACIFIC CHRISTIAN WRITERS CONFERENCE. Seattle, June 22-24, 1995. Keynote speaker: Madeleine L'Engle. Offers Mentoring Program, Process Sessions, Issues Forums, & Marketing Update Sessions. Contact: Linda Wagner, Humanities Dept., Seattle Pacific University, Seattle WA 98119. (206)281-2109. Attendance: 160.

*WASHINGTON CHRISTIAN WRITERS FELLOWSHIP SEMINAR. Seattle, February 1995. Speakers: Elaine Colvin, Myrtlemay Crane, Marilou Flinkman & others. Contact: Elaine Colvin, P.O. Box 11337, Bainbridge Island WA 98110. (206)842-9103.

WENATCHEE CHRISTIAN WRITERS MINI-SEMINAR. Wenatchee, September 1995. Contact: Shirley Pease, 1818 Skyline Dr. #31, Wenatchee WA 98801-2302. (509)662-8392. Attendance: 50.

WRITERS HELPING WRITERS. Spokane; March 16-18. This is not a conference, but a booth offering manuscript evaluation and help to writers during the annual Christian Workers Conference. Contact: Pat Pfeiffer, P.O. Box 104, Otis Orchards WA 97027-0140. (509)927-7671 or 226-3532 (evenings).

+WRITERS HELPING WRITERS AND SPEAKERS WORKSHOP. Spokane, April 22, 1995. Speakers: Kay David, Pat Pfeiffer and Dolly Meredith. Contact: Pat Pfeiffer, P.O. Box 104, Otis Orchards WA 97027-0140. (509)927-7670 or 226-3532 (evenings).

*WRITERS INFORMATION NETWORK (W.I.N.) SEMINARS. Various locations/dates. Contact: Elaine Colvin, Box 11337, Bainbridge Island WA 98110. (206)842-9103. Attendance: 75-150.

WRITER'S WEEKEND AT THE BEACH. Ocean Park, February 24-26, 1995. Speakers: Michael Whalin, Lauraine Snelling, Birdie Etchison, Pat Rushford. Contact: Pat Rushford, 3600 Edgewood Dr., Vancouver WA 98661. (206)695-2263 or Birdie Etchison, P.O. Box 877, Ocean Park WA 98640. (206)665-6576. Attendance: Limited to 45-50.

WRITERS WORKSHOP: FROM PEN TO PUBLISHER, Walla Walla Community College, March 4, 1995. Save $10 if you register before February 25. Contact: Marcia Mitchell, 835 Valencia, Walla Walla WA 99362. (509)529-4672. Attendance: 75.

WISCONSIN

*GREEN LAKE CHRISTIAN WRITER'S CONFERENCE. Green Lake, July 1995. Contact: Jan DeWitt, Program Dept., American Baptist Assembly, Green Lake WI 54941. (800)558-8898 or (414)294-3323. Attendance: 75+.

SWORD & LIGHT WRITERS' SEMINAR. Milwaukee, possible spring conference. Contact: Andrea Kuhn-Boeshar, 10605 W Wabash, Milwaukee WI 53224-2315. (414)355-8915.

THE WRITER'S TOUGHEST JOB - MARKETING. Menasha; October 1995. Instructor: Margaret Houk. Contact: Eugene Gibas, Dir. of Continuing Education, University of Wisconsin-Fox Valley, 1478 Midway Rd., Menasha WI 54952. (414)832-2636. Also classes in nonfiction writing and selling for the religious marketplace. Write for catalog.

*TIMBER-LEE CHRISTIAN WRITER'S CONFERENCE. Timber-Lee Christian Center/East Troy, February 1995. Contact: Gene Schroeppel, N8705 Scout Rd., East Troy WI 53120. (414)642-7345. Attendance: 30-40.

CANADA

*GOD USES INK WRITERS AT BRIERCREST SCHOOLS. Caronport, Saskatchewan, Briercrest Bible College; May 1995. Contact: Donna Lynn Erickson, 510 College Dr., Caronport SK S0H 0S0 Canada. (306)756-3214. Attendance: 100.

GOD USES INK WRITERS CONFERENCE/ON. Ancaster, Ontario; June 1-3, 1995; June 1996. Contact: Audrey Dorsch, Box 8800, Sta. B, Willowdale ON M2K 2R6 Canada. (905)479-5885. Attendance: 110-120. Offers a Professional Track for advanced writers.

+SWAN VALLEY WRITERS GUILD CONFERENCE. Swan River, Manitoba; October 21-22, 1995. Keynote speaker: Alma Barkman of Winnipeg. Contact: Marlene Hohne, Box 2115, Swan River MB R0L 1Z0 Canada. (204)525-4652.

WORDPOWER. Winnipeg, November 1995; Clearbrook, fall 1997. Contact: MB Herald, 3-169 Riverton Ave., Winnipeg MB R2L 2E5 Canada. (204)669-6575. Offers workshops for advanced and young writers. Attendance: 100-150.

FOREIGN COUNTRIES

*YWAM WRITING SEMINARS. Seminars pending in Egypt, Israel, Great Britain, Chile, Guatemala during 1995. Open to invitations. Contact: Beverly Caruso, 1621 Baldwin Ave., Orange CA 92665. (714)282-0496. Attendance 15-50.

AREA CHRISTIAN WRITERS' CLUBS, FELLOWSHIP GROUPS, AND CRITIQUE GROUPS

(*) Asterisk before a listing means the information was not verified or updated by the group leader.
(+) A plus sign before a listing indicates a new listing.

ALABAMA
*CHRISTIAN WRITERS CLUB OF WEST ALABAMA, Birmingham/Northport area. Contact: C. Joanne Sloan, 3230 Mystic Lake Way, Northport AL 35476. (205)333-8603. Membership open.

ARIZONA
*BETHANY CHRISTIAN WRITERS' CLUB. Phoenix. Contact: Rod Hugen, 2140 W. Nicolet, Phoenix AZ 85021. (602)995-1857. Membership (25+) open.

FOUNTAIN HILLS CHRISTIAN WRITERS. Contact: Rosemarie D. Malroy, 10413 N. Demaret Dr., Fountain Hills AZ 85268-5742. (602)837-8494. Membership (12) open.

+GRACE CHAPEL WRITERS CLUB. Scottsdale. Contact: Frances Klinkert, 4523 N. 34th St., Phoenix AZ 85018. Membership (11) open.

MESA CHRISTIAN WRITERS CLUB. Contact: Donna Goodrich, 648 S. Pima St., Mesa AZ 85210. (602)962-6694. Membership (20) open.

*PHOENIX CHRISTIAN WRITERS CLUB. Contact: Vic Kelly, 2135 W. Cactus Wren Dr., Phoenix AZ 85021. (602)864-1390.Membership (20) open.

*PRESCOTT CHRISTIAN WRITERS FELLOWSHIP. Contact: Barbara Spangler, Box 26449, Prescott Valley AZ 86312. (602)772-6263/778-7342. Membership (10-15) open. Sponsors one-day seminar (usually 4th Saturday in September).

SWEETWATER CHRISTIAN WRITERS GROUP. Glendale. Contact: Carla Bruce, PO Box 5640, Glendale AZ 85312. (602)978-5511/247-0174. Membership (12-15) open.

TEMPE CHRISTIAN WRITERS GROUP. Contact: Marsha Crockett, 1604 W. Barrow Dr., Chandler AZ 85224. (602)963-5637. Membership (15-20) open.

ARKANSAS
*NORTHEAST ARKANSAS CHRISTIAN WRITERS CLUB. Horseshoe Bend. Contact: Thelma McMillon, 1307 Park Lane, Horseshoe Bend AR 72512. (501)670-4477. Membership (3) open.

CALIFORNIA
+CASTRO VALLEY CHRISTIAN WRITERS GROUP. Contact: Pastor Jon Drury, 19300 Redwood Rd., Castro Valley CA 94546. (510)886-6300/881-5888. Membership (8-12) open. Sponsoring a Christian Writers Seminar, February 24-25, 1995.

CHRISTIAN WRITERS FELLOWSHIP OF ORANGE COUNTY. Huntington Beach. Contact: Louis Merryman, P.O. Box 538, Lake Forest CA 92630. (310)379-5646. Membership (90) open. Monthly newsletter. Sponsors critique groups in Costa Mesa, Fullerton, Fountain Valley, Huntington Beach, LaVerne, Mission Viejo, Torrance, Santa Ana, and Long Beach (contact critique group coordinator, Jessica Shaver 310-595-4162). Sponsors two Writers' Days: March and October 1995.

*CHRISTIAN WRITERS OF VENTURA COUNTY. Ventura. Contact: Karen Weldin, 851 Camelia Dr., Port Hueneme CA 93041. (805)486-0635. Sponsors February seminar. Membership (15+) Open.

DIABLO VALLEY CHRISTIAN WRITERS GROUP. Danville. Contact: Peggy Parker, 2275 Trotter Way, Walnut Creek CA 94596. (510)934-3221. Membership (8-12) open.

*GLENDALE CHRISTIAN SCRIBES. Contact: Stephanie Smedley, 10413 Oro Vista, Sunland CA 91040. (818)352-7017. Membership (8) open.

*HAYWARD CHRISTIAN WRITERS GROUP. Hayward. Contact: Wesley Sharpe, 29416 Providence Wy, Hayward CA 94544. (510)785-2049. Membership (8) open.

+HIGH DESERT CHRISTIAN WRITERS GUILD. Lancaster. Contact: Ellen Berg, 3600 Brabham Ave., Rosamond CA 93560-6891. Membership open.

HIS SCRIBES OF SOUTHERN CALIFORNIA (formerly **LONG BEACH CHRISTIAN WRITERS**). Sponsors groups in Long Beach, Mission Viejo, LaVerne, and others. Contact: Jessica Shaver, 186 E. Cameron Pl., Long Beach CA 90807-3851. (310)595-4162. Fax: (310)426-9978. Membership (50) open.

*INLAND EMPIRE CHRISTIAN WRITERS GUILD. Moreno Valley. Contact: Bill and Carole Gift Page, Unit 112, 23571 Sunnymead Ranch Pkwy., Ste 103, Moreno Valley CA 92557-2867. (909)924-0610. Membership (46) open. Sponsors twice-yearly seminars in February & September.

+LA CIN ACHIM 18:21. Associated with the Christian Afro-American Reeducation and Treatment - Braintrust. Christian philosophy, intellectual self-defense, intellectual-mastery and life-management. "We will match you up with writers as mentors or collaborators." Contact: Achim Rodgers, 6341 Johnson Ave., Long Beach CA 90805. (310)428-7349.

LODI WRITERS ASSOCIATION. Contact: Dee Porter, Box 1863, Lodi CA 95241. (209)334-0603. Membership (65) open. Sponsors one-day workshop.

+OAKLAND CHRISTIAN WRITERS CLUB. Contact: Sharon Haynes, 1068 - 85th Ave., Oakland CA 94621. (510)562-4743. Membership (20) open.

SACRAMENTO CHRISTIAN WRITER'S CLUB. Fair Oaks. Contact: Betsy Schwarzentraub,1402 Nutmeg Ln., Davis CA 95616. (916)756-0852. Membership (50) open.

SAN DIEGO COUNTY CHRISTIAN WRITERS' GUILD. Contact: Sherwood E. Wirt, 14140 Mazatlan Ct., Poway CA 92064. (619)748-0565. Membership (225) open. Sponsors fall seminar (September 23, 1995), Leslie H. Stobbe, keynote speaker; and spring awards banquet in March.

THE WRITE BUNCH. Stockton. Contact: Shirley Cook, president, 3123 Sheridan, Stockton CA 95219. (209)477-8375. Audrey Seitelman, secretary, (209)957-4977. Membership (7) open.

COLORADO

*CHRISTIAN WRITERS' CLUB. Ft. Collins. Contact: Martie McNeil, 6801 N. County Rd. 15., Fort Collins CO 80524. (303)490-2764. Membership (8) open.

*COLORADO CHRISTIAN COMMUNICATORS. Colorado Springs. Contact: Madalene Harris, 810 Crystal Park Rd. 23, Manitou Springs CO, 80829. (719)685-9432. Membership (30+) open. Sponsors fall seminar.

COLORADO CHRISTIAN WRITERS. Lyons. Contact: Debbie Barker, 67 Seminole Ct., Lyons CO 80540. (303)823-5718. Membership (10+) open. Sponsors an annual seminar and several critique groups.

CHRISTIAN WRITERS IN TOUCH. Lakewood. Contact: Chris Adams, 2573 Benton St., Edgewater CO 80214. (303)232-9470. Membership (6+) open. Sponsors April seminar.

DELAWARE
DELMARVA CHRISTIAN WRITERS' FELLOWSHIP. Dover. Contact: Candy Abbott, P.O. Box 777, Georgetown DE 19947-0777. (302)856-6649. Sponsors annual seminar.

FLORIDA
*ADVENTURES IN CHRISTIAN WRITING. Orlando. Contact: Mary Shaw, 350 E. Jackson St., Orlando FL 32801. (407)841-4866. Membership open.

SUNCOAST CHRISTIAN WRITERS GROUP. Largo. Contact: Elaine Creasman, 13014 - 106th Ave. N., Largo FL 34644-5602. (813)595-8963. Membership (30) open.

TITUSVILLE CHRISTIAN WRITERS' FELLOWSHIP. Titusville. Contact: Nancy Otto Boffo, 2625 Riviera Dr., Titusville FL 32780-5144. (407)267-7604. Membership (10) open.

WRITING STRATEGIES. Daytona Beach. Sponsors half-day seminars quarterly in January, February, May and October. Send SASE for brochure. Contact: Rosemary J. Upton, 1420 N. Atlantic Ave. #801, Daytona Beach FL 32118-3563. (904)253-6666. 100+ on mailing list.

WRITING STRATEGIES CRITIQUESHOP. Daytona Beach. Holds a workshop the second Tuesday of each month. Contact: Rosemary J. Upton, 1420 N. Atlantic Ave. #801, Daytona Beach FL 32118-3563. (904)253-6666. Membership (20) open.

GEORGIA
NORTHEAST GEORGIA WRITERS. Gainesville. Contact: Elouise Whitten, 660 Crestview Terr., Gainesville GA 30501-3110. (404)532-3007. Membership (25) open. Sponsors day and night groups, contests, critique groups, two all-day workshops and a biennial writers'conference.

IDAHO
CHRISTIAN WRITERS OF IDAHO. Post Falls. Contact: Sheri Stone, Box 1754, Post Falls ID 83854-1754. (208)667-9730. Membership (25) open. Sponsors an annual fall seminar.

ILLINOIS
*DECATUR BRANCH OF AMERICAN PEN WOMEN. Around Decatur. Contact: Martha B. Query, Rte. 1 Box 379, Maroa IL 61756-9503. (217)794-3796. Membership (10) open. Working group.

*JUVENILE FORUM. Moline. Contact: David R. Collins, 3403 45th St., Moline IL 61265. (309)762-8985. Membership (8-15) open to those writing for children or youth.

*TRUE VINE CHRISTIAN FELLOWSHIP. Springfield. Contact: Faith Logan, 813 S. 13th St., Springfield IL 62702. Membership (8) open.

INDIANA
CHRISTIAN WRITERS' GUILD. Crawfordsville. Contact: Aileen Karg, 1004 Cottage Ave., Crawfordsville IN 47933-1506. (317)362-9186. Membership (10+) open.

*CREATIVE WRITERS. Marion. Contact: Mary M. Cain, 631 Candlewood Dr., Marion IN 46952. (317)662-6222. Membership (14) open.

FORT WAYNE CHRISTIAN WRITERS CLUB. Fort Wayne. Contact: Linda R. Wade, 739 W. Fourth St., Fort Wayne IN 46808-2613. (219)422-2772. Membership (20) open.

+OPEN DOOR CHRISTIAN WRITERS. Westport. Contact: Janet Teitsort, Box 78, Westport IN 47283-0078. (812)591-2210. Membership (14) active.

*****SEYMOUR CHRISTIAN WRITER'S CLUB.** Contact: Anna Belle Stewart, Route 2 Box 29, Seymour IN 47274. (812)523-8178. Membership open.

THE WRITING ACADEMY. Contact: Rev. Benny Boling, 3600 W. Republic Rd., Springfield MO 65807-5402. Membership (56) open. Sponsors year-round correspondence writing program and annual seminar in August (held in Indiana).

IOWA

CEDAR RAPIDS CHRISTIAN WRITER'S CRITIQUE GROUP. Contact: Helen Hunter, 1132-21st St. SE, Cedar Rapids IA 52403. (319)362-4777. Membership (14) open. A day and a night group.

*****RIVER CITY WRITERS.** Council Bluffs. Contact: Dee Barrett, 16 Susan Lane, Council Bluffs IA 51503. (712)322-7692. Membership (4-6) open.

+SIOUXLAND CHRISTIAN WRITERS. Sioux City. Contact: William B. Tucker, 4711 Sergeant Rd., Sioux City IA 51106-4536. Membership (22) open.

KANSAS

*****CHRISTIAN WRITERS GROUP OF TOPEKA** Contact: Charles White, 4102 NW Dondee Ln., Topeka KS 66618. (913)286-0388. Membership (14) open.

*****CREATIVE WRITERS FELLOWSHIP.** Newton, Halsted, Hesston. Contact: Chester Osborne, 429 N Weaver, Hesston, KS 67062. Membership (15) open.

*****LAMPLIGHTERS CHRISTIAN WRITERS CLUB.** Andover. Contact: Sharon Stanhope, Box 415, Benton KS 67017. (316)778-1043. Membership (20) open.

LEARNERS CHRISTIAN WRITING CLUB. Medicine Lodge. Contact: Ruth E. Montgomery, P.O. Box 308, Medicine Lodge KS 67104-0308. (316)886-9863. Membership (12) open.

PITTSBURG CHRISTIAN WRITERS FELLOWSHIP. Pittsburg. Contact: LeAnn Campbell, 267 SW 1st Ln., Lamar MO 64759. (417)682-2713. Membership (12) open. Sponsoring an April 8, 1995 seminar.

PRAIRIE CHRISTIAN WRITERS. Larned. Contact: Marilyn Phemister, 206 E 10th St., Larned KS 67550. (316)285-6217. Membership (5-6) open.

KENTUCKY

JACKSON CHRISTIAN WRITERS' CLUB. Vancleve. Contact: Donna J. Woodring, KMBC, P.O. Box 10, Vancleve KY 41385-0010. (606)666-5000. Membership (9) open.

*****OHIO VALLEY FELLOWSHIP OF CHRISTIAN WRITERS.** Contact: Irmgard L. Williams, 434 9th St., Henderson KY 42420-2888. (502)826-4144. Membership open.

*****THE PRESBYTERIAN WRITERS GUILD.** No regular meetings. National writers organization with a quarterly newsletter. Dues $15 per year. Contact: Ann Barr Weems, 6900 Kingsbury Blvd., St. Louis MO 63130. (314)725-6290.

LOUISIANA
*LOUISIANA CHRISTIAN WRITERS GUILD. Various locations. Contact: Dr. Donald M. Aycock, 4754 N. Milnor Dr., Memphis TN 38128-4812. Membership (50+) open.

MARYLAND
ANNAPOLIS FELLOWSHIP OF CHRISTIAN WRITERS. Annapolis. Leader is Mark Littleton, 5350 Eliot's Oak Rd., Columbia MD 21044. Contact: Jeri Sweany, Box 411, Annapolis MD 21403. (410)267-0924. Membership (15) open.

MASSACHUSETTS
*WESTERN MASSACHUSETTS CHRISTIAN WRITERS FELLOWSHIP. Springfield. Contact: Barbara A. Robidoux, 127 Gelinas Dr., Chicopee MA 01020. (413)594-6567. Membership (50) open. Monthly newsletter.

MICHIGAN
SOUTHEASTERN CHRISTIAN WRITERS GROUP. Royal Oak. Contact: Audrey Perry, 255 W 14 Mile Rd. #1518, Clawson MI 48017-1955. (810)288-0913. Membership (15) open.

MINNESOTA
MINNESOTA CHRISTIAN WRITERS GUILD. Edina. Contact: Charette Barta, 5344 Ewing Ave. S., Minneapolis MN 55410. (612)922-4609. Membership (95+) open. Sponsors an annual spring seminar.

MISSOURI
*INSPIRATIONAL WRITERS WORKSHOP OF GREATER ST. LOUIS. St. Charles. Contact: Lila Wold Shelburne, 23 Blackberry, St. Louis MO 63301. (314)946-8533. Membership (2-3) open to writers.

*CHRISTIAN WRITERS WORKSHOP. St. Louis. Contact: Celeste Rhea, P.O. Box 87, Ironton MO 63650-0087. (314)645-5460. Membership (8) open.

*NORTHLAND CHRISTIAN WRITERS. Kansas City. Contact: Margaret Owen, 207 NW 67th St., Gladstone MO 64118. (816)436-5240.

SPRINGFIELD CHRISTIAN WRITERS CLUB. Contact: Owen Wilkie, 4909 Old Wire Rd., Battlefield MO 65619. (417)882-5185. Membership (10) open.

*UMC CHRISTIAN WRITERS GUILD. Columbia. Contact: Mike Kateman, 11640 E. Durk Rd., Centralia MO 65240-9716. (314)445-6533. Membership open.

MONTANA
*HELENA CHRISTIAN WRITERS. Contact: Lenore Puhek, 1215 Hudson, Helena MT 59601. (406)443-2552. Membership (12) open as space allows. Has one-day writers retreat for members.

*MONTANA CHRISTIAN WRITERS. Contact: Margaret Wilkison, 2007 Sweet Grass Rd., Helena MT 59061. (406)442-9939.

NEBRASKA
*LINCOLN WORD WEAVERS. Contact: Frenchy Dennis, 2212 Hanover Ct., Lincoln NE 68512. (402)421-3670. Membership (10) open.

NEW HAMPSHIRE

THE WORDSMITHS. Nashua. Contact: Cynthia Vlatas, 5 Jeremy Ln., Hudson NH 03051. (603)882-2851. Membership (20) open. May hold 1995 workshop. E-Mail addresses: America Online (JC Writers); Internet (jcwriters @aol.com).

NEW JERSEY

NEW JERSEY CHRISTIAN WRITERS FELLOWSHIP OF SCOTCH PLAINS. Scotch Plains. Contact: Fran Pasch, 165 Norwood Ave., North Plainfield NJ 07060. (908)755-2075. Membership (10) open.

NEW JERSEY SOCIETY OF CHRISTIAN WRITERS. Millville. Contact: Dr. Mary Ann Diorio, Box 748, Millville NJ 08332-0748. (609)327-1231. Membership (46) open.

*RAINBOW WRITERS. Bridgewater. Contact: Dr. Megan D. Simpson, 9 Iroquois Trail, Branchburg NJ 08876-5451. (908)231-9437. Membership (8) open.

*SOUTH JERSEY CHRISTIAN WRITERS FELLOWSHIP. Atlantic City. Contact: Sandi Cleary, 308 Clark Pl., Northfield NJ 08225. (609)646-5694.

NEW MEXICO

*SOUTHWEST CHRISTIAN WRITERS ASSOCIATION. Farmington. Contact: Kathy Cordell, 91 - Rd 3450, Flora Vista NM 87415. (505)334-0617. Membership (14) open. Sponsors annual one-day seminar in September.

+SOUTHWEST WRITERS. Albuquerque. Contact: JoAnn Hamlin, 1338 Wyoming Blvd. NE, Ste. B, Albuquerque NM 87122. (505)293-0303. Membership (1,000+) open. Sponsors conference at Hilton Hotel in Albuquerque; August 25-27, 1995; August 23-25, 1996.

NEW YORK

BROOKLYN WRITER'S CLUB. Contact: Ann Dellarocco, Box 184, Bath Beach Station, Brooklyn NY 11214. (718)837-3484. Membership (50+) open.

*NEW YORK CHRISTIAN WRITERS GROUP. New York. Contact: Sharita Hunt, c/o Calvary Baptist Church, 123 W. 57th St., New York NY 10019. (212)975-0170. Membership (20) open.

SYRACUSE CHRISTIAN WRITERS' GUILD. Liverpool. Contact: Pat Spencer, 108 Woodpath Rd., Liverpool NY 13090. (315)652-3178. Membership (25-60) open. Sponsors annual seminar.

NORTH CAROLINA

*CHRISTIAN WRITERS CLUB. Contact: David F. Browning, Box 4311, Rocky Mount NC 27801. (919)442-7119.

+COVENANT WRITERS. Lincolnton. Contact: Janice Stroup, 403 S. Cedar St., Lincolnton NC 28092. (704)735-8851. Membership (10) open.

OHIO

*AKRON MANUSCRIPT CLUB. Contact: Tom Raber, Box 966, Cuyahoga Falls OH 44223. (216)928-7268. Membership open. Sponsors annual writers'conference in May.

COLUMBUS CHRISTIAN WRITERS ASSN. Contact: Brenda Custodio, 3069 Bocastle Ct., Reynoldsburg OH 43068. (614)861-1011. Membership (50) open. Sponsors a fall workshop; October 5-7, 1995.

COLUMBUS CHRISTIAN WRITERS ASSN/PATASKALA. Contact: Melissa Morgan, P.O. Box 667, Pataskala OH 43062. (614)927-7773. Membership (25) open.

DAYTON CHRISTIAN SCRIBES. Kettering. Contact: Lois Pecce (secretary), Box 613, Dayton OH 45459-0613. (513)433-6470. Membership (40-45) open. Mara Curran, leader.

GREATER CINCINNATI CHRISTIAN WRITERS' FELLOWSHIP. Contact: Teresa Cleary, 895 Garnoa St., Cincinnati OH 45231-2618. (513)521-1913. Membership (25) open.

MARION AREA CHRISTIAN WRITERS. Marion. Contact: Irene M. Sprague, 603 Henry St., Marion OH 43302. (614)387-3047. Membership (10) open. May sponsor an April seminar.

NORTHWEST OHIO CHRISTIAN WRITERS. Bowling Green. Contact: Nancy Kintner, 4235 Lyman, Toledo OH 43612-1584. (419)478-1055. Membership (30) open. Sponsors a Saturday seminar in September.

*****OHIO FELLOWSHIP OF CHRISTIAN WRITERS.** Contact: John G. Hoffman, 233 W. Church St., Marion OH 43302. (614)387-6683. Membership open. Sponsors annual writers' conference.

+SET FORTH WRITERS GUILD. North Central OH/Mansfield area. Contact: Donna Caudill, 836 Delph Ave., Mansfield OH 44906. (419)747-1755. Membership (32) open.

*****STATELINE CHRISTIAN WRITER'S CLUB.** Celina. Contact: Shirley Knox, 54106 Club Island Rd., Celina OH 45822. (419)268-2040. Membership (10) open.

WESTERN OHIO CHRISTIAN WRITERS. Sidney. Contact: Alice Linsley, 231 N. Miami Ave, Sidney OH 45365. (513)663-4131/492-8584. Membership (43) open.

OKLAHOMA

*****TULSA CHRISTIAN WRITERS.** Contact: Vicki Musser, 14801 E. 111th St., Broken Arrow OK 74011-3904. (918)251-2706. Membership (65) open. Sponsors annual spring writers' conference.

+WORDWRIGHTS. Oklahoma City. Contact: Irene Martin. P.O. Box 300332, Midwest City OK 73140. Membership (10-20) open.

OREGON

+CORVALLIS CHRISTIAN WRITERS GROUP. Contact: Ken Himes, 3179 NW Greenbriar Pl., Corvallis OR 97330. (503)757-7227. Membership (4) open (especially to experienced writers).

+EMERALD CHRISTIAN WRITERS GROUP. Eugene. Daphne Killion, (503)343-9372. Membership (6) open.

+EUGENE CHRISTIAN WRITERS GROUP. Contact: Lois Erickson, 885 Pioneer Ct., Eugene OR 97401. (503)342-6896. Membership (5) open.

+GRESHAM CHRISTIAN WRITERS GROUP. Contact: Elsie Larson, 1541 SW Pleasant View Dr., Gresham OR 97080. (503)661-5358. Membership (5) open.

+LEBANON/ALBANY CHRISTIAN WRITERS GROUP. Contact: Rebecca Brown, 36135 Bohlken Dr., Lebanon OR 97355. (503)258-6978. Membership (4) open.

+MONMOUTH CHRISTIAN WRITERS GROUP. Contact: Cathy Verley, 14100 Kings Valley Hwy., Monmouth OR 97361. (503)838-0394. Membership (5) open.

+NEWBERG CHRISTIAN WRITERS GROUP. Contact: Betty Hockett, 1100 N. Meridian #38, Newberg OR 97132. (503)538-9871. Membership (5) open.

OREGON CHRISTIAN WRITERS. Contact: Kris Ingram, pres., 955 S. 59th St., Springfield OR 97478-5452. (503)726-8320. Meets three times annually: February in Salem, May in Eugene, and October in

Portland. All-day Saturday conferences. Membership (250) open. Sponsors annual conference in August (near Salem). Newsletter & critique groups.

THE RIGHT TO WRITE CRITIQUE GROUP. Salem. Contact: Marcia Mitchell, 4400 Bren Loop N.E., Salem OR 97305. (503)588-0372. Membership (6) open.

SMITH ROCK CHRISTIAN WRITERS. Redmond. Contact: Josephine Manes, 2135 NE O'Neil Way, Redmond OR 97756. (503)548-8872. Membership (5) open.

+TIGARD CHRISTIAN WRITERS GROUP. Contact: Ed Demaree, P.O. Box 23944, Tigard OR 97281. (503)620-7840. Membership (5) open.

WORDSMITHS. Gresham/East Multnomah County. Contact: Susan Thogerson Maas, 27526 SE Carl St., Gresham OR 97080-8215. (503)663-7834. Membership (6) open. Christian and secular writers.

PENNSYLVANIA

THE FIRST WORD. Sewickley. Contact: Shirley Stevens, 326 B Glaser Ave., Pittsburgh PA 15202-2910. (412)761-2618. Membership (12) open.

+GREATER JOHNSTOWN CHRISTIAN WRITERS' GUILD. Contact: Betty Rosian, 108 Deerfield Ln., Johnstown PA 15905-9406. (814)25-4351. Membership (15) open.

GREATER PHILADELPHIA CHRISTIAN WRITERS' FELLOWSHIP. Broomall. Contact: Marlene Bagnull, 316 Blanchard Rd., Drexel Hill PA 19026. (610)626-6833. Membership (40) open. Sponsors annual writers' conference; April 27-29, 1995.

HARRISBURG AREA CHRISTIAN WRITERS' FELLOWSHIP. Mechanicsburg. Contact: Georgia Burkett, 220 Dock St., Middletown PA 17057. (717)944-4427. Holds bi-annual conference; next one 1996. Membership (60) open.

MONTROSE CHRISTIAN WRITERS FELLOWSHIP. Contact: Patti Souder, 35 Lake Ave., Montrose PA 18801-1022. (717)278-4815. Membership (13) open. Holding a conference July 10-14, 1995.

YORK WRITERS. Contact: Rita Atwell-Holler, 100 Greenwood Rd., York PA 17404-5766. (717)792-0228. Membership (12) open. Sponsors annual one-day seminar; July 1995.

SOUTH CAROLINA

CHRISTIAN WRITERS FELLOWSHIP INTL. Contact: Sandy Brooks, Rt. 3 Box 1635, Jefferson Davis Rd, Clinton SC 29325. (803)697-6035. No meetings, but offers bimonthly newsletter (Cross & Quill), prayer fellowship, writing instruction, and consultations. Membership open.

CHRISTIAN WRITERS GROUP. Greenville. Contact: Nancy Parker, 150-12C Oak Ridge Place, Greenville SC 29615. (803)281-0876. Membership (8) open.

*SPARTANBURG WRITERS GROUP. Contact: Linda Gilden, 105 Pheasant Rd., Spartanburg SC 20302. Membership (6) open.

TENNESSEE

*CHATTANOOGA BIBLE INSTITUTE CHRISTIAN WRITERS WORKSHOP. Chattanooga. Contact: Barbara Tucker, 1902 Duncan Ave., Chattanooga TN 37404. (615)624-1346. Membership (10) open.

TEXAS

+AUSTIN CHRISTIAN WRITERS' GUILD. Contact: Jane Bryant, 703 Knollwood Cir., Austin TX 78746. (512)329-0617. New group. Membership open.

INSPIRATIONAL WRITERS ALIVE! Pasadena/Austin/Spring. Contact: Maxine E. Holder, 3606 Longwood Dr., Pasadena TX 77503-2221. (713)477-3716. Membership (105) open. Sponsors summer seminar, monthly newsletter, and annual contest. Note: This leader will be moving in spring 1995 and can be reached at the address listed below under Palestine Chapter after that.

INSPIRATIONAL WRITERS ALIVE!/AMARILLO CHAPTER. Contact: Helen Luecke, 2921 S. Dallas, Amarillo TX 79103-6713. (806)376-9671. Membership (25+) open. Sponsoring a seminar April 8, 1995.

+INSPIRATIONAL WRITERS ALIVE!/AUSTIN CHAPTER. Austin. Contact: Mike Rothman, (512)450-1836. Membership open.

INSPIRATIONAL WRITERS ALIVE!/HOUSTON CHAPTER. Houston. Contact: Wanda Shadle, (713)862-1115 or Pam Binkley, (713)467-2041. Membership (30) open.

+INSPIRATIONAL WRITERS ALIVE!/NORTHWEST HOUSTON CHAPTER. Spring. Contact: Claire Ottensteen, (713)376-7613 or Mary Ann Evans, (409)267-3287. Membership open.

+INSPIRATIONAL WRITERS ALIVE!/PALESTINE CHAPTER. Palestine. Contact: Maxine Holder, Rt. 4 Box 81H, Rusk TX 75785. Starting spring 1995; membership open.

INSPIRATIONAL WRITERS ALIVE!/TRINITY CHAPTER. Dayton. Contact: Mary Ann Evans, (409)267-3284 or Shelia Shook, (409)258-7961. Membership open.

+LOWER RIO GRANDE VALLEY CHRISTIAN WRITERS LEAGUE. Harlingen. Contact: Herschel Whittington, 2910 Treasure Hills, Harlingen TX 78550. 210-423-8048. Membership (30) open.

*SOUTHWEST CHRISTIAN WRITERS GUILD. Dallas. Contact: Jan Winebrenner, 2709 Winding Hollow, Plano TX 75093. (214)783-6319. Membership (60) open. Sponsors early October seminar.

UTAH

UTAH CHRISTIAN WRITERS FELLOWSHIP. Salt Lake City & suburbs. Contact: Kimberly Malkos, 117 W Park St., Copperton UT 84006-1134. (801)568-0939. Or Kate Mauch, (801)942-1803. Membership (25) open. Monthly newsletter $12.

VIRGINIA

+NORTHERN VIRGINIA CHRISTIAN WRITERS FELLOWSHIP. Vienna or Fairfax. Contact: Jennifer Ferranti, dir., P.O. Box 629, Dunn Loring VA 22027-0629. (703)698-7707. Membership (35 & growing) open.

S.O.N. WRITERS. Alexandria. Contact: Susan Lyttek, 2434 Temple Ct., Alexandria VA 23307-1524. (703)768-5582. Membership (5-6) open.

+WINCHESTER CHRISTIAN SCRIBES. Contact: Bernice M. Mercier, 104 Woody's Place, Winchester VA 22602. (703)678-1038. Membership (8-10) open.

WASHINGTON

*ADVENTIST WRITERS ASSOCIATION OF WESTERN WASHINGTON. Seattle area. Contact: Marion Forschler, 18115 - 116th Ave. SE, Renton WA 98058-6562. (206)235-1435. Membership (25) open. Newsletter $10/yr. Sponsors annual writers' conference.

*CHILDREN'S WRITERS CRITIQUE GROUP. Spokane. Contact: Pat Pfeiffer, P.O. Box 104, Otis Orchards WA 99027-0104. (509)927-7671 or 226-3532 (evenings). Or call Christian at (509)448-0593. Membership open.

CHRISTIAN WRITERS. Walla Walla. Contact: Dolores Walker, 904 Ankeny, Walla Walla WA 99362-3705. (509)529-2974. Membership (10) open.

*KITSAP COUNTY CHRISTIAN WRITERS SUPPORT GROUP. Bainbridge Island. Contact: Kay Stewart, 7584 Meadowmeer Ln., Bainbridge Island WA 98110. (206)842-4269.

NORTHWEST CHRISTIAN WRITERS ASSN. Bellevue. Contact: Agnes Lawless, 17462 NE 11th St., Bellevue WA 98008-3814. (206)644-5012. Meets monthly. Membership (90) open.

SPOKANE CHRISTIAN WRITERS. Contact: Niki Anderson. (509)448-6622. Membership (6-8) open.

SPOKANE NOVELISTS. Contact:Joan Mochel, 12229 Ruby, Spokane WA 99218-1924. Membership (7) open.

+SPOKANE WRITERS. Contact: Pat Pfeiffer, P.O. Box 104, Otis Orchards WA 99027-0104. (509)927-7671/226-3532. Membership (20) open by vote.

WASHINGTON CHRISTIAN WRITERS FELLOWSHIP. Seattle. Contact: Elaine Wright Colvin, Box 11337, Bainbridge Island WA 98110. (206)842-9103. Membership (350) open. Holds three annual meetings: January 28, April 29, and September 30, 1995.

WENATCHEE CHRISTIAN WRITERS' FELLOWSHIP. East Wenatchee. Contact: Shirley R. Pease, 1818 Skyline Dr. #31, Wenatchee WA 98801. (509)662-8392. Membership (35) open. Holds one-day seminar in September.

*WHATCOM CHRISTIAN WRITERS CLUB. Group does not meet regularly. Area contact: Judy Slotemaker, 840 E Pole Rd., Lynden WA 98264. (206)354-2636.

WRITERS INFORMATION NETWORK (W.I.N.). Meetings held in various states as announced (possibly Hawaii, Canada, Washington & Ohio). Contact: Elaine Wright Colvin, Box 11337, Bainbridge Island WA 98110. (206)842-9103. Resource and referral/marketing newsletter. Membership (1,000+) open.

WISCONSIN

*THE PRESBYTERIAN WRITERS GUILD. (Meets once a year where PCUSA General Assembly is held. Will be in WI this year.) Dr. Dale Robb, president. Contact: Jeanne Giles, 625 Illinois Pl., Box 160, Palmyra NE 68418. Gives two annual awards, one to a seminary senior and one to a Presbyterian writer. Membership (140) open.

SWORD & LIGHT/GREATER MILWAUKEE CHRISTIAN WRITERS' GUILD. Milwaukee/Waukesha. Contact: Andrea Kuhn-Boeshaar, 10605 W. Wabash Ave., Milwaukee WI 53224-2315. (414)355-8915. Membership (15) open. Tentatively planning a spring seminar.

*WISCONSIN FELLOWSHIP OF CHRISTIAN WRITERS. Janesville. Contact: Jean Marie Wuttke, 1710 Randolph Rd., Janesville WI 53545. (608)752-1323. Membership (6) open.

*WORD & PEN CHRISTIAN WRITERS CLUB. Menasha. Contact: Beth Grosek, 529 E. Cecil St., Neenah WI 54956-3818. (414)727-4753. Membership (18) open.

CANADA

ARTISTIC LICENSE (formerly WRITERS CHALLENGE & SUPPORT GROUP). Langley, BC. Contact: Christy Bowler, Box 56040, Valley Center PO, Langley BC V3A 8B3 Canada. (604)530-4314. Membership (30) open.

*FRASER VALLEY CHRISTIAN WRITERS. Clearbrook/ Abbotsford. Contact: Ingrid Shelton, 2082 Geneva Ct., Clearbrook BC V2T 3Z2 Canada (Box 783, Sumas WA 98295). (604)859-7530. Membership (30) open.

MANITOBA CHRISTIAN WRITERS ASSN. Winnipeg. Contact: Eleanor Bilsland, 201 - 177 Watson St., Winnipeg MB R2P 2P8 Canada. 697-4559. Membership (20) open.

SOUTHERN MANITOBA FELLOWSHIP OF CHRISTIAN WRITERS. Winkler or Roland. Contact: Isabel Allison, Box 208, Roland MB R0G 1T0 Canada. (204)343-2119. Membership (5) open.

*SPIRITWOOD SCRIBES. Meets 19X/yr. Contact: Richard W. Unger, Box 212, Spiritwood SK, S0J 2M0. (306)883-2462. Annual dues $5. Membership open.

SWAN VALLEY WRITERS GUILD. Manitoba. Contact: Marlene Hohne, Box 2115, Swan River MB R0L 1Z0 Canada. (204)525-4652. Membership (8-9) open. Sponsoring seminar October 21-22, 1995.

Note: If your group is not listed here, please send information to: Sally Stuart, 1647 SW Pheasant Dr., Aloha OR 97006. November 1st is deadline for the next year's edition.

EDITORIAL SERVICES

The following listing is included because so many writers contact me looking for experienced/qualified editors who can critique or evaluate their manuscripts. These people from all over the country offer this kind of service. I cannot personally guarantee the work of any of those listed, so you may want to ask for references or samples of work.

The following abbreviations indicate what kinds of work they are qualified to do: GE indicates general editing/manuscript evaluation; LC indicates line editing or copy editing; GH - Ghostwriting; CA - co-authoring; B - brochures; NL - newsletters; SP - special projects; and BC - book contract evaluation. The following abbreviations indicate the types of material they evaluate: A - articles, SS - short stories, P - poetry, F - fillers, N - novels, NB - nonfiction books, BP - book proposals, JN - juvenile novels, PB - picture books, BS - Bible studies, TM - technical material, E - essays, D - devotionals, S - scripts.

Always send a copy they can write on and an SASE for return of your material.

(*) Indicates that publisher did not return questionnaire.
(+) Indicates new listing.

ARIZONA

+CARLA'S MANUSCRIPT SERVICE/CARLA BRUCE, 4326 N. 50th Ave., Phoenix AZ 85031. (602)247-0174. GE/LC/GH. Does A/N/NB/BS. Charges $15-20/hour or will quote per page or project. Does ghostwriting for pastors & teachers; professional typesetting.

JOY P. GAGE, 2370 Rio Verde Dr., Cottonwood AZ 86326-5923. Send material with $25 deposit. GE. Does A/N/NB/BP/BS/E/D. Charges $25/hr.

*KAREN MARTELL, 5829 N. 81st St., Scottsdale AZ 85250. (602)991-1134. Fax: (602)949-1041. Call/write. GE/LC. Does A/SS/F/N/NB/JN/BS/TM/D. Charges $15/hr-$1.50/pg.

'LEEN POLLINGER, 12610 Westgate Dr, Sun City West AZ 85375-5137. (602)546-4757. Call/write. GE/LC. Does SS/F/N/NB/BP/JN/BS/D. Charges $12-35/hr depending on work done. Fee schedule available for SASE.

CALIFORNIA

CHRISTIAN COMMUNICATOR MANUSCRIPT CRITIQUE SERVICE, 3133 Puente St., Fullerton CA 92635-1952. (714)990-1532. Fax: (714)990-1952. Call/write/for entire book send material with $80-100 deposit. Staff of 11 editors. GE/LC/SP/book contract evaluation. Edits all types of material. Articles/stories $60. Three-chapter book proposal $80. Additional editing $20/hr.

DINA DONOHUE, 1633 Diamond St. #9, San Diego CA 92109-3161. (619)272-2890. Write. GE. Does A/SS/F/D. Articles/1,500 wds/$20, short stories/3,000 wds/$25; $5 each additional 1,000 wds; fillers/to 750 wds/$10.

*DIANE FILLMORE PUBLISHING SERVICES, 13776 Starhill Ln., LaPuente CA 91746-2733. (818)336-5899. Call/write. GE/LC/GH/CA/B/NL/SP. Does A/SS/F/N/NB/BS/D/small group or SS curriculum. Charges $15/hr.

GOOD NEWS LITERARY SERVICE/CYNTHIA WACHNER, P.O. Box 587, Visalia CA 93279. (209)627-6241. Send for rate sheet.

*VICKI HESTERMAN, PhD, P.O. Box 6788, San Diego CA 92166. (619)224-4549. Call/Write. GE/LC/CA/SP. Does A/NB/BP/TM/E/D. Specializes in helping people tell their personal stories. Charges standard rates.

DARLENE HOFFA, 512 Juniper St., Brea CA 92621. (714)990-5980. Write. GE. Does A/F/NB/BP/BS/D. Charges $35/article or short piece.; $65 for book ms up to 52 pgs, plus $1.25/pg.; or $15/hr.

DENELLA KIMURA, 785 Barton Way, Benicia CA 94510-3807. (707)746-8421. Write/$10 deposit. GE/LC. P/F/E/D. Line editing $10/page; poetry book proposals: 30-48 pgs with possible markets, $50. Produces chapbooks.

*LIGHTHOUSE EDITING/DR. LON ACKELSON, 13326 Community Rd., #11, Poway CA 92064. (619)748-9258. Write. GE/LC/revision. Does A/SS/BP/BS. Charges $25 for article/short story critique; $35 for book proposal; $25 + $3/pg for critique and revision.

MARY CARPENTER REID, 925 Larchwood Dr., Brea CA 92621. (714)529-3755. Write. GE. Does A/SS/N/BP/JN/PB/E. Charges $35/article or short piece.; $65 for book ms up to 52 pgs, plus $1.25/pg.

JANE RUMPH, 1130 Leonard Ave., Pasadena CA 91107-1746. (818)351-8703. Write. GE/LC. Does A/F/NB/BS/TM/E/D/theses/dissertations. Charges $15-20/hr.

*DR. WESLEY SHARPE, 29416 Providence Way, Hayward CA 94544-6416. (510)785-2049. Call/write/send material with $25. GE/LC/B/NL. Does A/F/NB/BP/D. Charges $30/hr. Contact for estimate.

LAURAINE SNELLING, 952 Marie Ave., Martinez CA 94553-3519. (510)372-9047. Fax: (510)372-3622. Call/write. GE/GH/CA/NL/SP. Does A/SS/N/NB/BP/JN. Charges $40/hr, or by the project after discussion with client.

COLORADO

COLORADO CHRISTIAN WRITERS CONFERENCE / DEBBIE BARKER, 67 Seminole Ct., Lyons CO 80540. Phone & Fax: (303)823-5718. Call/send material with deposit of $100. GE/LC. Does A/SS/F/N/NB/BP/JN/BS/TM/E/D/queries. Negotiable rates on a project basis.

*EDITH QUINLAN, 9030 W. 3rd Pl., Lakewood CO 80226. (303)237-8358. Call/write. GE/LC/NL. Does A/F/NB. Charges $10/hr.

FLORIDA

JULIA LEE DULFER, 705 Hibiscus Trail, Melbourne Beach FL 32951. (407)727-8192. Call. GE/LC. Does A/SS/N/NB/BP/JN/BS/E/D. Charges $20/hr for all functions.

EDIT, DESIGN, TYPESET/KISTLER LONDON, 325 Wilder Blvd. #302A, Daytona Beach FL 32114-6083. (904)255-8585. Write. GE/LC/CA/B/SP. Does A/SS/P/F/N/NB/BP/BS/TM/E/D/medical. Also organizes, transcribes, writes, rewrites, produces camera-ready copy. Will typeset on Quark Xpress (Macintosh). Send for rate sheet.

LESLIE SANTAMARIA, 4019 Cardinal Blvd., Daytona Beach FL 32127-6637. (904)788-7720 (fax the same). Write. GE/LC/GH/CA. Does A/SS/N/NB/BP/JN/BS/TM/E/D/S/query & cover letters/resumes. Charges $1/page for GE; $2/page for LC; $15 minimum.

IDAHO

+IN PRINT/KAY YOUNKIN, 9125 Edwards Rd., Rathdrum ID 83858. (208)687-1079. Fax: (208)687-1079. Write or send with deposit. GE/LC/GH/B/NL/SP/book contract evaluation. Does A/SS/P/F/N/NB/ BP/JN/PB/BS/TM/E/D. Fee is by the page or hourly with minimum deposit of $25.

ILLINOIS

DEBORAH CHRISTENSEN, P.O. Box 354, Addison IL 60101. (708)665-3044. Fax: (708)665-0372. Send with $20 deposit. GE/LC. Does A/SS/F. Charges $20 for first hour; $15 for each additional hour.

EDITECH/DOUGLAS C. SCHMIDT, 872 S. Milwaukee Ave., Ste. 272, Libertyville IL 60048. Write. GE/LC/SP. Does A/SS/F/BS/D; Sunday school curriculum. Charges $25/hr or negotiated flat fee.

+DAVE & NETA JACKSON, 917 Ashland Ave., Evanston IL 60202. (708)328-2561. Available for coauthoring, editing, writing and rewriting, design and typesetting. Authors of over 65 published books. Call or write for information and prices.

VIRGINIA J. MUIR EDITORIAL SERVICES, 130 Windsor Park Dr. #C205, Carol Stream IL 60188. (708)665-2994. Write. GE/LC/CA. Does A/SS/N/NB/JN/BS/TM/E/D. Charges $30/hr; $30 minimum, plus telephone, research expenses and postage.

*JIM RIORDAN, 4207 W. Josephine Dr., Kankakee IL 60901. Write. GE. Does N/NB/BP/TM. Book proposal $250; books under 200 pgs. $400; books over 200 pgs. $400 + $50/100 pgs.

WIGHTMAN WEESE, 1114 E. Wakeman, Wheaton IL 60187. (708)665-9064. Fax: (708)665-9079. Write. GH/CA only. Negotiable terms.

THE WRITER'S EDGE, P.O. Box 1266, Wheaton IL 60189. A subsidiary of Harold Shaw Publishers. Charges $45 to evaluate a book proposal and if publishable, they will send a synopsis of it to editors who might be interested. If not publishable they will tell how to improve it. If interested, send an SASE for guidelines and a Book Information Form.

INDIANA

DENEHEN, INC. / DR. DENNIS E. HENSLEY, 6824 Kanata Ct., Fort Wayne IN 46815-6388. Tel./Fax: (219)485-9891 (Fax 10 a.m-6 p.m., M-F). Call/write. GE/LC/GH/SP. Does A/SS/P/F/N/NB/BP/JN/ E/D. Rate sheet for SASE.

MICHIANA EDITORIAL SERVICES/GRACE PETTIFOR, Box 356, Granger IN 46530-0356. (219)272-7595. Write/call. GE/LC/SP/typesetting. Does A/SS/N/NB/JN/PB/BS/E/D. Rate sheet for SASE.

PMN PUBLISHING/GEORGE ALLEN, Box 47024, Indianapolis IN 46247. (317) 888-7156. Fax: (317)351-1772. Write. Various editorial services. Call or write for services available and charges. B/NL/SP. Does A/BS/D/book reviews.

KANSAS

+SHAUERS COMMUNICATIONS / MARGARET SHAUERS, 1411 - 12th, Great Bend KS 67530. (316)792-1683. Christian author with 1,000+ published children's stories will critique children's fiction: $20 and up for 6 double-spaced pgs; $3 for each pg. over. Market appraisal included. Send SASE.

ESTHER L. VOGT, 113 S. Ash, Hillsboro KS 67063. (316)947-3796. Write. GE/LC/GH. Does SS/N/JN. $15 for first chapter (to 20 pgs); $12 for each chapter thereafter.

LOUISIANA
BLUE-PENCIL SPECIALISTS/JOHN M. CUNNINGHAM, JR., Box 55601, Metairie LA 70055-5601. (504)837-4397. Send material with $10 deposit. GE/LC. Does A/SS/F/BS/T/E/D. Charges according to word count; rate sheet for SASE.

*GLORY ARTS/BARBARA NAUER, P.O. Box 82510, Baton Rogue LA 70884. (504)673-6481. Fax: (504)673-6330. Does editing, re-writing, ghosting, graphics, radio promo, and author advising. Charges by the hour. Send SASE for price list.

MARYLAND
NEE EDITORIAL SERVICES/KATHIE NEE, 7115 Varnum St., Landover Hills MD 20784. (301)577-9072. Call/write. GE/LC/B/SP. Does A/F/NB/BP/BS/E/D/tracts/pamphlets/resumes/job application letters/ biographical sketches. Charges $10-12/hr. Brochure available for SASE.

MASSACHUSETTS
AMELLIA PUBLICATIONS/BARBARA ROBIDOUX, 127 Gelinas Dr., Chicopee MA 01020. (413)593-4386. Fax: (413)594-4741. Send/$20 deposit. GE/LC/B/NL/book printing. Does A/SS/F/NB/TM/E/D. Fee negotiable; estimate given.

*MARION VUILLEUMIER, 579 Buck Island Rd., West Yarmouth MA 02673. (508)775-4811. Call. GE (readies mss for presentation to publishers). Does NB/BP. $60 for initial reading & consultation; $30/hr. thereafter. Also has an information service: Writers' Helpline, (900)988-1838x549. $2/minute (3 minute max.). Gives up-to-date market news and writing tips.

MISSOURI
+TIM PATRICK MILLER, 4131 Manchester Blvd., St. Louis MO 63110. Line edit, $1/pg; copy edit, $2/pg; structural edit, $7/hr; proofing, .95/pg. Literary consultations/new writers, $10/hr; literary consult-ations/published writers, $25-150/hr.

DEBI STACK, Box 11805, Kansas City MO 64138-0306. (816)763-5743. Write. GE/LC. Does NB/BP/BS/ E/D/customized marketing analyses & consulting. Send for rate sheet.

NEW HAMPSHIRE
*SALLY WILKINS, Box 393, Amherst NH 03031-0393. (603)673-9331. Write. GE/LC. Does A/F/JN/PB/ BS/TM. Rate sheet for SASE.

NEW JERSEY
DAYSTAR COMMUNICATIONS/DR. MARY ANN DIORIO, Box 748, Millville NJ 08332-0748. (609)327-1231. Fax: (609)327-0291. Call/write. GE/LC/GH/CA/B/NL/SP. Does A/SS/P/F/N/NB/BP/JN/PB/BS/ E/D/S/copy for ads and PR material/resumes/business letters; also translations in French, Italian and Spanish. Rate sheet for SASE.

NEW MEXICO
*K.C. MASON, 1882 Conejo Dr., Santa Fe NM 87501. Write for information, fees, and availability.

NEW YORK

+STERLING DIMMICK, 86 Route 34, Waverly NY 14892-9793. (607)565-4470. Write. GE/GH/CA. Does A/SS/P/F/N/NB/BP/JN/PB/BS/TM/E/D/S. Charges $15-20/hour or by the project.

WILLIAM H. GENTZ, 300 E. 34th St. (9C), New York NY 10016. (212)686-5737. Write. GE of book proposals/special projects/contract evaluation. Hourly rate or project fees negotiable.

OHIO

BOB HOSTETLER, 6687 Baker Rd., Somerville OH 45064. (513)726-6618. Fax: (513)726-6618. Send material with full payment. GE/LC/GH/CA. Does A/SS/P/N/NB/JN/PB/TM/Books. Rate sheet available for SASE.

OKLAHOMA

+KATHRYN FANNING, Critique Service, P.O. Box 18472, Oklahoma City OK 73154. N/NB; no poetry. Charges $3.50/page.

OREGON

NASIRA ALMA, 1631 SW Yamhill #108, Portland OR 97205. (503)221-4941. Call. GE/GH. Does A/SS/P/N/NB/BP/BS/E/D. For an initial overview, which includes a single-spaced report of not less than 10 pgs, charges $400 (for book of average size). Sometimes negotiates a flat fee for the project.

BEST SELLER CONSULTANTS/URSULA BACON, Box 922, Wilsonville OR 97070. (503)682-3235. Fax: (503)682-8684. Call or write. GE/LC/GH/CA/BCE. Does A/SS/N/NB/BP/JN/PB. Fees are quoted on a per project basis. Ms evaluation for 250-325 pgs starts at $550. Full report and chapter-by-chapter recommendations included. Secular, but handles Christian books.

*CHRISTIAN WRITING SERVICES/ED STEWART, 3540 SE Spring Dr., Hillsboro OR 97123. (503)640-2522. Call. LC/GH/CA. Does NB/BP. Charges by the project based on $35/hr.

GAIL DENHAM, Box 89, Newberg OR 97132. (503)538-4691. Call. GE. Does A/SS/P/F/JN/PB/E/D/brochures/newsletters. Has photos to go with articles or books. Charges $20/hour; $25 minimum.

MARION DUCKWORTH, 2495 Maple NE, Salem OR 97303. (503)364-9570. Call/write. GE. Does A/F/NB/BP/BS/D. Charges $10.00 for 1st 1,000 wds; $5 for each additional 1,000 or fraction. Contact for terms on other. Consultations or private lessons, $15/hr.

*LYON'S LITERARY SERVICES/ELIZABETH LYON, 2123 Marlow Ln., Eugene OR 97401. (503)344-9118. Call/write. GE/LC. Does A/SS/N/NB/BP/JN/TM. Variable rates, roughly $30/hr.

*PRIMA FACIE PUBLISHERS/BEN RIGALL, 534 NE 71st Ave., Portland OR 97213. (503)255-2199. Write or call. GE/LC. Contact for information and fees.

CONNIE SOTH, 4890 SW Menlo Dr., Beaverton OR 97005. (503)644-4972. Call/Write. GE/LC/SP. Does A/SS/N/NB/BP/D. Negotiable rates; by the hour, chapter or project.

SALLY STUART, 1647 SW Pheasant Dr., Aloha OR 97006. (503)642-9844. Call/write. GE. Does A/SS/N/NB/BP/JN/PB/E. Charges $20/hr. for critique; $25/hr. for consultations. Comprehensive publishing contract evaluation $50-75.

THE WRITE TOUCH/SALLY PETERSEN, 14815 SW 141st Ave., Tigard OR 97224. (503)590-2357. Fax: (503)590-0692. Call. GE/LC/B/N/SP. Does A/F/BP/TM. Will guide through self-publishing process. Makes bid based on hourly rate and estimate of job length (roughly $55/hr) for brochures, newsletters, etc; less for editing manuscripts.

PENNSYLVANIA
MARLENE BAGNULL, 316 Blanchard Rd., Drexel Hill PA 19026-3507. (610)626-6833. Fax: (610)626-6833. Call/write. GE/LC. Does A/SS/N/NB/BP/JN/BS/D. Charges $20/hr.

VAL CINDRIC EDITING & PUBLISHING SERVICES, 536 Monticello Dr., Delmont PA 15626. Tel/Fax: (412)468-6185. Call. GE/GH/CA/B/SP. Does N/NB. Free brochure sent on request. Charges $20-25/hr. Project estimate provided.

IMPACT COMMUNICATIONS/DEBRA PETROSKY, 11331 Tioga Rd., N. Huntingdon PA 15642-2445. (412)863-5906. Call. GE/LC/B/NL/SP. Does A/SS/F/N/NB/BP/BS/TM. Typesetting available. Charges $20/hr. Per page rates also available. Interested in promoting ministry of the local church through greeters packets, tracts, pastor's publicity, bulletin inserts, etc.; 10% discount for nonprofits.

SOUTH CAROLINA
CHRISTIAN WRITERS FELLOWSHIP INTL. / SANDY BROOKS, Rt. 3 Box 1635, Clinton SC 29325. (803)697-6035. Fax: (803)697-6035. GE/LC. Does A/SS/F/NB/BP/JN/PB/E/D. Charges $1/pg ($20 min.) for general editing; $3/pg ($35 min.) for line editing. Enclose payment.

TEXAS
*****SYLVIA BRISKEY**, P.O. Box 9053, Dallas TX 75209-9053. (214)521-7507. Call/send ms/full payment. GE/LC. Does SS/P/N/JN/PB/children's stories/secular articles. Poetry, charges $5.60 plus $1/line; fiction $30 to 2,000 wds, $2.50/page thereafter.

+JAN E. KILBY, P.O. Box 17494, San Antonio TX 78217-0494. (210)657-0171. Fax: (210)829-0732. Member of Assn. of Professional Writing Consultants. Call. GE/LC. Does A/SS/P/F/N/NB/BP/JN/PB/E/D/speeches/other material. Call for prices/information.

+LYNN POWELL, 10702 Stone Canyon #232, Dallas TX 75230. (214)696-8473. GE/GH/B/NL. Does A/NB/BP/BS/TM/E/D. Charges $10/hr for proofreading; $20/hr for editing/revision; and $25/hr for ghostwriting.

VIRGINIA
*****HCI EDITORIAL SERVICES/DAVID HAZARD**, Box 71, Lincoln VA 22078. (703)338-7032. Write or call. GE. Does N/NB/BP. Works with agents and self-publishers. Fees on request.

+PUBLICATIONS MANAGEMENT, INC. / JANETTE G. BLACKWELL, 6727 Gouthier Rd., Falls Church VA 22042-2706. (703)534-2949. Call/write. GE/LC/B/NL/SP. Does A/SS/N/NB/BP/BS/TM/E/D/biographies; will oversee design and printing. Charges $12/hr. for copy editing; $16/hr. for substantive editing and rewriting. Estimates given for other work.

WASHINGTON
BIRDIE ETCHISON, Box 877, Ocean Park WA 98640. (206)665-6576. Write. GE/LC. Does A/SS/F/N/BP/PB. Charges according to length, $15 minimum.

KALEIDOSCOPE PRESS/PENNY LENT, 2507 - 94th Ave. E., Puyallup WA 98371-2203. Tel./Fax: (206)848-1116. Call/write/send material. GE/LC/GH/CA/B/NL/SP. Does A/SS/P/F/NB/BP/PB/E/D. Also market analysis & subsidy publishing. Line item editing $3/pg; other projects negotiated individually.

AGNES C. LAWLESS, 17462 NE 11th St., Bellevue WA 98008-3814. (206)644-5012. Write. GE/LC/CA. Does A/SS/P/F/N/NB/BP/JN/BS/E/D. Send SASE for rate sheet; $15/hr.

*VIRGINIA A. MOODY, 17402 - 114th Pl. NE, Granite Falls WA 98252. (206)691-5402. Call/write. GE/CA/B/NL/SP. Does A/SS/F/N/NB/BP/JN/PB/BS/TM. Charges $1/pg. Very interested in co-authoring.

+PATRICIA H. RUSHFORD, 3600 Edgewood Dr., Vancouver WA 98661. (206)695-2263. Call/write. GE/B. Does A/SS/N/NB/BP. Fee $15-35/hr (negotiable). Offers private tutoring & consultations @ $15/hr or private week-end workshop for $150, plus meals and lodging.

PAULINE SHEEHAN, Box 801, Lake Stevens WA 98258. (206)334-7049. Write. GE. Does BP. Charges $15 for up to 2,000 wds, plus $2/pg after that.

SHIRLEY POPE WAITE, 1604 Pleasant, Walla Walla WA 99362. (509)525-5592. Write. GE. Does A/F/D/meditations. Charges $5-25 according to word count.

WRITE AWAKE EDITORIAL SERVICES/GLORIA CHISHOLM, 13115 NE 123rd Pl, #204, Kirkland WA 98034. (206)823-6008. Fax: (206)823-6008. Call or write. GE. Does A/SS/F/N/NB/BP/JN/E/D. Free estimates; generally $25-50 for article/short story, $100-250 for book proposal.

WRITER'S BLOC/SCOTT R. ANDERSON, 7372 Guide Meridian, Lynden WA 98264. (206)354-2398. Write. GE/LC/GH/CA/B/NL/SP. Does A/SS/N/NB/BP. Charges $35-60/hr or by the project (estimate given). Offers wide range of editorial & pre-press (design/layout) services.

WRITERS INFORMATION NETWORK/ELAINE WRIGHT COLVIN, Box 11337, Bainbridge Island WA 98110. (206)842-9103. Fax: (206)842-0536. Send material/deposit. GE/LC/CA/B/NL/SP. Does A/SS/P/F/N/NB/BP/JN/PB/BS/E/D. Send SASE for rate sheet & list of all services.

WISCONSIN

BETHESDA LITERARY SERVICE/MARGARET L. BEEN, South 63 West 35530 Piper Rd., Eagle WI 53119-9726. (414)392-9761. Fax: (414)547-8871. Write. GE/LC. Does A/SS/P/F/NB/E/D. Devotional & inspirational readings. Teaches writers'classes, workshops, seminars—all ages. Charges about $15/hour.

MARGARET HOUK, 514 S Buchanan, Appleton WI 54915. (414)739-4997. Call/write. GE/LC. Does A/NB/BP/BS. Charges $20/hr. or $2.50/pg. (minimum $10).

CANADA

*A. BIENERT, Box 1358, Three Hills AB T0M 2A0 Canada. 443-2491. GE/LC. Does N/NB. Charges negotiable.

BERYL HENNE, 541 - 56 Street, Delta BC V4L 1Z5 Canada (U.S. address: Box 40, Pt. Roberts WA 98281-0040). (604)943-9676. Write. GE/LC/B/NL. Does A/SS/NB/BS/TM/D. Charges $20/hr.

CHRISTIAN LITERARY AGENTS

(*) Indicates that publisher did not return questionnaire.

(#) Indicates that listing was updated from guidelines or other sources.

(+) Indicates new listing.

ALIVE COMMUNICATIONS, P.O. Box 49068, Colorado Springs CO 80949. (719)260-7080. Fax: (719)260-8223. Agents: Rick Christian and Greg Johnson. Well known in the industry. Est. 1989. Represents 56 clients. Open to unpublished authors in exceptional cases. Handles all types of books; short stories & articles; screenplay adaptations, film rights, and audio projects. Deals in both Christian and general market.

> **Contact:** Query with synopsis, author bio/list of credits, one sample chapter/SASE.
>
> **Commission:** 15%
>
> **Fees:** Only extraordinary costs with client's pre-approval; no review fee.
>
> **Tips:** "We look for fresh, creative ideas—ones that don't copy the success of others. Not only should the ideas be strong, the words have to sparkle on the page. Presentation is everything. Allow 3-4 weeks for review."

+AUTHOR AID ASSOCIATES, 340 E. 52nd St., New York NY 10022. (212)758-4213. Agent: Arthur Orrmont. Not known in industry but expanding Christian/religious client list. Est. 1967. Represents 10 Christian clients. Open to unpublished authors. Handles novels for all ages, nonfiction for all ages, and scripts.

> **Contact:** By mail or phone.
>
> **Commission:** 15%.
>
> **Fees:** Evaluation fees for new/unpublished authors.

BK NELSON LITERARY AGENCY, 84 Woodland Rd., Pleasantville NY 10570. (914)741-1322. Fax: (914)741-1324. Agent: Jennifer Nelson. Recognized in the industry. Est. 1979. Represents 2 clients. Open to unpublished authors. Handles adult fiction and nonfiction, motion picture and television scripts. Also CD-Rom authors, video material, motion picture stories and biographies.

> **Contact:** Send inquiry and SASE.
>
> **Commission:** 15%, foreign 25%.
>
> **Fees:** $320 to evaluate a manuscript up to 80,000 words, and $1/pg thereafter; $2/pg for proposals with sample chapter.
>
> **Comments:** "Allow us the opportunity to evaluate and if the material is saleable, we will give you the best representation in the publishing/literary field."

BRANDENBURGH & ASSOCIATES LITERARY AGENCY, 24555 Corte Jaramillo, Murrieta CA 92562. (909)698-5200. Agent: Don Brandenburgh. Recognized in industry. Est. 1986. Represents 24 clients. Open to some unpublished authors. Handles adult novels (limited) and nonfiction (for general market if related to education and/or psychology). Books only.

> **Contact:** Query/SASE (or no response).
>
> **Commission:** 10%; 20% for foreign or dramatic rights.
>
> **Fees:** $35 for mailing/materials when contract is signed.

PEMA BROWNE LTD., Pine Rd., HCR Box 104B, Neversink NY 12765. (914)985-2936. Fax: (914)985-7635. Agent: Perry Browne. Recognized in industry. Est. 1966. Represents 7 clients. Open to unpublished authors. Handles novels and nonfiction (preferred) for all ages; picture books, and scripts. Only wishes mss not sent previously to publishers.

> **Contact:** Query with credentials & SASE.
> **Commission:** 15%.
> **Fees:** No reading fees for Christian mss, juvenile or romance mss.

+THE CHANDELYN LITERARY AGENCY, P.O. Box 50162, Clayton MO 63105. (314)533-5692. Fax: (314)645-8057. Agent: Tim Patrick Miller. Est. 1990. Represents 4 clients. Open to unpublished authors. Handles all types of material.

> **Contact:** Query letter, synopsis, full manuscript or 3 chapters (for fiction), proposal (non-fiction); release for scripts. SASE.
> **Commission:** 10%; 20% if using sub agent.
> **Fees:** Our subsidiary agency (T. Patrick Miller) handles all editorial and marketing services.

+FRANCINE CISKY LITERARY AGENCY, P.O. Box 555, Neenah WI 54957. (414)722-5944. Agent: Francine Cisky. Handles secular and Christian. Fiction & nonfiction; no children's or poetry. Specializes in historical fiction.

> **Contact:** Query letter or synopsis with one chapter and SASE.
> **Commission:** 15%.
> **Fees:** None.

LOIS CURLEY ENTERPRISES, 18755 W. Bernardo Dr., Suite 1039, San Diego CA 92127-3010. (619)675-2031. Fax: (619)675-2026. Agent: Lois L. Curley. Recognized in industry. Est. 1979. Represents 24 clients. May be open to unpublished authors. Handles adult fiction and nonfiction. Books only. Currently has a waiting list of new clients.

> **Contact:** Query, fax, or call. Send SASE for submission guidelines.
> **Commission:** 15% on first 35,000 copies, 10% thereafter.
> **Fees:** Charges normal office expenses.
> **Comments:** "We have a waiting list of writers from which we select one or two new clients each quarter for representation."

*THE CURTIS BRUCE AGENCY, 3437 - 38th St. SW, Seattle WA 98126-2220. Agent: Bruce W. Zabel. Recognized in industry. Est. 1990. Represents 80 clients. 10% unpublished authors. Handles child/teen/adult novels; child/teen/adult nonfiction; picture books. Specializes in novels.

> **Contact:** Query with brief synopsis, sample chapter, resume, and return postage mailer. Responds in 3-5 weeks on query; 18-24 wks on mss.
> **Commission:** 15% on domestic fiction, nonfiction, dramatic & film sales; 20% on foreign sales. Offers a written contract.
> **Fees:** Related office costs. Also offers marketability evaluation service, $100-200; critique service, $500-$1,000.

*DEERING LITERARY AGENCY, 1507 Oakmont Dr., Ste. B, Acworth GA 30102. (404)591-2051. Fax: (404)591-0369. Agent: Charles Deering. Recognized in the industry. Est. 1989. Represents 23 clients. Open to unpublished authors. Handles novels and nonfiction for all ages, picture books, scripts, and poetry books. Book length material only.

> **Contact:** Query letter and synopsis.

Commission: 12%

Fees: Reading fee, plus expenses. i.e., postage, phone calls, faxing, etc.

Tips: "I see so many mss that are not in the appropriate format. Please edit for spelling, tense, sentence structure, etc. Good religious material is so needed in our society today. Write uplifting material."

JOYCE FARRELL AND ASSOCIATES, 669 Grace St., Upper Montclair NJ 07043. (201)746-6248. Fax: (201)746-7348. Agent: Joyce Farrell. Recognized in the industry. Est. 1985. Represents 15-20 clients. Open to new authors. Handles fiction and nonfiction for all ages, picture books, electronic books, issue books, scientific/psychological/theological books for a general audience. Contact: Mail or fax, with query. Include bio, outline and synopsis. If mailing, may include 2 chapters.

Commission: 15%

Fees: None

GOOD NEWS LITERARY SERVICE, Box 587, Visalia CA 93279. (209)627-6241. Fax: (209)627-6242. Agent: Cynthia A. Wachner. Recognized in industry. Est. 1986. Represents 12 clients. No unpublished authors. Handles novels and nonfiction for all ages; picture books; scripts; articles, photos.

Contact: By mail. Send query, brief outline & resume for book. Write for submissions guidelines on other types of material.

Commission: 15%; 20% foreign. Sliding percentage scale for magazine-length material.

Fees: $100 deposit toward out-of-pocket expenses. Charges reading fees.

HARTLINE LITERARY AGENCY, 123 Queenston Dr., Pittsburgh PA 14235. (412)829-2483. Fax: (412)829-2450. Agent: Joyce Hart. Recognized in industry. Est. 1992. Represents 16 clients. Open to unpublished authors. Handles adult novels and nonfiction, especially health, motivational, financial, and self-help.

Contact: Phone or query.

Commission: 15%.

Fees: Fee schedule available on request.

Tips: "Know the target audience for your book; research the market to find similar books in print. We also provide editing and consulting services for authors."

*HOLUB & ASSOCIATES, 24 Old Colony Rd., North Stonington CT 06359. (203)535-0689. Agent: William Holub. Recognized by Catholic publishers. Est. 1966. Open to unpublished authors. Handles adult nonfiction; possibly picture books; Christian living in secular society.

Contact: Query with outline, 2 sample chapters, intended audience, and bio.

Commission: 15%.

Fees: Postage and photocopying.

*JEAN V. NAGGAR LITERARY AGENCY, 216 E. 75TH St., New York NY 11201. (212)794-1082. Agent: Jean Naggar. Not recognized in industry. Est. 1978. Represents 5 clients. Open to unpublished authors. Handles adult/teen/children novels and nonfiction, picture books. Handles articles/short stories only if handling book-length as well.

Contact: Query letter/1-2 pg. synopsis.

Commission: 15%; 20% foreign.

Fees: No reading fee, but xerox, telephone & overseas mailing for clients.

*PEN & INK LITERARY AGENCY, 4319 Toll Gate Ln., Bellbrook OH 45305-1238. (513)434-0686. Agent: Theresa Freed. Recognized in industry. Est. 1993. Building client list. Open to unpublished authors.

Handles fiction and nonfiction for all ages, picture books, scripts, poetry books; informational, motivational and how-to. Books only.

Contact: Send SASE for information.

Commission: 15%; 20% foreign.

Fees: Charges a $90 reading fee that is refunded on receipt of advance from publisher; also office expenses and marketing fee.

Tips: "Please submit ms in proper form. This will save everyone time and money."

PUBLISHING IDEAS UNLIMITED, 804 Howard St., Wheaton IL 60187-4017. Tel./Fax: (708)668-4017. Agent: Mr. Leslie H. Stobbe. Recognized in the industry. Est. 1992. Represents 12 clients. Open to unpublished authors. Handles adult & teen novels and nonfiction.

A RISING SUN LITERARY GROUP, 1153 Alabama Rd., Ste. 106, Acworth GA 30102-2506. (404)924-2288. Fax: (404)924-7678. Agents: Lynn Watson & Dorothy Glancy. Recognized in the industry. Est. 1989. Represents 40 clients. Open to unpublished authors. Handles fiction and nonfiction for all ages, picture books, scripts, poetry books, and short story collections. Also edits texts and trade books.

Contact: By phone or mail.

Commission: 13%.

Fees: Reading fee $125. Contract fee varies depending on manuscript.

Comments: "We provide an indepth critique and professional marketing package."

+THE SHEPARD AGENCY, Pawling Savings Bank Bldg., Brewster (Rt. 22) NY 10509. (914)279-2900/3236. Fax: (914)279-3239. Agents: Jean or Lance Shepard. Recognized in the industry. Est. 1986. Represents 8 clients. Open to unpublished authors. Handles fiction and nonfiction for all ages; no picture books; especially business, reference, professional, self-help, cooking and crafts. Books only.

Contact: Query letter and sample material.

Commission: 15%

Fees: None except long-distance calls and copying.

*WILLIAM PENS, 342 Alden Cove Dr., Smyrna TN 37167. (615)355-4455. Fax: (615)355-9977. Agent: William D. Watkins. Recognized in the industry. Est. 1993. Represents 8 clients. Open to unpublished authors. Handles adult novels and nonfiction. Books only.

Contact: Phone, Fax or mail.

Commission: 10% to negotiate contracts only; 15% for full literary services.

Fees: Charges for telephone, copying, mail and travel expenses.

Tips: "Unlike most other agents, I provide writing and editing services as well as consulting services for authors, publishers, and ministries."

WOLGEMUTH & HYATT, INC., 8012 Brooks Chapel Rd., Ste. 243, Brentwood TN 37027. (615)370-9937. Fax: (615)370-9939. Agents: Michael S. Hyatt and Robert D. Wolgemuth. Well recognized in the industry. Est. 1992. Represents 30 clients. No unpublished authors. Handles only adult nonfiction.

Contact: By letter, phone or CompuServe.

Commission: 15%

Fees: Charges fees.

Other Services: Offers a manuscript evaluation service for unpublished authors to assist them in increasing their chances of getting published.

Comments: "We work with authors who are either best-selling authors or potentially best-selling authors. Consequently, we want to represent clients with broad market appeal."

THE WRITER'S EDGE - See listing under Editorial Services - Illinois.

ADDITIONAL AGENTS

NOTE: The following agents did not return a questionnaire, but have been identified as agents who handle religious manuscripts. Be sure to send queries first if you wish to submit to them.

(*) Indicates they are known in the industry.

Julian Bach Literary Agency
E. 71st St
New York NY 10021
(212)753-2605
nonfiction/fiction

Elizabeth H. Backman
P.O. Box 762
Pine Plains NY 12567
(518)398-6408
nonfiction/fiction

Michele Glance Serwach
Creative Concepts Literary Agency
5538 Hertford Dr.
Troy MI 48098-3235
nonfiction/fiction

Bonnie Crown
B R Crown Intl Literary & Arts Agency
50 E. 10th St
New York NY 10003
(212)475-1999
nonfiction/fiction

Carol Atwell
Diamond Literary Agency
3063 S Kearney St
Denver CO 80222
(303)759-0291
nonfiction/fiction

Al Hart
Fox Chase Agency Inc
Rm 930/Public Ledger Bldg
Independence Square
Philadelphia PA 19106
(215)625-2450
nonfiction

*Stephen Griffith
PO Box 3439
Boone NC 28707-0739
(704)262-3345

Nikki Cane
Gary L Hegler Literary Agency
Box 890101
Houston TX 77289-0101
(713)486-8478
nonfiction/fiction

Lawrence Jordan
Lawrence Jordan Literary Agency
250 W 57th St Ste 1527
New York NY 10107
(212)690-2748
nonfiction/fiction

Ned Leavitt
The Ned Leavitt Agency
70 Wooster St #4F
New York NY 10012
(212)334-0999
nonfiction/fiction

K. Allman
Literary Marketing Consultant
One Hallidie Plaza #701
San Francisco CA 94102
(415)979-8170
nonfiction/fiction

Pamela G. Ahearn
Southern Writers
635 Gravier St #1020

New Orleans LA 70130
(504)525-6390
nonfiction/fiction

Mark Sullivan
Mark Sullivan Assoc.
521 Fifth Ave. #1700
New York NY 10175
(212)682-5844
nonfiction/fiction

DENOMINATIONAL INDEX OF BOOK PUBLISHERS AND PERIODICALS

An attempt has been made to divide publishers into appropriate denominational groups. However, due to the extensive number of denominations included, and sometimes incomplete denominational information, some publishers may have inadvertently been included in the wrong list. Additions and corrections are welcome.

ASSEMBLIES OF GOD
Book Publisher:

Gospel Publishing House

Periodicals:

American Horizon

Advance

At Ease

CE Counselor

High Adventure

Junior Trails

Live

Maranatha

Memos

Paraclete

Pentecostal Evangel

Pentecostal Testimony (Canada)

Resource (Canada)

Teen Life

Take Five

Woman's Touch

Youth Leader

BAPTIST, SOUTHERN
Book Publishers:

Broadman & Holman

New Hope Publishers

Renewal Press

Southern Baptist Press

Woman's Missionary Union

Periodicals:

Baptist History & Heritage

Challenge

Christian Single

Church Administration

Church Media Library

Church Musician

Discipleship Training

Glory Songs

Home Life

Journey

Mature Living

Music Leader

Music Makers

Music Time

ParentLife

Pioneer

Proclaim

Search

Senior Musician

Southwestern News

Student, The

Young Musicians

BAPTIST, OTHER
Book Publishers:

Judson Press (American)

National Baptist (Missionary)

Periodicals:

American Baptist

Baptist Beacon

Baptist Informer (General)

Baptist Leader (American)

The Canadian Baptist

Certainty (Regular)

Challenge (Regular)

Co-Laborer (Free Will)

Conquest

Contact (Free Will)

The Five Stones (American)
Fundamentalist Journal
God's Special People (Independent)
Heartbeat (Free Will)
Impact (Conservative)
LIGHT...For/Christian Walk (Independent)
Link & Visitor
Messenger, The (Pentecostal Free Will)
Moments with God (North American)
Primary Pal (Regular)
Secret Place (American)
Standard, The
Writer's Forum

CATHOLIC
Book Publishers:
ACTA Publications Alba House
American Catholic Press
Ave Maria Press
Don Bosco Publications
Brown Publishing
Catholic University of America Press
Christian Classics
Cistercian Publications
Dimension Books
Franciscan Herald Press
Franciscan University Press
Harper SF (Cath. bks)
ICS Publications
Liguori Publications
Liturgical Press
Loyola University Press
Thomas More Press
Orbis Books
Our Sunday Visitor
Pastoral Press
Paulist Press
Regina Press
Regnery Gateway
Resurrection Press
Servant Publications
St. Anthony Messenger
St. Bede's Publications

St. Paul Books
Sheed & Ward
Tabor Publishing
Periodicals:
America
Annals of St. Anne
Arkansas Catholic
Arlington Catholic Herald
Bible Today
Canadian Catholic Review
Catechist
Catechumenate
Catholic Accent
Catholic Courier
Catholic Digest
Catholic Exponent
Catholic Forester
Catholic Health World
Catholic Heritage
Catholic Life
Catholic Near East
Catholic New York
Catholic Parent
Catholic Sentinel
Catholic Telegraph
Catholic Twin Circle
Chicago Studies
Columbia
Commonweal
Companion
Compass
Conscience
Critic, The
Ecumenical Trends
Environment & Art
Emmanuel
Eucharistic Minister
Family, The
Homiletic & Pastoral Review
Interim, The
Liguorian
Living Words
Marian Helpers Bulletin

Messenger/Sacred Heart
Messenger (KY)
Messenger/St. Anthony
Miraculous Medal
Montana Catholic
My Friend
National Catholic Reporter
New Covenant
New Oxford Review
N.A. Voice of Fatima
Oblates
Oblate World
Our Family
Our Sunday Visitor
Parish Family Digest
Pax Christi USA
Prairie Messenger
Praying
Priest, The
Queen of All Hearts
Religion Teacher's Journal
Review for Religious St. Anthony Messenger
Rural Landscapes
St. Joseph's Messenger
St. Willibrord Journal
Sisters Today
Social Justice Review
Spirit
Spiritual Life
This Rock
Today's Catholic Teacher
Today's Parish
Upsouth
U.S. Catholic
YOU! Magazine
Youth Update

CHRISTIAN CHURCH/CHURCH OF CHRIST
Book Publishers:
CBP Press (Disciples of Christ)
Chalice Press (Disciples of Christ)
College Press (Church of Christ)
Friendship Press (Church of Christ)

Pilgrim Press, The (United Church of Christ)
Periodicals:
Christian Chronicle
Christian Standard
Disciple, The (Disciples of Christ)
Four and Five
Lookout, The
R-A-D-A-R
Straight
Teenage Christian (Church of Christ)
Weekly Bible Reader

CHURCH OF GOD (Anderson, IN)
Book Publisher:
Warner Press
Periodicals:
Christian Leadership
Church of God MISSIONS
Pathways to God
Vital Christianity

CHURCH OF GOD (Cleveland, TN)
Book Publisher:
Editorial Evangelica
Periodicals:
Church of God EVANGEL
Lighted Pathway
Unique
Youth and CE Leadership

CHURCH OF GOD, OTHER
Periodicals:
Bible Advocate (Seventh Day)
Church Advocate
Church Herald and Holiness Banner (Holiness)
Gem, The
Pentecostal Messenger

CHURCH OF THE NAZARENE
Book Publishers:
Lillenas (music)
Beacon Hill Press

Periodicals:
Children's Church Exch.
Discoveries
Herald of Holiness
Level C Teacher
Level D Teacher
Listen
Power and Light
Preacher's Magazine
Resource
Standard
Table Talk
Teens Today
Together Time
Wonder Time

EPISCOPAL/ANGLICAN
Book Publishers:
Alban Institute
Forward Movement
Morehouse Publishing
Periodicals:
Acts 29
Cathedral Age
Episcopal Life
Interchange
Living Church
The Witness

FREE METHODIST
Periodicals:
Evangel
Light and Life
Light From the Word
Response (SPU)

FREE WILL BAPTIST
Periodicals:
Co-Laborer
Heartbeat

LUTHERAN
Book Publishers:
Augsburg Press (ELCA)
Concordia
Langmarc Publishing
Periodicals:
Canada Lutheran (ELC - Canada)
Christmas (ELCA)
Cresset
Diaconalogue
Esprit (ELCC)
Evangelism (MO Synod)
Lutheran, The (ELCA) Lutheran Digest
Lutheran Educ. (MO Synod)
Lutheran Forum
Lutheran Journal
Lutheran Laymen (MO Synod)
LutheranPartners (ELCA)
Lutheran Witness (MO Synod)
Lutheran Woman Today(ELCA)
Morning Glory
Northwestern Lutheran
Parenting Treasures (MO Synod)
Parish Teacher (ELCA)
Word & World (ELCA)
Teachers Inter. (MO Synod)

MENNONITE
Book Publishers:
Herald Press
Kindred Press
Periodicals:
Christian Living
Companions
Mennonite, The
Mennonite Brethren Herald
Mennonite Reporter
Mennonite Weekly Review
The Messenger
On the Line
Partners
Purpose
Story Friends

Story Mates

With

MISSIONARY CHURCH
Book Publisher:
Bethel Publishing
Periodicals:
Emphasis/Faith & Living
Ministry Today

PENTECOSTAL HOLINESS CHURCH
Periodicals:
ADVOCATE
CE Connection
Helping Hand, The
Worldorama

PRESBYTERIAN
Book Publishers:
John Knox Press
Presbyterian & Reformed
Westminster Press
Periodicals:
Covenanter Witness
Horizons (USA)
PCA Messenger
Presbyterian Outlook (USA)
Presbyterian Record
Presbyterian Survey

QUAKER/FRIENDS
Book Publishers:
Barclay Press
Friends United Press
Periodicals:
Evangelical Friend
Friends Journal

REFORMED CHURCHES
Periodicals:
Church Herald
Reformed Worship
Vision (MI)

SEVENTH-DAY ADVENTIST
Book Publishers:
Pacific Press
Remnant Publications
Review and Herald
Periodicals:
Cornerstone Connections
GUIDE Magazine
Insight (MD)
Insight/Out
Journal/Adventist Ed
Liberty
Message
Ministry
Our Little Friend
Primary Treasure
Signs of the Times
Vibrant Life
Young and Alive

UNITED METHODIST
Book Publishers:
United Methodist Publishing House
Imprints: Abingdon Press
Cokesbury
Dimensions Press
Discipleship Resources
Upper Room Books
Periodicals:
alive now!
Christian Social Action
Good News
Leader/Church School Today
Magazine/Christian Youth!
Mature Years
Methodist History
New World Outlook
Pockets
Quarterly Review
Response
Upper Room

UNITED PENTECOSTAL
Periodicals:
Conqueror, The
Pentecostal Homelife
Teen Life
Vision
Youth World

WESLEYAN CHURCH
Periodicals:
Changing Lives
Friend
In Touch
Vista (IN)
Wesleyan Advocate
Wesleyan World

MISCELLANEOUS DENOMINATIONS
Armenian Holy Apostolic
Pourastan
Brethren Church
Brethren Evangelist

Christian Missionary & Alliance
Christian Publications
Evangelical Covenant Church
Cornerstone
Covenant Companion
Evangelical Free Church
Evangelical Beacon
Pursuit
Fellowship of Christian Assemblies
Fellowship Today
Fellowship of Evangelical Bible Churches
Gospel Tidings
Foursquare Gospel Church
Foursquare World Advance
Open Bible Standard Churches
MESSAGE of the Open Bible
United Brethren in Christ
The United Brethren
United Church of Canada
United Church Publishing House
United Church Observer
United Church of Christ
United Church Press

GLOSSARY OF TERMS

NOTE: This is not intended to be an exhaustive glossary of terms. It includes primarily those terms you will find within the context of this market guide.

Advance. Amount of money a publisher pays to an author up front, against future royalties.

All rights. An outright sale of your material. Author has no further control over it.

Anecdote. A short, poignant, real-life story, usually used to illustrate a single thought.

Assignment. When an editor asks a writer to write a specific piece for an agreed-upon price.

Avant-garde. Experimental; ahead of the times.

Bimonthly. Every two months.

Biweekly. Every two weeks.

Book proposal. Submission of a book idea to an editor, usually includes a cover letter, thesis statement, chapter-by-chapter synopsis, market survey, and 1-3 sample chapters.

Byline. Author's name printed just below the title of a story, article, etc.

Circulation. The number of copies sold or distributed of each issue of a publication.

Clips. See "Published Clips."

Column. A regularly appearing feature, section, or department in a periodical using the same heading; written by the same person or a different freelancer each time.

Contributor's copy. Copy of an issue of a periodical sent to the author whose work appears in it.

Copyright. Legal protection of an author's work.

Cover letter. A letter that accompanies some manuscript submissions. Usually needed only if you have to tell the editor something specific, or to give your credentials for writing a piece of a technical nature.

Critique. An evaluation of a piece of writing.

Devotional. A short piece which shares a personal spiritual discovery, inspires to worship, challenges to commitment or action, or encourages.

Editorial guidelines. See "Writer's guidelines."

EPA/Evangelical Press Assn. A professional, trade organization for periodical publishers and associate members.

Essay. A short composition usually expressing the author's opinion on a specific subject.

Evangelical. A person who believes that one receives God's forgiveness for sins through Jesus Christ, and believes the Bible is an authoritative guide for daily living.

Feature article. In-depth coverage of a subject, usually focusing on a person, event, process, organization, movement, trend or issue; written to explain, encourage, help, analyze, challenge, motivate, warn, or entertain—as well as to inform.

Filler. A short item used to "fill" out the page of a periodical. It could be a timeless news item, joke, anecdote, light verse or short humor, puzzle, game, etc.

First rights. Editor buys the right to publish your piece for the first time.

Freelance. As in 50% freelance: means that 50% of the material printed in the publication is supplied by freelance writers.

Freelancer or freelance writer. A writer who is not on salary, but sells his material to a number of different publishers.

Free verse. Poetry that flows without any set pattern.

Genre. Refers to type or classification, as in fiction or poetry. In fiction, such types as westerns, romances, mysteries, etc., are referred to as genre fiction.

Glossy. A black and white photo with a shiny, rather than matte finish.

Go-ahead. When a publishers tells you to go ahead and write up or send your article idea.

Haiku. A Japanese lyric poem of a fixed 17-syllable form.

Holiday/seasonal. A story, article, filler, etc. that has to do with a specific holiday or season. This material must reach the publisher the stated number of months prior to the holiday/season.

Humor. The amusing or comical aspects of life that add warmth and color to an article or story.

Interdenominational. Distributed to a number of different denominations.

International Postal Reply Coupon. See "IRC."

Interview article. An article based on an interview with a person of interest to a specific readership.

IRC or IPRC. International Postal Reply Coupon: can be purchased at your local post office and should be enclosed with a manuscript sent to a foreign publisher.

Journal. A periodical presenting news in a particular area.

Kill fee. A fee paid for a completed article done on assignment that is subsequently not published.

Light verse. Simple, light-hearted poetry.

Mainstream fiction. Other than genre fiction, such as romance, mystery or science fiction. Stories of people and their conflicts handled on a deeper level.

Ms. Abbreviation for manuscript.

Mss. Abbreviation for more than one manuscript.

NASR. Abbreviation for North American serial rights.

Newsbreak. A newsworthy event or item sent to a publisher who might be interested in publishing it because it would be of interest to his particular readership.

Nondenominational. Not associated with a particular denomination.

Not copyrighted. Publication of your piece in such a publication will put it into public domain and it is not then protected. Ask that the publisher carry your copyright notice on your piece when it is printed.

On acceptance. Periodical pays a writer at the time an article is accepted for publication.

On assignment. Writing something at the specific request of an editor.

On publication. Periodical pays a writer when his/her article is published.

On speculation. Writing something for an editor with the agreement that he will buy it only if he likes it.

One-time rights. Selling the right to publish a story one-time to any number of publications (usually refers to publishing for a non-overlapping readership).

Payment on acceptance. See "On acceptance."

Payment on publication. See "On publication."

Pen Name. Using a name other than your legal name on an article in order to protect your identity or the identity of people included in the article. Put the pen name in the byline under the title, and your real name in the upper, left-hand corner.

Personal experience story. A story based on a real-life experience.

Personality profile. A feature article that highlights a specific person's life or accomplishments.

Photocopied submission. Sending an editor a photocopy of your manuscript, rather than an original. Some editors prefer an original.

Published clips. Copies of actual articles you have had published.

Quarterly. Every three months.

Query letter. A letter sent to an editor telling about an article you propose to write and asking if he or she is interested in seeing it.

Reporting time. The number of weeks or months it takes an editor to get back to you about a query or manuscript you have sent in.

Reprint rights. Selling the right to reprint an article that has already been published elsewhere. You must have sold only first or one-time rights originally, and wait until it has been published the first time.

Royalty. The percentage an author is paid by a publisher on the sale of each copy of a book.

SAE. Self-addressed envelope (without stamps).

SASE. Self-addressed, stamped envelope. Should always be sent with a manuscript or query letter.

Satire. Ridicule that aims at reform.

Second serial rights. See "Reprint rights."

Semiannual. Issued twice a year.

Serial. Refers to publication in a periodical (such as first serial rights).

Sidebar. A short feature that accompanies an article and either elaborates on the human interest side of the story or gives additional information on the topic. It is often set apart by appearing within a box or border.

Simultaneous rights. Selling the rights to the same piece to several publishers simultaneously. Be sure everyone is aware that you are doing so.

Simultaneous submissions. Sending the same manuscript to more than one publisher at the same time. Usually done with non-overlapping markets (such as denominational) or when you are writing on a timely subject. Be sure to state in a cover letter that it is a simultaneous submission and why.

Speculation. See "On speculation."

Staff-written material. Material written by the members of a magazine staff.

Subsidiary rights. All those rights, other than book rights, included in a book contract—such as paperback, book club, movie, etc.

Subsidy publisher. A book publisher who charges the author to publish his book, as opposed to a royalty publisher who pays the author.

Tabloid. A newspaper-format publication about half the size of a regular newspaper.

Take-home paper. A periodical sent home from Sunday School each week (usually) with Sunday School students, children through adults.

Think piece. A magazine article that has an intellectual, philosophical, or provocative approach to a subject.

Third world. Reference to underdeveloped countries of Asia and Africa.

Transparencies. Positive color slides, not color prints.

Trade magazine. A magazine whose audience is in a particular trade or business.

Traditional Verse. One or more verses with an established pattern that is repeated throughout the poem.

Unsolicited manuscripts. A manuscript an editor did not specifically ask to see.

Vanity publisher. See "Subsidy publisher."

Vitae/Vita. An outline of one's personal history and experience.

Work-for-hire assignment. Signing a written contract with a publisher stating that a particular piece of writing you are doing for him is "work for hire." In the agreement you give the publisher full ownership and control of the material.

Writers' guidelines. An information sheet provided by a publisher which gives specific guidelines for writing for the publication. Always send an SASE with your request for guidelines.

GENERAL INDEX

This index includes only periodicals, books, and greeting cards. Conferences, groups, and editorial services are listed alphabetically by state; secular newspapers are listed alphabetically by the name of the paper; agents are listed alphabetically by the name of the agency. Check the Table of Contents for the location of these supplementary listings.